DICTIONARY OF LITERARY BIOGRAPHY
YEARBOOK: 1981

Dictionary of Literary Biography

DICTIONARY OF LITERARY BIOGRAPHY YEARBOOK: 1981

Edited by
Karen L. Rood
Jean W. Ross
and
Richard Ziegfeld

A Bruccoli Clark Book
Gale Research Company • Book Tower • Detroit, Michigan 48226
1982

Manufactured by Braun-Brumfield, Inc.
Ann Arbor, Michigan
Printed in the United States of America

ISSN 0731-7867

Contents

New Entries

Preface

DLB Yearbook is divided into two main sections: Updated Entries and New Entries. Updated Entries are designed to complement the *DLB* series with current information about the literary activities of living authors and reports about the most recent scholarship on deceased ones. Each Updated Entry takes as its point of departure an already published *DLB* entry, adding primary and secondary bibliographical information, providing descriptions and assessments of new works, and, when necessary, reevaluating an author's works. Subjects of the entries are offered the opportunity to comment on their recent writings or to respond to previously published entries in *DLB*. The death of a major literary figure prompts a summation of his achievement. One of the functions of Updated Entries is to provide fresh, authoritative appraisals of the careers of recently deceased authors and to solicit comments from the authors' contemporaries. Newly published material that contributes significantly to the understanding of a deceased author's life or work—such as letters, journals, notebooks, or a biography—will also be discussed. The form of entry in Updated Entries is similar to that in the standard *DLB* series. Each Updated Entry is preceded by a reference to the *DLB* volume in which the basic entry on the subject appears. Readers seeking information about an author's entire career must consult the basic entry along with the Updated Entry for complete biographical and bibliographical information.

The second section is devoted to New Entries, on figures not previously included in *DLB*. Emphasis is placed on biography and syntheses of the critical reception of the authors' works. Bibliographies of the authors' writings and the critical writings about them are selective. The lists of books at the beginnings of entries are intended to give an overview of the subjects' book-length work in all genres; major books are included, but ephemeral works such as chapbooks or pamphlets are normally omitted. Primary bibliographies at the ends of entries are selected to include works other than original book-length writings, such as screenplays, translations, and contributions to books and periodicals. The most useful books and articles about the authors are selected for the secondary bibliographies. If there are significant public collections of an author's papers, the information is listed at the end of the entry.

Samuel Johnson's observation that "the chief glory of every people arises from its authours" was endorsed by the *DLB* advisory board, editors, and publishers in the first volume of the *DLB* series. *DLB Yearbook* is a further affirmation of that belief. *Yearbook* is designed to augment the *Dictionary of Literary Biography* so that the series may more fully realize its obligation to make the achievements of literature better understood and more accessible to students, while at the same time serving the needs of scholars and teachers.

Permissions

The following people and institutions generously permitted the reproduction of photographs and other illustrative materials: Thomas Victor, pp. 4, 5, 6, 20, 22, 25, 31, 35, 57, 82, 95, 111, 115, 120, 134; Wide World Photos, pp. 29, 100, 127; Glynn Robinson Betts, p. 45; Mark Morrow, pp. 67, 257; Princeton University Library, p. 76; E. Sands, p. 87; Culver Pictures, p. 103; Jerry Bauer, p. 105; Michael Kidd, p. 151; Ann Charters, p. 156; Pat Hill, p. 165; Wayne Barker, p. 183; The New York Public Library at Lincoln Center, Astor, Lenox and Tilden Foundations, p. 215; John Howard Griffin, p. 219; Bellarmine College Library, p. 224; Lotte Jacobi, p. 234; Damon Knight, p. 267; Kenneth Lee, p. 271.

Acknowledgments

This book was produced by BC Research.

The production staff included Mary L. Betts, Joseph Caldwell, Angela Dixon, Joyce Fowler, Karen Geney, Stacy Gibbons, Robert H. Griffin, Patricia S. Hicks, Sharon K. Kirkland, Cynthia D. Lybrand, Mary V. McLeod, Shirley A. Ross, Walter W. Ross, Robin A. Sumner, Cheryl A. Swartzentruber, Charles L. Wentworth, Carol J. Wilson, and Lynne C. Zeigler.

Anne Dixon did the library research with the valuable assistance of the following librarians at the Thomas Cooper Library of the University of South Carolina: Michael Freeman, Dwight Gardner, Michael Havener, David Lincove, Donna Nance, Harriet Oglesbee, Jean Rhyne, Paula Swope, Jane Thesing, Ellen Tillett, and Beth Woodard. Photographic copy work for this volume was done by Pat Crawford of Imagery, Columbia, South Carolina.

Finally, grateful acknowledgment is due the subjects of entries in this book who were kind enough to read their entries for accuracy. Without the assistance of all these people, this book would not have been possible.

Nelson Algren

(28 March 1909-9 May 1981)

Nelson Algren, author of *The Man with the Golden Arm* (1949) and *A Walk on the Wild Side* (1956) died of heart failure in Sag Harbor, Long Island, on 9 May 1981. His most recent novel, *The Devil's Stocking*, based on a murder-robbery in New Jersey for which middleweight boxer Rubin Carter was convicted, has gone unpublished in the United States, though a German translation has appeared in Europe. The seventy-two-year-old Algren lived alone and left no family. This tribute from Jack Conroy was received after *Yearbook: 1981* had gone to press. See also the Algren entry in *DLB 9, American Novelists, 1910-1945*.

A TRIBUTE *from Jack Conroy*

I had published two stories by Nelson Algren and met him in New York or Chicago several times before I went to Chicago in 1938 to work on the Federal Writers' Project and to join Algren in an effort to revive the *Anvil* as the *New Anvil*. This latter endeavor we eventually accomplished with funds raised by a series of benefit affairs and production of a melodrama called *The Drunkard's Warning, or Chicago by Gaslight*, in which Nelson, wearing a long gray wig and a marvelously woebegone expression, appeared as the wronged wife of the drunkard-villain, James T. Barrelhouse.

Nelson was living in one of several studios flanking an arcade on Cottage Grove Avenue—studios that once had served as shops to accommodate visitors to the World's Columbian Exposition in 1893. He had already published his first novel, *Somebody in Boots* (for which he had received the munificent sum of $100 in advance), and was working on short stories and his second novel, *Never Come Morning*.

Living with Nelson in his pad in Rat Alley (as we soon dubbed the arcade because of the fearless and ferocious rodents that infested it even in broad daylight), I soon became conscious of his fascination with Baudelaire. He was often seen reading the collection entitled *Baudelaire: His Prose and Poetry*, edited by T. R. Smith and published by Modern Library, containing the epilogue translated by Arthur Symons which, it often seems to me, embodies the leitmotiv of Algren's works:

> With heart at rest I climbed the citadel's
> Steep height and saw the city as from a tower,
> Hospital, brothel, prison and such hells
> Where evil comes up softly like a flower.

And the conclusion:

> I love thee, infamous city. Harlots and
> Hunted have pleasures of their own to give
> The vulgar herd can never understand.

The *New Anvil* died of malnutrition with the May-June 1940 issue. The writers project was disbanded. Nelson and I, refugees from the project, were enrolled as investigators for the Venereal Disease Control Project. Our job was to hunt down females who had infected servicemen with a venereal disease, with only their often-skimpy recollections of a good-time girl met in a bar to guide us. The women had to be brought in for treatment, but a good many (fearing "the law") considered it a kind of arrest. Nelson's sympathy for these "harlots and hunted" grew as he invaded their forlorn lives.

Nelson's reputation as a voice from the lower depths advanced in Chicago's literary community, but his regard for his "infamous city" was never of a booster or Rotarian flavor. When *Holiday* magazine wanted to publish a special Chicago edition, it commissioned Algren to write the lead article. The result was so unflattering that it was relegated to rear pages and Albert Halper was called upon to turn out a more felicitous lead story. The Algren article formed the basis for his slim book *Chicago: City on the Make*, in which, despite his reservations, he was moved to observe: "Yet once you've come to be part of this particular patch, you'll never love another. Like loving a woman with a broken nose, you may find lovelier lovelies. But never a lovely so real."

Algren fled east during his final years, and often said he never wanted to return to his "infamous city" even as a corpse. So he is buried in the little whalers' graveyard in Sag Harbor, New York. Official Chicago gave him belated recognition in death. A four-block stretch of Evergreen Avenue where he had lived for years in a third-floor walk-up flat was renamed Algren Street and newspaper photos revealed Mayor Byrne pointing coyly to the sign. Algren Day was duly proclaimed with a high-sounding declaration. But the outraged citizens of Evergreen Avenue resented the change in their street, likely to cause all sorts of complications with mail, etc. They circulated a handbill protesting the honor bestowed upon "the poet, Robert Algren," and Alderman Nardulli commented: "I didn't even know duh guy." So the signs came down. It was *all* Evergreen Avenue again. Chicago's "harlots and hunted" were again without an advocate, and the city's dominant trend was, as Algren described it in *City on the Make*:

Town of the small, cheerful apartments, the beer in the icebox, the pipes in the rack, the children well behaved and the TV well tuned, the armchairs fatly upholstered and the record albums filed: 33 rpm, 45 rpm, 78 rpm. Where the 33 rpm husband and proud father eats all his vitamin-stuffed dinner cautiously and then streaks to the bar across the street to drink himself senseless among strangers, at 78 rpm, all alone.

DICTIONARY OF LITERARY BIOGRAPHY YEARBOOK: 1981

A call to the American Writers Congress

Writers in America face a crisis. Rapidly advancing concentration in the communications industry threatens as never before to exclude and silence serious writers who are out of political or literary fashion. New writers find it more and more difficult to publish, and even established writers are subject to what novelist Mary Lee Settle has recently called "the censorship of slow-moving books." Government support for the arts is being slashed. Attacks on writers—libel suits, book bannings, censorship by government and special interest groups—are increasing all across the country.

More than the private interests of writers is at stake: there is also a vital public interest in the character, quality, and critical spirit of our literary culture.

Therefore, The Nation Institute, a nonprofit organization associated with *The Nation* magazine, hereby issues a call for The American Writers Congress, which will be held at the Roosevelt Hotel in New York City from October 9-12, 1981.

Through panels, workshops, roundtables, caucuses and plenary sessions, the Congress will examine writers' rights, bread-and-butter issues, and the role of writing and writers in the United States today. The Congress will provide a forum for writers of all descriptions—poets, playwrights, novelists, journalists, scholars, critics, and the associations, guilds and unions that represent them—to talk to one another and to the country at large, and to develop new ways of working together in defense of common interests.

The Writers Congresses of the 1930s were a reaction to the Depression at home and fascism abroad. The MORE conventions of the 1970s responded to widespread dissatisfaction with mainstream media. Today many writers are disturbed by the increasing commercialism that threatens their ability to survive as writers; others are concerned by the intolerance associated with the rise of the right; still others express alarm at the debasement of literary culture caused by recent political and economic developments. These issues pose fundamental questions for every writer—and reader—in America, and demand an active response. The American Writers Congress is not only a forum for airing all these concerns, but a first step toward doing something about them.

THE AMERICAN WRITERS CONGRESS
Working Agenda

October 9-12, 1981 • The Roosevelt Hotel • New York City

FRIDAY EVENING, OCTOBER 9th:
CONVOCATION

Opening Address
New York's Largest Literary Cocktail Party

SATURDAY, OCTOBER 10th:
THE ISSUES FACING WRITERS TODAY

A.M.

Keynote Panels:

- Writers and American Society in the 1980s
- Crisis in the Communications Industry

P.M.

Panels and Workshops

ACCESS TO MEDIA . . . Communications conglomerates and the blockbuster complex • Publishers and writers: where interests conflict, where they converge • Updates on the independent press, the progressive press, the labor press • The tastemakers: critics as cultural czars.

POLITICS AND AESTHETICS . . . Monoculture vs. multiculture: is there an "American" literature? • The politics of government funding cutbacks • Libel as a political weapon • Academic publishing: subsidy, ideology, and tenure • Updating Orwell: politics and the American language • Language and the visual media society: can literature survive? • The politics of literacy.

CENSORSHIP . . . National security and censorship • Local censorship: libraries, school boards, textbooks • Limits on the confidentiality of sources • The Freedom of Information Act: how to keep it and use it • The First Amendment and its boundaries.

INDIVIDUAL WRITERS . . . The writer engagé: writers as statesmen and activists • Writers and patrons: shifting sources of support • In the garret: the impact of isolation • Self-censorship: compromise or perish? • From pen to processor: writers and the new technology.

EVENING

Parties and Receptions Held by Sponsoring Organizations

SUNDAY, OCTOBER 11th:
COURSES OF ACTION

A.M.

Keynote Panel:

- What Can Writers Do?

P.M.

Panels and Workshops

SURVIVAL TACTICS . . . A writers union: problems and prospects • Health and libel insurance • How writers organize abroad • What to do if you're sued • New funding possibilities: a federal writers project, changes in tax laws, a library lending fee, a look at the Canada Council.

ALTERNATIVES TO THE MAINSTREAM . . . How to establish an authors' publishing cooperative • Self-publishing, distribution and promotion • Writing for TV and movie independents • Co-operative workspace and data services.

EVENING

Plenary Session:

Debates and Voting on All Resolutions Presented to the Congress.

MONDAY, OCTOBER 12th:
FOR THE FUTURE

A.M.

Meetings of Action Committees to Implement Decisions Taken at the Plenary Session.

 A Project of   The Nation Institute

Announcement for the American Writers Congress

Dictionary of Literary Biography

The American Writers Congress
(9-12 October 1981)

Jean W. Ross
Columbia, South Carolina

"Writers in America face a crisis. Rapidly advancing concentration in the communications industry threatens as never before to exclude and silence serious writers who are out of political or literary fashion. New writers find it more and more difficult to publish, and even established writers are subject to what novelist Mary Lou Settle has recently called 'the censorship of slow-moving books.' Government support for the arts is being slashed. Attacks on writers—libel suits, book bannings, censorship by government and special interest groups—are increasing all across the country." So began the call to the American Writers Congress held at the Roosevelt Hotel in New York City, 9-12 October 1981.

The congress, originated by the Nation Institute, a nonprofit organization associated with the *Nation* magazine, was the culmination of a year's work. The first writers' congress to convene since the 1930s, it was conceived by *Nation* editor Victor Navasky as a conference. "This matured into calling it a Writers Congress, on the theory that a congress is a forum for political action and maybe something useful could be done," Navasky told the *Village Voice*. At the invitation of an organizing committee, writers across the country formed local planning groups to articulate their concerns to its representatives. A general meeting in New York City on 12 September, a month before the scheduled congress, brought together spokesmen from many of these planning groups as well as special-interest groups that had earlier excluded themselves from the planning process. They represented a wide range of concerns, including an already well-organized effort to promote a writers' union. As Navasky

explained to *DLB*, this gathering finally addressed two problems: it created a plan designed to allot meeting space and advertising to special-interest groups within the larger framework of the congress, and it decided to end the congress with a plenary session in which delegates could vote on specific resolutions.

On 9 October, Toni Morrison, author of *Tar Baby* and an editor at Random House, opened the American Writers Congress with her keynote address to an audience far exceeding the anticipated 1,500-2,000. Noting the writer's diminishing status in the cultural life of the community, she called for organization. "The idea of the lone writer is a cherished one," Morrison said, "but that condition will keep us weak and vulnerable. Our work is not validated by our misery. We need collective power."

The aggressive tone of Morrison's speech was repeated throughout the congress as participants attended a variety of panel discussions, some organized hastily, some moved to other quarters to allow for badly needed additional space. Several panel topics reflected political concerns. "The Book Wars: Local Censorship of Language and Ideas" was organized by PEN American Center and moderated by Frances FitzGerald; "Libel as a Political Weapon" dealt with the increasing number of libel suits—many of them frivolous—against writers. One panel considered forms of censorship ranging from local banning to federal controls in the name of national security. Others confronted some of the strictly practical problems besetting writers. Prime examples were "Writers and Patrons," "Beyond the Hudson: Dealing with the Publishing Industry from Outside the Center of Gravity," and "Work-

Meridel Le Sueur and Victor Navasky at the opening of the American Writers Congress

Studs Terkel and Toni Morrison at the American Writers Congress

shop on Contracts, Taxes and Insurance." Such events as "An Evening of Solidarity with Silenced Korean Writers" reflected the interests of minority groups.

One West Coast participant wryly described the congress as 3,000 writers crying in unison. Despite the overlying political issues, the loudest and most frequently repeated cries had to do with survival in a tough marketplace. The figures generally quoted to describe the economic plight of the writer were from a survey conducted by Columbia University for the Authors' Guild Foundation. Based on responses from roughly half of the 5,000 published writers who were polled, this survey established the authors' median 1979 income from writing at $4,775, well below poverty level.

Publishers—largely not present to respond—were criticized for computerized selection of manuscripts, unfair contracts, failure to back writers sufficiently against libel suits, mismanagement in marketing and distribution, even lack of common courtesy in such matters as returning writers' telephone calls. Writers living in areas far from New York City contended that their problems with publishers were greater because of the geographical distance, though they were often contradicted by New York area writers.

Whatever their individual differences, writers at the congress were united in a sense of frustration that led them to vote overwhelmingly in the 11 October plenary session to endorse the principle of a national union. Since that vote, the Organizing Committee for a National Writer's Union has been meeting biweekly in New York, working with labor union attorney Lewis Steel to move the principle toward reality.

Work continues on other ideas raised at the congress. The executive committee of the Writers Congress is working toward an activist alliance of existing writers' groups. Other resolutions provided for committees to monitor and speak against threats to the First Amendment, including Reagan administration plans to exempt federal agencies from the Freedom of Information Act. Questions which were raised at the end of the plenary session but not clarified or acted on will be submitted to all participants in a packet now in preparation, as will a progress report from the union committee.

Shortly after the American Writers Congress was held in New York City 9-12 October 1981, *DLB* contacted a few writers to ask what they perceived as the most crucial issues facing their profession now and in the near future. We also wrote to several

Working session at the American Writers Congress

Voting on a resolution at the American Writers Congress

publishers, inviting their comments on some of the charges we heard most often during the Writers Congress: that publishing decisions are made by computer, that publishers fail to respond to authors' phone calls, that books currently being reviewed are often unavailable because of distribution breakdowns. And what about the idea of a national writers' union? Following are some of the responses from both groups.

GAY TALESE: I believe the publishers of books are not defending the written word sufficiently. We have too many lawyers in America today, and they are causing a great deal of trouble in areas where trouble would not exist if lawyers were not there to foment it. They're working on a retainer basis or getting a percentage of the take in settlements and charging enormous rates while doing so. This has brought to big business in general, and to publishing as well, a condition where lawyers are gaining increasing power to intimidate. Their power in the publishing business is offensive to writers and is a threat to the freedom of expression. As I said in one of my speeches at the Writers Congress, I think writers should get together and demand of our publishers that they will not force writers to share in

the expense of legal fees resulting from nuisance suits brought against books. Libel suits are brought against writers frequently these days when libel has *not* been committed. Even though a suit does not get to court, does not even make the newspapers, does not even warrant a serious examination, the publishers may summon a $200-an-hour lawyer to settle the case. They want to settle because it's cheaper to give a complainant ten, fifteen, twenty thousand, whatever, than to go through the whole expensive process of trying a suit. Magazine publishers and newspaper publishers defend the written word and reporters are not asked to share the legal fees. But book publishers want to settle and then stick the writer with half the bills, which are very, very high. I think that's unfair.

WALDO SALT: By far the most important aspect of the October Writers Congress was the almost literally overwhelming response to the call. The response was a clear demonstration of the need among writers to communicate, to share our anxiety, and to spread the alarm over the degenerate state of our culture. I am grateful to the *Nation* for initiating the congress. Whether the proposed writers' union would serve to unite writers or become yet another schismatic, jurisdictional teapot tempest, whether or not the panel discussion answered all the questions, seem less important to me than the fact that the questions were raised.

All over the world and throughout history writers have always been among the first victims of political persecution. During the 1947 Congressional hearing into un-American activities in Hollywood, Bertolt Brecht said to me, "In Germany, Hitler burned the books first. Here they burn the writers first; then the books take care of themselves."

The effectiveness of the Writers Congress will finally be judged by the extent to which writers—of the First, Second, or Third World—are able to survive, report, and affect the deepening moral crises of our times.

ROGER KAHN: Since the meetings, writers I've talked to seem to have special sources of rage: the de facto freezing of magazine rates for twelve inflationary years; the fact that auditing book publishers almost always turns up sales figures higher than reported; the book publishers' right of rejection which, when an editor is fired, can be sheer whimsy. Sheer though ghastly to the victim.

My own sense is a bit broader. Publishers, at least since I first experienced their contract departments in 1954, have maintained legal staffs. (Obviously they had lawyers long before that.) Writers, being poorer, have not. Thus over many decades, equity in publishing has been established by lawyers working for or representing publishers. That clearly is no equity at all.

Some salient points: publishers will commission works, reject them and demand and in many cases receive a return of the advance payment for the commission. Publishers demand a variety of warranties from the author but, except in very few cases, will not warrant size of printing, promotional, or advertising budgets. Publishers demand half of book-club rights and as much as they can get of paperback and magazine rights. Publishers try increasingly to get authors to bear all the risk of libel or privacy suits, while limiting the author to a royalty of at best 15 percent.

The ideal solution would be to throw out all such traditional "equity" and start fresh. What can happen if prosperous and hungry authors stick together in a congress or union is to chip away at this superstructure publishers and their lawyers have constructed for themselves. Practically, we could have real equity in publishing contracts within five years or at most a decade. . . .

WILLIAM TARG of Targ Editions: No, I don't think that decisions are being made by computers—not publishing decisions. But they are being made by blockhead (blockbuster obsessed) business-school graduates who don't know which side of a book is up. Marketing directors are deciding what is good to publish. The old-fashioned editor—who read manuscripts and worked closely with an author—is becoming obsolete. But most executives who call themselves editors don't know much about literature—except the best-selling titles and authors—and each one of them should be sentenced to a two-year apprenticeship in an antiquarian bookshop.

The lack of bookmanship and sensitivity to the book (the physical book, too) is a national disgrace. Amateurs are designing trade books today. The great traditions of book design and printing and binding are gone; most trade books today—despite high prices—are trash insofar as physical qualities are concerned. Knopf and Random House are among the half dozen exceptions. Atheneum is another maverick, doing well what most ignore: making good-looking and enduring books.

Countless good books are never stocked because they are not "merchandiseable." When a chain store buyer says *no* to a particular title, that means it may not appear in any of several hundred or more stores throughout the country. Censorship? Yes.

Agents and editors are getting lazy, uppity, and more and more it is not possible to reach them by phone or get replies to letters. "In conference—will call you back" is what secretaries tell authors. But the call rarely comes back. Editors read less and less, and they make decisions on the reports of their assistants or junior editors. I know of cases where a major book was declined because a "reader didn't like it." The editor didn't bother to check it out.

I think a writers' union is a constructive idea, although the agents are trying to help the authors with closer scrutiny to certain elements in contracts. I think an advertising budget should be included in all book contracts: SPACE ADVERTISING with the author's photo included! Knopf is outstanding in this respect.

DAN LACY, Senior Vice President at McGraw-Hill, Inc.: Ever since Gutenberg every unsubsidized publisher has had to base publishing decisions in large part on calculations as to whether he or she could sell enough copies at an acceptable price to meet editing, production, marketing, and administration costs. Those that generally calculated well stayed in business and published more books. Those that didn't went broke. Computers can help make those calculations more accurately and less expensively, and publishers who use them can do better by their authors. But, of course, computers do arithmetic; they do not judge the quality of manuscripts, and even the validity of their arithmetic depends on the validity of sales and costs estimates supplied them. There is still the need for sound judgment if there is to be sound publishing.

I am sure some publishers and agents are negligent in answering mail and returning calls. Authors should turn to other agents or publishers when they experience poor treatment. I suspect that the horror stories about mistreatment that can be related are all too often quite true, but I also suspect that they create so much justified resentment because they are exceptions to generally satisfactory relations. No publisher who does not deal with authors efficiently and courteously is likely to survive long.

It is unhappily true that books often are not available in bookstores when they are reviewed. But I expect that the principal reason is not a "distribution breakdown" on the publisher's part but rather that each of the thousands of bookstores in the country can stock only a tiny proportion of the more than 40,000 books published annually in the United States. Every publisher would, of course, like to have all his current trade books on the shelves of every bookstore; but the publisher does not control that decision.

As to a new authors' organization, I find it hard to conceive what can be added to the representation already given by agents and by the Authors' Guild, which has been a strong and needed voice for authors' rights and needs.

DONALD I. FINE, President of Arbor House: I really don't know what went on [at the American Writers Congress] and so do not feel it appropriate to comment on what I did not observe or hear firsthand.

I do not make generalized accusations or defenses about book publishing or book publishers or agents. I only speak for Arbor House, and its staff. In that context, the questions you raise about various criticisms are easily answered—Arbor House does not publish by computer, and respects and responds meaningfully to authors.

ASHBEL GREEN, Vice President and Senior Editor for Alfred A. Knopf, Inc.: I did not attend the American Writers Congress, so I cannot fairly comment on anything that took place there. And I can only speak to your questions in terms of my experience here. Publishing decisions at Knopf are made by editors and editorial management. I certainly respond to phone calls and to manuscripts submitted—in fact, I answer my own phone. Sometimes books are reviewed weeks or even months before publication date, and the review medium fails to inform the publisher's publicity director. As regards a writers' union, I think it ought to be asked what it could accomplish beyond the work already being carried on by the Authors' Guild.

CHARLES SCRIBNER III, Vice-President and Director, Charles Scribner's Sons:

We do not make publishing decisions by computer. Our computer can do many wonderful things, but it cannot evaluate the quality of a manuscript, whether fiction or nonfiction.

We respond to every phone call and manuscript—it's not only a matter of good publishing, but it's common courtesy.

Current books currently reviewed are almost never unavailable, except in that blessed instance when a title becomes a runaway best-seller before its publication date, in which case there may be a delay of a few days if the stores have not ordered sufficient stock.

The idea of a writers' union I leave to Hollywood. Is it productive there? If novelists would prefer union wages to royalties then perhaps the subject is worth further discussion.

See pp. 291-298 for "A Report on Continuing Business."

"Panic Among the Philistines": A Postscript
An Interview with Bryan Griffin

Jean W. Ross
Columbia, South Carolina

Bryan Griffin, an essayist and writer of short fiction, has long been a foe of literary hype. In "Panic Among the Philistines," a two-part article published in the August and September 1981 issues of *Harper's*, he writes: "It is becoming apparent that most of the well-known books of the last thirty-five years will have been swept up and forgotten by the turn of the century. They were, in large measure, the printed outgrowth of a particular and unrepeatable stage in the adolescence of a literary democracy, and that stage is beginning to pass into memory." Cheever, Updike, Styron, Roth, Oates, Capote, Mailer, and lesser-known writers come under attack in Griffin's article, as do the popular critics and reviewers who, in his opinion, have been trying to outshout each other in praise of the mediocre and even bad in contemporary writing in "an age when everything was Great precisely because nothing was very good."

Not surprisingly, Griffin's comments provoked a lively response from readers. "Panic Among the Philistines" raised questions among *DLB*'s editors; Mr. Griffin kindly agreed to answer them by mail.

DLB: Why do you set the beginning of our "suspended cultural adolescence" in the 1890s?

GRIFFIN: It seems to me that the stage was set for the first act of the "suspended cultural adolescence" in the late eighteenth century, which saw the beginnings of what the history professors like to refer to as "the loss of faith." It has been said that genuine art can arise only during ages of genuine belief (religious or otherwise), and surely there is a great deal of truth to this. (As Carlyle said in a letter to his brother, "How can we *sing* and *paint* when we do not yet *believe* and *see*?") We think of the great Victorians as men and women of great faith (and so they were, for the most part), but in fact their high moral and artistic seriousness was largely an effort to provide mankind with an alternative code—a framework and a rationale for "gentlemanly" life on earth without the certainty of God (or gods). They hoped

to show us why the Athenian virtues of beauty and truth and goodness were desirable things in and of themselves—why we should act as spiritual beings even if we were not religious beings. This effort—this "holding action"—defined the cultural life of the nineteenth century.

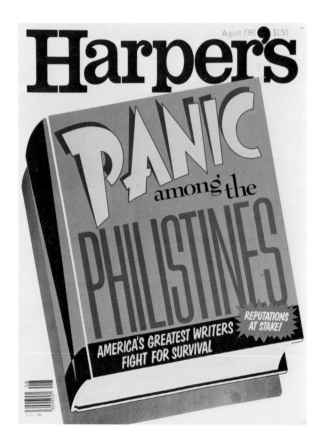

Cover for August 1981 Harper's, *featuring Griffin's indictment of contemporary literature*

But when the last of the old giants finally faded away—when first Schiller and then Goethe and Scott and then Carlyle and Emerson and Arnold (father and son) and Dickens and George Eliot and Tennyson and Gladstone and Tolstoy died—they had no intellectual or artistic heirs. They had failed to keep alive the values that had inspired and

The old giants: (top) Sir Walter Scott, Johann Wolfgang von Goethe, Thomas Arnold, Thomas Carlyle, Ralph Waldo Emerson, and Friedrich von Schiller; (bottom) Matthew Arnold, Count Leo Tolstoy, George Eliot, Charles Dickens, Alfred, Lord Tennyson, and William Ewart Gladstone

defined "art" for twenty-five centuries, and the artistic thunder—the "genuine belief," of one sort or another, that must feed a great culture—was gone. It was the supremely adolescent Oscar Wilde who ushered in the new age in 1890, when he said: "There is no such thing as a moral or an immoral book. Books are well written or badly written. That is all." It was, so to speak, an open-ended proposition.

We arrived at our present state by combining the Wildean principle with (a) the genuine cultural democracy that was part of the legacy of the first world war and (b) the collective psychological sickness—the cult of depravity—that has been the response of the artistic community to the spectre of the third and final world war.

DLB: Your criticism of certain contemporary writers often stresses the explicit sexuality of their work. Do you consider explicit sex in writing bad in and of itself?

GRIFFIN: If I seem to stress the "sex and gore" factor in contemporary Anglo-American literature, it is because contemporary litterateurs are so fond of stressing it themselves; and if I make fun of "the literary vulgarians"—writers who have never outgrown a postpubescent obsession with the mechanical aspects of human behavior, who still see the world through childhood's prism of physicality—it is only because the vulgarians take themselves, and their common obsession, so seriously.

In this context, I have frequently expressed the conviction that genuine artists do not write about explicit things, but about the implications and the consequences of explicit things. An artist (or a nonartist, for that matter) may legitimately deal with any worldly matter, but he must be greater than his world, or he is not an artist, or even a successful human. Though the subject may be corporeal and even uncomely, the artist must be beautiful, in the deepest Platonic sense of the word; and the literary exploitation of a writer's private physical fantasies, be they sweet or hideous, is not only not beautiful, it is brutalizing—to art, to love, to society, and to life.

That does not strike me as a controversial proposition; and in fact, it was not even a debatable one in any of the twenty-five centuries that built the Western cultural heritage. The easy option—the option we have chosen—was always *there*, of course: at any time in those 2,500 years, citizens in general, and artists in particular, might have chosen to shed their facades of civility and decorate their libraries

and their museums and their public squares with mechanical diagrams of the most elemental processes of digestion and reproduction and death (after all, Americans in the twentieth century don't feel anything that Mycenaeans and Victorians didn't feel). But no significant society—not even the most primitive—ever wanted to exercise that easiest of options. We must ask ourselves why not; and we must ask ourselves why the last thirty-five years have witnessed a retreat to prehistorical attitudes in such matters.

More to the point, we should ask ourselves why it is that we are so anxious to persuade ourselves that our repetitive diagrams of the elemental acts must necessarily be classified as "art" or "literature." What did literature do to deserve this bizarre burden? Why are these exercises in explicitness any closer to poetry than to, say, medicine, or animal husbandry, or plumbing, or—can we say it—pornography? What, in other words, is our rationale? We had better start thinking up a pretty good story, because our children are going to be asking some rough questions.

And so I would reverse your question, as our children will reverse it, and ask whether "explicit sexuality," or "literary physicality" of any sort, is ever good in and of itself? In other words, I think that critics and readers and editors should put the onus on the writer and insist that an "artist" who delights in violating and savaging an ancient, fundamental human feeling—in this case, the universal instinct to sanctify the procedures of birth and love and death by respecting their supremely private nature—be required to justify his or her savagery. For example: I recently read and enjoyed a very witty review by James Wolcott in which he properly criticized an exhibitionistic new novel (by John Irving) for its "sewer-happy grubbiness," but was careful to assure his readers that "obscenity and toilet humor don't usually bother me." Our question to such reviewers ought to be: "Why on earth not?" "Obscenity"—which we may define as that which is repulsive or loathsome to the senses—"usually bothers" all healthy, whole-souled men and women, and has done so since the beginning of recorded history; if it does not "usually bother" us as novelists and critics and editors, are we not *less* healthy and smaller souled than other men and women? And if we are lesser souls, what have we to do with art, or art with us? Can we be proud of the fact that Americans born after 1940 have learned to recognize as "art" anything that is just a bit more prurient, a bit more regressive, and a little less subtle than the rest of their nightmarish world? Is that really the reputation we wanted? And if so, why?

The novelist Sloan Wilson gave an interview a few years ago in which he spoke quite eloquently about the basic human sentiments. He said that he shared "the mystical feeling toward sexuality." "You can't handle it explicitly in your private life," he said, "and I don't think you can as an artist. If, in your private life, you became clinical with your spouse, it would all disappear. It is certainly an enormously powerful force in all our lives, but when you become clinical in writing about it, it becomes, among other things, ludicrous." Writers who cannot share that universal understanding, who cannot see the delicate beauty in the consummation of love (and the pity in the consummation of lust)—who are still, as so many of them would phrase it, "sexually hung up" on the mechanics of the thing—are ignorant of the deepest emotions of human life and should quit the literary arenas and take up more congenial work. As artists—as men and women of feeling—they are fakes. I await the exception that will prove the rule.

DLB: Do you think subsidies have generally helped or hindered the production of good literature?

GRIFFIN: I have no terribly strong views on this issue. If we may judge by the record of recent years and by the example of other countries, it seems clear that subsidized art is no more or less mediocre than unsubsidized art. Certainly history is full of examples of serious writers who were helped by a little extra money (in our own century, Forster enjoyed a small private income, Eliot was supported for a time by well-meaning friends, etc.); but there is also much truth in the old cliche that an exceptional artist is going to say what he or she has to say with or without financial encouragement (again, Carlyle comes to mind, as an example of a writer who refused to accept help even in his poverty). It seems to me that the crucial factor in all this is not the quantity of the art (there are so few worthy artists in any generation) but the quality of the benefactor. A patron may be a friend or the president of a corporation or a parent or a publisher or a descendant of the Medici, but unless that patron has a distinct artistic vision of his own and knows what he wants for his money—and no government agency in an unfinished democracy can possess such a vision—the whole exercise becomes a game of chance. In any game of chance, there are more losers than winners. But if citizens wish to subsidize a thousand losers (many of whom may be dreary and dangerous to art and life) in order to smooth the way for a

single genuine artist (who may or may not appear), surely that is their privilege.

However, I do feel strongly about the larger economic issue, i.e., the infusion of vast sums of corporate money into the various artistic arenas. When we turn literature into a business like any other we disenfranchise the real readers, the quiet men and women who really care about genuine books and ideas. Many of the writers and publishers and critics and editors who are responsible for our present sad state would stop tormenting us tomorrow if the financial rewards of their involvement were drastically reduced.

DLB: You mention very briefly in your article the names of several writers whose work you admire—among them J. I. M. Stewart, Gabriel Fielding, Evelyn Page, and Gerald Warner Brace. With the possible exception of Stewart (for his mysteries written under the pseudonym Michael Innes), these people are not well known even among quite literate readers. What do they have that makes them deserving of current and lasting literary recognition? Are there any better-known writers you like?

GRIFFIN: It is true that J. I. M. Stewart is known to American readers only for "his mysteries written under the pseudonym Michael Innes," and that is precisely the point I wished to make. Stewart is seventy-six years old. He has been Reader in English Literature at the University of Oxford for twelve years and Student of Christ Church for twenty-three years; he has taught at the University of Leeds in England, at Queen's University in Ireland, and at the University of Adelaide in Australia. He wrote the essay on modern English literature for a recent edition of the *Encyclopaedia Britannica*, and he is the author of the final volume (*Eight Modern Writers*) in the monumental *Oxford History of English Literature*. He is the author of *Character and Motive in Shakespeare*, he has written brilliant biographies of Kipling, Conrad, and Hardy, he edited the Nonesuch Edition of Florio's *Montaigne*, he writes frequently for the *Times Literary Supplement* and other publications, and last but not least, he is the author of fifteen novels (and two short story collections) under his own name. His fiction has been praised in extravagant terms by some of the worthiest writers of the past half-century. By any rational standard, Stewart must figure as one of the most accomplished men of letters of his time. And how is he treated in the largest English-speaking nation on earth? Well, some of us have discovered the pseudonymous detective tales he writes in his spare time. Which is precisely what I had in mind when I reprimanded the American literary authorities for neglecting—nay, obstructing—quiet, well-intentioned writers who had something "grown-up" to say.

Our shame is that we lavish our attention on the most recent "erotic epic" and reject the careful, consistent work of decent, intelligent twentieth-century men and women of dignity and compassion and learning. Everything that I say of Stewart could be said of the other people on my list, some of whom have had even more distinguished careers and some of whom have written things of rare beauty and uncommon insight. We need these people—these serious, thoughtful people—as we have never needed them before, and we aren't given the opportunity to listen to them.

In this context, it is interesting to note that when Morris Philipson of the University of Chicago Press saw the list you refer to, his reaction was to suggest that it was time to prepare reprints of good novels by the authors on that list (and this is now being done). His reaction was in striking contrast to the trepidation expressed by representatives of the former literary establishment, many of whom said, in effect, that (a) they'd never read any books by the writers on Griffin's list, so (b) books by writers on Griffin's list couldn't possibly be worth reading. (For example, a columnist at the *San Francisco Examiner* was annoyed by the implication that the writers on the list were "the *real* writers," and a columnist for the *Village Voice* unashamedly attacked the writers he hadn't heard of on the grounds that they were "obscure," and hadn't been "blessed with success.") It is this fan magazine mentality—this "a writer isn't a writer until we've all seen him singing with Mike Douglas on television" mentality—that did so much to wreck the reputation of the American literary community in the first place. And if the community is ever to experience an intellectual renaissance, its various representatives are going to have to start cultivating the attitude of Morris Philipson, which is the attitude of the genuine reader. In other words, the kids are going to have to start looking for—and reading—books again, instead of sales figures and publicity handouts. They are going to have to turn down the televisions and the radios and the stereos and rediscover the libraries and the secondhand-book shops, and the people in the libraries and the shops. They are going to have to rediscover the sort of people who know who J. I. M. Stewart is, and the people who would *like* to know who he is: the people who respond to a new name—or a new idea—with inter-

est and hope rather than with fear and hatred.

Are there any better-known writers I like? Well, I thought that some of the writers on my list—Gerald Warner Brace, for instance, or Gabriel Fielding—*were* fairly well known (though I confess that I did not learn of Brace's death until after I'd composed the passage). I could list twenty other names, but I suspect that all would be equally obscure. I can think of dozens of perfectly *literate* writers—even John Updike can put words together prettily—but I am always being disappointed by their books. Which is to say that I could point to lots of very good books written by famous living writers who later succumbed to prevailing winds and went on to write not-so-good books (Angus Wilson has written some good novels, and so have Graham Greene and William Golding and Iris Murdoch and Gore Vidal and Piers Paul Read and many others); but I cannot think of many active, well-known writers who seem to possess a large, commanding vision of life or behavior that shines through all their work so that one can say, "Here is a man or woman who wants to show us something good that he or she has seen" (if there were many such writers alive today, I would not have needed to write my bad-tempered articles). I cannot even think of many very well-known writers who are capable of producing civilized entertainment (as opposed to enlightenment) without savagery. Our well-known writers specialize in mood rather than intellectual, psychological, or spiritual revelation; and the truth, I suppose, is that good books by confused men and women are only accidentally good: they give us a false, momentary impression of force and purpose where none exists.

But certainly Graham Greene and John Le Carre are eminently "readable" (and occasionally provocative), and I still read them. I like Louis Auchincloss, with occasional reservations. I like some of William Trevor's short stories. And I am enthusiastic about Mary Renault, if only because she offers (in the words of the *Washington Post* critic Rita Mae Brown) "a profound commentary on the emotional shabbiness of 20th-century life." Her earlier "contemporary" novels (from the 1930s, 1940s, and 1950s) should be reprinted.

DLB: Are there critics or reviewers whose opinions you respect?

GRIFFIN: In an era of mass literacy, I am unenthusiastic about reviewers who are merely talented phrase makers, or worshippers of other phrase makers. My greatest respect is reserved for writers

Neglected moderns: (top left) Gabriel Fielding, (bottom left)
Gerald Warner Brace, and (above) J. I. M. Stewart

who are philosophers in the Athenian sense; which is to say that I respect citizens who employ language as a means of revealing and honoring their separate understandings of the highest human and social purposes—citizens who are completed humans first and writers second. Accordingly, I admire many essayists and columnists and journalists and writers of general nonfiction who occasionally turn their attention to books (George Will and Meg Greenfield of *Newsweek*, the English critic Martin Green, Malcolm Muggeridge, Lewis Lapham, the biographer Frances Donaldson, Joseph Sobran and Ellen Wilson of the *National Review*, Judith Martin of the *Washington Post*, to name a few at random), but not many professional book reviewers.

James Wolcott of *Esquire* is an independent thinker. I think he could be even more effective if he would stop being so frightened of his moralistic instincts (we could use a few intelligent moralists). Jonathan Yardley of the *Washington Post* dislikes my own writing (which he has described as "arrogant" and "singularly irritating"), but I like his because he is an enemy of cant and back scratching in the literary fraternity, and because he is a fount of common sense. He deserved his Pulitzer. Gore Vidal has also wielded a sharp critical razor in his time. The tragedy of Vidal's criticism is the tragedy of his fiction: he recognizes the symptoms of the contemporary literary disease in others—and perhaps in himself—but he is ignorant, or distrustful, of the only known treatments. I have great (and increasing) respect for Jack Beatty of the *New Republic* because I believe he sees the truth clearly, and tells it, and because he is a good writer to boot. And of course I always read John Simon if only because he has, as he himself once wrote, "endeavored to remain absolutely independent in [his] criticism, recognizing no call of coterie, friendship, pity, or established reputation."

I should also note that there are particular literary periodicals that appeal to my iconoclastic tendencies. The criticism in R. Emmett Tyrrell's *American Spectator* is almost always fresh and intelligent and unorthodox, and I like to write for that magazine because I like the literary company. The occasional reviews in the new national version of the *Yale Literary Magazine* have real weight to them and seem to echo the aesthetic judgments of the past and (we must assume) the future (I suppose it's only proper to note that I have recently joined the magazine's advisory committee, but obviously my admiration precedes my involvement). I often feel that I have come home when I read the reviews in the *New Republic*, and, as you might guess, I find

much that is worth reading in *Harper's*.

But having said all that, I must say that I don't know of a literary critic who shares my fury. My aim—not to put too fine a point on it—is to do my bit to smash the intellectual *context* within which we have been thinking and writing and publishing for thirty-five years. If there are critics and reviewers who share that purpose, I have yet to see their work. Granted, the literary winds are shifting, and many critics are adopting a more rigorous tone, which is all to the good. I like more and more of what I am reading these days, but I am suspicious: I can't help remembering that these are the same people who helped to create the literary monster in the first place. One recent novel (by John Irving) has been properly savaged by publications—*Newsweek*, *Esquire*, the *Washington Post*, even the *Nation*—who were seen swooning over the same brew (*Garp*) a couple of years ago. And when the authorities at the *Washington Post* refer to John Updike's latest novel as "pornography," are they forgetting that they once honored Mr. Updike as "America's finest novelist"? What's going on here? Do our literary mandarins mean what they say now, or did they mean what they said then? Do they ever mean anything, or are they merely eager to hitch a ride on the latest trend?

DLB: In analyzing our literary state, you blame writers, publishers, critics, teachers, and the larger reading public. They form a chain; where can it be broken? Given the marketplace conditions under which they labor, can publishers realistically be expected to change their means of choosing what they will publish?

GRIFFIN: No. On the contrary, in our lifetimes there will always be more people who want to sell or read *Beyond Jogging* than there will be people who want to sell or read Dante. It has always been so—though, as your question implies, the collapse of the old class systems and the gradual emergence of true economic (and therefore cultural) democracy has made the problem more acute. Whatever their economic and ethical faults, the old class divisions ensured that there would always be a genuine cultural "elite," a small but fairly stable class of wealthy, educated citizens who could and did preserve the cultural heritage of the West in their schools, their thought, their behavior, and their art.

But if the patrons and the sponsors are gone, the *audience* for real books and real ideas is still out there, and it is potentially huge. Its members can be discovered in the libraries and in the used-book shops and hovering over the remainder tables (where one finds the good books that were so impossible to find—or even hear of—when they were new). The audience exists, but it has been disenfranchised and brutalized and humiliated for so many years that its members have become furtive, afraid to stand up and declare themselves. The task, in my view, is to rally these quiet people, to encourage them to reassert themselves *as* an audience, or, if you will, as a "market." Until the literary democracy reaches its ideal state—which is to say, until a large majority of men and women are educated, responsible citizens, in the Athenian sense—the audience for real books and ideas cannot be the dominant audience in terms of numbers or buying power. But such an audience can pack enough of an economic punch to exert an influence on the sales charts—to get equal time for itself and its interests.

Authors can help by refusing to write for shabby publications (it ought to be a source of shame to us that "serious" writers like Cheever and Greene write primarily for pornographic magazines such as *Playboy* and *Rogue*) and by giving their books to editors and independent publishers of proven integrity. Publishers can help by reassuming their responsibility for the contents of books that appear on their lists. Critics can help by paying attention to what they genuinely admire—in books and in humans—and by refusing to participate in the literary riot of the moment. A determined "literary aristocracy" can support publishers and magazines and authors of integrity and civility and good intention, and in time it can re-establish itself as a cultural—if not an economic—directorate.

Such an "aristocracy" need not become isolated and ingrown and self-congratulatory (as have certain literary cliques of our own day) any more than the students at the Platonic academies became isolated from Greek life. Genuine culture is, after all, the one universal language simply because it survives by tapping the deepest human feelings and aspirations; and an elite that remains true to those feelings and aspirations—that remains true to its cultural heritage—can never become socially or intellectually narcissistic. Our present difficulties have come about not because contemporary art is being created for the common man in the street— there is nothing wrong with popular art—but because contemporary art is being created *by* the common man, by the nonartist. Given half a chance, and a little encouragement from the uncommon men and women (in this context, the artists), the vast majority of free souls will value the good and the true, and reject the charlatans.

Numbers, after all, aren't everything. How many humans ever heard Pericles speak? How many souls spoke with Socrates? What proportion of the population in 1643 was in a position to read Sir Thomas Browne's *Religio Medici*, let alone purchase it? How many Victorians read Carlyle? And yet Pericles and Socrates and Browne and Carlyle and their peers made us what we are today. "Moral, aesthetic, spiritual and intellectual splendor" can triumph over current marketplace conditions just as those same qualities triumphed over Sparta and Hemlock and war and poverty and the industrial revolution. The history of mankind is the history of that triumph.

DLB: Why do you hold out the hope that the "cultural minority" will someday become the "literary majority"? What signs of change do you see?

GRIFFIN: It's an ancient battle—between those who would celebrate and extend the values of civilization and those who would fill their own pockets (actual and psychological) by savaging those values—and I can't believe that it will be won or lost in our lifetimes (unless our lifetimes are the last human lifetimes, in which case we've lost). Still, we may draw hope from the knowledge that the battle is once again being fought. I need only look at my own mail to know that: hundreds of letters from quiet readers and writers and editors (and even a few reviewers, I'm delighted, and astonished, to note) who invariably begin by saying, "I thought I was all alone," or "I've never written to a magazine before," or "I thought there must be something wrong with *me*." In greater and greater numbers, readers are beginning to realize that it's safe for them to get up and start acting as human beings again. What I find most encouraging about these letters (and I am not the only writer who receives them) is that so many of them come from younger scholars and writers and publishing officials. By the same token, it is worth noting that many of the most exciting new publications (some of which I referred to earlier) are edited and written by very young people. This is not an accident. The long-overdue literary rebellion—and there is no better phrase to describe it—is in large measure a rebellion of youth.

There is a healthy element of anger—even savagery—in the movement. The anger proceeds, I think, from a profound sense of betrayal. It is important to remember that those of us who are under the age of, say, forty, were born into the literary squalor. The members of the younger generations are the walking wounded, so to speak. They were raised on the sickly fantasies of which I have spoken: their tutors poured the brew down their throats in the schools and the universities, and the children actually tried to base their dreams and their lives on the ugly diet (alas, you've only to look at some of us to see that). And then the cultural authorities wondered why so many of their young charges were less than eager to spread the Western gospel in Southeast Asia (it is one thing for Alcibiades to suffer for the code of Athens, but it is another thing to give up an arm or a life in order to make the world safe for the democratic social visions of John Updike). The point is that cultural failure is also social failure. We know now what the postwar literati did to us and to the fabric of the only civilization we've got: our "artists" failed us just when we—and by "we" I mean humanity in this century—needed them most desperately, and we bear a legitimate grudge against them. A society that represents the culmination of 2,500 years of culture should have been able to feed its children on something better than Norman Mailer. And the society ought not to be too surprised when the recipients of such a diet finally begin to regurgitate with unusual force, even savagery.

In other words, we must place our trust in and draw our hope from the essential nature of humanity. Mankind will not forever suffer an artistic regime that despises and oppresses life itself, and a century is a very long time. Something fundamental in us rebels after a while. In the end, I suppose, it is one more case of hunger: our souls are starved, and we will feed them, whether the representatives of the old guard like it or not. When we realize that, we begin to hope.

Updated Entries

John Ashbery

John Ashbery

(28 July 1927-   )

Dana Yeaton
Middlebury, Vermont

See also the Ashbery entry in *DLB 5, American Poets Since World War II*.

NEW BOOK: *Shadow Train* (New York: Viking, 1981).

John Ashbery's poetry has always presented a challenge, and in *As We Know*, published in November 1979, that challenge was clearly stated in the author's note to the first poem: "The two columns of 'Litany' are meant to be read as simultaneous but independent monologues." What follows is a poem of over 3,000 lines which is both more elusive and more accessible than anything Ashbery has offered his readers to date. The critical reaction to *As We Know* confirms what many have suspected since 1976, when the poet won three major awards—a Pulitzer Prize, a National Book Award, and a National Book Critics Circle Award—for *Self-Portrait in a Convex Mirror*: that is, if John Ashbery is not the most important, innovative, and provocative living American poet, he is at least the most controversial.

Ashbery's earliest and most influential supporter, Harold Bloom, found the two columns of "Litany" bewildering and preferred to think of them as separate poems, reflecting two parts of the same psyche, with the right-hand column "much the better" of the two. Helen Vendler, who has only recently begun "Understanding Ashbery" (the title of her 16 March 1981 *New Yorker* article), found "Litany" "a somewhat trying imitation of the bicameral mind." Both critics agreed with Peter Stitt of the *Georgia Review* in preferring the short poems which comprise part 2 of *As We Know*, though neither seemed as frustrated by part 1 as Stitt, who wrote that "in 'Litany,' arbitrariness and absurdity are established and demonstrated at the very start, but we still have sixty-five pages to go, sixty-five pages of arbitrary nonconversation conducted by two characters who seem to speak neither to one another nor to us. A disheartening prospect."

In short, none of these critics seemed to believe Ashbery when he called the monologues "simultaneous but independent." Though it may be natural to look for formal relationships between the two columns, the purpose of Ashbery's note is to discourage this tendency. The confusion which results from trying to find such links can be seen in the praise of "Litany" as well as in the criticism. Following the 1981 publication of *As We Know* in the United Kingdom (where Ashbery's popularity has recently soared), Helen McNeil of the *Times Literary Supplement* called "Litany" a "magnificent long poem" with which "Only late Wallace Stevens and the Auden of 'In Praise of Limestone' can stand comparison. . . ," but she also treated the two columns as the voices of two characters in a dialogue. Borrowing a premise put forth by David Bromwich in the *New York Times Book Review*—a premise which Ashbery has called "completely false"—she named the left column "Brass" and the right "Silver." As Ashbery explained to interviewer Piotr Sommer during a reading tour of Poland in the spring of 1980, Bromwich used "a short fragment from my poem 'Litany' which talked about living in different ages, the Golden Age, the Silver Age, the Bronze Age, etc., and he decided that that was the *topic* of the book. He was able to deal with it, perfectly satisfactorily from his own point of view; it just happens that it's not true that this is the subject of the book. It's one of the many subjects which appears briefly and then is replaced by something else."

Though it is probably often true that criticism reveals more about the critics than the text, it is no coincidence that this is so often the case with Ashbery's work. Composed, as he says, "of what the day provides," his poems become grab bags of postures, attitudes, and possibilities. In the past, Ashbery's hospitable mind, "taking in everything like boarders," has been generous with his critics, and the fact that such an unopinionated person has raised such controversy remains the central paradox of his career. When "Litany" first appeared, Ashbery recalls, he felt "a little apprehensive and sort of embarrassed about annoying the same critics who are always annoyed by my work. I'm kind of sorry that I cause so much grief." His art criticism, appearing most recently in *Newsweek* and *New York*, is a lesson in the compassionate, humanistic criticism he calls for in "Litany." As a critic Ashbery avoids both the cutting wit and cloudy jargon which often appears in art reviews. And his perennial suspicion of the avant-garde should give his critics pause before they dismiss his work as the latest in literary fashion. "Confronted with a cord stretched taut between the ceiling and floor of a gallery," he assured readers of *New York* in 1978, "I tend to step around it, rather than reexamine my conception of 'space.' "

Yet Ashbery *is* a poet of the avant-garde, who as Helen McNeil pointed out, "experiments in order to live, breaking traditional forms as a prerequisite for knowledge." Keith Cohen described this tendency in "Ashbery's Dismantling of Bourgeois Discourse" (one of the many persuasive essays in David Lehman's *Beyond Amazement*, 1980) as "a frontal attack on the fundamental props of bourgeois discourse—continuity, utility, and closure." But Ashbery claims only that he experiments because "I'm always trying not to repeat myself."

In his new book, *Shadow Train* (1981), Ashbery has "not repeated" himself by writing fifty poems, each of sixteen lines. The book is a departure both because in the past Ashbery has scarcely produced two, much less fifty, poems of equal length and because it does not include the one long poem characteristic of earlier books. Ashbery explained, "Since I'm known for writing very long ones, I thought I'd just see what it's like if I don't. It's as simple as that really."

But Ashbery knows that "Nothing is very simple." Habitually on the lookout for "Paradoxes and Oxymorons" (*Shadow Train*'s original title), he is fascinated by the inconsistencies and contradictions in systematic knowledge. The false premise from which one infers true conclusions, the "deeper outside" things—these are the cracks in language which he continuously stalks, and which provide the fireworks in his verse. The title poem from *Shadow Train* begins with "smooth violence," the oxymoron which sets the poem in motion:

> Violence, how smoothly it came
> And smoothly took you with it
> To wanting what you nonetheless did not
>   want.
> It's all over if we don't see the truth inside that
>   meaning.
>
> To want is to be better than before. To desire
>   what is
> Forbidden is permitted.

Here, as the paradox of "wanting what you nonetheless did not want," turns into the mock aphorism, "To want is to be better than before,"

John Ashbery

Ashbery is taking his customary steps both toward and away from assertion. Again with "To desire what is / Forbidden is permitted," he uses the syntax of an ethical pronouncement to make a simple declarative statement. Some may be frustrated by this playfulness, reading it as a sign of indifference, of the hedonism in contemporary art which Ashbery has come to represent in poetry. As always, Ashbery runs the risk that even those who enjoy his "mild effects" will at some point feel the butt of his joke: toying with the structures of language, he cannot always avoid making the reader feel that he too is being toyed with.

As slippery and equivocal as Ashbery can be, his reluctance to stake out and hold a position should not be taken for a lack of one. He is committed to the idea that "a poem which is in effect a sermon, telling one how to behave correctly, is a kind of veiled insult to the reader; it's preaching to the converted. Because I believe that most readers of poetry are not likely to turn out to be Richard Nixon or Henry Kissinger, or people who need to have their viewpoint corrected so that they can behave in a more wholesome way." The inconclusiveness of Ashbery's verse is not due to a lack of conviction but to an instinctive distrust of anything certain. For him poetry is an investigation, and every statement a conjecture which must be interrogated, and perhaps discarded, leaving readers often with more questions than answers. Ashbery would not disagree and might be complimented by Peter Stitt's complaint that in "Litany," "the reader feels lost in the middle of a world he cannot quite comprehend." Ashbery sees understanding as "a sort of Penelope's web that's constantly being taken apart when it's almost completed, and that's the way we grow in our knowledge and experience." Similarly, Ashbery's poems have a way of coming apart just when the reader feels on the verge of mastering them. The intent is not to lose the reader and gain advantage because, the poet says, "I'm quite puzzled by my work too."

The impossibility of completely mastering any text has long been the subject of Ashbery's work, and the scope alone of his longer poems has kept most critics from trying. But *Shadow Train* has presented a special temptation. Never has Ashbery produced a book of poems which *look* so easily tamed. Already Helen Vendler has tried her hand at explicating one of these brief poems and not without some encouragement from Ashbery himself. "Paradoxes and Oxymorons," for example, begins and ends with assurances to confused readers:

> This poem is concerned with language on a
> very plain level.
> Look at it talking to you. You look out a win-
> dow
> Or pretend to fidget. You have it but you
> don't have it.
> You miss it, it misses you. You miss each
> other.
>
> The poem is sad because it wants to be yours,
> and cannot.
> What's a plain level? It is that and other
> things,
> Bringing a system of them into play. Play?
> Well, actually, yes, but I consider play to be
>
> A deeper outside thing, a dreamed role-
> pattern,
> As in the division of grace these long August
> days
> Without proof. Open-ended. And before you
> know
> It gets lost in the steam and chatter of type-
> writers.
>
> It has been played once more. I think you
> exist only

> To tease me into doing it, on your level, and
> then you aren't there
> Or have adopted a different attitude. And the
> poem
> Has set me softly down beside you. The poem
> is you.

Yet Ashbery's message is not as simple or consoling as the impression it leaves. "What's a plain level?," he asks, as if to call his own bluff. How can the poem set him "softly down beside you," when "you aren't there / Or have adopted a different attitude?" Still, "Paradoxes and Oxymorons" is one of the more accessible poems in this collection, and it shows Ashbery's method at its most transparent and, consequently, the poet at his weakest. Most of his poems, he admits, are written "all at once, at one sitting, and pretty fast." Though he used to rework them extensively, he claims, "I somehow trained myself not to write something that I'm going to have to revise a great deal." For Ashbery then, each poem is a performance which must go on, incorporating its mistakes and contradictions, revising itself as it proceeds. At times in *Shadow Train* Ashbery's ability to connect disparate images—making non sequiturs seem to follow from each other—becomes strained and the writing automatic. Occasionally the confusion appears to exist for its own sake.

But these are small reservations in the face of Ashbery's enormous accomplishment. With each achievement his reputation for innovation increases. Since *Shadow Train* appeared he has reaffirmed his commitment to experimentation by producing "Description of a Masque," a prose piece of twelve typescript pages which takes its name and subject from a seventeenth-century text by Thomas Campion. At least two other prose pieces will appear in the next book, along with a poem written in rhymed couplets. Even in his twentieth book, John Ashbery seems to have found a new way not to repeat himself.

Periodical Publications:
"Picasso: The Art," *New York*, 13 (12 May 1980): 28-31;
Introduction to "A Folio Of Poets Chosen By John Ashbery," *American Poetry Review*, 10 (March/April 1981): 28.

References:
David Lehman, ed., *Beyond Amazement: New Essays on John Ashbery* (Ithaca & London: Cornell University Press, 1980);
Piotr Sommer, "John Ashbery in Warsaw: America's most celebrated living poet talks to his translator," *Quarto*, no. 17 (May 1981): 13-15.

William S. Burroughs

(5 February 1914-   )

Robert E. Burkholder

Pennsylvania State University, Wilkes-Barre

See also the Burroughs entries in *DLB 2, American Novelists Since World War II* and *DLB 8, Twentieth-Century American Science-Fiction Writers*.

NEW BOOK: *Cities of the Red Night* (London: Calder, 1980; New York: Holt, Rinehart & Winston, 1981).

"A good rule is never ask the general public to experience anything they cannot easily experience. You don't want to scare them to death, knock them out of their seats, and above all, you don't want to puzzle them," said William S. Burroughs recently. But despite this statement, Burroughs continues to confound and terrorize his audience with his fantastic, violent vision of the world and his experimental fictional techniques. Now approaching the age of seventy, Burroughs has managed to maintain the cutting edge in his work by refusing to compromise on either his message or the way he chooses to present it. The proof of this statement is in Burroughs's latest novel, *Cities of the Red Night* (1980). Although it may have more plot than the plotless *Naked Lunch* (1959), *Cities of the Red Night* relies upon the same montage technique and the same theme of escape from the forces of control that distinguishes that earlier work.

Perhaps because of this similarity and its function as a symbol of Burroughs's unwillingness to change despite past criticism, the critics continue to attack or dismiss his work. While Rob Schmieder in *Library Journal* claims that *Cities of the Red Night* represents "some of Burroughs' most impassioned and accessible writing," the majority of critics find it to be a work of little merit. Most severe is Thomas M. Disch, who in the *New York Times Book Review* dubs *Cities of the Red Night* an "anemic clone" of *Naked Lunch*. Disch claims that the novel's appeal is limited to opium addicts and homosexuals with hanging fetishes, and he indicts Burroughs's entire career on the basis of his view that Burroughs's work is amoral and without art: "Forget morality! Forget art! What Mr. Burroughs offered the rubes back in 1959 and what he offers them today, in somewhat wearier condition, is entrance to a sideshow where they can

view his curious id capering and making faces and confessing to bizarre inclinations." In *Atlantic,* Phoebe-Lou Adams admits that in *Cities of the Red Night* "Mr. Burroughs writes single scenes brilliantly," but she qualifies her praise by concluding that the novel "requires a high tolerance for bloodshed, black magic, and buggery."

Writing in the *New Republic,* Julia M. Klein seems most dismayed that Burroughs "teases us" with two intertwined coherent narratives in the first half of *Cities of the Red Night* and then forsakes all sequence about halfway through the book. She concludes, "Maybe intelligibility is too much to expect of the author of such wildly disordered works as *Naked Lunch* and *Nova Express*." But despite Klein's observation that *Cities of the Red Night* is as "wildly disordered" as the rest of Burroughs's work, she softens her criticism by expressing something akin to pity for Burroughs, whom she views as a tortured and misunderstood writer: "his fictional world is never recognizably our own, even at its war crazed worst. The demons he depicts in novel after novel seem to be his personal tormentors. Burroughs's prose is pungent, lyrical, abrasive, but the vision it projects remains irretrievably a private one." Klein is perhaps correct in assuming that Burroughs's vision in *Cities of the Red Night* is "a private one," but it is intended as a private vision for *all* of his readers, to be interpreted by each in a singularly personal way. Such freedom from the control of the traditional concepts of plot, setting, and character has been Burroughs's goal since the mid-1950s, and there is little reason to believe that he is turning his back on that goal now.

Because Burroughs is so concerned with control of the individual in the modern world and the concomitant loss of freedom, at the beginning of *Cities of the Red Night* he returns to the time when that freedom was lost. As in his earlier work, Burroughs demonstrates his fascination with outlaws by telling the story of the pirate Captain Mission, which he has taken from Don C. Seitz's *Under the Black Flag* (1925). According to Burroughs, Mission, who lived in the latter half of the seventeenth century, was the progenitor of "The liberal principles embodied in the French and American revolutions and later in the liberal revolutions of 1848." Mission codified these principles when he founded a republic called Libertatia on the coast of Madagascar. Included in the articles he drew up for the governance of his colony were the ideas that all governing decisions were to be placed in the hands of the colonists, that slavery and the death penalty were to be abolished, and that religious freedom would exist without sanction or molestation. However, the colony and its ideals were wiped out in a surprise attack by natives, and according to Burroughs, "Your right to live where you want, with companions of your choosing, under laws to which you agree, died in the eighteenth century with Captain Mission. Only a miracle or a disaster could restore it."

Since the publication of *Naked Lunch,* Burroughs has been indicted for failing to provide some rational context or background which might add perspective to the wild, science-fiction-like imaginings and random selection of image blocks that are the mainstay of his aesthetic philosophy, a philosophy at least partially justified by his notion that we need to escape the constructs of Aristotelian logic and the declarative sentence to free ourselves from the false reality and authorial control that traditional fiction has always presented. The reader must grapple, sometimes in vain, with the paradox that Burroughs represents. Surely, even in the randomness of Burroughs's structure and certainly in his very dependence upon language as a tool for communication, he is asserting some control over

William S. Burroughs

the minds of his audience. This paradox is, unfortunately, a problem with which Burroughs does not deal.

However, in supplying both an underlying concept that binds the novel together and some straightforward narrative, Burroughs seems to be saying to his critics that even with such conventional devices the "reality" of his fiction is just as false or difficult to perceive, the identity of the characters is just as fluid, and the book is ultimately as far beyond understanding in the traditional sense as *Naked Lunch, The Soft Machine* (1961), *The Ticket That Exploded* (1962), and *Nova Express* (1964). In fact, it is apparent that Burroughs wants us to understand his work in a more basic way than we understand traditional fiction in which we are asked to "see" the events of the novel and to consciously accept the order of reality the author has created for us. In Burroughs's work this order is usually lacking, and the reader is required to sense the reality, at an almost unconscious level, which is more often than not created in terms that de-emphasize the sense of sight and emphasize the sense of smell—the odor of ozone associated by Burroughs with time travel or the stench of the decaying bodies of people who have died from an uncontrollable disease—and the tactile sense—which is most important in the numerous scenes describing hangings and the ac-

companying autoejaculation or in descriptions of various types of homoeroticism. To Burroughs the senses of touch and smell are a way of creating a different perspective on fictional reality for his reader.

Another problem in understanding *Cities of the Red Night*, and all of Burroughs's work for that matter, is the paradox that while he is essentially pessimistic about existence in the modern world, he is at heart an optimist and an idealist. The very act of creating a canon that attempts to free the mind of the reader from the control of logic and accepted order is inherently an optimistic act, and Burroughs's ideal is clearly delineated in the tale of Captain Mission which begins *Cities of the Red Night*. Juxtaposed with this ideal, at least for the first half of the novel, are the narratives of Noah Blake, an eighteenth-century gunsmith, and Clem Snide, the "private asshole" who figures prominently in *Exterminator!* (1973). The Blake narrative is the first-person tale of how Blake and a group of friends sign on as deckhands on *The Great White*, captained by the somewhat forbidding Opium Jones. They are eventually shanghaied by pirates and taken to Port Roger on the coast of Panama, where they are enlisted in the cause of some pirate partisans led by Captain Nordenholz. It is soon clear that the cause is really the same as Captain Mission's (there

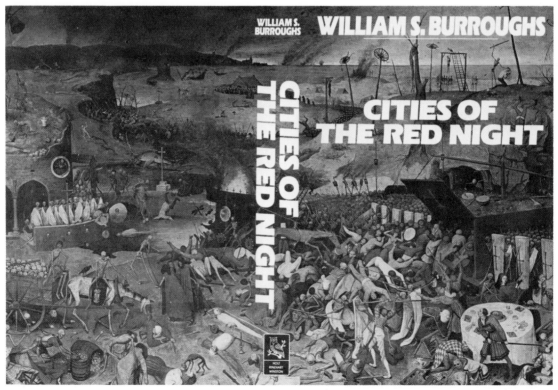

Dust jacket for the American edition of Burroughs's "vision of apocalypse"

is the suggestion that Blake and his friends were openly scorned in the American colonies because of their homosexuality, something that would be impossible under Mission's articles), and Blake contributes to that cause by inventing a cartridge gun and an exploding cannonball. Armed with these advanced weapons, the partisans become involved in a guerrilla war with the forces of control, which in this narrative are represented by Spain, seeking to add to its colonial empire.

Interspersed with this narrative, so that one chronological plot is constantly interrupted by another, is the story of Clem Snide, a twentieth-century detective, who is hired by a wealthy family to locate their lost son. Snide's search leads him and his assistant, Jimmy Lee, to the Greek islands, Mexico City, and finally Lima, Peru. Snide follows a trail of decapitated bodies and the strong odor given off by victims of a strange red virus, which causes a fiery red rash around the genitals of its sufferers, who ultimately die in a sexual frenzy. This trail leads Snide to a group of men who want to find certain picture books which once belonged to Captain Mission. Snide accepts a check for $200,000 to find these lost books, although he believes the money is actually to be spent on producing forgeries. So Snide becomes an artist of sorts, writing scripts and producing pornographic films and books.

Even though they are ostensibly separated in time by nearly 300 years, there have been from the beginning subtle suggestions of overlap in the Blake and Snide stories in the use of certain characters (notably the otherworldly Iguana twins) and images in both narratives. At a point nearly halfway through the novel, Burroughs chooses to introduce a more fantastic, and at times incoherent, narrative involving the six Cities of the Red Night—Tamaghis, Ba'dan, Yass-Waddah, Waghdas, Naufana, and Ghadis—which existed "in an area roughly corresponding to the Gobi Desert, a hundred thousand years ago." It is in this setting and through this narrative that the Blake and Snide narratives coalesce into a vision of apocalypse. The reader searching for meaning in the chronology of the Blake and Snide narratives is finally thwarted because Burroughs's characters have actually been moving indiscriminately through time and space confounding any sense of linear progression the reader has been foolish enough to place his faith in. This notion that any sense of linear progression is undesirable is supported by Burroughs's description of his writing: "it's more poetic messages, the still sad music of humanity, my dear, simply poetic statements."

The narrative involving the six Cities of the Red Night concerns the battle between the partisans, fighting in the spirit of Mission's pirates to escape systems of control, and the forces of control lead by the Countess de Gulpa and the Countess de Vile, the two evil matrons responsible for the ultimate control weapon, the red virus. The narrative spins forward through parodies of Western novels with cowboys and Venusians and nightmarish image blocks which echo parts of the Blake and Snide narratives, toward a war of control between the opposing forces that Burroughs finally does not resolve. Instead he chooses consistently to undercut his vision with reminders that it is all artificial. Burroughs suggests at one point that the battleground where the warring factions meet "looks like Hollywood gone berserk," with Roman legionnaires battling French riot police, Vikings and pirates fighting Texas Rangers, and Hannibal's elephants charging a train of 1920s marines. All of time is merged in this absurd and frightening battle, which may even be a scene in one of Clem Snide's filmscripts. And perhaps Burroughs's point is that whether artifice or not, the escape from time he offers is "real" in the truest sense, since he suggests that entering the "gate in time" he has created in *Cities of the Red Night* and his other work is the only way to escape from the inevitability of the "great mushroom-shaped cloud" that was his childhood nightmare and is the final dark image of this latest novel.

Perhaps the most important source book on Burroughs yet to be published is Victor Bockris's *With William Burroughs: A Report From the Bunker* (1981). Bockris followed Burroughs with a tape recorder for seven years (1974-1981), and the result is a thoroughly entertaining and informative set of transcripts, arranged thematically rather than chronologically, of Burroughs's conversations with friends—notably Allen Ginsberg, publisher Maurice Girodias, Christopher Isherwood, Susan Sontag, Terry Southern, and Andy Warhol. Bockris's book is filled with Burroughs's thoughts on women, drugs, music, writers, and writing. The anecdotes about his meetings with Beckett in Berlin or Céline in Paris or Mick Jagger in London are sometimes humorous and always informative.

Bockris also chronicles the details of Burroughs's life since he left London in 1974. In the summer of 1973 Allen Ginsberg had traveled to London primarily to spend time with Burroughs.

While there, Ginsberg suggested to Burroughs that he return to the United States to deliver a course of lectures on writing at City College of New York between February and May 1974. Since Burroughs had never lectured for a full term and had never lectured at an American university he felt some initial skepticism, but arrangements were made, and he arrived in New York in January 1974. Soon after his arrival, Ginsberg introduced Burroughs to James Grauerholz, from Coffeyville, Kansas, who soon became Burroughs's companion, full-time assistant, and secretary. Grauerholz was an invaluable help to Burroughs during the preparation of the manuscript of *Cities of the Red Night* and was instrumental in organizing the Nova Convention, which was held 30 November-2 December 1978 to honor Burroughs. However, after the two men completed work on *Cities of the Red Night*, Grauerholz returned to Kansas.

The lecture series at City College of New York; stints at the Naropa Institute in Boulder, Colorado; appearances at international conventions on psychoanalysis in Milan in January 1980 and New York in the spring of 1981; a brief reading from his works on the television show *Saturday Night Live* in November 1981; and participation in the Nova Convention attest to Burroughs's new attitude concerning his role as a public literary figure. According to Barry Miles, "William's had an absolute rebirth since he came back to the states. He's a very different person now, much more confident in his position as some kind of literary celebrity and I think it was moving back to New York that enabled him to do that." Burroughs himself freely admits that he views his lectures, readings, and public appearances as a form of show business which provides a valuable source of income.

When Burroughs first returned to New York in 1974, he lived in a third-floor walk-up flat at 77 Franklin Street. Here he worked on his university lectures, spending as much as seven or eight hours on each, and began work on *Cities of the Red Night*. In late 1975, Burroughs moved to a bizarre but secure apartment on the Bowery which he has named The Bunker, probably because, as the converted locker room of an old gymnasium, it has no windows. Burroughs, usually impeccably dressed, now prowls the Bowery armed with a cane, a blackjack, and a can of teargas, and he has even proposed the formation of the "Order of the Grey Gentlemen," a select society that would go on mugger hunts in the subway, armed with canes and Mace.

Surely the highlight of Burroughs's present stay in New York was the 1978 Nova Convention, a series of lectures, panels, films, exhibitions, theater performances, readings, and concerts in honor of Burroughs, which was conceived by Grauerholz, Sylvere Lotringer of Columbia University, and the New York poet John Giorno. The list of participants, who ranged from Ginsberg and Sontag to the heavy-metal rock singer Patti Smith and Keith Richards of the Rolling Stones (who did not show up), attests to Burroughs's strange cultural position as a major figure of contemporary avant-garde fiction and the so-called Godfather of Punk.

For Burroughs, his stay in New York has been productive. Besides spending his time searching for a piece of property where he can build a country house, Burroughs continues to write, working on essays, a series of European lectures and readings, and a new novel tentatively entitled "The Johnson Family." According to Bockris, Burroughs is "extremely concerned with death, talking and writing about it all the time." Despite apparent good health, Burroughs has recently stated that "I may or may not have ten years." However, Burroughs's own sense of mortality should be viewed from the perspective of his work, of which Sylvere Lotringer says, "Not many writers can survive being burnt alive like Burroughs has. His consequent irony gives his writing essential distance. For me, Burroughs writes from a distance beyond death."

References:

Phoebe-Lou Adams, Review of *Cities of the Red Night*, *Atlantic*, 247 (April 1981): 126;

"Avant-Garde Unites Over Burroughs," *New York Times*, 1 December 1978, C11;

Victor Bockris, *With William Burroughs: A Report from the Bunker* (New York: Seaver, 1981);

Carole Cook, Review of *The Third Mind*, *Saturday Review*, 6 (6 January 1979): 56;

Thomas M. Disch, "Pleasures of Hanging," *New York Times Book Review*, 15 March 1981, pp. 14-15;

Michael Barry Goodman, *Contemporary Literary Censorship: the Case History of Burroughs' "Naked Lunch"* (Metuchen, N.J.: Scarecrow, 1981);

Julia M. Klein, Review of *Cities of the Red Night*, *New Republic*, 184 (18 April 1981): 39-40;

Richard Kuczkowski, Review of *The Third Mind*, *Library Journal*, 103 (1 September 1978): 1637;

Donald Palumbo, "William Burroughs' Quartet of Science Fiction Novels as Dystopian Social Satire," *Extrapolation*, 20 (Winter 1979): 321-329;

Rob Schmieder, Review of *Cities of the Red Night*,

Library Journal, 105 (15 November 1980): 2430-2431;

William L. Stull, "The Quest and the Question: Cosmology and Myth in the Work of William S. Burroughs, 1953-1960," *Twentieth Century Literature*, 24 (1978): 225-242.

Paddy Chayefsky
(29 January 1923-1 August 1981)

Paddy Chayefsky died of cancer in New York City. See also the Chayefsky entry in *DLB 7, Twentieth-Century American Dramatists*.

A TRIBUTE *from ARTHUR CANTOR*

Paddy Chayefsky's death on 1 August 1981, at the age of fifty-seven, marked the end of a major writing career.

His list of credits and honors is impressive. A prolific and distinguished writer of television drama in the early days of that medium—almost all of his plays were produced in the 1950s in the aptly named "golden age of television"—he won admiring reviews and wide audiences. He had four plays produced on Broadway: *Middle of the Night* (1956), *The Tenth Man* (1959), *Gideon* (1961), and *The Passion of Josef D.* (1964). He wrote eight films, three of which—*Marty* (1955), *The Hospital* (1971), and *Network* (1976)—won Academy Awards.

When he died he was rich and famous, respected internationally, and well on his way to being an elder statesman for writers, actors, directors, producers, and other members of the colorful and restless literary, theatrical, and cinematic subcultures of New York and Hollywood.

Despite all this he was clearly unfulfilled in one area—the professional theater—which he found both stimulating and frustrating. He was convinced that Broadway's drama critics had done him wrong, particularly in the case of his last Broadway work, *The Passion of Josef D.*, a picaresque, startlingly original play about Stalin and the Russian Revolution. This unconventional production, which opened early in 1964, ran only a few weeks, was unappreciated by the press, and left with Chayefsky a gnawing residue of resentment and anger about the New York stage which he was never able to overcome. For the last seventeen years of his life he gave almost all his time and energies to film.

Chayefsky's early work—most of it, as observed earlier, in television—was largely autobio-

Paddy Chayefsky at the 1978 Academy Awards ceremony

graphical, good-naturedly sentimental, and warmly humorous. He drew richly on his memories of middle-class Jewish family life and turned out plays like *The Catered Affair* (1955), *The Bachelor Party* (1953), *Marty* (1953), *Middle of the Night* (1954), *The Mother* (1954), and *Holiday Song* (1952). The first four of these later became films. As popular as these teleplays were, they were reviewed by a few critics in patronizing fashion, and some of the phrases—"plays about little people," "Chayefsky has a tape-recorder ear"—rankled the playwright and led to his pursuing larger-than-life themes and uncommon language in subsequent writings.

He decided to tackle major issues and established institutions. A disciplined researcher, he never finished a play without becoming an authority on the subject. In the play *Gideon* he took a section of the Bible, the story of Gideon from the Book of Judges, and made the Lord Jehovah one of his characters. In *The Passion of Josef D.* Lenin, Trotsky, and the Bolshevik bureaucracy were his subjects. In the film *The Hospital*, he tore into the untidy bureaucracy of America's hospital network, exposing the hypocrisy, insensitivity, and materialism of much of the medical profession. In the film *Network* he did much the same for the people who run America's TV cartels. The renowned Chayefsky ear for dialogue served him especially well in these arenas. Unafraid to attack the sacred cows of society, he wrote with neo-Shavian paradox and bitingly funny irony. He was able to express a consistent impatience without seeming petty. He

could be savage without also being peevish. And he was able to pinpoint areas for social satire long before those areas became commonplace sitting-duck matter.

The Chayefsky personality was as fresh and uncompromising as his work. Gregarious, talkative, wittily opinionated, he was an angry man with a bedrock of authentic sentiment.

Those who were lucky enough to work with him—and I was one, as a producer of three of his plays—earned the right to profit from the Chayefsky legacy of achievement and the qualities which shaped his career: the courage to deflate pretension, a love of life and language, and a willingness to work hard, very hard, to achieve his literary goals.

Evan S. Connell, Jr.
(17 August 1924-)

Brooks Landon
University of Iowa

See also the Connell entry in *DLB 2, American Novelists Since World War II*.

NEW BOOKS: *A Long Desire* (New York: Holt, Rinehart & Winston, 1979);
The White Lantern (New York: Holt, Rinehart & Winston, 1980);
Saint Augustine's Pigeon (San Francisco: North Point Press, 1980).

The description on the dust jacket of *Saint Augustine's Pigeon* (1980) calls him "an assiduous collector of historical absurdities, coincidences, contradictions, artifices, outrages, and insanities." Certainly, the sixteen stories in Evan S. Connell's most recent book would alone explain and justify such a claim, but then his writing has always demonstrated a profound fascination with the odd particulars of human experience. Connell's *Notes from a Bottle Found on the Beach at Carmel* (1963) and *Points for a Compass Rose* (1973) were enigmatic prose poems that brimmed with curious odds and ends of information. More recently, Connell has devoted two collections of essays, *A Long Desire* (1979) and *The White Lantern* (1980), to exploring moments of history when the best or the worst of human nature crystallized in someone's singular obsession. As one

of Connell's characters in a story in *Saint Augustine's Pigeon* observes: "Each age does produce its folly—some scheme, project, or fantasy toward which the blood drains—economic, political, religious. Always."

A Long Desire contains eleven essays that celebrate the courage and the folly of some of the great explorers and travelers of history, uncommon men and women who, as similar people are described in *Saint Augustine's Pigeon*, "follow dim trails around the world hunting a fulfillment they couldn't find at home." Connell's searchers range from Stephen, the twelve-year-old shepherd boy who led the first Children's Crusade, to explorers Columbus, Martin Frobisher, Mary Kingsley, and Richard Halliburton. In some essays, the searchers are of secondary interest to the search itself—whether for El Dorado, for the Seven Cities, for Atlantis, or for the alchemist's dream of the Philosopher's Stone. Easily among the most intriguing of Connell's explorers are Isabella Bird Bishop, Marianne North, Fanny Bullock Workman, Kate Marsden, and Mary Kingsley—sensible, prim Victorian ladies who suddenly realized their strong desires to explore Africa or Siberia or the Himalayas. "The most unlikely travelers the world has ever known," Connell calls them, reflecting later in *The White Lantern* that

Evan S. Connell, Jr.

"faced with such people, one can't help thinking that the nineteenth century English must have been utterly bonkers." "It is the singular person," he explains in *A Long Desire*, "inexplicably drawn from familiar comforts toward a nebulous goal, lured often enough to death—it is he, or she, whose peregrinations can never be thoroughly understood, who is worth noticing."

Connell notices not just the contours of time and place recorded by standard histories but the ludicrous, the tragic, the intriguing small details of legendary lives. He reminds us that for every Henry Hudson or Martin Frobisher there also sailed, and usually suffered, crews of men with forgotten names, names like Sydrack Fenner or Abacuck Prickett. He notes that Columbus kept two sets of log books, one recording distances actually sailed, one recording smaller distances to mollify edgy crew members. Connell is quick to call attention to the unexpected realities of adventuring. In describing a voyage of Martin Frobisher, he points out: "Authorities on shipbuilding agree, contrary to what you might expect, that sixteenth-century English vessels were not as reliable as tenth-century Viking ships, and perhaps not as safe as a Mediterranean bireme of the fourth century B.C." It is important to observe, however, that these essays are more than just collections of little-known facts: pervading them is Connell's interest both in what makes these adventurers so uncommon and in what ties them to the smaller desires of the people who stay behind. "Magellan. Columbus. Marco Polo. Ibn Batuta. Hsuantsang. Captain Cook. There's no end to the list, of course, because gradually it descends from such legendary individuals to ourselves when, as children, obsessed by that same urge, we got permission to sleep in the backyard."

Connell's career has been studded with linked works: *Mrs. Bridge* (1959) and *Mr. Bridge* (1969), *Notes from a Bottle Found on the Beach at Carmel* (1963) and *Points for a Compass Rose* (1973), *The Connoisseur* (1974) and *Double Honeymoon* (1976). Each of these pairings suggests that Connell likes to return to an idea or form to consider it from a different angle, and this pattern holds true for *The White Lantern*, the

companion volume to *A Long Desire*. While the first book focuses most often on searchers for fame or riches, *The White Lantern* deals more with seekers of knowledge. Gold more often than not obsessed and impelled Connell's first group of subjects; the desire to understand more about who and where we are, about our origins and about our nature, drives his second group. The seven essays in this volume have to do with theories ranging from evolution to astronomy, with archaeologists' discoveries about Etruscans and Vikings, and with the scientific exploration of Antarctica. *The White Lantern* considers obsessions of a more abstract and complicated order than those in *A Long Desire*, but Connell's handling of his subjects is equally deft. Terming the book "a brilliant browse," John Leonard wrote in the *New York Times* that Connell "seems to be saying that we

Dust jacket for Connell's most recent short-story collection

are what we were, odd, brave, dangerous, bemused, hanging ourselves on our own curiosity as though question marks were hooks or nooses."

The most gripping of these pieces, indeed, one of the most gripping accounts any reader is likely to encounter anywhere, reconstructs the hardships and tragedies suffered by early Antarctic expeditions led by men such as Sir Douglas Mawson, Robert F. Scott, and Roald Amundsen. Yet it also records the more mundane side of their undertakings. "An adventure is merely an interruption of an explorer's serious work and indicates bad planning," huffed Amundsen, first man to reach the South Pole. In the same phlegmatic vein is Amundsen's reaction to his first meal of sled-dog cutlets: "I must admit that they would have lost nothing by being a little more tender, but one must not expect too much of a dog."

Connell even lists the names of the sled dogs for Sir Douglas Mawson's ill-fated 1912 expedition: Haldane, Ginger, Pavlova, Mary, George, and Johnson. He does so not from a love of trivia, but from a fierce determination to preserve the immediacy of history for his readers. "Those damn textbooks. . . . They ruin everything," complains a Connell protagonist in "The Walls of Avilla," one of the stories in *Saint Augustine's Pigeon*, and Connell must surely feel the same. An essay in *The White Lantern* details the tedious struggle to translate ancient hieroglyphics. Connell singles out the achievement of George Smith, a philologist at the British Museum, who one day, exulting over his translation of the story of Gilgamesh, began inexplicably to take off his clothes. "What happened next?" Connell asks, only to lament: "We don't know because whoever kept the records in those days didn't think it was important. It was, though. Such details, like fine plums, ought to be plucked and tenderly boxed." Both *A Long Desire* and *The White Lantern* represent Connell's finely crafted efforts to do just that.

In what must now be seen as a classic understatement, Connell told an interviewer several years ago that he "read a lot of nonfiction: archeological, anthropological, historical" (the bibliography for *A Long Desire* lists over 120 works). He then explained why he liked such books, citing an example that became the subject of one of the essays in *The White Lantern*: "The overtones are often so much greater than in fiction. They've recently found some Viking cemeteries in Greenland. The skeletons were almost dwarfs. Apparently they were suffering from rickets and malnutrition, but when the European ships came in, they had to have the latest European fashions. They were practically starving to death, but were dressed in the latest styles. You can go through a three-hundred page novel and never find anything as substantial as that. Of course, you can find it in Tolstoy or Melville, but there aren't many of them around."

Connell's fascination with information of this nature has long spilled over into his fiction: readers of *The Connoisseur* can learn as much about pre-Columbian art as they can learn about Muhlbach's obsession with that art. *Saint Augustine's Pigeon*, Connell's selected stories, reveals more in common with his two preceding nonfiction works than might be expected. The book opens with "The Yellow Raft," a tightly written description of the disappearance at sea of a naval aviator in World War II. It closes with "A Brief Essay on the Subject of Celebrity: With Numerous Digressions and Particular Attention to the Actress, Rita Hayworth." There, Connell suggests that celebrity, symbols of affluence, and achievements themselves all serve a simple purpose, existing "to perpetuate our name just as children do, notifying the future that we are worth at least a minor celebration." The stories in *Saint Augustine's Pigeon* are mostly about people who deserve, but do not seem likely to receive, the minor celebrations of posterity—a drowned aviator, a strangely Christlike Chihuahuan fisherman, an old woman dying at a bus stop with only a tramp to witness her passing. Other stories feature characters frustrated by denials of any form of celebration in their own lives, people desperate for change but locked into the conventions of sameness.

Two of the most thoughtful of Connell's stories, "The Walls of Avila" and "The Palace of the Moorish Kings," scrutinize the life of a restless world traveler, a lover of the unusual and poetic, through the resentful, staid eyes of the small-town friends he left behind. "Another decade and the world's going to be as homogenized as a bottle of milk," worries the traveler, while his friends criticize him for not being like them. Three stories feature Karl Muhlbach, the frustrated and disappointed protagonist of Connell's *The Connoisseur* and *Double Honeymoon*. Of the sixteen stories in this collection, four come from Connell's *The Anatomy Lesson and Other Stories* (1957), five come from *At the Crossroads* (1965), and seven have not before been published in books. Writing in the *New York Times Book Review*, Barry Yourgrau cited some of the particular strengths of Connell's style: "Mr. Connell is distinguished by his precision with dramatic and physical detail; he hears the delicate modulations of mood, and he construes language with a special firmness and grace, a masterly authority."

At present, Connell is working on a book about General Custer, of which he says, "It started out as an essay. I had planned a book of essays about the Old West, beginning with the cliff dwellers, progressing to the Indian wars, outlaws, etc., but got so interested in the Little Bighorn fiasco that I could not stop reading about it and writing about it. So far I have perhaps 300 pages, no end in sight." The book is tentatively called "Son of the Morning Star"—that being what the Cheyennes called Custer. North Point Press has just republished Connell's classics *Mrs. Bridge* and *Mr. Bridge*.

Connell's works have been successful with critics and have enjoyed respectable sales, but his impressive writing still remains one of America's best-kept literary secrets. Perhaps his uncompromising sensibility and the crisp straightforwardness of his prose have somehow worked against him in a time when flamboyance often passes for style. Certainly Connell has not courted larger audiences: he pursues his own interests in his writing with no attention to current literary fashion, and his life remains almost aggressively private. By republishing his classics *Mrs. Bridge* and *Mr. Bridge* as well as publishing *Saint Augustine's Pigeon*, North Point Press has given readers a new chance to savor Connell's talent.

Interviews:

Dan Tooker and Roger Hofheins, "Evan S. Connell, Jr.," in *Fiction! Interviews with Northern California Novelists* (New York: Harcourt Brace Jovanovich/William Kaufmann, 1976), pp. 54-69;

Patricia Holt, "PW Interviews Evan S. Connell," *Publishers Weekly*, 220 (20 November 1981): 12-13.

Robert Coover
(4 February 1932-   )

Larry McCaffery and Sinda J. Gregory
San Diego State University

See also the Coover entry in *DLB 2, American Novelists Since World War II*.

NEW BOOKS: *Hair O' the Chine* (Bloomfield Hills, Mich.: Bruccoli Clark, 1979);

After Lazarus (Bloomfield Hills, Mich.: Bruccoli Clark, 1980);

A Political Fable (New York: Viking, 1980);

Charlie in the House of Rue (Lincoln, Mass.: Penmaen Press, 1980);

Spanking the Maid (Bloomfield Hills, Mich.: Bruccoli Clark, 1981).

In 1979 Robert Coover moved back to the United States after spending most of the previous ten years living in Spain and England. It may seem paradoxical that a writer whose works have often focused on American culture, speech, and habits of thought should spend so much of his time overseas, but as Coover explained in a 1981 interview in *Genre* there are a number of advantages in being an expatriate writer: "A writer needs isolation, a cell of his own, that's obvious, but distance can also help. It has a way of freeing the imagination, stirring memory. Fewer localisms creep in, less passing trivia, transient concerns." Coover's move to the United States was actually the culmination of several years of constant relocation: he spent 1976 in Virginia, teaching at V.M.I.; in 1977 he returned to Barcelona, where he had met his wife, Pilar, in order to see what life in the post-Franco era was like in Spain; and in 1978-1979, he lived in London and Kent in England. In 1979 they decided to move to Providence, Rhode Island, and Coover was hired as an adjunct professor at Brown University.

There had been other disruptions for Coover during the late 1970s. In 1977 he had published *The Public Burning*, a massive, ambitious novel which had occupied much of his attention for nearly a decade. The circumstances surrounding the creation and publication of *The Public Burning* had proved to be frustrating and disheartening. Coover's editor, Hal Scharlatt, died in mid-project. Because the book deals with the controversial Rosenberg case and one of its narrators is a character named Richard Nixon, his original publisher, Knopf, abandoned it at the last moment (Coover

Robert Coover

had hoped to have the book published in 1976 as a kind of Bicentennial gift to America); because of his publisher's concern over possible libel suits, lawyers were at times present with Coover during the final editing of the book. Critical response to the book was mixed, but the book made the *New York Times Book Review*'s best-seller list. Coover then decided to lay aside temporarily "Lucky Pierre," another huge project of which he had already written some 100,000 words in the early 1970s before his attention had become completely occupied with *The Public Burning*, and to concentrate on writing shorter works including a novel of moderate length (150,000 words) tentatively titled "Gerald's Party," which Viking will publish in late 1982 or early 1983.

Work on this book and on various radio plays and stories, combined with a visiting professorship at Brandeis University from 1981 to 1982 (his classes there included writing workshops and an examination of the ancient exemplary fictions), has made the period since Coover's return to the United States a busy one indeed. Also during this period a number of shorter works, written at various times during his career, have been published. *Hair O' the Chine* (1979), *After Lazarus* (1980), *Charlie in the House of Rue* (1980), and *Spanking the Maid* (1981) were published in limited editions while *A Political Fable* appeared in a trade edition.

Beginning in 1977 there also appeared a number of critical studies dealing with Coover's work, which had been relatively neglected until this time. These studies, which considered Coover's fiction, with its many experimental, reflexive, and self-conscious formal features, within the context of other postmodern experimentations, include several important articles in the major scholarly journals devoted to contemporary literature, Larry McCaffery's more lengthy study in *The Metafictional Muse* (1982) and Richard Andersen's *Robert Coover* (1981).

The differences among Coover's recently published short works suggest the way that Coover's work has evolved during the past twenty years. Both *After Lazarus* and *Hair O' the Chine* were written nearly twenty years ago, in the late 1950s, when Coover was writing dozens of highly experimental "exemplary fictions" (several of which were eventually included in *Pricksongs and Descants*, 1969). *A Political Fable*, on the other hand, written roughly in the middle of Coover's career to date (it originally was published as "The Cat in the Hat for President" in the *New American Review* in 1968), is representative of the type of experimental fiction he was producing in the late 1960s, when he was completing pieces like "The Babysitter" and "The Magic Poker" that would anchor *Pricksongs and Descants*. Finally, *Charlie in the House of Rue* and *Spanking the Maid*, works of considerably more complexity than the other three, are indicative of certain new directions in Coover's fiction—a turn away from reflexive fiction, for example, and a de-emphasis on the oral quality of the text.

As different in intent and achievement as these five works are, they do exhibit certain tendencies common to nearly all of Coover's writing. In a general sense, for example, all five can be seen as reworkings or reinvestigations of familiar mythic or pop-cultural materials. Throughout his career Coover has used this kind of familiar subject matter precisely because of the possibilities it offers to reshape his audience's prior expectations. These works also share with Coover's other fiction preoccupations with transformation and metamorphosis, the eternal processes of death and rebirth, sorrow and joy, dread and hope. As an extension of his interest in change, Coover's fascination with punning (a form of verbal transformation) remains evident, as does his use of what he has referred to as "structural puns"—the juxtaposition within a story of two unexpected elements. Finally, these stories also demonstrate Coover's consistent examination of the major fictional modes through which society organizes its response to reality. For Coover the dogmatic perspectives created by religion, politics,

myth, literature, historical views, or any of society's communal narratives need to be constantly reevaluated, the ironies and paradoxes contained within them explored for new complexities and fresher modes of perception. Offering his own reshaping of these materials as an analogy for the process available to us all, Coover explores the relationship between imagination and reality, writer and text, experience and metaphor with the same remarkable powers of linguistic play, wit, philosophical and aesthetic complexity, and narrative power that characterizes all his work.

Both *After Lazarus* and *Hair O' the Chine* take the form of film scripts (both, in fact, were written during approximately the same period in which Coover wrote the "Sentient Lens" stories in *Pricksongs and Descants*), and each exploits a tension between the reader's expectations about a familiar story (the story of Lazarus in the Bible and "The Three Little Pigs," respectively) and an ongoing disruption of these expectations by a narrative consciousness. Thus, like a number of Coover's other fictions written in the 1960s ("The Magic Poker," "Klee Dead," "The Marker," "The Hat Act," and *The Universal Baseball Association*), *After Lazarus* and *Hair O' the Chine* are works which examine who and what the artist is. The rationale behind Coover's choice of biblical and fairy-tale materials is quite evident, since both produce what he has called "mythic residues" which evoke a rich series of associations. As Coover noted in the *Genre* interview, he often uses such familiar stories as a starting point: "If some stories start throwing their weight around, I like to undermine their authority a bit, work variations, call attention to their fictional natures." The Bible is, for Coover, an obvious source of dogmatic thought, simply because it has so often been viewed as literal rather than metaphorical truth; but Coover also shares with Barthelme, Barth, Pynchon, and other postmodernists a conviction that pop culture is just as likely a source for dogma. As he explains, "The pop culture we absorb in childhood—and I'd include all the pop religions as well—go on affecting the way we respond to the world or talk about it for the rest of our lives. And this mythology of ours, this unwritten Bible, is being constantly reinforced by books and newspapers, films, television, advertisements, politicians, teachers, and so on."

Coover's use of a film-script format also deserves comment, for he has been fascinated by the cinema and other visual media for most of his artistic life. Before he firmly decided on writing as a career, he had studied painting under Leroy

Nieman at the Art Institute of Chicago, and he also produced, wrote, and directed a film, *On a Confrontation in Iowa City*, while he was at the Iowa Workshop in 1969. Thus it is not too surprising when Coover admits in the *Genre* interview that "I work with language because paper is cheaper than film stock. And because it's easier to work with a committee of one. But storytelling doesn't have to be done with words on a printed page, or even with spoken words. Probably, if I had absolute freedom to do what I want, I'd prefer film." Coover's interest in film has been evident in his fiction, which often relies blatantly on cinematic techniques. He finds interesting the notion of cinematic montage or juxtaposition, the ability of cinema to manipulate time, its great sense of immediacy, its mixture of what he calls "magic and documentary power"—all of which have potential applications in fiction. More directly, writing fictions in the form of film scripts allows Coover to explore still another form which has had a particular impact on the modern sensibility. Indeed, Coover shares with McLuhan and others the view that television and the cinema have begun to affect the way we perceive the world around us. In presenting a narrative supposedly from the viewpoint of a mechanical instrument—the camera—Coover also subtly reinforces his point that there is no such thing as a realistic, objective perspective; the objectivity in these two books is wholly undermined by the presentation of the emotions and anticipatory feelings of the human subject who controls the operations of the camera (and, in the case of *Hair O' the Chine*, by the responses of the scholarly commentator who projects himself into the film).

After Lazarus opens with "gradually augmenting, a hollow voice" crying out, "I have risen! I have risen!" These words, presumably uttered by Lazarus, mark the beginning of a cyclic psychodrama played out in an unnamed mysterious village where all identities seem gradually to merge. At first there appear to be a number of clearly identifiable characters in the plot—an old woman dressed in black, whom we follow on her way to a cathedral; a priest who leads a funeral procession of women mourners; a dead man in a coffin—but all the women look alike, as do all the men, and gradually there is a merging of plot elements into a series of cyclic gestures. For example, an old woman turns into a pallbearer, who in turn becomes the old woman, so that distinctions between male and female characters break down. Even the corpse in the coffin participates in this process of transformation: at one point he digs himself out of his grave only to be thrown back by one of the pallbearers;

later, however, one of the pallbearers climbs into the coffin to take his place, and the rest of the pallbearers hurl the casket at the onlooking camera.

After Lazarus is a strangely disturbing story. Although its ambiguities can be interpreted in several ways, it is clear that the book examines man's relationship to the ever-present cycles of life and death, dread and hope, creation and destruction. Coover appears to be suggesting that man at once fears the inevitability of change, metamorphosis, and death and yet depends upon these basic cycles for his sense of stability. Like moviemaker George Romero, Coover knows there is something archetypal about man's fear of disrupting this cycle—a cycle which is publicly acknowledged and rigidified through the ritualized formulas that surround birth, marriage, and death. Still, if this fear of disruption is natural—and it has analogous applications for the artist, the politician, or for anyone who relies on specific patterns for a sense of order—it also tends to deny or even destroy attempts to create new patterns and new life.

Unlike the somber mood of *After Lazarus*, Coover's other film-script fiction, *Hair O' the Chine*, is a comic piece that mixes bawdy, outrageous sex with a mock-serious literary analysis of "The Three Little Pigs." In a shifting series of scenes presented as film shots, two stories emerge: one involves the sometimes violent, sometimes slapstick courtship of a woodcutter and a maid; the other concerns the wise little pig who built his house of brick and the ominous wolf who has come to devour him. In the midst of these two stories is an off-screen voice who provides commentary on the story of the pig and the wolf. The subject of his analysis is actually confined to a single tableau—the pig at the window of his house, looking out with an "indefinable expression" at the wolf, whose face suggests "greed, or hunger, or perhaps mere weariness." This static scene, recreated in an illustration by Robin McDonald, is relatively straightforward, but the voice in *Hair O' the Chine* finds nuances of meaning in the most obscure gestures as he turns to psychology, semantics, literature, sociology, and history to comment upon it. The narrator's heavy-handed pedantry is further mocked by the fact that while he is lavishing a ridiculous amount of scholarly analysis on this fairy-tale image, a more vigorous, exciting drama is being played out before him. Through the first half of the story, the voice ignores the maid and the woodcutter as they tumble about in sexual combat, hurl gooey mortar at each other, and smear butter on each other's body. The scenes with the woodcutter and the maid contain a bit of

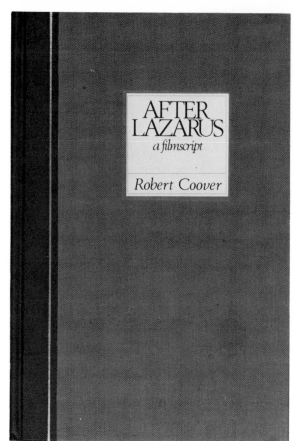

Front covers for recent books by Coover

everything—sex, violence, burlesque comedy, suggestions of fertility rituals—but the voice (the parodic scholar and exegete) passes over their more significant actions in favor of a scene with far less potential for analysis.

Frontispiece by Robin McDonald for Hair O' the Chine

Eventually, however, the vitality and passion of the woodcutter-maid scene break down the voice's concentration on his textual analysis: as corn juice and saliva dribble down the chin of the maid after she has bitten into an ear of corn, the voice begins to swallow with a "forced chuckle" and nervously clears his throat. Further and further distracted, the disembodied voice finally *becomes* the woodcutter and is literally projected into the scene he has previously ignored. At the same time he continues his analysis, which becomes increasingly incoherent and finally breaks down completely. Thus, Coover suggests, the vitality of life and art always outstrips the critic's analysis. Although Coover's parody of the critical imagination is at times rather labored, *Hair O' the Chine*'s humor, veiled scholarly allusions, and metafictional self-commentary provide a good example of his early experimental concerns.

In many respects *A Political Fable* is a kind of warm-up exercise for *The Public Burning* (both works were conceived at approximately the same time); certainly both books appear to be reactions to the general antiwar, antipolitical atmosphere that was sweeping America in 1968. Published in book form by Viking to coincide with the 1980 election year, *A Political Fable* remains a dazzling, often hilarious spoof of America's circuslike political operations. Coover presents the rhetoric of American political thought as a system of outworn, conventional metaphors which the public accepts because of its lack of imagination. The novella is narrated by Mr. Brown, the rather dull, colorless chairman of the minority party, who, when the book opens, is preparing for his party's national convention. Brown is the book's middle-of-the-road politician, a pragmatic skeptic about absolutes who is highly self-conscious about the metaphorical nature of politics but who also fears anarchy, admitting that he "needed the familiar as much as anyone else and so found comfort in the traditional." Brown is aware of the fictional nature of political dogmas, anticipating many of the views that Coover worked out in considerably more detail in *The Public Burning* by asserting, "Theoretically, politics is all issues: the word used to describe the conflicts arising in men's efforts to suffer one another. But practically, of course, there are no issues in politics at all. Not even ideological species. 'Liberal,' 'conservative,' 'left,' 'right,' these are mere fictions of the press, metaphoric conventions to which politicians sooner or later and in varying ways adapt. Politics in a republic is a complex pattern of vectors, some fixed and explicable, some random, some bullish, some inchoate and permutable, some hidden and dynamic, others celebrated through flagging, usually collective sometimes even cosmic—and a politician's job is to know them and ride them." An eminently successful politician with a fiercely competitive nature and a limited sense of humor, Brown resists the Cat-in-the-Hat's highly unorthodox, anarchist approach to politics. Just before the party's convention, however, Brown is persuaded to support the cat's candidacy for presidency. Soon the cat's wild antics have captured the fancy of America to such a degree that he appears a shoo-in for election.

The cat's message is much the same as a point that Coover returns to repeatedly throughout his fiction: "We've been living in a shutdown world. We're opening it up. It's worth it." Or, as the cat puts it in one of his many poetic ditties: "Now you see what I can do! / I can give you something new! /

Something true / And impromptu! / I can give you a new view!" The cat's personal manager, Clark, provides the best summary of what the cat represents in a conversation with Brown: "We have a terrible need for the extraordinary. We are weary of war, weary of the misery under our supposed prosperity, weary of dullness and routine, weary of all the old ideas, weary of all the masks we wear, the roles we play, the foolish games we sustain. The cat cuts through all this. We laugh. For a moment, we are free." Throughout the book Clark articulates a number of Coover's points about the subjective nature of society's systems of beliefs and values, pointing out the need to demolish prior systems in order to institute the new, while at the same time recognizing the comfort and assurance which these systems provide. He points to "The mystification of history produced by our irrational terror of reality," and asserts, "The Cat breaks the rules of the house, even the laws of probability, but what is destroyed except nay-saying itself, authority, social habit, the law of the mother, who, through violence in the name of love, keeps order in this world, this household? Ah no, mess-making is a prerequisite to creation, Mr. Brown. All new worlds are built upon the ruins of the old." Yet he also admits, "The structures we build to protect us from reality are insane, Mr. Brown, but they are also comforting. A false comfort, to be sure, but their loss is momentarily frightening." This last comment proves to be prophetic. In all his works Coover not only presents the need to tear down outmoded habits of thought but also the fear which leads the public to resist this dismantling of its systems. Most of the public want to keep playing the same old games, governed by the same old rules; and they are unaware that they are engaged in a game. Even Brown, who is fully aware of the gamelike nature of all conventions (including national political conventions), finds it difficult to accept the cat's flaunting of the rules. More important, he is never able to embrace the more radical suggestion to abandon the current game and start up an entirely new one. As the Cat-in-the-Hat sings, "Come along! / Follow me! Don't be afraid! / There are many more games / That we haven't played." Not surprisingly, the cat's call for "a total violent disruption" of the system is unacceptable to the powers that be. Threatened by a military coup should the cat win, his campaign managers set him up to be murdered by a mob of reactionaries. What follows is a wild orgy, reminiscent of the cathartic public rituals that conclude Coover's full-length novels. At first glance the cat's martyrdom does not appear to be in vain, for his

party reconvenes, and with the cat as its somber symbol it creates a platform whose promise is "The New View." But this gesture is surely an ironic presentation of the way the world always tries to contain and stifle the genuinely creative act by reconstituting it within its own familiar framework. The hope remains, however, that the cat may not have exhausted all its nine lives, that there are more hats from which it may later emerge.

A Political Fable is a brilliant and effective satire not only of the infantile sensibilities that seem to dominate the American political process but also of what the cat refers to as "the madness of normalcy." This madness, suggests Coover, underlies the very fabric of the American consciousness; our inability to respond to this madness with fresher forms and creative alternatives has been largely responsible for the sorry state of the nation. Presented in Coover's typical manner, blending elements of comedy and the grotesque with an impressive display of verbal and philosophical pyrotechnics, *A Political Fable* is a bold denunciation of political, intellectual, and artistic inertia.

In *Charlie in the House of Rue* Coover explores the territory between what horrifies us and what makes us laugh. Its point of departure is the character and cinematic conventions found in Charlie Chaplin's Little Tramp films—an ideal context in which to examine the relationship between comedy and tragedy since Chaplin's films, for all their humor, so often skirt the boundaries of genuine pathos and despair. Although the story is not narrated in the film-script form of *After Lazarus* and *Hair O' the Chine*, its development relies extensively on cinematic conventions. As Charla Gabert suggests in the *Chicago Review*, "The unique characteristics of silent films—absence of dialogue, and exaggerated gestures approaching pantomime—particularly dominate our expectations and shape the text. . . . Coover has also drawn upon familiar conventions of horror films to reiterate the connection of his text to film." Indeed, the House of Rue through which Charlie wanders in this tale owes its existence almost solely to the world of silent films, with its absence of speech, its colorlessness, its surreal notions of causality, its flickering shadows, and other peculiar lighting effects. After meticulously describing Chaplin in the guise of the Little Tramp on the story's opening page ("slapshoes splayed, baggy trousers bunched around his waist and tattered jacket fastidiously buttoned, hands gripping the two ends of his bamboo cane, black derby set square on his head"), Coover puts Charlie through a familiar comic routine: he challenges a hat tree to a fight, blows his nose on a tapestry, doffs his hat politely to a suit of armor, offers the armor a cigar, selects a cigar for himself, asks the suit of armor for a light, gets no response, and so on. By the time the reader enters very far into the story, however, he realizes that he is as much in the surreal, grotesque world of Luis Bũnel and Salvador Dali's film *Un chien Andalou* (1928), where characters and objects are unexpectedly transformed into other things, time and causality are wholly out of joint, and orderly events have nightmarish analogs. Charlie begins a series of adventures in different parts of the house, encountering in separate rooms seemingly familiar stock characters—a sad-faced old man, a sexually provocative maid, a lovely but unapproachable young woman, and a policeman.

Charlie's engagement with these characters is at first comic. Later, however, his adventures begin to take on truly ominous overtones. Dabbing at the old man's tearful eyes, Charlie accidentally knocks one of his eyeballs loose. The scene has been transformed from the silly, slapstick world of silent comedy into the realm of a ghoulish nightmare: "Slowly [the eye] bulges forward, oozing out of its socket, pops suddenly free, and slides down his withered cheek, hanging there by a slippery thread. Desperately, Charlie tries to push the eyeball back in, but it is difficult even to hang on to it: it keeps popping and oozing out of his grasp. And then the other one begins to emerge from its socket."

The remainder of the novella focuses mainly on Charlie's frantic efforts to save the beautiful woman in white. As she dangles helplessly from a noose, Charlie desperately runs from room to room searching for a means to cut the rope, encountering the other characters in situations which have by now lost any semblance of comedy, although many of the specific elements of these scenes are the ones which in other situations produce laughter. Under different circumstances, one might laugh as Charlie struggles to hold up his pants, or as the policeman repeatedly slips on a bar of soap, but the context of these events now precludes amusement. Although the story may be seen as a Kafkaesque vision of man helplessly entrapped in a mysterious, threatening world, Coover's main intent seems to be an examination of the way in which contexts change the implications (or "meanings") of the elements contained within them. In the process Coover manipulates the familiar gestures of comedy—slipping on a banana peel, the hot foot, a custard pie in the face—to reveal the violence, sadism, and pain inherent in them.

Despite its relative brevity, Coover's most recent novella, *Spanking the Maid*, is one of the most complex, compelling, and perfectly executed works of his career. It is a story composed of the same scene repeated with only slight variations, slight additions, and slight deletions: a maid enters her master's bedroom, where he is stirring from the past night's dreams. She tries to perform her duties; she fails; she is spanked. The sequence begins anew each day as she enters once more, fails once more, and again suffers her punishment. There is little if any development of character, no real evolution of the plot; it is a story that revolves around variations on a single image that might initially seem trite and conventional. Yet Coover turns this cliche of sexuality into a vibrant and passionate examination of stasis and mutability, order and disorder, the freedom of our minds and the enslavement of our bodies. In the *Genre* interview Coover remarks that his fiction usually begins by his attempt to open up a metaphor in much the same way that a flower exfoliates, allowing all the potential beauty and meaning to expose itself to view. *Spanking the Maid* is a tribute to Coover's remarkable ability to explore an image to its fullest, until it comes to speak of those unspeakable matters for which metaphors can be our only entry.

It is typical of Coover's desire to resurrect tired conventions that the literal level of this metaphor is so insignificant. Despite all the elements of sexuality and pornography, *Spanking the Maid* is less concerned with male-female relationships or the sociology of the authoritative male and the submissive female than it is with a more complex, universal working out of the metaphor. In one sense, this story is an exploration of the writer's relationship to his art—the maid ("made") being the medium that is worked/spanked by the master/artist. Thus, as the man looks at her upturned bottom, "he thinks of it as a blank ledger on which to write," and he further "finds himself searching it for something . . . a message of sorts." But just as the writer can never dominate or enslave his medium, the master in this piece is no more in absolute control than the maid: both are caught up in the ceaseless, repetitious process of becoming; both are bound—she to her duty to care for him, he to his duty to preserve the system that regulates and defines their roles. Finally, the maid and master are equally fearful of "bodily punishment," a phrase which implies not just spanking but the ultimate, inevitable punishment which every body submits to—death. Thus we are told that "every animal is governed by [punishment], understands and fears it, and the fear of it keeps every creature in its own sphere, forever preventing . . .

or even scouring out the tub or toilet,
for she knows that only in giving herself
(as he has told her) can she find herself:
true service (he doesn't have to tell her!)
is perfect freedom. And so, excited by the
songs of the birds, the sweet breath of morning,
and her own natural eagerness to please, she
turns with a glad heart to her favorite
task of all: the making of the bed. Indeed,
all the rest of her work is embraced by it,
for the opening up and airing of the bed
is the first of her tasks, the making of
it her last. Today, however, when she
tosses the covers back, she finds, coiled
like a dark snake near the foot, a bloodstained leather belt. She starts back.
The sheets, too, are flecked with blood.
Shadows seem to creep across the room
and the birds fall silent. Perhaps, she
thinks, her heart sinking, I'd better go
out and come in again . . . .

o o o

12

A manuscript page from Spanking the Maid

Illustration by Rikki from Spanking the Maid

that natural confusion and disorder that would arise without it." When the master, weary of the continual cycle which defines his existence, says, "Why bother at all when it always seems to turn out the same?," he could as easily be lamenting human mortality as his maid's repeated failures. This ultimate fear, Coover implies, makes us slaves to the systems (such as religion and art) we construct to take our minds off our own approaching deathly punishment. *Spanking the Maid* asks that the reader accept the scary but exhilarating sense of liberation that comes from facing the "natural confusion and disorder" that defines existence, breaking free of one's individual sphere and living "life to the full sense of the word . . . not to exist or subsist merely, but to make oneself over, to *give* oneself to some high purpose, to others, to some social end, to life beyond the shell of ego." The master's sense of duty and the maid's willing submission to what is required of her exhibit this desire to "live life in the full sense of the word." So, too, do painful duties, such as the author's attention to his text, allow one to organize his existence and momentarily defy "this dark little pocket of lingering night" that is said to remain "no matter how much sunlight and fresh air" the maid lets in her master's bedroom.

Periodical Publications:
"The Tinkerer," *Antaeus*, 24 (1976): 111-112;

"Ground Hog Hunt," *American Review*, 25 (October 1976): 1-32;
"The Master's Voice," *American Review*, 26 (November 1977): 361-388;
"In Bed One Night," *Playboy*, 27 (January 1980): 150-152.

References:
Richard Andersen, *Robert Coover* (Boston: Twayne, 1981);
Judith Wood Angelius, "The Man Behind the Catcher's Mask: A Closer Look at Robert Coover's *The Universal Baseball Association*," *Denver Quarterly*, 12, no. 2 (1977): 165-174;
Neil Berman, "Coover's *The Universal Baseball Association*: Play as Personalized Myth," *Modern Fiction Studies*, 24 (1978): 209-223;
Charla Gabert, "The Metamorphosis of Charlie," review of *Charlie in the House of Rue*, *Chicago Review*, 32, no. 2 (1980): 60-64;
Jessie Gunn, "Structure as Revelation: Coover's *Pricksongs and Descants*," *Linguistics in Literature*, 2, no. 1 (1977): 1-42;
Kathryn Hume, "Robert Coover's Fiction: The Naked and the Mythic," *Novel: A Forum in Fiction*, 12 (Winter 1979): 127-148;
Susan Kissel, "The Contemporary Artist and His Audience in the Short Stories of Robert Coover," *Studies in Short Fiction*, 16 (Winter 1979): 49-54;
Larry McCaffery, *The Metafictional Muse* (Pittsburgh: University of Pittsburgh Press, 1982);
McCaffery, "Robert Coover's 'Cubist Fictions,' "*Par Rapport*, 1, no. 1 (1978): 33-40;
McCaffery, "Robert Coover on His Own and Other Fictions," *Genre*, 14 (Spring 1981): 45-64; reprinted in *Interviews with Contemporary American Novelists*, edited by Thomas LeClair and McCaffery (Urbana: University of Illinois Press, 1982);
Brenda Wineapple, "Robert Coover's Playing Fields," *Iowa Review*, 10, no. 3 (1979): 66-74.

Malcolm Cowley

(24 August 1898-   )

Donald G. Parker
Orange County Community College,
State University of New York

See also the Cowley entry in *DLB 4, American Writers in Paris, 1920-1939.*

NEW BOOKS: *The Dream of the Golden Mountains: Remembering the 1930s* (New York: Viking, 1980);
The View from 80 (New York: Viking, 1980).

RECENT AWARDS: National Magazine Award for "The View from 80," 1979; Connecticut Medal for Excellence in the Arts, 1979; Penney-Missouri Journalism Award, 1979; Jay B. Hubbell Medallion (Modern Language Association), 1980; Gold Medal for Criticism and Belles Lettres, American Academy and Institute of Arts and Letters, 1981.

Malcolm Cowley is now an octogenarian—or an "octo," as he puts it in his recent short book, *The View from 80,* an expansion of his award-winning essay published in *Life* in December 1978. From the bourn of an essentially undiscovered country, he paused in his travels, invited by one of the senior editors of *Life,* to write an essay about "how it feels to be old." Then, because of reader response ("an astounding number of letters from many parts of the country"), an expanded version including further reflections, anecdotes, quotations, and responses to and quotations from readers' letters was published in September 1980.

What comprises *The View from 80* is best summed up by Cowley: "To enter the country of age is a new experience, different from what you supposed it to be. Nobody, man or woman, knows the country until he has lived in it and has taken out his citizenship papers. Here is my own report, submitted as a road map and guide to some of the principal monuments." Of all the temptations of old age, the most tempting, according to Cowley, is not "whiskey or cooking sherry but simply giving up. . . . Poet or housewife, businessman or teacher, every old person needs a work project if he wants to keep himself more alive." Cowley himself has not lacked projects since "growing old"; in a recent interview he pointed out, "I've published more books since I was

seventy years old than I published before I was seventy. That's rather unusual, isn't it?"

Malcolm Cowley and his second wife, Muriel, whom he married in 1932, live in Sherman, Connecticut, in a two-story converted barn on seven acres of land "seventy miles north of Grand Central Station." He purchased the site in 1936 thinking that there he "could fish and hunt in season, grow a big garden, and still spend three days a week at the *New Republic* office." The barn is an immaculately kept and comfortable home containing a great many books and works of art; among the latter are pieces by Peter Blume and Alexander Calder. The house is eighteen miles from Brewster, New York, the location of the nearest train station. Cowley still commutes on occasion to New York City, where he is a consulting editor at the Viking Press.

Sherman is a small, quiet town located in a hilly, heavily wooded section of western Connecticut near the New York border. Cowley first came to the area in 1926 to be near his friends Hart Crane and Slater Brown as part of a "Connecticut migration" that also included in those days Allen Tate and Caroline Gordon Tate, Matthew and Hannah Josephson, Peter Blume, Robert Coates, and Nathan Asch. Since then the area has been a retreat for writers and artists, especially those linked, however strongly or warily, to New York City.

Though once an extensive traveler and lecturer, as well as a frequent visiting professor, Cowley is now more or less in permanent residence at Sherman, for at this point, he explains, he is "portable with difficulty." However, he does make appearances. In April 1981 he was at Harvard, his alma mater, to address those associated with the *Harvard Advocate,* which he edited more than sixty years ago, and also visited his granddaughter, Miranda, an undergraduate at the university. (His son, Robert, is an editor at a leading publishing house in New York City.)

Despite Cowley's limited mobility, he is not out of touch with a world that continues to seek him out for numerous reasons. At a Modern Language Association Convention special event entitled "Malcolm Cowley Talks about the Lost Generation," held during December 1978 in New York City, he captivated a huge standing-room-only audience in a hotel ballroom with his charm, his forthrightness, his lack of pretension, and his eloquent, informed presentation. He has also made occasional television appearances. Especially noteworthy have been televised interviews with him for programs about Hart Crane and William Faulkner. Most recently he appeared on NBC's "Prime of Your Life" to discuss *The View from 80.*

He mildly complains about having become a "national literary or scholarly resource" for those desiring information about the writers and artists he has known. Speaking not long ago he commented, "Sometimes, you know, I feel as if I was the last person who spoke some extinct language, like Cornish or Mohegan, as if I'm the last person remaining who knows the grammar and vocabulary. So that often I get questioned on the vocabulary, which doesn't ring bells to me. The questions them-

selves show the questioner doesn't know much about the field. So in those cases I generally avoid answering at all. But I do answer a lot of letters."

Television is one source of enjoyment for the Cowleys. When asked by Diane U. Eisenberg in 1979 what he and Mrs. Cowley find most pleasurable these days, he replied, "We enjoy watching television serials and features and we enjoy meeting friends. . . . The pleasure reading that I do has to do with one of our family pleasures at night sometimes. . . . watching the serial as novel on TV. When they put Trollope on TV, we read Trollope. . . . 'I, Claudius' set us to reading 'I, Claudius' or 'The Twelve Caesars,'. . . . Now that they're putting on *Anna Karenina,* I started reading Tolstoy again. Trollope, Tolstoy, Dickens. I like the serials but they are mostly on public television and mostly imported from England."

A primary concern, as ever, to Cowley is his trade, which he discusses from various vantage points in one of his recent books. –*And I Worked at the*

Malcolm Cowley

Writer's Trade (1978) is what its subtitle states, *Chapters of Literary History, 1918-1978.* The book is made up of chapters rather than essays, the author explains in his preface, because the parts tell a chronological story, part of an unfinished history of modern American letters. Or as Cowley told Eisenberg, "I have always been interested in doing a history of American letters and the literary life in my own lifetime; this book picks up some aspects of it that I'd neglected before. It deals with friends whom I haven't written about; it deals with sudden surges of emotion in the literary world, changing fashions, and finally with the sixties and with the resurgence of the religion of art in the 1970s. It is in many ways autobiographical. I love to write memoirs. In fact, the easiest parts of a book for me are the parts when I'm really collecting my own memories of something that happened."

Cowley's prose in *–And I Worked at the Writer's Trade* is, as John Leonard described it in the *New York Times,* characteristically "lean and sinewy. His moral metronome, as usual, ticks away. His acumen and liberal sympathies are, as ever, manifest. . . . There is not a page here without the watermark and signature of intelligence." Beginning with his friendships at Harvard in 1918, the book is primarily a series of appreciations of such writers of renown as Hemingway, Aiken, Faulkner, and Caldwell and of such forgotten or never well-known writers as novelist Robert M. Coates and poet S. Foster Damon. According to Reed Whittemore the discussion of "these lesser figures . . . will perhaps be the chief attraction of the volume. . . . He makes a good case for the talents and integrity of the neglected ones he deals with."

As with most of Cowley's literary history, *–And I Worked at the Writer's Trade* is to some extent "memoiristic," including details from his years at Harvard, in Greenwich Village, in Paris, at the *New Republic,* and as a member of the National Institute and the American Academy of Arts and Letters. It is also in part a sequel to *The Literary Situation* (1954) in that it further discusses Cowley's theory of literary generations and addresses such matters as the circumstances surrounding literary reputation, the importance of personal ethics, and the fictional necessity of "story" as opposed to the "anti-story" or metafiction. In this volume Cowley succeeds again in providing qualitative, at times definitive, critical judgments grounded in a confident sense of the necessity of moral and aesthetic "accountability."

The Dream of the Golden Mountains: Remembering the 1930s, published in March 1980, is yet another astutely perceptive addition to his continuing criti-cal and social (as well as autobiographical) history of American literature. The volume confirms his eclectic, cosmopolitan literary interests and the value of his vigorous, uncompromising approach to writers and writing. As always, a civilized persona moves through this work in a controlled, compassionate, lucid manner, alert to the shifting trends and spirits of the writers, the works, and the era under scrutiny.

In Eisenberg's 1979 interview, Cowley said of the forthcoming *The Dream of the Golden Mountains:* "I am trying to extend *Exile's Return*, or that sort of book, through the 1930s. But it's going to be a very different sort of book because I can't any longer use 'we' so freely as I did in *Exile's Return*. [There] I was conscious of speaking for many other people I knew. In the 1930s there was more difference of opinion and I have to be a great deal more objective."

In his writing Cowley discovered that the era of the 1930s "broke in two" about 1936, and so he concluded the book at that point. (He decided to write about the second "half" of the period in another book.) Cowley sees 1930 as "a watershed between two ages." The difference between the artistically explosive 1920s and the Depression decade was indeed acute; of the 1930s Cowley writes in his preface, "There has never been a period . . . when literary events followed so close on the flying coattails of social events." In fact, he focuses so intently on political concerns that literary matters frequently fade well into the background.

The "dream" of the title refers to the "daydream of revolutionary brotherhood" that haunted the early Depression years. Despite the Wall Street crash, despite the financial, personal, and professional stumbling of American society, Cowley felt at the time that "there was hope as well, the apocalyptic hope that a City of Man would rise on the other side of disaster. By surrendering their middle-class identities, by joining the workers in an idealized army, writers might help to overthrow 'the system' and might go marching with comrades, shoulder to shoulder, out of injustice and illogic into the golden mountains. That was the dream in an exalted form; I remember reading it in the shining eyes of younger people."

Cowley worked for the *New Republic* from 1929 to 1940, and many memories of his experiences there are included in *The Dream of the Golden Mountains*, but he also offers numerous examples of the discontent and bewilderment that swept the nation during the first half of the decade, none more telling than the pitiful "Bonus march" on

Washington in 1932, when unemployed World War I veterans who had gone to Washington to seek payment of their bonuses were forcibly dispersed by government troops. His personal participation in such confrontations was limited to his experience in the coal fields near Pineville, Kentucky, where he went in February 1932 with Edmund Wilson, novelist Waldo Frank, and editor Quincy Howe to express support for the striking miners.

Many Americans during the Depression were converted to a homegrown sense of radicalism, and writers and artists were especially attracted to the "daydream of revolutionary brotherhood." Many even turned to communism because, according to Cowley, the problems facing the nation were moral and religious as well as financial and political. Feeling increasingly threatened from all sides, they embraced a sanitized, watered-down brand of communism. However, the contradictions inherent in an artist's search for individualism within a mass or attempting to create lasting art out of temporary political upheavals were but two of the reservations that kept Cowley from joining the Communist party. He devoted his energies to completing *Exile's Return* instead.

For Alfred Kazin "the most telling part" of *The Dream of the Golden Mountains* "deals not with the Communist religion but with the empty American countryside and a ravaged people." Both are memorably evoked by Cowley's "unforgiving details" in a most telling, even poetic, manner. In fact, as the narrative closes in 1936, a series of withdrawals culminates in Cowley's return to rural Connecticut, and R. W. B. Lewis notes, "Cowley always writes an uncommonly agreeable prose, easy, lucid, . . . but his prose rises toward the fabulous and the poetic when he goes back to the country. . . . The poignant fading of the dream of the golden mountains was . . . somewhat mitigated by the reality of the green Connecticut hills and woodlands."

Cowley is now at work on a book that will, in effect, be the last volume of a trilogy about American literature and society between the world wars, a trilogy begun with *Exile's Return* and continued in *The Dream of the Golden Mountains*. The new book will cover the period 1936-1942, years during which his life "changed decisively," politically, socially, and artistically. Though the writing goes slowly in his eighty-third year, such labor had been a constant in his life, an all-abiding challenge. As he told Eisenberg: "The writer's trade is a laborious, tedious but lovely occupation of putting words into patterns. I love that trade, profession, and vocation. And that is something that persists over time."

Cowley's latest books are reminders of the overall importance of his career, of the fact that he has been a highly influential figure in American literature since 1929. If he has been overshadowed by contemporaries who possessed more flamboyant personalities or who limited themselves to writing in one genre, Cowley has always had impressive supporters and admirers, from those who praised his early promise as a poet to the likes of R. P. Blackmur, Allen Tate, and Stanley Edgar Hyman, who have acknowledged his importance as a literary critic. Surely few would disagree with a recent appraisal by Wallace Stegner: "He is certainly our best and wisest student of American writing. . . . No student of our literature can afford not to know everything he writes." As John Leonard expressed it, Cowley is "a hero of the culture we breathe."

Other:
The Portable Emerson, edited by Cowley and Carl Bode (New York: Viking, 1981).

Periodical Publications:
"A Response (concerning Crane's *Supplication to the Muses on a Trying Day*)," *Hart Crane Newsletter*, 2 (Fall 1977): 15-16;
"*The New Republic* Moves Uptown," *New Republic*, 178 (20 May 1978): 27-30;
"1935: The Year of Congresses," *Southern Review*, 15 (Spring 1979): 273-287;
"Two Views of *The Bridge*," *Sewanee Review*, 89 (Spring 1981): 191-205.

Interviews:
George Plimpton, "Malcolm Cowley . . . Talking," *New York Times Book Review*, 30 April 1978, pp. 7, 16, 18, 20;
Diane U. Eisenberg, "A Conversation with Malcolm Cowley," *Southern Review*, 15 (Spring 1979): 288-299;
Warren Herendeen and Donald G. Parker, "An Interview with Malcolm Cowley," *The Visionary Company: A Magazine of the Twenties*, 1 (Summer 1981): 8-22.

References:
John W. Aldridge, "Malcolm Cowley at Eighty," *Michigan Quarterly Review*, 18 (Summer 1979): 481-490;
Hans Bak, "Malcolm Cowley: The Critic and His Generation," *Dutch Quarterly Review of Anglo-American Letters*, 9 (1979): 261-283;

Please Return to MC

Malcolm Cowley--A Hasty Chronology

1893, Aug. 24. Born in a thunderstorm near Belsano, Pa., 70 miles east of Pittsburgh.

1904-1911. Public school in Pittsburgh. In the 8th grade at Liberty School (as also in high school) a classmate was Kenneth Burke.

1911-1915. Peabody High School in Pittsburgh, with an interlude of four months at Bryn Athyn Academy (1912), a Swedenborgian school near Philadelphia (father was Swedenborgian).

1915-1917. Harvard. class of '19. Ranked second in class as a freshman.

1917, April. Went to France to drive an ambulance for the American Field Service, but drove a munition truck instead, TMU 526.

1918. Back at Harvard for spring semester. In the fall went to Field Artillery Officers' Training Camp just before the Armistice.

1919. Greenwich Village. Half starved. In August married Marguerite Frances Baird.

1919, fall, to Feb., 1920. Back at Harvard for a final semester.

1920-21. Greenwich Village again, first freelancing, then a copywriter for Sweet's Architectural Catalogue.

1921-1922. To France on an American Field Service fellowship. Attended Université de Montpellier. Diplôme d' Études Française.

1922-23. Fellowship renewed. Lived in Giverny, fifty miles west of Paris. Met the Dada crowd. Helped to get out Secession and Broom.

1923-1925. New York again, and back to work for Sweet's Catalogue.

1925. Moved to Staten Island, then resigned from Sweet's to see if I could now earn a living by freelancing. Could, just.

1926. Moved to Sherman, Ct., renting a house for $10 a month.

1928. Bought an abandoned farm near Sherman, but on the New York side of the state line. 70 acres, $2800, which I didn't have. Made the downpayment with a prize of $100 from Poetry.

1929, October. Went to work for The New Republic.

1930. Invited to join the editorial board. Served as literary editor, 1930[1940.

1931. Peggy goes to Mexico for an amicable divorce. MC gives her the farm in NY State.

1932. Expedition to Pineville, Ky. MC marries Muriel Maurer, June 18, Communist election campaign.

1933. Springtime in Tennessee.

1934. Exile's Return published. (A first book, of poems, Blue Juniata, had appeared in 1929.) Son born, December.

1936. The Cowleys move to a remodeled barn in Sherman, CT.

1937. World congress of writers in besieged Madrid.

1940, December. Earthquake at The New Republic. MC loses post as literary editor and becomes the weekly book reviewer.

Cowley's autobiographical chronology

2---Chronology

1941, Dec., to March 1942. MC works in Washington for the Office of Facts
    and Figures. Is attacked by the Dies Committee. Resigns post in
    March; returns to Sherman (and to reviewing for The New Republic).

1943-1948. MC receives five-year fellowship from Mary Mellon; spends
    much of his time studying American literature. The Portable Faulkner
    (1946) was a first fruit of the study. In 1948 he resigned from The
    New Republic, when it moved to Washington.

1948. MC joined the Viking Press as a literary consultant.

1949. Elected to the National Institute (president, 1956-59 and 1962-65).
    Testified at both trials of Alger Hiss.

1950. Walker-Ames Lecturer at University of Washington, his first teaching
    assignment. Later assignments were at Stanford (four times, beginning
    in 1956), Michigan, Cornell, Minnesota, Hollins College (twice), and
    University of Warwick (England, 1973, the last).

1951. Exile's Return revised and reissued.

1954. The Literary Situation.

1962. Black Cargoes (with Daniel P. Mannix), a history of the Atlantic
    slave trade.

1966. The Faulkner-Cowley File.

1967. Think Back on Us.

1968. Blue Juniata: Collected Poems.

1970. A Many-Windowed House, essays on American literature.

1971. The Lesson of the Masters (with Howard E. Hugo), an anthology of
    great novels that had no success. (I mean the anthology hadn't.)

1973. A Second Flowering: Works and Days of the Lost Generation.

1978. And I Worked at the Writer's Trade.

1980. The Dream of the Golden Mountains. Also, in September, a short book,
    The View from 80.

----Of the books listed here, seven, or more than half, were published
after the author was 70.

George Core, "Malcolm Cowley 1898-," *American Writers*, Supplement II, Part I (New York: Scribners, 1981), pp. 135-156;

Benjamin DeMott, "Malcolm Cowley Writing . . . ," *New York Times Book Review*, 30 April 1978, pp. 7, 77;

Alfred Kazin, "Writers in the Radical Years," *New York Times Book Review*, 23 March 1980, pp. 7, 24;

John Leonard, Review of *–And I Worked at the Writer's Trade, New York Times*, 28 April 1978, p. 25;

R. W. B. Lewis, Review of *The Dream of the Golden Mountains, New Republic*, 182 (15 March 1980): 28-30;

Lewis P. Simpson, "Cowley's Odyssey," *Sewanee Review*, 89 (Fall 1981): 520-539;

Simpson, "The Decorum of the Writer," *Sewanee Review*, 86 (Fall 1978): 566-571;

Reed Whittemore, Review of *–And I Worked at the Writer's Trade, New Republic*, 178 (29 April 1978): 29-31.

AN INTERVIEW *with MALCOLM COWLEY*

DLB: About two and one-half years ago at a Modern Language Association convention you mentioned that you had become a national literary or scholarly resource, against your will, and that many people who wanted information straight from "the horse's mouth," so to speak, were seeking you out. Are you still besieged by such requests?

COWLEY: Indeed I am. Anybody who wants to write a book about the 1920s, particularly, sends me a letter and says, "Would you please answer this questionnaire of only six typewritten pages, single-spaced? Do you remember so and so?" A great deal of my time is taken up just answering letters. I don't *always* answer them. If they're interesting, if they ask interesting questions, I try to. I find that that cuts into my time for writing. I should like to retire as a national scholarly resource. But I do answer a lot of letters and it costs a great deal for postage. I'm always grateful to people who enclose a self-addressed, stamped envelope.

DLB: Could you give an idea of what, most recently, people are asking you about?

COWLEY: It's generally figures, people, that they

ask about. Others, though, ask about the present: "What is the difference between our generation and the generation of the 1920s?" That seems to be a favorite question. "Are we like them, the so-called lost generation authors, or are we a different breed?"

DLB: We would like to know some of the things you are doing now. For instance, we know that you were at Harvard this week, giving a talk. Could you tell us about it?

COWLEY: I read poems to them; I spoke about my theory of what a poem should be and how I had revised poems, and then picked up a little bit about being a national scholarly resource, how I hated it . . . read another poem and let it go at that.

DLB: Do you plan to give any talks or readings the rest of this year?

COWLEY: No, I have no schedule for talks. I am beginning to be "portable with difficulty." Somebody wants me to give a talk, I say, "All right, if you send somebody to my house to get us and deliver us to the hall and then take us home again, I'll consider it."

DLB: Is there something you would like to deliver a talk about?

COWLEY: Not at the present moment. I'm more interested in continuing my memories from the years 1936 to 1942, when my life changed decisively. . . . I found that the 1930s broke in two about the year 1936; the second half of the decade made a different story. So I'm starting out to write as much of that now as I have material on. Some of it I think is quite interesting.

DLB: Will this be a fairly long book?

COWLEY: About as long as *The Dream of the Golden Mountains*. I hope not longer. It's awfully hard to get time for writing.

DLB: And that's the major project . . . ?

COWLEY: That's the major project, at present. I'd like to write more poems. I don't want to do, at present, too much reviewing.

DLB: Are you writing creatively also now?

COWLEY: Creatively . . . I'm writing, shall we say, "memoiristically."

DLB: How about poetry? At the end of the twenties you were known primarily as a poet.

COWLEY: Indeed I was. Yes. I'd been writing reviews but I'd been publishing a great many poems. My first book of poems came out in 1929, and when I went on the staff of the New Republic I found I had less time for writing poems. There was another dash of poetry-writing activity in the year 1968 in reference to Blue Juniata: Collected Poems. I revised a great many old poems completely and wrote a number of new ones.

DLB: Have you written many new ones in, say, the past two or three years?

COWLEY: No, I'd like to get back to it.

DLB: There's a rather interesting tone at the end of The Dream of the Golden Mountains: Remembering the 1930s. It seems to come to a kind of extraordinarily tentative moment, as if some decisions were about to be made historically. Is this the beginning of the next memoir?

COWLEY: Yes, the period from '36 to '39 is the period of the People's Front when the effort was to create an alliance against Hitler and stop the march of fascism, and then that came to a dramatic halt with the Hitler-Stalin Pact on August 23, 1939.

DLB: Then this memoir will conclude in 1942?

COWLEY: Yes, I came back to the country with the decision that I was no longer going to sign anything, make statements, endorse statements made by others, that I was out of politics.

DLB: Do you project a work after this next work that will take you beyond 1942?

COWLEY: At the age of eighty-two going on eighty-three it is very dangerous to project too many books. Maybe if I did it would keep me alive forever because I wouldn't get them finished.

DLB: Flaubert says you are known by your omissions. In your writing career you have written many different things—poems, reviews, and history. Have you ever been tempted by the novel?

COWLEY: Tempted, but I managed to resist the temptation. No, I am really not by essential talent a novelist. I don't remember properly what people said.

DLB: In the beginning, in high school, didn't you intend to be a playwright?

COWLEY: Oh yes, I had that idea for a while, but I gave it up quite early.

DLB: Your true genre is poetry, is it not?

COWLEY: I think so. My true genre, much more than you might think, is "feeling." Considering that very often I don't feel, that's a surprising thing to say, but when I do feel, the surge of emotion makes me think, yes, this is the point where I should begin.

DLB: –And I Worked at the Writer's Trade and The Dream of the Golden Mountains, your most recent books besides The View from 80, were very well received by the critics, didn't you think?

COWLEY: Yes, the last three books have all been received better than I expected them to be.

DLB: Almost all the critics said they were well written, and Alfred Kazin said the book Malcolm Cowley had been writing all his life is The Lives of the American Poets. Do you have any comment on Mr. Kazin's comment?

COWLEY: I think I ought to get credit for writing well, but that is always a two-edged compliment, because if someone says of a writer that he writes well, that means that he is perhaps more impressed by the style than he is by the substance.

DLB: You seem to have a high opinion of writers who have a very good prose style, and you speak of yourself at one point as a "wordsmith," someone who worked very hard at the development of a prose style. Do you have some reflections on the nature of a prose style?

COWLEY: The basis goes very much back to two things. One is simple logic: Does this statement make sense logically? That combines with whatever feeling one has for the graded series. If you have three events in a series, make sure that the last event is more dramatic than the two that preceded it; that's an old, old principle. The other thing is simply the narrative principle: to engage your readers' interest, to arouse their expectation, and then in some unexpected way to fulfill the expectation. So much of our work comes down to "story," whereas story has been looked down upon during the past thirty or forty or fifty years. It seems to me that anything that a story can't be made of lacks something in vividness and force.

DLB: Another thing in reference to prose style: you have linked it in some degree to morality, and in one of your recent comments, which is becoming a famous one, you said (in one of your books) that "no complete son-of-a-bitch ever wrote a good sentence."

COWLEY: That is an overstatement, but on the other hand a writer can't afford to be a complete son-of-a-bitch. There's something false in a complete son-of-a-bitch, whereas the writer eventually has to lay himself bare. If there's any insincerity in his doing that, the sentence isn't good. Or you can take something that Kenneth Burke once said on the subject, that an author can make his words lie but can't make his prose lie, because when he's telling a lie the whole rhythm and the whole imagery of his prose are different from when he's telling the truth about himself.

DLB: In the 1940s you withdrew from New York City to Sherman, Connecticut. Various people have wondered about that and about your responsiveness to the countryside, . . . as if you were going back to your roots.

COWLEY: Well, you remember I had moved to the country in 1936, but I went in three days a week until there was a revolution at the *New Republic* in November-December 1940, and I was no longer an active editor; instead I was a weekly book reviewer. I could do that from here in Sherman, going into New York only one day a week. Besides, I'd always been a countryman, and I became very content with not taking part in New York life. What got me were the antagonisms, the gossip, the little wars that are still going on. I wanted no part of them.

DLB: Just recently R. W. B. Lewis, writing about *The Dream of the Golden Mountains*, praises your style and says it rises toward the poetic when you speak about the countryside. He suggests at the end of his review that the "dream of the golden mountains"

was "mitigated by the reality" of the Connecticut countryside.

COWLEY: I was always somewhat of a solitary. My real great pastime was walking in the woods.

DLB: Would you say something else about your current work for Viking?

COWLEY: I'm technically retired now, and my post is literary consultant. I go to Viking about twice a month. I usually have some book that I'm working on as a project. The last big editing job was a book that will come out next fall, *Waldo Emerson* by Gay Wilson Allen, which I think is a very good life of Emerson. I worked on the Emerson Portable, choosing the contents of it, although I didn't write the introduction. I have part of the editorial job on other portables as they come out, and sometimes I read manuscripts if they seem to fall within my field.

DLB: You are a past president of the National Institute of Arts and Letters. Do you remain active in that organization?

COWLEY: Oh, yes, I remain active in the Institute and the Academy. That is, I get down to their dinners—about three dinners a year and two luncheons. Sometimes I serve on a committee.

DLB: In *The Dream of the Golden Mountains*, and really in all your books, isn't there a search for "character," maybe a search for an American character, for what an American should be like in a given historical period?

COWLEY: I don't think that I have really searched for "character." I've admired character when it came to the fore, but I don't think I ever set out consciously to look for it.

DLB: You have written that you consciously avoided fame early in your career because you felt that might have something to do with a threat to integrity.

COWLEY: You know, this is true. It's not an exaggeration. I questioned the effect fame had on people I knew who had been snatched into fame—its effect on their characters and lives. I thought that what I wanted to do was just to hold out without being corrupted. In fact, I had a couple of definite chances to become a "widely known" author when I was younger—what they used to call "being circused"—and I just wouldn't follow through on them—they didn't arouse my interest.

DLB: You have nevertheless become famous, at this point, don't you think? You are usually referred to as one of the most distinguished critics of modern American literature. Recently John Cheever, whom you know very well, said, "Malcolm Cowley's uncompromising dedication to the importance of literature is unequaled in our time, as is the depth and breadth of his view of the literary landscape." However, some recent reviewers and commentators on your writing have noticed what they call a sense of "wistfulness" in your writing, a sense of regret about the past. Do you think that is there in any way?

COWLEY: Wistfulness, no. There *is* that regret for the past, which I think is a dangerous thing to have, and yet I can't escape the conclusion that this was a more pleasant country in 1910 than it is in 1981. In many ways American life *was* freer and more open in 1910. But we have achieved a certain moral freedom in 1981 that we didn't have in 1910, 1920. Nobody goes to Paris now to be free. You can be just as free in Chicago or even in Dubuque.

DLB: Is there anything you regret about the past, in particular, in reference to your career?

COWLEY: I regret that I didn't get more work done.

–Donald G. Parker

Robert de Graff
(9 June 1895-1 November 1981)

Richard Layman
Columbia, South Carolina

Robert Fair de Graff, the visionary publisher who founded Pocket Books, the first successful mass-market paperback imprint, died on Sunday, 1 November 1981, at his home in Mill Neck, Long Island. He was eighty-six.

Wallis E. Howe, Pocket Books' first sales manager and a longtime employee of de Graff's, described his boss in 1962 as "a tall, patrician, even courtly gentleman . . . who is equally beguiling to the ladies at the helm of one of his four foreign cars or in impeccable flannel shorts on the grass courts of the Piping Rock Club. . . . I have never known him to read a book for pleasure, but I have rarely seen him err in judging the sales potential of a book."

De Graff began his publishing career in 1922 as a salesman for Doubleday, Page. Three years later, in 1925, he became a vice-president and director of the firm's reprint subsidiary, Garden City Publishing Company. Feeling that retail book prices were too high, even for cut-rate hardback reprints, de Graff began searching for ways to sell books more cheaply. At Doubleday, Page he created the successful, inexpensive line of nonfiction reprints called Star Dollar Books.

In 1936, de Graff left Doubleday, Doran (Doubleday, Page had merged with Doran in 1927) to become president of the reprint publishing company Blue Ribbon Books. There he had full freedom to test his innovative ideas about merchandising. Early in 1937, he managed a takeover of the fifty-year-old reprint house A. L. Burt, with its list of some 2,000 titles. He also began testing distribution through chain department stores. De Graff's market tests showed that books priced at thirty-nine cents sold twelve times as rapidly as those priced at seventy-five cents, so early in 1938, he launched Triangle Books, a clothbound line reprinted from Blue Ribbon's reprint lists and priced at thirty-nine cents. Triangle Books were designed to compete directly with popular magazines in department stores.

Buoyed by his perception of a new method for distributing low-priced books, de Graff resigned from Blue Ribbon Books in February 1938 to plan his own publishing company, a paperback reprint house that would sell quality books for a quarter. To achieve such a low retail price, he would reduce the discount to retailers from the customary 30-35% to 20%; distributors' discounts were dropped to 36%

Robert de Graff

July 1943 advertisement for Pocket Books

from the normal 46%; and authors' royalties, which had been at least 10%, were reduced to 4% for Pocket Books. He planned to take advantage of the latest printing and binding technology and the most economical page size (pocket size—about four inches by seven inches) to reduce production cost; he would set up his own distribution system, concentrating on efficiency, customer service, and point-of-sale advertising. By utilizing the distribution techniques of magazine wholesalers and selling directly to chain department stores, he could reduce costs while increasing direct sales contact with his retail outlets.

De Graff received little encouragement in his new venture. The impossibility of selling paperbacks "had almost become an axiom in publishing . . . because there had been so many failures in the last 30 or 40 years," he recalled. "Possibly it was my persistent nature that urged me to prove once and for all that it really *wouldn't* work that tempted me to try it. . . . I felt that if a first-class book, editorially and physically, could be made, the turnover would be sufficiently rapid that the wholesaler and retailer would not require the usual large margin."

De Graff found support for his ideas at Simon and Schuster, where Leon Shimkin, Richard Simon, and Max Lincoln Schuster went into partnership with him and provided him with an office space for his three-person staff in the Simon and Schuster building. De Graff owned 51% of the new company, called Pocket Books, which had a capitalization of $30,000. On 19 June 1939, after test marketing 1,000 copies of Pearl Buck's *The Good Earth*, Pocket Books published ten titles in printings of 10,000 copies each (except for *Enough Rope*, of which 7,600 copies were printed). The first ten titles were James Hilton, *Lost Horizon*; Dorothea Brande, *Wake Up and Live*; William Shakespeare, *Five Great Tragedies*; Thorne Smith, *Topper*; Agatha Christie, *The Murder of Roger Ackroyd*; Dorothy Parker, *Enough Rope*; Emily Brontë, *Wuthering Heights*; Samuel Butler, *The Way of All Flesh*; Thornton Wilder, *The Bridge of San Luis Rey*; and Felix Salten, *Bambi*. The success of the line was immediate and in 1935 Marshall Field, a master merchandiser with a special interest in mass communications, bought the company for $3 million with the stipulation that de Graff would remain as president and that Field would not interfere with his operation of the business.

In 1949, when de Graff became chairman of the board of Pocket Books, leaving the presidency to Leon Shimkin, annual sales were 180 million books and the principles of mass-market paperback publishing which he had innovated had already revolutionized the publishing industry. De Graff retired before Pocket Books' twenty-fifth anniversary (by which time sales were 300 million copies annually), devoting his last years to philanthropy and community service.

In 1961 he saw the company he had founded go public, offering stock worth $72 million. Since 1966, Pocket Books has been a subsidiary of Simon and Schuster.

References:

Thomas W. Ennis, "Robert F. de Graff dies at 86; Was Pocket Books Publisher," *New York Times*, 3 November 1981, p. 11;

Piet Schrenders, *Paperbacks, U.S.A.* (San Diego: Blue Dolphin, 1981), pp. 18-30;

John Tebbel, *A History of Book Publishing in the United States*, volumes 3 and 4 (New York: Bowker, 1978, 1981).

Joan Didion

(5 December 1934-)

Margaret A. Van Antwerp
Columbia, South Carolina

See also the Didion entry in *DLB 2, American Novelists Since World War II*.

NEW BOOKS: *Telling Stories* (Berkeley, Cal.: Bancroft Library, 1978);
The White Album (New York: Simon & Schuster, 1979; London: Weidenfeld & Nicolson, 1979).

In recent years Joan Didion has emerged as a prominent yet enigmatic literary personality. Since the 1977 publication of her best-selling novel, *A Book of Common Prayer*, works by Didion have been included with increasing frequency in anthologies, a bibliography of her writings has appeared, and scholarly articles investigating various aspects of her prose have become more numerous. This critical acclaim for Didion's work has been accompanied by enormous popular success. Mass-circulation magazines such as *Ms.*, *People*, and *Self* have featured interviews with the author, and she has often been a television talk-show guest. Despite this wide exposure Didion remains, as one interviewer suggests, "more than *slightly* enigmatic." Her life, in the words of another, seems "a wealth of contradictions." And her work, as reviews of her most recent book indicate, is becoming in some ways controversial.

Didion lives in Los Angeles with her husband, John Gregory Dunne (the author of *Delano*, *The Studio*, *Vegas*, *True Confessions*, *Quintana & Friends*), and her fifteen-year-old adopted daughter, Quintana Roo. Since 1977 two collections of Didion's short works have been published. The first, *Telling Stories* (1978), was a limited-edition keepsake volume prepared for contributors to the Bancroft Library of the University of California at Berkeley, Didion's alma mater. This slight volume contains the only three short stories Didion ever wrote: "Coming Home," "The Welfare Island Ferry," and "When Did Music Come This Way? Children Dear, Was It Yesterday?" All of them were written in 1964, a crucial year in Didion's literary career, the year after her first novel, *Run River*, was published. Didion recalls 1964 as a time of fear that she might never write another novel: "I sat in front of my typewriter, and believed that another subject would never present itself. I believed that I would be forever dry. I believed that I would 'forget how.' " For this reason Didion wrote the three stories collected in *Telling Stories*, as what she has called "a kind of desperate finger exercise."

The stories, because of their limited printing, received very little critical attention. They are interesting, however, because in them Didion rehearses themes that have now become hallmarks of her prose: the loss of one's home and one's past and entrapment in an alien and often debilitating present.

The White Album (1979), Didion's second book since 1977, is a collection of twenty journalistic pieces written between 1968 and 1978. Many of them appeared originally in the *Esquire* column "The Coast," written alternately by Didion and Dunne from February 1976 through December 1977. Some are based on Didion and Dunne's experiences as screenwriters in Hollywood, where in recent years they have worked together on a screenplay entitled "Water" and completed the screenplay for *True Confessions* (1981), from Dunne's 1977 novel of the same name. Most notably, all of the essays of *The White Album* are intimate memoirs of Didion's personal and professional life during the last years of the 1960s and the first of the next decade.

Despite her prominent place in the most fashionable literary circles of New York and social circles of Hollywood, Didion is by her own admission an introvert, an outsider. Dunne screens all Didion's telephone calls and often sits in on the interviews she gives, while Didion manages all of the couple's business dealings like the "fragile little stainless-steel machine" one friend has called her. "I'm really too shy," Didion once told an interviewer for *Ms.* magazine. "I don't talk much. I am not articulate. I don't make judgments. . . . I'm only myself in front of my typewriter."

This feeling of ease in front of the typewriter is perhaps Didion's most remarkable feature. As one of her former editors, Ralph Graves, observes: "Joan gives everyone the impression of being very private. Then she'll turn around and write the

inside-of-the-stomach stuff that you'd think you'd
need to know her five years to find out." For Didion,
however, "inside-of-the-stomach stuff" is an essential part of the writer's contract with readers: "If you
want to write about yourself," Didion has remarked,
"you have to give them something." And this, precisely, is what Didion has done in the most forceful
of the essays collected in *The White Album*, a work
which is in many ways a sequel to her 1968 collection, *Slouching Toward Bethlehem*.

The White Album takes its title from the 1968
Beatles album (which has no name but only a plain
white jacket). Didion found the record "ominous
and disturbing, an album inextricably connected to
the Manson murders and the dissonance of the
60s." The Beatles album was one of the last collaborations of the rock group before its fragmentation.

The record was also a kind of "catechism" for
Charles Manson and his followers: after the brutal
murder of actress Sharon Tate Polanski and six
others, the title of a song from it, "Helter Skelter,"
was found written in blood on the refrigerator. All
of these facts related to the record seemed somehow
symbolic to Didion, corollaries of her own physical
and psychic disintegration of the time. The title
essay, "The White Album," is a bold and often
moving working out of those corollaries.

In the essay, Didion uses what she terms the
cinematographic technique of the "flashcut" to alternate between evocations of her personal crisis
and the national crises of the late 1960s. Of Didion,
one learns that she suffered a breakdown during
the summer of 1968, around the time that she was
named a *Los Angeles Times* Woman of the Year,

Joan Didion

during the summer of Robert Kennedy's assassination and of the violence at the Democratic convention in Chicago. Didion's experience was characterized by "an attack of vertigo, nausea, and a feeling that she was going to pass out"—facts which Didion claims to record verbatim from the psychiatric report filed on her by a private clinic in Los Angeles. "By way of comment," she writes, "I offer only that an attack of vertigo and nausea does not now seem to me an inappropriate response to the summer of 1968."

Throughout "The White Album" Didion is able to maintain a perfect balance between her personal anguish and her account of the social and political upheaval of the 1960s. As one reviewer notes, "there are many reasons for the effectiveness of 'The White Album,' [but] the most striking has to do with the use to which personal neurosis has been put. Joan Didion . . . gives the impression of having refined it to the point where it vibrates in exquisite attunement to the larger craziness of the world she inhabits and observes." In the essay the "maniacal desire" for order and control that Didion describes elsewhere comes into contact with the chaos of the student strikes that rent San Francisco State College in 1968—strikes in which, Didion observes, "disorder was its own point." She recalls interviewing Black Panther Eldridge Cleaver and speaking with him about the commercial prospects of his book *Soul on Ice*—"not an unusual discussion between writers, with the difference that one of the writers had his parole officer there and the other had stood out on Oak Street and been visually frisked before coming inside." And, along with many other of her experiences as a reporter that seemed to suggest the nature of the breakdown she was about to suffer, she remembers buying the dress for Linda Kasabian, one of Manson's followers, to wear to court to testify against her one-time leader.

Didion's house at the time figures importantly in the essay as a tangible symbol of the disintegration she senses both around and within her: "This house on Franklin Avenue was rented, and paint peeled inside and out, and pipes broke and window sashes crumbled and the tennis court had not been rolled since 1933, but . . . during the five years that I lived there, even the rather sinistral inertia of the neighborhood tended to suggest that I should live in the house indefinitely." Didion's interest in the symbolism of house and home is one that runs not only through the title essay, but through the entire collection as well. It surfaces in "Many Mansions," suggestive of America's political and moral decline. Here Didion compares the ostentatious, never-

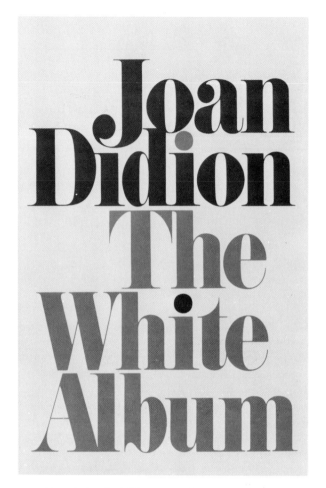

Dust jacket for Didion's second collection of essays

inhabited California governor's mansion that Ronald Reagan built with the modest apartment of his successor, Jerry Brown, and the old, "extremely individual house" in Sacramento that belonged to the forerunners of both. It surfaces again in "The Getty," Didion's account of her visit to the "seventeen-million-dollar villa built by the late J. Paul Getty to house his antiquities and paintings," and makes a final appearance in the concluding essay of the book, "Quiet Days in Malibu." In this essay, Didion writes of the house to which she moved, after her breakdown as if to suggest quiet acceptance of that experience and all that it implied: "When I first moved in 1971 from Hollywood to a house on the Pacific Coast highway I had accepted the conventional notion that Malibu meant the easy life. . . . By the time we left Malibu, seven years later, I had come to see the spirit of the place as one of shared isolation and adversity, and I think now that I never loved the house . . . more than on those many days when it was impossible to leave it when fire or flood had in fact closed the highway."

Another preoccupation that recurs in the essays of *The White Album* is Didion's suggestion that the boundaries between literature and life are indistinct: fictional characters possess the same authenticity as those of flesh and blood. She cites Cecelia Brady, a character in F. Scott Fitzgerald's *The Last Tycoon*, as an authority in the essay "In Hollywood," and says that Evelyn Waugh might have created the students at San Francisco State. James Pike, the controversial Episcopal bishop featured in "James Pike, American," seems "the shadow of a great literary character, a literary character in the sense that Howard Hughes and Whittaker Chambers were literary characters."

In the essay "In the Islands" Didion suggests that places become real only when they become a part of literature: "Certain places seem to exist mainly because someone has written about them. Kilimanjaro belongs to Ernest Hemingway. Oxford, Mississippi, belongs to William Faulkner. . . . A place belongs forever to whoever claims it hardest, remembers it most obsessively, wrenches it from itself, shapes it, renders it, loves it so radically that he remakes it in his own image."

To interviewer Linda Kuehl, Didion admitted that this sense of confusion and even the dependence of life upon art has been for her a constant concern: "I was one of those children who tended to perceive the world in terms of things read about it. I began with a literary idea of experience, and I still don't know where all the lies are." She further revealed that her penchant for living "life on the edge" is a "literary idea," one that "derives from what engaged me imaginatively as a child." It is this life on the edge that is evident on nearly every page of *The White Album*.

Interestingly, reviewers of the collection paid little attention to Didion's preoccupation with the reality of literary ideas. Most agreed that *The White Album* represented a more mellow, more widely ranging collection than *Slouching Toward Bethlehem*, which Didion herself terms a much less "tentative" work. Praise was nearly unanimous for Didion's style—"a fine steel framework that gives these . . . pieces a unity"—and for her incisive and demanding eye for detail. In these regards, the comments of reviewer Robert Towers are typical: "All of the essays—even the slightest—manifest not only her intelligence, but an instinct for details that continue to emit pulsations in the reader's memory and a style that is spare, subtly musical in its phrasing and exact. Add to these her highly vulnerable sense of herself, and the result is a voice like no other in contemporary journalism."

Most of the critical complaint that surfaced in reviews of *The White Album* has to do with the highly personal, confessional tone of many essays, especially those in which Didion describes her breakdown ("The White Album"), her bouts with migraine headaches ("In Bed"), and the threatened disintegration of her marriage to Dunne ("In the Islands"). Didion's comment, as she announces the possibility of divorce from Dunne, is typical of those that aroused protest: "I tell you this not as aimless revelation but because I want you to know, as you read me, precisely who I am and what is on my mind. I want you to understand exactly what you are getting: you are getting a woman who for some time now has felt radically separated from most of the ideas that seem to interest other people. You are getting a woman who somewhere along the line misplaced whatever slight faith she ever had in the social contract, . . . in the whole grand pattern of human endeavor."

Reporter Hillary Johnson summarizes negative critical reaction to such unburdenings with a revealing anecdote. Johnson met Didion at a 1977 publisher's party to celebrate the appearance of *A Book of Common Prayer*: "Though the space was filled with small groups of New Yorkers chatting loudly and amiably, Didion stood alone, near the iced shrimp and crudités, her face bearing an expression of dread lest anyone approach her. Few did approach her, possibly because they had read some of her magazine essays and articles, which have now resurfaced in a collection called 'The White Album.' " Despite an awareness that it is "Didion's ultrasensitivity that has made her such a unique, perceptive reporter" in *The White Album*, Johnson concludes that "One just wishes the woman wasn't in so much pain." Lance Morrow, reviewing for *Time*, laments especially Didion's inclusion in the collection of thoughts on her own divorce, previously published as "a disagreeably calculated column she wrote for *Life* in 1969." Rosemary Dinnage for the *Times Literary Supplement* focuses upon the *"Despair"* of Didion's insistent message, *"It doesn't matter,"* while Ann Hulbert for the *New Republic* feels that "we . . . want to know *why* Didion wants to expose such raw, private experience, to feel that we are walking around with her bad dreams for some other reason than that she's self-indulgent and we're morbidly curious."

A small group of critics demonstrated concern over Didion's sincerity in the essays. In an article for the *Nation* Barbara Grizzuti Harrison spoke of the author's "covertly political messages" in *The White Album* and elsewhere, called her style "a bag of tricks . . . (I don't know why they have evoked so much wonder)," and declared that most episodes of *The White Album* "put me more in mind of a neurasthenic Cher than of a writer who has been called America's finest woman prose stylist." "Entrepreneurs of Anxiety" John Lahr titled his article on Didion and Dunne for a recent issue of *Horizon*. She is the "Princess of angst"; he is unable to "see the hellishness behind the vulgarity he enjoys"; together they are "the Lunts of the Los Angeles literary scene," "pretenders to the throne of high culture; and only a society indifferent to literature could tolerate their pretensions to excellence." Critics sharing a strong inclination toward feminism similarly found fault with Didion's essay "The Woman's Movement," which describes the movement as a "curious historical anomaly" based on a Marxist vision of women as the proletarian class. As Martha Duffy summarized it from a feminist point of view, the essay errs in its examination of "only threadbare documents of the movement." Of Didion Duffy writes, "One can almost hear Hemingway cheering her on."

The most academic of the discussions among critics of *The White Album* centered on the question of where Didion's greatest talents lay, in the writing of fiction or nonfiction. Ironically, for Didion "never wanted to be a journalist or reporter," it is for her nonfiction that the critical accolades are more willingly given. It is Morrow who best summarizes the current case for the superiority of Didion's reportorial work: "Didion's novels," he writes, "are less interesting than her collections of magazine pieces; paradoxically, the novels do not exert the dramatic force of her journalistic essays."

Work that Didion has promised for the future may prolong this discussion. Her work in progress includes the novel "Angel Visits," with which she has been concerned for several years. The title, Didion has announced, comes from a Victorian expression meaning "pleasant visits of short duration." The novel, set in Honolulu where Didion has spent much time, began to take form in her mind as the story of "an extended dinner party in which the lives of a family are revealed," but the work has been continually changing. Didion spoke to Kuehl about the literary idea of the "dark journey" that has been associated with the novel in her mind and about the evolution of her idea for "Angel Visits": "I can recall [as a child] disapproving of the golden mean, always thinking there was more to be had from the dark journey. The dark journey engaged me more. I once had in mind a very light novel, all surface, all

conversations and memories and recollections of some people in Honolulu who were getting along fine. . . . Well, I'm working at that book now, but it's not running that way at all. Not at all."

In addition to her current work as novelist, journalist, and screenwriter, Didion is a frequent contributor to the *New York Times Book Review* and the *New York Review of Books*. She is also at work on "Fairytales," a volume of nonfiction based on her childhood in California. It seems likely that she will remain an important and provocative writer, perhaps most remarkable in the way noted by Walter Clemons in his review of *The White Album* for *Newsweek*: "The presence of brilliantly capable writers whose best work is not that in which they themselves take most pride is a phenomenon of our time. Edmund Wilson yearned to be honored as a novelist. So do Mary McCarthy, Norman Mailer, Gore Vidal, Elizabeth Hardwick and Susan Sontag. All of these look like permanent writers; each aspires to an eminence their essays have already secured for them. Joan Didion joins them: 'The White Album' is her best book since 'Slouching Toward Bethlehem' eleven years ago." However Didion's future works affect the opinion set forth by Clemons, there seems little doubt that her name will continue to be associated with such impressive literary company as this.

Screenplay:

True Confessions, by Didion and John Gregory Dunne, United Artists, 1981.

Periodical Publications:

"Meditation on a Life," Review of Elizabeth Hardwick's *Sleepless Nights*, *New York Times Book Review*, 29 April 1979, pp. 1, 60;

"Letter from Manhattan," *New York Review of Books*, 16 August 1979, pp. 18-19;

"I Want to Go Ahead and Do It," Review of Norman Mailer's *The Executioner's Song*, *New York Times Book Review*, 7 October 1979, pp. 1, 26, 27;

"Nuclear Blue," *New West*, 4 (5 November 1979);

"Mothers and Daughters," *New West*, 4 (12 December 1979);

"Boat People," *New West*, 5 (25 February 1980);

"The Need to Know," by Didion and John Gregory Dunne, *New West*, 5 (5 May 1980);

"Without Regret or Hope," Review of V. S. Naipaul's *The Return of Eva Perón with the Kill-*

ings in Trinidad, *New York Review of Books*, 12 June 1980, pp. 20-21;
"Honolulu Days," *New West*, 5 (14 July 1980).

Interviews:
Susan Braudy, "A Day in the Life of Joan Didion," *Ms.*, 5 (February 1977): 65-68, 108-109;
Digby Diehl, "A Myth of Fragility Concealing a Tough Core," *Saturday Review*, 4 (5 March 1977): 24;
Linda Kuehl, "Joan Didion," in *Writers at Work: The Paris Review Interviews*, Fifth Series, edited by George Plimpton (New York: Viking, 1981), pp. 339-357.

Bibliography:
Fred Rue Jacobs, *Joan Didion–A Bibliography* (Keene, Cal.: Loop Press, 1977).

References:
Barbara Grizzuti Harrison, "Joan Didion: The Courage of Her Afflictions," *Nation*, 229 (26 September 1979): 277-286;
John Lahr, "Entrepreneurs of Anxiety," *Horizon*, 24 (January 1981): 36-39;
C. L. Westerbrook, Jr., "Coppola Now," *Commonweal*, 106 (28 September 1979): 531-532;
Mark Royden Winchell, *Joan Didion* (Boston: Twayne, 1980).

F. Scott Fitzgerald
(24 September 1896-21 December 1940)

W. R. Anderson
Huntingdon College

See also Fitzgerald entries in *DLB 4, American Writers in Paris, 1920-1939* and *DLB 9, American Novelists, 1910-1945*.

NEW BOOKS: *Correspondence of F. Scott Fitzgerald*, edited by Matthew J. Bruccoli and Margaret M. Duggan, with Susan Walker (New York: Random House, 1980);
Poems 1911-1940, edited by Bruccoli (Bloomfield Hills, Mich. & Columbia, S.C.: Bruccoli Clark, 1981).

NEW BIOGRAPHY: Matthew J. Bruccoli, *Some Sort of Epic Grandeur: The Life of F. Scott Fitzgerald*, with a genealogical afterword by Scottie Fitzgerald Smith (New York & London: Harcourt Brace Jovanovich, 1981; London: Hodder & Stoughton, 1981).

Zelda Sayre Fitzgerald:
Scandalabra: A Farce Fantasy in a Prologue and Three Acts (Bloomfield Hills, Mich. & Columbia, S.C.: Bruccoli Clark, 1980).

Throughout his professional life, F. Scott Fitzgerald practiced a detailed and meticulous, if somewhat disorganized, self-historiography. That he was an inveterate keeper of records, lists, correspondence, and notes is evidenced in the publication during the last two decades of four volumes of letters, his *Ledger* (in which he recorded invaluable biographical and professional information), his *Notebooks*, and material from the Fitzgeralds' scrapbooks. His biographers have benefited from this habit—indeed, compulsion—but the depth of Fitzgerald's self-examination and self-knowledge, as revealed in these documents, has at times not been fully understood. Matthew J. Bruccoli's *Some Sort of Epic Grandeur*, the most recent biography of Fitzgerald, draws extensively on Fitzgerald's records to supplement other biographical research. Throughout its pages, a dual voice speaks: that of the biographer, recording, commenting, and evaluating; and, equally valuable, that of the subject, struggling to comprehend, order, and preserve the meaning of his life and work as well as to understand the two important decades of American history and culture in which he worked.

With the publication of *Some Sort of Epic Grandeur* and *Correspondence of F. Scott Fitzgerald*, we probably now know as much about Fitzgerald as posterity can know about a literary figure. As his records inform biography and criticism, it is no longer possible to discount him as an immensely talented but careless and frivolous playboy of the Jazz Age. The Fitzgerald who steps forth from the pages of *Some Sort of Epic Grandeur* as well as from material in his *Correspondence*, which brings to print more than 600 pages of heretofore unpublished letters from and to Fitzgerald, is much more detailed and complex. The *Selected Letters of Ernest Hemingway* adds some further illumination in its references to Fitzgerald.

Some Sort of Epic Grandeur both enlarges and corrects the record of Fitzgerald's life. By meticulous correlation of the documented facts about that life with the short stories, novels, drama, and nonfiction pieces Fitzgerald wrote, it emphasizes his hard work and craftsmanship. From its pages emerges a record of his struggle with the growing awareness of the price one must pay to exploit life's possibilities to the utmost. For Fitzgerald, that price always included dedication, labor, and, most important to a true understanding of his achievement, moral responsibility. *Some Sort of Epic Grandeur* recognizes the Fitzgerald around whom myths were built: the symbolic figure of golden talent and instant success who came to typify the glory of the 1920s in the minds of much of the public—and perhaps in his own mind. At the same time, however, *Some Sort of Epic Grandeur* painstakingly and persistently examines the complex truth at the center of the Fitzgerald myth. No longer is it possible for a student of Fitzgerald's career to remain unaware of the consistent growth in his sense of moral responsibility and his awareness of moral failure as they develop both in his life and his work. In the process, the biography provides complete histories of the composition of all five of Fitzgerald's novels. One of its most important contributions is its full and perceptive treatment of Fitzgerald's relationship with the film industry in Hollywood, especially during the last years of his life. In the process of tracing his determined efforts to succeed as a screenwriter, it offers the fullest record of that phase of his career. Fitzgerald in Hollywood is shown as an intelligent, hardworking craftsman. Unlike earlier books such as Budd Schulberg's fictional *The Disenchanted* (1950) or Aaron Latham's biographical *Crazy Sundays* (1971), *Some Sort of Epic Grandeur* does not attribute Fitzgerald's relative lack of success as a screenwriter to alcoholism or failure to understand Hollywood. Rather, it shows that he was in many ways sensitive to and appreciative of the artistic potential of moving pictures. His failure to become a major screenwriter resulted rather from a combination of personal difficulties—his

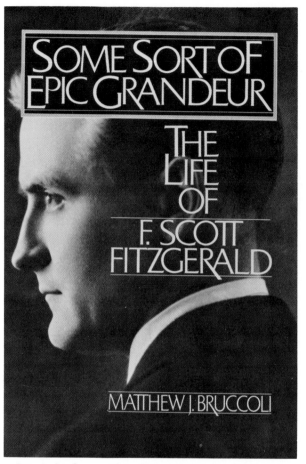

Dust jacket for recently published biography of Fitzgerald

wife's mental illness, his own physical illness (complicated by occasional bouts of drunkenness), emotional strain resulting from the breakup of his family, and the financial pressure inherent in all of these. Fitzgerald came to see that he would be unable to adapt to the team-writing system prevalent in Hollywood and returned to his real medium, the novel. Nevertheless, he learned much about the craft of screenwriting. It was not simply an easy way to make money for him, and *Some Sort of Epic Grandeur* shows the reader a conscientious and competent craftsman who, under other circumstances, might well have made a permanent contribution to the history of film composition.

In their examination of the private life, if such a term can be applied to Fitzgerald, *Some Sort of Epic Grandeur* and *Correspondence* are both honest and compelling in documenting Zelda and F. Scott Fitzgerald's struggles to survive economically and artistically. Fitzgerald fought continually to provide economic stability for his family. He was unable to do so, despite literary success that certainly placed him solidly in an upper-middle-class income group. His struggles to live on an income that was lavish by average standards—he earned between $15,000 and $40,000 a year during most of his career, at a time when many Americans were making do on as little as $1500—would seem comic if they were not so strongly identified with the central dilemma of his life. From almost the beginning, he and Zelda sought grace and stability in a world where those were increasingly rare commodities, particularly for individuals who sought to forge them from their own artistic labors. The effort, complicated by his alcoholism and poor health and her mental collapse, was doomed. Yet their lives, as they now can be understood, were for the most part valiant and honest struggles, far from the frivolity and superficiality of the popular mythology long associated with them.

Indeed, one of the important contributions of these new Fitzgerald studies is the extent to which Fitzgerald and (to a lesser degree) Zelda Fitzgerald can be understood not as victims of the 1920s/1930s boom and bust, but as individual representatives of the rich and complex social history of their era. They epitomize their times not as examples of the cost of Jazz Age hedonism, the hollowness beneath the glittering bubble, but as examples of the American spirit struggling naively but idealistically with the newfound wealth and power of the period between the world wars, when the agrarian republicanism of the American Dream was forced to adapt to world power and responsibility as well as to success and wealth. The adjustments were difficult, for the culture and for the individual. It is one of the lasting strengths of Fitzgerald's art that he seems from the beginning to have recognized that his life was intrinsically American, of its time. Given that recognition, and the talent to blend personal experience with historical process, he was able to create fiction of lasting beauty and tragic significance from his own successes and failures, aspirations and anguish. Fitzgerald rarely wrote mere disguised autobiography, but his own experience, beliefs, and sense of values were deep in the fabric of characterization as well as in incident and detail in most of his work. Thus, as *Some Sort of Epic Grandeur* demonstrates, the study of his fiction contributes to an understanding of his life. More important, the study of his life and those of his family is basic to a full understanding and appreciation of his fiction.

Fitzgerald's *Correspondence* and *Some Sort of Epic Grandeur*, as they place in print virtually all the hitherto unpublished documents of his life, make clearer than earlier scholarship the closeness and the bitter struggles of the Fitzgerald family relationships. Some of the material these books contain emphasizes the agony and failures of that family life, particularly in correspondence associated with Zelda Fitzgerald's insanity. There are letters in which the Fitzgeralds blame each other and strain for self-justification. Yet there is also correspondence full of mutual dependence, respect, and love. Toward the end of Fitzgerald's life, when they were living on opposite ends of the continent—he in Hollywood, she in North Carolina and Alabama—they accepted essentially separate lives. Yet neither would abandon the other, for to do so would be to deny the value of their mutual past, as well as to abandon responsibility. Theirs was a heartrending marriage, but despite their lapses and failures, it remained a marriage—another evidence of commitment, particularly on his part, to responsibility.

In presenting the facts of the Fitzgeralds' lives as completely as possible, *Some Sort of Epic Grandeur* constantly sets straight the record. Fitzgerald did not make a drunken fool of himself at Edith Wharton's tea at her house outside Paris in July 1925. Her formality so inhibited him that he tried telling a slightly risque story to enliven the party, but he was not drunk, nor was she shocked; in fact, she seems not to have understood the point of the anecdote and simply to have dismissed it without reaction. According to a companion, Fitzgerald showed no evidence of guilt or embarrassment on his return trip to Paris. Thus one of the most well known of the anecdotes of Fitzgerald's drunken social excess is not true. There are, to be sure, more accurate records of his alcoholic antisociability.

The most persistent false perception of Fitzgerald, that he was a sycophantic and naive worshiper of wealth and the wealthy, has been exposed as false by most of the Fitzgerald scholarship of the past decade. The myth has nonetheless persisted. *Some Sort of Epic Grandeur* should be the final denial of that myth, as it patiently reiterates that such legendary encounters as the one between Fitzgerald and Hemingway over the magic of wealth never happened. In "The Snows of Kilimanjaro" (1936) Hemingway wrote about "poor Scott Fitzgerald," who had begun a story, "The very rich are different from you and me" (a line from Fitzgerald's "The Rich Boy," though not its beginning), and who had been put in his place by the retort, "Yes they have more money." Although Bruccoli's earlier *Scott and Ernest* (1978) had already thoroughly exposed the fallacy of that exchange, *Some Sort of Epic Grandeur* should ensure that Fitzgerald's romance with money will be seen as critical examination rather than simply infatuation.

The new biographical material in *Some Sort of Epic Grandeur* provides a measured and objective context within which to read the Fitzgeralds' work and against which to measure critical studies. Its broad and detailed perspective permits useful application of more specific and directed studies such as Thomas J. Stavola's *Scott Fitzgerald: Crisis in an American Identity* (1979), which traces Fitzgerald's struggle toward artistic maturity through a "psychohistorical study" based on Erik H. Erikson's theory of life cycles. It stresses the formative influence of childhood pressures as shaping both the Fitzgeralds toward rebellion, conflict, and self-doubt and follows that influence through Fitzgerald's four completed novels. The temptation toward psychoanalysis through literature is strong with the Fitzgeralds, but a balanced knowledge of their biographies will permit the careful reader to avoid the more obvious pitfalls of bending their fiction to fit a theory about their lives.

Brian Way's *F. Scott Fitzgerald and the Art of Social Fiction* (1980) is a balanced and thoughtful consideration of Fitzgerald's writing which separates the careful craftsman from the romantic mythology. It concentrates on *The Great Gatsby*, *Tender Is the Night*, and a few of the stories, attempting to place them in the tradition of perceptive social analysis typified by the works of Henry James and Edith Wharton. While the scope of Way's study is severely restricted, his intelligent reading of the novels and his tendency to question some of the old assumptions of Fitzgerald criticism—notably that Fitzgerald's work should be read only as social mythology in the vein of James Fenimore Cooper—make *F. Scott Fitzgerald and the Art of Social Fiction* a useful tool to understanding one of the more important qualities of Fitzgerald's achievement: his awareness of the nuances of social behavior as they shape character and define experience in a particular time and place. Way's book lends credence to Bruccoli's depiction of Fitzgerald as a sensitive and conscientious artist at work.

In the context of Fitzgerald biography, new publications of Scott Fitzgerald's poems and Zelda Fitzgerald's play *Scandalabra* become useful literary documents, though neither of them is of particularly high artistic merit. Like most potential writers, Fitzgerald tried his pen on poetry as well as fiction in his formative years. Beginning with those early efforts, *Poems 1911-1940* traces Fitzgerald's lifelong flirtation with verse. About half of the collected poetry belongs to two major groups—the librettos

he wrote for the Triangle Club musicals while he was at Princeton and the poetry and verse he included in his first novel, *This Side of Paradise*. Some of the rest was printed in college publications such as the *Princeton Tiger* (a humor magazine) and the *Nassau Literary Magazine*. Others appeared in his preparatory school's magazine and in commercial magazines, including the *New Yorker*. Many survived in his *Notebooks* and other papers.

Fitzgerald's command of figurative language, imagery, and verbal nuance is generally recognized as a major factor of his literary skill. The haunting lyricism of Fitzgerald's prose style, enriched by his capacity for electrifying the reader with its rightness of cadence or precision of detail, is an attribute justly renowned as poetic. One assumes that the writer of such prose would also be a good poet. In fact, though he began writing verse early and continued until the end of his life, and though he was an avid and sensitive reader of English poetry (he adored Keats, revered Shakespeare and Wordsworth, and admired and understood his contemporary Eliot), Fitzgerald was not himself a good poet. Much of his verse is pedestrian. The serious poetry is rarely inspired, and the humorous verse lacks the satiric thrust or rowdy vitality Hemingway achieved in some of his efforts. Nevertheless, Fitzgerald's poetry is a measure of his interest in the writing of others and of his growing literary craftsmanship.

The librettos he provided for three of the Triangle Club's annual musicals—*Fie! Fie! Fi-Fi!* (1914), *The Evil Eye* (1915), and *Safety First!* (1916)—are sprightly and clever and excellent apprentice work for one who would develop an outstanding ear for the rhythms and cadences of sophisticated speech. They were a demanding discipline, requiring inventiveness with rhyme and flexibility in adjusting meaning to the musical score. The Triangle presentations were not amateurish. The Gilbert and Sullivan quality of their productions demanded fluency, sophistication, and wit, as is demonstrated by these lines from "A Slave to Modern Improvements" in *Fie! Fie! Fi-Fi!*:

There's the scientific question of the power of
　　　　　　　　　　　　　　　digestion,
　It worries some, it doesn't worry me.
　And of course my father's dictum was that I
　　　　　　　　　　　　　should be a victim,
　Get tested for my true capacity.
　So they told me at the table,
　"Eat as much as you are able,

So that we can find out what we want to
                                    know."
And they brought me in, a platter,
What it bore, it doesn't matter,
And then producing watches told me "Go."

Fitzgerald's satire "To My Unused Greek Book," from the *Nassau Lit* of June 1916, weakens at the end but evidences an early appreciation for the rhythms and images of Keats, whose "Ode on a Grecian Urn" it parodies. More competent poetic

Dust jacket for first collected edition of Fitzgerald's poems

apprenticeship is manifested in "Princeton—The Last Day" (*Nassau Lit*, June 1917). Its cadences and lush, subdued imagery are tributes to Tennyson: "The last light wanes and drifts across the land, / The low, long land, the sunny land of spires." Its complex form—the final line of each nine-line, iambic-pentameter stanza an Alexandrine (iambic hexameter) and the *abbabcbcc* rhyme scheme—is a slight modification of the demanding Spenserian stanza. Another poem first published in the same issue of the *Nassau Lit*, "On a Play Twice Seen," is

also a tribute to the demands of traditional poetic structure, a classic Petrarchan sonnet. Both are competent poems written in difficult forms. Fitzgerald, perhaps under the tutelage of his friend John Peale Bishop, was developing a strong interest in the intricacies and disciplines of literary craftsmanship. Another poem of the same period, "Rain Before Dawn" (*Nassau Lit*, February 1917), contains hints of the imagistic and metaphoric power of Fitzgerald's fiction to come:

                                    Now the dawn
Tears from her wetted breast the splattered
blouse
Of night; lead-eyed and moist she straggles
o'er the
                                    lawn
Between the curtains brooding stares and
stands
Like some drenched swimmer—Death's
within the
                                    house!

"The Pope at Confession" (*Nassau Lit*, February 1919) is an early expression of Fitzgerald's sense of moral responsibility and the weight of moral dread, manifested as an almost symbiotic relationship between pontiff and wraithlike confessor. "Our April Letter," from Fitzgerald's *Notebooks*, would seem to be a later work, judging from an evident debt to the conversational free verse and haunting imagery of T. S. Eliot: "April evening spreads over everything, the purple / blur left by a child who has used the whole paint-box." "One Southern Girl," also from the *Notebooks*, is rich in Keatsian sensuosity and drowsy timelessness, as well as in biographical reminiscence:

Still does your hair's gold light the ground
        And dazzle the blind 'till their old ghosts
                                    rise;
Then, all you cared to find being found,
        Are you yet kind to their hungry eyes?
Part of a song, a remembered glory—
        Say there's one rose that lives and might
Whisper the fragments of our story:
        Kisses, a lazy street—and night.

Other later poems also reflect concerns in Fitzgerald's life, as in the echoes of lost youth which sound through "Thousand-and-First Ship" or the pangs of uncertain love evoked in "Some Interrupted Lines to Sheilah," written for Sheilah Graham. At the end of his life, he was still concerned with sharpening his appreciation of form and sound, as shown in his translation-adaptation of Rimbaud's "Voyelles," first published in Sheilah Graham's *College of One* (1967).

In his introduction to *Poems 1911-1940*, poet James Dickey wrestles with the irony that Fitzgerald, among the most lyrically poetic of novelists, was unable to raise his poetry above derivativeness and mediocrity. Dickey's insight into the nature of poetic creativity leads him to conclude that Fitzgerald's particular talent required the narrative framework of the novel to bring out its most haunting and perceptive poetic qualities: "Fitzgerald's lyricism is deeply embedded in a sense of drama, and to employ it he has need of situations in which the drama has been built up by the preceding interaction between people. . . .The paradox is this: Fitzgerald's lyric gift, his gift of the heartbreak phrase, the unforgettable, intrinsically poetic choice of words, needed not the structures and formal manipulations peculiar to versification, but those of the novel and story." As Dickey's observations indicate, Fitzgerald was an artist of fiction, but his lifelong absorption in poetry served him well as a means for honing his critical judgment and as finger exercises in technique and form in preparation for his poetic fiction.

Another recent Fitzgerald publication is Zelda Fitzgerald's 1932 play *Scandalabra*. An airy farce in the tradition of Oscar Wilde, it was written while she was undergoing treatment in Baltimore for her second breakdown. Fitzgerald encouraged her to turn to brief, light composition both as therapy and to turn her interest away from more serious fiction, his exclusive province, he felt. Until it was finished, he apparently took no hand in *Scandalabra*. Then, after a dress rehearsal ran five hours, Zelda Fitzgerald prevailed on him to assist in cuts and revision. Working all night, Fitzgerald helped the author and the production company, the Junior Vagabond Players, to make the play effective for its run from 26 June to 1 July of 1933. Zelda Fitzgerald had intended the play for Broadway, but a disappointing reception doomed it to the single run in Baltimore.

Despite its trivial plot and ephemeral quality, the play is another useful document in Fitzgerald studies. It is a product of Zelda Fitzgerald's determination to find a place for herself as a creator. Yet, placed in the biographical context of Fitzgerald's fear that her writing would interfere with or undercut his own career, its very frivolity is a commentary on her efforts to find an outlet which would not threaten him. The plot follows the struggles of a serious and moral young couple to live down to the demands of an absurd legacy which requires that they engage in a risque and deliberately debauched existence in order to inherit a fortune. They are guided in their attempt by a comic gentleman's gentleman called Baffles. The plot is thus an ironic reversal of that of Fitzgerald's second novel, *The Beautiful and Damned*, with its relentless revealing of the destructive effects of inheritance on two frivolous people. Through a series of sleight-of-hand plot complications, including a reverse surprise ending, the couple earns the inheritance without actual loss of virtue, but the delicate hints of sexual suspicion which color the play also reflect the Fitzgeralds' tortured marriage, as do both *Tender Is the Night* and Zelda Fitzgerald's novel *Save Me the Waltz*.

Zelda Fitzgerald's dialogue is witty and sprightly, but she, like her husband, wrote better fiction than drama. *Scandalabra*, like Fitzgerald's poetry, is worth preserving less for its artistic merit than as a useful document in literary history. Like the letters and biographical writing which have recently been published, they illumine and complete the context of the lives which produced some of the best fiction of the twentieth century and two novels, *The Great Gatsby* and *Tender Is the Night*, which are among the principal achievements of American literature.

References:

Ernest Hemingway Selected Letters 1917-1961, edited by Carlos Baker (New York: Scribners, 1981);

Thomas J. Stavola, *Scott Fitzgerald: Crisis in American Identity* (New York: Barnes & Noble, 1979);

Bryan Way, *F. Scott Fitzgerald and the Art of Social Fiction* (New York: St. Martin's, 1980).

William Price Fox

(9 April 1926-   )

George Garrett
York Harbor, Maine

See also the Fox entry in *DLB 2, American Novelists Since World War II.*

NEW BOOK: *Dixiana Moon* (New York: Viking, 1981).

William Price Fox's latest novel, which was mentioned as being in progress at the time of the earlier *DLB* entry about him, appeared in 1981 with strong supporting statements by writers as respected and as various as Kurt Vonnegut, Richard Yates, Pauline Kael, and John D. Macdonald. And like each of his other works since the celebrated *Southern Fried* (1962), *Dixiana Moon* was moderately successful at the marketplace and yet mostly ignored by the reviewers and critics who have and exercise the power to make or break literary reputations. There is something of a mystery about Fox's reputation; for, clearly, his work has been appreciated by many readers over the years. And his fellow writers have long since recognized him as a vital and original storyteller. People such as Vonnegut, Yates, and Macdonald seldom write blurbs for anyone and have reputations for great and serious probity. That they should choose to speak out for Fox and his work is a matter of real consequence. But the support of neither readers, writers, nor even the regional book reviewers in his native South—and these have been, by and large, generous in their appreciation of Fox's work—has been able to give Fox the kind of national recognition that he seems justly to deserve. There are, perhaps, reasons behind, if not for, this injustice. And *Dixiana Moon*, a novel which shows Fox at his best, all his gifts in order, all his professional skills brought to bear on a pertinent and interesting (and, as always, highly amusing) story, is a good place to examine the discrepancy between his limited literary reputation and his considerable achievement.

It should be said at the outset, however, that this problem has not deterred Fox from continuing his own creative work. And he continues to live in Columbia, South Carolina, teaching creative writing to students at the University of South Carolina.

Recently he realized a long-held dream when he, together with his wife and son, bought and moved into a fine house on Wheeler Hill, the highest spot in Columbia, a residential neighborhood of large old houses richly shaded by ancient live oaks and other hardwood trees. But he has not lost touch with the other side of life in Columbia, that side made

William Price Fox

most familiar in his novels and stories. For he still holds frequent and energetic court at the Capitol Cafe on Main Street, where one can easily see many characters who appear to have emerged full-blown from the pages of a Fox novel.

The typical Fox story may push itself to the hyperbolic, humorous boundaries of the credible, may end on the wild and woolly near edges of the purely fabulous. But, unlike the fictions of many contemporary writers, it never begins there. Instead it grows and then flowers out of the plain, gritty specificity of the familiar. The roots of his fables are real. And so it seems relevant that he has chosen to return to and remain at the place of his beginnings, to live close to his own roots. It is likewise significant that even when dealing with characters who are in many details distinctly different from himself, Fox tends to draw directly from the capital of his own experiences to invest imaginary figures with the breath of life.

For instance, Joe Mahaffey, the delightfully complex and indefatigable narrator of *Dixiana Moon*, is a salesman for a printing and packaging company. So, for a time, was William Price Fox. Mahaffey, in effect, runs away with a circus. So did Fox, once upon a time. But we are not dealing with anything so commonplace as a portrait and celebration of the artist as a young man or, for that matter, with a simple rejection of the hard-grabbing way of life in America in this last quarter of the century. True, Mahaffey gives up his career as a salesman to join the amazing mud-circus world of Buck Brody. But it is not an obvious and easy choice for him to make, and it is the cumulative experience of the entire story which allows him to make that choice. It is a natural choice, for love and for life, but we arrive at the wisdom of it at the same time that Joe does. It is not the typical situation of waiting for the protagonist to discover the obvious. We are not entitled to condescend to Joe Mahaffey (or, for that matter, to any of the others among the crew of major and minor characters). And we are not allowed to anticipate or outguess him. And therein lies one important difference between the fiction of Fox and that of many of his more prominent contemporaries. It lies in the fullness and richness of characterization. Again and again his characters surprise us, and sometimes even themselves, by their capacity to be something more than the stereotypical sum of their parts.

Joe Mahaffey is a case in point. Happy and unhappy, he loves the performing craft of selling. And he does it well. He is a good salesman. One reason is that he has a real enthusiasm not merely for the business of selling a product but also for the product itself. He knows printing and packaging inside and out, and he knows and admires quality work even as he rejects the cheap and the shoddy and the phony. As a narrator in this first-person story, he is able to articulate, gracefully enough, both his enthusiasms and his ethical and aesthetic

Dust jacket for Fox's most recent novel

standards. A good con man himself, he is able to persuade us, more or less, to share them. Similarly and simultaneously, thanks to the lifetime experience of his own father, a dreamer and a schemer and always a loser, he is equipped to understand and, more important, to see through the scams of his Southern buddy, Buck Brody, and also to recognize the rich self-delusions which serve to give life and breath to the con man's dreams. He knows well enough "how all they needed was a little time and a little money and a little break and it was going to be a brand new horse race." Yet, knowing and understanding, Joe freely chooses that way of life in the end.

What we are talking about here is unusual dimensionality of character, of characterization in the classic and dramatic sense—classic in that the author is equally involved, or equally disengaged if you prefer, with each and all of the characters, even with Joe as first-person narrator; who, after all, speaks only of and for himself and not for Fox; dramatic in that events occur and forces collide without other inference or commentary than that of the narrator, who, after all, is continually changing as he experiences the events of the story. This dramatic quality is almost purely Jamesian. Fox is often compared by other writers to Mark Twain, and justly so. There is much of the finest spirit of Twain in Fox's full range of humor and in his mastery of the living American vernacular and, as well, in the kind of story he tells. Here, for instance, the journeys and tribulations of Joe Mahaffey and Buck Brody deliberately evoke recollections of the archetypal Duke and Dauphin in *Huckleberry Finn*. But, perhaps because the dazzling surfaces of his work divert us, we miss the truth that Fox is just as much in the moral tradition of Henry James where both ambiguity and the power of resolution are derived, first, from a many-sided view of things and, secondly, from an insistence upon the free will of characters who must make moral decisions. That is to say, in the case of *Dixiana Moon*, no matter how much we, the readers, may *wish* for Joe Mahaffey to choose the life of the circus over the corporation and no matter how much he may favor the former over the latter, the choice, to have any meaning, must be a real one involving a weighing and sifting of good things and bad. Joe, a great maker of lists, is fully aware of that. And it must be a free choice; Joe must at least perceive himself to be judging, then acting freely. Now, add to this the fact that Joe Mahaffey is an "irrepressible optimist," that neither angst nor heebie-jeebies nor routine blues can keep him down or hold him back for long, and you can

begin to see how far the world of Fox's fiction is from much recent American fiction. He writes comedy (though, like all good comedy, it hovers always on the edge of real disaster, even tragedy) at a time when comic fiction is rare. He creates dimensional characters at a time when the conventions of characterization are more ignored than honored. Intellectually, thus ideologically, he is at least a skeptic of the age's dominant, deterministic, Marxist-Freudian secular tradition or its offshoot—behaviorism. The kind of story Fox likes to write simply will not work if the characters are merely puppets manipulated by huge, invisible social and economic forces. These forces may or may not exist, like ghosts and other psychic phenomenon. But his characters must at least preserve the freedom allowed by Boethius in *The Consolation of Philosophy*. That is, they perceive themselves to be both free and responsible and try to act accordingly.

Finally, Fox's work is socially distinct from the prevailing contemporary mode (one is tempted to call it the Establishment) in American fiction. Fox accepts America, with all its ambiguities and contradictions intact, just as he accepts his characters and they accept their world, with an absolute minimum of judgmental posturing. Thus, politics, political answers and solutions to problems do not enter into his fiction very much except at a remove and by inference. At a time when much serious fiction in America—think of Roth, Heller, Mailer, Vonnegut, Malamud, Updike, etc.—is riddled with politics, Fox has chosen to deal with the subject only insofar as it may legitimately impinge upon the lives of his characters. Which is to say not very much. Pop culture—the movies, songs, television shows and commercials—is far more influential in their lives than the sound and fury of political action. Finally, at a time when national critics and reviewers have declared the Southern literary renaissance and flowering to be over and done with, Fox is uncompromisingly Southern, part of the Southern literary tradition going back to Mark Twain and beyond him to Twain's roots, to the frontier and backwoods storytellers whose persistent haunting is the chief spirit of the Southern tradition.

Among the moderns he is closer to Erskine Caldwell and to some of Faulkner, especially Faulkner's comic novels (including *As I Lay Dying*) than to the more decorous Fugitive-Agrarian school. Among his contemporaries he is at least kin to Calder Willingham and Harry Crews, though never so emphatically sardonic as the former and nowhere so trendy and fashionably surreal as the latter. And in *Dixiana Moon* Fox offers a new twist to the Southern novel; for Joe Mahaffey is not a Southerner, nor is his off-again-on-again girl friend, Monica. Choosing each other at last, choosing the life of Buck Brody's mud circus, they also choose the South for a home place. So, in one sense, *Dixiana Moon* is a story of conversion. Conversion from one way of life to another and from one place to a new one. For *this* to work within the strict demands Fox makes upon himself as craftsman, Mahaffey must be at once sensitive to and appreciative of place in general, the sense and feel of it. Which he is. And so, interestingly, some of the most sensitive renderings of the particular beauties and excitements of present-day Manhattan are to be found here in *Dixiana Moon*. Fox handles the city as well and as easily as and much more lovingly than any of the Eastern urban writers for whom it is the chief locus of wonder and danger. Weighing the pros and cons, Joe perceives most of the faults of the South, old and new, and there is much about his life in New York that he loves without reservation: "But most of all I missed the action. Winter was half over now and in a few more weeks it would warm up and the balloon men and the Italian-ice vendors would be out at Central Park, and Monica and I would be cruising through the zoo and heading over for the Tavern on the Green." What he chooses, though, and in so choosing follows the great national migration of the past two decades, is positive. Not some-

thing preserved from the past, but rather something else. "Something bigger and wilder and better, with more money and more fun and more everything of everything. And right there, steering the Olds down the Dixiana Highway, with the elephants blocking out the sun and the guitar sound and that great smell of cold beer, I knew exactly what I was going to do."

There is much more to single out for praise in William Price Fox's mature fictional art, as witnessed here in *Dixiana Moon*—the wonderfully clear and vivid and witty style, the economy and graceful pace of his story, the sensuously realized surfaces of places and things, his refusal to settle for easy labels and cliches, this refusal resulting in a continuing sequence of little surprises, his perfect-pitch ear for American speech of our time, his own irrepressible good humor and optimism, and, perhaps most of all, the pure fun of his invention. Very few of our good, serious novelists—and we must certainly number Fox among them; he has earned his way and right, with or without critical recognition—are as much *fun* to read as Fox is. If, as seems likely, he keeps on in the directions indicated by *Dixiana Moon*, the problem of critical recognition may prove to be irrelevant. Readers have already found him, and it seems only a matter of time before they will come together to offer the one kind of recognition that is irrefutable.

Herbert Gold
(9 March 1924-   )

Brooks Landon
University of Iowa

See also the Gold entry in *DLB 2, American Novelists Since World War II.*

NEW BOOKS: Slave Trade (New York: Arbor House, 1979);
He/She (New York: Arbor House, 1980);
A Walk on the West Side: California on the Brink (New York: Arbor House, 1981);
Family: A Novel in the Form of a Memoir (New York: Arbor House, 1981).

Herbert Gold speculates that he "may be the only middle-aged Jewish novelist from Cleveland, Ohio, ever to contribute a Jaguar to the Zen Buddhist order," and he is probably right. Undoubtedly, he is also among those American novelists and essayists best attuned to life in California and to the agonizing dynamics of contemporary male-female relationships—most sadly, divorce. Gold has long been a prolific writer, as a novelist, an essayist, a short-story writer, an autobiographer, and a journalist. His recent work suggests that, if anything, his output is speeding up: since 1979, he has produced three novels, *Slave Trade*, *He/She*, and *Family*, and a collection of essays, *A Walk on the West Side: California on the Brink.* "I can't help telling stories," Gold explains. "In fact, most of my critics would say I tell too many stories." Conscious of the fact that in some critical circles to be prolific is to make the quality of one's work suspect, Gold persuasively argues, "The prejudice against writing a lot is like saying love is too important to do it all the time—you should only make love four or five times in your lifetime and make sure it's terrific. It doesn't work that way."

Gold's recent work signals both a turn and a return in his career. After writing several novels that drew heavily from his Midwestern and Jewish roots—*The Prospect Before Us* (1954), *The Man Who Was Not With It* (1956), *Fathers* (1967)—in the late 1960s Gold shifted his focus to California, where he had moved in 1963. The novels *The Great American Jackpot* (1969), *Swiftie the Magician* (1974), and *Waiting for Cordelia* (1977) are all set in California and respond to the prevailing concerns of 1960s

Herbert Gold

and 1970s California, particularly San Francisco. This California is again celebrated and satirized in Gold's 1981 collection of essays, *A Walk on the West Side*. There, Gold looks at California with a kind of bemused tolerance totally lacking in the writings of more insistent chroniclers such as Nathanael West and Joan Didion. "California is less a country of the mind than one of the playful imagination—a story which ends with another story," he notes in "Some Misconnections of Soul in California," and he concludes that "California is special, typical, hopeless, and still full of hope." In another essay, Gold quotes William Saroyan as telling him, "I'm growing old! . . . I'm falling apart! And it's VERY INTERESTING!" Something of Saroyan's spirit infuses Gold's essays, as they seem to suggest that to "ride with the flow" makes good sense, even if the cliche and many of its worshipers grate on the sensibility. One cannot read these essays without agreeing with Laura Freid, who recently characterized Gold as "a man who fits into the mobile twentieth-century American lifestyle with remarkable ease, while at the same time damning it for the visible wreckage it leaves." The nineteen pieces in *A Walk on the West Side* should further cement Gold's well-deserved reputation as a skilled writer-of-all-trades. Some years ago, Gold noted of his nonfiction, "There's a high in doing journalism because you do have this power to manipulate reality. . . . I like to deal with the real world, so I think information is important. The journalism I do helps to keep me in touch with what's going on."

Gold's essays and his fiction both indicate that one thing going on is the complete breakdown of marriage as an American institution. One of his essays in *A Walk on the West Side* begins with the observation that "in San Francisco most marriages seem to be in escrow, most relationships in a state of sustained title search," and two of his most recent novels, *Slave Trade* and *He/She*, suggest that he sees this condition as general. Both novels also signal a turn away from California: while its action opens in San Francisco, *Slave Trade* moves to Europe and Haiti and across the United States; *He/She* is as vague in its setting as it is in the personal-pronoun "names" of its two major characters.

Slave Trade, Gold's eleventh novel, is also his most enigmatic: written in the general manner of a hard-boiled detective novel, it follows the involvement of Sid Kasdan, a "defrocked" San Francisco private eye, in an international scheme for supplying young Haitian boys to wealthy perverts. As would be expected of a book purporting to follow the detective formula, Gold's novel features first-person narration, slowly unraveling mysteries, a knockout scene or two, various colorful villains, and a twisting plot. However, the substance of *Slave Trade* departs completely from the detective pattern. While he literally sells his services to the Haitian slave traders, escorting the young boys from their "school" to their buyers, Sid is himself a slave to the memory of his former wife who has cheerfully and efficiently divorced him. All of Sid's energy goes toward missing his ex-wife, and his scruples are as enervate as his spirit. Of his almost zombielike pandering of young boys, he reflects, "Well, I'd abolished morality in California, like so many others, as a way of staying young. I was making it from boyhood clear into middle age without ever taking on the duties of a man, whatever they were. And I was broke. And I was stuck. And I was curious. So I might want to ride with this, too, until it didn't feel good anymore."

Finally, after delivering Lucien, a particularly intelligent and sensitive boy, into the sadistic hands of a rich California veterinarian, Sid decides that it indeed does not "feel good anymore." He frees the boy and sets out on a cross-country drive toward Miami, hoping to return the boy from there to his native village in Haiti. Sid's belated efforts in Lucien's behalf, however, prove hopelessly quixotic: once in Haiti, Sid discovers that his former wife now works for the slave traders. They murder Lucien, and the novel closes with Sid's negotiations to save his own life. The result of these negotiations remains unknown. Unlike recent "soft-boiled" detectives such as Thomas Berger's Russel Wren or Richard Brautigan's C. Card, Sid is no joke: he kills to avenge Lucien's murder and he is so completely "hard-boiled" that he is almost impervious to suffering and injustice in the world around him. The only suffering he recognizes is his own; the only injustice, that done to him by his wife. Although surrounded by the trappings of the detective story, Sid is essentially a man paralyzed by divorce. "What slavery is: is not being in possession of yourself," his ex-wife reminds him, and while Sid can escape the possession of his employers, he cannot escape possession by his love, his dream of his marriage.

Slave Trade did not fare well with reviewers, but Gold's twelfth novel, *He/She*, a book explicitly concerned with divorce, had them scrambling to find new superlatives. *He/She* chronicles the agonizing dissolution of a marriage, as both husband and wife struggle to find words for their complicated and contradictory feelings. "Their marriage was tender, practical, playful, and finally its body was obscured to both of them by the birth of their child and the convulsions of the time. People need freedom, at least I do, she said. Neither of them had expected this. Their divorce was amicable and mysterious."

He (the characters are never named) likes to think of marriage as a "festival," even though he admits to himself that he has been disappointed and bored by his wife. She, so efficient in other matters, fumbles to make him understand her quiet rage, her determination to seek a life of "unboredom." "I can't divorce myself," she explains. "I can't even divorce our child. I've got to divorce someone." When he desperately tries to hold on to their marriage, she snaps, "You used me when we were married to make yourself happy, and you're still using me to keep yourself unhappy." He resolves to keep calm and patiently tries to put things together again; she declares, "I didn't marry you for your patience."

No reader of Gold's recent writing, fiction or nonfiction, will underestimate the impact of his own two divorces on his sensibility. His 1948 marriage to Edith Zubrin ended in 1956, and more recently he was divorced from Melissa Dilworth, whom he married in 1968. In *He/She* he meticulously charts the disintegration of a marriage with the discipline of a dedicated researcher viewing his own cancer cells though a microscope. Larry McMurtry, himself a writer much concerned with the breakup of relationships, claimed that Gold's focus in *He/She* was so tight "that one is reminded of those little lights doctors use when they need to peer up a nose or in an ear." Describing the novel as a "primal moan," McMurtry said in the *New York Times Book Review*, "Some readers will find it riveting, and others claustrophobic, depending on what stage they're at in their own marriages." Joyce Carol Oates found *He/She* riveting. "So magnified is Gold's domestic drama," she wrote in *Mademoiselle*, "so minutely dissected his struggling, unhappy, confused husband and wife, that the reader comes to feel he has witnessed a real marriage in its combative deterioration." Anatole Broyard called *He/She* Gold's best novel and, referring to van Gogh's phrase "the brokenhearted expression of our time," summed up the book as "not abject or pathetic or sentimental—just brokenhearted."

Although She in Gold's novel initiates a divorce that He does not want, the book derives much of its strength from refusing to judge motives. Gold's subject is always the dynamics of a relationship, the tenacity of the idea of marriage, an idea that continues to haunt one after the death of the

22

She had counselled patience to me before, but never claimed it for herself. She had never counselled disappointment. Her hands looked empty and weary. Usually they were sewing, cooking, admonishing. She had always promised hard work would be rewarded. But maybe a marriage isn't supposed to be just hard work after all, her marriage or mine.

"I met your father" -- I already knew this -- "we were ice skating at the rink on Euclid, City Ice and Fuel. He was funny and smart and my sister knew him, she recommended him, a good provider." Her skin emitted the smells of damp grass and the wet earth of a garden -- a healthy old woman's smell. In this garden of puffy ankles and swollen joints there had once been an ice skater's grace. "We was first married, your father used to take out the rubbish without I had to ask him. You adjust to everything, son, and this zero darkness we got here, too." She reached across the table to touch my face. She let her hand fall when I was startled. "But there got to be advantages someplace. Your stomach, I'm glad it's better."

###

Herbert Gold
November 1980

"Mothers and Man," typescript page from a work in progress

actual marriage. A recent interviewer, Laura Freid, accurately notes that Gold "reacts to women's concerns neither with fear nor with compensatory tolerance." "I haven't fallen in love in two years," Gold told Freid. "Maybe I'm at the point where the women's movement wants me to be." Certainly, his portrayal of the woman in *He/She* shows remarkable depth and understanding. As Joyce Carol Oates concluded her review of the novel, "Gold's language is so swift, lean and brutal, his character's exchanges so absolutely convincing, that *He/She* will probably emerge as one of the most convincing (and painful) documents of the era in which, for the first time, and stridently, the *she* in American marriage screams her discontent."

Gold's latest novel, *Family*, is a blend of fact and fiction that returns to his concern with his heritage. Like his 1967 best-seller, *Fathers*, this is "a novel in the form of a memoir," and like *Fathers*, it is compelling. Gold has described *Fathers* as "a novel in which I have used real names and the sense of some real people in order to make a particular bridge between history and the shaping imagination." He was careful to add, "It did not happen like this, but it might have. Perhaps it once happened *almost* like this." The same caveat applies to *Family*, where Gold reconstructs the life and style of Frieda Gold, his mother.

Frieda, her sister, Anna, and their determined mother, Hilda, wrested their family from the turn-of-the-century Ukraine to the beckoning splendors of Cleveland, Ohio. "In America," Hilda reasons, "you can prefer one thing to another, and then you can do the thing you prefer, unless you have to do the other thing." Faced with a husband who refuses to do anything but play chess in the new land, Hilda takes control of the family. She and her daughers "created their world by acts of will and defiance as men were said to do." The early history of the family, then, is a history of a mother and of daughters who become mothers, women who "could not fail to make themselves the center." Indeed, *Family* was originally to be titled "Mothers," and it remains a work dedicated to and dominated by Frieda Gold, who learned from her mother that "life is not just what we make it. It's also how we can finagle."

Frieda displays all the comic and cloying aspects of the archetypal Jewish mother: she has "an impeccable smiling rage to make things right." Her truce with the English language is fragile (she berates her son for "studying the literal arts in the Ivory League"); her unshakable conviction that proper nutrition can solve any problem can turn her dinner table into a small war over a helping of salad. But Gold's characterization exposes the strength beneath the stereotype, revealing the fierce hopes, fears, and sadness that give rise to her actions: "She tried to control everything, but matters of mortality lay beyond her insistence. She knew the essential pains reached deeper than her kitchen skills, her household management, and yet she never stopped trying."

Family is the third of Gold's books to try explicitly "to tempt out the truth" from the facts of his life. *Fathers* explores the conflict between a son who values security and a father who has survived so much that he knows security to be chimerical. In his autobiography, *My Last Two Thousand Years* (1972), Gold tried to discover what it means to be a Jew and a writer in America. Together, these three books are like map overlays for the territory of Gold's life, each book developing different aspects of the same personal history, with the two novels searching for "something truer than history." The publication of *Family* continues to confirm that Gold finds in the particulars of his life the truths of universal experience. To his mother's belief that "family was all," that "life is clear, painful, confused, and busy," Gold adds his sad recognition that "family can become a ward; it's everything, and yet it confines." Through the stories of large and small conflicts with his mother, of the loving tension of his relationship with his father, of marriages and divorces, of children, and finally of grandchildren, Gold's reconstruction of five generations not only captures the familiar sounds of fathers, mothers, and children in inevitable, loving conflict, but also the silences. At one point, Gold watches his mother: "She was sad beyond what we said to each other. This is a characteristic of sadness between friends and lovers or among family, no matter how the poets and complainers try to put things right, no matter how mothers wail and sons grumble and lovers demand. There is a sadness which is utter, irreducible, and the words which comfort are also claws that deceive and wound."

In this always appealing and frequently moving chronicle of a family, Gold raises many troubling questions and arrives at only one satisfying answer: "Only history is a sure winner. My mother and father living after me in my children and grandchildren—that's a thing to count on."

All of his work, but particularly his last three books, distinguishes Gold as one of our most serious contemporary authors, a writer equally attuned to the problems of society and the possibilities of literature. Avoiding formalistic and confessional extremes, he consistently tries to make sense of the painful vagaries of American life. Both as a novelist and as a low-keyed, commonsensical critic of culture, Gold merits attention and respect.

Interviews:
Laura T. Freid, "The 'He' of *He/She*: Herbert Gold,"

Columbia (Summer 1980): 28-29;
Dan Tooker and Roger Hofheins, "Herbert Gold" in *Fiction! Interviews with Northern California Novelists* (New York: Harcourt Brace Jovanovich/William Kaufmann, 1976), pp. 111-123.

Caroline Gordon
(6 October 1895-11 April 1981)

Ashley Brown
University of South Carolina

See also the Caroline Gordon entries in *DLB 4, American Writers in Paris, 1920-1939* and *DLB 9, American Novelists, 1910-1945*.

NEW BOOK: *The Collected Stories of Caroline Gordon* (New York: Farrar, Straus & Giroux, 1981).

Caroline Gordon died on 11 April 1981 in San Cristobal de las Casas, Chiapas, Mexico, in her eighty-sixth year. She had spent her last three years there with her daughter and son-in-law; it was the final stage in a lifelong journey that had taken her back and forth across North America and much of Western Europe. And yet one never thought of her as a wanderer like her friend Katherine Anne Porter. She used to say of Miss Porter, who was descended from Daniel Boone, that you could always see a restless gleam in her eye as soon as she was settled in *anywhere*; she had to move on. Caroline Gordon always gave the impression, sometimes in rather unlikely circumstances, of carrying on from where her grandmother left off at their ancestral farm in southern Kentucky. She was a natural matriarch and loved to be surrounded by people younger than herself. In 1973 Donald and Louise Cowan, who were then president and graduate dean of the University of Dallas, started a special master's program in creative writing for her to direct. When I was invited out in 1977, there was Caroline with an entire small university at her feet. She was already in her eighties and still going strong. When she was not on the campus, she could be found at home in a sort of apartment complex called The Old Mill Stream with her dogs (she always kept dogs and cats) and a few familiar pieces of furniture and pictures that had followed her

around the country. She was, almost to the end, the mistress of the plantation who somehow didn't seem displaced.

Caroline left Kentucky in 1924 to live in New York City; that was the place to live if you were going to be a writer. And she had recently met Allen Tate through their young friend Robert Penn Warren; by the end of that year she and Allen were married. Thus began a literary partnership that lasted thirty-five years. In the New York and Paris of the 1920s the Tates were near the center of a brilliant new literary generation. In retrospect one is impressed by how young they all were; if they had come to an end in 1930 (when most of them were hardly more than thirty), their achievement would still be considerable. Caroline was a late starter by comparison with most of them. Her first story, "Summer Dust," came out in Yvor Winters's little magazine the *Gyroscope* in 1929; her first novel, *Penhally*, was published in 1931 when she was thirty-six. It was an altogether accomplished novel; she had thought through the problems of technique that some writers take several books to work out.

By this time the Tates had returned from their years in New York and Paris to live in an old house which they called Benfolly, perched above the Cumberland River near Clarksville, Tennessee. Their original literary friends—John Crowe Ransom, Warren, Donald Davidson, Andrew Lytle, and others in the old Fugitive group at Vanderbilt— lived in the vicinity, mostly in Nashville, and for a few years they had a literary community of their own. It was the so-called Agrarian period in their lives, a period of furious creativity for them as it was for their Southern contemporaries such as Faulkner. None of them was more energetic than

Caroline Gordon and Allen Tate at the University of North Carolina at Greensboro, 1938

Caroline, who produced four novels and quite a few stories between 1931 and 1937. The Tates were often poor, but they lived with a certain style at Benfolly, which soon became a mecca or a least a stopping point for many of their friends from the old days in New York and Paris. I suppose the climax of this period came in the summer of 1937, when their house guests included Ford Madox Ford and his wife, Janice Biala, Ford's secretary, and the twenty-year-old Robert Lowell, who pitched a tent in the front yard. Caroline necessarily had to do most of the entertaining at the same time that she was finishing a novel. Janice Biala rendered the whole affair, as Ford would say, in a painting which used to hang in Caroline's kitchen in Princeton. Many years later Caroline wrote a novel, *The Strange Children* (1951), about their life at Benfolly during

the 1930s. By 1950 she had become a Roman Catholic; looking back on this earlier period of their lives, she seemed to say that there was a certain futility in their effort to perpetuate an order of Southern history that had already passed. But her later Christian emphasis, which informs such novels as *The Malefactors* (1956), in no way diminishes the achievement of her novels and stories of the 1930s.

Aleck Maury, Sportsman (1934), which was recently reprinted by the Southern Illinois University Press, is an American classic which at first glance seems just a prolonged fishing and hunting story. The central figure was based on James Morris Gordon, Caroline's father, who had gone to Kentucky from Virginia as a tutor and eventually married his student, Caroline's mother. As classicist and sportsman, Aleck Maury, who has only the memory of a civilization to perpetuate, can still act the Aeneas who will never found another Troy, and his life is based on his sportsman's instinct for ritual as a barrier against the onslaught of time. It is a sometimes poignant book. This novel and several related stories (the best known is "Old Red") occasionally remind one of certain stories in Hemingway's *In Our Time* (1925), but a better analogy is with Turgenev's *A Sportsman's Sketches* (1852), as Ford pointed out many years ago. Even more impressive among Caroline's novels is *None Shall Look Back*, published early in 1937: her tragedy of the Civil War which has for its model nothing less than *War and Peace* (1864-1869). Her young hero, Rives Allard, dies; his private tragedy is caught up in the larger action of which the Confederate commander, Bedford Forrest, is the representative. *None Shall Look Back* yields nothing to the popular taste that made a sensational best-seller of *Gone With the Wind*, published in 1936; and in a sense Caroline's novel, with its fine austerity, is an index to her high standards. Other readers have admired *Green Centuries* (1941), which deals with the migration westward through the mountains at the time of the Revolution, and it is unquestionably the most intelligent novel to have been written about this subject. I myself prefer the long story called "The Captive" (1932), a masterpiece of sustained style about the pioneer woman Jinny Wiley, captured by Indians on the same frontier.

Caroline Gordon's novels and stories build up an impressive image of Western man and the crisis which his restlessness has created. We can see one instance of this in Rion Outlaw and his dream of infinite space in *Green Centuries*. But there are scarcely any institutional forms to restrain him. Chapman, the modern historian in *The Women on the Porch* (1944), is the latest version of Rion Outlaw, and *his* dream of infinite space is a nightmare. Nearly all of Miss Gordon's heroes are aware of the general plight, but Chapman, Stephen Lewis (Aleck Maury's son-in-law in *The Strange Children*), and Tom Claiborne in *The Malefactors* are intensely conscious of a failing in their lives, and their meditations take the form of an interior drama.

Caroline's *Collected Stories*, long overdue, was published by Farrar, Straus and Giroux the week after she died; a pity that she didn't live to see the first enthusiastic reviews. Although she was primarily a novelist, this volume of her short fiction might be a good place for the interested reader to experience the range of her work: the Aleck Maury stories, "The Captive," "The Brilliant Leaves," quasi-comic tales like "The Ice House," the short

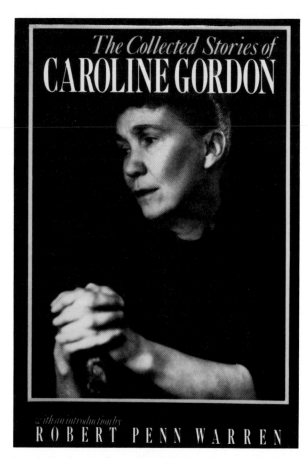

Dust jacket for the first collected edition of Caroline Gordon's short stories

novel called "Emmanuele! Emmanuele!" based on Andre Gide in North Africa. It may seem astonishing that the same person who wrote one story should have written the others. But in these stories she shows herself to be a true follower of Flaubert, whose *Trois Contes* (1877) was the first book of short fiction that created a special prose texture for each subject. Like Flaubert, she could write about different worlds because they are projected from a single vision.

Each of us who knew Caroline and remember her fondly will have his own image of her, no doubt isolated and intensified by the passage of time. I see her in the garden back of The Red House, a little eighteenth-century farmhouse in Princeton where she lived for twenty years; she is withdrawing her dark, flashing eyes from the conversation and directing them up to the trees in the late afternoon sunlight. This is something that a number of her characters do, and so I quote her from *The Malefactors* to describe her action at this moment: Claiborne "stared at the copper beech tree as if he could find the answer there," and "he had felt that those dusky boughs harbored Presences." The tree as a symbol of "wholeness" yields a meaning to him who contemplates it lovingly, Caroline is saying; it could be an intimation of something timeless, perhaps divine.

A TRIBUTE *from HOWARD BAKER*

Caroline Gordon was born in Todd County, Kentucky, 6 October 1895. Although she was not a resident of Kentucky while writing her books, she and her husband, Allen Tate, lived sporadically in their historic Southern house in Tennessee, a couple of score of miles to the south of Caroline's birthplace. But more often than not they found themselves established at one strange place or another. Caroline, as the wife of a restless, young intellectual, and then wholly independently, ventured forth year by year "to see the townlands and learn the minds of distant men"—in order the better to understand, I am convinced, the ways of her native Kentuckians. After New York there was Paris, then the Mediterranean coast . . . the valleys at the end of the Oregon Trail; Nauplia in Greece; Davis, California; Irvine, Texas. . . . She died in Chiapas, Mexico, 11 April 1981, and was buried with appropriate Catholic Indian rites in the cemetery under the brow of the mountain at San Cristobal de las Casas.

In all of these places she was of a disposition to nurture the sentiment expressed by the child in her first short story, "Summer Dust." "I am who I am," to paraphrase the thoughts of the little girl, "I am the only one here who is a Kentuckian!" But for the grown woman, the novelist, there was a problem. How does one reconcile the confident fact of being a unique person, a Kentuckian, with the disturbing fact that "a serpentine red thread" marks the fabric of all lives, no matter how variegated the stuff of which they are made? The undisguisable thread attaches the bold patterns of disparate lives to a common denominator, death. This is the inevitable, the shaping form, to which every character in fiction must be true, each in his own way.

Penhally, the earliest novel, though looking back to Kentucky, was written in Paris. The red thread that marks the members of the family depicted in it resembles a Sophoclean family curse. The disaster, however, which emerges in this story is not Greek so much as it is decadent feudalism, which in the American South had taken the form of the entailment of property. Distorted rights of in-

heritance in one Todd County family, along with entangled bloodlines, lead from half-hidden acts of violence to open fratricide. In Paris, the very old churches such as Saint-Julien-le-Pauvre, huddled in deep shadow, a Byzantine shadow in this instance, are causes enough to make one brood deeply, as the author of *Penhally* certainly did, on a belated, gilded materialism inherited in her homeland from the Middle Ages.

Later in her career she explained that in her mind a novel contains within its structure two patterns of action. There is "the upper pattern," which is to say, the reasonable account of the events which occur in the narrative. But beneath its surface there is "a lower pattern," which boils up from time to time from the subconscious mind of the protagonist. It makes flashes when it appears, like "a meandering red thread" on the surface material. In *Penhally* the lower pattern becomes visible in dreams, intuitions, spontaneous actions, Jungian in character, all harkening back to an inbreeding of family passions. Very often these upsurges in subsequent novels appear to have their source in classical mythology.

A fascination with Heracles goes back to the first short story. It persisted in the author's preoccupations until finally it furnished the complete form and substance for the last novel, *The Glory of Hera*. The last stage of preparation for work on this novel occurred in Nauplia, Greece, during Caroline's protracted visit there with her cousin Cary Peebles. The choice of Nauplia, I think, is extremely interesting. From that decayed port all of the upper reaches of Greece, from Thebes to Mycenae and out through the Gulf of Corinth—the scenes of the exploits of Heracles—seem to arise distantly but vividly in the imagination. The shrunken city itself demands a necessary suspension of disbelief, just as myth does. Here are the small clear monuments left from the spectacular, and brief, conquests of the Romans, the Byzantines, the Franks, the Venetians, and the persistent Turks; here was the first capital under modern independence, here the quiet place for the retirement of official hangmen.

The Glory of Hera is confined to a lower pattern of events, in which Heracles pursues a serpentine course through the labors that were forced upon him. They are as they are recorded in mythology but with Jungian overtones. But now the flashes that emerge from the action are the bright flashes that belong to the upper pattern. Heracles, in his many sacrifices of himself for the benefit of mankind, foreshadows the Christ of the Christian religion. Yet he is always something of a Kentuckian in his bearing, something of the stubborn, undaunted, naturally gallant frontiersman.

There was to have been an upper-structure transcription of the story, in which the author would have turned an autobiographical account of herself into a history of a heroic, myth-tinged ancestry, which included most prominently Meriwether Lewis. Unfortunately, the project was still a fragmentary manuscript when she died. The unfinished book however could hardly have added to what we already know. Caroline Gordon was a stylist of the highest order. The forms which she devised for presenting mythic substance are of the greatest importance. Her work has patterns, or levels, of interest which make it incomparable.

A TRIBUTE   *from BRAINARD CHENEY*

Caroline, as I have said before, was committed to an incredible quest. *Committed* is the word, the circumstance, I think, that most nearly describes her life and her career. And they were incredible!

I remember her with awe, as well as with affectionate devotion. And when I speak of her as my literary godmother, it is no byword of belles lettres. Whatever the limitations of my fiction, its achievements are the results of her influence, guidance, and instruction, more than all other tutelage, or any other example.

I came to her of a dubious and bobtailed literary background. My most notable academic mark was that I was a dropout of three colleges and only completed my junior year at Vanderbilt. From which I (having been fired from a better-paying bank job) wayfared into the police run on a Nashville newspaper. And my reportorial vocabulary suffered from all of the half-baked, over-anxious, ill-assorted categorizing given to the trade. I might add, plus an unhappy academic overlay of Latinesque polysyllables.

The first kindly literary light of my early journeyman days was a sometime Vanderbilt English instructor and Fugitive poet, casually in the lists of the *Nashville Banner* staff by reason of a campus explosion over a novel he had written called *The Professor*, allegedly satirizing the head of the English department. But Stanley Johnson was patient with this would-be writer, and even sympathetic. Sufficiently so, to read some of my verse and give me elementary instruction in fiction writing.

My aims were humble at that time and rose no higher than the hope of eventually making the commercial magazine market. Who remembers Thomas H. Uzzell's *Narrative Technique?* I slept with it under my pillow—to no exciting inspiration, I may say. But Stanley read my stuff for several months over the limited time of his wayside excursion into journalism, before he went on to the University of Tennessee. He removed beyond my orbit, and I did not see him again for several years.

In 1930, another literary influence came my way, Robert Penn Warren, teaching English at Vanderbilt, his alma mater, for a year. And my wife and I enjoyed his good company. "Red," as he is called by his friends, took some tactful interest in my literary endeavors and was basically helpful. And a decision of his then, casually confided to me, bore fortuitous and far-reaching results for me. He said that the short-story market was so precarious and its rewards so skimpy that he was turning from this form to give his attention to a novel. The publishing of a novel had more impact on the market and the literary world generally. In fact, he had already suited the deed to the word and was into the throes of a major work. He even let me see some of the manuscript.

My short-story writing efforts a la Uzzell had been so discouraging that hope must lie in some other direction, and why not a novel, so I followed Red's example. In unlikely support of which, may I add that my first published prose did take the form of a novel.

But the greater good fortune Red brought me in that year in Nashville, before he went on to a greater future elsewhere, was to introduce us to the Tates—Caroline and Allen were living at Benfolly, near Clarksville.

I had just read "The Captive," and my horizon on the possibilities of fiction had been enlarged. This was the greatest bloody Indian story I had ever read. (After fifty years, I have recently reread "The Captive" and I still think it is the greatest bloody Indian story I ever read, and, in its way, worthy of the company of such masterpieces as *None Shall Look Back* and *The Malefactors*.)

My literary efforts then came under Caroline's influence. Allen was immersed in writing poetry, biography, and criticism then. He did, in time however, read my novel manuscript and advise me. But I was too much in awe of him then to seek his help.

It was Caroline who sympathetically and indefatigably read my stuff. Saw something in it. Read it, and took it apart, line by line. It was Caroline who made me aware of the atrocious categoric conveniences of my newspaper jargon. (She had been a newspaper reporter briefly once.) It was Caroline who breathed upon me some sense of the integrity of narrative prose, the particularity of fictive expression. It was Caroline who patiently and persistently overwatched my rewriting of that grievous first novel of mine, brought it into fictional form. It did not make publication, happily; but it put me on my way, under her continued guidance to my next and successful effort. Indeed, a thing that seemed marvelous to me then, my novel got runner-up place in Houghton Mifflin's contest for first published fiction that year. And brought me a Guggenheim the next year.

It was soon after the publication of that first novel that I encountered again my early mentor, Stanley Johnson, on a visit to Nashville. We were having lunch together at the old Hermitage Hotel. Stanley congratulated me on my accomplishment, said he thought it a superior novel. In fact, he said he was astonished by it. He added, extravagantly, even envious! Then he turned to me wryly: "Who in hell taught you to write that smooth, simple, telling prose?"

A TRIBUTE *from ANDREW LYTLE*

Reading Miss Gordon's fiction, you are rarely conscious of the sex of the writer. This is the definitive measure of her craftmanship and of her devotion to its practice. Given an equal talent and luck, the major artist is distinguished from the minor by energy. And Miss Gordon was endowed with all of energy's properties. I only know of one other who sustains the same kind of extravagant display of vitality. I can hear the gallop of her typewriter in correspondence. She rarely paused for typing errors. In action her mind could not delay. As in her fiction the drive of her sentences delights the eye. The untidy page of the letter is a part of its form. She used to complain that it takes as much time to write a letter as it does a page of fiction. She further said if you waited long enough, you didn't have to answer. Her letters all had the quality of her fiction. Wherever the word was concerned, she showed herself a devoted, committed writer. The master was Henry James, introduced probably by Ford Madox Ford, who worked with her on her first novel, *Penhally*. Ford himself was such an artist, but no one could have suffered the act as did she. Allen Tate, her husband, in the fierce concentration upon his craft, whether verse or criticism, or his one novel, sustained in her presence this ancient practice. But she was more vocal about it. Flaubert was usually her example, and her fervor was catching, despite her complaint that it was like being on the chain gang.

I have not mentioned her generosity to other writers, particularly beginners with a sure talent. To their work she brought the same attention that she would bring to her own. The great example of this patronage is Flannery O'Connor. Letter after letter of instruction and advice passed between them. Nothing was withheld on the one part, nor did false pride show on the other. Indeed, it could be said that fundamentally their subject was the same: what a society, materialistic and mechanical, does to the human psyche. They were both Roman Catholic, Miss O'Connor by cradle, Miss Gordon by choice. This distinction made the difference in their work. They were both Southern to the marrow of their bones. Being set apart by her formal religion gave to Miss O'Connor a perspective on the Prostestant world about her. Miss Gordon was born into that world but understood better the range of its hierarchy. She had a peculiar sense of it as it was before its defeat and degeneration. But her view was historic and tragic. The defeat of the Confederacy and the consequent destruction of Southern, that is the transplanted segment of European, society, its effect upon the succeeding generations, gave her the substance for her earlier fiction. Her later fiction concerns the damage into the third generation of what cracked and broken forms do to human beings. Her actors belong to a different category from Miss O'Connor's. Most of her work was done before she joined the Roman church, and it seems to me that the fiction whose complications derive from her immersion in the new faith is less satisfactory. A universal church that in her known society is not universal cannot find the concrete images or manners to deliver a satisfactory fiction. She must have felt this, as she turned to the Greek-Roman world of myth and fable for her last book, which was to be completed by another book laid among her family in Kentucky. This book was never completed. Presumably it would reveal in the disparity of time the same constant myths but with forms composed of differing mores. Now that she is elsewhere, in a place or condition where presumably all things are known and all hearts clarified, if I have misunderstood her intentions, I can feel reasonably exempt from a scarifying descent upon any imprudence of statement. I hope.

A TRIBUTE *from WALKER PERCY*

Caroline Gordon was one of the most generous people I have ever known—as well as one of the best writers. When I took advantage of my acquaintance with her to send her a manuscript of the first novel I wrote, she replied with a thirty-two-page, typed, single-spaced letter, which began:

"You've made every mistake it is possible for a beginner to make. . . ."

As one of the modern masters of the short story, she does not need my testimony. But I will cite a recent experience with her fiction. Recently I re-read *Aleck Maury, Sportsman* in a new edition. What a delight! One is again struck by the cleanness and economy and beauty of her writing—and by the feat she pulled off in getting inside another person's skin—a man at that, a hunter-fisherman!

Mary Gordon
(8 December 1949-)

John R. May
Louisiana State University

See also the Mary Gordon entry in *DLB 6, American Novelists Since World War II*, Second Series.

NEW BOOK: *The Company of Women* (New York & Toronto: Random House, 1980; London: Cape, 1981).

Critics' responses to Mary Gordon's second novel, *The Company of Women*, have seemed more mixed than those to *Final Payments*, her impressive first novel published in 1978. Susan Lardner, writing in the *New Yorker*, said that *The Company of Women* "turns out to be a bluff of a novel—a brave show of sentiment and phraseology covering the collapse of a farfetched ambition." Emilie Griffin, in one of three review-essays on the novel in the 11 July 1981 issue of *America*, called it "flawed," but then added that to her its flaws are "necessary and even providential."

There had, of course, been criticism mixed with praise for *Final Payments*. David Lodge in the *Times Literary Supplement* noted how the "novel, so firmly and freshly written at the outset, threatens to turn soft at the core." Paul Ablemen found it "theology posing as fiction, a hybrid form which compounds the tedium of the former with the imprecision of the latter to the advantage of neither." James M. Rawley and Robert F. Moss, writing jointly in *Commonweal*, described the novel as "a sturdy hybrid: a relatively trashy plot, marked by

contrivance and sensationalism, but handled with the tools of high art, specifically a technical sophistication and an allusive, savagely ironic tone."

Praise and blame and their inevitable mixture aside, one thing is abundantly clear about this promising young novelist: Mary Gordon is attracting more attention as a Catholic writer of serious fiction than any other American after Flannery O'Connor and Walker Percy. Francine du Plessix Gray, reviewing *The Company of Women* for the *New York Times*, put it this way: "If there was any doubt that Mary Gordon was her generation's preeminent novelist of Roman Catholic mores and manners when she published her remarkable first novel, *Final Payments*, it is dispelled by her new book."

Gordon, like both of her heroines, grew up "among radically conservative Catholics." Her father, a Jewish convert to Catholicism in 1937 (twelve years before her birth), was a scholarly, "right wing" Catholic like Isabel's father in *Final Payments*. Gordon was extremely close to her father and has vivid memories of him, even though he died when she was eight. Her mother, born of Irish-Italian immigrant stock, though she had been stricken with polio as a child and was crippled, worked for a law firm to support the family. Charlotte Taylor, "the resilient, tough-talking, supportive and strongest woman" in *The Company of Women*, is modeled, Gordon admits, on her own mother, and Gordon's parents met through a Roman Catholic priest in much the same manner the principal characters of this second novel do. Gordon's only child, Anna, born in 1980 of her second marriage (to Arthur Cash, a biographer of Laurence Sterne), is named for Gordon's mother.

From interviews with Gordon and from Gordon's 1978 *Harper's* article on dissident Catholics, "More Catholic than the Pope: Archbishop Lefebvre and the Rome of the One True Church," it is possible to piece together a picture of the Catholic past and present that have shaped Gordon's viewpoint. Asked by Le Anne Schreiber in 1981 whether she was "still a believing Catholic," Gordon responded: "I consider myself a Catholic. I have a real religious life in a framework which I think of as Catholic. But I don't think John Paul II would be real pleased with it." Her willingness to acknowledge a disparity between her own beliefs and the official teachings of the church may have been unheard of in the Catholic world of her youth, but it is nonetheless typical of Catholicism in the late 1970s and early 1980s. She confessed in the same interview to an indebtedness to Flannery O'Connor's brand of tough allegiance to the church: "I think one of the things that helped me in life is Flannery O'Connor's statement that you must remember that in this day and age one must suffer because of the church and not for the church." If she was being quoted accurately, however, her memory had played a revealing trick on her. O'Connor's observation, in a 1955 letter, which Gordon quotes in her review of O'Connor's collected letters for the *Saturday Review*, was actually: "It seems to be a fact that you have to suffer as much from the Church as for it." The passage of more than twenty years, including the tumultuous experience of modernization within the Catholic church brought about by the Second Vatican Council, accounts perhaps for the implied difference in Gordon's and O'Connor's attitudes. What Gordon values about the church "is that it does seem there is an essential core that seems to last and to go on, to retain its language, to retain its ritual, to retain—I like to think—some central values that are immutable." An especially illuminating source of insight into Gordon's attitude toward the church is her report in *Harper's* on her visit to the Oyster Bay, Long Island, headquarters of French Archbishop Marcel Lefebvre, the leader of the major right-wing dissident group of post-Vatican II Catholics. Gordon's reasons for her disappointment in her Oyster Bay experience suggest what she herself would like to find in the church: "I was looking for miracle, mystery, and authority; I was interested in style, in spirituality, in a movement that combined the classical ideal of the Gregorian

Mary Gordon

Mass with the romantic image of the foreign life, suggesting illegitimacy."

Finally, in an interview with Diana Cooper Clarke for *Commonweal*, Gordon admitted that only Wilfrid Sheed's review of *Final Payments* was "instructive" to her. It is impossible to tell what Gordon found specifically instructive, but Sheed, himself a Catholic writer, seemed especially perceptive in pointing out that *Final Payments* is a new kind of Catholic novel that "does show brilliantly the effects of the new dispensation on American Catholic fiction. It gives a picture of certain Catholic lives . . . more ambiguous than anything either a loyalist or a heretic would have had a mind to produce a few years ago. In the European manner, the Church is seen not as a good place or a bad place, . . . but as a multilayered poem or vision which dominates your life equally whether you believe it or not: which doesn't even seem to need your belief once it has made its point." At any rate, the significant difference between the recent Roman Catholic renewal and the Protesant Reformation is that in this century the reformers, often apparently heterodox, have remained within the church—and been accepted, or at least tolerated.

What makes a novelist Catholic is, of course, the achieved Catholic novel itself, which is much more than a novel that appeals to religious elements or merely uses Catholic settings. George Hunt, in an effort to characterize what he apparently considers is Gordon's minimal achievement, implies that her novels adhere only to "Catholic surfaces." "Gordon has taken evident pains," he writes, "to insert all the odd Catholic artifacts." Even more favorable critics, such as Madonna Kolbenschlag, note "a heavy ballast of nostalgia in Gordon's perception of Catholicism." For a novel to be Catholic, it must have an overall world view, reflected in the dramatic conflict the protagonist experiences, that is typical of Roman Catholicism.

Gordon's understanding of Catholicism is both true to tradition and reflected in her novels, most successfully in *The Company of Women*. Of all the branches of Christianity, Catholicism has been conservative in the root meaning of that word. It has persevered in its tradition, even ironically in the midst of change. It is the most structured of Christian churches, both in doctrine and hierarchy, and it has in its liturgy preserved a ceremonial style that sets it apart, for example, from Protestant Christianity's emphasis on the Word. That these qualities of Catholicism—permanence, structure, and style—illumine the world view in Gordon's novels can be demonstrated.

David Lodge sees in *Final Payments* something of the "high-cultural equivalent of the Catholic ghetto—the 'Catholic novel' of Greene, Mauriac, Bernanos, Bloy, with its characteristic fondness for aphorisms that are subversive of liberal, materialistic assumptions." Isabel Moore, the protagonist of *Final Payments*, who, after spending eleven years nursing an invalid father, finds herself at the age of thirty on the threshold of a life she is ill prepared to live, if not one she has despaired of ever experiencing, just as often turns her aphorisms against reactionary, spiritualistic assumptions—those inescapable cultural graves that tend to get confused with living belief—and so her critical eye reflects a balanced conservatism.

Reminiscing with her friend Eleanor about their Catholic high-school days and their devotion to the sacraments, Isabel comments, "We were concerned with the perfection of the outward form." They also learned the "trick of comedy instead of intimacy, the endlessly entertaining routine that can deflect sexual advances, declarations of love or hatred, talk of death, fear of aging." If Isabel and Eleanor are in any sense normative—and in the world of this novel they clearly seem to be— intelligent Catholic girls, after they have discarded the sacraments and their outward form, certainly persevere in the discipline of "comedy instead of intimacy."

There is, however, a dark side to the novel's vision of the Catholic family. Isabel's father's love, the only genuine love she may ever experience (as her friend Liz says), is also the love that effectively enslaves. Her sacrifice for her father can be taken as a metaphor for the church's determination to keep "certain scenes intact," namely to keep its members children always (the Roman church would seem to be alone among the Christian churches in preserving the image of "Holy Mother the Church"). Thus if Isabel is more than rare type and if her experience is to be read as universal, the novel offers little hope that the structure of filial piety will ever become, in Catholicism, adult interpersonal communion.

Final Payments shows flashes of brilliance for a first novel and reaches a peak of poignant irony—in Isabel's work for the aged in foster homes—then it lapses into Dickensian melodrama. The guilt money she pays finally is far less convincing than her account of the psychological debt we must all pay the past. Yet in its affirmation of freedom over stagnation, it is certainly a deeply Christian novel, if not in this respect specifically Catholic.

The company of women in Gordon's second novel is a circle of widowed, separated, and unmarried women whose center is an arch-conservative Catholic priest so disaffected by the changes in his monastic order occasioned by the Second Vatican Council that he has left his religious community and become a diocesan priest. His lonely life is partially filled by regular monthly visits from five women— Charlotte, Clare, Elizabeth, Mary Rose, and Muriel—that his itinerant ministry has previously touched. Although Cyprian is the leader of the company of woman that gives the novel its name, he is not the novel's protagonist. There is another circle that Cyprian himself is a part of, and its center is Felicitas, the daughter of the widowed Charlotte Taylor (the only mother among the older women). Felicitas alone is the heir to their faith, and their special hope for her is that she will transmit it intact (that is, as *they* have lived it) to future generations. Thus, *The Company of Women* begins with a kind of Catholic joke that also projects the novel's ultimate irony: "Felicitas Maria Taylor was called after the one virgin martyr whose name contained some hope for ordinary human happiness." The name Felicitas is, of course, the Latin word for happiness.

The novel is divided into three parts, each covering a crucial period of Felicitas's life, beginning in 1963, her fourteenth year, with the events surrounding a nearly fatal accident caused by Cyprian's distracted driving. Felicitas's brush with death occasions an adolescent passage toward life in the spirit—toward independence. Part 2, by far the longest of the three, is set in 1969-1970 and treats Felicitas's awakening to a world apart from (she would think subversive of) the intimacy (read *suffocation*) of the company of Cyprian and his faithful women. Felicitas leaves the private world of a small Catholic college and matriculates at Barnard College (which Gordon herself attended against the wishes of the principal of her Catholic girls' high school). There she is exposed to the ruthless insensitivity of a subcultural academic: Robert Cavendish is a professor of political science who is as unbending in the cause of liberalism as Cyprian is for religious orthodoxy. Felicitas conceives a child either by Robert or Richard, whom Robert callously passes her on to after he tires of her. She decides to have an abortion, but during a harrowing experience at an illegal clinic, she changes her mind and returns to the company of women to have her child. Part 3 is set in 1977 in Orano, New York, where the entire company has moved to support Cyprian in his last years. Linda, Felicitas's daughter, has quietly replaced her mother as the hope of the group (though Felicitas is still dearly loved). Having reached the age of reason, Linda is the perfect child of her mother's ideological liberation; in the absence of a father, she has been taught by Felicitas to say, "My father is one of two people."

Part 3, slightly shorter even than part 1 and a series of monologues by each of the principal characters, is by far the richest section of the novel. It is concerned with new life (Linda's), impending death (Cyprian's), and a planned marriage. Felicitas has decided to marry Leo Byrne, a stolid but dependable hardware dealer. Her reasons for marriage reveal a more realistic acceptance of nature's forms and certainly her rejection of unadulterated feminism ("it is for shelter that we marry and make love"); her delay in marrying though is typical of her independence of the church's ways.

Asked in a 1981 interview whether she had been exposed to "any framework of values in her adult life with the resonance of Catholicism," Gordon responded, "No. But feminism comes closest to it." *The Company of Women* pays a minor debt to feminism; yet it owes much more to the genuinely Catholic tradition that celebrates the sanctity and permanence of friendship over the exclusiveness of married love. Francine du Plessix Gray gives Gordon's debt to this tradition precise historical perspective: "She rebels against the idealization of romantic, sexual and marital love that has inspired much of the novelistic form for over two centuries. She values instead the 2,000-year-old notion (unquestioned from Aristotle's time to the Enlightenment, and only dethroned by the Romantics) that sees friendship as an infinitely more central ingredient of human happiness than any bonding of sexual affection." Inclined at the end of his life to feel that he has failed his priestly vocation because he is doomed "to the terrible ringed accident of human love," Cyprian comes to understand the meaning of "the incarnation for . . . the first time." Alone on a walk through the night, weary with self-pity, he stops at an all-night diner. A matchbox on the counter announces, "ACE 24-HOUR CAFE: WHERE NICE PEOPLE MEET," and he confessed, "Tears came to my eyes for the hopefulness, the sweetness, the enduring promise of plain human love." What Cyprian is inclined one moment to call a "terrible ringed accident" is of course no accident at all. Friendship's ring is an awe-inspiring refraction of mystery itself—the human structure that corresponds to the community of Persons in the Trinity; its permanence, a transcendent gift. It is appropriate, then, that the prevailing imagery of the novel relates to durability, a variation on the theme of permanence. Elizabeth, for example, understands what the adolescent Felicitas senses as she rides with Cyprian in his truck: "the extreme pride, the hard, durable pride of such company." The circle of friendship as enduring community reflects perfectly the Catholic sense of structure and permanence; the style characteristic of a Catholic world view is found in Felicitas's preferred vocation as a woman within the church.

The flatness in the presentation of the principal male characters, if indeed Robert can be compared to Cyprian at all, seems purposeful here, or at least understandable, although Gordon admits difficulty in creating believable men, a failure that is often clear in *Final Payments*. It is important that Felicitas awakens initially to the fact that Cyprian and Robert are both unyielding, selfish men— Cyprian in the name of God and religion, Robert in the service of mindless liberalism. What Cyprian has that Robert will never apparently possess, which is at the heart of the novel's meaning and the implied justification for Cyprian's selfishness, is a learned instinct for that saving bond of trust and love every human yearns for and needs. The novel's touching irony is that Felicitas and Cyprian acknowledge the grace of human friendship at the same time, and apparently separately, though the reader knows Felicitas has come to the realization *through* Cyprian and his company of women.

Most of the focal women of Gordon's two novels have become "eunuchs for the kingdom of God," whether willingly or through circumstances, even if the kingdom they serve is not easily recognized or readily acceptable in biblical terms. They are all "virgins" of the spirit, if not wholly of the body. Felicitas, in name and in the intention of her creator, seems to typify the sort of wedding of feminism and Catholicism that would suit Gordon the most, both in fiction and reality. "That ideal of unencumberedness, of commitment, of passion, is very very much with me," Gordon admits, "and very much came out of those images of the virgin martyrs." The perfection of style that Felicitas, and Gordon, yearn for, a feminist ideal with undeniable roots in Catholic tradition, is an "unencumbered, devoted, directed singular life."

Whereas *Final Payments* has a more explicit and pervasive Catholic imagery, *The Company of Women* is more Catholic in its world view. Moreover, even though the first-person narrative voice of *Final Payments* is generally quite successful (except perhaps in the novel's confused, melodramatic final chapter) and its central conflict more dramatic, intense, and suspenseful, *The Company of Women* is a better novel: more subtle in imagery, less strained in dramatic effect, and more appealing and plausible in character motivation and setting.

Periodical Publications:

"More Catholic than the Pope: Archbishop Lefebvre and the Rome of the One True Church," *Harper's*, 257 (July 1978): 58-69;

"The Habit of Genius: Flannery O'Connor, *The Habit of Being*," *Saturday Review*, 6 (14 April 1979): 42-45;

"Woman's Friendships," *Redbook*, 153 (July 1979): 31ff.

Interviews:

Diana Cooper Clark, "An Interview with Mary Gordon," *Commonweal*, 107 (9 May 1980): 270-273;

Barbara A. Bannon, "PW Interviews Mary Gordon," *Publishers Weekly*, 219 (6 February 1981): 274-275;

Le Anne Schreiber, "A Talk with Mary Gordon," *New York Times Book Review*, 15 February 1981, pp. 26-28.

References:

Francine du Plessix Gray, "A Religious Romance," review of *The Company of Women*, *New York Times Book Review*, 15 February 1981, pp. 1, 24, 26;

Emilie Griffin, "Man, Woman, Catholic III," *America*, 145 (11 July 1981): 8-9;

George Hunt, "Man, Woman, Catholic II," *America*, 145 (11 July 1981): 6-8;

Madonna Kolbenschlag, "Man, Woman, Catholic I," *America*, 145 (11 July 1981): 4-6;

Susan Lardner, "No Medium," review of *The Company of Women*, *New Yorker*, 57 (6 April 1981): 177-180;

James M. Rawley and Robert F. Moss, "The Pulp of the Matter," *Commonweal*, 105 (27 October 1978): 685-689.

Paul Green

(17 March 1894-4 May 1981)

Rhoda H. Wynn
Paul Green Dramas

See also the Green entries in *DLB 7, Twentieth-Century American Dramatists*, and *DLB 9, American Novelists, 1910-1945*.

Paul Green was a writer, a teacher, a champion of peace and justice, a humble man who loved the soil, and a man of warmth, good humor, and caring. All of us who admired him, respected him, learned from him, and loved him are grateful that he was active and in possession of these traits until the hour of his death on 4 May 1981.

Paul Green enjoyed writing—with all the innate pain and frustration of striving to reach the high standard he set for himself, pushing that standard ever higher. He wrote and rewrote his works, seeking always to improve their quality, and said on many occasions that while he was often unhappy when writing, he was even more unhappy when he was not.

He was a voracious reader and a good student at every age level, so it was not surprising to his peers that in 1914 he became teacher-principal of a three-room school to earn the money necessary to attend the University of North Carolina at Chapel Hill. In 1916-1917 as a first-year student at the university, he taught freshman English and during that year wrote *Surrender to the Enemy*, which, when produced on the campus, was the first play this playwright ever saw. After service in World War I, he returned to Chapel Hill in fall 1919 and wrote one-act plays that were produced by the Carolina Playmakers.

His major academic interest was philosophy, which he pursued in graduate work at Cornell University during 1922-1923 and as a professor in the philosophy department at Chapel Hill from 1923 to 1939. But even as a graduate student and professor in philosophy, Green could not deny his urge to write plays and would find himself at the typewriter all night readying a one-act for possible publication. Paul Green also found joy in teaching, serving later as a professor of dramatic art (1939-1944) at Chapel Hill and, bringing his experience as a Hollywood screenwriter to the UNC department of radio-television-motion pictures in 1962-1963. Beyond these formal commitments, he seized every oppor-tunity to teach informally—the names of trees and common weeds as one walked with him through the woods, the philosophies of Aristotle, Plato, and Kant in seemingly casual travel conversation, or composers' lives and works with the help of the auto's tape playback as one drove with him to New York or to the distant amphitheaters, in which sixteen symphonic dramas were produced in various seasons. To work with him on research was to be overwhelmed with the amount of knowledge he had already accumulated and the eagerness with which he sought more in libraries and historic places. In an essay for teachers he once wrote, "Life is like a tree forever growing," and it could be said he was always a student and always a teacher.

Mankind and "where we are going" were prime interests and constant concerns. Although he grew up on the family farm in racially divided eastern North Carolina, for him racial prejudices had to be overcome. One finds his frustration over man's inhumanity to man in his poignant story about Rassie, the Negro playmate of his childhood, in the powerful plays *White Dresses* (1923), *In Abraham's Bosom* (1926), and *Hymn to the Rising Sun* (1936), and in his 1932 screen adaptation of *Cabin in the Cotton*. The list is long, for all of his life he championed the removal of prejudicial barriers. In his later years Paul Green was cautiously pleased that discrimination was fading, permitting a man or woman to set goals without limitation by the skin into which he or she had been born.

This writer from a Southern turn-of-the-century farm who traveled the world as a lecturer for the Rockefeller Foundation, also hoped for a day when the states of the world might become a nation of nations—one world—growing out of the United Nations concept. "Where are we going in this world?," he would often ask when violence, nuclear proliferation, war, and the talk of war were loudly evident. Frequently he wrote to senators, U.S. presidents, and others in whose hands that future was being molded, pleading for leadership in cooperation and peace.

Green recognized the value of humor in life and found it even in serious moments. His smiling blue eyes, which sustained the reading demands of eighty-seven years without spectacles, and the natural up-turning of his lips were evidence that he had laughed often.

He was a man on whom eight universities bestowed honorary degrees while numerous other groups recognized his achievements in drama, history, literature, and civil rights, but among these numerous and diverse honors his most cherished one, because he had had to earn it, was his Phi Beta Kappa membership.

higher ideals of man and never succumbing to box-office exploitation.

His dreams of a "people's theatre" wherein the history and folktales of the people might be told in theaters at which all the people would feel welcome prompted him to create the form he called "symphonic drama." For a large part of his later years he wrote primarily in this dramatic form, meeting with boards, helping to design amphitheaters to accommodate the dramas' needs, and always reminding

Paul Green

As a screenwriter, Paul Green was never willing to compromise his principles to the almighty dollar of the Hollywood studios. He observed early that depicted violence in movies and television would be reflected in imitated violence, and while not ignoring the place of love, passion, struggle, and hurt in his dramas, novels, short stories, and essays, insisted on maintaining the proper relationship of these to his plots and characters, emphasizing the

the local, state, and national financial supporters that the facilities also should include provisions for dance recitals, graduations, concerts, and religious observances, such as Easter sunrise services. This theater of the people must also adhere to the highest literary and dramatic standards, he insisted. He would not tolerate easily written, amateurishly produced stage pieces. To serve as a guiding force to this growing movement, then, he founded the Institute of Outdoor Drama. He was often called "the Father of Outdoor Drama," which was also fitting, for he was an indefatigable worker for the movement and perhaps its strongest critic from within.

In his own words, Green was "always crazy about music," to which he was introduced in childhood when his mother played the organ in church and purchased a piano with hard-earned money from the sale of eggs and butter from the farm. He listened to and learned the songs of the Negroes and whites with whom he chopped cotton in the fields and came to enjoy the good close harmony of the quartet in which he sang tenor. Though he could pass a happy hour playing his violin, picking out melodies on the piano, and even notating the music he composed for specific needs in his plays, Green never became proficient at playing an instrument. Music, though, was a vital part of his being, and his dramas, movie scenarios, and novels were laced with folk songs, hymns, narrative dances, martial music, and original melodies and lyrics. To his children and grandchildren he passed on this love of music—perhaps another evidence of his informal teaching—so that each of them finds personal pleasure in music, while still others are professionally accomplished musicians.

Paul Green was subjected in his youth to narrow Southern religious practices, which offended his sensibilities. He knew the Bible well from numerous readings beginning at age ten, and he believed in the philosophy of Jesus—nonviolence, forgiveness seventy times seven, the brotherhood of all men, and the exalted position of women. Although he married the daughter of an Episcopal minister, he did not subscribe to any organized sect but kept his communion with man and nature, and identified his faith as "humanist." Before one gets the impression that Paul Green was saintly, let the writer note that he liked a good poker game, a good wine, and a good earthy story, and in his earlier days was the giver of "wild parties."

He revered the body as "our only home" and

often used this image in talking with young interviewers, actors, newsmen, and others who smoked or were obese or careless in their habits. Working in the "garden," a generous planting of an acre and more, was his daily exercise. One sensed that it was not only the exercise itself he sought but a joyful renewed acquaintance with the soil and with the vast sky of his youth when, plowing with the reins of the mule in one hand and a book of poetry in the other, he had memorized great passages to make "that great ball of fire which seemed to hang in the sky go down." He liked "to get up a good sweat," and never did he lose his broad, straight shoulders, his determined stride, or his firm handshake.

Early in January 1981 Paul entered in his journal a list of eleven writing and publication projects he planned to complete in the year, including two manuscripts nearing readiness.

So it was on the day before his death Paul Green wrote letters in a strong, steady hand, inscribed some copies of his newest edition of *The Lost Colony*, several hundred of which he had contributed to every North Carolina school and college, phoned his older sister who had raised the family following the early death of their mother, talked with two grandchildren who had been invited to perform on cello and piano at the university, walked in the garden with Elizabeth, his wife of nearly sixty years, drove his tractor to its shelter, and no doubt read during the night from one or more of the books on his bedside table.

Hundreds of neighbors, friends and "fellow-workers" gathered in the Paul Green Theatre on the University of North Carolina campus before his burial to celebrate his life and all it had meant to them individually with selections from his writings and his compositions.

As he lived, so he died—a writer, a teacher, a man of the soil, a humble man whose work and ideals earned for him the highest recognition his state, his profession, and his peers could and did bestow on him.

Ernest Hemingway

(21 July 1899-2 July 1961)

Scott Donaldson
College of William and Mary

See also the Hemingway entries in *DLB 4, American Writers in Paris, 1920-1939* and *DLB 9, American Novelists, 1910-1945*.

NEW BOOK: *Selected Letters 1917-1961*, edited by Carlos Baker (New York: Scribners, 1981; London: Granada, 1981).

The 1981 publication of nearly 600 letters in Ernest Hemingway's *Selected Letters 1917-1961* opened a fresh perspective on a man whom Carlos Baker, editor of the volume, rightly called "one of the most commanding personalities of the age."

In the two decades between Hemingway's death in 1961 and publication of his letters, biographers and critics were reduced to paraphasing the contents of his letters, rather than quoting them directly, and in the process they lost much of the original flavor. The reason was a 1958 note in which Hemingway instructed his executors as follows: "It is my wish that none of the letters written by me during my lifetime shall be published. Accordingly, I hereby request and direct you not to publish or consent to the publication by others, of any such letters." The decision to override this prohibition was made by Mary Hemingway, the author's widow, for several reasons. Many of those who might have been hurt by seeing these letters in print were no longer alive. Much that Hemingway might have wanted kept secret had since come to light. Eventually it became clear that not to publish a judiciously edited selection of these letters would only serve to deprive scholars in particular and the reading public in general of a keener insight into the makeup of one of the major figures in twentieth-century literature.

Actually, the almost 600 letters represent only about 10 percent of Hemingway's epistolary output. An inveterate correspondent, he wrote letters to avoid the harder writing that went into his prose, or to transmit and receive gossip, which, he admitted, went "in one ear and out my mouth," or to exhibit his knowledge in several fields, or to get rid of debilitating emotions by talking about them, or, fi-

nally, to seek approval by others of his own behavior. In correspondence he often spelled badly, uttered obscenities, and resorted to private lingo. Sometimes, he aimed to shock his reader. He wanted to be thought a man who had been around and knew the answers. Yet he also wanted to do the right thing. He had his own ideas about what constituted the properly conducted life, and was unforgiving to anyone, not excluding himself, who failed to live up to his standards of conduct.

In his introduction Baker asserted that Hemingway's shortcomings "were balanced by qualities that more than tipped the scale in his favor." Perhaps so, yet even in a volume which omits some of his more outrageously nasty letters, the picture that emerges is of a man who took excessive delight in venting his scorn upon other people, collectively and individually.

Like most others of his generation who stemmed from Middle-Western, middle-class Protestant roots, Hemingway grew up with a strain of anti-Semitism and ethnocentrism. At its most innocent his anti-Semitism took the form of his calling himself "Hemingstein" as a joke about his carefulness with money. But the word *kike* appears disconcertingly often in his letters, and so do other slurring references to Jews. Similarly, the British are condemned on several counts, including their performance in the Spanish civil war. Their soldiers were "cowards, malingerers, liars and phonies and fairies," Hemingway insisted; "What a degenerate people the English are." He had no more tolerance for Canadians. He and Hadley Hemingway and baby Bumby were "the only nice people in Canada," he wrote Sylvia Beach in 1923.

Hemingway's intolerance extended to individuals as well as groups, and in particular to individual writers. He consistently wrote scurrilous things about writers who might have been regarded as his rivals for reputation, the more so as he grew older. For example, the "more meazly and shitty the guy, i.e. Joyce, the greater the success in his art." If Hemingway "wrote as sloppily and shitily as that freckled prick [Sinclair Lewis]," he could write

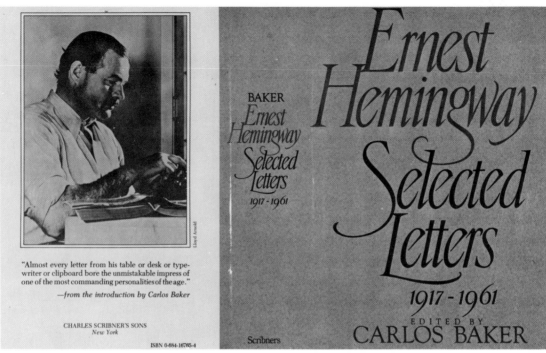

Dust jacket for the first collection of Hemingway's letters

5,000 words a day. Thomas Wolfe "was a one book boy and a glandular giant with the brains and the guts of three mice." Edmund Wilson "has strange leaks" in his integrity and his knowledge; leaks so bad "that if he were an aqueduct he would be dry." Sherwood Anderson "was like a jolly but tortured bowl of puss turning into a woman in front of your eyes." Gertrude Stein was nice "until she opted for fags and fags alone." He suggested facetiously that William Faulkner may well have been vouchsafed religious revelations over his breakfast grits, but added that "people who talk about God as though they knew him intimately . . . are frauds." Remember, he cautioned, "never to trust a man with a southern accent." James Jones, who admitted in the promotional copy for *From Here to Eternity* (1951) that he had deserted in 1944, "is an enormously skillful fuck-up and his book will do great damage to our country." Hemingway took particular satisfaction, he wrote Sara Murphy, in knocking down Wallace Stevens, who was "6 feet 2 weighs 225 lbs and . . . when he hits the ground it is highly spectaculous."

Yet at the same time these letters demonstrate Hemingway's capacity for tenderness, friendship, and love. When Gerald and Sara Murphy's son Baoth succumbed to tuberculosis in 1935, Hemingway sent a moving message of condolence. Anyone "who dies young after a happy childhood, and no one ever made a happier childhood than you made for your children, has won a great victory," he wrote the Murphys. Now, Hemingway said, they were all on a boat together, a good boat that they'd made but that would never reach port and since there would be no landfall "we must keep the boat up very well and be very good to each other." Hearing that Margaret Anderson, who had published his early fiction in the *Little Review*, was stranded in Paris without funds in 1941, Hemingway sent Solita Solano $400 for Anderson's passage and a message, "don't ever worry because as long as any of us have any money we all have money." He also joined in the campaign to free Ezra Pound from confinement in 1957 on the grounds that "great poets are very rare and they should be extended a measure of understanding and mercy." To prove his support, he offered $1500 to help Pound resettle in Italy, and sent him a check in that amount upon Pound's release in 1958.

Pound had encouraged Hemingway during the early 1920s in Paris. He's teaching me to write, Hemingway said of the poet, and I'm teaching him to box. Boxing, like fishing and hunting, was one of the things men could enjoy together, and after settling in Key West and later in Cuba, Hemingway repeatedly encouraged friends to come down to fish the waters of the Gulf Stream. Trolling for marlin, hunting elk in Idaho, savoring the bullfights in

Spain, skiing in Austria, betting the horses in France—in such activities Hemingway welcomed the company of other men, including writers. Among the writers who visited were friends such as John Dos Passos, Archibald MacLeish, and Donald Ogden Stewart. In time each of these friendships foundered when Hemingway would suffer through a period when, as he confessed to MacLeish, he became "too awful for anybody to stand."

The most complicated of Hemingway's literary friendships was with F. Scott Fitzgerald, and several previously unavailable letters shed new light on that relationship. Hemingway turned against Fitzgerald, he said, when the latter's drinking made him objectionable. But even then, as he made clear in letters to Maxwell Perkins, Harvey Breit, and others, he remained very fond of Fitzgerald. He also communicated his critical judgments of Fitzgerald's work. Fitzgerald's best novel, Hemingway commented in November 1941, was *Tender Is the Night*: "it has all the realization of tragedy that Scott ever found. Wonderful atmosphere and magical descriptions and none of the impossible dramatic tricks that he had outlined for the final book." *The Last Tycoon*, he felt, was a pale book-in-the-making, the product of that "emotional bankruptcy" Fitzgerald acknowledged in himself: "in the things between men and women, the old magic was gone. . . ." The novel-in-progress contained some "very fine parts . . . the part about Stahr was all very good." But he did not see how Scott could have finished the book working "with that gigantic, preposterous outline. . . ."

Hemingway placed the blame for what he regarded as Fitzgerald's decline on his wife, Zelda. She had driven her husband to drink, he believed, by encouraging his dissipation and by challenging his manhood. "I often wonder," he wrote Perkins in 1928, "if [Fitzgerald] would not have been the best writer we've ever had or likely to have if he hadn't been married to some one that would make him waste *Everything*." Other friends, such as Waldo Peirce and Evan Shipman, were afflicted with woman trouble too, according to Hemingway. Closer to home, he was convinced that his mother had emasculated his father. Women were the serpents in his garden, with but one lasting exception. The tenderest letter in the book is one he wrote to Hadley Richardson Hemingway, his first wife, in November 1922. She was feeling ill, and Hemingway, in Lausanne to cover a conference on the Greco-Turkish dispute, desperately missed his "sweet little feather kitty with the castorated oil and the throwing up. . . ."

In 1926, when he left Hadley Hemingway for Pauline Pfeiffer, Hemingway suffered terrible pangs of remorse. "I'm perfectly willing to go to hell after I'm dead rather than now," he wrote Pauline Pfeiffer. The trouble was that "now it looks like both." He could not bring himself to write home about the breakup with Hadley until a year after it happened, and when he did, Hemingway made it seem as if she had decided on the divorce. "Don't feel responsible for what I write or what I do," he wrote Dr. C. E. Hemingway back in Oak Park, Illinois. "I take the responsibility, I make the mistakes and I take the punishment." Then plaintively, he added, "You could if you wanted be proud of me sometimes—not for what I do for I have not had much success in doing good—but for my work." Unlike his parents, Hadley Hemingway approved of his work, and as a parting gift Hemingway insisted on signing over to her the royalties from *The Sun Also Rises*. He never forgot her, and in times of loneliness—as during 1942 when he stayed in Cuba and Martha Gellhorn, who was then his wife, went off to war as a correspondent—he wrote Hadley that he loved her very much and that he could not help it, it was "just untransferable feeling for early and best Gods."

In selecting and editing these letters, Carlos Baker was able to call upon his vast fund of information about Hemingway. He also exercised tact and judgment. The names of a few living persons who might have been hurt by seeing themselves mentioned in print have been omitted. Entire letters, including some that deal with family problems, have also been left out of the volume on the grounds of good taste and of possible invasion of privacy or libel. Explanatory notes are used sparingly; some of the more obscure people Hemingway referred to in letters, for example, go unidentified. Despite such intentional and unintentional omissions, Baker's collection presents much material for the first time, including letters to Archibald MacLeish, Bernard Berenson, and the men at Scribners who became Hemingway's friends as well as publishers, especially the legendary Perkins and Charles Scribner, Sr. Where it seems appropriate, Baker supplies notes referring the reader of these letters to pertinent sections of his definitive biography of Hemingway.

The letters constitute a kind of biography between the lines and are particularly useful in illuminating Hemingway's young manhood and his last years. His early show of bravado, for example, fails to conceal his youthful vulnerability to love and war. In writing back to Oak Park after his wounding in World War I, young Hemingway maintained a remarkably stiff upper lip. He joked about the experience and demonstrated a nineteen-year-old's pride in his rank and honors. They could address him as "either 1st Lieut. or Tenente as I hold the rank in both the A.R.C. [American Red Cross] and Italian Army. I guess I'm the youngest 1st Lieut. in the Army," he wrote his father in September 1918. The silver *medaglia valore* was "on the way," he added.

The course of his romance with Agnes von Kurowsky, the nurse he met and fell in love with while recuperating in the Red Cross hospital in Milan, can be traced indirectly through his letters to male friends. In December 1918 he enthusiastically wrote Bill Smith, "Bill this is some girl and I thank God I got crucked so I met her. Damn it I really honestly can't see what the devil she can see in the brutal Stein but by some very lucky astigmatism she loves me Bill. So I'm going to hit the States and start working for the Firm. Ag says we can have a wonderful time being poor together." Later in the same letter, he adds, "Why man I've only got about 50 more years to live and I don't want to waste any of them and every minute that I'm away from that Kid is wasted." This exuberance plummeted into depression four months later when, after Hemingway's return to the United States, she called off their engagement. In confronting this disappointment, as he had when he was wounded, Hemingway tried to present the best possible face to the world. In April 1919 he wrote to Lawrence Barrett "that all bets with any of the women either wild or tame are off definitely. I am a free man! That includes them all up to and including Ag. My Gawd man you didn't think I was going to marry and settle down did you?"

In reaction to such hurts Hemingway adopted a facade of cast-iron insensitivity that is often reflected in the tough talk of his letters. But the vulnerability remained, and in his later correspondence, which grows increasingly long-winded and dull, he resorts to bragging about his accomplishments, insists upon his expertise in any number of fields, and finally descends into paranoia. In December 1960 he set down an open letter absolving his wife Mary of any complicity in the supposedly illegal acts for which, Hemingway believed, the FBI and IRS were pursuing him. While hospitalized at the Mayo Clinic during these last months, his weight dropped rapidly from 200 to 170 pounds, and his spirits sank accordingly. Yet he took time in his deepening depression to write his

doctor's nine-year-old son a cheerful get-well note on 15 June 1961. Less than three weeks later he shot himself.

Perhaps Hemingway's most persistent complaint during the last ten years of his life was against critics and would-be biographers, who he thought were poaching on his literary territory and invading his personal privacy. "What difference does it make if you live in a picturesque little outhouse surrounded by 300 feeble minded goats and your faithful dog Black Dog? The question is: can you write?" Thus there is a certain irony that these letters have a good deal more to say about Hemingway as a man than about Hemingway as a writer. For the most part, he did not discuss his writing in correspondence, other than to indicate how many words he had turned out in any given day or week. Still, the places where he does talk about his writing are among the most interesting in 900-plus pages of Baker's selection.

In August 1923, for example, he insists to Ezra Pound that the vignettes that make up *in our time* (1924), later used as interchapters between the stories of *In Our Time* (1925), "hook up" when read all together and goes on to explain why. In November 1924 he wrote Robert McAlmon that he had cut out the last nine pages of "the long fishing story" (which was later published as "Big Two-Hearted River") since "all that mental conversation" interrupted the flow "just when I was going good and I could never get back into it and finish it." "Wouldn't it be funny," he speculated, "if some publisher accepted it because of the stuff that I've got to cut?" In December 1925 he told Fitzgerald that "Cat in the Rain wasnt about Hadley," but that "Out of Season" represented "an almost literal transcription of what happened" after the two of them had a row. Hemingway had reported the drunken fishing guide depicted in that story to the hotel owner, the guide was fired, and he consequently hanged himself. At the time, Hemingway explained, he "wanted to write a tragic story *without* violence" so he did not include the hanging. And yet another example of the thing happily left out occurs in an August 1940 letter to Perkins, where he asks "What would you think of ending [*For Whom the Bell Tolls* (1940)] as it ends now without the epilogue?" Hemingway eventually did delete this epilogue, but unfortunately one cannot know from these letters what Perkins replied. It would probably be useful to read a two-way correspondence between Hemingway and Perkins.

Only rarely did Hemingway expound upon

literary principles in his letters. When he did, it was worth reading. Thus he wrote Perkins that a book the editor had sent him was "monumental, but dull. Eschew the monumental. Shun the Epic. All the guys who can paint great big pictures can paint great small ones." The secret of reading *The Old Man and the Sea* (1952), he told Berenson, was that there was no symbolism: "The sea is the sea. The old man is an old man. The boy is a boy and the fish is a fish. The sharks are all sharks no better and no worse. All the symbolism that people say is shit. What goes beyond is what you see beyond when you know. A writer should know too much." He did not like Malcolm Cowley's rearrangement of *Tender Is the Night* into chronological order. Hemingway wrote Edmund Wilson in 1951: "I read it all

through and it seemed to take the magic out of it. Nothing came as a surprise and the mystery had all been re-moved. I think it was one of those ideas Scott had sometimes, like his titles that Max Perkins kept him from useing, which was not too good." In 1940 Hemingway explained to Charles Scribner about keeping daily word counts: "I don't know as many words as a guy like Tom Wolfe and so it is a hell of a thing for me to get anything over five hundred of them down in a day. Then at the end of the week I always add them up so that I can think even if I am a no good son of a bitch I wrote, say, 3500 words this week. It's wonderful to be a writer." And at moments like these, when Hemingway discussed the intricacies of his craft in correspondence, it is wonderful to read his letters.

George V. Higgins
(13 November 1939-   )

Hugh M. Ruppersburg
University of Georgia

See also the Higgins entry in *DLB 2, American Novelists Since World War II.*

NEW BOOKS: *A Year or So with Edgar* (New York: Harper & Row, 1979; London: Secker & Warburg, 1980);
Kennedy for the Defense (New York: Knopf, 1980; London: Secker & Warburg, 1981);
The Rat on Fire (New York: Knopf, 1981; London: Secker & Warburg, 1981).

Since the publication of *Dreamland* in 1977, George V. Higgins's career has followed an uncertain path. The quality of his writing has remained high; his skills in reproducing the idiosyncracies of human speech and dialect have improved; and his ability to create tight, economical episodes of energy and tension has not diminished. His reputation as a crime novelist has never been greater. On the other hand, the nature of his most recent work suggests that he may feel unsure about the kind of fiction he wants to write. In *Dreamland*, Higgins seemed to have found his natural metier: a fusion of detective and philosophical fiction employing a contempla-

tive, introspective narrator and a novelistic structure relying primarily on dialogue to bring about the gradual uncovering of a truth about one or more of the main characters. In *A Year or So with Edgar* (1979), Higgins retained this essential form, but in his last two books he has abandoned it almost entirely, returning to methods characteristic of the earliest period in his career. Higgins's recent work, however, does make abundantly clear his intention to continue the use of narration through dialogue—which gives his fiction its distinctive mark as well as its power to delineate human character.

The narrator of *A Year or So with Edgar* does very little talking and a great deal of listening. In fact, Higgins's eighth novel contains more talk and less action than anything he has written. The narrator is Peter Quinn, a highly successful Washington lawyer in his late forties, who thinks himself a fairly stable and responsible man, slightly timeworn and rather cynical about his marriage and the ideals of his youth. The Edgar of the title is a friend from his college days at Fordham University. After they graduated, Quinn entered law school, Edgar Lannin became a reporter with a Boston newspaper, and they drifted apart. Over the years, they have run into each other only occasionally, but after Edgar divorces his wife and begins visiting Washington regularly, he begins seeing Quinn more often. It is at this point that the novel begins. Virtually the entire narrative—with the exception of the introduction, one chapter, and a few other short sections—occurs at a table or desk on either side of which sit Quinn and Edgar, one listening and the other talking.

The two main characters are diametrical opposites. Quinn is a sober, responsible, conservative lawyer, who learned early enough that he would have to play by the rules to prosper in his profession. He has played sufficiently well to establish himself in a prominent Washington practice and to win a temporary position as special adviser to a U.S. president (Lyndon B. Johnson). Edgar, on the other hand, is a hard-drinking womanizer, cynical and pessimistic, apparently not very ambitious, ever ready with a joke or witty retort, unwilling to take himself or anyone else seriously. Most of his old college friends (including Quinn) think him a reprobate. He usually initiates the meetings with Quinn. Yet when they get together, usually for a drink and a meal, Quinn listens sympathetically as Edgar regales him with accounts of his divorce, his friends' problems, and political and private scandals. At first Quinn almost pities his friend, believing that Edgar seeks him out merely as an audience, and perhaps also for a free meal, but he comes gradually to entertain other suspicions.

In the course of explaining Edgar, Peter Quinn also explains much about himself. More than a series of rowdy anecdotes told by an outrageous middle-aged drunk, *A Year or So with Edgar* explores the so-called mid-life crisis, which many people encounter during their forties. For men such as Quinn and Edgar, these years mark a crisis in identity—they are years of self-doubt, divorce, affairs, career changes, alcoholism, or worse. Edgar and Quinn often discuss friends who are having such problems, and the narrative reveals early on that Edgar, with his divorce, alimony problems, drinking, and general physical decrepitude, is experiencing such a crisis himself. Not so evident is Quinn's own mid-life crisis, clearly apparent to many of his friends but not apparent at all to him. In fact, Edgar begins visiting Quinn because he suspects that his friend's marriage is collapsing and that Quinn might need some help extricating himself from the ruins. Because Quinn is the narrator, the reader remains unaware of his problems and of Edgar's altruistic motives almost to the novel's end, though Quinn's habitually sarcastic remarks about his own marriage and the divorces of his friends might arouse some suspicions. In effect, as Quinn listens to Edgar talk about life after divorce, he is unwittingly being prepared to cope with the changes he himself is about to encounter.

Edgar Lannin, a humorous character with a knack for telling funny stories, is responsible for most of the novel's humor. Because he is a journalist and Quinn a lawyer, the narrative contains a considerable amount of often-tiresome trade talk, mainly in the book's first half. This aspect of the book was soundly criticized by reviewers. Martin Levin in the *New York Times Book Review* briefly described the book's conversational form but then noted, "All of this is interesting but quite often irrelevant. Lannin and Quinn do help each other out of scrapes and they share the same lady friend for a spell. But the story in which they interact has no visible narrative thread." The *New Yorker* reviewer reacted even more negatively: "Edgar talks and talks and talks. . . . He ruminates, he recollects, he elaborates, he is routinely vilely obscene, he affects a yokel accent, and the harder he tries to be obscene, the more deadly tedious he becomes. . . . There is no story, no movement, only Edgar, smirking and droning."

Despite these criticisms, typical of the novel's lukewarm reception, Edgar's stories and Quinn's reminiscences fit well into the narrative. In general, *A Year or So with Edgar* is Higgins's most deceptively casual work. The two friends' discussions of their college days, former girl friends, jobs, wives and children, friends and acquaintances, and their own experiences ultimately return to the unspoken double theme of time and disillusionment that penetrates the book. Like many of Higgins's protagonists, both Edgar Lannin and Peter Quinn have been disillusioned by the passing of the years and their failed marriages and disenchanted with their careers. Both have to cope with their shattered ideals and do the best they can to recover confidence and continue with their lives.

In *Kennedy for the Defense* (1980) Higgins returns to the subject of crime, but he retains the lawyer's perspective through the first-person narrator, Jeremiah F. Kennedy, whose wife calls him "the classiest sleazy criminal lawyer in Boston." Kennedy is not a wealthy or powerful man; he belongs solidly to the middle class, living with his wife and daughter in a modest home in Braintree, Massachusetts. His clients include car thieves, pimps, prostitutes, murderers, and the like. Hence, the

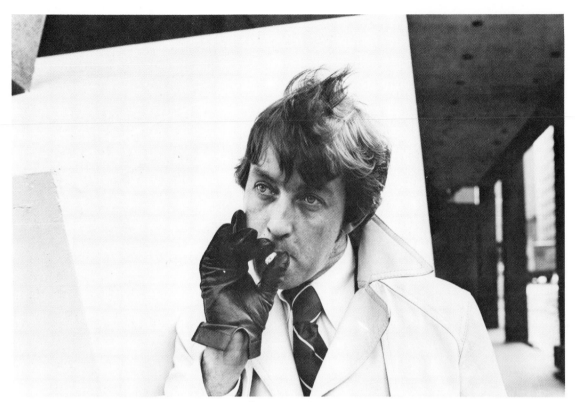

George V. Higgins

irony of his last name particularly irritates him: "While my name is Kennedy, I am not related to the bastards. I don't even know the bastards. For all I know, they may be very nice people. For all I care, they can treat each other like wolves. What they do or don't do is no concern of mine; I only wish they would go at it a little less famously—*had* gone at it, a little less famously, a long time ago—because I happen to have the same name and I get sick and tired of explaining to people that I am a poor working stiff who ended up with the same name because the first guy who had it was the horniest man in Sligo, or some bogtrotting place."

Though Kennedy regards himself as a "man with few illusions," beneath his cynical veneer he is devoted to his own ideals: the support of his family and defense of his clients. When his wife chides him for accepting money from a client who happens to be a pimp, he explains, "Trouble is, the Constitution says every man's entitled to counsel of his choice. He chooses me, I have my living to consider. The Constitution doesn't say that I can't consider my living. Doesn't say anything about it. Because not eating is unpleasant, I generally take the case."

Most of *Kennedy for the Defense* takes place while the narrator is vacationing with his family in Green

Harbor, Massachusetts. During the span of a week he is called away on three cases. In the first Teddy Franklin, "one of the best car thieves on the Eastern Seaboard" and a longtime Kennedy client, has been stopped by Massachusetts State Patrolman Torbert Hudson, who proceeded to eat his temporary driving permit and to arrest him for driving without a license. Several days later Hudson pulled over Franklin's wife, devoured her auto registration papers, and arrested her for driving an unregistered vehicle. Franklin never appears physically in the novel; he usually calls Kennedy on the telephone late at night and talks at length. The second case involves a dandyish young homosexual named Emerson Teller arrested for proposing fellatio to a state trooper. Emerson is clearly guilty; the best Kennedy hopes for is a probated sentence until he discovers that Emerson's father, a former alcoholic, once bribed Torbert Hudson into filing a false report on an accident in which two teenagers died. Thus, Kennedy succeeds in having the charges against Emerson dropped in return for remaining silent about the corrupt patrolman, who is quietly dismissed from the police force.

The third case takes up much of the book's second half. A dim-witted boat mechanic named

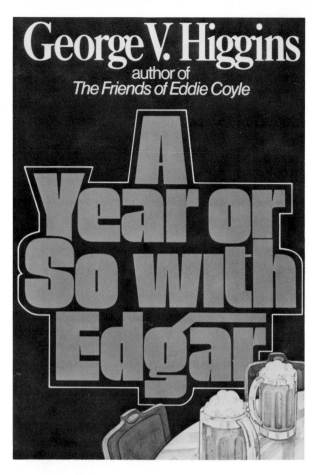

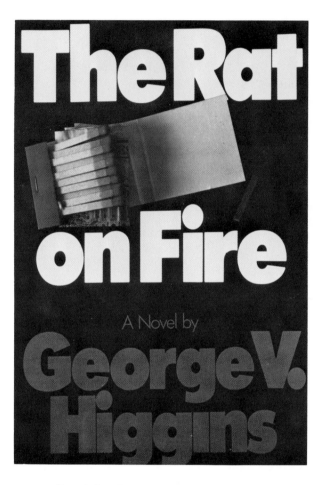

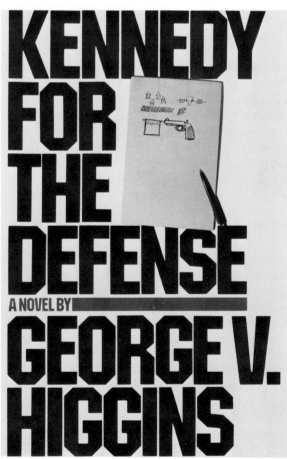

Dust jackets for Higgins's most recent novels

Donald French appears unannounced in Kennedy's office and reports that he thinks he is about to get in trouble but that he is not sure why. A man named Warren Gould, he says, has been asking about him. Kennedy becomes interested in the case because he believes French is too stupid to lie about having done anything wrong. He learns that French's girl friend, a part-time prostitute named Jill Candelaria, is also a paid informant working with a fanatical FBI agent to set French up for arrest as part of a drug-smuggling raid. Kennedy spends much of his time trying to discover the agent's plans and identity.

Although the *New Yorker* reviewer complained that the novel "is not, unhappily, a very lively piece of entertainment," other notices were more laudatory. Noting Higgins's "increasingly deft touch" as a writer, Peter Stoler wrote in *Time* that despite the book's untidy plot, "its tangled cast is instantly credible and permanently delightful. From the opening wisecrack, Kennedy and his world seem so real that when, at novel's end, the lawyer finally relaxes on the 'Irish Riviera,' readers may feel a slight sense of resentment. The fault is Higgins's for providing so much merriment in so brief a space." Evan Hunter, himself a crime novelist, agreed in the *New York Times Book Review*: "George V. Higgins writes very good books. 'Kennedy for the Defense' is one of his best. . . . Higgins has created a genre of his own. . . . He is the le Carre of classy sleaze, and that is classy indeed." Hunter also praises the novel for its dialogue, humor, and rich variety of character.

Kennedy for the Defense is Higgins's funniest book. Much of the humor surfaces in Kennedy's discussions of his clients and in their own words to him. The sketchy plot does not weaken the novel but rather keeps the focus on the dialogue and Higgins's wide variety of interesting and vividly human individuals. Kennedy is clearly the novel's unifying force—a man of ideals and integrity despite his choice of clients, not perfect yet doing his best for the people who rely upon him as lawyer, husband, and father—the most likable and down to earth of Higgins's protagonists.

In *The Rat on Fire* (1981) Higgins resurrects the character types and methods of such early novels as *The Friends of Eddie Coyle* (1972) and *The Digger's Game* (1973). There is no central protagonist or first-person narrator. Its short chapters focus upon small groups of characters talking in a diner, a law office, or a bar. The subject is arson. Jerry Fein, a slumlord, has hired two hoodlums, Leo Proctor and Jimmy Dannaher, to burn his run-down apartment building; Billy Malatesta, a state

fire marshall is on Fein's payroll. Detective Lieutenant Inspector John Roscommon of the Massachusetts State Police is investigating rumors that Proctor has been hired to burn down another building. Mavis Davis and her worthless son Alfred live in this slum building, whose tenants are represented by Wilfrid Mack, state senator and successful black lawyer, who charges them well for his time.

The novel's title tersely describes Proctor's method of arson. He captures several rats and places them in a small cage, which he douses at the proper time with gasoline. Placing it against a hole in the wall of the building's basement, he sets it afire and releases the burning rats. The resulting fire is usually attributed to faulty wiring. Moreover, since Malatesta works for Fein, it is unlikely that the fire's true nature will be discovered.

The episodic structure of *The Rat on Fire* employs a three-part focus: usually the chapters alternate between the meetings of Jerry Fein and his arsonists—either in his office or in a pastry shop of which Proctor is particularly fond—and the rantings of Lieutenant Roscommon, who strongly suspects that Proctor plans to commit arson but does not know the intended method or building. Other chapters deal with Mavis Davis and her son Alfred and their requests for help from Lawyer Mack. Higgins interweaves these three plot strands skillfully: Roscommon suspects that arson is to be committed, and Fein and his men have no idea they are under police surveillance. Mavis Davis is the archetypal innocent victim; oblivious to the danger which threatens her, she complains justifiably over the decrepit condition of her building. The narrative's real interest lies not so much in the conspiracy's final outcome as in how Fein and Proctor plan it and in how Roscommon tries to thwart it.

Dialogue serves the usual prominent role in this Higgins novel, but with an ingenious twist. In several of the chapters in which Proctor and his coconspirators meet in the Scandinavian Pastry Shop, the arsonists sit talking in a booth while two truck drivers, named Don and Mickey, talk at the counter. Higgins deftly intermixes the two conversations without obscuring the sense of either. The result humorously evokes a sense of life and its simultaneity. But there is also another reason for the intermixing dialogue: late in the novel Roscommon hints that "sources" have kept him informed about Proctor's plans. These sources are none other than Mickey and Don, undercover policemen, who have invariably been present when Proctor, Dannaher, and Malatesta meet in the shop.

The Rat on Fire includes other moments of humor. Jimmy Dannaher, whom Proctor has hired to assist him, is afraid of prison, the dark, and rats. Alfred Davis has fallen into the bad habit of committing assault in the presence of numerous witnesses. Jerry Fein, despite his utter lack of conscience, is an oddly congenial fellow who admires Mavis Davis for her integrity and covers his office walls with pictures of Elvis Presley, Milton Berle, Henny Youngman, and the Inkspots. He can be diplomatic and humane, and he contributes frequently to charities, but his real mettle shows when his own financial welfare becomes an issue.

Like *Kennedy for the Defense*, *The Rat on Fire* illustrates how justice gets done—not only through the persistence of policemen and detectives who investigate and try to prevent crime, but also through the incompetent duplicity of the crooks who try to commit it. Though Higgins's latest novel is highly entertaining and readable, it lacks the energy and vigor of many of its predecessors. It does possess, however, a compensating lucidity of dialogue and characterization as well as an economy of structure, which keeps the novel always in motion. Despite its return to the methods of the early novels for which Higgins has been so often praised (and scorned for abandoning), *The Rat on Fire* did not meet with a good reception. Phoebe-Lou Adams of the *Atlantic Monthly*, praising its accurate depictions of the Boston criminal world, called it "compact, cruel, and bitterly funny—Mr. Higgins at his best." Other critics, however, disliked its reliance on dialogue. "Fein jaws at a 10-page clip and so does his secretary," wrote Michael Malone in the *New York Times Book Review*, and, he added, "Mr. Higgins has been highly and rightly praised for a capacity to capture the tough funny argot characteristic of [the crime-novel genre]. But all this praise seems to be giving his characters logorrhea." Peter Lewis in the *Times Literary Supplement* agreed: "Reading a Higgins novel is rather like facing a firing squad armed with high-velocity rifles.... Higgins' unvarying style, so refreshing at first, eventually tends to develop into a predictable monotone, and when that happens the momentum of the book slows down dramatically. The stylist is ultimately the victim of his own style."

Higgins's most recent fiction convincingly demonstrates his versatility as a writer. After *Dreamland*, a confessional, philosophical work, he conflated humor and psychology in *A Year or So with Edgar*. *Kennedy for the Defense* combines humor and crime, while *The Rat on Fire* returns to the straightforward crime formula of *The Friends of Eddie Coyle*. George V. Higgins is probably capable of producing any type of novel he wants, and he will probably continue to vary the sort of fiction he writes during the next few years. Yet in *The Rat on Fire*, he may have considered too much the tastes of the readers who lauded him for *Eddie Coyle* and complained when *Dreamland* and *A Year or So with Edgar* abandoned the subjects which drew them to his work in the first place. Nonetheless, *Dreamland* established Higgins's potential as a serious novelist. Whether he decides to develop that potential or to continue as a popular crime writer, or perhaps to do both, he is sure to remain prominent in contemporary American literature.

Meyer Levin
(8 October 1905-9 July 1981)

Daniel Fuchs
Los Angeles, California

Meyer Levin died of a stroke in Jerusalem at the age of seventy-five. Daniel Fuchs's review of *The Architect*, Levin's last novel, first appeared in the *New York Times Book Review* on 3 January 1982. See also the Levin entry in *DLB 9, American Novelists, 1910-1945*.

NEW BOOK: *The Architect* (New York: Simon & Schuster, 1981).

For Frank Lloyd Wright, who is the subject of Meyer Levin's novel *The Architect*, the enemy was "they," so designated as a matter of convenience; at one point in his autobiography, Wright drew up a partial list of the people afflicting him: reporters, cameramen, editors, immigration officers, judges, federal officials, county officials, lawyers in Chicago, in Milwaukee, in Baraboo, Wis. Levin, who died this year, was similarly beset. He believed he was the victim of a conspiracy of silence; that hostile, left-wing critics unfairly dismissed his work as "too Jewish," as sentimental; that he was systematically persecuted and then ridiculed because he was persecuted, since his detractors, when he fought back, had a chance to make him out "a complainer, a loser, a freak." He was caught in a maze.

Some months before the publication of his novel *The Settlers* in 1972, to protect himself, he sought out a new psychoanalyst. "I wanted to be under some sort of control during those months," he wrote, "to make certain that I wouldn't do anything rash in this critical prepublication period that could prove damaging to the reception of the book." In the case of his earlier novel *Compulsion*, he took his editor's advice to go away. "The enemies you tell of are undoubtedly real," another of his analysts, Dr. Bychovsky, said to him. "The question is, are they worth all the trouble you give yourself over them?"

Levin couldn't contain himself. In writing to one of his adversaries, he used a phrase so inexcusable and hideous that he later didn't want to believe that he had mailed the letter; he actually convinced himself that he didn't know whether or not he had

sent it. "To prevent further evil, I declare that all I have written should perish, let my name be erased from eternity," he wrote in response to a bad book review in a magazine, in another enraged letter which he must have regretted and wished he could recall. "I ask only that others, particularly members of my family (incurable Jewish sentiment) should not be blamed for my errors. I acted alone."

I met Meyer Levin once in California. This was at his home, at a Sunday morning party he and Mrs. Levin were giving for some friends and their children, the party as much for the children as for the grown-ups. The Levins had a house in the Hollywood Hills, a little distance west of the Cahuenga Pass leading into Burbank and the San Fernando Valley. Southern California in those days was relatively undeveloped, a half-dozen years from the great rush that came with the ending of the Second World War. There were yucca stalks and Joshua trees standing by themselves in the sandy soil of the hills, the valley had fields of walnut groves instead of the blocks of homes that were to come, and the pace was slow and easy.

Levin was in Hollywood for a spell of movie work, under short-term contract at Columbia Pictures. I knew him only as the author of his successful Chicago novel, *The Old Bunch*, and as someone who had once brought out a collection of Chassidic tales. He was of medium height, not stocky, but gave the impression of having reserves of strength. There was no side to him. He was open and cordial. He was interested at that time, so I was told, in marionettes and wanted to do, or had already done, O'Neill with life-size puppets playing the roles. I was told he loved to be with people and was always having parties and gatherings. The famous dancer Katherine Dunham was in the city with her troupe, giving a series of performances, and Levin had them at his Sunday morning party. I remember seeing the girls in their colorful offstage dresses, moving among the guests and smiling at the children. We stood talking about pictures and the studios—pleasant, unhurried talk. Two mothers went looking for their children. Mrs. Levin had taken a group on a hike in the hills, they had been gone awhile, and the young mothers were worried.

When Levin, in the beginning, wrote stories about non-Jews (so that his fiction in those early years, the late 20's and 30's, would be salable and possible), he felt he was "passing." When he faithfully kept to his own people, he not only met the editorial resistance of the times, he also stirred up the Anti-Defamation League and had sermons preached against him in the temples. For any writer, at the outset, the problem is to find out what he wants to say that will make his mark and justify him. The miles of reading matter we stuff ourselves with day by day in a lifetime, enough to go around the globe a hundred times—the writer has this always in the back of his head somewhere, that there is enough and plenty without him, and so it is a vexation to him to search out his subject, his own way, his tone, or "voice," as it is called nowadays. The writer has to be on his guard, because ideas are hard to come by, and he is so grateful when he has one that he quickly works it up and uses it, not realizing that it may be a bad idea, a bad image or invention. He asks himself what he wants to do for the reader and then has to watch out for soap opera, which his story may easily become. He wants to outrun his critics and reviewers and not be mortified, to make his work organic, needed, something of its own kind, and irrefutable.

Levin was a war correspondent in Europe, representing the Overseas News Agency and sometimes the Jewish Telegraphic Agency, and, as the Allied armies went spreading eastward after the invasion, he followed along in the uproar of battle, bent on his own special purpose and anxiety, looking to see what he could learn of the Jewish survivors. In a synagogue in Paris he found an exhausted, shrunken Jew, who stayed with him and told him stories containing names of places that Levin had not heard of and that were also new to the world: Drancy, Treblinka, Ravenswood, Auschwitz. (Drancy was a prison barracks outside of Paris and was the assembly point from which the Jews of France went on to Auschwitz in Poland.) With the meeting with the Jewish survivor in the Paris synagogue, Levin had his theme. He knew the guise he wanted for his work, and he had his voice. He had his own subject, set down for him almost as if by providence, firm and authentic, unassailable, and he adopted it with the ardor of the possessed, together with the perils that go with such a devotion.

He kept forward with the troops and hastened to the camps as fast as they were liberated. Levin was among the first Americans to go into Buchenwald, Dachau, Bergen-Belsen and Theresienstadt. The abominations, the bodies stacked like cordwood, the mass graves, which he was among the first, through both his news agencies, to reveal and report on, ate into his bones. He immersed himself in the lore of the camps—their management, the mechanics and bureaucracy of these establishments, the life that went on there, the senseless savagery and insult—and it irked him that he couldn't do enough to make these enormities as clear and compelling as he

Meyer Levin

wanted them to be, that people even then didn't like to listen.

Levin got wind of a brilliant tank commander, a major general in the boldest American military tradition, with an amazing record of combat victories, the first to break through the Siegfried line. The general came from an immigrant Jewish family background; his father was an aged Hebrew teacher in Denver. Levin wanted to use this story. But when he made his way into the Aachen sector, where the general's division was fighting, and the junior officers around the general saw the drift of Levin's intention, there was a certain holding back and silence. Levin wrote directly to the general, who replied flatly that he didn't want his Jewish origin mentioned.

A short time later, by chance, Levin heard of another brilliant tank commander, a colonel, Creighton Abrams. Levin caught up with the colonel in the field, trying out a new Sherman tank and enjoying himself with it. Levin told him he wanted to do a story on him, that he was specifically interested in the Jewish angle. The colonel barely heard him or cared; it was a matter of indifference to him. He invited Levin along, swept him up into the tank with him, went swooping off on the trial run, churning up slopes, doing turns and figures of eight—and it wasn't until much later that Levin discovered the colonel wasn't Jewish at all, that Abrams was an old Scottish family name. In 1950, in his autobiographical *In Search* Levin wrote of the Jewish major general without the least understanding or feeling for the general's needs and situation; in the case of the magnificent Creighton Abrams, with an even more startling lack of humor.

This selfless, single-minded streak in Levin was to become more pronounced in the years that followed. He was now immersed in the aftermath of the camps, in the refugees, the illegal landings, the recalcitrance of the British and the shootings. He gave a good part of a lifetime to the continuing struggles of Israel as it labored to set itself up as a new nation, and it was a torment to him, a bewildering disappointment that became more exasperating with each of his publications, to see his books, produced in good conscience and serving important causes, given poor space in the reviews or no space, passed over and denied the recognition that he knew they deserved. He felt something was amiss, that there must be some hidden opposition, an enmity derived from old political or literary quarrels, that people were acting in concert against him.

Levin read *The Diary of Anne Frank* in France when it came out there, translated into French from the original Dutch. He identified with the book at once. For him, the eerie voice out of the past would make real, in ways that people would not be able to forget, the meaning of the Holocaust, and do at last what he had been straining to accomplish ever since he had entered the concentration camps. He saw *The Diary* from the start as a play and film, and arranged to do the dramatization. He was active in

the American publication of the book, had helped choose the American publisher, wrote the major New York City newspaper review. He completed his dramatization, found a Broadway producer agreeable to the parties involved, was told his work was good, began discussing directors and casting. And then, because of the normal alarms and uncertainties of theatrical productions, because of machinations or honestly felt differences, reservations began to arise, and the play eventually was taken away from him. It was more than he would put up with. He was convinced a political clique was agitating against him behind closed doors. He believed the new people were determined to commercialize and betray the story when they complained that his version was "too Jewish" and oppressive. He fought back in a deranged fury of lawsuits, public appeals and outcries, committing excesses and holding on, until people wondered at him, until his friends became distressed and avoided him and he couldn't stand himself.

In the 1950's, Levin filmed a number of Frank Lloyd Wright's structures. The film, we are told in an author's note that Levin appended to *The Architect*, was "inexplicably lost," but the remembrance of those buildings and the footage he shot stayed in his mind, and he kept feeling for years that his work on Wright was still to be done. Then, finally, he set himself to the task. Wright, who took for a family crest the Druid symbol signifying "Truth Against the World" and who went into battle without planned retreats, lived in a tumult of strife on a scale much larger than the troubles Levin had brought on himself.

Levin was completely absorbed in the writing of *The Architect*. He was restoring the Chicago that had meant a great deal to him in his young manhood, the Chicago of Louis Sullivan, Dankmar Adler, Charles Tyson Yerkes, Adelina Patti, John Altgeld, Clarence Darrow, Harriet Monroe, even the boy Hemingway. Levin took sly, affectionate digs at Sandburg, at Dreiser. There is a lightness in the book, a humor and freedom. He frankly juggled certain events around in time and place, combining, for example, Wright's first two wives into one so that he could make a better triangle with Wright and the architect's third lady, a better truth or at least a more artistic and entertaining one.

Proust, in writing of the death of Bergotte, tells of "his books arranged three by three" as if keeping watch over the novelist who was gone. So Meyer Levin's books might be grouped, in pairs or three by three, in a gesture to a man who took on the most painful themes of our times, who was on the scene throughout, and who worked to the limits of his strength in a long and honorable writer's career.

A TRIBUTE *from IRVIN FAUST*

Meyer Levin was a tough, resilient man whose life in letters reflected these qualities. He fought for his books as he would fight for his children, which indeed his books were. In his later years he wasn't

fashionable in the world of criticism, but he continued to drive ahead until the end in ways that were meaningful to Meyer Levin. His personal vision touched millions of readers, and this contact, this communication, was for him, I believe, a vindication for his courage and tenacity and belief in self.

A TRIBUTE *from NORMAN MAILER*

After all these years, *The Old Bunch* is still the best novel about Jews in America.

Anita Loos
(26 April 1893-18 August 1981)

Alden Whitman
Southampton, New York

Anita Loos, who died in New York on 18 August 1981, was a screenwriter, playwright, novelist, and memoirist. Most notably, she is remembered as the author of *Gentlemen Prefer Blondes*, a 1925 novel that poked fun at a romance between a professed sophisticate and a mindless blonde.

A pithy satire of romantic emotionalism, the minor classic ran through eight-five editions and translations in fourteen foreign languages. A short book of seven chapters cast in diary form, it detailed the adventures of Lorelei Lee, the blonde from Little Rock, Arkansas, her friend Dorothy Shaw, and Gus Eisman, the Chicago Button King, through whose kindness Miss Lee is enabled to tour Europe's Ritz Hotels. Lorelei Lee, the archetypal vamp, epitomizes women sensitive to the material values of romance and the durability of diamonds.

In December 1949, a Broadway musical, starring Carol Channing, was adapted from the novel; it ran for two years. Two films were adapted from *Gentlemen Prefer Blondes*: Alice White and Ruth Taylor played in a 1928 movie of the book, and a musical in 1953 featured Marilyn Monroe and Jane Russell.

Before Anita Loos added Lorelei Lee to American culture, she had acquired a formidable reputation as a screenwriter, going back to 1912, when she wrote for D. W. Griffith at American Biograph. She once estimated she produced some 200 silent film scripts for such stars as Mary

Pickford, Lillian and Dorothy Gish, Douglas Fairbanks, Mae Marsh, Francis X. Bushman, and the Talmadge sisters, Constance and Norma. Some of her silent films were *A Virtuous Vamp* (1919), *The Perfect Woman* (1921), *Dangerous Business* (1921), and *Learning to Love* (1925). In addition, she was among the first to prepare screen captions, and her subtitles for *Intolerance* (1916) are considered especially noteworthy.

Versatile as well as prolific, Anita Loos wrote two Broadway comedies in the 1920s—*The Fall of Eve* (1925) and *The Whole Town's Talking* (1926). Loos took a vacation from writing in the late 1920s to enjoy her international celebrity and to bask with her friends, who included H. L. Mencken; George Jean Nathan, theater critic; Joseph Hergesheimer, novelist; Ernest Boyd, Irish essayist; and Tallulah Bankhead, actress.

Resuming her screen career in 1931, she wrote, among other sound films, *Biography of a Bachelor Girl* (1935), with Anne Harding as the star; and *San Francisco* (1936), a musical with Clark Gable and Jeanette MacDonald.

Loos once remarked that she had "lost all track" of how many films she wrote. One of her most praised scripts was *The Women* in 1939. Based on the Clare Boothe Luce play, it featured Norma Shearer, Joan Crawford, Mary Boland, Rosalind Russell, and Paulette Goddard. She also wrote or adapted *Susan and God* (1940), *They Met in Bombay*

Anita Loos

(1941), *When Ladies Meet* (1941), *Blossoms in the Dust* (1941), *I Married an Angel* (1942), and the musical version of *Gentlemen Prefer Blondes*. The distinguishing feature of these and her other films is her flair for bright satiric comedy and crisp dialogue.

Toward the end of her film career, Loos turned again to the stage, writing *Happy Birthday*, a Saroyanesque comedy for Helen Hayes, which opened in 1946 and ran for 564 performances. This story of a prim librarian who lost her inhibitions in a bar was followed by *Gigi*, an adaptation from the French of Colette's witty story about the rearing of a *grande cocotte*. Opening in 1951, *Gigi* ran for 219 performances; a Hollywood musical version starred Maurice Chevalier.

Loos's other novels include *A Mouse Is Born* (1951), whose heroine gives a misspelled account of her movie career; and *No Mother to Guide Her* (1961), a Hollywood novel that Edmund Wilson liked, but that many other critics did not. In addition, she wrote an anecdotal account of her own film career,

Kiss Hollywood Good-by (1974), that was a companion to an earlier memoir, *A Girl Like I* (1966). In 1977, *A Cast of Thousands*, a picture book with candid yet affectionate commentary about her many show business friends, was published. Her final book, another memoir, was *The Talmadge Girls* (1978). Between books, Loos wrote occasional magazine articles of reminiscence.

To her skillful writing in all the genres she essayed, Anita Loos brought her perky personality, a bright tongue, and a keen mind. Her scripts radiate insouciance. Self-schooled and a prodigious reader, she was elfin-quick to satirize contemporary fads, foibles, and pretensions. To her life, as to her art, she brought an almost gamine joie de vivre that belied the high degree of discipline that went into her work. From silents well into the sound era, she was one of Hollywood's most productive script writers, completely professional. Strangely, she rarely looked at the completed movies she wrote. She would rather read, she said.

Mary McCarthy

(21 June 1912-   )

Joseph M. Flora
University of North Carolina at Chapel Hill

See also the McCarthy entry in *DLB 2, American Novelists Since World War II*.

NEW BOOKS: *Cannibals and Missionaries* (New York: Harcourt Brace Jovanovich, 1979; London: Weidenfeld & Nicolson, 1979);
Ideas and the Novel (New York: Harcourt Brace Jovanovich, 1980; London: Weidenfeld & Nicolson, 1981);
The Hounds of Summer and Other Stories (New York: Avon, 1981).

After Hannah Arendt heard her good friend Mary McCarthy lecture on "Art Values and the Value of Art" at the University of Aberdeen, she told her that she should draw on those ideas for a novel. The "germ" for *Cannibals and Missionaries* (1979) seems not to have been character or plot, but ideas—ideas that Mary McCarthy had mulled over for a long time. Knowledgeable about the visual arts as well as the literary arts, she can speak with authority about artifacts as she raises philosophical questions about their ultimate worth. Although often accused of casting a cold eye on the human predicament (despite her liberal political connections), McCarthy went on undaunted with her plan for a novel in which characters debate about art and revolution. She probably anticipated that her critics would again find her characters unappealing and lacking in warmth.

If art is long and life is short, the political moment of McCarthy's novel (the impending collapse of the Shah's regime in Iran) counterpoints the significance of artistic achievement against the terror of repression and revolution. At the end of McCarthy's story, a revolutionist (in a moment of despair) destroys himself by blowing up the house in Holland where he holds as "hostage" several great paintings and some well-meaning liberals who had intended to make their way to Iran to investigate reports about the brutality of the Shah's secret police, SAVAK. Instead, they find themselves hijacked to a remote "polder" in the Netherlands, along with a group of rich art collectors bound for Iran to inspect art treasures there. The hijackers

later ransom the parasitic collectors for their art treasures, their leader aware of the gigantic symbolism of this exchange. The destruction of the revolutionist, the art, and many of the liberals raises questions about the value of art in the contemporary world. Should a worthy person care greatly for art? Is the philosophy *ars longa, vita brevis* not to be tolerated in a world of social injustices? McCarthy also wanted to show, she explained, "how terrorists paint themselves into a corner because their aims are impossible."

The title of McCarthy's novel comes from a match game some of the hostages play during their captivity. Three cannibals and three missionaries are on one side of a river. The puzzle is to ferry all three missionaries safely across in a boat that holds only two people, never allowing the cannibals to outnumber the remaining missionaries; all of the missionaries can row, but only one of the cannibals can. There is appropriate symbolism here: will these hostages be released or rescued? And there is another puzzle: who are the cannibals and who are the missionaries in this novel? There is a great deal of waiting in most hijackings; time can be ponderous but also useful for reflection and discussion of ideas. But for various reasons, McCarthy's novel does not have the degree of suspense that the match game suggests.

As well as referring to a specific game, McCarthy's title also refers to many of the characters. And that is part of the challenge that McCarthy faced in writing her novel. She has a compelling device for bringing people together; the question is whether she can maintain her readers' interest in them as characters. She begins by introducing the novel's "missionaries," the liberals who are distressed at accounts of injustice in Iran. This is the group of characters McCarthy knows best, the type she has most often portrayed. The novel starts as a genial Episcopal rector takes leave from his normal and attractive family before beginning his trip to Iran. The rector picks up a bishop, an old friend, and together they journey to the airport. The challenge of their journey is caught up in the rector's silent construction of a sermon on the book of

Jonah, one that may well remind readers of the sermon in *Moby-Dick*, which also raises fundamental questions about the action to come. At the airport these clerics are joined by other "missionaries"—the female president of a women's college, a U.S. senator who is very like Eugene McCarthy, a journalist, and others. As the reader begins to meet new travelers, the others tend to go too much to the edges of his consciousness. Familiar characters are sacrificed to new characters. Eventually the reader comes to the conclusion that, despite her title, it is not character that engages Mary McCarthy in this novel. She is interested in ideas, in issues, and in telling her readers about Holland.

new paragraph for each speaker. In McCarthy's long paragraphs the illusion of speech dissipates.

The character that Mary McCarthy seems to like best is Van Vliet de Jong, a Dutch parliamentarian of reasonable attitudes and furthermore a better poet than the U.S. senator. And she seems also to admire Joeren, the chief of the terrorists, who is also Dutch. One of her primary aims is to make her readers understand better the plight of the Dutch (the terrorists are demanding that the Dutch leave NATO and withdraw recognition of Israel) and to celebrate Holland. As a small nation, Holland is put in a precarious position by global politics, making it "an imaginary country" in real ways. In her

Mary McCarthy

The novel of ideas has a history and some appeal. Usually the frame is less dramatic than that of *Cannibals and Missionaries*; usually the characters who are brought together in such novels get to talk more than McCarthy's do and probably more naturally. McCarthy has preferred to take her reader into the minds of select individuals, who reveal themselves and their ideas only minimally through their conversations. When McCarthy's characters talk, McCarthy does not always make the dialogue believable. Too often it seems condensed dialogue. Sometimes, too, McCarthy writes an extended paragraph in which many characters speak. The reader's response to such a paragraph is psychologically different from what it would be if the dialogue had been printed traditionally, with a

acknowledgments McCarthy says that she believes that her love for the Netherlands shows through the text. As it happens, the non-Dutch characters receive more of McCarthy's satirical bite. Most objectionable perhaps is Aileen Simmons, president of Lucy Skinner College. At first cast as a "missionary," Simmons will later strike most readers as a "cannibal," for she is the one most concerned with saving herself, perhaps more of a "cannibal" than the hijackers. She could easily fit into the cast of *The Group*.

Because Mary McCarthy is an important writer, *Cannibals and Missionaries* was widely reviewed, but many reviewers, as much as they might have tried, did not find the book very satisfying. Joseph Epstein's judgment is representative: "*Cannibals and*

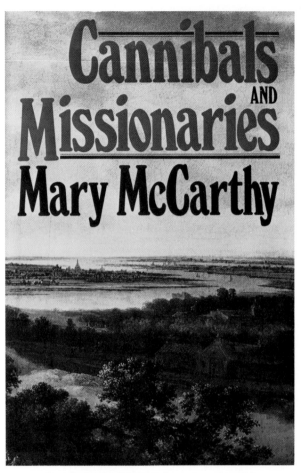

Dust jacket for McCarthy's most recent novel

Missionaries seems a novel less written than willed into being—and one which it takes a certain amount of will to continue reading." He declared the book "neither entertaining nor profound." Diane Cole explained the difficulty with the novel: "It's not so much the act of terrorism as the idea of terrorism that has caught hold of McCarthy's imagination." McCarthy herself seems to have sensed certain weaknesses in *Cannibals and Missionaries* even before the reviewers had their say. She announced that it would be her last novel, explaining, "Something I've observed is that one loses one's social perceptions, they get blunted and dimmer as one gets older—it's partly a matter of eyesight. You can continue writing poetry and essays and so on, but to be a novelist you have to have this alert social thing." It is unlikely that *Cannibals and Missionaries* will enhance McCarthy's reputation as a novelist; her earlier novels will be more widely read.

McCarthy sought a measure of revenge against her reviewers in her next book, *Ideas and the Novel* (1980). Originally presented as the 1980

Northcliffe Lectures at University College, London, the four chapters make a spirited defense of the "old-fashioned" notion that ideas have a place in novels. The book is thereby also a defense of the theory that underlies all of her fiction. The prejudice of critics and teachers is against such fiction. Quoting the young T. S. Eliot's famous observation about Henry James—"He had a mind so fine that no idea could violate it"—McCarthy sees James as the fount of a doctrine that fiction should be concerned not with telling but with showing, not with expressing the author's opinions and ideas, but with depicting life. Before James it was not so. Readers looked to novelists to provide them with information about many things, but a society with movies, television, newspapers, and magazines of every description seems to want something else from its writers of fiction. The same society does not value the long passages of setting that were standard in the novel before it became "art." Before James, a writer was not obligated to "refine himself out of existence" (as Joyce's Stephen Dedalus described the goal of the writer) and could intrude into his narrative to inform his readers in his own voice about many things. McCarthy envies these earlier writers their freedoms. Obviously she overstates her case, but she makes lively pronouncements: "Ideas are held not to belong in the novel; in the art of fiction we have progressed beyond such simplicities. The doctrine of progress in the arts is a hard doctrine, imposing itself even on those who are fervent non-believers. The artist is an imitative beast, and, being of my place and time, I cannot philosophize in a novel in the good old way, any more than I can write 'we mortals.' A novel that has ideas in it stamps itself as dated; there is no escape from that law." The reviewers of *Cannibals and Missionaries* agree that the law is very much in effect. One could argue, however, that ideas per se do not spoil that novel; rather McCarthy fails to handle them as effectively as she might.

Nevertheless, Mary McCarthy is an engaging teacher, and part of the pleasure of *Ideas and the Novel* is listening to McCarthy discuss novels of other writers for their ideas. She gives most of her attention to continental novelists (Victor Hugo, Stendhal, Dostoevski), for, she says, "the English novel is seldom searching, at any rate on the plane of articulated thought." As a study of ideas in novels, McCarthy's book is hardly complete, nor was it intended to be so. It is certainly, however, a challenge to further reflection on the subject. The hesitancy of others to discuss the novel of ideas is striking. McCarthy notes her failure even to find the

IDEAS AND THE NOVEL

4

You could say that <u>Crime and Punishment</u> was a novel about the difference be-

tween theory and practice. Well, if you were a philistine, you could. <u>The Possessed</u> also

deals with ideas and their execution and on a wider scale, <del>but</del> such without any reassuring

conclusion. In the earlier book there was just one theory, Raskolnikov's, which he fails

to prove, owing to his own half-heartedness in applying it—an indication of a possible
weakness
<del>flaw</del> in the theory itself. In The <u>Possessed</u>, there is a whole band of theorists, each

possessed by a doctrinaire idea, and a whole innocent Russian town to practice on. But in

the outcome there is no divergence between idea a nd reality; in most cases they have fused,
the superannuated old liberal,
which is what makes the novel so frightening. The exception is Stepan Trofimovich, an idealist

in his writings and something more abject in his daily conduct, who naturally holds no

terrors for his fellow-citizens.

It is possible to see <u>Crime and Punishment</u> as a prophecy of <u>The Possessed</u>. There is

the seed of a terrorist in Raskolnikov, which cannot come to fruit since he lacks a prime

essential: organization. He is isolated, and his having a devoted mother and sister who

bring out the "good" in him makes him feel all the more cut off. He appears to believe in

socialism, yet his only friend, the former student Razumihin, is a conservative and dis-
is lumped together with Raskolnikov
quietingly thick with functionaries of the law. A minor figure, Lebezniatikov, by <del>#######</del>
a spiteful
person as one of a pair of "notorious infidels, agitators, and atheists." Lebezniatikov,

who keeps talking about a commune and regards Sonia's being forced into prostitution as

"a vigorous protest against the organization of society," is certainly a socialist, but

Raskolnikov, who has no time for idiots, consistently gives him a very wide berth. He is

reserved, proud, and unsociable and, despite his boldness in theory, <del>##</del> never had any plan

to commit more than a single murder (the second was unplanned and regretted), obviously not

a chain of crimes. A final liability is the difficulty he has in making up his mind.

In <u>The Possessed</u>, all these deficiencies are made up. There is determination in

Pyotr Verhovensky, an organizing gift, complete absence of scruple. He thinks large, in

sweeping arcs, not one faltering step at a time. He is highly sociable, almost convivial,

has no pride; when we first meet him, he is described as "an ordinary young man, very lively

A page from the typescript of Ideas and the Novel

term *novel of ideas* in her dictionary of literary terms, though she could find such entries as *novel of the soil*. Her own book should help to reverse the trend, even as McCarthy hopes that the form of the novel may be revitalized—by making, she argues, ideas once again acceptable. She sees some hopeful signs in several works, such as John Updike's *The Coup* (1978) and Robert Pirsig's *Zen and the Art of Motorcycle Maintenance* (1974)—and authors who deal with ideas. McCarthy admits that to make it acceptable to deal with ideas in fiction other strategies may have to be employed "to disarm and disorient reviewers and teachers of literature, who, as always, are the reader's main foes." That, the final sentence of the book, is her knockout blow.

Mary McCarthy's work of the last decade has held no surprises. Her place as critic and essayist has seemed more assured than her place as a novelist. Her criticism is always engaging though unsettling to some because of her tendency to assert her positions so authoritatively. Katherine Anne Porter once called McCarthy "in some ways the worst tempered woman in American letters." Reviewing *Ideas and the Novel*, William H. Pritchard warned that the reader has to beware of McCarthy's ideas precisely because she writes with "absolute ease" and "speaks always with nothing less than confidence." Nevertheless, it is good to have studied with McCarthy. One should expect that her earlier fiction will attract new readers.

In 1981 Avon published *The Hounds of Summer and Other Stories*. In the title story vacationers at an Italian seaside find their tranquility disturbed when German tourists make their appearance. Only one other story in the book, "The Appalachian Revolution," was previously uncollected. The others previously appeared in *Cast a Cold Eye* (1950). The slight percentage of new work further suggests that McCarthy has indeed turned from the writing of fiction, short stories as well as novels.

If McCarthy is mainly skeptical about the future of the novel and about reviewers and educators as she gets older, she also becomes increasingly skeptical and pessimistic about other matters. There is little to cheer her on the American political scene, and she finds the lack of capable leadership in the Democratic party particularly disheartening. She finds the "conservative" ascendence misnamed, for the "conservatives" are really only "capitalists." If they were truly conservatives, she declares, they would wish to conserve resources and would be against the development of nuclear energy. She despairs of socialism "with a human face" ever get-

ting a chance to be developed, but she is most optimistic about Poland. The only political causes in which she takes an active interest are in Poland and Czechoslovakia.

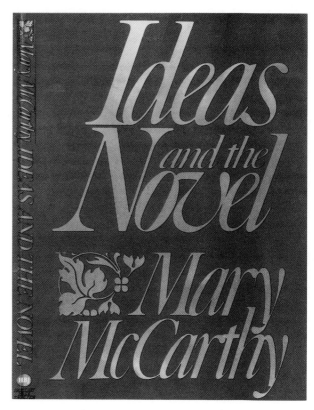

Dust jacket for McCarthy's most recent collection of essays

McCarthy continues to believe in marriage; divorced three times, she says that for her a divorce is always like a murder. She has been married to James West, her fourth husband, for over twenty years and gets great pleasure in domesticity. (She finds the women's liberation movement a bore, and the positions of the extremists futile.) McCarthy and West divide their time between their home in Castine, Maine, and Paris, where West, who has recently retired, served as a diplomat for many years. When the Wests are in Maine they live essentially private lives. In her younger days McCarthy thrived on controversy. Now her public appearances are rare although she gives an occasional lecture or reading. But she is not exactly docile; in January 1980 on the *Dick Cavett Show* she aroused the ire of Lillian Hellman by calling her a liar. McCarthy said that Hellman is "a bad writer and a dishonest writer" and that "every word she writes is a lie, including 'and' and 'the.'" Hellman sued, and the case, representing an enmity of many years, is still pending.

Although McCarthy has said that she would write no more novels, it is unthinkable that she would cease writing. As soon as she was finished with *Cannibals and Missionaries*, she was at work on a new book which she calls "an intellectual autobiography." It will be read with keen interest by everyone who wants to know more about her varied and eventful life. She knows, of course, that many reviewers will be waiting; a writer previously dubbed "Contrary Mary," she will seem fair game to many.

Despondent because her faith in socialism seems incapable of realization, McCarthy does not cease to care or to work. Although she does not believe in God ("that is not an act of will," she says; "I can't even conceive of God"), she recognizes that Christianity was the major shaping force of her life. Her experience in North Vietnam, which she wrote about in *Vietnam* (1967) and *Hanoi* (1968), made her realize how Christian she is: "But ethics came to me in the frame of Christian teaching, and even though I don't believe in an afterlife I'm still concerned with the salvation of my soul." Her new book will be a part of her attempt to achieve that salvation.

Interview:

Miriam Gross, "A World Out of Joint," *Observer*, 14 October 1979, p. 35.

References:

Diane Cole, Review of *Cannibals and Missionaries*, *Georgia Review*, 34 (Spring 1980): 228-231;

Joseph Epstein, "Too Much Even of Kreplach," review of *Cannibals and Missionaries*, *Hudson Review*, 33 (Spring 1980): 97-110;

Francis Gillen, "The Failure of Ritual in 'The Unspoiled Reaction,'" *Renascence*, 24 (Spring 1972): 155-158;

Darrel Mansell, "Unsettling the Colonel's Hash: 'Fact' in Autobiography," *Modern Language Quarterly*, 37 (March 1976): 115-132;

Wendy Martin, "The Satire and Moral Vision of Mary McCarthy," in *Comic Relief: Humor in Contemporary American Literature*, edited by Sarah Blacher Cohen (Urbana: University of Illinois Press, 1978), pp. 187-206;

Cathleen Medwick, "Mary McCarthy: an American Classic," *Vogue*, 171 (November 1981): 283, 291-292, 295, 297;

Mitzi Myers, "You Can't Catch Me: Mary McCarthy's Evasive Comedy," *Regionalism and the Female Imagination*, 3, no. 2-3 (1977-1978): 58-69;

William H. Pritchard, "Criticism as Literature," review of *Ideas and the Novel*, *Hudson Review*, 34 (Spring 1981): 117-124;

Gordon O. Taylor, "Cast a Cold 'I': Mary McCarthy on Vietnam," *Journal of American Studies*, 9, part 1 (1975): 103-114.

Wright Morris

(6 January 1910-   )

Michael Adams
Louisiana State University

See also the entry in *DLB 2, American Novelists Since World War II.*

NEW BOOKS: *The Fork River Space Project* (New York: Harper & Row, 1977);
Earthly Delights, Unearthly Adornments: American Writers as Image-Makers (New York: Harper & Row, 1978);
Plains Song: For Female Voices (New York: Harper & Row, 1980);
Will's Boy: A Memoir (New York: Harper & Row, 1981);
The Wright Morris Portfolio (New York: Witkin-Berley, 1981).

RECENT AWARDS: Distinguished Achievement Award, Western Literature Association, 1979; American Book Award for *Plains Song*, 1981; Robert Kirsch Award, *Los Angeles Times*, 1981.

"Neglect is increasingly a necessity, not just an accident," said Wright Morris in discussing, on the *Dick Cavett Show* (13 February 1980), the fact that he remains perhaps America's least-known major writer. "I feel that increasingly [for] the man who has a private preoccupation with what he's doing and who is engaged, to his own gratification, in what he's doing, neglect is increasingly crucial to what he's doing." Morris believes that his lack of fame keeps him from being distracted from his aesthetic objectives and helps maintain the consistent quality of his work, a quality which must eventually be recognized more widely. "I am confident," Morris told Cavett, "there are five million people in this country who would like my books if they read them, if they knew they were there. . . . I simply require that you read me on my own terms."

Morris has become even more available, in the sense of the quantity of his work. Since his retirement from teaching at San Francisco State University in 1975, he has had his twenty-sixth, twenty-seventh, twenty-eighth, and twenty-ninth major works published. *The Fork River Space Project* (1977) and *Plains Song* (1980) bring his total number of novels to twenty. *Earthly Delights, Unearthly Adorn-*ments (1978) is his third volume of literary criticism, and *Will's Boy* (1981) is his first—and apparently last—memoir. His subjects remain the American dream and its effect on typical Americans, especially the residents of the plains of Nebraska. Morris, who has lived in Mill Valley, California, for the past twenty years, continues to examine the manners and morals of the Midwest he left almost a half century ago.

The Fork River Space Project is Morris's fourth consecutive short, lyrical, primarily whimsical novel, following *In Orbit* (1967), *Fire Sermon* (1971), and *A Life* (1973). Kelcey, the narrator of *The Fork River Space Project*, writes "humorous, fantasy-type pieces" for magazines under the pseudonym Serenus Vogel and lives near Lincoln, Nebraska, with his young wife Alice. Their lives are calm and uneventful until Kelcey hires plumber Harry Lorbeer and painter O. P. Dahlberg, "Two oddballs that manage to roll into the same pocket." Lorbeer and Dahlberg are the sole residents of Fork River, Kansas, which suddenly became a ghost town in the early 1940s after being hit by a mysterious tornado. Dahlberg has written a science-fiction book inspired by the experience, and he and Lorbeer preside over the Fork River Space Project where crowds gather each weekend to celebrate the mysteries of outer space at the site, where they believe aliens have been. The two oddballs' goal is "to restore awe." As Alice and Dahlberg gradually fall in love, Kelcey tries to adjust to the changes in his life that he knows are coming: "They were young. What could they do with their feelings but have them?"

While so many previous Morris protagonists are concerned with exorcising the past, Kelcey has to reconcile himself to the future, deciding that the best way to confront matters is with amused detachment. Delving beneath his own surface eccentricities and those of the people around him, Kelcey learns not to be surprised by anything: unidentified flying objects would be as understandable to him as departing wives. Kelcey's efforts to explain his fellow earthlings make *The Fork River Space Project* the most epigrammatic of Morris's novels: "People do have their place if we can just determine what it is";

"People are crazy. If we admit to that, we can do pretty well"; "The people we are comfortable with are fictions: if the real person speaks up we're shocked." The most amusing part of the novel is Kelcey's memories of two other eccentrics, Tuchman and Taubler, whom he met in Paris in 1939. Taubler, an avant-garde artist who never speaks, lets his art, which consists of commonplace objects, do his talking for him. In this way he resembles Morris, whose skillful use of and insight into the ordinary make him the distinctive artist he is.

Wright Morris

The Fork River Space Project is perhaps more subtle and eccentric than is usual even for Morris, and the reviewers for the major periodicals ignored it for the most part. Those who liked the novel gave it qualified praise. In the *New York Times Book Review*, Anatole Broyard said that the novel "is full of attractive speculations, adequately embodied in characters our imaginations can willingly entertain, even if we cannot wholly accept them." Writing in *Book World,* William Logan was even less enthusiastic: "The novel's difficulty is that it throws off ideas

like sparks . . . but examines them cursorily. Morris has often been called underrated, but his fiction, though pleasurable and wry, seems limited in means, as if he cannot render his ideas in plot and character." While the characters in *The Fork River Space Project* are less vivid than is typical with Morris, he has never been concerned with plot, and it seems unjust to suggest that the novel's lack of a unified plot line results from any technical weakness on Morris's part.

Earthly Delights, Unearthly Adornments: American Writers as Image-Makers (1978) continues the explorations of American writers, their subject matter, and their styles which Morris began in *The Territory Ahead* (1958). Morris reexamines writers he dealt with in that study—Herman Melville, Walt Whitman, Mark Twain, Henry James, F. Scott Fitzgerald, William Faulkner, and Ernest Hemingway—and adds several more: Stephen Crane, Willa Cather, Gertrude Stein, Sherwood Anderson, Ring Lardner, T. S. Eliot, Katherine Anne Porter, John Dos Passos, Richard Wright, James Agee, and Carson McCullers. Morris looks at the images these writers have created and suggests, "The telling imagery of our memorable writers is rooted in memory and emotion. The whiteness of the whale, the lineaments of death, the speech of groping hands, water purling over rocks, the recurrent voices of impotence and rage provide us with the clues to the writers' obsessions, the chimed notes of their emotion. In this wise, reader and writer are joined in a profound yet impersonal comprehension."

As in *The Territory Ahead,* Morris is able to evoke vividly other writers' qualities. William Faulkner, he says, "writes with his damper wide open, sucking in more air than the occasion warrants . . . but without this draft there might have been no fire, only clouds of smoke." Of Ring Lardner he observes, "People seldom sound as good as he reports them, but they would if they could." Morris is at his best as a critic when analyzing style: "The meandering James sentence, with its snaglike punctuation, grew out of the need to gather a *total* impression, now tripping forward, now tilting sideward, or pausing to take a step rearward, graphically indicating, as in an artist's mock-up, the complications of a full-scale portrait." As Benjamin DeMott wrote in the *New York Times Book Review,* "Wright Morris has a gift for metaphors that translate other writers' styles into physical experiences." While not all of Morris's observations are original, most are memorable and even entertaining. "The result," DeMott observed, "is something close to an astonishment: a lively book of literary criticism."

Women characters in Morris's fiction have been relatively insignificant. They have usually been more important for their relationships with his men than for their own roles in his fictional world. *Plains Song: For Female Voices* (1980), another short, poetic novel, reverses this situation as Morris presents four generations of Nebraska women from the early twentieth century to the present, offering his usual examinations of the loneliness and alienation of the inhabitants of the plains from a new perspective. The result is his most highly praised book in twenty years and the winner of the second American Book Award for fiction presented by the Association of American Publishers.

Cora Atkins bites through her hand during the consummation of her marriage, and she and her husband Emerson, a man so self-reliant he cuts himself off from those around him, barely communicate for the remainder of their long marriage. (Just before Emerson dies, the narrator comments "It shamed her to look at him with his eyes closed, feeling in her soul he was a stranger to her, and she to him.") Emerson's brother Orion, who talks to Cora much more than her husband does, grows quiet after his wife Belle dies in childbirth and becomes even less communicative after being gassed in World War I. The Atkins women cannot communicate with each other either. Cora is unable to understand Belle's strange Ozark ways—"More and more, it seemed to Cora, Belle's prattle was less an expression of her high animal spirits than a need to break the silence around her"—and Cora's daughter, Madge, fat and complacent, is satisfied merely to watch Belle's daughter, Sharon Rose.

Cora and Sharon emerge as the protagonists. The reader comes to admire Cora for her ability to endure the hardships of farming and the solitude of the plains and Sharon for her ability to see what the others cannot about their listless existences. Cora has the strength to persist in her endeavor to make the most of a bad thing, while Sharon leaves to make something of herself, first as a piano student in Chicago and later as a music teacher at Wellesley College. Sharon tries to rescue Madge's daughter, Blanche, as well but fails to overcome the passive, cowlike side of the girl's nature.

Morris, as in his other fiction, is writing not only about life on the American plains, but about any life carried on without feeling, imagination, or apparent purpose. Yet he sees this kind of life as being most predominant in the rural Midwest. Sharon cannot understand why anyone lives in such a place: "Numbed by the cold, drugged by the heat and chores, they were more like beasts of the field than people." She has to escape from "the ceaseless humiliations, inadmissible longings, the perpetual chores and smoldering furies, the rites and kinships with half-conscious people so friendly and decent it shamed her to dislike them." The fact that these people are so often friendly and decent even if they are only half-conscious makes their lives so disturbing for Morris, their inability to come completely alive so sad. In this novel Morris presents women as the main victims of such bleak, empty existences; plainswomen like Cora have been expected to endure in silence.

Plains Song probably received more enthusiastic reviews than any other books by Morris since *The Field of Vision* (1956), which received the National Book Award, and its sequel, *Ceremony in Lone Tree* (1960), which is generally considered his best novel. Brad Owens, in the *Christian Science Monitor,* called *Plains Song* "a beautiful, subtle novel that accomplishes the rare effect of presenting history from the inside out," adding that "Rather than measure gigantic social changes, the weight with which earth-shaking events rests on individuals . . . Wright Morris carefully records the quiet equivocations of the human heart." In *Saturday Review,* Jack Sullivan wrote that Morris's Plains "are brought to life with an appropriate sparseness and exactness of detail that make their very monotony haunting. The effect of this eloquent novel is hallucinatory." Larry McMurtry, in the *New York Times Book Review,* said, "The triumph of the book, in terms of craft, is that we experience the sense of the slow passage of time so necessary to such a story. Yet it is told subtly and with economy. . . . The textures of emotional, social and physical experience merge; the sense of experience is precise, satisfying and complete."

According to Morris, "The writer has to discipline the imagination and deal with the nucleus of memory. My raw material was the first thirty years of my life, and I had to learn how to organize it in fictional terms." *Will's Boy: A Memoir* (1981) presents this nucleus of memory, the first twenty years of Morris's life, in nonfictional terms, and interspersed throughout the memoir are brief extracts from nine previous books as examples of how Morris has transformed the raw material of his life. At the center of *Will's Boy* is his changing relationship with his father, William Henry Morris, who raised him mostly alone. (Grace Osborn Morris died six days after her son's birth.) *Will's Boy* is also a story of the promise of the American West and the way men such as Will Morris failed to take advantage of this promise.

Will Morris, a station agent for the Union Pacific Railroad in Central City, Nebraska, made his most serious effort to attain the American dream after his second marriage, to a girl young enough to be his daughter. Like Will Brady, the protagonist of *The Works of Love* (1952), he started a chicken farm in order to supply fresh eggs for dining cars, but most of his chickens died. The Morrises moved to Omaha for a fresh start, but Will's new egg business also failed, and his wife left him. Morris had developed a brother-sister relationship with his stepmother and began to feel estranged from his father: "It was us against him." Morris then went to live with the Mulligans, the family of a classmate, and after having to suffer the shame of his father's writing bad checks for his support, he made his first move toward independence by getting a paper route to help pay his way: "Making real money like that restored my self-esteem." Every time Morris saw his father, Will Morris claimed to be trying to find a new mother for him so that they could be a family again because he considered himself and his son superior to the Mulligans, an idea that both "pleased and puzzled" Morris "since he was not a good provider, as Mrs. Mulligan never tired of saying, and I knew he ran around with loose women even as he talked about a new mother for me." Morris and his father eventually moved to Chicago.

In Chicago the teenaged Morris drifted away from his father, spending most of his time at a YMCA, where he discovered talents for Ping-Pong, leadership, and drawing. For the first time Morris "fell under the spell of art. Little it mattered that I showed little talent for it. This fever, which did not abate, persuaded me that I was destined to be an artist, with my drawings on the front pages of newspapers." Morris and his father got back together when Will Morris proposed a trip to California by car. Will felt that Chicago had not lived up to his expectations, while for Morris, "it was Chicago that had given me the expectations that I was now looking up to—but it was easy for me, if given the chance, to shift them over to California. I would just feel stronger what I had been feeling all the time." The 1927 trip to Los Angeles in several broken-down vehicles with a colorful collection of passengers and the similar return trip after the coast also fell short of Will's dreams form the basis of Morris's first novel, *My Uncle Dudley* (1942). Will's sense of adventure throughout these travels raised Morris's sagging opinion of his father.

Morris felt restless back in Chicago because "seeing the world had given me ideas. I forget what they were, but almost everywhere I looked the grass looked as green as Christmas jewelry." He graduated from high school and enrolled at the City College of Chicago, but when his grandfather, Wright Marion Osborn, a devout Seventh Day Adventist, offered to send him to an Adventist college in California, Morris accepted: "What inspired me was *flight*." The account of his brief stay at Pacific Union College in Angwin, California, is the comic highlight of *Will's Boy*. Morris was shocked to discover that his fellow students were literal interpreters of the Bible, and when he tried to show them their error, he was expelled for creating disorder and confusion.

Morris next spent several weeks working on the Hereford, Texas, ranch of his Uncle Dwight Osborn. This experience inspired his short story "The Rites of Spring," and his freethinking uncle is the model for Uncle Fremont Osborn of *Cause for Wonder* (1963) and Floyd Warner of *Fire Sermon* and *A Life*. After a final stay in Chicago, Morris went to Pomona College in Claremont, California, whose beautiful campus surrounded by orange groves had attracted him on his trip to Los Angeles. *Will's Boy* ends with Morris's leaving Pomona with a firm optimism about the future to travel in Europe: "My considerable experience of the world had not as yet inspired me to try to change it, nor did the way I perceived it depress or disturb me. I accepted things as I found them. If one day I proved to be deserving, I firmly believed I would be rewarded."

Will's Boy offers, without sentimentality or nostalgia, the sources of Morris's feelings about the promises America, especially the West, offers as it shows how American dreamers such as Will Morris fail to achieve their own expectations. Will Morris is the prototype of all those characters in Morris's fiction who chase success while trying to maintain their peculiar brands of individualism. Morris has no plan to continue writing this autobiography at the present, saying that a writer's youth is the most interesting part of his development and anything thereafter is "just gossip." Morris began working on his next book in the spring of 1981.

Morris has also had several recent exhibitions of his photographs, including two in New York: at the Prakapas Gallery in the spring of 1977 and at the Witkin Gallery in early 1981. These photographs, taken between the late 1930s and early 1950s, are collected in *The Inhabitants* (1946), *The Home Place* (1948), and *God's Country and My People* (1968). The photographs from the Witkin Gallery exhibition were published as *The Wright Morris Portfolio* (1981). Hilton Kramer, reviewing the Prakapas exhibition in the *New York Times,* said it "leaves us in no doubt that he would have achieved great eminence in this medium had he chosen to pursue it." Morris writes in his 1979 essay "Photographs, Images, and Words," "Mirror, window, or wall, the photograph exists; it is a piece of the world's substance, and it is more than the source of our self-serving impressions. The true photograph confronts us with all the ambiguities of life itself." Morris's continuing efforts—as novelist, critic, memoirist, and photographer—to confront the ambiguities of life and art solidify his status as one of America's most versatile and productive artists.

Periodical Publications:
"In Our Image," *Massachusetts Review,* 19 (Winter 1978): 633-643;

"Hail to Thee, Blithe Man! Bird Thou Never Wert!" *New York Times,* 5 February 1978, V: 17;

"Crazy Rhythm," *New York Times,* 13 May 1978, p. 23;

"Odd Balls," *Atlantic Monthly,* 241 (June 1978): 90-93;

"Photographs, Images, and Words," *American Scholar,* 48 (Autumn 1979): 457-469;

"Where the West Begins," *Prairie Schooner,* 53 (Summer 1980): 5-14;

"The Lover and the Beloved," *New Yorker,* 57 (13 July 1981): 26-27.

Interviews:
"An Interview with Wright Morris," *Book Forum,* 2 (1976): 36-38, 40;

Robert Dahlin, "PW Interviews Wright Morris," *Publishers Weekly,* 217 (22 February 1980): 6-7.

Bibliography:
"First Editions of Wright Morris," *Bancroftiana,* 77 (January 1979): 5-6.

References:
Randall K. Albers, "Female Transformation: The Role of Women in Two Novels by Wright Morris," *Prairie Schooner,* 53 (Summer 1979): 95-115;

Jack Brenner, "Wright Morris's West: Fallout from a Pioneer Past," *University of Denver Quarterly,* 10 (Winter 1976): 63-75;

G. B. Crump, "D. H. Lawrence and the Immediate Present: Kurt Vonnegut, Jr., Ken Kesey, and Wright Morris," *D. H. Lawrence Review,* 10 (1977): 103-141;

Robert D. Harper, "Wright Morris's *Ceremony in Lone Tree*: A Picture of Life in Middle America," *Western American Literature,* 11 (1976): 199-213;

Ginny Brown Machann, "*Ceremony in Lone Tree* and *Badlands*: The Starkweather Case and the Nebraska Plains," *Prairie Schooner,* 53 (Summer 1979): 165-172;

Raymond L. Neinstein, "Wright Morris: The Metaphysics of Home," *Prairie Schooner,* 53 (Summer 1979): 121-154.

Toni Morrison
(18 February 1931-   )

Elizabeth B. House
Augusta College

See also the Morrison entry in *DLB 6, American Novelists Since World War II, Second Series*.

NEW BOOK: *Tar Baby* (New York: Knopf, 1981).

Toni Morrison's fourth novel, *Tar Baby*, is a departure from her previous work in two important ways. First, the book's setting is more exotic than the American small-town atmosphere found in *The Bluest Eye* (1970), *Sula* (1973), and *Song of Solomon*

(1977), Morrison's three earlier novels. More significant, though, *Tar Baby* contains this author's first fully realized white characters. In her earlier books, Morrison portrays small-town cultures which undoubtedly have been affected by whites, but which are peopled almost solely by blacks. White figures, when they appear, do so only peripherally. In *Tar Baby*, however, while she again uses the myth, magic, and poetic language which figure so largely in her first three novels, Morrison moves her setting deftly from Paris to a Caribbean island to New York, and instead of keeping her characters in racially closed societies, she juxtaposes white and black people.

To note such shifts, however, is not to say that this author or her life-style has radically changed. Morrison is still a senior editor at Random House, a teacher at Bard College, and a busy mother who combines her career with caring for two sons. And, as any gifted writer does, she tells universal truths using whatever materials suit her purpose. Understandably, Morrison is particularly irritated by those who try to pigeonhole writers or their work and thus deny the universal appeal of good literature. For example, in the 30 March 1981 issue of *Newsweek*, which features her picture on its cover, Morrison explains that the Jane Austen novels she read as a youngster "were not written for a little black girl . . . but they were so magnificently done that I got them anyway—they spoke directly to me out of their own specificity." Then, in a *Vogue* interview, Morrison details her annoyance with people who classify her own books too rigidly: "People . . . say, 'I know you're writing black novels, but I was really in-

Toni Morrison

terested.' It used to offend me very deeply. I said, 'Well, I read a little Dickens, I thought it was wonderful.' " And to a person who complained that he had trouble understanding her books because his experience was so different from the black one her novels portray, Morrison says she retorted, "Boy, you must have had a hell of a time with *Beowulf*!"

Morrison dedicates *Tar Baby* to five women who, she says, always "knew their true and ancient properties," and the book's preface carries a quotation from Corinthians, "For it hath been declared unto me of you, my brethren . . . that there are contentions among you." These two bits of prose aptly introduce the novel's two major themes, the difficulty of settling conflicting claims between one's past and present and the destruction which abuse of power can bring. As Morrison examines these problems in *Tar Baby*, she suggests no easy way to understand what one's link to a heritage should be, nor does she offer infallible methods for dealing with power. Rather, with an astonishing insight and grace, she demonstrates the pervasiveness of such dilemmas and the degree to which they affect human beings, both black and white. Much of the novel's power and clarity comes from Morrison's careful craftsmanship, especially her symbolic use of names and precise juxtaposition of characters and settings. *New Republic* reviewer Maureen Howard observed that *Tar Baby* is "as carefully patterned as a . . . poem," and, indeed, the book's themes are integral parts of a finely wrought and artistic design.

The familiar story of Brer Rabbit and the Tar Baby provides a frame for the patterns of Morrison's fourth novel. In a pre-Uncle Remus version of this tale, a farmer (rather than Brer Fox) devises the tar baby to lure and then trap Brer Rabbit, who has been raiding gardens. As the farmer expects, Brer Rabbit is entranced by the tar decoy and tries to engage it in conversation, but when the lure refuses to answer, the rabbit becomes angry, hits the tar baby, and entangles himself in its sticky surface. Eventually, of course, Brer Rabbit outsmarts his captor by begging not to be thrown back in the briar patch, which, in reality, is his only place of safety. The outwitted farmer tosses the wild creature back into the brambles, and the sadder but wiser animal scurries away.

Morrison has said that the tar baby of her fourth novel is the black woman who attracts the black male, and Jadine Childs, the book's protagonist, is indeed enticing. A graduate of the Sorbonne, the young black American is also a sought-after model; she has had a small part in a movie; and

Cover for 30 March 1981 Newsweek

as one might expect, she is showered with the attentions of suitors. However, in the midst of all her successes, Jadine feels "inauthentic," and she finally leaves Europe to decide whether or not to accept a wealthy white man's offer of marriage.

One of the many orphans in *Tar Baby*, Jadine has been raised by her Aunt Ondine and Uncle Sydney Childs, both longtime servants of Valerian Street and his wife, Margaret. Valerian, now seventy, has retired as head of the family's Philadelphia candy business and moved with his wife and two faithful servants to Isle des Chevaliers, a Caribbean paradise named for mythical black horsemen who are said to roam the island. Before white men invaded the paradise, Isle des Chevaliers had been a lush rain forest, but now its tropical greenery has been tamed and to a large extent destroyed by civilization's "improvements." As his last name suggests,

Valerian has helped pave the forest and thus destroy the island's natural beauty, but that offense is perhaps offset by his unusually generous nature. In addition to other philanthropic labors, the candy magnate has sent Jadine through school and financed her European travels. Thus, when the exquisite young woman must decide whether or not to marry, she comes to Isle des Chevaliers to spend Christmas with her foster parents, Ondine and Sydney, and her friends Valerian and Margaret. Unfortunately, Jadine's island holiday only exacerbates her indecision about whom and where she wants to be. Part of the conflict she must resolve is occasioned by her unique position as the servants' relative and the employers' protegee. Another unsettling fact of Jadine's life at Isle des Chevaliers is the older Childses' belief that their adored niece neglects her duties as their foster daughter and thus fails to live up to her last name. The old couple's greatest fear, and the notion to which they have become accustomed, is that Jadine will be too busy to make funeral arrangements for them when they die.

Once Jadine is on the island, she and her hosts await the arrival of the Streets' son, Michael, a twenty-nine-year-old man who is described alternately by his mother as someone who helps others preserve their heritages, and by his father as a "cultural orphan" who seeks societies he can live in without ties and thus without risk of pain. As a youth, Michael had urged Jadine to leave the posh school where she was studying art history and go out into the world with him to "help her people." Jadine demurred, and since that time, Michael has apparently drifted from studying poetry and anthropology to working on Indian reservations and aiding migrant workers. In fact, the only people he seems reluctant to associate with are his parents. Valerian was seven when his own father died, and perhaps because of this loss, the candy magnate particularly wants to pass the family business on to Michael. However, unlike the third-century Roman emperor for whom Valerian is named, the candy manufacturer's son will not carry on his work. When Emperor Valerian took the throne, he gave half his land to his son, Gallienus, to rule. But when twentieth-century Valerian tries to give Michael the candy business, the boy refuses to enter into the family endeavor.

Predictably, Michael never appears on Isle des Chevaliers, but the man who does come for Christmas dinner, a young black drifter named William "Son" Green, proves to be a catalyst for an explosion of pent-up conflicts. An American, Green has jumped ship and survived on the island by foraging for food and stealing chocolate from the Streets' kitchen, and he is first discovered in Margaret's closet. From there, ever-dutiful Sydney promptly drags his fellow black man before the head of the household. Perhaps saddened by Michael's absence or perhaps only to show his own power, Valerian then shocks both blacks and whites by inviting the intruder to sit down to dinner rather than turning him over to the police. Son accepts the invitation, and eventually, to the group's further amazement, Valerian installs him in the guest bedroom for a visit of indefinite length.

Son's presence upsets the household's equilibrium not only because he enters their lives in a strange manner, but, most clearly, because he observes none of the rules of social hierarchy to which they are accustomed. In fact, Son Green is different in most ways from every other character in *Tar Baby*. Except for him, all of *Tar Baby*'s characters, both black and white, are either in some sense orphans or lonely parent figures who have been deserted by their children. In both cases, cultural links between parents and child, between generations, have been broken, and continuity of a life-style is threatened. Also, except for Son, all the people in *Tar Baby* are either agents of or accede to the hierarchy of power and "progress" which controls the modern business world and has helped destroy Isle des Chevaliers's natural beauty. Jadine has been a willing and apt student of Valerian's life-style, itself an exemplum of the imperial ease which money and power can bring. And Sydney and Ondine's social standing places them well above the Streets' other servants. In contrast, Son Green, as his name suggests, is closely tied to his heritage and to the earth. Rather than despoiling the land as Valerian and his kind have done, Son has an extraordinary talent for making plants bloom, and he sees no value in artificial social barriers which ensure that some people will control others. He shocks Sydney, for example, by cheerfully saying "hi" to the solemn butler as he serves a formal meal. And only Son takes the trouble to learn that Gideon and Thérèse are the real names of two black servants whom Sydney and Ondine, along with the rest of the household, know only as "Yardman" and "Mary," the name given to every baptized black female on the island.

The household's facade of order and tranquility finally crumbles at Christmas dinner when Valerian casually mentions that he has dismissed Yardman and Mary for stealing apples. At first only Son questions Valerian's right to fire the two, but the young man's audacity sets off a sequence of events which alters each character's life. Following Son's retort, Valerian orders the man to leave his house, but Son quietly refuses to do so. This conflict of wills between host and guest leads to a release of Ondine and Sydney's long-closeted frustrations, and in the heat of recriminations which follow, Ondine reveals a damning truth—that as a young woman she had seen Margaret obsessively sticking pins into young Michael's flesh. After Ondine details this terrible secret, Margaret explains to Valerian that she tortured their son, "because I could . . . and I stopped doing it or wanting to do it when I couldn't. . . . When he was too big, when he could do it back, when he could . . . tell." Although no other person in the novel uses power with malevolent intentions equal to Margaret's, every character except Son does use power over another person simply because it is possible to do so. Objectively, Margaret's aberrations can be seen as merely another embodiment of the power with which Valerian rules his household: Jadine controls her aunt and uncle; Sydney and Ondine direct other servants; and white men impose their wills upon nature.

In the emotional chaos which follows Ondine's revelations, Jadine finds herself torn between her Parisian jet-set life and her almost primeval attraction to Son Green, who, now clean and well-fed, proves to be a gorgeous reminder of simpler times. Almost inevitably, Son and Jadine become lovers, but they move in two different worlds even when residing in the same house. The pair first travels to New York, where Jadine thrives but where Son feels kinship only with the concrete lion on the library steps. The situation reverses, however, when Son and Jadine visit his small, rural hometown, Eloe, Florida. There Son is in complete harmony with himself and his heritage, while Jadine is an alien, an intruder from a busier, more world-wise, more dominant culture. Jadine attempts to pull Son into her world by having him enroll in college, but he wants no part of lessons in what he sees as the white man's view of life. Conversely, Son tries to show Jadine the heritage that she has thrown away by assimilating Valerian's customs and values, his money, power, and privilege, but she sees no future in returning to life as it is lived in Eloe.

Unable to reconcile their differences, Jadine and Son part. Following the pair's separation, Jadine visits Isle des Chevaliers, and then rumors suggest she has left the Caribbean on Air France, accompanied by a handsome white man. Son still loves Jadine and vows to find her, but at a crucial point in his search, Thérèse guides him, not to Valerian's dock as he had asked but rather to the wild backside of Isle des Chevaliers. When Son questions her, Thérèse replies that Jadine is not worthy of him and that on this beach he can choose either to walk to Valerian's house on the island's opposite side or to join the free black horsemen who, she believes, still inhabit this unspoiled portion of Isle des Chevaliers. After Thérèse's instruction, Son begins to walk away from the shore, and then, in the novel's last words, he is described as running toward the woods, "Lickety-split. Lickety-split. Lickety-lickety-lickety-split."

Morrison does not specify whether Son chooses to join the mythical horsemen or continue his search for Jadine. However, in light of the book's folktale frame and the storybook words with which it ends, she seems to suggest that the rabbit has escaped to the briars, that Son will not attempt to join Jadine's fast-paced life. Whatever choice he makes, though, the novel's ending is not happy. For all his virtues, Son can be part of Jadine's life only if he rejects his true self, his ancient properties. But living in the briar patch is not a perfect choice either, for the past, the world of myth and story books, cannot be the sole habitat of a mature person. Similarly, while Jadine is suffocated by Eloe's provincialism, Paris offers only superficial pleasures which will continue to make her feel inauthentic. Ultimately, the tale Morrison weaves is about problems rather than solutions.

Tar Baby has garnered Morrison a good deal of media attention, but the novel itself has received surprisingly mixed reviews. Negative critics' most valid complaints touch upon the book's plot structure and are exemplified by Darryl Pinckney's insistence in the *New York Review of Books* that "picking out what happens in *Tar Baby* is like trying to keep one's balance in a swamp." In contrast, more satisfied reviewers such as *Newsweek*'s Jean Strouse argue that the book's merits far outweigh any flaws it may have. Strouse writes that some readers may find *Tar Baby*'s plot "too consciously wrought, but if there are flaws in the novel's construction they don't matter: Morrison's voice, with its precision and musical cadence, is so original, she has so much to say about modern life and she creates such indelible characters that she leaves you affected, astonished, and appalled." In a similar positive vein, Maureen Howard labels *Tar Baby* "a fine new novel," lauds the author's character descriptions as a "series of stunning performances," and adds that "thematically, this novel is much tighter than Morrison's earlier works."

Unquestionably, Toni Morrison is an important novelist who continues to develop her talent. Part of her appeal, of course, lies in her extraordinary ability to create beautiful language and striking characters. However, Morrison's most important gift, the one which gives her a major author's universality, is the insight with which she writes of problems all humans face. In his Nobel Prize speech, William Faulkner notes that a writer's only true subject is "the human heart in conflict with itself." Morrison, who wrote a master's thesis on Faulkner and Virginia Woolf, seems to agree, for at the core of all her novels is a penetrating view of the unyielding, heartbreaking dilemmas which torment people of all races. The new directions she takes in

Tar Baby show Morrison's versatility in treating such conflicts and make anticipating her future work an extreme pleasure.

References:
Thomas LeClair, "The Language Must Not Sweat:

A Conversation With Toni Morrison," *New Republic*, 184 (21 March 1981): 25-29;
Cathleen Medwick, "Toni Morrison," *Vogue*, 171 (April 1981): 288-289, 330-332;
Jean Strouse, "Toni Morrison's Black Magic," *Newsweek*, 97 (30 March 1981): 52-57.

Joyce Carol Oates
(16 June 1938-   )

Holly Mims Westcott
Florence, South Carolina

See also the Oates entries in *DLB 2, American Novelists Since World War II*, and *DLB 5, American Poets Since World War I*.

NEW BOOKS: *Son of the Morning* (New York: Vanguard, 1978; London: Gollancz, 1979);
The Step Father (Northridge, Cal.: Lord John Press, 1978);
Sentimental Education (Los Angeles: Sylvester & Orphanos, 1978);
All the Good People I've Left Behind (Santa Barbara: Black Sparrow Press, 1979);
Queen of the Night (Northridge, Cal.: Lord John Press, 1979);
Cybele (Santa Barbara: Black Sparrow Press, 1979);
Unholy Loves (New York: Vanguard, 1979; London: Gollancz, 1980);
Lamb of Abyssalia (Cambridge, Mass.: Pomegranate Press, 1979);
A Middle-Class Education (New York: Albondocani Press, 1980);
Bellefleur (New York: Dutton, 1980; London: Cape, 1981);
Three Plays (Princeton: Ontario Review Press, 1980);
A Sentimental Education (New York: Dutton, 1980; London: Cape, 1981);
Contraries: Essays (New York: Oxford University Press, 1981);
Nightless Nights (Concord, N.H.: Ewert, 1981);
Angel of Light (New York: Dutton, 1981; London: Cape, 1981).

Joyce Carol Oates, now approaching her mid-forties and a writer nearly all of her life (her first stories were drawings, she says), has continued her steady pace of writing and publishing through the late 1970s and early 1980s. Since the 1978 publication of *Women Whose Lives Are Food, Men Whose Lives Are Money*, nine books by Oates have been published in trade editions and six briefer works have been published in small limited editions. There have been two changes in her life, however. The first is her move in 1978 (with her husband Prof. Raymond Smith) from the relative isolation of the University of Windsor in Ontario to Princeton University, where she is closer to and more nearly a part of the literary community whose hub is New York City. At Princeton, she has a much lighter teaching load, giving her more time to attend to her writing and to the activities which feed her writing. The second is a change in publishers. Though Louisiana State University Press and the Black Sparrow Press continue to publish that work she intends for only a limited audience, she has ended her association with Vanguard Press and gone to E. P. Dutton, a larger publishing house, which now publishes those novels and short-story collections for which Oates hopes to find a wide audience. Fawcett Books, which has published all of her novels in paperback, is participating with Dutton in an effort to promote her work to a larger readership, in a conscious move to make Oates a better-known figure on the American literary scene and to achieve greater popular acceptance of her work.

Since 1978, at least five critical works on Oates have been published and a number of dissertations have been written about her work, suggesting her increased acceptance by literary scholars despite some continued criticism of her prolificity. Oates herself makes no promise of slowing down and speaks defensively: "It may be the case that we all must write many books in order to achieve a few lasting ones—just as a young writer or poet must have to write hundreds of poems before writing his first significant one." Each book, she says, is "a world unto itself, and must stand alone and it should not matter whether a book is a writer's first, or tenth, or fiftieth."

There have also been changes in Oates's writing habits in more recent years. While her "first novels were all written on a typewriter, first draft through, then revisions, then final draft," the more recent novels, beginning with *The Assassins* (1975), have been written in longhand. She says, "As I get older, I find I can't write as fast, and I have to rewrite again and again, sometimes as much as 17 times." She often holds the rough draft of one novel in abeyance while she works on short stories or another novel. "The rhythm of writing, revising, writing, revising, etc., seems to suit me. I am inclined to think that as I grow older I will come to be infatuated with the art of revision, and there may be a time when I will dread giving up a novel at all," she comments. One central thing has not changed: at the core of Oates's life is the act of writing. "If you are a writer," she told one interviewer, "you locate yourself behind a wall of silence and no matter what you are doing, driving a car or walking or doing housework, which I love, you can still be writing, because you have that space."

The material for Oates's writing comes from everywhere. One interviewer, speaking of her "magnitude of attention," says that she "creates the impression of a creature equipped with antennae that continuously scan the environment." Though her characters are admittedly composites of real people, she has never used her husband in any of her work and has used her parents (and herself, as a child) in only one brief bit of *Wonderland* (1971).

Eden County, her fictional equivalent of Erie County in western New York, where she grew up, remains a favorite setting, providing the background for *Son of the Morning* (1978), which Oates describes as "a first person narration by a man addressing himself throughout to God.... the whole novel is a prayer." The title of the novel comes from the book of Isaiah in which Satan is called "son of the morning." In Oates's novel, the son of the morning is Nathan Vickery, a charismatic preacher conceived during the gang rape of a virgin. Though, unlike Satan, Nathan does not willfully bring about the downfall of others, his one-sided view of life has evil effects. He has seven visions of God, the first at the age of five, and these

Joyce Carol Oates

become his obsession. Each chapter begins with Nathan's "prayer," but there are shifts to a third-person point of view as the novel presents the various characters who enter and then leave Nathan's life: his mother, who is too young and too immature to mother him; his grandmother, who nurtures his spirituality; his grandfather, a skeptical intellectual; the various preachers who attempt to act as mentors in his youth; Leonie, a young woman whom he first desires and then rejects; and Japheth, the theology student who becomes his disciple but later attempts to murder him.

One of the most dramatic moments in *Son of the Morning* occurs when Nathan, remorseful over having felt lust for Leonie, puts his eye out before a congregation. Rather than repulsing his followers, this act strengthens his appeal to them. He goes on to lead a group called the Seekers of Christ, attracting hangers-on who hope to profit personally from his powers of leadership. He, however, is detached from their desires for money and power, as he is from all things worldly. After Japheth's attempt to murder him, Nathan is changed. There is a final apocalyptic downfall, but only symbolic death. At novel's end, he returns to Yewville, the town where he was born, having renamed himself William Vickery and divorced himself from his evangelistic past. However, he still searches for God, and his despair in this search permeates the novel.

"I wanted to write about religious experience from the other side, about interior experience," Oates said about *Son of the Morning*. "I've been interested in it for many years, and I think religious experience is real and possible to everyone." Because she believes that religion "becomes fossilized when it's put into an exterior form," Oates aimed to show in this book "how interior experience becomes modified and can't be controlled as it is taken over by the evangelical church." While writing this novel, Oates devoted hours each day to reading the Bible in an attempt to put herself "in the place of a fundamentalist Protestant who could go to the Bible every day for guidance and would not have any critical or historical preconceptions. . . .Getting into that frame of mind was a very shattering experience. The world of the Bible is a world of intense drama. Every day is a battle between good and evil, between God and the devil. I spent many hours . . . in that world, like Nathan, my hero. You get so caught up in it you feel that in just a few minutes there will be revelation." *Son of the Morning* was generally well received by critics, who admired both its ambition and what they saw as its varying achievements.

All the Good People I've Left Behind (1979), a volume of short stories, was published by Black Sparrow Press, an indication that this handsomely produced book is not intended for a wide audience. For Oates, short-story writing provides a break between novels and often a means of moving from one novel to another. The stories about which she is serious, she preserves in book form; the others she prefers to be forgotten. "Each of the story collections is organized around a central theme and is meant to be read as a whole," she says and describes the arrangement of the stories within each volume as a "rigorous one, not at all haphazard."

All the Good People I've Left Behind includes ten stories, many dealing with people in academic life. One character, Annie Quirt, appears in several—in some as a main character and in others as a peripheral character. The last story, which gives the volume its title, traces the history of two couples from graduate school, when they are good friends, to mid-life when the ties of neither friendship nor marriage bind them, for each has become alienated from the others. Never really losing their inno-

cence, they move from one wrong idea of life to another. Their happiness at the beginning of the story is destroyed, yet they neither learn nor grow. Near story's end, Maxine reads on the tag of a Celestial Seasonings teabag, "Wisdom comes through suffering." Talking to Fern shortly before committing suicide, she drunkenly muddles it: "Suffering comes through wisdom." Knowledge and experience bring only pain; all the stories in the book carry out this essential idea. The characters by and large are intelligent, neurotic sufferers. Unable to learn from their mistakes, they simply go on to other, more disastrous mistakes. And they are unable to sustain the relationships which might support them in their despair.

Cybele (1979), named for an ancient bisexual goddess who was celebrated in orgiastic rites by eunuch priests, tells the tale of a man who is sexually powerless, but who nevertheless is doomed by his sexual desires. Sexual obsession, like any other obsession, can be futile and defeating, leading, Oates indicates, to sterility, an inversion of its natural purpose. *Cybele* focuses on a man to whom we are introduced in a chapter called "In Memoriam: Edwin Locke." The speaker, a former lover, describes Locke, who died at the age of forty-six, as successful and attractive, with a wife, two children, and a good education—all the requisites for a happy life. The point of view shifts to third person for the remaining chapters, which tell of the mid-life crisis that leads Edwin to engage in a series of affairs, each more disastrous than the last.

First he pulls Cathleen, a married woman from his own social circle, into an affair; she is followed by Risa, a swinging gold digger who takes him for his money and then leaves with a former lover; and finally, after attempting reconciliation with his wife, Cynthia, he becomes involved with Zanche, an artist with a strange daughter, who introduces him to bohemian life. Edwin is impotent; sex therapy is expensive and offers no help. Everyone seems to want only Edwin's money, and there is the suggestion that money is all he has to give. His sons, with whom he has never spent much time, are estranged from him, and his attempts to win them over fail. Cynthia is at first vindictive, but by the end of the tale she has built a new life for herself. Edwin, however, is more miserable than ever.

The final scene of the novel is characteristically Oatesian in its grotesqueness and violence. Edwin attempts to make love to Zanche's nine-year-old daughter, Chrissie, only to discover that the daughter has a penis. He hurts her and begins to tear apart the apartment. Zanche returns with friends, who attack Edwin. He manages to get away from them, but they catch up with him later, and his decaying body is eventually found near the expressway. In the last paragraphs, which flash back to an earlier moment, Rok, one of the killers, is trying to get his lighter to work so he can set fire to Edwin's body.

Though the reader is struck by the violence of Edwin's death, he feels no pity for him because Edwin's prime concern has always been for himself and his image. Edwin's lovers may mistreat him, but since he sees each one primarily as a reflection of himself, he deserves no better. *Cybele* reiterates effectively a favorite theme of Oates's, the moral bankruptcy of the upper-middle class. Edwin's fate is of his own making, and he has no redeeming nobility to earn the reader's respect.

Oates's next novel, *Unholy Loves* (1979), takes a different turn, though its characters, like most Oates characters, have the same tinge of desperation. Here the setting is Woodslee University in upstate New York, an expensive and prestigious school for Ivy League rejects. Covering faculty politics and personal lives during one school year, the plot focuses on the social occasions which bring the faculty together. The catalytic event of this novel is the arrival of Albert St. Dennis, a distinguished elderly poet, for a year's residence. A number of the faculty immediately begin to jockey for his favor. He is alcoholic, possibly senile at times, and near the novel's end, he dies in a fire he has accidentally started after an evening's revelry.

The most important of the novel's many characters is Brigit Stott, who is having a difficult time writing her third novel. A member of the English department, as are many of the characters, she is separated from her husband and feels she is a failure both as an artist and as a woman. At a party to introduce St. Dennis to the faculty she is led into an affair with Alexis Kessler, a brilliant but erratic pianist and composer who is in danger of being fired from Woodslee, largely for his temperamental and bizarre behavior. The affair between Brigit and Alexis is at first idyllic, then stormy, violent. The novel's last scene brings them together briefly, but their relationship is over. The affair, however, has helped to push Brigit beyond the stalemate she has reached; she is considering leaving Woodslee for a job nearer her family, from whom she has previously felt estranged, and she is back at work on a new novel. This conclusion provides a sense of optimistic completion and the implication that one may gain a degree of control over one's own life. Brigit says, "But whatever happens to me for the rest of my life . . . won't be inevitable. I think that's why I feel so optimistic." However, Alexis has the novel's last sentence, introducing an element of doubt: "But surely, my love, that won't last?"

A subordinate plot concerns itself with the rivalry between Lewis Seidel, an English professor, and Oliver Byrne, the dean, who leaves Woodslee at novel's end for a college presidency. Seidel, in the meantime, has an affair with Sandra Jaeger, the wife of a young English professor who is first hired, then fired, and ultimately rehired, thanks to his wife's having gained favor with Seidel. The Jaeger-Seidel affair could well provide material for a sequel were Oates a novelist to take advantage of spin-offs. One has the sense that the next year at Woodslee—indeed, each year at Woodslee—could provide material for a whole new novel.

Much of *Unholy Loves*'s third-person omniscient narration presents the insides of the characters' minds. The reader finds himself flitting from character to character and from thought to thought within each character's mind. However, the style is appropriate for the subject matter. Two of the characters—Brigit and Sandra—keep journals, and in presenting the mental journals of the various characters, the book itself takes on a kind of journallike quality. (Oates herself keeps a formal journal which she says "resembles a sort of on-going letter to myself, mainly about literary matters.")

Oates claims that there has been "humor of a sort in my writing from the first, but it's understated or deadpan." *Unholy Loves* is probably a good example of that humor, but in this novel it sometimes seems intentionally catty, the laughter often closer to sneering. It is probably no accident that this novel was published after she left the University of Windsor. Critics recognized the novel's achievement while noting that this was not one of Oates's major efforts.

Bellefleur (1980), the first of Oates's novels to be published by Dutton, is a major effort, an ambitious novel dealing with six generations of the Bellefleur family. Jean-Pierre Bellefleur has established an empire whose power is made visible by the sixty-four-room castle built by his nephew. The castle, called Bellefleur after the family, provides a suitably gothic background for the strange beasts, transformations, and prophetic events which provide the fabric of the novel, including such oddities as a half-wit boy who seems to turn into a dog, a captured gnome who becomes a devoted servant, a strange beast that is actually a housecat, and a giant bird that steals a baby. The story jumps back and forth from generation to generation, but focuses most strongly on Gideon Bellefleur and his beautiful wife, Leah, who attempts to restore the decaying Bellefleur empire to its former grandeur. In the end her hopes are quite literally crushed when Gideon crashes his airplane into the castle, destroying himself and his family. It is left to Jedediah, the holy man of the family who has made his hermitage on the mountain, to come down from the mountain and found a new Bellefleur line. "The point," John Gardner writes in his review of the novel, "is one made in *Son of the Morning* and elsewhere. Loving God completely, one cares nothing about the world, not even about people whom one sees, rightly, as mere instances; on the other hand, completely loving oneself or the world, one loses one's soul and becomes (as Gideon in the end) a figure of death."

A rich and complex story, *Bellefleur* creates in Oates's usual corner of New York a weirdly gothic setting against which strange occurrences seem normal. Gardner notes that "what is known in Shakespeare criticism as 'sliding time' becomes a calculated madness" in *Bellefleur*. Though there are realistic details and a genealogical chart, no dates are given and one feels that specific time is deliberately obscured in order to create a not-of-this-world feeling.

Oates says she attempted to write *Bellefleur* for years: "I would collect images along the way—a clavichord I saw, a snatch of conversation I heard—but I never could find the right voice." She finally began the novel after suddenly envisioning a woman sitting beside a baby in a cradle in a shabby but lushly overgrown walled garden. Oates felt an urge to be there, and the urge carried her through intensive writing which began in the summer of 1978, after her move to Princeton, and ended the following May. The novel took possession of her and she attempted to write a chapter a day. She calls *Bellefleur* her "vampire" novel. "Even talking about it still drains me," she says. "I've had many such psychic vampire experiences in the past." Writing this novel helped her to develop theories about nineteenth-century gothicism: "Using the werewolf, for instance, is a way of writing about an emotional obsession turning into a kind of animal." In *Bellefleur* the half-wit who becomes a dog is demonstrating his essential brutality. Finishing the novel left her with a kind of homesickness, "like loving a place you know you will never go back to."

Critics responded to *Bellefleur* much as they did to *Son of the Morning*, applauding its ambition, seeing much that is good and a little that is not. They were generally enthusiastic, but did not find the novel flawless.

Three Plays (1980) includes three plays which were produced Off Broadway during the 1970s: *Ontological Proof of My Existence* (1972), *Miracle Play* (1973), and *Triumph of the Spider Monkey* (1979). Described by Oates as "rites of sacrifice," they are interesting as thematic footnotes to her prose fiction and have some merit of their own. They were published by the Ontario Review Press, a small firm which operates as an offshoot of the *Ontario Review*, a literary journal which Oates founded with her husband in 1974 and which he edits.

E. P. Dutton published, also in 1980, *A Sentimental Education*, a collection of six stories, including "The Tryst," which was previously published in *All the Good People*. The volume received mixed reviews. One of the stories, "The Precipice," could easily have given the book its title, for all six stories reflect the statement that Wesley quotes in that story: "We run carelessly to the precipice, after we have put something before us to prevent us seeing it." All the characters shield themselves in some way from truths they prefer not to see; the ultimate revelation of that truth is the climax of each story. The word *education* in the title of the collection is also appropriate, but most of the characters learn too late.

The title novella is about Duncan Sargent's murder of his cousin Antoinette. Duncan, a bright nineteen-year-old who has dropped out of Johns Hopkins in the second semester of his freshman year because of a nervous breakdown, is spending the summer in Maine with his mother, her widowed sister, and the sister's two daughters, the older of whom is fourteen-year-old Antoinette. A secret affair develops between Duncan, who indulges in alternate fantasies of tender love and sadistic treatment of Antoinette, and Antoinette, who is also caught by mercurial sexual impulses which frighten her. During a secret meeting on a rocky area of the beach, Duncan at last penetrates Antoinette. She is scared by the pain, and, when she threatens to tell, Duncan pounds her head against the rocks, killing her. Circumstances lead everyone to believe strangers are guilty of the murder; Duncan is not suspected at all, and the family cannot understand why he grieves so much over the death of a cousin he has seemingly ignored. Although his mother tries to reassure him, Duncan knows that he is still unable to cope with his feelings. In the past he suppressed them rather than trying to deal with them, and when they were let go, murder resulted. He sees the precipice too late, and there is nothing he can do now to turn time back.

Contraries (1981), a collection of seven essays written over a period of about twenty years and intermittently revised, were originally stimulated, Oates tells the reader, "by feelings of opposition and, in two or three cases, a deep and passionate revulsion." Her initial responses to such varied works as Oscar Wilde's *The Picture of Dorian Gray*, Dostoevski's *The Possessed*, and D. H. Lawrence's *Women in Love* provoked questions to which she responds with close attention to specific texts.

assistant, Nick Martens, who is the actual lawbreaker. His daughter Kirsten, an anorectic, drugusing boarding-school student, cannot accept her father's guilt. Though she has no hard evidence otherwise, she is too aware of his great integrity to believe that he would accept a bribe. She is persuaded that his death was somehow caused by her mother, Isabel, and Nick, who have been in love since shortly after Isabel's engagement to Maurice. Kirsten's monomania eventually draws in her brother Owen, a success-oriented Princeton senior bound for Harvard Law School and a career like his father's. Their determination to kill Isabel and Nick

Dust jacket for Oates's most recent novel

Angel of Light (1981) takes its title from the name Thoreau gave to John Brown, some of whose descendants are the central characters of this novel. The book is loosely based on the fall of the House of Atreus, brought about when Orestes, at the urging of his sister Electra, avenged the murder of his father Agamemnon, by killing his mother Clytemnestra, and her lover Aegisthus, who have killed Agamemnon in his bath. In Oates's novel, Maurice Halleck, director of the Commision for the Ministry of Justice, apparently commits suicide by driving his car off the road into the deep water of a swamp. He leaves a note, confessing his involvement in a bribery scandal, which clears his old school friend and

ultimately brings their own downfalls as well, in scenes of Oatesian violence that leave Owen and Isabel dead and Kirsten and Nick, who now confesses his guilt, in self-imposed exiles.

Thomas R. Edwards writes that "In her portrayal of the Halleck children, Miss Oates achieves a fresh and frightening picture of a desire that exceeds any available attainment. Owen and Kirsten . . . strive to reconstruct reality in the image of their dream of justice, as [John Brown] had once also tried to do, with equally shattering effect."

Though most of the novel is set in Washington, D.C., *Angel of Light* is not the kind of book one reads as an "inside" story of the nation's capital. Still, the setting reminds the reader that justice and betrayal are national issues in post-Watergate days. The novel goes beyond the contemporary Washington scene, bouncing back and forth in time and space through the lives of Maurice and Isabel and Kirsten and Owen, so that one comes to know its characters well before one sees their ultimate downfall. Edwards speaks of *Angel of Light* as "another chapter in Joyce Carol Oates's ongoing exercise of the imagination, but . . . also a strong and fascinating novel on its own terms. Coming after her haunting fantasy *Bellefleur*, which in effect levitates above the history and geography of the known world to report that its larger moral contours remain deeply mysterious, *Angel of Light* gravitates back towards the terra firma of a novel like Miss Oates's *them*, where social circumstances and personal fate are closely and realistically linked." He adds, however, that "enough mystery persists in *Angel of Light* to suggest that this prolific and various novelist is staking out new fictional ground." Some other critics were not so generous with their praise, seeing in the novel more soap opera than human drama, but the fierceness of their criticism is nevertheless a measure of the serious consideration with which Oates's work is met.

With Oates's ever-expanding canon, she is indeed staking out new fictional ground year by year. Edwards, commenting on her prolific output (as every critic feels compelled to do), notes that Oates "recalls an old-fashioned idea of the novelist who does not occasionally unveil a carefully chiseled 'work of art' but who conducts a continuous and risky exercise of the imagination through the act of writing." Oates may yet create a fictional world of the dimensions of Balzac's, or Dickens's, or Faulkner's. In any case, the books she has had published over the short span of four years represent an energetic and impressive effort toward that goal.

Other:

Best American Short Stories, edited by Oates and Shannon Ravenel (Boston: Houghton Mifflin, 1979).

Interviews:

Judith Applebaum, "PW Interviews Joyce Carol Oates," *Publishers Weekly*, 213 (26 June 1978): 12-13;

Robert Phillips, "Joyce Carol Oates: The Art of Fiction LXXII," *Paris Review*, 20 (Fall 1979): 199-226.

Bibliographies:

Douglas M. Catron, "A Contribution to a Bibliography of Works by and about Joyce Carol Oates," *American Literature*, 49 (November 1977): 399-414;

Donald C. Dickinson, "Joyce Carol Oates: A Bibliographical Checklist," *American Book Collector*, 2, new series (November/December 1981): 26-39; 3, new series (January/February 1982): forthcoming.

References:

Joanne V. Creighton, *Joyce Carol Oates* (Boston: Twayne, 1979);

Thomas R. Edwards, "The House of Atreus Now," review of *Angel of Light*, New York Times Book Review, 16 August 1981: 1, 18;

Lucinda Franks, "The Emergence of Joyce Carol Oates," *New York Times Magazine*, 27 July 1980, pp. 22-23, 26, 30, 32, 43-44, 46;

Ellen G. Friedman, *Joyce Carol Oates* (New York: Frederick Ungar, 1980);

John Gardner, "The Strange Real World," review of *Bellefleur*, New York Times Book Review, 20 July 1980, pp. 1, 21;

Mary Kathryn Grant, R.S.M., *The Tragic Vision of Joyce Carol Oates* (Durham: Duke University Press, 1978);

Linda W. Wagner, ed., *Critical Essays on Joyce Carol Oates* (Boston: G. K. Hall, 1979);

G. F. Waller, *Dreaming America: Obsession and Transcendence in the Fiction of Joyce Carol Oates* (Baton Rouge: Louisiana State University Press, 1979).

William Saroyan

(31 August 1908-18 May 1981)

William Saroyan died of cancer in the Veterans Administration Hospital in Fresno, California. See also the Saroyan entries in *DLB 7, Twentieth-Century American Dramatists*, and *DLB 9, American Novelists, 1910-1945*.

A TRIBUTE *from HERBERT GOLD*

The daring young man has jumped off the trapeze. At nearly three-quarters of a century, he was still flying. Full of anger and fun, full of spite and frolic, resentful of too many things but lover of everything, William Saroyan carried an awful burden in his old age—the burdens of unrequited love, ambition, and the intention to make masterpieces.

And yet why should he have itched and raged so when he had more love, adulation, fulfillment, and pleasure than almost any ten men, even ten Armenians?

To the end he was writing books, and writing marvelous ones. So what if his admirers howled in the wilderness about neglect—his own howls were louder, angrier, and more likely to end in roaring laughter.

Like a sage young man keeping old-fashioned roots in his past and his ambition, he divided his time between Fresno and Paris.

In Paris, in a gloomy walk-up, he ate off the newspaper while he read it; he bought his vegetables and cheese and brought them home and made tea and wrote. He talked to people in the market, people he met on the street, and occasionally to old friends.

In Fresno, in a middle-class tract, with a few fig trees growing in the backyard, he rode his bicycle, he went to the market, he gossiped with his cousins, and he wrote. When he talked, his voice boomed because he wanted to be heard, and he knew that the world, like himself, had grown a little deaf. He kept another house next door, in case his son or daughter might choose to visit him. It was filled with books, records and manuscripts.

When I passed through Fresno with my son Ari, they discussed yogurt, old typewriters, the condition of being young and being a son, the vocation of writing. When he came to San Francisco he wanted to meet Ari's twin brother, Ethan, and they discussed the origin of names, the condition of twinship, the art of storytelling.

He gave them the manuscript of a fable about a man and a child and the difficulty of being parent and child. His wonderful late book, *Obituaries* (1979), had just come out. He offered my sons and me good advice: Don't die, he said, it will do no good, it doesn't pay, people won't really appreciate you for it.

"Don't die, figure out how and stay put, there is plenty of time, let it go for this summer and next winter, and give the matter your best thought, even if you go about on your feet and your shoes and enjoy the business of looking and moving, it is right that you should not die, so don't do it. . . ."

A few months later, in Paris, I called to invite him to dinner. He wanted to know who else would be there. He wasn't sure he wanted to spend an evening with my other guests, but he would come at five, we could have a walk and a visit to the bookstore, Shakespeare & Co., we could drink some tea, we could have a serious talk. And then he might go home and do some writing he had in mind. There were a couple of books and plays pressing on him.

But at eight, after our walk, talk, and tea, he sniffed the food, the guests seemed okay; he decided to stay, and he talked, we all talked and laughed and complained with him, and he clattered down the stairs with the promises to do this every night for the rest of the century.

A few weeks before the end, I called him in Fresno. He was fine, writing, writing lots. When would I visit with my sons? How were they? He had a couple of books ready to go. Sure, he would be in San Francisco soon to check up on the boys.

The amazing thing about literary fame is that he was the most famous writer around when I was in junior high school. His book *The Human Comedy* (1943), was a best-seller and was made into a movie. His plays *The Time of Your Life* (1939) and *My Heart's in the Highlands* (1939) were successes on Broadway.

He turned down the Pulitzer Prize because he didn't believe in such honors. Perhaps he didn't mind the honor that came to him for turning it down.

But in recent years, though his books got fun-

William Saroyan, 1977

nier and deeper—especially that—sadder and funnier and deeper, people wondered if he was still alive.

He even wrote a book called *Not Dying* (1963), in which he cited, in order to remind us, Tolstoy's repeated words in his last diaries: "Still Alive."

He wrote new plays. He directed them. He wrote for newspapers and magazines. He grieved for the loves he had lost. He celebrated figs, melons, good bread, friendship. He remembered and he imagined.

He didn't want to be the greatest Armenian-American writer in the world. He wanted, very boyishly, just to knock everyone's eyes out with beauty and fun and delight and sadness.

Somehow people didn't want to hear about the melancholy that lay beneath all the playfulness. He lived alone and was lonely and wrote furiously.

Now he didn't figure out, any more than anyone else can, how to stay put. There was no more time, but there are books yet to be discovered—manuscripts in Fresno and at his sister's in San Francisco and in the rue Taitbout in Paris. He enjoyed the business of looking and moving more than almost anybody; it was right that he should not die, but he did.

The last sentence of his last published book, *Obituaries*, reads: "I did my best, and let me urge you to do your best, too. Isn't it the least we can do for one another?"

So he never let up. He wrote a story a day, two, three, a chapter a day of a novel, or two, or three, but there is nothing truer than the note he struck at the end of his first published story, "The Daring Young Man on the Flying Trapeze." The would-be writer was hungry, he demanded to be noticed, and he ended like everyone else—"dreamless, unalive, perfect."

William Saroyan (1908-1981). Rest in Continued Turbulence.

Budd Schulberg
(27 March 1914-   )

Richard A. Fine
Virginia Commonwealth University

See also the Schulberg entry in *DLB 6, American Novelists Since World War II, Second Series.*

NEW BOOKS: *On the Waterfront: A Screenplay* (Carbondale & Edwardsville: Southern Illinois University Press, 1980);
Moving Pictures: Memories of a Hollywood Prince (New York: Stein & Day, 1981).

After a five-year silence following the publication of *Swan Watch* (1975), Budd Schulberg has produced three books in the past two years. *Everything That Moves* (1980), a slight novel which disappointed even his admirers (see *DLB 6*), has been followed by two more significant books. The first, *On the Waterfront* (1980), is Schulberg's best screenplay and the basis for Elia Kazan's much discussed and feted 1954 movie, and the second, *Moving Pictures: Memories of a Hollywood Prince* (1981), is Schulberg's long-awaited reminiscence of his childhood and adolescence among moviemakers in Hollywood and New York during the 1920s and early 1930s. To his occasional annoyance, Schulberg has been closely associated in the public mind with Hollywood since the publication of his first novel, *What Makes Sammy Run?*, in 1941. Yet these two recent books strengthen this identification.

Given the reputation of Kazan's *On the Waterfront*, it is surprising that twenty-five years passed before the publication of Schulberg's screenplay. Released in 1954, *On the Waterfront* was the rarest of Hollywood phenomena—a somber, even bleak, black-and-white picture, keenly analyzed and often lavishly praised by critics, which nevertheless attracted millions of moviegoers to the box office. In his ten-page afterword to the book, Schulberg describes the circumstances surrounding the making of *On the Waterfront*, "a story with more ups and downs than the plot of the movie itself." Schulberg was living comfortably on a farm in Bucks County, Pennsylvania, in the early 1950s when he was approached by Kazan, then at the height of his fame for his work both on Broadway and in Hollywood. Schulberg had resolved to abandon the forced and often frustrating collaborations involved in writing screenplays in order to concentrate on writing novels, but he was intrigued by, and eventually accepted, Kazan's proposal that together they script and shoot a movie entirely in the East, removed from the usual front-office interferences of Hollywood. The two men considered doing a film on a case of racial persecution in Trenton before they settled on the theme of exploitation and corruption on the docks and in the warehouses of New York Harbor.

Along with consulting Malcolm Johnson's Pulitzer Prize-winning articles for the *New York Sun* about union corruption on the waterfront in New York, Schulberg conducted his own yearlong investigation on the docks and in the waterfront neighborhoods. There he discovered "At least 10 percent of everything that moved in and out of the harbor" eventually lined the pockets of mobsters and corrupt union officials, and "if you were one of the 25,000 longshoremen looking for work, either you kicked back to a hiring boss appointed by mob overlords with the connivance of 'legitimate' shipping and stevedore officials, or they starved you off the docks." Schulberg spent months listening to longshoremen's conversations in dockside taverns and bars: "Sometimes it seemed as if everybody I talked to on the waterfront said something usable. I had left Hollywood because there were too many collaborators. Here I was surrounded by them—and welcomed every one of them."

He also learned that a handful of men were fighting the corruption and exploitation on the docks. The most prominent of these men was the "waterfront priest," Father John Corridan, "a tall, fast-talking, chain-smoking, hardheaded, sometimes profane Kerryman." Father Peter Barry, the character played by Karl Malden in *On the Waterfront*, is based on Corridon, and Schulberg reveals in his afterword that he used nearly verbatim Corridan's often preached "Sermon on the Docks" in the scene where Father Barry climbs into a ship's hold to deliver the last rites to a murdered insurgent longshoreman and makes a speech about "Christ in the shape-up" in which he compares the man's death to the Crucifixion.

Once Schulberg had completed a first draft of the script, he and Kazan traveled to Hollywood in search of studio financing. Darryl Zanuck, Twentieth Century-Fox's production chief, became the first in a long line of Hollywood executives to turn them down, complaining, "Who's going to care about a lot of sweaty longshoremen?" The two had exhausted seemingly every possibility when independent producer Sam Spiegel, who used the name

Budd Schulberg

S. P. Eagle, agreed to the project, provided that Kazan worked with a low budget and a short shooting schedule. Kazan then recruited Marlon Brando, whom he had worked with previously on *Streetcar Named Desire*, as well as Lee J. Cobb, Karl Malden, Rod Steiger, Martin Balsam, and Eva Marie Saint, who made her screen debut in this film. They settled on Hoboken, New Jersey, for location shooting, and completed filming in just thirty-five days during the dead of winter. Kazan and Schulberg also agreed to an arrangement—rare in the American film industry—whereby the author reported daily to the set to work on rewrites and script changes necessitated by "practical and creative

exigencies." As Schulberg says in his afterword, "just for once, getting a script to the screen in the spirit in which it had been conceived—thanks to that rare director who refused to make a distinction between playwright and screenplaywright—was victory enough. Find me a director who respects the *play*, as Kazan respected . . . this one. . . , and the *auteur* theory [of film directing] will float away like the hollow, gaseous thing it is."

Against all studio predictions, *On the Waterfront* opened to enthusiastic audiences and was a great commercial success. Moreover, the New York Film Critics voted it the best movie of the year, and it received an unprecedented eight Academy Awards, including awards for best production, best direction, and best original screenplay. Twenty-five years later, *On the Waterfront* continues to be screened frequently in revival houses and in college film courses and discussed in journals devoted to American cinema and culture. Perhaps the most provocative recent examination of the movie appears in a 1979 issue of the *American Quarterly*, where Kenneth Hey argues that Terry Malloy's agonizing decision to inform on the mob mirrors Schulberg's and Kazan's own difficult decisions in the early 1950s to testify as friendly witnesses before the House Un-American Activities Committee investigating Communist influence in Hollywood. According to Hey, ambivalence is the essential theme of *On the Waterfront*. "The film argues openly that injustice can be remedied through existing political institutions," Hey maintains, "but it grafts onto this basically liberal position the suggestion that individuals are frequently casualties of the conflict between right and wrong, and that the individual's response to the clash of absolute moral standards is ambivalent."

On the Waterfront: A Screenplay actually marks the second time Schulberg's story of union corruption appeared in print; he had earlier rewritten his screenplay as a novel, *Waterfront* (1955), which framed the story of Terry Malloy's confrontation with Johnny Friendly with much more sociological analysis and historical commentary. Whereas the novel is discursive, Schulberg's 140-page screenplay is characterized by a tautness of structure, which brilliantly conveys the claustrophobic atmosphere in which the action takes place and in which the characters must make crucial moral decisions. This economy, along with the vivid street language of the longshoremen, dialogue as accurate and profane as Hollywood would allow in the 1950s, has been recognized as Schulberg's greatest accomplishment as a screenwriter.

Dust jacket for Schulberg's award-winning screenplay

Schulberg worked intermittently for about five years on his most recent book, *Moving Pictures: Memories of a Hollywood Prince*. His progress was delayed by the tragic illness and premature death of his first wife, actress Geraldine Brooks, in 1977. (Two years later, in the home of Elia Kazan, he married Betsy Ann Langman.) *Moving Pictures* deals with Schulberg's childhood and adolescence as the son of one of Hollywood's most powerful producers, Benjamin P. (B. P.) Schulberg. It is at once an insider's glimpse of the American film industry, a chronicle of Schulberg's father's career, an examination of one second-generation American family's determined pursuit of success and the toll that pursuit eventually took, and a recollection of Schulberg's own privileged yet often painful upbringing within that family. Aided greatly by his father's unpublished autobiography and his own childhood diaries, Schulberg approaches each of these subjects—the film industry, his father, his family, and his own emotional development—with candor and clearheadedness.

The opening chapters of *Moving Pictures* focus on Schulberg's father, a Hollywood tycoon of whom little has been written until now. Schulberg builds a convincing case for placing his father in the front ranks of American film-industry pioneers. Before he was twenty, B. P. Schulberg had worked for director Edwin S. Porter, "truly the father of the American motion picture." By 1914, when Budd Schulberg was born, B. P. Schulberg was writing scenarios and publicity for Adolph Zukor, head of Famous Players Company and soon to be one of the most influential men in the industry; in his capacity as a publicist B. P. Schulberg coined the famous phrase "America's Sweetheart" to describe Mary Pickford and helped make her the first bona fide movie star. After World War I, B. P. Schulberg tried to convince the industry's four major talents—Mary Pickford, Douglas Fairbanks, D. W. Griffith, and Charlie Chaplin—to form a production company with Schulberg serving as chief administrator. The idea came to fruition as the highly successful United Artists Company but without Schulberg's participation. Undaunted, Schulberg formed his own company, Preferred Pictures, before eventually taking charge of Zukor's Paramount Pictures studio in the mid-1920s. Under Schulberg's guidance, Paramount—together with Metro-Goldwyn-Mayer—dominated the industry.

Budd Schulberg's account of his father's contributions, large and small, to the development of the American film industry is accurate and sensible. By all other accounts as well, B. P. Schulberg was one of the most intelligent, creative, and shrewd producers of his day. He many times tried, and often succeeded in, making movies which were a cut above typical Hollywood fare. Yet Budd Schulberg is not blind to his father's failings: his pathological gambling, his frequent womanizing, and his often misplaced faith in business associates. "Father was so intelligent in some ways. . . ," Schulberg comments. "But so crazy-dumb in other ways."

The elder Schulberg allowed his son access at an early age to the film sets, back lots, and conference rooms of the movie industry. It was a privilege Budd Schulberg occasionally abused. He remembers hiding in a huge fig tree on the MGM lot and lobbing ripe fruit through an open window at unsuspecting matinee idols and studio executives: "Who else can boast of scoring a direct hit with a ripe fig on the most luminous star in the Metro heavens? Greta Garbo!" Over the years Schulberg came to know a great many of Hollywood's leading producers, directors, writers, and actors, and *Moving Pictures* includes anecdotes and vignettes of some of the film industry's most celebrated figures: Louis B. Mayer, Adolph Zukor, Gary Cooper, Greta Garbo,

Sam Goldwyn, and David Selznick, among others. But Schulberg focuses his attention and sympathy more often on those whose fame was brief (like the genius-director Marcel DeSano, who directed his only hit, *The Girl Who Wouldn't Work*, for B. P. Schulberg in 1925), those who are forgotten (like the original Hollywood antihero, George Bancroft, star of such early gangster films as *Underworld*, 1927, and *The Dragnet*, 1928), or those who became victims of their own success and whose lives ended badly (like Clara Bow, the "gum-chewing, g-dropping" It Girl of the 1920s). Sensitive to the

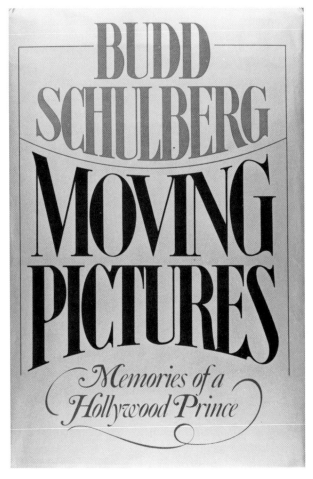

Dust jacket for Schulberg's Hollywood memoir

fleeting nature of success in America, Schulberg reacted soberly to the news of Bow's death in 1965 after thirty years of obscurity and poverty: "I thought of the vibrant Clara I had known in my youth. And although I had never met her, I thought also of Zelda Fitzgerald, who was *the* flapper of the literate international set during the same riotous period over which Clara had presided. They were like the opposite sides of the same shiny coin—let's call it Zelda for heads and Clara for tails—and when the coin fell dead on the dance floor both sides came up losers."

Schulberg learned much about the process and machinations of moviemaking. He came to share B. P. Schulberg's insistence that "unless the writer's structure is sound, the plot has its own logic and power, and its characters are believable, intriguing and *vital*," even the best director would be hard pressed to make an honest movie. He also came to believe that "the glamor capital of the world was as tough a company town as could be found." Both beliefs would influence Schulberg's career as a screenwriter, making him naturally suspicious of the Hollywood establishment and causing him to accept few assignments without the assurance his work would be respected by producers and directors.

During his childhood, Schulberg's family worshipped fervently the American success ethic, and he devotes much of *Moving Pictures* to analyzing his parents' tireless pursuit of wealth, culture, and social acceptance. Schulberg remembers his family's moves to larger quarters in better neighborhoods with each successive advancement in B. P. Schulberg's career. He describes his mother, Adeline, as striving for self-improvement, "reaching up for every intellectual branch she could close her little hands around." She was a devotee of the then popular French psychoanalyst Emile Coué and required her son to recite at bedtime Coué's famous dictum, "Every day in every way I'm getting better and better."

Much was expected of the Schulberg children; failure or weakness was shunned. "Parental love...," Schulberg laments, "was expressed not in terms of physical touching—embraces and kisses—but in educational and artistic prodding." When Schulberg began to show first promise as a writer, he remembers being "overpraised and overstimulated to achieve. Some of the fun of growing up was stolen from me by the realization that before I had published anything except in highschool journals and local sports pages, my career had already been chosen for me.... It was as if Mother had already made me a success and there was no margin for failure."

The psychological strains of such high expectations surfaced in various ways. Schulberg stammered, despite an endless succession of visits to expensive therapists; he had "an embarrassing tendency to faint" when confronted with unpleasantness; and he was puritanically priggish, objecting to his father's taste for highballs and his mother's for cigarettes. He was as a child, to an extent which amazes him as an adult, "a Billy Sunday in knickers."

Schulberg had cause to be concerned about his parents; their marriage did not withstand the pressures of success and notoriety in the movie colony. When in spring 1932 his father would not end his affair with his protegee Sylvia Sidney, his parents separated in acrimony and for good. His mother set up a talent agency, which soon became successful, but by 1932 his father's power in the industry was waning, and in the late 1930s he was reduced to taking out a full-page ad in a trade paper asking for any job. *Moving Pictures* ends in autumn 1932 with Schulberg's departure from Los Angeles to attend Dartmouth College. He recalls with sadness that while his entire family came to see him off at the train station, his parents left in separate cars. He knew at once that his childhood was over.

Most critics agree that *Moving Pictures* is the fullest and most incisive account of Hollywood written to date by a native son. Like many of Schulberg's other books, it has been praised for its honesty but criticized for its stylistic lapses. Film critic and historian Janet Maslin, for instance, while noting that "Mr. Schulberg's candor serves him well," complains of the book's "rambling" narrative and "overblown" prose. It is clearly, however, Schulberg's most accomplished work since *The Four Seasons of Success* (1972). Budd Schulberg continues to live most of the year on Long Island and plans to write more volumes of reminiscences.

Periodical Publication:

"What Makes Hollywood Run Now?," *New York Times Magazine*, 27 April 1980, pp. 52-58, 63-64, 74, 76, 81-82, 84, 86, 88.

References:

Kenneth Hey, "Ambivalence as a Theme in *On the Waterfront* (1954): An Interdisciplinary Approach to Film Study," *American Quarterly*, 31 (Winter 1979): 666-696;

Janet Maslin, "Home Sweet Hollywood," *New York Times Book Review*, 6 September 1981, pp. 9, 22.

AN INTERVIEW *with BUDD SCHULBERG*

DLB: *Moving Pictures*, a partial memoir of your growing up as the son of an important figure in the movie industry, is the book people have been expecting you to write for years. Why didn't you write it sooner?

SCHULBERG: I had certain work I wanted to finish before I got to this book. I knew that once I sat down to it, it would take a very long time, as it did—maybe five years on-and-off with research and trips back to Hollywood and writing and rewriting. I wanted to be sure I had that chunk of time to myself.

DLB: In addition to your screenplays and the memoir, you've written two Hollywood novels, *What Makes Sammy Run?* and *The Disenchanted*. Do you think of yourself as a Hollywood writer?

SCHULBERG: More, I would say, as a writer from Hollywood and of Hollywood and interested in Hollywood but not really as a Hollywood writer. For one thing, I've lived away from what was my home practically all of my adult life. I look at it but from something of a distance.

DLB: It surely would have been very easy for you to stay in Hollywood. Was it difficult to make the decision to move East?

SCHULBERG: I've joked about that in the past because so many of the writers around me at that time were saying, "Oh, if I could only get out of here, if I could only get back and write my play or write my book," and they never did leave. So now they never *could* leave. It's a story that I became fascinated with. I think it was easier in one way for me to leave because I had been raised there; so many people finally want to leave their hometown, like Tom Wolfe and F. Scott Fitzgerald. That was part of it. Another part of it was somewhat taken out of my hands by the fact that *What Makes Sammy Run?* caused such a strong reaction against me from the Hollywood Establishment that my staying on and working at that time became virtually impossible. So I sort of burned my own bridge then. Of course, by the time I wrote that I was wanting to leave, and I wrote a major part of it back in the East, up and around Dartmouth College. I was ready emotionally to leave Hollywood. The book just pushed me over the brink—the kind of book it was and the reception it got—if I had any doubts about wanting to linger. It helped in that way.

DLB: It's been generally believed that the book is a roman a clef. To what extent is Sammy Glick a fictional character?

SCHULBERG: I would say he's a fictional character in the sense that almost all fictional characters evolve from actual people. At the time it was something of a scandal because everyone on the Hollywood scene seemed to think it was one particular person. That bothered me because I didn't want it to be a thinly disguised biography. I really had five or six people in mind whose characteristics overlapped.

DLB: Most Hollywood novels are bad. Is it a coincidence that two of the *best* are F. Scott Fitzgerald's *The Last Tycoon* and your novel *The Disenchanted*, which is about Fitzgerald in Hollywood?

SCHULBERG: It was something of a coincidence, I think. It was a strange happening that I should be put with Scott in 1939 to write a rather silly winter-carnival movie story at a time when both of us obviously were thinking of writing about Hollywood. I had written a series of short stories with the same central character of Sammy Glick, and I really didn't know until after we got back from our trip to Dartmouth that Scott was also planning to write a Hollywood novel. I think there was clearly interplay between the two of us which was not completely coincidental, although somewhat inadvertent. He was very interested in my background and my father's experiences. Some of the things that I said to Scott are said by Cecilia in *The Last Tycoon*. So in a sense I think he undoubtedly drew something from our relationship. And that decade later when I wrote *The Disenchanted*, I of course drew on our trip and on our conversations.

DLB: Are you planning to continue the memoir that you've begun in *Moving Pictures*?

SCHULBERG: Yes, I do expect to continue the memoirs. I'm not working on them at the moment except for preparing notes. I'll do one film in between, the remake of *A Face in the Crowd*. After that's done, sometime in spring or summer, I hope to go into the second of what may be three books; I'm not sure yet.

–Jean W. Ross

Richard Yates
(3 February 1926-   )

Brooks Landon
University of Iowa

See also the Yates entry in *DLB 2, American Novelists Since World War II*.

NEW BOOKS: *A Good School* (New York: Delacorte/Seymour Lawrence, 1978);
Liars in Love (New York: Delacorte/Seymour Lawrence, 1981).

RECENT AWARD: National Magazine Award for Fiction for "Oh, Joseph, I'm So Tired," 1978.

"I think it probably *is* the hardest and loneliest profession in the world, this crazy, obsessive business of trying to be a good writer," Richard Yates told DeWitt Henry and Geoffrey Clark in a 1972 *Ploughshares* interview. More recently, in an article in the *New York Times Book Review*, Yates has written: "Time is everything. I am 55 now, and my first grandchild is expected in June. It has been many years since I was a young man, let alone an apprentice writer. But the eager, fearful, self-hectoring spirit of the beginner is slow to fade. With my 8th book just begun—and with deep regret for the desolate wastes of time that have kept it from being my 10th or 12th—I feel I haven't really started yet. And I suppose this rather ludicrous condition will persist, for better or worse, until my time runs out." While Yates may feel like a beginner, his fiction always shows the mark of a veteran craftsman, someone who quietly pursues and achieves the traditional goals of fine fiction. In his thoughtful reassessment of Yates's career, novelist Jonathan Penner has explained in the *New Republic*: "Yates's creative instincts owe much to tradition, little to fashion. In an age embarrassed by story-telling, half-persuaded by the chic critics that fiction should repel innocent belief, he tells stories we believe."

Yates's most recent accomplishments include *A Good School* (1978), a novel, and a collection of short stories, *Liars in Love* (1981). One story in this collection which first appeared in the *Atlantic Monthly*, "Oh, Joseph, I'm So Tired," won the prestigious National Magazine Award for Fiction in 1978. Judges praised "Oh, Joseph, I'm So Tired" for "sensitivity and superb simplicity that make it a joy to read." Their phrase not only focuses on two of the great strengths of Yates's fiction, but also serves as a reminder that this writer, so frequently cited for the sadness of his stories, can indeed be a joy to read.

another story, "Regards at Home," all concern stages in the life of William Grove, an autobiographical character who seems to overlap Yates's earlier character Robert Prentice, protagonist of *A Special Providence* (1969) and of the story "Builders" in *Eleven Kinds of Loneliness* (1962). Yates has called "Builders" "a direct autobiographical blowout," and William Grove, like Prentice before him, seems much shaped by the author's personal history. "Oh, Joseph, I'm So Tired" shows Grove as a boy of seven in 1933, and "Regards at Home" shows him at twenty-three as the young writer leaves for France

Richard Yates

Somewhat frustrated by comments on the "unrelieved sadness" of his books, Yates shrugs: "It's always seemed to me that a lot of my stuff is as bright and funny as anybody else's—but this, of course, gets into areas of critical evaluation that are not for me to discuss." Certainly, Yates's philosophy is not tied to the doleful. "Easy affirmations are silly and cheap, of course," he notes, "but when a tough, honest writer can look squarely at all the horrors of the world, face all the facts, and still come up with a hard-won, joyous celebration of life at the end, in spite of everything, that can be wonderful."

A Good School, "Oh, Joseph, I'm So Tired," and

"to take up the business of my life." *A Good School*, described by one reviewer as "a short novel that reads as swiftly as a stolen diary," covers the formative period from 1941 to 1944, when Grove was a floundering student at a failing prep school, Dorset Academy.

Dorset is a "funny school" by prep standards, only twelve years old, fielding no interscholastic athletic teams, and accepting students no other school would take. Its campus is picturesque to a fault, composed of self-consciously rustic red stone and sagging-roofed buildings claimed to be "Cotswold" architecture. Years after his stay there,

Grove realizes "what brighter people seemed to notice right away, that there was something fanciful and even specious in the very beauty of the place—a prep school that might have been conceived in the studios of Walt Disney." This observation and others appear in Grove's retrospective, first-person foreword and afterword to *A Good School*, but the balance of the book's narration is third person, with point of view shifting among various students and faculty members.

Although Dorset Academy folds after Grove's class of '44 graduates, and although its teachers are as unexceptional as its students, it is "a good school" for William Grove, who, despite failing grades and chronic awkwardness, becomes editor of its paper. "It saw me through the worst of my adolescence, as few other schools would have done," he recounts, "and it taught me the rudiments of my trade. I learned to write by working on the Dorset *Chronicle*, making terrible mistakes in print that hardly anybody ever noticed." Grove's apprenticeship, however, is in more than writing: he endures the physical harassment and social arrogance of his peers, maturing to perceptions that let him begin to understand himself and those around him. In chronicling Grove's growth, Yates reveals again his genius for portraying the treacherous dynamics of friendship and the painful processes by which we learn to live with ourselves.

Readers of Yates's earlier work will find much in the life of William Grove familiar. "Like a great jigsaw puzzle, the territory of Yates's work knits together as it expands," Jonathan Penner notes: "Certain experiences have emerged as central to his fiction—World War II and its scars; growing up with a bohemian mother divorced from a plodding father; prep school education; a stifling job in public relations or advertising or sales; physical and mental illness. Increasingly, too, the books are moored one to another by the threads of shared particulars—persons, places, events." Yates accomplishes this intricate interweaving of material without falling into self-pity or self-aggrandizement, which he has specified are "the two terrible traps that lie in the path of autobiographical fiction."

In his *Ploughshares* interview Yates discussed at some length the autobiographical content of his fiction, finally isolating its particular challenge: "Anybody can scribble out a confession or a memoir or a diary or a chronicle of personal experience, but how many writers can *form* that kind of material? How many writers can make it into solid, artistically satisfying fiction?" What "artistically satisfying fic-

tion" means to Yates can be better understood in light of his recent article, "Some Very Good Masters," in the *New York Times Book Review*. There, after crediting the movies of the 1930s for getting him "into the habit of thinking like a writer," he

Dust jacket for Yates's most recent novel

acknowledges his profound admiration for F. Scott Fitzgerald's *The Great Gatsby* ("a short piece of work that gains range as it gathers momentum, until the end of it leaves you with a stunning illumination of the world"). But he reserves his greatest praise for Gustave Flaubert's *Madame Bovary*: "I wanted *that* kind of balance and quiet resonance on every page, that kind of foreboding mixed with comedy, that kind of inexorable destiny in the heart of a lonely, romantic girl." Yates continues: "Another thing I have always liked about both *Gatsby* and *Bovary* is that there are no villains in either one. The force of evil is felt in these novels but is never personified— neither novelist is willing to let us off that easily." Nor is Yates, as his fiction consistently refuses to supply villains to account for the disappointments and tragedies of his characters. "I much prefer the kind of story," he explains, "where the reader is left wondering who's to blame until it begins to dawn on him that he himself must bear some of the responsibility because he's human and therefore infinitely fallible."

From his comments about his writing and certainly from the writing itself emerges Yates's absolute commitment to the tradition of literary realism. "I think it's a cop-out to say that our times are too hectic or frantic or confusing for good, traditional, formal novels to emerge," he insists, continuing: "I've tried and tried, but I just can't stomach most of what's now being called 'The Post-Realistic Fiction.' . . . I know it's all very fashionable stuff and I know it provides an endless supply of witty little intellectual puzzles and puns and fun and games for graduate students to play with, but it's emotionally empty. It isn't *felt*." Yates dedicates his own writing to finding felt material in the commonplaces of daily life, prompting Penner to note that "few other writers dare trust themselves for so long with everyday life, unrelieved by thrilling action, clamant sex, or shocking Gothic twists."

Steering between the extremes of what he calls "stylistic fooling around" and writing that is "merely realistic," Yates delights in simple, vernacular dialogue through which his characters give themselves away. The appeal of his style has never been more clear than in "Oh, Joseph, I'm So Tired" when William Grove's sister explains to him what it means to hear a whole city: "I don't mean just the loud sounds, she said, like the siren going by just now, or those car doors slamming, or all the laughing and shouting down the street; that's just close-up stuff. I'm talking about something else. Because you see there are millions and millions of people in New York—more people than you can possibly imagine, ever—and most of them are doing something that makes a sound. Maybe closing doors, maybe putting their forks down on their plates if they're having dinner, or dropping their shoes if they're going to bed—and because there are so many of them, all those little sounds add up and come together in a kind of hum. But it's so faint—so very, very

faint—that you can't hear it unless you listen very carefully for a long time."

Liars in Love, published in October of 1981, was greeted with great enthusiasm. Reviewers not only praised its seven stories but also took the opportunity to praise Yates's earlier writing. *Liars in Love* continues the autobiographical thrust and general concerns of Yates's work. Its stories present a variety of relationships (always poignant, usually doomed) between lovers, brothers and sisters, and mothers and children. While his protagonists are men and women of widely varying ages who live in many different places, their experiences all could have been in the life of William Grove. The collection includes Yates's prize-winning "Oh, Joseph, I'm So Tired," "Regards at Home," and "A Compassionate Leave," which was first published in *Ploughshares*. Other stories appear for the first time.

Yates now lives in Boston, where he is working on a novel he hopes to finish before 1983, but which he is not yet ready to describe or title. He remains one of our most able and serious writers, a man whose works strongly bid to withstand the challenge he feels so keenly of "the terrible, inexorable indifference of time itself."

Periodical Publications:
FICTION:
"Oh, Joseph, I'm So Tired," *Atlantic Monthly*, 241 (February 1978): 52-63;
"Regards At Home," *Atlantic Monthly*, 246 (August 1980): 38-54.

NONFICTION:
"Some Very Good Masters," *New York Times Book Review*, 19 April 1981, pp. 3, 21.

References:
DeWitt Henry and Geoffrey Clark, "An Interview With Richard Yates," *Ploughshares*, 1 (December 1972): 65-78;
Jonathan Penner, "The Novelists: Richard Yates," *New Republic*, 179 (4 November 1978): 42-45.

New Entries

To read contemporary literature is not only a pleasure, but a duty. In our proper anxiety to be familiar with "the best that is known and thought in the world," we must certainly endeavor to be familiar with the best that is known and thought in our own time. The culture that confines itself to the literature of the past is an imperfect culture.

George Sampson
Concise Cambridge History of the English Language

T. J. Bass
(Thomas Joseph Bassler)
(7 July 1932-   )

John Ower
University of South Carolina

BOOKS: *Half Past Human*, as T. J. Bass (New York: Ballantine, 1971);

The Godwhale, as T. J. Bass (New York: Ballantine, 1974; London: Eyre Methuen, 1975);

The Whole Life Diet (New York: Evans, 1979).

Writing under the pseudonym T. J. Bass, Thomas Joseph Bassler has produced in his novels *Half Past Human* (1971) and *The Godwhale* (1974) two of the best works of science fiction to be published during the 1970s. Both of Bassler's novels are notable for their relatively sophisticated narrative technique. They are also outstanding for their intellectual richness, presenting many interesting ideas about science and technology and the future historical development of human society. In their treatment of these subjects *Half Past Human* and *The Godwhale* are works of genuine consequence for two important streams in their genre. First, Bassler's novels provide fine examples of so-called hard science fiction. That is, they are characterized by their emphasis on the accurate use of scientific and technological fact both in itself and as a basis for extrapolating future developments in these areas. *Half Past Human* and *The Godwhale* likewise constitute additions of real importance to the distinguished tradition of dystopian fiction. In this regard, Bassler's depiction of the human and ecological costs of extreme overpopulation presents a negative vision of man's future all the more daunting for its plausibility. Bassler's considerable achievements as a science-fiction writer have been appropriately honored by the nomination of both *Half Past Human* and *The Godwhale* (in 1971 and 1974 respectively) for the prestigious Nebula Award. These nominations, made by the Science Fiction Writers of America, show the respect that Bassler's work has earned from fellow practitioners in his literary field.

Bassler was born 7 July 1932 in Clinton, Iowa. He was the first of four children. His father was Louis Bassler, a shoemaker, and his mother was Faustina Slattery, a registered nurse. Bassler married Gloria Napoli in 1960 and has six children.

(The name of the fifth, Karl, is an acronym for Komputerized Aerospace Research Laboratory.) That Bassler enjoys a happy, rich, and stimulating relationship with his family is indicated not only by the many activities that the author pursues with his wife and children, but also by his emphasis in his two novels on the domestic as a means of achieving human fulfillment.

Bassler took his M.D. degree from the State University of Iowa, Iowa City, in 1959 and completed his internship at Los Angeles County-Southern California Medical Center in 1960. In the same year, Bassler began his residency in pathology at the University of Maryland in Baltimore. His residency was continued at the Los Angeles County-Southern California Medical Center from 1961 to 1964, when he was certified in anatomic and clinical pathology. Bassler then served in the United States Army from 1964 to 1966, attaining the rank of captain. During his military service, he was chief of the histiopathology section of the Third Army Medical Laboratories in Fort McPherson, Georgia. His work involved directing a school for medical technology and doing general pathology in the laboratory at the headquarters of the Third Army. Bassler presently practices his medical specialty at several hospitals in the Los Angeles area. In addition, since 1966 the author has lectured at the School of Medical Technology, Centinela Hospital, where he has taught, among other subjects, hematology, parasitology, and chemistry. He has also had three years of forensic experience with the Los Angeles County Medical Examiner's Office, where he studied hundreds of cases of "sudden death."

In addition to Bassler's varied career as a medical practitioner, he is likewise a medical scientist, with a number of professional publications to his credit. These include not only articles in journals and volumes that are directed toward Bassler's fellow physicians, but also his lively popular book *The Whole Life Diet* (1979). The latter work, like Bassler's medical articles, reflects his strong interest in the relationship of diet and exercise to physical health and to longevity. Bassler strongly believes that the use of tobacco, a rich diet of refined food, and the lack of strenuous exercise all contribute to the most prevalent causes of aging and death (the commonest of these being atherosclerosis) in advanced urban industrial countries. As preventive measures against such "diseases of civilization," Bassler advocates a combination of healthy diet and healthy exertion. Concerning the former, Bassler lays particular stress upon the nutritional value of natural, unprocessed foodstuffs such as eggs, fruits, and nuts. He also sees special benefits in regular long-distance walking and running, especially on a daily basis. He suggests that such a regimen will radically improve a person's physical condition and through its demands on his body ensure that he eats properly. Bassler is himself an avid long-distance runner, having completed more than 100 marathons. Bassler's concern with exercise is further expressed in his editorship of the *American Medical Joggers Association Newsletter,* which he founded in 1969. He has also participated in marathon clinics around the United States.

Bassler believes that a healthy diet combined with appropriate physical exertion can overcome "most of the problems of Olde Age," and can result in life spans of 100 years or more. He has even described aerobic exercise as an "experiment in immortality." As evidence for such assertions, Bassler cites the cardiovascular youthfulness that is revealed in autopsies of those who have pursued a healthy life-style. He also points to the absence of atherosclerosis and to instances of remarkable longevity among primitive populations where "the diet is unprocessed and exercise level is high." Bassler's special medical interests are of course in keeping with the emphases on life-style and preventive health care that have become increasingly prominent during recent years. In this regard, Bassler can be characterized as a bold and yet scientifically responsible pioneer. He is not afraid to challenge the conventional wisdom of his profession and to advance controversial ideas and recommendations if he thinks they have a sound basis in medical fact. For instance, Bassler maintains that the natural aging process can be greatly slowed by a person's keeping fit enough to walk as many miles as he is years old! Similarly, Bassler refuses to be bound by conventional categories of medical thought and practice. He employs in his writing such relatively innovative concepts as "sports" and "orthomolecular" medicine (concerned respectively with the physiological effects of exercise and dietary biochemistry). In general, Bassler feels that the

T. J. Bass

1960s and 1970s were revolutionary years with respect to an understanding of human physiology and that this revolution demands a corresponding change in outlook by the medical profession. Such thinking may perhaps be seen in part as a product of that romantic, experimental, and at times radical mentality that has come to be associated especially with Bassler's adopted state of California. The creative, speculative, intellectually innovative tendencies that are revealed in Bassler's medical thinking are in accord with his literary vocation as a science-fiction writer. However, Bassler's professional publications, like his novels, reveal a scientific intellect that is lucid and disciplined, both well and widely informed.

As might be expected, Bassler devotes much of his leisure time to hiking and running. He engages in such exercise not only for the sake of his physical health, but also for the recreational opportunities it affords. Bassler and his family take advantage of the stimulatingly diverse environment of Southern California, with its varied possibilities for outdoor activity. Thus, Bassler states that "The ecosystem is reflected in my books. . . . I enjoy the mountains, the ocean and (even) the cities." Together with his wife and children, Bassler "does the John Muir Trail from Mt. Whiteney [*sic*] to Yosemite (210 mi)." He and his family likewise make good use of their proximity to the sea. Bassler himself enjoys "Hiking 20 or 30 miles a day through the cities along the beach[,] . . . a fun way to see things and to eat your way through . . . various menus." Similarly, Bassler finds in urban marathoning an enjoyable means of exploring his environment and of socializing: "MARATHONING allows me to cover a great deal of distance on foot and see everything up close while chatting with training partners." Besides expressing his outgoing personality and his obvious zest for living through pastimes connected with exercise, Bassler also has a keen interest in the study of whales: "My partner, J. C. Roberts, MD . . . is one of the early men to explore Cetacean Research, here, at Marineland of the Pacific. We do a lot of whale 'watching' both in the sea and under the microscope—thus, my book, GODWHALE, is a natural result." Bassler also raises goats for milk and meat, a practice which he advocates in *The Whole Life Diet*.

Bassler's reputation as a science-fiction writer is based on his two novels, *Half Past Human* and *The Godwhale*. These books display considerable skill and sophistication in their narrative technique and are likewise outstanding as novels of ideas. Concerning the first of these matters, Bassler makes particularly effective use of narrative discontinuity. In both novels he subdivides relatively long chapter units into a number of discrete episodes. Frequently, two of these units when contiguous will involve the same character and only a small jump in space and/or time. On some occasions, however, Bassler will move without transition from one of his dramatis personae to another. Similarly, many narrative breaks entail sudden shifts in location, while the opening chapter of *The Godwhale* takes the reader in a single leap over a number of centuries with the cryogenically suspended Larry Dever. While Bassler's discontinuities can on a first reading of his novels be confusing, they do allow him a great deal of narrative flexibility. Moreover, Bassler's fragmentation of his chapters into separate, relatively brief subsections permits him to employ an interesting variety of plot lines, personalities, episodes, and scenes. In this way he is able to give a representative cross section of his dystopian future society. Bassler can likewise by means of his discontinuities place side by side different facets of his future world for thematic and symbolic comparison. The novelist weaves through these juxtapositions a subtle, rather complex network of interrelationships among various ideas and images. Such a pattern in turn provides a matrix which ultimately helps the reader to understand better any particular aspect of *Half Past Human* or *The Godwhale*. Bassler's

contextual structure, which is analogous to a collage or a montage, recalls the "mosaic configuration . . . for insight" created by John Brunner in his science-fiction classic *Stand on Zanzibar* (1968).

Bassler's narrative discontinuities and his multiplicity of plot lines and characters make his two novels harder to follow and more intellectually demanding than is usual with science-fiction novels. Another factor which contributes to the relative difficulty of *Half Past Human* and *The Godwhale* is Bassler's practice of plunging us abruptly into a future world very different from our own. *Half Past Human* offers at least some introductory explanation of Bassler's dystopian Hive society and of the relict aboriginal populations remaining outside the Hive's underground shaft cities. However, the opening scene of *The Godwhale* makes no such concessions to its audience in presenting Larry Dever's future milieu. The reader who begins the latter novel for the first time feels as if he had been instantly transported over many centuries to greatly changed surroundings which he finds highly unfamiliar and confusing. Surmounting such initial disorientation, which combines the experiences currently termed "culture shock" and "future shock," involves among other things understanding a strange physical environment, mastering a new vocabulary, and comprehending unaccustomed social phenomena. The reader of Bassler's novels accordingly needs some patience, application, and persistence to familiarize himself with the author's fictional future.

The demands Bassler makes upon his audience by his proliferation of story lines and characters and by his plunging readers into a largely alien milieu adversely affected the initial reception of *Half Past Human*. For example, Mike McQuown, writing in the "fanzine" *Luna Monthly*, complained that the novel has "too many characters and too many subplots." McQuown was also turned off by what he stigmatized as Bassler's "jargon": that is, the new vocabulary which the reader must master as he encounters Hive society and the aborigines. Similarly, the anonymous reviewer for *Publishers Weekly* asserted that the "characters are so numerous and so weird, and the plot so labyrinthine, that only the most determined puzzle solvers will stick with the novel to the end." However, the reviews of *The Godwhale* displayed a more sympathetic and intelligent appreciation of the work on its own terms. *Publishers Weekly* praised Bassler's second novel as "marvelously inventive," while T. A. Shippey stated in the *Times Literary Supplement* that "*The Godwhale* is . . . full of splendid side-issues and its plot is too inventive to be summarized, too full of wayward and independent life." Obviously, these two reviewers found Bassler's narrative technique a literary asset rather than a hindrance.

Bassler's narrative discontinuities and the multiplicity of his story lines and characters make it impossible to provide simple plot summaries of his novels. It is therefore best to approach them through their rich intellectual content. To begin with, Bassler's professional background and interests are reflected by *Half Past Human* and *The Godwhale* in a number of ways. As a medical researcher and practitioner, with competence in several fields and a special regard for relevant technologies, Bassler is naturally a proponent of hard science fiction. Thus, his novels are characterized by an abundance of varied scientific and technological data. Bassler not only presents such information in liberal doses, but also employs it as an intellectually sound basis for extrapolation in creating his future milieu. In this regard, Bassler's scrupulous concern with factual accuracy and with speculative plausibility has led him to consult a variety of specialists outside his own areas of knowledge. His "hardware consultant" was the engineer "who literally put the legs on the moon module of Apollo 11," his "electronic consultant" designed a thermometer to measure lunar temperatures, and his "software consultant" conducted a school for digital-computer operators. As a writer of hard science fiction, Bassler demands a certain degree of scientific and technological literacy for a full comprehension of his work. However, although the average reader will doubtless find Bassler's novels dauntingly technical in places, the author certainly does not intend his work only for a scientifically sophisticated elite. Rather, his fiction can be seen as attempting to bridge in a twofold manner the gap between the trained specialist and the interested layman. On the one hand, Bassler's novels should raise the intellectual level of the layman by stimulating him to acquire the necessary background information. On the other, following a tradition established by Jules Verne and H. G. Wells, Bassler's fiction presents scientific and technical material to the ordinary reader in a fashion which is generally comprehensible and interesting and often imaginatively striking. Bassler's literary vocation as a scientific popularizer is indicated by his account of how his career as a fiction writer began during his army service: "a general asked me to prepare a report on the causes of malaria. . . . The report had to be written in non-technical language for laymen, and when I finished, the whole thing sounded so much like science fiction, I decided to try my hand at that."

In attempting to further the scientific and technological education of his readers, Bassler quite naturally lays particular stress on medicine. Thus, *Half Past Human* and *The Godwhale* are liberally sprinkled in places with technical medical vocabulary. The two books present information from a variety of medical specializations, including genetics, anatomy, biochemistry, and psychology. Bassler's concerns with diet and exercise appear indirectly but significantly in his two novels. Both works illustrate the contrast which he draws in his medical articles between sedentary urban man, who lives on a diet of highly refined food, and those primitive peoples who are healthy, strong, and long-lived thanks to natural foodstuffs and to rugged exertion. The citizens of Hive culture, which is the descendant of our urban, industrial, and technological society, live on overprocessed fare that is deficient in essential nutrients. The bad diet of the Hive dwellers and (at least in cases like that of fat old Walter from *Half Past Human*) lack of sufficient exercise are largely responsible for bodies which are weak, soft, and in other ways decidedly privative. The denizens of the Hive also tend to obesity, and they have a normal life span of only thirty years. Such sorry physical specimens are sharply contrasted in Bassler's novels with the healthy and vigorous aborigines. In part because the latter have a natural diet and ways of life that require exercise, they are far more robust than the Hive dwellers and can reach a much more advanced age. The physical superiority of the aboriginals over the Hive "Nebishes" parallels and largely explains the generally greater capacities of the primitives on a mental, spiritual, and moral plane.

As hard science fiction, *Half Past Human* and *The Godwhale* are also notable for their extrapolations from current developments in electronics and other fields so as to explore the positive and negative potential of man's technology. In this regard Bassler's thinking centers on the romantic opposition between the organic and the mechanical. On the affirmative side, Bassler believes that progress in cybernetics and other areas will effectively erase the distinctions between the living organism and the machine, between the human being and technology, as obviously subhuman. The bridging of these antitheses is particularly apparent with Larry Dever in *The Godwhale*. Larry is involved (especially through the accident that leads to the amputation of the lower half of his body) in a series of intimate physical, mental, and emotional relationships with complex and often sentient devices. In Larry's case, we have not an opposition of man and machine, but rather a positive synthesis on all levels of human life, including even the sexual. Similarly, Bassler sees cybernetic engineering as eventually being able to create intelligent, "living" personalities in some ways superior to those of human beings. In both of Bassler's novels, such electronic devices become full-fledged characters, functioning as companions, mentors, and even as quasi divinities for man. The first of these roles is performed by Toothpick and Ball in *Half Past Human*, while the part of the beneficent deity is played by the extraterrestrial colonization vehicle *Olga*; the deity in *The Godwhale* is the plankton-harvesting vessel *Rorqual Maru*. All four of Bassler's "cyberpersonalities" once again render essentially meaningless the distinctions between the human and the subhuman, the organism and the machine. Concerning the first of these dualities, even the small companion robots Toothpick and Ball possess mentalities that may well be superior to those of the men whom they guide. The opposition between the organic and the mechanical is blurred in connection with Bassler's four electronic characters by his sexual symbolism. Toothpick and Ball are associated with the male genitalia, while *Olga* and *Rorqual* are both feminine-maternal symbols, acting as "wombs" of new birth.

Bassler draws a clear-cut antithesis in *Half Past Human* and *The Godwhale* between the fulfillment of the positive potential of man's technology and the realization of its negative possibilities in the Hive. The latter outcome involves a pejorative contrast between the organic and the mechanical, together with a reduction of men to a subhuman level by the technological violation of their physical and psychic integrity. Regarding the first of these two motifs, Hive society in several basic areas superimposes the mechanical and the artificial upon the organic and natural. Thus, Hive agriculture involves large-scale central planning, is highly mechanized, and makes heavy use of chemical fertilizers and pesticides. The yields of such industrialized farming (which are supplemented by the even more artificial methods of hydroponics) are in turn processed almost beyond recognition, being distributed as virtually synthetic food and clothing by mechanical dispensers. Just as in Hive agriculture and its end products, the organic and the natural have to a large extent been superseded by the mechanical and artificial, so the Hive technologically manipulates and controls human reproduction. The most outstanding example of such intervention is the "baby factory" in *The Godwhale*, which is strongly reminiscent of the Hatchery of Aldous Huxley's *Brave New World*

(1932). Moreover, the Hive has interfered artificially not only with the natural and organic processes of reproduction, but also with those of dying. Citizens who become terminally ill are kept alive indefinitely in a chilled "suspension" by a sophisticated support apparatus. Bassler's second motif of the Hive's reducing people to a subhuman level through technology is stressed especially in *The Godwhale*. For instance, the envoy Drum unknowingly has incorporated into his body a bomb, meant to destroy those with whom he is supposed to negotiate. Similarly, the Hive warrior ARNOLD's sexuality is, in order to make him a more enthusiastic fighter, oriented by psychological programming toward violence. In cases like those of Drum and ARNOLD, the Hive citizen is treated not as a personality to be respected in his own right, but rather as a machine or tool existing for the ends of his society. In this degraded capacity, the individual is ruthlessly used and if need be sacrificed by the Hive authorities.

Bassler's concern with science and technology is interwoven in his novels with the historical and sociological interests that are likewise central defining characteristics of mainstream science fiction. These last two preoccupations are combined in Bassler's extrapolation from present undesirable trends in the developed urban and industrial countries to create the frightening dystopia of the Hive (or, as it is alternatively called, "Big Earth Society," abbreviated as "Big ES"). The Hive, with its overcrowded subterranean shaft cities and intensive, mechanized agriculture, represents especially a plausible extension of present developments in Southern California. Significantly enough, it is in this region, transformed by Big ES from a potential paradise to an underground urban hell, and, on the surface, to an overexploited wasteland, that much of the action of Bassler's novels occurs.

The author sees Hive civilization as resulting from a complex historical process that involves biological, socioeconomic, and technological factors. Fundamental to the future development of Hive culture is the tendency of man's population once freed from natural checks to expand to the very limits of available resources. Since the vastly increased number of mouths renders it essential that every square foot of arable land be cultivated, the swarming human masses are forced underground into high-rise shaft cities. Overpopulation also contributes to the rise of a rigid bureaucratic tyranny through the need to allocate perennially scarce resources and to manage three trillion people. These ends are achieved largely by the creation of a worldwide network of electronic devices which together form an intelligent master computer called the "Class One." Since only the Class One has any overall comprehension of Big ES with its millions of cities, the computer becomes the single dominant factor in Hive government. In its overriding concern with the collective "good" of Big ES, the Class One has little regard for individuals, who are routinely sacrificed when their electronic overlord deems it necessary.

To survive the new conditions created by overpopulation, man must adapt both to crowding and to various deprivations. The necessary bodily and psychological changes in humanity are brought about partly through genetic engineering by the Hive and partly through the harsh pressures created by its physical and social environment. These latter forces, working together with deliberate policies of Big ES, push out or destroy those unsuited to Hive existence. The combined result of these various agencies is the "Nebish," a new human species whose lack of a fifth toe is a Freudian emasculation image suggesting both its corporeal and psychic degeneracy. Perhaps the most prominent psychological attribute of the typical Nebish is his complacent and lethargic docility. This is produced not only by genetic changes, but also by the policies of Big ES, which keeps most of its members sexual neuters and further indoctrinates its subjects with a passive "Good Citizen" mentality. However, despite the blandness of the average run of Nebishes, there likewise occur among Hive dwellers a number of nasty character traits, which include ruthless self-centeredness, power seeking, sadism, and perfidy. For example, the well-developed streak of cruelty in Hive psychology is displayed by a gruesome practice connected with the "Hunt" (in which drug-stimulated Nebishes track down and kill the aborigines who pilfer and trample Big ES crops). If successful, the hunter ritually cuts a "trophy" from his victim.

The dystopian quality of Hive culture can be further highlighted by considering some important specifics of the day-to-day existence of the typical Nebish. His living quarters, like his diet, show how Big ES must tightly ration a general scarcity of basic necessities. Thus, the shortage of dwelling space in the crowded shaft cities means that their inhabitants must occupy small cubicles, often shared by five or more persons. Such domestic groupings in turn constitute a travesty of the traditional family (for Bassler, one of the chief means of true human fulfillment) that reflects especially the gross interference of the Hive with sexuality and procreation. Not

only are children produced by a variety of artificial means which are more or less divorced from natural parenthood, but the Hive household must accommodate the "neuts" who make up the majority of Big ES population. Largely as a result of these factors, monogamous marriage resulting in "normal" childbearing has been all but superseded by non-reproductive units like the "family-5" of old Walter in *Half Past Human*. In such associations, the strong emotional bonds created by sexual relations between husband and wife and by parental love for children are at best replaced by weaker affections less likely to detract from loyalty to Big ES. The relative attenuation of the personal attachments within the Hive family results partly from its substitution for heterosexual union of the "meld," a grotesque "group grope" supposed to bring about the spiritual fusion of its participants. This sterile travesty of the sexual communion of man and woman, in which erotic passion and pleasure are sadly diluted, cannot produce a genuine love. Rather than being united by true devotion, the Hive family is held together by sheer economic necessity. This causes a parasitism and predation among family members in which each individual pursues his own self-interest. For example, when Jo Jo from Walter's household jumps to "shaft base" in a drug-induced fantasy, one of his associates rushes to obtain before his death his remaining allotment of food. Jo Jo's "calories" are then consumed by his family in a feast that has obvious cannibalistic overtones.

On his trips between his cubicle and work, the Hive dweller often is forced by his society's lack of energy for commuter transportation into prolonged and wearisome journeys on the spiral walkway of his shaft city. He may also have to push through underground tubeways that are packed, reeking, and dirty. While he is traveling to his workplace (where he will probably have to put up with worn-out equipment and other hindrances created by the perennial scarcity of resources and technical personnel), it is possible that he will be murderously assaulted by one of the many psychotics created by the pressures of Hive life. Even more frequent than such violence among Nebishes is suicide. This is sometimes caused by the adverse effect upon cerebral functioning of an allergic reaction to house-mite dust (the mites being only one of several parasites and scavengers that thrive in the shaft cities). A second cause of suicide is "Molecular Reward," a hallucinogenic drug dispensed by the Hive authorities with an apparently cynical knowledge of its dangers. Another officially

Netted Hulk

[Arnold spins web net

stiff   *Back arched, eyes open*

The hulk reeked of brine. It lay still in the tangled
net while the alarm rang. A fat dwarf rustled up in wrinkled
coveralls, stared bug-eyed for a moment and then turned off the
clanging alarm. *He clutched the switch for support.*

"Netted a Fisheye." he shouted over his shoulder. "Looks
like a dead one."

Behind him several fat little forms appeared in the
corridor. They huddled together. Their large, dark sun goggles
added to their tremulous *wide-eyed* appearance.

Fat Arnold limped up and put a gloved hand on the cold,
greasy gritty skin. "Looks dead, alright, but we'd better tie off his
dominant carotid anyway. His right hand has the heaviest callouses.
Call the sharps committee."

Three dwarfs hesitantly left the group and inserted their
keys into the cabinet locks and opened the drawers. They carried the
tools to Arnold and stepped back. He walked around the body and
sliced into the left neck. A layer of muscle was separated...
uncovering a white, rubbery artery.

"Carotid has some gas and clots in it. The inner lining
is stained raspberry. This one's dead, alright---been dead for
a couple days." *muttered Arnold* he said tieing a thick ligature around the vessel.

Waving the crew of obese little nebishes forward he
ordered the body placed in the cooler for dissection.

"The Lab boys will be happy to see that one---and there's
be lots of good protein *left over,*" there too." he smiled.

Page from an early draft of The Godwhale

approved recreation even more risky than "tripping" on Molecular Reward is the Hunt for aborigines. Not only does the Nebish hunter stand a good chance of being killed by his quarry, but his inadequate physique is badly damaged in the chase by drug-stimulated exertion. The Hunt accordingly illustrates the ruthless way that Big ES uses its citizens, its callous treatment of the individual as expendable. The hardness of the Hive government in dealing with its subjects is seen also in the case of the retired. Like Drum and Ode in *The Godwhale*, the nonproductive senior citizen may have his pension suddenly frozen if the annual harvest is poor. The retiree is then forced to choose between suspension or one of society's most undesirable jobs.

The degenerate and all too often demonic Hive stands in sharp pejorative opposition in Bassler's novels to the relict primitive populations of five-toed Homo sapiens. These aboriginals in *Half Past Human* are land dwellers called "buckeyes." In *The Godwhale*, the primitives are termed "Benthics" and inhabit air-filled subaqueous domes in coastal waters (built by Big ES for recreational purposes and subsequently abandoned). Much of the life of the aborigines is negatively determined by the dominance of Earth's major land areas by Big ES and more narrowly by the ever-present danger of Hive hunters. Thus, the buckeyes lead an economically marginal and physically hazardous existence as raiders of Hive crops, as do the Benthics until their life is revolutionized by the return of Earth's marine biota. Due largely to their limited food supply and/or living space, the aboriginals are relatively few in number as compared with the trillions of Big ES. Moreover, the technology of the buckeyes is forced to remain for the most part at a stone-age level because metal artifacts could easily be spotted by the Hive's electronic detectors. The social organization of the land-dwelling primitives is likewise kept at a rudimentary level by the surveillance devices of Big ES and by the constant patrols of its hunters. These are more likely to detect a group, however small, than a solitary individual. Accordingly, even nuclear families generally do not exist among the buckeyes, the males as a rule being driven away by their mates after the conception of a child. Only on the remote and uncultivated summit of Mount Tabulum in the California Sierras does a small village of buckeyes exist. The Benthics are able because they are partially protected from Big ES by the sea to evolve a more sophisticated culture, but they too remain basically primitive. Thus, regarded superficially, the aborigines would seem to have been reduced by the Hive to the status of an unimportant side issue in human history.

However, the primitives are in fact of fundamental importance to man's future. Thus, in both *Half Past Human* and *The Godwhale*, there eventually takes place through the aborigines a rebirth of humanity from the degeneracy represented by the Hive. Such a renewal illustrates Bassler's belief that man's physical and instinctual life forms the basis for his higher nature, a healthy and vigorous body being necessary for a healthy and vigorous psyche (a truth exemplified negatively by the average Nebish). Because the buckeyes and Benthics have escaped the biological degeneration of the Hive dwellers, they likewise preserve the emotional, intellectual, moral, and spiritual capacities that allowed humanity to achieve greatness for a period before the decay leading to the Hive. Moreover, the conditions created by the Hive and its hunters have led to the survival of only the physically and mentally fittest of the aborigines, thereby maintaining and perhaps improving man's original endowments. The bodily and instinctual vigor of the buckeyes and Benthics together with the higher life that these produce are seen especially in connection with the full-blooded sexuality of the aborigines. In keeping with the physical vitality it expresses, the passionate eroticism of the primitives is inseparable from procreation. This is because the aboriginal females have evolved an estral cycle and are receptive only when fertile. Paradoxically enough, such an apparently animal level of sexual expression is in its very primitive power all the more effective in generating a specifically human psychic life. Thus, the reproductive urge arising from the estrus of the aboriginal females produces toward their mates a genuine and deep (if unenduring) love. Similarly, the primal sexual vigor of the aborigines is in good part responsible for the spiritual vitality that is manifested in their religious faith. Bassler underlines the connection between the erotic and the religious in aboriginal life through the buckeye shaman Hip. Not only does his name have obvious sexual overtones, but he derives his oracular powers from the testicular cyber Ball. The emotional and spiritual vitality which the primitive peoples derive largely from their instinctual energies are important among the human endowments that make them the vehicles of an eventual racial rebirth.

The antithesis in Bassler's novels between the racial degeneracy represented by the Hive and the enduring human potential preserved by the aborigines is connected with a plot motif important both in *Half Past Human* and *The Godwhale*. This is the exodus from Big ES and subsequent association with the primitives of a select few Hive dwellers who still retain at least some of man's original endowments. These capacities are carried by the five-toed gene, which has not yet been entirely bred out of all of the citizens of Big ES. In *Half Past Human*, the two most significant characters to leave the Hive are Tinker and Moses Eppendorff. Both belong to genetically engineered castes of skilled technologist-handymen who must to perform their duties retain abilities bestowed by the five-toed gene. Tinker's latent humanity is awakened through his sexual polarization by the Hive authorities. In keeping with the connection that Bassler sees between man's instincts and his higher psychic life, Tinker becomes through his burgeoning libido capable of deep feelings. He is soon involved in a monogamous love relationship with the polarized female Mu Ren, with whom he fathers an unauthorized child. When the infant is threatened by the Hive authorities, Tinker escapes with his family to the buckeyes of Mount Tabulum. There he finds true human fulfillment through his family life, and by expressing his creative gifts as a technologist and a craftsman. That Moses Eppendorff also retains the five-toed gene and its resulting human traits is indicated by a gesture of self-assertion contrary to Good Citizen attitudes. This is Eppendorff's naming after himself an economically valuable species of slime mold he has discovered. Subsequently, while Moses is on a mountain-climbing expedition, he encounters Old Man Moon, a member of the original human stock made virtually immortal by biological experiments with the aging process. Moses joins Moon and for a time lives with him the life of the buckeyes. In this connection, Eppendorff begins to realize through his loving sexual involvement with aboriginal females a spiritual "potency" later expressed in his role as a latter-day counterpart of the biblical Moses.

The thematic and narrative pattern of a Big ES citizen's retaining a human potential which he fulfills by leaving the Hive and becoming associated with the primitives is important also in *The Godwhale*. Thus, the Hive warrior ARNOLD possesses as a modified genetic copy of Larry Dever the latter's relatively pristine human endowments. It is accordingly not surprising that ARNOLD rebels against Big ES as a consequence of sexual involvement with the Benthic female White Belly. He then joins the aborigines. ARNOLD acts not only as a heroic defender in relation to the primitives (saving them from the depredations of the newly created Hive navy) but also as a patriarch, accumulating a harem of surplus Benthic females. In these ways,

the misdirection of ARNOLD's libido by the Hive is overcome, his sexual energies being channeled to positive human ends. ARNOLD's revolt from Big ES is paralleled in *The Godwhale* by the escape from the Hive of the warrior's "ancestor" Larry Dever, who once again becomes connected with the Benthics. The way in which characters in *Half Past Human* and *The Godwhale* realize their humanity by leaving Big ES and becoming variously linked with the aborigines constitutes a sort of rebirth that foreshadows the eventual rejuvenation of mankind through the primitives.

The opposition of the degenerate Hive to the aborigines with their potential for a racial renewal is central to Bassler's rather complex view of man's future. On the one hand, Big ES will undergo a slow but steady degeneration resulting finally in the extinction of Nebish humanity. The Hive will indeed remain relatively stable over millions of years and is even capable of minor resurgences, such as the building of an oceangoing navy in *The Godwhale*. However, these small-scale renewals cannot reverse an overall decline that is apparent in a number of ways. On a physical level, Big ES cannot keep up with maintenance and repairs, the decay of the Hive being manifested in the breakdown and wearing out of equipment, in the mounting piles of unfixable junk with which the shaft cities are littered. Intellectually speaking, Big ES is gradually losing both knowledge and the ability to retrieve its remaining information in a meaningful order. As a consequence, the Hive has suffered considerable scientific and technological regression from the peak period of human culture. Emotionally and morally, the decay of Big ES is manifested in an already terminal stage by the crowds of the shaft cities. These are completely lacking even in awareness of the individual person, let alone in compassion or responsibility for him. The emotional and moral deadness of the crowds in the Hive underlines how overall Big ES is moving inexorably to its demise.

In contrast with the Hive in its decline toward a final extinction, the buckeyes and Benthics become the vehicles of a historical rebirth for humanity. The potential for racial renewal inherent in the primitives is at once suggested and fulfilled in *Half Past Human* by the interstellar colonization vessel *Olga*. The spaceship was constructed at the technological high point of mankind's past civilization before its lapse into Big ES was well under way. As a product of such an important peak in man's intellectual and cultural development, *Olga* suggests the human capacities preserved by the aborigines, which will presumably be realized once again after humanity is rejuvenated. This renewal is effected by *Olga* with the aid of Hip and Ball, who together gather the scattered buckeyes. *Olga* then transports them (together with a quarter million five-toed cancer patients whom Toothpick has revived from long suspension and cured of their illness) to the planet Tiercel in the constellation Sagittarius. Here, the relatively small number of colonists are planted in scattered and somewhat primitive settlements on a world less hospitable to man than Earth. In such circumstances the new arrivals will for a considerable time at least be free from the negative effects of too great a population density and its concomitant "civilization." Bassler further implies that the relative adversity of the colonists' environment on Tiercel will creatively stimulate and challenge the innate competitiveness and adaptability of five-toed humanity. The combined result of these factors will be at least a temporary rebirth for mankind. Moreover, Tiercel does not represent the only hope for the future of five-toed Homo sapiens. As long as suitable worlds are available, humanity can continue to found new colonies, thereby effecting an indefinite succession of racial rejuvenations. In addition, aboriginal populations which preserve man's potential can survive on Hive-dominated planets like Earth. Thus, with some help from Gitar, a cybernetic servant of *Olga*, the terrestrial buckeyes replenish their numbers after *Olga*'s departure for Tiercel. While the resurgence of Earth's aborigines does not challenge the dominance of the Nebish, the primitives do contribute to humanity's renewal by providing *Olga* with suitable settlers for fresh colonies.

Bassler's view of man's future in *Half Past Human* implies a cyclical-organic vision of racial history as repeating indefinitely a rhythm which parallels the biological lifetime of the individual. Thus, human civilization on Earth has developed from a primitive "childhood" recalled by the buckeyes toward a maturity which, through the technological achievement represented by *Olga*, enables mankind to "reproduce" itself on other planets. Unfortunately, however, the very advancement of humanity on Earth has given rise to the conditions which bring about a decline of the race into the "old age" of Hive society. The rhythm just described will in turn presumably be reiterated for the foreseeable future by the extraterrestrial settlements.

There is in *Half Past Human* no indication of a cyclical recurrence of the racial lifetime on Earth itself. However, such an idea is implied in *The God-*

whale by a rebirth of man on his home planet. This rejuvenation takes place chiefly through the Benthics but also involves five-toed settlers landed by the gigantic spaceship *Dever's Ark* (a product of man's past technological achievements like *Olga* and possessing the same thematic significance), which has returned from a colonizing mission to Procyon. *Dever's Ark* likewise "seeds" Earth's now sterile oceans with their former biota, a renewal of terrestrial nature which at once parallels and makes economically possible humanity's renascence. Also important with regard to man's resurgence is *Rorqual Maru*, a huge plankton harvester built before Earth's seas became barren. Fighting together, *Rorqual* and ARNOLD save the Benthics from the navy of Big ES. The harvester also works along with ARNOLD and Larry Dever to establish and to foster five-toed populations on Earth's islands. Finally, *Rorqual* helps to effect mankind's rebirth by providing a secure home for the numerous family of ARNOLD.

As powerful and benevolent "cyberdeities," *Rorqual* and *Dever's Ark* are intended to suggest both the existence of a divinity who created the cosmos and also his beneficence toward man (that is, five-toed Homo sapiens, who must during the following discussion be clearly distinguished from the four-toed Nebish). God's loving regard for humanity is indeed so great that he has made his universe specifically as an abode for our species. Such a providential intention is revealed by the divinity's "signing" of his cosmic work with the formula $gy = c$ (in the case of a planet habitable by man, its gravitational acceleration expressed in meters/second^2 times its orbital period in seconds equals the speed of light in meters/second). It is particularly significant that $gy = c$ applied precisely to Earth itself at the very time humanity's prosimian ancestors emerged. For Bassler, this remarkable coincidence cannot be accidental. Rather, it is God's way of indicating that he has destined mankind to dominate first its home planet, and then the universe. Bassler's belief that humanity is its creator's chosen species does not of course lead the novelist to sanction the sort of racial aggrandizement exemplified by the Hive, which exercises a destructive tyranny over Earth's environment. Instead, Bassler sees man's cosmic ascendancy as properly involving a beneficent stewardship over God's other works. This idea is implied in *The Godwhale* by *Dever's Ark*, which preserves Earth's nonhuman life forms for propagation on other worlds.

Seen in historical perspective, Bassler's two science-fiction novels are most evidently outgrowths of the counterculture of the sixties. Both books illustrate the proclivity of that decade for various forms of dissent. For instance, Bassler's dystopian Hive reflects the widespread rejection during the sixties of the urban, industrial, and bureaucratic civilization of modern America. *Half Past Human* and *The Godwhale* were likewise obviously influenced by the environmental movement of the sixties, with its reaction against the despoliation of nature. Finally, Bassler's two novels register an indirect protest against the Vietnam War. Thus, certain of the methods used by Big ES in hunting the aborigines recall the procedures of the American army in Vietnam (for example, the employment by the Hive of electronic detectors and of aerial "huntercraft" that perform like helicopters). The elements of dissent that mark Bassler's novels as offshoots of the sixties grow in turn from an idealistic, religiously toned romanticism also characteristic of that decade. Such an outlook is seen in Bassler's depiction of the aborigines, which in large part represents a latter-day form of romantic primitivism, of the cult of the "noble savage." The "sixtiesh" aspects of *Half Past Human* and *The Godwhale* may now seem dated to the unsympathetic observer. However, as Marilyn Ferguson suggests in *The Aquarian Conspiracy* (1980), the counterculture of the sixties is still at work in America as a force for creative change. Both Bassler's medical work and his science fiction are very much part of the "aquarian conspiracy." As such, they may gain increased recognition during the 1980s.

AN INTERVIEW *with T. J. BASS*

DLB: What would you say are your one or two most important priorities as a medical practitioner?

Bass: My primary interest is the problem of aging. I was a deputy medical examiner for three years and got a very clear impression of what caused people to get old. So now I give life-style advice to try to prevent things like heart attacks, strokes, emphysema, and arthritis. We're pretty heavy into marathon running (family marathoning, which involves children and parents); sensible dieting, something your grandmother could make in the kitchen; and avoiding tobacco smoke, either primary smoking or a room full of secondary smoke.

DLB: What science-fiction writers have influenced you most or what writers do you most admire?

Bass: Well, I'm very poor on names. I read a story with no conscious effort to recognize who the author is because that could ruin it since I know so many personally. So the type of writer I enjoy is somebody who keeps the whole story in what I call "hard science"—he may be projecting into the future and postulating some hard-science advances, but he will not do anything that has to do with time travel and teleporting or anything that is obviously impossible. I don't have any special authors: I just enjoy real stories.

DLB: What do you think is the most important function of a science-fiction writer?

Bass: I don't have any opinion about that. I think that anybody who does anything in the fields of the arts should do what he wants to do, what he enjoys, and if he gives a second thought to what he's going to earn from it, either in terms of cash or popularity, then he ruins it by compromising in some way. So if you're talking about art, you have to separate it from business. What we've seen lately is a lot of combining art with business, and the result is really half-and-half and I don't enjoy it, so I can't endorse that type of activity, although it's probably getting very common. I think it was Ray Bradbury who once said he hated MGM and he hated Russia, but he hated Russia more because it's bigger. What he was referring to was the period when he "sold his soul" to advise. He was working on movies, and after a period of working "for money" in science fiction, he went back to try to create and found that he had lost a lot of his ability to create. Then he had to spend some time "purifying" himself and getting away from income problems of the art.

DLB: You have said *The Godwhale* (1974) is a religious novel. What is your religious background?

Bass: I think that *The Godwhale* is my personal effort at exploring proof of the deity in science, but it's a lighthearted effort, of course. I'm a Catholic, my family's Catholic, and we're very conservative Catholics, but I think when you sit down to write a hard science-fiction story about "deity," you have to capitalize some of them and use small letters for some of them, and you have to appreciate the relationship between humans and nature as being quite close to that between a human and a deity. So I'm not into supporting organized religion, because that again is like combining art with business.

DLB: Are you satisfied with the reception of your

novels by critics and readers?

Bass: Well, I'm not really too aware of that. I've been sent some reviews by fellows who really enjoy science fiction and they seemed to enjoy my work, but reviews don't seem to be related too much with being accepted by the market, which I really wasn't too concerned with, again because I write sort of because I have to write. It's not a business with me—it's more or less a hobby. So when I read something by a critic, it's because somebody sent it to me and then it's usually very, very good. I haven't read anything bad because the fellows who wouldn't like it probably didn't read it.

DLB: Do you have another major science-fiction novel underway since *The Godwhale*?

Bass: Well, I think we all have a few unwritten ones. I do have close to forty file drawers at home. Right now I'm really heavy into following some heart pa-

tients, about a hundred and eighty of them who have done marathons, and my family. Most of my writing and research concern the aging process in humans as affected by, not science so much, as by habits of eating right and running.

DLB: So you believe that science fiction is of secondary importance, for the time being at least?

Bass: Yes. It would be different if one of my editors cried a lot and pressed me. Then I might change the order of what I'm doing, but the way it is now I'm all fired up by the concept of small children starting out life-styles that may prevent them from suffering what we consider old age. This really excites me, because we've got about ten years of this type of life-style on a lot of neighborhood children who now are in college, and I'm observing them to see how they fare. And then we've got the heart patients running; there are a lot of them we're watching. It's really exciting.

—*John Ower*

M. F. Beal
(6 September 1937-   )

Ann Charters
University of Connecticut

BOOKS: *Amazon One* (Boston: Little, Brown, 1975);
Safe House (Eugene, Oreg.: Northwest Matrix, 1976);
Angel Dance (New York: Daughters, Inc., 1977).

The radical feminist writer M. F. Beal was born in New York City on 6 September 1937, the daughter of Edwin F. and Mary Peer Beal. She received her B.A. from Barnard College in 1960 and her M.F.A. from the University of Oregon in 1970, the same year that she began teaching writing and literature as an associate professor at California State University in Fresno. In recent years she has been living in Oregon, where she was a founding member of the Women's Resource Center of Lincoln County, Oregon.

M. F. Beal's first fiction, the story "Gloria Mundi," was published in the Barnard College magazine *Focus*. In the 1960s several of her stories were published in the *Atlantic Monthly* and the *American Review*, and in 1972 her work was included

in the annual *Best American Stories* volume. Beal became interested in writing short stories, she says, "for three reasons at least. The formal considerations provide a challenge in craft. Traditionally, the genre offers an opportunity for high quality communication. Nobody else was writing the short stories I thought needed to be written.

"Fiction attempts to satisfy a human hunger to experience life's events as connections in a larger scheme. We learn things we would not otherwise be likely to know about even those people we live with and we identify ourselves as human based on the models literature provides. Individual acts and transits which seem trivial nonetheless touch us all and the story is a sounding board whereon reverberations arrive from our lives and the fiction we have experienced. To read is to be involved in a uniquely private and at the same time immemorially collective activity.

"The form of the story—how it is framed, focused and revealed—is of utmost importance to me. I desire to present the material in a straight-forward manner so the reader does not become preoccupied with the method of exposition and my 'art,' and can move into the content freely with little thought how the construct was deliberately devised. All of this arises from desperation. There are human events which must find their way into our literature. The intrinsic pedagogic or affective 'worth' of events does not assure them a place in fiction, however, and there is only one person who can reveal what I experience in my life and observe in the lives of others."

The intense texture of Beal's fiction reflects her "desperation," her concern for documenting the conditions of violence that she observes pervading American society. *Amazon One* (1975), her first published novel, is a chronicle of a decisive month in the lives of a group of radical activists, the Weatherman Underground, in Berkeley, California, during the early 1970s and the subsequent breakup between the women and men in that organization. *Safe House* (1976) is a "Casebook Study of Revolutionary Feminism in the 1970's," feminist reportage of the last days of the Symbionese Liberation Army just before their shoot-out with the police in Watts, California, after the kidnapping of Patricia Hearst. *Angel Dance* (1977) is a detective novel about Kat, a lesbian Latina detective in love with her client Angel Stone. The hard-boiled narrative describes an odyssey through California scenes of rape and sadism that parallel larger conditions of brutality and oppression in American society: "When the rapist hissed *one more chance* he was being paramilitary for someone somewhere with his finger on the trigger of a bigger gun." The common theme of all these books is violence, "the conditions of American life which breed and approve of violence from domestic relations to foreign policy." Charlotte Mills's introduction to *Safe House* states her theme more specifically: "Women and violence—the most controversial and taboo subject in American society today." Other radical feminists, like Kate Millett and Marge Piercy, have written about women and violence in novels like *Sita* (1977) and *Vida* (1979), but neither communicates the passion and rage of Beal's fiction.

Amazon One is probably Beal's most accessible book. Its publisher, Little, Brown, awarded her the Atlantic Grant award, the first given in four years, as recognition of the novel's "literary merit" and its contribution to a little-known segment of our social history. *Amazon One* tells the story of a month in the history of a small group of Weatherman anarchists planning to bomb the Bank of America and other establishment buildings in the San Francisco-East Bay area. When their bombs explode in the basement of the house they are renting, killing three of the men, the women go into hiding to avoid the police, scattering to various places with friends and family on the West Coast and in New York City. The

M. F. Beal

desperate quality of their lives on the run is a menacing saga of encounters with hostile or unloving parents and untrustworthy friends, reliance on drugs for ragged stretches of endurance or euphoria, and a prevailing paranoia until the remnants of the group meet again at a demonstration on the Berkeley campus, and one of the women shoots a male survivor of the group believed to have set off the basement explosion. The lack of a larger ideological and social framework dooms the radicals at the start, especially since the anarchist women were powerless to change the male domination of the group. One of the heroines, Marina, thinks about an early lover, Mort, who introduced her to radical politics in 1960 in college in New York City: "She knew he was no Galahad and was ashamed for

Perhaps what he regretted the ~~most~~ *worst* was that he had
never been able to tell her the things which bothered him
~~worst.~~ *most.* Somehow it seemed, growing up, that he would either
be able to confide in his woman, or that he would not need
to if he couldn't. Yet it didn't happen that way in pra-
tice. For one thing, ~~the~~ women knew when you were having
trouble. They did not respect it in that they moved into
trouble like a storm into a vacuum. Sitting on the edge
of the bed, feeling lousy, *you* ~~could~~ look up to find your
wife's face, an expression of bewilderment on it, like
you didn't know who she was, or she didn't know who you
were, which was probably worse. Her lips, colored according
to the season, might in this kind of extremity seem like
the cloaca of some alien animal, her eyes might suddenly
resemble the eyes of a deer you killed the year before in
the woods, or conversely, like hawk's or tiger's or snake's.
Predatory, fascinated with your mortality, the eyes searched
while you tried to dredge even enough words to call the
spell, pick up your socks and put them on your ~~cold~~ pur-
pling feet so you could slide the lot into your boots and
get out on the daily road. To? Work, earn, come home
to the eyes, hers and the children's this time, they having
as much or more need of whatever it was he was supposed to
have/do. He could understand why his own father had been

— M.F. Beal, *FAMILY MATTERS*

"Family Matters," revised typescript

her innocence. He was a man, planning in full consciousness a thing he decided must be done, yet she felt honored he had picked her, as if that made her a woman. She realized utterly what he meant by 'revolutionary discipline' but she could never free herself from the knowledge she was *his woman* enough to protest the drudgery which fell when they began to live together: feeding of endless faces anykind of food she had been able to scrounge, the washing up, cleaning, endless bedchanges, trips to laundry. . . . She raged at Mort, demanding to be let out of the apartment to do some *real* work. And that turned into typing, proofreading, distributing informational material to delivery people, or running an angry letter of reply to an editorial in the student newspaper. And endless purchases of Chock-Full-O-Nuts coffee and wholewheat brownies To Go. Mort, Ross, the other steadies and a skinny, slight boy named Sol who looked like a rabbinical student, comprised the strategy and tactics group. She got one foot in the door while passing through food and drink; then it closed."

After the success of *Amazon One*, Little, Brown contacted Beal to do a story on the Symbionese Liberation Army, but as the manuscript of her book began to take shape, it became obvious that it was "neo-journalism," which Mills defines as different from conventional journalism in that it "denies any reporter's ability to be completely objective and defies any of the media to adequately translate to the public the complexities of any story." The manuscript, titled "Safe House," was returned by Little, Brown with apologies, the comments indicating that the text's implications of feminist leadership in the SLA and the manuscript's revolutionary and lesbian overtones were unacceptable for mass readership.

In answer, Beal wrote an essay, "What Men Fear," an analysis of what she thought was threatening about feminist politics to male establishment publishers. This essay was included with *Safe House* when it was published as the first book by the feminist press Northwest Matrix, which Beal helped to start in Eugene, Oregon. Mills wrote in her introduction to *Safe House*, "According to a *Journalism Quarterly* report, there are 560 feminist presses and publishing houses. Why have women started their own publishing network? One reason is the difficulty women have met in getting their serious work accepted through the establishment publishing houses. How high does the conspiracy

against women's literature go? It starts in the grade school classrooms and goes to the editorial penthouses of Madison Avenue." As a "Casebook study of Revolutionary Feminism in the 1970's," *Safe House* is both a description of the fiery last hours of the SLA in Watts and a collection of documents pertaining to the subject of women and violence, including "Exhibits" of quotations by such male revolutionary leaders as Gandhi, Mao Tse-Tung, Ché Guevara, and Malcolm X, as well as women revolutionaries such as Sarah Grimké, Emma Goldman, Susan B. Anthony, Rosa Luxemburg, Angela Davis, Monique Wittig, Susan Stern and Emily Harris. The book concludes with the SLA slogan, "You May Kill Revolutionaries, But You Won't Kill Revolution."

Beal's next book the following year was the detective fiction, *Angel Dance* (1977), whose lesbian heroine has adventures modeled on the popular mystery novels about hard-boiled California detectives. If she had the idea of using a detective novel to help spread her ideas about radical feminism (in the manner of Per Wahloo and Maj Sjovall, who collaborated on the highly successful series of Swedish mystery stories featuring the policeman "Martin Beck" to spread their ideas about radical socialism), then *Angel Dance* falls short of the mark; its affected narrative line is difficult to unravel and its characters are not sufficiently realized. The book is the weakest of Beal's efforts, since it is furthest from the kind of writing she does best: factual documentation of places and events, dramatic creations of scenes as in the vignettes about the Weatherman group in the opening chapters of *Amazon One*.

The novelist Lois Gould, writing on *Amazon One* in the *New York Times*, perceptively commented that "M. F. Beal . . . discovers both heroism and violence in women and makes the fatal connection—with love." Beal's three published books, despite her promising beginning, have been in three completely different literary forms, and it is too soon to assess her contribution to American literature. Nonetheless it is evident that she is one of the foremost documenters of revolutionary feminism in our time.

Periodical Publication:
"Joining Up," *Atlantic Monthly*, 218 (December 1966): 102.

Paul Blackburn

(24 November 1926-13 September 1971)

George F. Butterick
University of Connecticut

BOOKS: *The Dissolving Fabric* (Palma de Mallorca: Divers Press, 1955; Toronto: Mother/Island Press, 1966);

Brooklyn-Manhattan Transit (New York: Totem Press, 1960);

The Nets (New York: Trobar, 1961);

16 Sloppy Haiku and A Lyric For Robert Reardon (Cleveland: 400 Rabbit Press, 1966);

Sing-Song (New York: Caterpillar, 1966);

The Reardon Poems (Madison, Wis.: Perishable Press, 1967);

The Cities (New York: Grove, 1967);

In. On. Or About the Premises (London: Cape Goliard, 1968; New York: Grossman/Cape Goliard, 1968);

Three Dreams And An Old Poem (Buffalo: University Press at Buffalo, 1970);

Gin: Four Journal Pieces (Mt. Horeb, Wis.: Perishable Press, 1970);

The Assassination of President McKinley (Mt. Horeb, Wis.: Perishable Press, 1970);

Early Selected Y Mas: Poems 1949-1966 (Los Angeles: Black Sparrow, 1972);

The Journals, edited by Robert Kelly (Los Angeles: Black Sparrow, 1975);

Halfway Down the Coast (Northampton, Mass.: Mulch Press, 1975);

By Ear (New York: # Magazine, 1978);

Against the Silences (London & New York: Permanent Press, 1980).

Paul Blackburn was born in Saint Albans, Vermont, though he is most identified with New York City. M. L. Rosenthal, his most consistent academic champion, whom he succeeded as poetry editor of the *Nation* in 1962, called him "our finest poet of city life since Kenneth Fearing." Like Frank O'Hara, Blackburn had many friends, who sustained his reputation after his death. He worked tirelessly on behalf of fellow poets, setting up readings, providing an audience, and running a "Poet's Hour" on radio station WBAI in New York. One of his greatest contributions was to encourage the tape-recording of public readings. From Ezra Pound, who first brought him into contact not only with the medieval troubadours, but with poets of his

own generation such as Robert Creeley, Blackburn learned that poetry has to be served in the most practical of ways. His mother, Frances Frost, to whom he was devoted, was a widely published minor poet. Blackburn was known for his translations—of the troubadours, of García Lorca, and of contemporary South American writers such as Julio Cortázar. Since he was unassuming, his reputation suffered somewhat from the unavailability of editions of his own work: his long poem "The Selection of Heaven," which he considered a major work, has yet to be published. Cats, very much a part of his life, occur throughout the poems, although the gull was his totem. The speaker of his poems has a catlike personality, or, as he himself described it, "untrustworthy, independent." In an autobiographical statement written toward the end of his life, Blackburn said with typical modest good humor: "Poor fellow, tho a New Englander by birth, a Westerner by accident, and a New Yorker by trade, he is Mediterranean by adoption and lusts after French food, Greek wines, Spanish coñac, and Italian women. His tastes are broad and indelicate: he would gladly settle for Italian food, French wines, Spanish coñac and Greek women." He was married three times—to Winifred Grey McCarthy in 1954 (divorced 1963), to Sara Golden in 1963 (divorced 1967), and to Joan Miller in 1968, with whom he had a son, Carlos T.

Blackburn's first book was not a presentation of his own writing but a translation of selected Provençal troubadour poets, published by Robert Creeley's Divers Press in 1953. *Proensa* (literally, Provence) sets the tone for all of Blackburn's own verse, which is playful, colloquial, familiar, wryly sardonic, and melancholy, all about love and the immediate world. Following the stimulation and lead of Pound, with whom he corresponded, having encountered fragments of the troubadours in Pound's early *Cantos*, Blackburn undertook a study of Provençal at the University of Wisconsin, from which he graduated in 1950. He continued his studies and by 1953 was able to publish the small volume of a dozen translations with facing texts. Two further years of study and research at the University of Toulouse, made possible by a Fulbright scholarship in 1954, were followed by a stay in Málaga, Spain, and Bañalbufar, Mallorca—where living was less expensive—reading, translating, and making constant revisions. At the same time he was writing his own poems, which made their way into many magazines and small, interspersed collections. The basic work for the troubadour anthology was completed by 1958, although plans for a long introduction were interrupted by the dissolution of his marriage. He returned to the work repeatedly thereafter through the 1960s, revising, adding notes, seeking to perfect it. It was as complete as possible at the time of his death, after which his friend George Economou, a classicist and poet himself, prepared it for publication by the University of California Press.

Blackburn's translations sound very much like the street tradition common to the beat generation, or, in the words of the twelfth-century poet Arnault de Marueill, whom he quotes, "The open manner / which I cannot put from my mind." It was the music of the ubiquitous vernacular that he honored, although unlike Pound, his translations are decidedly on the side of speech rather than music. Robert Kelly writes: "Though he worked with all the resources of scholarship, his translations do not smell of the library; he caught the dance and brought it to new places." Translating the troubadours was a preoccupation that lasted throughout Blackburn's life, reflecting a set of attitudes he never abandoned (including a perhaps hopeless romanticism) and which served him as a touchstone, a source of guidance and refreshment. His fondness for cats, perhaps, was romanticism; smoking thickly scented Gauloises and Picayunes was certainly so (he died of throat cancer); and even his drinking, possibly. But his good fellowship, attested to by countless friends among poets, was not a mannerism; it was from the heart.

As a poet, Blackburn has been associated with Robert Creeley and Charles Olson (although they had very decided differences, which included open quarrels). His poems appeared with theirs in Cid Corman's *Origin*, and he also was published in three issues of the *Black Mountain Review*, so that he has sometimes been called a "Black Mountain Poet," although he never set foot on the college's grounds until long after its demise and lived beyond its sphere of influence for many years. His original loyalty was to Pound and then William Carlos Williams, and his ultimate identity was with urban living, especially in New York City. He did gain immeasurably from Olson's "Projective Verse" essay (1950) and was one of the most conscientious prac-

titioners of techniques it fostered, but he was more akin in spirit to Creeley and especially Williams. Finally, it was his own sense of steadiness and kindness, sad love and unique devotion, bright eye and a knowing wink that upheld his verse.

Blackburn's first book of his own poems, *The Dissolving Fabric*, had actually been ready for publication as early as 1952 but did not appear until 1955. The poems are characterized by the same directness and simplicity of diction as the Provençal translations—excellent poems such as "The Birds," "Committee," "The Assistance," "The Mirror," "The Search," and "The Return." Close to speech, they are not intricately wrought verbal icons. They are not heavily laden with images or decorative devices. The images are there when the poet needs them, however—"The lazy dragon of steam issues / from manhole cover"—but he is not primarily interested in poetic snapshots. There is a sense of confidence and control throughout, although, granted, the risks taken are not unusual. Despite an awareness of tension—"the trap of will / will trip it snap shut like brass"—the view is naturally placid. Blackburn appears to prefer the traditional simplicity of troubadour song or Pound's classicism, though without the startling or chiseled image. There are no gestures of extravagance, no surrealistic virtuosity or impacted symbolism. His is a personal, shareable poetry.

Blackburn's habit of adding extra meaning by way of the title is begun early. The poet seeks to dramatize by headings, as in "The Sudden Fear." More successful is "Committee," about his cats and the poet himself waiting for his beloved to come home, forming, with playfully exaggerated formality, the "committee" of the title. In "The Assistance," the commonplace—vulgar, in that sense—is teased out and hardly given away by the title. A man afoot in the city needs to relieve himself after a night's drinking. The narrator carefully and wittily refrains from naming the act outright, while still presenting the ready truth how "On the farm it never mattered . . . But in a city of eight million, one / stands on the defensive," until the resolution is reached:

> But in the shallow doorway of
> a shop on Third Avenue, between
>   the dark and the streetlight,
> it was the trail of the likewise drinking-man
>   who preceded me
>   that gave me courage.

Another fine poem in the volume, "The Search," intentionally or not, summarizes nicely

Paul Blackburn

Blackburn's poetics. A common hamster, "mammal and sure," serves as a metaphor for the poet, answering his quest for self-fulfilling meaning. A poem, like the mammal, must wear a "mixture of attitude": "sublime trust and disdain, careless, sure." Paradoxical as they may seem these are the qualities of the poet's own greatest success. Still another poem, "The Return," is a fable, the meaning of which grows more complex as it draws to its close. It is at least about the demands of poetry, the compromises expected of the poet by his art, but also the demands which love and society make. A poet, a cowboy, a western hero (there are later photos of Blackburn in a cowboy hat) returns to the "net" of society's "shaded streets," his achievement told in an image not entirely pleasant (the strain evident in the forced transitive "staggered"): "his love pinched / and staggered his ankles down thru the warm dust / to speech / casting at dice to buy his loss." The result—the net which has all along been an entrapment, the ultimate compromise and sacrifice of will, the inevitable necessity for uncertain commitment—becomes a constant theme for

Blackburn. One need only see "The Purse-Seine," the title of his subsequent book, or poems like "The Decision" in *Against the Silences* (1980).

In retrospect, *The Dissolving Fabric* is an entirely auspicious first book. Overall in the volume there is the sense of the craftsman who chooses to work in open patterns, not one pushed there by haste or disregard or by current fashion, not lured by laziness or pretense. Blackburn employs the metric of meaning: the words, and after them the phrases, the lines, are placed upon the page where they fall in speech and thought. They are not subjugated by preexistent form or subjected to a prior inspection of reason. Thus they are without traditional rhyme or reason, though not without a delicate metric of their own, the logic of natural necessity. Such a meter does not bind, subdue, or hold up the intention, but shares the occasion of it equally. Creeley and Williams, as well as Olson, have shown the way. Very often a Blackburn poem will have the same subject matter, and tone, even, of a poem by Creeley or Williams, but is allowed to hang looser on the page. His is not always the deepest wit, but a ready one, and just such obliquity of distinction is charactertistic of the poems as well. He lacks the musical preciosity, the insinuation and whiplike resolve of a contemporaneous Creeley poem. Rather, he proceeds at a less trying pace. Whereas Creeley conveys tension, intellectual control, and tightness in his musicality, Blackburn's line gives the impression of being relaxed—almost to the point of distraction and drift and almost, at times, inconsequentiality—although the needs behind them are no less meaningful than Creeley's deliberate anguish or Olson's thundering down the pike in a conveyance of his own devising.

Brooklyn-Manhattan Transit, which did not follow until 1960, is a book of only five poems, but superbly chosen ones. These include the classic subway poem, "The Once-Over," concerning the attentions drawn by a statuesque blonde standing in the center of the train, told in Blackburn's classic understatement, and the equally delightful "Clickety-Clack," a tale of a ride to Coney Island (during which the speaker reads aloud from a copy of Lawrence Ferlinghetti's collection *A Coney Island of the Mind* to his fellow passengers) and an encounter with "some girl sitting opposite me with golden hair," reported with an exquisite sense of timing and a comical use of traditional injunction:

Watching her high backside sway and swish
down that

street of tattoo artists, franks 12 inches long,
                                                             past
        the wax museums and a soft-drink
        stand with its white inside,
I stepped beside her and said: "Let's
fling that old garment of repentence, baby!"
    smitten, I
hadn't noticed her 2 brothers were behind me

    clickety-clack

    Horseman, pass by

(Although effective here in its own right, the final entreaty is also a playful literary allusion to Ferlinghetti's "Reading Yeats I Do Not Think.") Some of Blackburn's best poems, such as these two or the later "The Yawn" and "The Slogan," while not voyeuristic themselves, are about the visual stimulation offered by life casually encountered in the everyday movements of the city. Others, such as "Meditation on the BMT," are chastisements for living badly. The collection is subtitled grandly "a bouquet for Flatbush," and all the poems were written on or about travels by that specific New York subway line. They are like the newspapers one might read on such short trips between the boroughs; as popular and immediate as a city gossip column and as concise and full of wit as the best of cartoons.

With *The Nets* (1961) the poet enters realms more exotic and in some cases mythological, such as "Venus, The Lark Flies Singing Up . . ." and "The Vine . The Willow / Lurch To and Fro," both owing, like the later "The Watchers," directly to Robert Graves's *White Goddess* (1948). The poems in the volume were all written before those in *Brooklyn-Manhattan Transit*, during his stay on Mallorca (where in fact he met Graves) and shortly thereafter, upon return to New York and the dissolution of his first marriage. (Blackburn's books are not chronological in the usual sense.) Experience is diffused with a Mediterranean light, as in "Banalbufar . . ." where "The mind / is filled with flower smell and sun / even when sun is not." The structures also grow in complexity. Most successful is "The Purse-Seine," a poem praised by James Dickey ("a real poem, and all Blackburn's"), concerning the fatalism of love that encloses all. Clayton Eshleman finds it "a very strange poem—it feels like a masterpiece yet it also keeps its action at one remove so that at the end of it one has the feeling of not knowing what really happened. . . ." The purse-seine, a net that can ensnare entire schools of fish, is a fairly straightforward symbol. It is the love which binds.

The deepest professions of love, as the end of the poem suggests, may already be part of the trap. Images of danger abound, although as the poet points out in an interview, "none of the resistances are explicit in the poem. But there are lots of images of resistance in there. I've had a bad experience in love and had one marriage rocked on me and I'm afraid to get into another thing. I don't trust myself. I don't trust her or the incredible attraction that there is literally, physically, between two people. . . ." He is not content with pure description, though the poem begins magnificently so, its lines following the movement of representative gulls "flung by wind" and "hung" in the air before tuning. The lines ride out on the breath of the poet. In the last stroke of description, however, the gulls ride the wind as if it were a larger dimension, "the conditions of civilization" itself, which certainly love also is. But it is a soaring, rapacious love. And while the description itself is breathtaking, beyond is the bitter lesson of a man who knows better:

                        their cried falls, bitter
        broken-wing graces crying freedom, crying
                                            carrion, and
        we cannot look one another in the eye,
                that frightens, easier to face
        the carapace of monster crabs along the
                                    beach . The empty
        shell of death was always easier to gaze upon
        than to look into the eyes of the beautiful
                                    killer . Never
                look a gull in the eye

For a number of years the chief source of Blackburn's writing was *The Cities* (1967), although the published version contains less than half the poems Blackburn intended in his original manuscript. As the title anticipates, the poems shift between his home base of New York and temporary outposts like Barcelona and Málaga. The book itself, meanwhile, is composed carefully to relieve the reader's possible boredom: "The thing was to set up the volume in terms of a rhythm, so that the reader didn't get bored with too many of one kind of poem all in a row. My intention was not to put all the idea poems together and all the love poems together and all the hard object things together, but to keep a rhythm going among them that would be a kind of ground base. In other words, you can read that book from beginning to end and not get bored at any point with any particular kind of poem." It is a modesty and consideration typical of Blackburn, and he succeeds accordingly.

There are such admirable pleasantries as "The Unemployment Bureau," told like an Old World fable, and "The Game: 1960 Series," concerning the great American ritual of baseball, with its concluding pun, "Yanquis, come home," reflecting current politics as well. These are positive glimpses of the immediate environment. The poet is also capable, however, of the scathing denunciation of a satirical "Sirventes," authentic in its stinging tongue, with Blackburn himself a "maddened double" of the troubadour Peire Vidal: "Whole damn year teaching / trifles to these trout with trousers. . . ." More often there is the tender thoroughness of "The Tides," which presents the argument of human need for sexual love, concluding with the undeniable regularity of "What the man must do / what the woman must." This is followed by the poignancy of "Phone Call to Rutherford," a tribute to the stricken, stalwart William Carlos Williams. There is also the well-paced "laurel" written "For Mercury, Patron of Thieves," with its catlike sense of timing and sly wisdom, and again the timing of "Out" and "Hands," and the fulfillment of "The Routine." All these claim status for Blackburn as a significant poet.

Another special poem is "The Yawn," in which the speaker recalls the yawn of a beautiful girl on the morning subway to work and finds himself "yawning" both in fact and in retrospective marvel. It may be said to be as much about the artistic process, the transference of sensibility and suggestibility, as it is about the particular incident described.

Blackburn is an occasional poet, taking full advantage of the same "casual intensity" that Cid Corman observed he found in the cats with which he always surrounded himself. Corman, who published Blackburn's work in *Origin*, writes of his "love of the casual fall of language, in speech, the music of chatter, of cliche, a love of people talking . . . the words likewise jostling, falling upon a page. They are all only love songs." Blackburn's greatest loyalty is to common speech; his mastery is the same. There is no insistent beat, no closely held or tightly curled enjambment, no domineering, irreversible thunder of sounds. The risk is inconclusiveness and torpor, although timing and resolution are perhaps his principal concerns rather than depth of meaning or attractive surface patterning. The progression of his images is soft, mutable, easily yielding its consistency, although not a mere mixture or mess of metaphor, because in Blackburn's assured, laconic manner there is no sense that the responsibility for a poem's success falls more heavily on metaphor or any other representation than the subject in the act of telling itself. This is true whether in the intentional splicing of separate "tracks" (a term Blackburn favors, perhaps owing to his fondness for tape recorders) in "How To Get Up Off It," where a parallel is drawn between mountain climbing and the fluttering presence of pigeons in front of the New York Public Library, or in this exemplary passage from "For Mercury, Patron of Thieves":

> At dawn,
> all places equal :
> Athens, Paris, Brighton Beach and Arizona.
> The trap.
> The bear
> dies in the trap : Mercury too a thief,
> the cat's walk lives . The difference
> is feet

This depiction seems something of an excuse to lead the poet to his proper destination (there are no other mentions of bears before or afterward in the poem), achieved in the final stanza: "The sidewalks of spring / love us as we love them, no better, caress the feet / the way the feet press them. . . ." It is an image of the tension in balance which is also love. Grace and poise and productive resistance—the poet walks catlike but in no straight line.

Blackburn's next collection, *In. On. Or About the Premises* (1968), reflects the poet's commonly acknowledged loyalty to place. The volume is in two sections—poems written in New York's landmark McSorley's Ale House, which Blackburn was fortunate enough to have as his neighborhood tavern, and those written in a bakery-restaurant farther uptown, near Funk & Wagnalls, the encyclopedia publishers, where he worked for a time as a copy editor. Among the best of these works is "A Dull Poem," which is anything but. Dedicated to Louis Zukofsky, who lived in nearby Brooklyn, it is a meditative landscape, a camera's eye focusing on that slice of life observed within the bakery and without its window during lunchtime on Saturday—a brief natural history of neighborhood New York, unpretentious yet complete and flavorful. Told without artifice or borrowed drama, monotony, too, is part of the picture, as is the nonchalant but all-seeing eye of the poet, watching life in the street, as flames, ever moving, ever random, absorbing and fascinating.

Girlwatching, also, reaches its peak in "The Slogan," one of Blackburn's most perfectly constructed and delightful poems. Poems like these, describing the scene as work stops at a construction site while the men pause to appreciate a passing blonde, earned Blackburn a reputation of machismo. The volume concludes with "The Watchers," Blackburn's longest published poem, a meditation prompted by letters on the side of a construction company's crane leading to an association with an old Roman legend which Blackburn knew from Robert Graves's *The White Goddess*, about how Mercury invented the alphabet after watching the flight of cranes. That kind of pun, which Blackburn favors, was delightfully successful in "The Slogan," where the Consolidated Edison Electric Company's semiapologetic boast, "Dig We Must," familiar to every New Yorker as the city is perpetually transformed underfoot, is punned with "dig" in the more recent sense of "attend to"—in this case the "wellknit blonde" jiggling her way across the street. "The Watchers," using the pun as an opportunity, becomes a poem on the construction of civilizations, the information drawn from Graves freely intermixed cross-culturally with the on-the-spot observations of the poet as "sidewalk engineer." It becomes a cultural summarization of the sort familiar to readers through Olson's "The Kingfishers" or Robert Duncan's "Poem Beginning with a Line by Pindar," and has been praised by Rosenthal, among others, who comments that if "The Watchers" is any indication, Blackburn "is better able to sustain a long poem with a theoretical bearing akin to that of Olson's 'The Kingfishers' than any of his Black Mountain fellows, because [he is] better able to sustain a complex pattern of motifs without losing rhythmic and emotional momentum anywhere along the line."

Blackburn left behind at his death a great many uncollected and unpublished poems, and an effort has been made to make these available. *Early Selected Y Mas* (1972), the first of the posthumous volumes, reprints ephemeral earlier books and includes previously uncollected work. Among the latter, "The Continuity" from around 1953 can be said to set forth Blackburn's poetics as clearly and simply as anything he ever wrote more directly on the subject. Men in the street discuss a liquor store holdup; the poet writes it down, yet preserves all the character of the oral tale:

> Yeah? I was in there early tonight.

> The continuity. A dollar forty-
> two that I spent on a bottle of wine
> is now in a man's pocket going down Broad-
> way.

Thus far the transmission is oral.

> Then a cornerboy borrows my pencil
> to keep track of his sale of newspapers.

There is an irony involved, but one degree removed, so that the continuity—the poetic process itself—is preserved, even though the poet's attention is interrupted by the newsboy's request, thereby ending the poem. It is a perfect embodiment of Blackburn's sense of what a poem should be as he later stated it for the Paterson Society: "the poet must find and heighten his reality, make it / so exact that every reader will recognize himself / somewhere in the poem." Furthermore, the poet in making that reality "deduces the myth and sets it down, / so carefully attentive to the quality of the action, / the thing," that the reader actually "become[s] his poem for him."

The lure of love, his persistent theme, makes its appearance once again swiftly and graphically in the very brief "Venus," in language immediately accessible:

> This star, see,
> she comes up and leaves
> a track in the sea.

> Watcha gonna do, swim
> down that track or
> drown in the sea?

As if there were a choice! The star is evanescent, unobtainable, and beauty slays one way or another. The colloquial tone, somewhat rough, seems at odds with the classicism of the theme and the splendor of the visual image, but maybe not. With the addition of refrains, the poem could be a classic blues. Also in the volume is "Cabras" ("Goats"), Blackburn's most political early poem. In it he declares his independence from politics, celebrating neither democratic man nor Marxist man, and honoring not patient burros, who walk "very carefully, without resentment," nor sheep, who "die silently, pleading with their soft eyes," nor pigs, "who scream under the knife, and for a long while." He prefers the goats in the next field:

> The goats in the next field, however, are
>   hobbled,
> being otherwise difficult to catch,
>   they are so quick and stubborn
> and full of fun.

These are more true to the condition of poetic man.

Halfway Down the Coast (1975) is the slightest of Blackburn's posthumous collections, with few sustaining poems, mostly minor work written during a Guggenheim year in France and Spain in 1967 and 1968. There are occasional intermittent gleams such as two poems from the "Ritual" series, both subtitled "It Takes An Hour" (the second, "Ritual XVII," also to be found in *The Journals*), but most are uninspired, lacking in vitality, familiar in theme and manner. *By Ear* (1978) continues with previously unpublished work, poems of sensual experience and sexual praise, and an assortment of mostly observational commentaries, including a funny, irreverent dismissal of old bugbears: "Allen Tate, John Crowe Ransom, and / sixteen other writers of the southern school," entitled "An Instance of Criticism."

The last of Blackburn's posthumously published collections, before a comprehensive assessment which will yield a complete selected poems, is *Against the Silences* (1980). The manuscript had been kept separately in a looseleaf binder by the poet, although the title is publisher Robert Vas Dias's addition. The focus of the fifty poems, written between 1962 and 1968 in New York and Colorado where Blackburn had been poet-in-residence at the Aspen Writers' Workshop, is on the dissolving relationship with his second wife, Sara, which ended in divorce in 1967. Robert Creeley speaks of the painfully personal nature of the poems in his preface to the volume. Although some are simple praises of love and payings of respects, most concern sexual frustration and, progressively, jealousy, the despair of a Mexican divorce, and loneliness.

Some, such as "The Infield Hit," deal with private lovers' squabbles, but not all are that restricted. The depths of the poet's feelings toward his mother can be seen in the preliminary poem, "The Line," written on her dying of cancer, as he himself would die twelve years later. He writes in this unwittingly prophetic passage:

> Cancer grows in a womb where I grew once
> and swells as much.
> Only she carries death in her now . silent .
> will yield
> only to further silence / the skin
> stretches tight across her forehead
> as her father's did, as also mine someday
> will.

"Ritual VI" and "The Decisions" are among his best poems. If the theme of the book has been confined to a relationship, then these poems are about those choices which sustain relationships. The tightly controlled "Ritual VI" is a poem of perceptions which make a place for feelings. It begins with the attractive couplet, "Grids and lines / keep all our melting time." In his interview in *Contemporary Literature*, the poet expresses no sense of being threatened or overwhelmed by the "grids" of life, including the urban ones of streets and architectural angles. Here, the natural processes continue within man's limits and delineations: there is a thaw outside, "the roof dissolves under the sun / a map melting and changing like Africa / only it is snow and the continents shift." From the opening couplet, sounds link: "lines" and "time," now "shift" and in the next stanza "A *shimmer* hardly to be *shook* off." There is a regular transfer of pattern, whether from consonance to consonance, as above, or from perception to perception, as in the "shimmer . . . assails the birds" as the birds in their turn "assail the air." There is a transfer of energy, a natural continuance, maintained in the sounds that follow—from "assail" and "air" to "complaints." The delicacy of off-rhymes and linking assonance is masterful, reflecting the full inheritance of Blackburn's Provencal preoccupation.

In this world of natural harmony, the measure of love is kept. The poet turns from the world beyond the window, a world of rooftops and patterns of melting snow like maps of drifting continents, to a portrait of the beloved, sitting in the same sun within the room, and within her own lines:

> the sweet line of
> mouth, smoke rising, cigarette
>   moving with the hand
>   table to a mouth and down
> my fingers reach and trace the loving line it
>   makes at me. . . .

All leads to self-mockery in the classic manner, the happy irony of the question: "Who is this madman / who wishes for a subdued life of leisurely gestures?" It is himself, of course; a "madman" not unlike Williams's "happy genius" of his own household. The movement is from the objective world through feeling to ultimate self-awareness, from external perception to internal knowledge, from objectivity to the deeply subjective, from sight to insight: it is a well-constructed poem, without being hobbled by blind obedience to predetermined form.

"The Decisions," which follows, is not narrowly about the poet's relationship with his wife but, as the title implies, commitment itself. It ends with

22 July

Travelling ahead again
in my head again
which cannot know that I'm dead
again.

Besht, fathered, and Magnificuidly

am I?

People to talk to in these streets
delight me
Spicer I am not afraid,
Olson as gigantic cherub
garbed in nightgown thinking
Steve Jonas reeling trippily
for once in angel dust,

Kerouac writing the true novel
of the Golden Eternity on a
ribbonless typewriter, without
paper, never revising

Some time finally to talk with Dr.
Williams, tho it seems I stammer,
he don't

if you like it, we
like it too,
we cluded ē you

and I, beyond all likelihood, get
to that grove before Ezra, walk
abt saying, "I must prepare, I must
prepare."

Entry from Paul Blackburn's journal

the clear Zen wisdom that is also Yankee pragmatism: "You / Lift it, / I'll saw." In other cases, titles are intended to give a dimension to a poem that the poem in its own words does not already possess. Such is not always to the poem's advantage, as in "O Painters," or even "Collage" from 1964:

> Hand on her
> shoulder
> I kiss her, she
> grins her pleasure .
>
> Hand on my shoulder
> she kisses me as I
> kiss her . The consciousness
> is in the bodies now .

This is a perfectly balanced poem, far simpler and more natural than the title would allow, making it seem more a technique or a style than a natural evolvement, more art than truth. One case where

the title does contribute to necessary uncertainties, however, is "Getting the Call." Complexities are packed into its brevity:

> "Are you in the kitchen, honey?" she
>   calls.
>   from the livingroom.
> "I'm afraids o," I answer, not
>   quite noncommittal.
>   —Cooking what.
>   My own sausages.
>   like as not

Neither exactly petulant nor self-pitying, it is nevertheless bitter and ambiguous. All in all, a bit of psychological accuracy from the domestic arena, though whether a slight tremor of irony, or subdued rage, one can never be sure.

The Journals (1975) is the form Blackburn's work took in its final years, representing his writings from November 1967 up to six weeks before his death. The volume is what he promised when he summarized his poetics for the New American Poetry Circuit publicity brochure in 1970: "Sound counts. Total music counts. Large and inclusive forms are coming." Verse and prose are freely intermingled; prose passes in and out of poetry as the need arises, and visually there is no difference between the two on the page. Finding sufficient coherence and continuity in the open chronological form, Blackburn had assembled the manuscript himself, although it was later edited by poet Robert Kelly for publication. The day's occurrences might include typing a poem on a borrowed typewriter in a Barcelona bank, having to break the news to his wife that her father has just died, or giving elaborate directions to a friend how to reach his home in Cortland, New York, where he had been teaching at the state college since September 1970. Interspersed with journal jottings and identified as such are titled poems, many bearing the date of composition. The poem or entry titled "17.IV.71" is equal to Blackburn's best poetry. The fact that he is dying of cancer—mentioned briefly in the poem, but without a single trace of self-pity—makes it only the more poignant, as it ends:

> "Anything you want?"
>   she asks, heading out the door, leading
>   downstairs, get the bicycle out of the
>   cellar.
>   —No, nothing, thanks. The slacks are
>   brown, she is
>   carrying anything I want downstairs to
>   take it for
>   a ride on the bicycle.

The "anything" and "it" are perhaps the most intimate way the father can speak—or can dare speak—about the beloved two-year-old son he will shortly never see again, likewise his wife, the "she" in brown slacks that are almost a metonym—so intimate and familiar she can be summarized by such details—a simple pronoun, a "third person singular," very singular. So complete is the coming loss that the objective and matter-of-fact is the only way to spare them all. The poet has checked his language and his feelings, but the reader shares the pang.

The final assessment of Blackburn's achievement will come when his collected poems or complete selected poems are assembled—considerably higher than the present poetry world realizes, somewhat less than his friends would have. Paul Blackburn is not major (few poets are), but he is

indispensable. He knew the ways of men and how they spoke. No poet is great by his ear for speech alone, but Blackburn does touch our most human chords, and for that we will not forget him.

Translations:

Proensa (Palma de Mallorca: Divers Press, 1953);

The Cid (New York: American R.D.M. Corporation, 1966);

Julio Cortázar, *End of the Game and Other Stories* (London: Collins, 1968; New York: Pantheon, 1967);

Pablo Picasso, *Hunk Of Skin* (San Francisco: City Lights, 1968);

Cortázar, *Cronopios and Famas* (New York: Pantheon, 1969);

Peire Vidal (New York & Amherst, Mass.: Mulch Press, 1972);

Antonio Jiménez-Landi, *The Treasurer of the Muleteer and Other Spanish Tales* (Garden City: Doubleday, 1974);

Guillem de Poitou: His Eleven Extant Poems (Mt. Horeb, Wis.: Perishable Press, 1976);

Proensa: An Anthology of Troubadour Poetry (Berkeley: University of California Press, 1978);

Lorca/Blackburn: Poems of Frederico Garcia Lorca Chosen and Translated by Paul Blackburn (San Francisco: Momo's Press, 1979).

Periodical Publications:

"Das Kennerbuch," *New Mexico Quarterly*, 23 (Summer 1953): 215-219;

"A Sad Story," *Black Mountain Review*, 5 (Summer 1955): 193-201;

"Writing for the Ear," *Big Table*, 4 (Spring 1960): 127-132;

"The International Word," *Nation*, 194 (21 April 1962): 357-360;

"The American Duende," *Kulchur*, 7 (Autumn 1962): 92-95;

"The Grinding Down," *Kulchur*, 10 (Summer 1963): 9-18.

Interviews:

David Ossman, *The Sullen Art* (New York: Corinth Books, 1963), pp. 22-26;

"Craft Interview with Paul Blackburn," *New York Quarterly*, 2 (Spring 1970): 9-14;

"An Interview with Paul Blackburn," *Contemporary Literature*, 13 (Spring 1972): 133-143.

Bibliography:

Kathleen Woodward, *Paul Blackburn: A Checklist* (La

Jolla: Archive for New Poetry, University of California at San Diego Library, 1980).

References:

Paul Carroll, "Five Poets in Their Skins," *Big Table*, 4 (Spring 1960): 133-138;

Paul Christensen, *Charles Olson: Call Him Ishmael* (Austin: University of Texas Press, 1979), pp. 194-198;

Cid Corman, "Paul," *Sixpack*, 7-8 (Spring-Summer 1974): 105-109;

Michael Davidson, " 'By ear, he sd': Audio-Tapes and Contemporary Criticism," *Credences*, new series, 1 (1981): 103-118;

Fielding Dawson, "A Little Memoir of Paul Blackburn," *Sixpack*, 7-8 (Spring-Summer 1974): 112-116;

James Dickey, "Toward a Solitary Joy," *Hudson Review*, 14 (Winter 1961-1962): 607-613;

Clayton Eshleman, "The Gull Wall," *Sixpack*, 7-8 (Spring-Summer 1974): 761-773; reprinted in his *The Gull Wall* (Los Angeles: Black Sparrow, 1975), pp. 37-49;

Eshleman, "A Mint Quality," *Boundary 2*, 2 (Spring 1974): 640-648;

Ross Feld, "It May Even All Be Alright," *Parnassus*, 2 (Spring-Summer 1974): 73-86;

Stephen Fredman, "Paul Blackburn The Translator," *Chicago Review*, 30 (Winter 1979): 152-156;

Annalisa Goldoni, "La Poesie di Paul Blackburn," *Studi Americani*, 15 (1969): 383-394;

Lee Harwood, "Second Thoughts on Paul Blackburn's THE JOURNALS...," *Poetry Information*, 17 (1977): 36-37;

William Heath, Review of *The Journals*, *Open Places*, 23 (Spring-Summer 1977): 55-57;

Seymour Krim, "See You in Hell, Later, Paul Blackburn," *Evergreen Review*, 95 (Fall 1972): 18-21;

Eric Mottram, "The Ear and Muscle under Music," *Sixpack*, 7-8 (Spring-Summer 1974): 182-199;

M. L. Rosenthal, *The New Poets* (New York: Oxford University Press, 1967);

Rosenthal, "Paul Blackburn, Poet," *New York Times Book Review*, 11 August 1974, p. 27;

Rosenthal, *Poetry and the Common Life* (New York: Oxford University Press, 1974), pp. 40ff.;

Sixpack, special Blackburn issue, 7-8 (Spring-Summer 1974);

Gilbert Sorrentino, "Paul Blackburn (1926-1971)," *Sixpack*, 7-8 (Spring-Summer 1974): 242-244;

Sorrentino, "Singing, Virtuoso," *Parnassus*, 4 (Spring-Summer, 1976): 57-67;

Michael Stephens, "Common Speech & Complex Forms," *Nation*, 223 (4 Septembr 1976): 189-190;

Robert Vas Dias, "THE JOURNALS by Paul Blackburn," *Poetry Information*, 17 (1977): 38-39, 106.

Papers:

Blackburn's papers and his extensive tape collection are in the Archive for New Poetry, the University of California at San Diego Library.

Ben Bova
(8 November 1932-   )

J. D. Brown
University of Oregon

SELECTED BOOKS: *The Star Conquerors* (Philadelphia & Toronto: Winston, 1959);

The Milky Way Galaxy: Man's Exploration of the Stars (New York, Chicago & San Francisco: Holt, Rinehart & Winston, 1961);

The Weathermakers (New York, Chicago & San Francisco: Holt, Rinehart & Winston, 1967);

Star Watchman (New York, Chicago & San Francisco: Holt, Rinehart & Winston, 1968);

Out of the Sun (New York, Chicago & San Francisco: Holt, Rinehart & Winston, 1968);

The Dueling Machine (New York, Chicago & San Francisco: Holt, Rinehart & Winston, 1969);

In Quest of Quasars: An Introduction to Stars and Starlike Objects (New York: Collier, 1969);

Escape! (New York, Chicago & San Francisco: Holt, Rinehart & Winston, 1970);

The Fourth State of Matter: Plasma Dynamics and Tomorrow's Technology (New York: St. Martin's, 1971);

THX 1138 (New York: Paperback Library, 1971);

Exiled from Earth (New York: Dutton, 1971);

The New Astronomies (New York: St. Martin's, 1972; London: Dent, 1973);

Flight of Exiles (New York: Dutton, 1972);

As on a Darkling Plain (New York: Walker, 1972);

Forward in Time (New York: Walker, 1973);

When the Sky Burned (New York: Walker, 1973);

The Winds of Altair (New York: Dutton, 1973);

Gremlins, Go Home (New York: St. Martin's, 1974);

Workshops in Space (New York: Dutton, 1974);

Survival Guide for the Suddenly Single, by Bova and Barbara Berson (New York: St. Martin's, 1974);

Notes to a Science Fiction Writer (New York: Scribners, 1975);

Science–Who Needs It? (Philadelphia: Westminster, 1975);

The Starcrossed (Radnor, Penn.: Chilton, 1975);

End of Exile (New York: Dutton, 1975);

Through Eyes of Wonder: Science Fiction and Science (Reading, Mass.: Addison-Wesley, 1975);

Millenium (New York: Random House, 1976);

The Multiple Man (Indianapolis & New York: Bobbs-Merrill, 1976);

City of Darkness (New York: Scribners, 1976);

The Seeds of Tomorrow (New York: McKay, 1977);

Colony (New York: Pocket Books, 1978);

Kinsman (New York: Dial, 1979).

As essayist, lecturer, novelist, and consummate editor, Ben Bova is a leading spokesman for expanded scientific research and the application of new technologies to solve present and future problems. He has argued his case in a series of distinguished science books and science-fiction novels for young adults and perhaps most forcefully as editor of *Analog Science Fiction/Science Fact* and *Omni* magazines. His recent speculative novels, moreover, are succinct, dramatic expressions of his optimistic vision of man's extraterrestrial destiny.

Ben Bova was born in Philadelphia in 1932 to Benjamin and Giove Caporiccio Bova. As a teenager in Philadelphia, he often traveled to the Hayden Planetarium in New York and developed a keen interest in astronomy. However, feeling that his lack of mathematical ability precluded a career in science, Bova pursued a degree in journalism at Temple University, which he received in 1954, and he worked as editor-reporter on the *Upper Darby News* from 1953 to 1956. While covering the politics, personalities, and scandals of the time, he met members of the aerospace community, which soon led to his first position in the scientific field. As a technical writer for the Martin Aircraft Company in Baltimore, he translated the data of the Vanguard Project into readable prose. In 1958, Bova accepted a position at the Massachusetts Institute of Technology, where he worked with leading scientists to write the screenplays for an outstanding series of instructional films produced by the MIT Physical Sciences Study Committee. In 1960 he moved on to the Avco-Everett Research Laboratory, first as a science writer, then as manager of marketing until 1971. At Avco-Everett Bova dealt with research, often classified, on new technologies, including laser applications. During this period he became a member of the American Association for the Advancement of Science, the National Association of Science Writers, and later a charter member of the National Space Institute. A skilled explicator and proponent of scientific research, Bova had a special interest in the American space program, which he had advocated even before Russia's Sputnik pushed it into high gear.

While working with scientists in the 1960s, Bova also established himself as a significant writer for younger readers. His first book, *The Star Conquerors* (1959), is a science-fiction novel for the young, as is his most popular work, *Escape!* (1970). As a science writer of nonfiction for young adults, however, Bova has been even more prolific and successful. He has written on such topics as reptiles, magnetism, quasars, weather control, and lasers. Two of his science fact books, *The Milky Way Galaxy* (1961) and *The Fourth State of Matter* (1971), were honored by the American Library Association as among the best such works of the year.

During this time Bova also contributed a number of short stories—the best collected in *Forward in Time* (1973)—to science-fiction magazines. When John W. Campbell died in 1971, Bova was the ideal choice to assume the editorship of *Analog* magazine. With an extensive background in science fact and science fiction, Bova was able to maintain the balance between speculative science and speculative fiction which Campbell had established. At the same time, Bova left his own distinctive stamp on *Analog*, which became the leading science-fiction magazine of the decade under his tenure. He granted more license to his writers on sexual topics; more significantly, he broadened the range of speculative fiction appearing in the magazine and heightened its quality. Bova's principle of selection was his belief that imaginative fiction had a special mission: to put a human face on the skeleton of a scientifically plausible future. He defined science in a general manner, including anthropology as well as astrophysics. For six consecutive years, 1973-1979, Bova received the Hugo Award for science fiction for best editor in his field.

Although an extremely dedicated editor, Bova eventually tired of *Analog*'s format and its apparently insurmountable identification as a magazine out of the mainstream. He resigned in 1978 to pursue his own writing but was soon convinced by the owner of *Penthouse* magazine to become, on a temporary basis, fiction editor of a new periodical, tentatively titled "Nova." The magazine, eventually called *Omni*, was not to be a "*Penthouse* in outer space," but a serious, mainstream magazine of science fiction and science fact. *Omni* was an attractive project to Bova, an opportunity to capitalize on the increasing interest in science fiction and present new developments in scientific technology to a mass audience. The present circulation of *Omni* is close to

one million, yielding a readership of some five million monthly. Bova is now executive editor of the magazine, overseeing its every aspect. Long believing that scientists and technologists have failed to make a strong case for the benefits of their research and that such discoveries and applications are the only realistic means to solve the mounting problems of life on the planet, Bova has made *Omni* a popular, distinguished forum in which to analyze and proliferate these views.

Bova's own creative fiction does much the same but in a more dramatic form. Actually, only a few of the fifty titles Bova has published over the past twenty years qualify as serious speculative narratives. Besides the popular science books and novels for young readers, Bova has written such diverse volumes as a hasty novelization of a screenplay by George Lucas and Walter Murch, *THX 1138* (1971); *Survival Guide for the Suddenly Single* (1974), a treatise on divorce in which Bova's chapters on that topic alternate with those by Barbara Berson, whom he later married; *The Starcrossed* (1975), a wild satire of television and Hollywood based on Bova's misadventures with Harlan Ellison during a doomed TV series; and *The Seeds of Tomorrow* (1977), an extended essay detailing the scientific and technological remedies now available for such problems as overpopulation and declining

Ben Bova

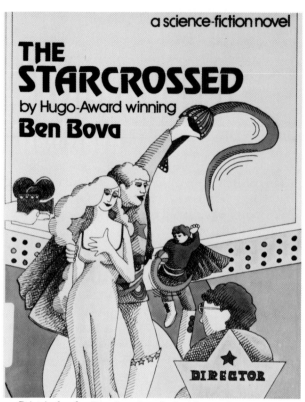

Dust jacket for Bova's satire of television and Hollywood

energy sources. These and other diverse works, however, have not kept Bova from an active career as a novelist. *Millenium* (1976), *Colony* (1978), and *Kinsman* (1979) are fine imaginative works, soundly crafted, entertaining narratives of adventure and idea, addressing political, moral, and technological topics from the standpoint of civilization's probable future. Bova's goal as a novelist is the same as his goal as an editor, which can be traced to his intent as a science writer in the aerospace industry years earlier: to convince the skeptical that proposed research programs result in gains in knowledge which ultimately yield enormous practical benefits. His science fiction is distinctive for its use of plausible advanced technology and convincing projections of imminent geopolitical disintegration—as well as the argument that it is the development of space which can solve the problems that the earth now faces. Bova's fictions are therefore set in the near future. Current political and economic problems are stretched to the breaking point. The essential struggle is between those who hold on to the traditional, but inadequate solutions of today and those who push for the colonization of space. Mankind's savior in this epic confrontation is usually a believable (because fallible and complex) individual who

fulfills the wish for a better future.

In *Kinsman*, Bova creates a hero for the space age, Chet Kinsman, an astronaut who becomes a leader of the future. Kinsman is in some ways a projection of the author himself. Both are from Philadelphia, both have fencing as a hobby, and both are more inclined toward politics than swashbuckling. (Chet Kinsman has been a figure of Bova's imagination since the late 1940s, the central character of many of his short stories, the young hero of *Kinsman*, and the older hero of *Millenium*. Both novels are more concerned with politics than adventure.) *Kinsman* details the intricate political maneuvers required to establish an American base on the moon. At the same time, it records its hero's journey from innocence to experience. Raised a Quaker, Kinsman is haunted by a murder he committed in space while on a military mission. The victim was a young female Russian cosmonaut. The year is 1999, and Kinsman is in charge of the American base on the moon. The American base is linked by passages to the nearby Russian base, and residents of both have transcended the confines of nationalism which have driven the nations of the earth to the brink of war. Earth, "choked by too much population and too few resources," must face increasing competition for its energy reserves. The arms race has accelerated and entered a new orbit—American and Russian satellites are fitted with nuclear weapons. The novel is a countdown to doomsday, which is averted only when the American and Russian moon bases unite, declare independence, seize the network of military satellites, and enforce a worldwide truce.

The psychological and political conflicts of this situation are treated more fully in the sequel, *Millenium*. While *Millenium* is a melodramatic work—one man saves the world against great odds—it is Bova's most taut, absorbing novel, a deft and convincing blend of geopolitics, space technology, and complex human actions. It does not simply argue that the colonization of space will solve today's pressing problems; it demonstrates that this process is not simple, nor is it without a price. The bright future will require revolution, and perhaps blood, and its toll will be human and individual as well as broadly political and cultural.

Essentially, *Kinsman* and *Millenium* are narratives of a likely future in which the disease of nationalism, the decay of the cities, and the depletion of natural resources precipitate the collapse of present social and economic systems. The new order of civilization is born in space and is restorative. As individuals are allowed to explore a new frontier, a freer and more productive empire begins, a second chance, perhaps, for pioneers to create a more perfect New World in fact as well as vision.

This quest and its attendant themes are also treated in *Colony*, Bova's best-selling novel to date. Although hastily composed to meet the publisher's demand for the "first novel of colonies in space," it is the author's grandest and most detailed narrative exposition. The novel chronicles eight months of Earth's turbulent history in 2008 A.D. as seven billion inhabitants tremble on the brink of cataclysm. The "gray authoritarianism and sameness" of a world government is attacked on two major fronts—one headed by multinational corporations which fear they will be put out of business, the other headed by violent revolutionary groups dedicated to fomenting the collapse of a desperately overcrowded, impoverished world. None of these groups possesses a sufficiently deep, workable vision of the future to save the planet; but the novel champions a fourth possibility—enlightened technology, represented by *Colony One*, a space vehicle constructed from lunar materials, large enough for millions of colonists in space orbit. The

Dust jacket for the first of Bova's Chet Kinsman novels

argument of the book is that such extraterrestrial labs are man's best hope, that the key to Earth's survival is dispersal of its population throughout the solar system. *Colony One* is a first step. It will be followed by many self-contained space communities which make use of the untapped raw materials and energy sources in space, supplying Earth with the basic needs which overpopulation and political conflict deny and thereby averting the disasters Bova and many others foresee. With a full, unrelenting commitment to space exploration and technologies, the human race can not only survive but prosper.

Colony presents a convincing view of the future by departing only slightly from the conditions of the present. *Skylab* and the space shuttle are not far removed from the satellite colony that Bova imagines: today's political events resemble the violent revolutionary actions, hostage takings, and corporate interventions in political developments which the novel portrays; and the poverty, overpopulation, and energy and resource depletion of the near future hardly seem exaggerated. In effect, *Colony* is a complex narrative argument for technological development and space exploration. The events and characters are an imaginative translation of Bova's essays and science books over the last two decades. The writing is straightforward and concise, and the marriage of action and argument in an epic narrative of plausible scientific advance pays homage to the writer who Bova feels influenced him the most, Robert Heinlein.

Ben Bova is an articulate man of extraordinary wit and vigor, a tireless exponent of the view that science can supply—in fact, has already supplied— the answers to the perplexing questions of man's survival. Insisting that the planet can become an Eden if man makes a concerted effort to colonize and exploit the deeper reaches of space he has already opened up, envisioning industrial production, energy creation, and waste disposal handled safely and efficiently elsewhere, he speaks of Earth as a potentially rich and pleasant "residential zone" of the solar system.

The possibility not simply of a future for man, but of a glorious future, has driven Bova to special achievements on many fronts—technical writing, science writing, lecturing, imaginative narrative, and editing. His angle of vision is a consistent projection of the present into the future. From this standpoint, he is obliged to press the limits imposed from many quarters. Not the least of these restrictions is the label publishers, critics, and audiences usually confer on him—science-fiction writer. As editor of *Omni*, Bova has begun to dissolve the narrow and confining distinctions between speculative and mainstream ideas. A major statement on scientific fact and the future, aptly titled *The High Road*, will be published soon. A mainstream novel is in the works, one which Bova hopes will not be summarily sentenced to the science-fiction-only shelves of the nation's bookstores. Bova has consistently pushed beyond formal restrictions and sought new forms to render in human terms the potential meaning and experience of science in the future, a bright, humane future, as opposed to the dark collapse of civilization which Bova regards as inevitable if we refuse to pursue fully all the new avenues of scientific research and technological application.

Other:
The Many Worlds of Science Fiction, edited by Bova

(New York: Dutton, 1971);
Analog 9, edited by Bova (Garden City: Doubleday, 1973);
The Science Fiction Hall of Fame, edited by Bova (Garden City: Doubleday, 1973);
The Analog Science Fact Reader, edited by Bova (New York: St. Martin's, 1974);
Analog Annual, edited by Bova (New York: Pyramid, 1976);
Aliens, edited by Bova (London: Futura, 1977);
Exiles, edited by Bova (London: Futura, 1977);
The Best of Analog, edited by Bova (New York: Baronet, 1978).

Papers:
Bova's papers are in the David C. Paskow Collection of the Temple University Libraries, Philadelphia.

Jerry Bumpus
(29 January 1937-   )

Sinda J. Gregory and Larry McCaffery
San Diego State University

SELECTED BOOKS: *Anaconda* (Western Springs, Ill.: *December* Magazine, 1967);
Things In Place (Fiction Collective, 1975);
The Worms are Singing (Ellensburg, Wash.: Vagabond Press, 1979);
Special Offer (Pomeroy, Ohio: Carpenter Press, 1981).

"Small things hide whole mysteries," says the narrator of Jerry Bumpus's wonderfully unsettling story "Our Golf Balls." In a body of work which includes one novel, *Anaconda* (1967), two collections of stories, *Things in Place* (1975) and *Special Offer* (1981), and dozens of uncollected stories, Bumpus plunges his readers into the mysteries of ordinary life. He is occasionally funny and whimsical, but more often startling, disquieting, even frightening, in a manner which may bring to mind Franz Kafka, William Faulkner, or Luis Buñel. Ranging from vivid naturalistic renderings to highly experimental approaches which break down the interface between reality and illusion, the waking and dream worlds, the various strategies of Bumpus's fiction are designed to strip away the comforting, civilized layers of human personality in order to force a

confrontation with the fantastic, irrational, animalistic aspects of ourselves which we normally keep hidden. Almost completely ignored by critics and the public during the first fifteen years of his career, Bumpus's work gradually began to be recognized and admired during the latter part of the 1970s as his stories were gathered into collections and his fiction began appearing in such journals as the *Partisan Review* and the *Paris Review*.

Jerry Bumpus was born on 29 January 1937, the son of Carl and Opal Gibbs Bumpus. He grew up in Mount Vernon, Illinois, a rural farming community in the south-central part of the state whose fortunes began to decline during the Depression when the railroad service to the area was discontinued. His father was a part-time operator of a grocery store, and although Bumpus's family suffered no real financial hardships during the late 1930s, he was witness at an early age to deprivation and hunger. This rural atmosphere with its own peculiar language, mythology, mood, and sense of isolation and futility would work its way into the fabric of nearly all of Bumpus's fiction. In 1945 when Bumpus was eight, his father was killed in the Battle of the Bulge, a traumatic experience which undoubtedly contributed to another of his major fictional motifs: the violent, destructive nature of an indifferent universe which constantly threatens to disrupt human relationships and mocks our efforts to find love and understanding.

After the death of his father, Bumpus's mother remarried. Theirs was not a particularly literary household, but Bumpus recalls that his Uncle Zip Clinton read and passed along to him *For Whom the Bell Tolls* and *The Old Man and the Sea*; these books, as well as *From Here to Eternity*, got him interested in literature at an early age. When he was twelve, his parents gave him for Christmas a Royal typewriter, which he would keep for twenty years, and although James Jones's character Robert E. Lee Prewitt had inspired him to become a soldier, he began to write as well. When he was sixteen, his family moved to Saint Louis, where he finished his last year of high school. By this time, his stepfather had convinced him not to pursue an army career, and in the summer between his junior and senior years of high school, Bumpus wrote his first novel, a book about the trials of a traveling salesman. Partially due to the encouragement of his high school English teacher—who had also interested him in the works of William Saroyan—Bumpus entered the University of Missouri in 1954, where he studied writing under William Peden and Thomas McAfee. He received his B.A. degree in 1958 and his first rejection slip—a note from Jarvis Thurston at *Perspective* informing him that his story "had no literary merit whatsoever." His parents were very supportive, however, and urged him to continue his writing. In the fall of 1958 Bumpus entered the University of Iowa Workshop, where he worked with Vance Bourjaily and eventually received his M.F.A. degree in 1960. After staying in Iowa City to teach part-time at the workshop, Bumpus took a position in the fall of 1961 in the English department at Northern Arizona University at Flagstaff. He had met Bettie McShane in Iowa City, and after their marriage in 1961 Bumpus and his family (which soon included two daughters, Margot and Prudence) began an odyssey which would take them to such places as the Canadian Academy in Kobe, Japan (1962-1963), Midwestern University in Wichita Falls, Texas (1963-1966), the Colorado School of Mines in Golden (1966-1967), Eastern Kentucky University at Richmond (1967-1968), Eastern Washington State College at Cheney (1968-1971), and finally to San Diego State University, where Bumpus is now a professor of English.

During this decade of constant moving and relocating, Bumpus also had his first stories published (mostly in *December*, a magazine published in Western Springs, Illinois) and his first novel, *Anaconda* (also published by *December*, as a special issue in 1967). Bumpus's early fiction was influenced by Faulkner and Nelson Algren, both of whom he had read extensively during his school years, but even these first works of fiction reveal a literary imagination not easily categorized. Like many other writers whose forms are nontraditional and whose subject matter resists paraphrase, Bumpus has had frustrating, often disheartening experiences trying to get his work published. For instance, although he wrote at least a dozen novels during the 1960s—and abandoned numerous other projects—the only book he had accepted during that period was *Anaconda*, and it was published in a small magazine only after he had received rejection notices from twenty-four publishers. In an interview conducted as part of a *Chicago Review* essay dealing with the Fiction Collective, Bumpus explained why editors at major publishers and magazines have rejected his work so consistently; speaking of *Anaconda*, he notes: "Several of them [editors] said that it just wasn't the kind of book that would have a wide enough appeal, that it wouldn't sell even though they personally liked it. Some also said they felt it was a little 'too grim, too morbid.'" Speaking of his lack of success with popular magazines, he adds: "I've published with *Esquire*, but that's the only one I've had any luck with. I send my stories to *Atlantic* and *Harper's* and occasionally to the *New Yorker*. . . . But I try them just out of perseverance, I guess. . . . An editor at *Harper's* said that she felt my stories were 'too special.' Slick magazines have to consider what they feel are the expectations of their readership—though I think they are often wrong in their assessments." At any rate, Bumpus was fortunate in having his work championed by Curt Johnson, the editor at *December* who was himself a writer of experimental fiction and hence willing to take risks for a writer like Bumpus.

Written in a basically naturalistic style which combines both an eye for realistic detail and hallucinatory, almost surreal effects, *Anaconda* is a brutal, intense account of an old man's anguished last days. In one of the few critical essays about Bumpus's fiction, G. E. Murray quotes from a note written by Bumpus to Curt Johnson in 1970 which gives some insight into the psychic history of *Anaconda*'s development: "I started writing *Anaconda* one summer morning at 2 o'clock after I had been drinking beer at Kenney's bar in Iowa City— July in 1958. I was 21 years old . . . the book that night when I started off wasn't supposed to be what it turned out to be—just in mind my grandfather, Alonzo Bumpus, who died in 1950, aged 70, of stomach cancer. He was a dry, small good man who supported his children's families during the Depression by hauling coal in Mt. Vernon, then in the 40s his spirit sank. . . . That night I started to think about Lon, but it turned out to be something else." As Bumpus indicates, the character who emerges in *Anaconda*, Lon McCaferty, is someone very different from the affectionate rapscalion in the author's memory. Indeed, the sixty-eight-year-old McCaferty is a man who we are told "had given up his work and the life he had grown accustomed to . . . and had spent the last fifteen years on the bum, tramping around the midwestern and southern parts of the country. Movement had been the story of his life." *Anaconda* tells a raw and painful story, but it is a work that evokes, above all, an almost palpable sense of atmosphere and mood; the fact that the mood evoked is linked to isolation, suffering, death, and man's powerlessness to alter his destiny does not lessen the beauty of its telling. Indeed, as G. E. Murray indicates, "the most attractive feature of *Anaconda* is the non-stop verbal electricity Bumpus courses through the book."

The oppressive mood of the novel is, of course, directly a result of plot since *Anaconda* certainly tells a painful story. It opens with McCaferty emerging soggy from a river, on his way home to die in familiar territory. The Spring Garden, Illinois, of the book's setting is an imaginative reconstruction of the area where Bumpus spent his childhood. Once a successful actor, whose profession was creating personae, affecting emotions, and engaging in communication with people who are likewise wearing masks, McCaferty comes back to the scene of his boyhood an alcoholic bum who drinks to numb himself to his own pain and to that of those around him. During these last days of tramping around, he meets others whose sad, miserable lives confirm what McCaferty sees as the ultimate tragedy in human affairs: the isolation of the individual. *Anaconda* is in part a picture of a hell in which human consciousness is trapped within its own painful, guilt-ridden, and frightened confines. McCaferty inhabits this hell, filled with the self-loathing and guilt of a man who has done his best to avoid attachments with others, in part because he fears their pain. In a key passage late in the novel, McCaferty confesses to a young, sympathetic woman who has momentarily befriended him: "I've done a million bad things. . . . I've watched a young man be killed and I didn't do a thing and I've got

drunk and been like a wild dog so many times that I can't remember how many times, and I've always been so afraid of people for some reason that I can't understand and I paid for an abortion for my wife who wanted to have a baby but I didn't, and I didn't care and it didn't bother me when my very own father died and when my only brother asked me for money I told him he wasn't really my brother and besides that I'm just a man named Lon McCaferty."

A man whose life has constantly been spent on the run (from himself and others), McCaferty is now slowed down by age, alcohol, and bad health—slowed down to the point where he can no longer avoid the awful "burden of himself." Unable to escape as he once could, McCaferty is slowly but inevitably crushed in this novel—literally by a bull at the conclusion, figuratively by the "anaconda of life that crushes good and bad alike." Alone, delirious, and near death after being struck by the bull, McCaferty undergoes an ironic rebirth into a life of responsibility and human communion. Although he can effect no real change in his circumstances, McCaferty finds himself thinking that "he would struggle to live as long as he could. The old urge for self-destruction that had directed at least half of the actions of his life, driving him to drinking, causing him to torment himself and the people near him, forcing him to destroy that happiness that he knew was happiness because he felt some demonic need for unhappiness, the old urge for self-destruction was gone." Finally forced into an ultimate corner and unable to shrink from responsibility, McCaferty is "finally living" just before he dies.

Although *Anaconda* is essentially a realistic novel, there are indications of the techniques Bumpus uses in his later fiction. One of the most noticeable connections between this work and wilder, more fantastic fiction Bumpus would later produce is his almost obsessive use of animals and animal imagery. Beginning with the anaconda of the novel's title and concluding with the bull of the final scene, both of which represent the absolute, primitive, unthinking power which rules us all, Bumpus uses animals both metaphorically and literally in this book to suggest the thin line which separates man from beast. In Bumpus's fictional world man, for all his elaborate social strategies, his complexities of language, his aspirations toward the spiritual realm, and his grandiose philosophizing, remains very much at one with the natural world around him. As Bumpus insistently erases distinctions between man and animals, he denies that man is superior to the world around him; all life shares death at the hands of the same indifferent force, and, ultimately, we treat each other with the same callousness and brutality that animals exhibit.

A major concern in all of Bumpus's fiction is to portray the interconnectedness of life. Rejecting the common belief that humans exist on a plane different from other living beings around them by virtue of intellect or soul, Bumpus insists that the only real human truth is that there are not *human* truths but only natural connections. Thus in *Anaconda* the closer McCaferty comes to his own end, the more those external qualities that man affects in order to put himself beyond nature fall away, until finally McCaferty is described as being "an old stiff grayhound, its eyesight failing, no longer able to see its tail to chase." As McCaferty's veneer of human qualities wears off, others begin to treat him with the same indifference they display for their animals and for each other: "People often looked at him as Jimmy was looking now—as if he was less than a human and a little more than a dog. But they talked

to him as if he was a dog, not waiting for or expecting a reply to what they said." The effect of this insistence on man's absolute entrapment in nature is an emphasis on the basic urges which control humans and animals alike. Both share primeval qualities beyond the reasoned, rational level of language. Indeed, in Bumpus's fiction of the 1970s one of his main aims was to devise fictional strategies to delve into the operations of this recessed, prerational aspect of existence.

The 1960s was a decade in which Bumpus concentrated on the writing of novels; the 1970s was devoted mainly to the creation of short fiction. Although he had received little if any critical attention during the 1960s, Bumpus's career took a turn for the better when his short fiction began to appear regularly in respected literary journals and magazines during the 1970s. Several of his stories were republished in such prestigious annual publications as *The Best American Short Stories* ("Beginnings" in 1974 and "Desert Matinee," later reprinted as "Things in Place," in 1975); *Prize Stories: The O. Henry Award* ("Idols of the Afternoon" in 1976); and *The Pushcart Prize: The Best of the Small Presses* ("Lovers" in 1977). This was a period in which Bumpus was also rethinking some of his views about writing and, like many other writers of the period, devising narrative strategies which often ignored realistic norms. In interviews, Bumpus explained some of the rationale behind his move away from realism by saying, "Part of it, of course, was discovering some of the great experimental works written during the 60s; I remember that reading Burroughs's *Naked Lunch* and Nabokov's *Pale Fire* in the late 60s had a big impact on my thinking, opened up a whole avenue of thought about how fiction could work; and reading Vonnegut's work, especially *Slaughterhouse Five*, was a continuing source of inspiration and interest for me. At any rate, I found myself becoming increasingly absorbed in my work with the formal aspect. In *Anaconda* I wanted to be 'natural' in my approach—as direct and honest and crude, even as unsophisticated, as possible; but during most of the 70s I found myself endlessly working and reworking the formal structures of my fiction, trying to create exactly the right means to present things about my characters that straight realistic treatments don't get at." Another, more mundane influence on Bumpus's work during this period was probably the long hours he spent analyzing and discussing student writing for his creative writing classes (a four-course load) at San Diego State: "I suppose my work has also been influenced by all the teaching I've done to support myself during my career—not in the sense of learning or borrowing from my students' work but from what happens in the classroom situation: listening to students analyze each others' work and doing so much thinking about the process of reading and analyzing fiction probably made me become more preoccupied with form and analysis than I had been previously. Certainly my fiction does get more formally extreme in its methods during the 70s, maybe even to the detriment of my work."

As Bumpus's stories began to appear widely in the "underground" circuit of small magazines and literary journals, it was almost inevitable that other writers (though still not the public at large) would begin to take notice of his work. In 1974 Ronald Sukenick and several other members of the recently formed Fiction Collective, impressed by what they had seen of Bumpus's work, agreed that the collective should urge him to submit a collection of stories. The collective, a writers' cooperative in which all editorial and promotional decisions are handled by the writers themselves, was organized specifically to publish struggling nontraditional writers such as Bumpus. Bumpus sent a selection of thirteen stories written mainly from 1971 to 1974, which was published in 1975 as *Things in Place*. The appearance of this collection marked the first stirrings of public and critical recognition of Bumpus's work: not only was the book widely and favorably reviewed in such places as the *New York Times Book Review* and the *Nation*, but it also generated critical analyses by critics like G. E. Murray and Tony Tanner in essays devoted to recent fiction. These critics were almost unanimous in praising Bumpus; one critic, John Agar in the *Carolina Quarterly*, went so far as to say, "Bumpus, above any writer I've read, captures the deepest level of common human experience . . . each of Bumpus's stories reveals the power of perceptions put into the right word. They are stories to read, mull over, and then read again. For despite his sometimes bizarre plots, Bumpus never falsifies."

Things in Place is an uncommonly rich and diverse collection which is challenging, puzzling, repelling, frightening, and funny. The stories range in style from relatively realistic tales such as "A Song of Old Fangles," "Selling," "Satisfaction," "Patsy O'Day in the World," and "Victims" to surreal stories like "Things in Place," "Our Golf Balls," "A Northern Memoir," "Idols of the Afternoon," and "In the Mood of Zebras." Overall the strength of this collection probably resides in Bumpus's extreme experiments in form, which allow his exotic

imagination free rein to seek out the darkest nightmares, the most glorious or the ugliest human desires.

The title story of the collection immediately introduces many of the book's typical themes, motifs, and formal peculiarities. The story, one of Bumpus's most disturbing creations, concerns Haskel, a reclusive inhabitant of a desolate, eerie desert area outside Lordsburg, New Mexico. It opens with Haskel confronting a wild band of motorcyclists who have come to the desert to raise hell in a fit of senseless, animalistic passion and fury. As is the case with many of the major characters in Bumpus's short fiction, none of the usual background information about Haskel is provided to assist us in understanding his psychology and motivation; rather, our only means of penetrating his psyche is through an objective narrator's description of his actions and thoughts. Haskel appears to be a man who has sought safety in the solitary life of the desert in order to avoid precisely the kind of situation he finds himself in as the story begins: alone, defenseless, facing a marauding pack of violent, cruel renegades who are said to be "big, long armed, etched with tattoos" with mouths "slashed with the obscene eagerness of wolves." In a plot that grows increasingly ugly, violent, shocking, and surreal, Haskel survives his initial encounter with the gang by silently driving through their midst in his pickup truck. Later he picks up one of the gang (named Hopalong) and his girl friend, Lily, and in response to their request for assistance (Hopalong's pants are soaked in blood) he takes them back to his cabin. The next day Hopalong, crazed with pain and shock, runs naked out into the snow. When Haskel runs after him, the motorcyclist turns, and in a passage typical of the shocking, visceral intensity of Bumpus's best prose, Hopalong reveals his mysterious wound: "Hopalong swung around, reared, rising and opening his arms like a bear turning on dogs, and Haskel saw the huge wide chest, the stomach black with hair wedging down to the bush at the base of the stomach, as if pointing to what Haskel didn't see. For there was not the big thrusting cock Haskel expected. Instead, a gash grinned blood over a white sprig of tendon. Running pumped fresh blood over what had dried on Hopalong's thighs, ringing the snow red around his knees."

Soon after, Hopalong dies, and Lily seduces Haskel in a scene that is both funny in its grotesqueness and typical of Bumpus's presentation of empty, animallike sexuality. Following the consummation—"Lily squatted like a frog, her knees wide

18

concerned. He spent more time gazing at Rochelle, but (surprise!)

he didn't try any you know what. Evening: dining, off to another club

for drinks, some dancing, and more friends. Richard certainly had a

lot of friends and they were all alike.

The fourth day ~~Day 4~~ Rochelle got her caps and partial bridge. She grinned

idiotically out the corner of her mouth when the dentist's reception-

ist said, "Are we all finished now?" which of course didn't mean ~~"Let~~

"Let me be the first to see" ~~me see~~ your ~~new teeth~~ *new teeth,"* but ~~instead~~ "How are you going to pay this

huge bill?" which of course Richard understood ~~and~~ *He* told the reception-

ist to ~~put the balance of the bill~~ *bill him for the balance* ($2,387 after Rochelle's $263)~~, on~~

~~his account.~~ "Thank you, Mr. Mills," the receptionist said, smiling

her face at Rochelle but with her eyes turned to Richard. That even-

ing Richard and Rochelle stayed home and he talked about his ex-wife,

Cherie, and his five ex-roommates ~~(not one by one, thank God, but~~ *(as he brought them out, all fine, one by*

~~globbed together in a composite in which it was easy for Rochelle~~ *one, and on, Rochelle globbed them one into*

~~not to have to get to actually know any of them),~~ *a composite the rest & this spared herself + them).* and Maxine. He

rambled on and on, and when he came to the end he said he was

interested in getting married again. "I believe in letting women

know from the beginning, when we're dating or living together. But

my writing is the most important thing ~~for me~~. Everything else must

take backseat to that. Though Maxine is very important in a different

way."

And he looked at Rochelle with something in his eyes that said

she was supposed to ask in _what_ way. Or she was to tell Richard

how she felt about Cherie and the five ex-roommates. Or Rochelle was

to begin ~~with~~ her own parade of exes. She asked if she could take a

look at some of Richard's fiction. ~~(He had never showed anything to the writing class)~~

"Huh?" ~~What? his lips whispered~~ *fell out of his mouth* before he caught ~~up with~~ himself, ~~closed~~

~~his mouth, and~~ *He* went into what he called The Library, *when he* returned with *it*

a literary magazine, ~~a copy of The Chicago Review~~ *Ploughshares magazine.* Rochelle opened to the table of contents

and there was Richard's name. She turned to his story, *"The Lithium Wars,"*

Revised typescript from a short story in progress

apart, and leaped. She sailed through the air and landed on Haskel. . . . 'There! Gottum Daddy's whanger' "—Haskel drives her to the highway, where she gets a ride, and then he continues to Lordsburg, where he watches a parade of "twenty or thirty women wearing white ten-gallon hats and white leather jackets and pants with long fringe," all riding palominos. When he returns to his cabin that night after having checked on Hopalong's body, which is propped up in a shed awaiting burial, he begins to make coffee. A noise is heard, Haskel looks out the window to see the same women he had seen earlier in Lordsburg on horses, and as he reaches for his coffee pot, he sees, as the story concludes, "the first of them leaning forward to clear the doorway as she rode into the cabin. The horses' eyes were huge, dazzled by the light."

"Things in Place" offers a good indication of the evolution of Bumpus's style since *Anaconda*. Whereas *Anaconda*, for all its pessimism and nightmarish qualities, depicts a recognizable world, quite clearly the world inhabited by Haskel *is* a nightmare. With its coolly dispassionate tone and the absolute horror of its content, "Things in Place" shows Bumpus's ability to articulate those feelings that arise from our nightly excursions into our subconscious, where we are all defenseless and where our evasions and self-deceits no longer protect us. Bumpus has indicated that the reader could view most of the scenes in the story as a series of "dreams but not hallucinations" experienced by Haskel, in which his secret anxieties about the world are projected into the episodes with Hopalong, Lily, and the palomino riders. Viewed in this way (though there is inadequate textual evidence to delineate reality and reverie), "Things in Place" becomes a story about the power of the subconscious to transform and transmute reality, creating a world whose content, cause and effect, logic, and mood are dictated by the inner mind. Many of the best stories from *Things in Place* and from Bumpus's next collection, *Special Offer*—stories like "Idols of the Afternoon," "Away in Night," "Our Golf Balls," "A Very Modern Home," and "On the Emperor's Birthday"—similarly describe powerful emotions of the subconscious overwhelming the conscious mind so that the distinction between the real and the imagined is eliminated. Thus, although we know very little about Haskel's "real life," we are given a portrait of his subconscious which, Bumpus implies, is the nonverbal primal reality we all share. Having come to the desert to escape people and the literal and psychic violence they inevitably bring, Haskel brings into imaginative being scenes and characters

that epitomize his, and our own, most basic fears: fears of being powerless, of being invaded, of being castrated. Haskel creates out of these fears men of such brutishness that they can rip the penis off one of their followers, women who watch their lovers die at one moment and shuffle a deck of cards the next, a world that violates the individual at will. But he also creates a sort of "resolution" of these fears, for the procession of women astride the palominos is presumably a symbol of the libido tamed, brought under control.

Clearly Haskel's "dream" is not merely a literal one to which we apply Freudian standards. And, in fact, Bumpus has indicated that "The Freudian notion of sexuality as the ultimate level of understanding and perception in our subconscious is inaccurate; there is a great dark pool in all of us beneath sex." This "great dark pool" makes a literal appearance in another story in *Things in Place*, "Our Golf Balls." This story is composed of a series of imaginary reflections related to us by an unnamed but obviously deranged narrator. In one of these scenes, the narrator describes a man who sneaks out onto a golf course at night intending to slip into a pond and retrieve lost golf balls. The pond, however, is not the placid, picturesque water hazard it appears to be in daylight; at night it is a treacherous, formless pool of dark, mysterious drop-offs which entrap the unwary poacher and drown him.

Even more than with Haskel we know nothing about the ordinary daily life of the narrator of "Our Golf Balls." Instead we grow to know him through the episodes he describes and through his choice of language; these episodes reveal a mind obsessed with the specter of nuclear holocaust, a specter which underlies a more fundamental fear that things in this world cannot hold together, that any sense of order must soon come unraveled. Secretly the narrator suspects that only "the magical marvel of regeneration" keeps things running smoothly, insures that each morning we confront the same reality as when we went to sleep: "All day he's aware of the placid jury of clocks looking on, he feels the homage of desks and swivel chairs, and with acquaintances all day he gets and gives, and has careful conversations with strangers. Things usually stay put and when there's a slip he looks the other way. But nights in bed he closes his eyes and gives over—it all must end and begin again!" His nightly dreams, however, recreated for us in prose of hallucinatory vividness, embody the ultimate fear in our atomic age that everything will soon explode: "Grinning, he skids down the long cloud hill and attacks the camps of friend and foe alike, ripping and tearing. Instantly the rampage widens, across the land people stagger forth in pajamas. The sky is burning, and all the streets and rooms and people, so laboriously put together, come undone. Every meaning and scrap of sense is scattered in trembling hunks. Poor fellow! Till dawn he tries to find his way home, stumbling through such debris it's as if the soup of the universe had sloshed out some of its logic for him to study."

Although Bumpus's fiction often suggests this notion of the inevitable disintegration of all that we hold dear—friendship, love, reason, even physical reality—he is not without hope, or good humor, about humanity's situation. As he has put it: "Each individual goes through the same process of living—all the world is a falling away; and yet human beings have vitality and joy in the face of knowing death. I hope I capture some of that vitality and joy in my work as well as the other, more negative things." In perhaps his most famous story, "The Heart of Lovingkind," a man suffers through an ill-fated romance with a kangaroo that ends disastrously, as it must, not because such a union is biologically impossible, but because all relationships are fragile and because we can never truly "possess" those we love as we would like to. When Ernie watches Gigi tragically leap to her death from a cliff, he realizes what most of Bumpus's characters eventually understand: "In that long moment Ernie realized he could never have Gigi—*all* of her." Since Bumpus's characters usually share Ernie's belief in the inevitable separation of individuals from those they love—indeed, since as one character says, "It's difficult to get satisfaction" of any kind in the world of ordinary experience—they typically can only hope to find joy and consolation in the world of the mind, in their dreams, in their memories, in the products of their imaginations. Thus the two elderly ladies in "Idols of the Afternoon" find solace not in the disappointing world of experience, where real excitement and sexuality and love have long since passed them by or never existed at all; instead they involve themselves in each other's imaginative lives, both creating through memory and imagination fantasies of fulfillment and passion that provide them with satisfactions unavailable in their daily lives.

In many of the stories in Bumpus's next collection, *Special Offer* (1981), this distinction between the real and the imagined is even more fluid. With the total abandonment of the logical and rational comes a celebration of the unlimited possibilities of the imagination. Such a celebration is dramatically acted out in "Mr. Spoon's Visit," in which the title character remarks, "We so ruthlessly dedicate ourselves to limits, we can't taste life . . . we can't breathe." To illustrate what going beyond limits involves, he astonishes two proper, rather smug society women by plucking from one's hair "a bright red rat with a quivery nose" and from the other's "a sky blue frog." *Special Offer* is filled with similarly startling, fantastic scenes and gestures, for in focusing on the life of the imagination Bumpus can give all concepts and actions equal credibility. One story, "Pizeop," ends with this notion: after having put up with her mad husband for years (he has, for example, invented his own private gibberish, which includes the word "pizeop"), a woman discovers he has left her. But instead of feeling grief, she giggles and dances around the room until she "collapsed and lay panting, staring out the window at the sky, the shallows of the universe, where all things, including pizeop, swirled in constant, relentless meaning."

After looking back through these stories, Bumpus said, "I realize they're all about the pain that comes with all relationships. Since we can't ever really connect with another person the way we want, we have to find an abstraction that we can share—something to allow us to come together in our minds since physical death always threatens any other sort of communion." The final story of *Special Offer*, "On the Emperor's Birthday," illustrates this idea, as a reclusive writer who has lived alone for years on an island finds himself sharing—or imagines that he is sharing—a ship with Japanese soldiers still loyal to their emperor. As he reads one of his stories to them, the fiction and the writer seem to merge until he is "caught up in the story—caught up by the sounds of the words amplified across the sea, and that implacability of things happening as they must." By the end of his lengthy narration, the writer is worried that the soldiers have been bored, that communication has once again broken down. But when one soldier asks, "Is that all?" the author's faith in his art is reaffirmed.

Although *Special Offer* was published in 1981, it is composed mainly of stories written by Bumpus before 1975. The uncollected stories which have appeared since 1975 indicate Bumpus's continued interest in fantasy and other forms of experimental structures. Indeed, perhaps the three most important works of his recent period—"Chums," "The Outdoorsman," and "The Happy Convent" (all published in *Partisan Review*)—are as formally innovative as anything Bumpus has written. Bumpus has suggested, however, that the fiction he has been working on the past year or two shows a new direction—a renewed interest in more realistic narrative formulas. This return to more conventional storytelling grew out of his recognition that formal considerations had perhaps taken precedence in his art at the expense of readability: "I had come to the point where I'd gone as far as I could in that direction, and I also began to suspect that it was difficult to keep reader interest in pure fantasy forms—readers need something they can more immediately recognize as part of a shared reality." Yet, given the dimensions of Bumpus's imagination, it seems unlikely that he will ever return to mimetic norms in any narrow sense. In fact, his latest published work, "The Attack on San Clemente" (in the *Paris Review*), a kind of cloak-and-dagger adventure story involving Richard Nixon and novelist Robert Coover, could be labeled "traditional" only in contrast to the extremities of his previous work. Bumpus's fiction constantly reminds us that our public personae are only facades, and that what lies beneath these facades, for all its grotesqueness, brutality, and occasional fantastic beauty, is something we all share.

Periodical Publications:
"Adolph Hitler, Judy Mauritz, and The Clear Blue Sky of Japan," *December* (Fall 1965);
"The Season of Deep Water," *Minnesota Review*, 2 (Summer 1968);
"Beginnings," *Tri-Quarterly*, 26 (Winter 1973);
"A Morning in Arcadia," *Kansas Quarterly*, 9, 3 (Summer 1977);
"Chums," *Partisan Review*, 44 (Fall 1977);
"The Outdoorsman," *Partisan Review*, 44 (Fall 1977);
"Heroes and Villains," *Epoch*, 27, 1 (Fall 1977);
"The Happy Convent," *Partisan Review*, 48 (Summer 1981);
"The Attack on San Clemente," *Paris Review*, 79 (1981).

References:
Larry McCaffery, "The Fiction Collective," *Contemporary Literature*, 19 (Winter 1978): 106-107;
McCaffery, "The Fiction Collective: An Innovative Alternative," *Chicago Review*, 30 (Autumn 1978): 107-126;
G. E. Murray, "Unmapped Places," *Fiction International*, 6/7 (1978): 140-146.

Lin Carter
(9 June 1930-)

Bill Crider
Howard Payne University

SELECTED BOOKS: *Sandalwood and Jade* (St. Petersburg, Fla.: Sign of the Centaur, 1951);
The Wizard of Lemuria (New York: Ace, 1965); revised and enlarged as *Thongor and the Wizard of Lemuria* (New York: Berkley, 1969);
Thongor of Lemuria (New York: Ace, 1966);
The Flame of Iridar (New York: Belmont Books, 1967);
King Kull, by Carter and Robert E. Howard (New York: Lancer, 1967);
Thongor Against the Gods (New York: Paperback Library, 1967);
Giant of World's End (New York: Belmont Books, 1969);
Tolkien: A Look Behind "The Lord of the Rings" (New York: Ballantine, 1969);
Lost World of Time (New York: Signet Science Fiction, 1969);
Lovecraft: A Look Behind the "Cthulhu Mythos" (New York: Ballantine, 1972);
Under the Green Star (New York: DAW, 1972);
Jandar of Callisto (New York: Dell, 1972);
The Man Who Loved Mars (Greenwich, Conn.: Fawcett Gold Medal, 1973);
The Black Star (New York: Dell, 1973);
Imaginary Worlds: The Art of Fantasy (New York: Ballantine, 1973);
The Valley Where Time Stood Still (Garden City: Doubleday, 1974);
Lankar of Callisto (New York: Dell, 1975);
Zarkon, Lord of the Unknown, in Invisible Death (Garden City: Doubleday, 1975);
Zarkon, Lord of the Unknown, in The Volcano Ogre (Garden City: Doubleday, 1976);
The City Outside the World (New York: Berkley, 1977);

Tara of the Twilight (New York: Zebra Books, 1978);
The Wizard of Zao (New York: DAW, 1978);
Journey to the Underground World (New York: DAW, 1979);
Darya of the Bronze Age (New York: DAW, 1981).

Linwood Vrooman (Lin) Carter, now one of the most prominent names in the field of fantasy, began contributing to amateur magazines in the late 1940s. Since then, he has collaborated with other writers, published numerous novels and stories of his own, written collections of verse, edited anthologies, served as general editor of the Ballantine Adult Fantasy Series and provided introductions for each book in the series, has written books of nonfiction and criticism, novels in the style of the hero pulps in the 1930s, and an erotic fantasy. He has also composed a fairy tale and war game rules. By late 1981, he had by his own count 108 books to his credit.

Lin Carter was born to Raymond and Lucy Carter in Saint Petersburg, Florida, where he grew up and received his education through high school. All his early reading, Carter now says, led him to fantasy, and the books he liked best were all fantasies: the Greek and Norse myths, Andrew Lang's fairy tales, *The Wind in the Willows*, *Peter Pan*, the Doctor Dolittle books, the Mary Poppins novels, and particularly the Oz books of L. Frank Baum. Carter's first novel (unpublished), written after his discharge from the army in 1953, was an Oz book.

It was when he was twelve years old that Carter first encountered the writer who influenced him perhaps as much as any other, Edgar Rice Burroughs. Having read most of the books in the children's section of the library, Carter checked out *The Master Mind of Mars* and took it home. In his "Author's Note" to his own novel, *Under the Green Star* (1972), Carter says that when he started reading Burroughs's book, he was "a helpless captive from the first page on," and much of Carter's writing today reflects a strong Burroughs influence.

While still in his teens Carter began contributing fan letters to the professional science fiction and fantasy magazines, and his work first began to appear in the "fanzines" (amateur publications) as early as 1947 with a poem entitled "Canal" in *Canadian Fandom* (September 1947). In addition to verse, Carter's fanzine work included articles, cartoons, and stories ("awful ones, too," Carter now says of the latter). Eventually he made over one hundred appearances in the amateur periodicals

and published a number of fanzines of his own, including *Spaceteer* while he was still in high school; *The Saturday Evening Toad*; and *Spectrum*, an all-review magazine which had a run of five issues dating from November/December 1962 to Winter 1964.

Some of Carter's fanzine articles formed the basis for works later published professionally. His "Notes on Tolkien" appeared in three issues of *Xero* (November 1961, May 1967, September 1962), edited by Richard A. Lupoff. These articles were the first draft of *Tolkien: A Look Behind "The Lord of the Rings"* (1969). The sonnet sequence which begins the Arkham House collection entitled *Dreams from R'lyeh* first appeared in *Amra*. Carter's first professional sale, "Masters of the Metropolis" (*The Magazine of Fantasy and Science Fiction*, 1957), a short story written in collaboration with Randall Garrett, was originally published in the fanzine *Inside* (January 1956).

After high school in Saint Petersburg, Carter worked in movie theaters in that city. In 1951 Carter himself published his first book, *Sandalwood and Jade*, a collection of verse influenced by such writers as Robert E. Howard and Clark Ashton Smith. Also in 1951, he was drafted into the army. He took his basic training at Fort Dix and then attended leadership school at Camp Breckenridge, Kentucky. After leadership school, he was shipped to Korea, where he spent a year as a company clerk. He served in both North and South Korea and saw action twice. Discharged as a corporal, Carter was eight months in grade and would have made sergeant except for a freeze on non-com promotions.

Carter went to New York in 1953 and took writing courses at Columbia University. In 1957 he began his career in advertising and copywriting, talking his way into the job on the strength of some of his work in the fan magazines. In the course of this career, which lasted until 1969, Carter wrote direct mail advertising for books, record clubs, teaching machines, dictionaries, and so on. He believes that the experience he received in writing such copy "contributed materially to making [him] a professional fiction writer" by teaching him to trim down his work "to lean, exciting prose" and "to eliminate the little dull gray words."

While working as a copywriter, Carter continued to write fiction. Prior to the publication of his 1965 novel, *The Wizard of Lemuria*, Carter wrote six other novels, five of which remain unpublished. The sixth, *The Flame of Iridar*, was sold to Belmont Books in 1967. It was during this phase of his career that Carter was married, twice. His first marriage, in 1958, was to Judith Ellen Hershkowitz. This marriage lasted for one year. In 1963 Carter married Noel Vreeland with whom he worked at Prentice-Hall. They separated in 1974 and were divorced in 1975. Carter has no children from his marriages, but he has two daughters born out of wedlock to different mothers: Michelle Chambers, born in August 1980, and Courtney Thompson, born in August 1981.

Carter's real career as a professional writer and editor began in 1965 with the Ace edition of *The Wizard of Lemuria,* though Carter did not become a full-time writer until 1969. In that year, having lost his job with the Albert Frank-Guenther Law Agency, Carter found himself with a number of writing contracts to fulfill and realized that he could not afford to take another job. He now devotes himself exclusively to his writing and editing.

When *The Wizard of Lemuria* appeared, one critic, John Boardman, wrote that the book was like "the result of a head-on collision between Burroughs and Howard." To appreciate Carter's fiction, it is necessary to understand his feelings about both these writers. According to Carter, Robert E. Howard is the creator of that subgenre of heroic fantasy known as "Sword & Sorcery." This term, coined by author Fritz Leiber, is defined by Carter in "Of Swordsmen and Sorcerers," his introduction to *Flashing Swords! #1 and #2* (1973): "*We call a story Sword & Sorcery when it is an action tale derived from the traditions of the pulp magazine adventure story, set in a land, age or world of the author's invention–a milieu in which magic actually works and the gods are real–a story, moreover, which pits a stalwart warrior in direct conflict with the forces of supernatural evil.*" From Burroughs, on the other hand, Carter derives the tradition of an Earthman transported to another planet where he encounters marvelous adventures with strange creatures and societies and wins the love of a beautiful princess. It is probably also from Burroughs that Carter received his fondness for series characters and books with cliff-hanger endings. Most of Carter's stories are continued from book to book, and even some of the books which now stand alone, such as the Atlantis novel, *The Black Star* (1973), and *Lost World of Time* (1969) seem to have been intended as the first books of series.

Lin Carter

Carter's first series, which began with *The Wizard of Lemuria,* features as its "stalwart warrior" Thongor the Mighty, who encounters machines, societies, and adventures reminiscent of those in the works of Edgar Rice Burroughs, as he fights his way with sword and fist across the lost continent of Lemuria. The series has been continued through six novels from three different publishers and in numerous short stories and even comic books. The first book in the series is still in print.

Carter also became involved in carrying on two series originally created by Howard, who had at his death in 1936 left behind numerous fragments, outlines, and incomplete stories. L. Sprague de Camp, a friend of Carter's who had critiqued the manuscript of *The Wizard of Lemuria,* was involved in getting Howard's stories of Conan the Barbarian into new paperback editions and completing the fragments of other Conan stories left unfinished by Howard. Too busy to work on Howard's King Kull tales at that time, de Camp recommended Carter to the agent for Howard's estate, Glenn Lord. Carter "touched up, tightened a bit, completed, or revised" the stories, which appeared in book form as *King Kull* (Lancer 1967). Carter and de Camp later joined in posthumous collaboration with Howard, wrote collaborative and separate pastiches, and extended the Conan saga.

Carter continued his own series books with the "World's End" tales, beginning with *Giant of World's End* (1969), featuring Ganelon Silvermane. The series is similar to the Thongor books; but instead of having a lost continent of the past as its setting, it takes place on Gondwane, a far-future supercontinent, formed when the present continents have drifted together.

Series in which the Burroughs influence is more strongly felt than that of Howard include the "Jandar" books, the "Green Star" cycle, and the "Zanthodon" novels. In the first two, as in Burroughs's John Carter tales, an Earthman finds himself on a strange planet, battling for a kingdom and the love of a princess. In the latter, a modern-day adventurer accompanies an eccentric professor to an underground world populated by prehistoric monsters and primitive men, a world reminiscent of Burroughs's Pellucidar. Of all the books in these series, perhaps the most notable is *Lankar of Callisto* (1975), sixth book of the Jandar series, in which Carter himself becomes the major character, accidentally transported to Jupiter's moon through the "Gate between the Worlds" by the same force which carried Jon Dark (Jandar) there. The book shows Carter in a playful mood, and not above self-

parody, as he depicts himself ("a lazy, self-indulgent, unathletic science-fiction writer nearing forty and of sedentary habits") trying to cope with dangers similar to those faced by his sturdy heroes in other novels. In narrating the story himself, Carter also has the opportunity to compare his predicaments with those faced by characters in his favorite books and movies. The result is a style different from others which Carter adopts and a unique point of view with an author caught up in the workings of one of his own fantastic creations.

Yet another series, and one of Carter's most entertaining to those who relish the hero pulps of the 1930s, features Zarkon, Lord of the Unknown, and his associates: "Scorchy" Muldoon, Nick Naldini, "Ace" Harrigan, "Doc" Jenkins, and "Menlo" Parker. Zarkon and his men face volcano monsters and master criminals with as much verve as Doc Savage; indeed, Carter's books are clearly influenced in both style and content by Lester Dent, who wrote most of the Doc Savage adventures published under the Kenneth Robeson pseudonym.

Of Carter's nonseries works, two titles stand out, *The Valley Where Time Stood Still* (1974) and *The Man Who Loved Mars* (1973). Both are set on Mars, and both deal with the same mythology of an age-old civilization, its lost cities, and its nearly forgotten gods, though they are otherwise not connected. The former deals with the search for a fabled lost valley where life on Mars is supposed to have begun, while the latter concerns a search for a lost city and the valuable treasure it is supposed to contain. Both novels comment on brotherhood, humanity, and understanding, though *The Man Who Loved Mars* is more pointed and contains a scathing commentary on colonialism at the same time.

Another book which must be mentioned is *Tara of the Twilight* (1978), different in its way from anything else Carter has done. *Tara* is a first-person story told from the point of view of its heroine rather than from that of a barbarian warrior. It is also a Sword & Sorcery tale that is at the same time what Carter calls in his introduction, "an intensely erotic work of fiction," quite a change from Carter's usual clean-cut action/adventure suitable for young boys.

Carter's professional nonfiction began with *Tolkien: A Look Behind "The Lord of the Rings"* (1969, although as has been pointed out above an early version had appeared in the fan press). In a very good introduction to Tolkien's work, Carter briefly discusses Tolkien's life, gives a summary of the *Lord of the Rings* trilogy and *The Hobbit,* investigates Tolkien's sources, and gives a concise history of fantasy

Dust jacket for an adult-fantasy anthology edited by Carter

literature. *Lovecraft: A Look Behind the "Cthulhu Mythos"* (1972) is a study of the invented myths used over a period of years by H. P. Lovecraft to give his stories a portion of their atmosphere and fascination. Lovecraft's followers are also analyzed, and Carter provides a complete bibliography of Cthulhu Mythos stories written by Lovecraft and others between 1921 and 1971. There is in addition an appendix which compares the differing opinions of various Lovecraft scholars and fans regarding the Mythos. The Lovecraft book in particular has been criticized for its subjectivity and its informal, chatty style. Carter himself admits that many of his value judgments are personal opinion, but the book remains a repository of valuable information for anyone interested in Lovecraft's work or its influence on later writers.

It was Carter's writing of *Tolkien: A Look Behind "The Lord of the Rings"* that led to his becoming general editor of the Ballantine Adult Fantasy Series. The publishers of Ballantine Books, Ian and

Betty Ballantine, were intrigued by Carter's obvious enthusiasm for the works discussed in the portions of the Tolkien study which described Tolkien's sources and related the history of fantastic literature. The Ballantines hired Carter as a consultant, and the result of his efforts was the Adult Fantasy Series which began with the publication of Fletcher Pratt's *The Blue Star* in 1969. As general editor, Carter was able to rescue some notable books from obscurity, such as Evangeline Walton's *The Island of the Mighty* (1970) (originally published in 1936 as *The Virgin and the Swine*). In the case of Ms. Walton, Carter was also able to bring into print a hitherto unpublished work, *The Children of Llyr* (1971), and to encourage her to produce more of her fine novels based on the *Mabinogion*, such as *The Song of Rhiannon* (1972). Carter also brought back into print the early works of well-known writers, such as Poul Anderson, whose first novel, *The Broken Sword*, was reprinted in the series in 1971. Carter also made available to the mass market the fantasies of authors best known for their writing in other areas, as with *Kai Lung's Golden Hours* (1972) by Ernest Bramah, most famous for his stories of the blind detective Max Carrados. As an anthologizer for the series, Carter edited books such as *Dragons, Elves and Heroes* (1969) in which he gathered fantastic episodes from varied sources of world literature ranging from *The Kalevala* and *The Volsung Saga* to the poetry of Browning and Tennyson. Finally, Carter published the work of young writers who have since contributed materially to the literature of fantasy. Examples are Joy Chant (*Red Moon and Black Mountain*, 1971) and Katherine Kurtz (*Deryni Rising*, 1970). Moreover, Carter brought back into print numerous works by William Morris, William Hope Hodgson, Lord Dunsany, James Branch Cabell, Clark Ashton Smith, H. Rider Haggard, and George MacDonald.

It would be difficult to overestimate Carter's influence as editor of Ballantine's Adult Fantasy Series. Poul Anderson, writing in Loay Hall's fanzine *Valhalla #1* (1979), compares Carter with legendary golden-age science-fiction editor John W. Campbell. Carter's "absolute distinction," says Anderson, "his complete irreplaceability, lies in what he has done and is doing for fantasy literature in his capacities of editor and consultant." Carter continues as an editor with his annual *Year's Best Fantasy Stories* and has recently revived the *Weird Tales* pulp title for a series of "paperback magazines." Zebra Books has also billed a 1981 collection of Robert Bloch's Cthulhu Mythos stories as "A Lin Carter Fantasy Selection."

As Carter's importance and ability as an editor have become firmly established, his fictional writings have been more severely criticized by readers and reviewers. Some accuse Carter (and all writers of Sword & Sorcery fiction, for that matter) of looking backward, of writing in a worn-out genre that resists innovation and evolution. While admitting that he has no real desire to change Sword & Sorcery, Carter does point out several of his own innovations, which include mixing the trappings of science fiction (lightning weapons and flying airboats) with fantastic action in primitive Lemuria in the Thongor series. He also introduced the erotic element into such fiction with a feminine narrator in *Tara of the Twilight*. It might also be pointed out that the theme of much Sword & Sorcery literature, including Carter's, that of Order versus Chaos, is not an ignoble one.

At the same time, one should not overlook the entertainment value of Carter's work. Carter has no pretensions to literary greatness, nor does he intend to deal at length in his fiction with important contemporary problems. He apparently does not believe that a writer should be "an improbable combination of Ralph Nader and Dostoevsky," as he puts it in his study of fantasy *Imaginary Worlds* (1973). Instead, he intends to devote himself to fast moving action/adventure stories in the manner of Burroughs and Howard, as in his latest novel, *Darya of the Bronze Age* (1981), in which Eric Carstairs returns to the underground world of Zanthodon. Carter has a clear talent for such tales, as well as enviable ability for descriptive scene setting, perhaps best exemplified by the fine opening paragraphs of such books as *The Man Who Loved Mars* and *Journey to the Underground World*. He has the ability to make the reader believe in the strange, the remote, and the fantastic. It is evident that he will continue to do so, as he works on his long-term projects: *Khymyrium: The City of a Hundred Kings, from the Coming of Aviathar to the Passing of Spheridon the Doomed*, an epic fantasy planned for a length of 500,000 words; *The Book of Eibon*, a posthumous collaboration with Clark Ashton Smith, drawing on Smith's unpublished notes and manuscripts; and a compilation of the complete text of the imaginary *Necronomicon* of Abdul Alhazred, to be made up of the quotations from the text found in the works of H. P. Lovecraft, August Derleth, Clark Ashton Smith, Frank Belknap Long, Robert E. Howard, Brian Lumley, Ramsey Campbell, and others.

As an industrious editor and a prolific writer, Lin Carter has established himself as a figure of the first importance in the field of fantasy. He has the ability to entertain and the ability to inform, and he has preserved and caused to be published volumes of importance to any scholar interested in the fantastic in literature. For these reasons his position is secure, and it seems quite likely that he will solidify that position in the years to come.

Other:

Dragons, Elves, and Heroes, edited by Carter (New York: Ballantine, 1969);

The Magic of Atlantis, edited by Carter (New York: Lancer, 1970);

New Worlds for Old, edited by Carter (New York: Ballantine, 1971);

The Spawn of Cthulhu, edited by Carter (New York: Ballantine, 1971);

Flashing Swords! #1 and #2, edited by Carter (Garden City: Doubleday, 1973);

Sonnet Sequence in *Dreams from R'lyeh* (Sauk City, Wis.: Arkham House, 1975);

The Year's Best Fantasy Stories, edited by Carter (New York: DAW, 1975);

Flashing Swords! #3, edited by Carter (New York: Dell, 1976);

Realms of Wizardry, edited by Carter (Garden City: Doubleday, 1976);

The Year's Best Fantasy Stories: 2 and *3,* edited by Carter (New York: DAW, 1976 & 1977);

Flashing Swords! #4, edited by Carter (Garden City: Doubleday, 1977);

Weird Tales #1 and #2, edited by Carter (New York: Zebra Books, 1980).

Reference:

Poul Anderson, "Concerning Lin Carter," *Valhalla #1* (1979): 15-16.

Jack Conroy

(5 December 1899-   )

Jon Christian Suggs
John Jay College, City University of New York

BOOKS: *The Disinherited* (New York: Covici-Friede, 1933; London: Wishart, 1934);

A World to Win (New York: Covici-Friede, 1935);

The Fast-Sooner Hound, by Conroy and Arna Bontemps (New York: Houghton Mifflin, 1942);

They Seek a City, by Conroy and Bontemps (Garden City: Doubleday, Doran, 1945); revised and expanded as *Anyplace But Here* (New York: Hill & Wang, 1966);

Slappy Hooper, The Wonderful Sign Painter, by Conroy and Bontemps (Boston: Houghton Mifflin, 1946);

Sam Patch, The High, Wide and Handsome Jumper, by Conroy and Bontemps (New York: Houghton Mifflin, 1951);

The Jack Conroy Reader, edited by Jack Salzman and David Ray (New York: Burt Franklin, 1980).

On a trip to England during the 1950s, Jack Conroy stopped in at a London bookstore to browse. When he asked the proprietor if he had *The Disinherited* (1933), Conroy's first novel, in stock, the fellow said he had not. "By the bye," the proprietor asked, "what do you suppose ever became of Conroy? I heard he was dead." On his way to the door by then, Conroy turned. "No, I think he's alive and living in Chicago."

True enough, Conroy had been living in Chicago since 1938 and continued to do so until 1966. In 1963 *The Disinherited* was "rediscovered" and republished in paperback; it has remained in print since. Still, Conroy has been one of the least celebrated, and yet most authentically talented, of the leftist American writers of the 1920s and 1930s.

Born John Wesley Conroy in Moberly, Missouri, he was the son of a miner's widow and her second husband, a renegade Catholic priest cum union man who had converted to Methodism. Although Conroy's father was educated and an orator of considerable skill, it was his mother's frustrated ambition to be a writer that stimulated his early interest in literature. For the most part, however, Conroy grew up in a hardscrabble mining camp and absorbed all its lessons. He learned how to work, how to tell tall tales, and, from the pages of *The*

Appeal to Reason passed around camp by workers, he learned radicalism early.

He learned even more from the diverse titles published as Little Blue Books by the Haldeman-Julius Company just over the state line in Girard, Kansas. Haldeman-Julius and his wife printed classics, humor, and radical tracts in five-cent booklet form; their small books were often the only texts in a worker's education. But Conroy read widely and as an adolescent was profoundly impressed by Macaulay's *Lays of Ancient Rome* (1842). Although he soon forewent the nineteenth-century ornateness of Macaulay's style, he never abandoned his respect for the breadth and intensity of learning that could produce such a work. In both his fiction and nonfiction, from his "proletarian" novelist days through the 1,000 book reviews he wrote in the 1940s and 1950s while living in Chicago, it was clear he was among the most erudite worker-writers of his time.

As a worker-writer, Conroy was the "real goods"—a working-class stiff, mostly self-educated (except for one semester at the University of Missouri, after which he left to escape the restrictions of ROTC and its uniforms), who could write. He missed World War I because of a heart murmur, married in 1922, and spent the early 1920s working around Moberly: haying, doing construction, laying brick streets ("The hardest job a man can do," he remembered), and generally making ends meet while trying to write. His fortunes, artistic or economic, changed very little until the closing years of the decade.

In 1929 Conroy joined the Rebel Poets, an international group loosely associated through its founder, Ralph Cheyney, with the Industrial Workers of the World. Cheyney had coedited an indictment of the Sacco-Vanzetti case entitled *America Arraigned* (1928) and had started the Rebel Poets as a focus for the radical interest the case had aroused. In the winter of 1930, Conroy and Ben Hagglund, both Midwestern members of the organization, decided to put out a literary magazine bearing the group's name. Their editorial policy was to publish any radical material that appeared—the angrier the better. Talent was not always necessary; Conroy would do a little editing, and Hagglund would then set the type and print it.

Conroy was still working in fields, mills, and factories as well as writing while he edited the *Rebel Poet* from January 1931 to October 1932. In 1931, H. L. Mencken saw a piece of his and asked Conroy to write something for the February 1932 issue of his *American Mercury*. Mencken liked Conroy's account of the bitter winter of 1931 and encouraged him to write more in the same vein. These sketches, and others published elsewhere, became the basic material for *The Disinherited*. Conroy had at first wanted to collect the pieces for a book-length autobiography, but Mencken thought a fictionalized account would be more salable and urged him to try for a novel. He liked Conroy's first attempt and tried to convince Knopf, his own publisher, to bring the book out. However, they refused, saying that the manuscript, while fictional, was not "novelistic."

Every major publisher in New York and Boston rejected the book until Conroy's agent returned to Covici-Friede, the fourteenth that had turned it down, with the proposal that Conroy would rewrite the work to include a central character whose presence would tie the episodic adventures of various workers and hoboes together. Covici-Friede agreed, and Conroy created the character of Larry

Donovan who appeared in every episode and whose decision to become a labor organizer marks the logical and emotional end of the novel.

Through Donovan, Conroy recreated the difficult, itinerant life of early twentieth-century working-class America. From coal mine to steel mill to foundry to tire plant and eventually to a Midwestern farm, Larry Donovan's picaresque life introduced the reader to radicals and hoboes, good women and bad men, bosses and finks, young men full of hope and old men ground under by an oppressive economic system. Donovan's decision to seek a solution for the workers' plight, through labor agitation and organization influenced by the example of a successful collective stand by his farmer friends, echoes a common theme found in proletarian "conversion" novels. But Conroy's skill was sufficient to make the decision believable and moving. Donovan's conversion was not just a revolutionary addendum to a collection of stories about work.

The Disinherited was well received, critically and popularly, selling more than 5,000 copies and going through two printings. Most reviewers, of both the political Left and Right, liked the stories and the style, but there were, as was usual during the period, complaints about the revolutionary propaganda

Jack Conroy

implicit in the lives and struggles of the working-class characters. Nevertheless, *The Disinherited* was mild in its call to social justice compared with other proletarian fiction of the day.

Still, it was a political book, for Conroy was a political man. Although there is no indication that he ever joined the Communist party or was even much of a fellow traveler, Conroy realized the Communists were doing more to open art and society to the working class than any other group in America in the 1930s. He tried not to let his distaste for their clumsiness and often self-defeating dogmatism obscure the goals he shared with them.

But it was difficult for Conroy. In the early 1930s he became president of the Rebel Poets and soon found himself in a struggle for control of the New York chapter. There, Philip Rahv, a young Communist party member (later to become a founder and editor of *Partisan Review*), attempted to seize control of the chapter and its publication, the *Rebel Poet*. Conroy's response to what he saw as an attempt to use the chapter as an outlet for the party's line on literature and art was to dissolve the New York organization and expel Rahv and his adherents.

Within months, the entire Rebel Poet movement began to collapse under other pressures, primarily the disappearance of its original Wobbly base and the deepening of the Depression. At this point the Communist party stepped in to fill the vacuum created by the demise of the Rebel Poets by sponsoring the establishment of John Reed clubs across the country. In New York the chapter was headed by Rahv, who also edited its journal, *Partisan Review*.

Conroy continued to write throughout this period. In May 1933 he and Hagglund had begun a new magazine, the *Anvil*, a journal of fiction and poetry by and for workers, to replace the *Rebel Poet*, which had folded in October 1932. At the same time, encouraged by the reception of *The Disinherited*, he began a second book, but he was working under difficult conditions. Money was still scarce in Moberly, and Conroy wrote hurriedly. The book, which he called "Little Stranger," was finished in less than a year, whereas *The Disinherited* had been the product of years of crafting and polishing. Conroy was also hampered by the fact that he was making a conscious attempt to write a traditionally structured novel, so it lacked the ideological fervor and personal identification he had brought to *The Disinherited*. Conroy had never truly felt himself to be a novelist, realizing that he had always lacked the ability to create believable situations or bring his

characters to life; he only attempted, as he liked to say, "to vivify the contemporary fact."

There was little contemporary fact in "Little Stranger." Conroy attempted to meld memory and invention by inserting fictitious characters into episodes from his Missouri childhood and adolescence. In a familiar structure of fraternal conflict, he traces the youth and manhood of a vagabond's children in the years before and after World War I. The children are half-brothers, different in temperament, and Conroy clearly was most interested in the development of the sensitive youth, the more obviously autobiographical of the two. Although the book contained more studied imagery and a less rigidly controlled use of "realism" in speech and narrative than did *The Disinherited*, its appeal lay in its early passages wherein the countryside of rural Missouri is the setting for childhood adventures and tragedies told in a style reminiscent of Mark Twain, a writer Conroy greatly admired.

Nevertheless, in 1935, *A World to Win*, as "Little Stranger" had been retitled by Covici-Friede, appeared to less than enthusiastic reviews, and did not sell well. There seemed little interest in the story of the two half-brothers and their particular responses to American working-class and bohemian life.

Conroy and Hagglund, however, were still publishing the *Anvil*, which was a popular success by the standards of the day: workers read it and good writers wrote for it, among them Richard Wright, Nelson Algren, Langston Hughes, and Erskine Caldwell. As before, Conroy did most of the editing in Moberly, accepting pieces rejected by other magazines because of their political outlook or the frankness of their portrayal of human relationships. He would then send the copy to Hagglund, wherever that itinerant printer might be working at the time, and soon another issue of the *Anvil* would emerge. It was this decentralized method of production, the absence of real working capital, and Conroy's ties to Moberly through family and poverty that eventually doomed the magazine.

In New York, *Partisan Review* had become first among publications of the councils of leftist literary theorizing. Rahv and William Phillips ran the magazine well, and it was especially exciting to young critics and writers. But the party apparently felt it lacked a creative component, so in late 1935 "invited" Conroy to merge the *Anvil* with *Partisan Review*. The offer was a shared title, *Anvil and Partisan Review*, shared editorial responsibilities, and a fairly clear threat to exclude the *Anvil* from all party bookstores and distribution routes if Conroy did

-34-   34 22705

coal-oil flame when Mother had whirled to see what
was happening. The room was in darkness and the
air was pungent with powder fumes. Mother groped
for the lamp and dropped the chimney with a sharp
exclamation when it burned her fingers. She ignited
the wick with a trembling hand.

Madge tumbled out of bed and hurried down the
stairs. Tim and I were goggle-eyed. Father
grasped each of us by an arm, crying passionately:

"Boys! Boys! Listen to me! If you must be
one, be a thief, a murderer, anything, but don't
ever be a scab! You hear me? Don't ever be a scab!"

"We won't never, pappy," we promised solemnly.

My father was not an unkindly man. On such a
night his enemy's dog, though it had bitten a hunk
out of his leg and the seat out of his pants, might
have stood beside his fire.

But not a scab.

The Monkey Nest never gave Tim a chance to stray
from his vow, because he cushioned the fall of a
bell rock before he was sixteen. But I have never
forgotten that night or the promise exacted.

The strike came to an end somehow. Reminiscing
about it, it is hard to say definitely just how it
did end or whether it was won or lost. Somehow the
miners seemed to lose the individual strike, but
steadily to progress along the far-flung battle line
of their goal. The history of the miners' union of

A page from the typescript of The Disinherited

not agree. After discussions with friends who had provided the *Anvil* what financial support it had, he agreed to the party's terms.

Within weeks the magazine began to slip from Conroy's grasp. The new title became *Partisan Review and Anvil*, and Conroy's small editorial staff was dismissed. He had no money for a trip to New York to fight for control and soon relinquished his remaining editorial authority to Rahv and Phillips. In late 1936 they broke with the party and suspended publication of the magazine. When they began to publish again in December 1937, Phillips and Rahv had returned to the format and title of the *Partisan Review*. The *Anvil* had ceased to exist.

Conroy was still languishing in Moberly without work and with a family to support when Nelson Algren suggested that he come to Chicago to work on the Writers' Project of the Works Progress Administration. Algren promised to get him into the WPA and even arranged for him to do a book review for a leftist weekly, the fee from which paid for his ticket to Chicago. But another reason Conroy left Moberly was as close to his heart as the prospect of work: Algren had suggested that they bring out another literary magazine for workers, the *New Anvil*.

The *New Anvil* was published in Chicago from March 1939 to August 1940, but eventually died along with proletarian enthusiasms in general. As the decade closed, leftist energies were directed toward the fight against fascism; there was no time for a workers' revolution. So Conroy stayed at the WPA, wrote book reviews, and met Arna Bontemps, with whom he wrote a very successful juvenile book, *The Fast-Sooner Hound* (1942); and two versions of the story of black-American migration, *They Seek A City* (1945) and *Anyplace But Here* (1966, a revised and expanded version of *They Seek A City*). He also wrote pamphlets for the war effort and worked with Algren to track down syphilitic prostitutes for the Public Health Service.

Two years after his wartime service ended, Conroy edited a popular collection of regional humor, *Midland Humor: A Harvest of Fun and Folklore* (1947), and became a senior editor for *The New Standard Encyclopedia*, a position he held for twenty years, retiring in 1966 when he returned to Moberly. In the intervening years he had published more juveniles, the most successful being *Sam Patch, The High, Wide and Handsome Jumper* (1951).

Jack Conroy was exactly what the proletarian literary movement was looking for. He was a white Anglo-Saxon Protestant working-class fellow who could write movingly and clearly about the in-

iquities of capitalism. He wrote a good book about working-class life and wrote another that might have been good if he had had the time to polish it. He was a principled editor of working-class fiction and poetry, and he was, for better or worse, an independent, radical voice in support of both.

Other:

Unrest, edited by Conroy and Ralph Cheyney (London: Stockwell, 1929);

Unrest, edited by Conroy and Cheyney (London: Studies, 1930);

Unrest, edited by Conroy and Cheyney (New York: Henry Harrison, 1931);

Midland Humor: A Harvest of Fun and Folklore, edited with an introduction by Conroy (New York: Wyn, 1947);

Writers in Revolt: The "Anvil" Anthology, 1933-1940, edited by Conroy and Curt Johnson (Westport, Conn.: Lawrence Hill, 1973).

References:

Daniel Aaron, "Introduction," in *The Disinherited* (New York: Hill & Wang, 1963), pp. vii-xiv;

Aaron, *Writers on the Left: Episodes in American Literary Communism* (New York: Harcourt, Brace & World, 1961;

James B. Gilbert, *Writers and Partisans: A History of Literary Radicalism in America* (New York: Wiley, 1968);

Frederick J. Hoffman, Charles Allen and Carolyn F. Ulrich, *The Little Magazine: A History and a Bibliography* (Princeton: Princeton University Press, 1946).

AN INTERVIEW *with JACK CONROY*

DLB: The common catch-all term for leftist literature in the 1930s was proletarian literature. Can you suggest what that term was supposed to mean to a writer?

CONROY: Ideally it meant "about the working class." But during the 1930s, there were stories about middle-class people and their troubles, that sort of thing. Leftist literature wasn't exclusively about the proletariat. It should be the worker writing about the troubles and the problems of a working-class man. But it didn't work out that way because not many of the writers were actually proletarians, members of the working class. I was one of them, being a miner's son—a genuine proletarian. But proletarian literature in the broad sense came to mean writing *about* the working class, and it wasn't always written by workers. Workers, if they have sufficient learning, like to write about things that they don't know anything about, like comfortable living or swashbuckling or fighting wars or things like that.

DLB: Who was the intended audience for proletarian literature?

CONROY: The workers, of course, who make up the majority of people but don't make up the majority of readers. I fear that no large segment ever read the literature that was intended for them. There was a core of intellectuals and workers who actually did take some interest in reading. I think of the United Mine Workers, which my father belonged to. They came over—a great many of them to Monkey Nest Camp, where I was born—from Europe. They were capable of intellectual development and had some. In England or Wales or wherever they came from, they had debating societies where they took an active interest in literature and philosophy. So they weren't entirely unlettered; the miners weren't, at any rate. But, by and large, the working class was illiterate, as it is today. Oh, they can read and write, but, as H. L. Mencken once said, "The Americano has a stupendous capacity for believing; particularly in believing that which is palpably untrue." So you see that I've inherited, or rather imbibed, some of Mencken's cynicism. I regard him as my literary godfather.

As I approach his age, I don't feel like mounting the barricades anymore because I wouldn't know which way to go! In our day, when we wrote our proletarian stories, there seemed to be only one enemy: capitalism. But who is the enemy now? In China they'll tell you that Russia is. In Russia they'll tell you that China is. And we have four or five distinct sects preaching marxism, showing the way to a marxist heaven much as Christians divide about the proper approach to get into the Christian heaven. So it's a very confusing situation today.

DLB: You claim to have written to bear witness to the times, and "to vivify the contemporary fact"; that's your phrase. But one gets the impression that most proletarian fiction was written to bring about change, even revolutionary change.

CONROY: I suppose mine was, by pointing out

these conditions. Of course, *The Disinherited* is the best example of my work. It did have a sort of revolutionary flavor, with the farmers organizing. But that actually happened. John Chamberlain, who later, I think, became pretty reactionary, was very enthusiastic about *The Disinherited* in the *New York Times*. He pointed out that the ending might seem tacked on or artificial for the sake of proletarian emphasis. But, he said, farmers *were* organizing and holding these penny option sales. That is historically true.

DLB: Can literature bring about that kind of social change?

CONROY: I think it can; it always has. Literature has inspired action and brought about social change. Think of Upton Sinclair's *The Jungle*, for example, which really brought about some reforms in the packing houses.

DLB: I was trying to gather whether, in the 1930s, people who were writing to bring about revolutionary change were disappointed to find out that their fiction didn't do that.

CONROY: I was disappointed, of course. We lived in a climate of excitement and fever then. Capitalism seemed to be collapsing; there was evidence of that. And the bottom had fallen out of the financial market. There was so much unemployment. And Roosevelt came along with his reforms, which sort of patched up the capitalist system. It's ironic that the man who saved, or certainly bolstered, the capitalist system was vilified by the ones he saved.

DLB: What effect did the Communist party have on American writing?

CONROY: They were for more drastic social change. They wanted "soviets" in the United States. They advocated a lot of excessive things which were unrealistic because the Russians who prescribed these things were deceived. They didn't know the actual situation or the temper of the American people, as Socialists before them had. The Socialists had been pretty powerful up to World War I. World War I crushed the Socialist party. But the Socialists and the agrarian reformers, like Sockless Jerry Simpson in Kansas, were much closer to the temper of the American people than the Communists.

DLB: Did the Party really attempt to influence leftist writers?

CONROY: Oh, yes indeed. And they were very, very foolish and very dictatorial about it. They did a lot of foolish things. But they did a lot of good things, too. I'm not one who wholeheartedly condemns the Communists for their role in the 1930s. They did things like organizing unemployment councils and moving furniture back into a house where people had been evicted. They had a system of literature distribution; they had some of the old Jimmy Higgins working-class bookstores. They would go into a factory and they would have ten copies of my magazine, the *Anvil*, whose slogan was "Stories for Workers," and they'd hawk them about. Meridel LeSueur, herself an author, once told me how the writers would sell the *Anvil* that way. So there were things like that being done in the 1930s which I think were beneficial.

DLB: How about the John Reed clubs? Were they good?

CONROY: The John Reed clubs were wonderful. I know Richard Wright acknowledged that and said so. They brought together aspiring artists and writers. The writers were pretty terrible sometimes, but they were earnestly trying to do something. And the clubs provided a meeting place and a forum for them. Richard Wright's dissatisfaction with the Communist party began when the party ordered John Reed clubs to be disbanded. They more or less replaced them with the League of American Writers.

DLB: That was an outgrowth of the first writers congress, in 1935, if I remember correctly.

CONROY: Oh yes, I was there.

DLB: The writers congresses in the 1930s were very political in their intent, and the League of American Writers wasn't a union. Is that correct?

CONROY: In the real sense it wasn't. They made some gestures about the inequities of royalty and all that sort of thing. But I'm afraid their main thrust was political.

DLB: There's been a recent writers congress with the suggestion that writers unionize.

CONROY: Oh, I've been reading about it. Parts of Meridel's talk were published in the *Daily World*. I've seen the first installment; I haven't managed to get the second. But it seems all to the good if it's emphasizing the financial crisis for writers. And it's about time, too. The writer gets the short end of it all, as you know, in the publishing scheme. I think from what I've read of it, it was really a step forward and something sadly needed.

DLB: Do you think the time will ever come when writers will try again to use their writing in a concerted way to bring about radical social change? The 1930s seem a unique period in American history.

CONROY: Yeah, well, I don't know. You know what Shelley said? Shelley said "Poets are the unacknowledged legislators of the world." I think that was a slight exaggeration, but to some extent it's true. I think that writers do have some impact on the times and on political movements, more than is commonly realized. And I feel that the writers will let their voices be heard again against injustices. They haven't so much lately. Certainly the "slumber years," as they're referred to, were the Eisenhower years. But, of course, there was a flurry during the Vietnam period. I don't know what'll happen in the 1980s, but I feel that something will, some sort of rebellion. "Boobus Americanus," when you tread on him too much, will turn.

–Jon Christian Suggs

Michael Crichton

(23 October 1942-)

Robert L. Sims
Virginia Commonwealth University

SELECTED BOOKS: *Odds On*, as John Lange (New York: New American Library, 1966);

Scratch One, as John Lange (New York: New American Library, 1967);

Easy Go, as John Lange (New York: New American Library, 1968);

A Case of Need, as Jeffery Hudson (New York: World, 1968);

Zero Cool, as John Lange (New York: New American Library, 1969);

The Venom Business, as John Lange (New York: World, 1969);

The Andromeda Strain (New York: Knopf, 1969);

Five Patients: The Hospital Explained (New York: Knopf, 1970);

The Terminal Man (New York: Knopf, 1972);

The Great Train Robbery (New York: Knopf, 1975);

Eaters of the Dead (New York: Knopf, 1976);

Jasper Johns (New York: Abrams, 1977);

Congo (New York: Knopf, 1980).

John Michael Crichton was born in Chicago, Illinois, the oldest child of John Henderson and Zula Crichton. His family moved early in his life to Roslyn, Long Island, where he grew up with his two sisters, Kimberly and Catherine, and his brother Douglas. His father, who died in 1977, was the president of the American Association of Advertising Agencies, and one of the primary topics of conversation at dinner in the Crichton household was English usage. Crichton started writing at an early age. He recalls that at age fourteen "I sold an article to the travel section of the *Times* and got 60 dollars. It kept me in money for a year." He always enjoyed mystery stories and movies, and among his favorite authors were Edgar Allan Poe, Sir Arthur Conan Doyle, and Alfred Hitchcock. These influences played an important role in his own writing career.

After earning a B.A. degree summa cum laude in anthropology at Harvard College of Harvard University in 1964, Crichton conducted anthropological and ethnological field work in Europe on a travel fellowship. While in England, he read Len Deighton's *The Ipcress File* (1962), which impressed him greatly. In 1965, while still in Europe,

he married Joan Radam. (They were divorced in 1970.) When he returned in 1965 to Harvard, where he had been accepted in the medical school, he began writing mystery novels to earn money. Using the pseudonym John Lange, he churned out *Odds On* (1966), *Scratch One* (1967), *Easy Go* (1968), *Zero Cool* (1969), and *The Venom Business* (1969).

He also produced a more carefully written mystery story, *A Case of Need* (1968), under the pseudonym Jeffery Hudson. Reviewers praised it, and he received the Edgar Allan Poe Award of the Mystery Writers of America for the best mystery of the year, and in 1972 MGM produced a film from the novel. The story concerns Dr. Arthur Lee, an obstetrician and benevolent illegal abortionist, who is unjustly accused and arrested for causing the death of Karen Randall, teenage daughter of a prominent Boston surgeon. Lee's close friend, pathologist John Berry, sets out to track down the real culprit, and his search earns him the enmity of those who wish to conceal the truth. In the framework of a tautly strung novel, Crichton examines the highly volatile question of abortion and makes a plea for a more rational approach to the problem.

In 1969 as a postdoctoral fellow at the Salk Institute for Biological Studies in La Jolla, California, Crichton finally decided that he was not dedicated enough to practice medicine: "These people were professionals of a very high order, and I was a pottering amateur." Since then he has applied his anthropological and medical training to his fictional creations.

Critical reaction to Crichton's novels has typically classified his work as popular fiction. Peter Andrews in the *New York Times Book Review* wrote that a "Crichton novel is always entertaining enough to pass a pleasantly idle hour, and if you lose it or someone swipes it, you're not out much." Another critic sums up his novels as having "a suspenseful plot that strains our credulity just beyond the breaking point, a few raffish characters who keep our interest, enough background information to indicate that the author has given the narrative his personal attention, and there you have it."

Crichton's approach to writing is consistent

from work to work. He fully exploits the techniques available to the omniscient author, controlling every facet of his plots, which are constructed as suspensefully as a Hitchcock film. He has said that the older he becomes, "the more it seems that Hitchcock is the major influence" in his work. His plots also reflect another Hitchcock concern—the constant concern with entertaining his readers. Crichton's characters are one-dimensional figures whose psychological makeups are determined by the particular drama in which they are involved. By and large, his characters tend to be exceptional people (scientists, psychiatrists, doctors, etc.) possessing specialized skills, who find themselves in extraordinary situations. Crichton often uses flashbacks to develop his characters. Although his plots are more memorable than his characters, the success of his fiction depends on human fallibility. In general, he has achieved his greatest success with fast-paced, plausible novels that combine elements of the fantasy and science-fiction genres (as in *The Andromeda Strain*, 1969, *The Terminal Man*, 1972, *The Great Train Robbery*, 1975, and *Congo*, 1980).

Crichton writes in a clean, concise prose. He usually works in short spans of a week or two, turning out 10,000 words during each sixteen-hour work day. His sentences are generally elliptical and convey essential information. There are few if any contemplative moments or long descriptive passages, except in those cases where Crichton assumes the role of medical, scientific, or social historian. Since 1979 he has written everything on a word processor, which allows him to compose and correct rapidly and efficiently. His fast-moving, visual style and his plots are readily adaptable to film, a medium Crichton likes; he has already written a variety of screenplays. "I'm interested in exposure," he says. "If there's something you want to say, no matter how wild, the best way is television. More people will see one lousy television show in a night than will see a good movie in a year. More people will see a lousy movie in a week than read a good book in a year."

Crichton prefaces his novels with scientific, medical, and historical introductions and adds minidigressions which establish verisimilitude and promote suspension of disbelief in his readers. As one critic put it, his novels are "both a backward look to the nineteenth-century realistic novel (written to transmit social and industrial information) and a projection into the future when the novel will organize and synthesize the findings of technology and science." Crichton uses these elements to strengthen his plots. His medical training undoubt-

edly plays a crucial role in reader acceptance of not so much the accuracy as the plausibility of his novels. He subordinates everything to plot, for his primary purpose is to tell a good story: "What I do is entertain people—that's all Dickens ever did, or Robert Louis Stevenson. They got made into artists by subsequent generations, but at the time all they were saying was 'Hey, do you want to hear a good story?' "

In 1969, while still in medical school, he finished *The Andromeda Strain* after collecting newspaper clippings and research articles and writing several drafts. Influenced by *The Ipcress File* and H. G. Wells's *War of the Worlds*, the novel was very problematic because, as he says, "I was up against the very considerable absurdity of the idea of a plague from outer space. When I finally learned that a complicated quarantine procedure really existed for the United States moon program, it was a considerable boost, and then I knew I could do the book." *The Andromeda Strain* was a best-seller. The Dell paperback edition sold over 3,000,000 copies, and the novel was chosen as a Book-of-the-Month Club selection. In 1971, Universal Pictures released

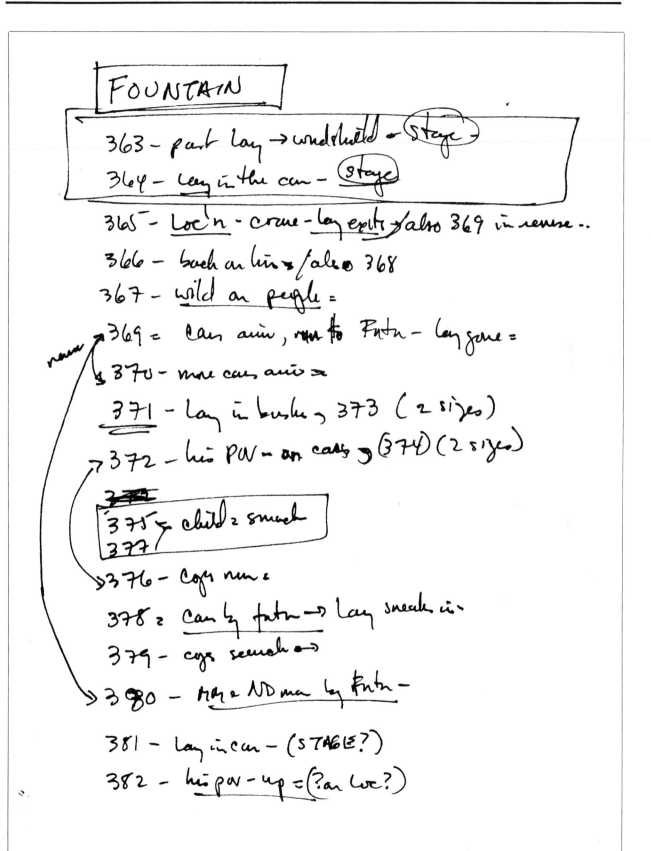

Shot list for a sequence in the film Looker

the popular movie version under the same name. (The screenplay was written by Nelson Gilding.)

The Andromeda Strain is a key novel to understanding Crichton's work method. He writes about fictional situations as if they had already transpired: "I found you could make something more believable if you pretended not that it might happen or was happening, but that it had happened. You are not there, it is over." This ploy allows him to control the flow of the narrative and insert related material. *The Andromeda Strain* recounts with documentary verisimilitude the story of Project Wildfire, the top secret project of the United States government to gather organisms from outer space for use in biological warfare research. When an unmanned space probe from Project Scoop returns to earth mysteriously, lethally contaminated, and lands in an isolated section of Arizona, Project Wildfire is mobilized to combat the threat of worldwide contamination by a virus, called the "Andromeda Strain." In Nevada, four scientists engage in a race against time to find an antidote to the unknown microorganism which has inexplicably killed all but a baby and an old derelict in the isolated town of Piedmont, Arizona. Stone, a Nobel Prize-winning bacteriologist; Leavitt, a clinical microbiologist; Burton, a pathologist; and Hall, a practicing surgeon-physician, wage their war against the virus in their supersophisticated, supersterile, underground laboratory.

Crichton's narrative focuses on the scientific, social, and political issues created by our constantly expanding technology. Technological innovations are introduced at such a dizzying pace that the average person is incapable of understanding them; thus, the responsible use of technology lies in the hands of a relatively small group of people. Even these specialists are capable of oversights, miscalculations, and poor judgment, partly due to their own technological tunnel vision.

Crichton expresses his continuing interest in contemporary medical and ethical problems in a nonfictional yet characteristically dramatic format in his next book, written during his last months in medical school in 1969. Crichton spent much of his time at the Massachusetts General Hospital, where, with the cooperation of its director, Dr. John Knowles, he researched *Five Patients: The Hospital Explained* (1970). He was named the 1970 Medical Writer of the Year by the Association of American Medical Writers for his work.

In *Five Patients: The Hospital Explained*, Crichton examines the health care profession by showing how a modern medical center functions.

Using five case studies as points of departure, he posits the idea that "medicine has become not a changed profession but a perpetually changing one. There is no longer a sense that one can make a few adjustments and then return to a steady state, for the system will never be stable again. There is nothing permanent except change itself." As always, his presentation of each case pulsates with drama, but he also explores such topics as expanding, changing medical technology, the spiraling costs of medical care and running a hospital, and the relationships between patients and doctors, and doctors themselves. He scrutinizes the traditionally conservative posture of the American Medical Association and criticizes what he sees as its irresponsible opposition to measures designed to benefit both patients and doctors. Crichton also studies the hospital in relation to society at large and provides a global view of the hospital's evolution from a custodial institution for the sick to its present-day role as an arena of crises. The book is written by a doctor who prefers writing about medicine to practicing it. As Crichton has stated, "I don't think I would have made a good doctor. It bored me silly."

The Terminal Man, like *The Andromeda Strain*, is a fictional work with a scientific basis. It was a bestseller and Book-of-the-Month Club selection, and a movie version was released by Warner Brothers in 1974. The novel involves an attempt at behavior modification through psychosurgery. Harry Benson, whose mind has been damaged in an automobile accident and who is subject to epileptic seizures during which he becomes violent, is implanted with electrodes to prevent these attacks. Predictably enough, the mechanism goes awry and Benson goes on a violent rampage during which he is pursued by neurosurgeons eager to defuse him. As Crichton has declared: "I've always wanted to rewrite *Frankenstein*, and this is it."

The book raises the same questions, though in a less sophisticated manner, as *The Andromeda Strain*, about the uses and abuses of technology in the hands of specialists whose judgment is suspect. Though *The Terminal Man* contains Crichton's customary dose of semiscientific data, charts, computers, and microhistories which expand the reader's horizons, it is ultimately a work of popular fiction. Theodore Sturgeon declared that "one regrets that so careful a piece of work should thereby remove itself from art into the arena of entertainment."

The Great Train Robbery (1975) and *Eaters of the Dead* (1976) mark a departure for Crichton from the world of science, and both qualify as pure entertainment. *The Great Train Robbery*, loosely based

```
SHOOTING SEQUENCE - LOOKER ROOM

1.  MASTER ON ALL ACTION.  From beside door, they remain R as
they enter.
1A.  TRACKING POV - INTO ROOM - as door opens and we go in
2.  STATIC POV - LARRY AND CINDY RIDE IN, jump off.
3.  WIDE SHOT - MASTER - PAN OVER TO MM hiding.  PAN UP TO LARRY
AND CINDY in position at screens and monitors.
4.  CLOSE ON L AND C as they get off, switch lights.
5.  THEIR POV - LIGHT CHANGE.  TRACK TO MANUAL
6.  2 SHOT MASTER - MISSING SCREENS - LARRY AND CINDY
7.  REVERSE 2 SHOT MASTER - MISSING SCREENS - L and C  LOCKED
CAMERA.
8.  CLOSE ON LARRY - UP AT HIM AS HE LOOKS AT MANUAL
9.  CLOSE ON CINDY - RAKING HER AS SHE LOOKS AT SCREENS
0.  FACING MM as he rises, with gun.
11.  DISAPPEARANCE - L and C, LOCKED CAMERA.
        FROM NOW ON ALL HANDHELD SEQUENCES
12.  CLOSE ON LARRY, TURNING AROUND
13.  LARRY'S POV, THE ROOM (360) and push toward cross hatch
panels and
14.  LARRY STRIKES CROSSHATCH PANEL, FALLS.
14A.  TRACK TOWARD GLASS, and
15.  LARRY STRIKES THE GLASS, FALLS.  (bleeding lip)
16.  PROTECTION : OVER LARRY to MONITOR, SHOWING MM on closed
circuit TV.
17.  LARRY MOVES TO FIRST TABLE, takes tumble.
18.  LARRY FALLS BEHIND TABLE.  EXTREME CLOSE UP, like Psycho.
One eye.  Gets to feet.
19.  POV LARRY - FEET - MULTIPLE TILTS  (not handheld)
20.  LARRY RISES - ALONE
21.  POV LARRY - THE ROOM
22.  LARRY FLUNG AGAINST WALL, COLLAPSES.  (wire pull)
23.  LARRY BACK TO THE TABLES.
24.  LARRY FLIES OVER 2 TABLES.  (pole gag)
25.  LARRY HITS BETWEEN TABLES.  GETS TO FEET.
26.  POV LARRY - CINDY.
27.  LARRY - SEES HER, does not move toward her.
28.  LARRY - BACKS UP - TO WALL.
29.  LARRY AT WALL - CAVES IN.
30.  LARRY FLUNG FORWARD TOWARD PIT.
31.  LARRY LANDS AT PIT EDGE, lights flicking.
32.  HIGH ANGLE DOWN on his predicament.
33.  LARRY BACKS OFF, goes deeper.
34.  LARRY SEES VIDEO SCREEN
35.  VIDEO SCREEN - PUNCH COMING
36.  LARRY GOES THROUGH GLASS
37.  LARRY INSIDE BOOTH - RECOVERING.  SEES MONITOR showing
Moustache Man approaching.
38.  LARRY LOOKING UP AT ROOM
39.  HIS POV - NOBODY THERE.
40.  LARRY EXITS - PUSHES CHAIR.  STRIKES MM, TOPLES OVER.
41.  LARRY RUNS TOWARD GLASSES, grabs a pair.  Gets hit.  PAN TO
MM pushing him away.
```

Working continuity for a fight sequence in Looker

on a little-known train robbery in Victorian England, became an immediate best-seller and was a
Book-of-the-Month Club selection. He also wrote
the screenplay of the enormously successful movie
released in 1979. Crichton did not do extensive
research for the book: "I didn't go to England. I sat
right here. I never looked up any court records; I
don't know that any exist. It wasn't a famous story.
At least, nobody ever heard of it till now. To me, the
appeal of doing a book like this is that you get to
make up what the world should have been like."
The novel involves a train robbery of gold bullion
masterminded by the aristocratic, wealthy, and
mysterious criminal Edward Pierce. Crichton

weaves an intricate plot punctuated by minidigressions on Victorian trains, burial customs, slang, technology, and mores.

Eaters of the Dead, a retelling of *Beowulf*, constitutes a fictional voyage into the land of the Vikings in medieval times. It is the first-person account of a clever tenth-century Arab diplomat, Ibn Fadlan, who, while on a delicate mission to the king of the Bulgars, is waylaid by the Viking barbarians. They take him to the far reaches of the Volga where he encounters the mysterious, murderous creatures, called Wendols, who are ravaging the Vikings' homeland. *Eaters of the Dead* again conforms to Crichton's writing formula—a good story infused with enough plausible detail so as to make it acceptable to the reader—but, contrary to his previous novels, it is applied to the remote past. The novel also demonstrates his apparent fascination with depicting unusual and sometimes gory ways of dying, as the Wendols' successive attacks are described in great detail.

In his latest novel, *Congo*, Crichton returns to the technological frontiers of the not-so-distant future, but here technology is put to quite different uses than before. Three adventurers cut through the rain forests of the Congo in search of the diamonds of the Lost City of Zinj which will revolutionize computer technology. Peter Elliot, a young Californian who is a primate specialist, accompanied by his intelligent gorilla, Amy; Karen Ross, a beautiful young genius from the Houston-based Earth Resources Technology Services, which is determined to find the valuable industrial diamonds before its ruthless Euro-Japanese rival; and Captain Charles Munro, an experienced "white hunter," join forces to overcome pygmies, killer hippopotamuses, ferocious tribal warfare, volcanoes, the rival global consortium, and an intelligent but murderous species of jungle gorilla in order to find the prized diamonds.

Congo is a well-told story exposing the reader yet again to complex issues related to technological advance; moreover, it reveals the merits and inadequacies of Crichton's fiction. Peter S. Prescott summed up his view by stating: "Scientists know that the genus trash comprises four distinct species three malignant and one benign: boring trash, meretricious trash, fallacious trash and entertaining trash. Most trashy novels are one or the other, but

Michael Crichton's distinction is that his latest romance combines the latter two." Harold Hayes regards *Congo* as "Michael Crichton's pop-science offering to Hollywood's World of Tomorrow—to the mythology of a future so close and yet so unsettling as to be perceived safely only through imaginings formed first by comic strips." While Prescott and Raymond Sokolov felt that Crichton had gone too far in portraying an ape who could use language, Harold Hayes was undisturbed, and Eugene Linden, who studies primate language, felt that objections to Crichton's depiction of Amy were unfounded. Yet both Prescott and Hayes touch upon an important question concerning Crichton's fiction; namely, the extent to which the popularization of his works detracts from his attempt to disseminate scientific information and address the related moral, social, political, and human issues.

Crichton has been a tremendous popular success, and his critics have praised him primarily for his ability to tell a good story based on quasi-factual data. His importance lies in his capacity to tell stories related to that frontier where fiction and science meet and, as in *The Andromeda Strain*, to increase public understanding of the technological world. His fiction is perhaps a reflection of the new version of the American Dream—this time a technological dream. In the vacillating struggle between a periodical return to displaced spiritual values and a renewed confidence in man's new technological gods, Crichton's best novels (*The Andromeda Strain* and in certain parts *Congo*) demonstrate that, for the immediate future at least, technological innovations offer the same possibilities and limitations as their human creators. *Congo*'s visual, fast-moving style and plot reveal Crichton's cinematic approach to fiction, and it could easily be made into a film. He says that "it may not seem 'literary,' but a great deal of my time is now devoted to making films that I have written, and I consider this as important as anything else I do. In any case, my film work is what differentiates me from most writers."

Screenplays:
Extreme Closeup, National General, 1973;
Westworld, MGM, 1973;
Coma, United Artists, 1978;
The Great Train Robbery, United Artists, 1979;
Looker, Warner Brothers, 1981.

Frederick Exley

(28 March 1929-   )

Michael Adams
Louisiana State University

BOOKS: *A Fan's Notes* (New York, Evanston & London: Harper & Row, 1968; London: Weidenfeld & Nicolson, 1970);

Pages from a Cold Island (New York: Random House, 1975).

Autobiography, fiction, confession, psychotherapy—whatever they are, Frederick Exley's books are remarkable works. *A Fan's Notes* (1968), *Pages from a Cold Island* (1975), and his work in progress, "Last Notes from Home," depict a character gone mad at a time when his country has perhaps gone even madder. Frederick Exley is hard on the narrator he calls Exley, who frequently seems content to drink, sleep, fornicate, and whine his life away, but he is equally hard on the age in which Exley has lived without using it to justify his character's paranoia. He is outraged at "the obscene spectacle America has become" but realizes that to remain alive a man must confront this America and try to understand it, even at the risk of insanity and self-destruction. Exley attempts a great deal in his books, fails occasionally, but writes beautifully and amusingly about the horrors he has seen, the horror he has lived.

Born in Watertown, New York, the son of Earl Exley, a telephone lineman, and Charlotte Merkley Exley, Exley briefly attended Hobart College before transferring to the University of Southern California, where he majored in English, graduating in 1953. As *A Fan's Notes* vividly recounts, he spent the next fifteen years failing at a series of jobs, including public relations work in New York, Chicago, and Los Angeles and high school teaching in rural New York, twice undergoing treatment at a mental institution, and trying to write. His marriage to Francena Fritz, 1967-1970, produced a daughter, Pamela Rae, and his second marriage to Nancy Glenn, 1970-1974, another daughter, Alexandra.

Exley embellishes the events of his life, exaggerating or underplaying them, making composites of real people, inventing characters. *A Fan's Notes* is subtitled *A Fictional Memoir*; Exley explains in his preface: "Though the events in this book bear similarity to those of that long malaise, my life, many of the characters and happenings are cre-

ations solely of the imagination. . . . I have drawn freely from the imagination and adhered only loosely to the pattern of my past life. To this extent, and for this reason, I ask to be judged as a writer of fantasy." *Pages from a Cold Island*, however, he calls "a work of nonfiction": "I have in some cases, to save them and me embarrassment, changed the names of real persons, their physical descriptions, in other instances even the locations where the action occurs." What is or is not factual is usually irrelevant, for what Exley the writer does with Exley the character is what matters. Although Exley comes close to being a self-pitying confessional writer at times, especially in *Pages from a Cold Island*, he usually presents his fictional Exley with objectivity and irony and seems as amazed as the reader at what this character says and does. If Exley is a great writer, it is not for his public self-torment but for what he reveals about success and failure in contemporary America.

A Fan's Notes opens sometime in the 1960s when Exley suffers what he takes to be a heart attack and is surprised to learn that he wants to live. The book goes on to reveal what has caused him to reach his nadir. His main problem is that he wants success and fame, a need instilled in him by his father, famous in and around Watertown for his athletic exploits and beloved by all who know him. Exley both loves and resents the father whose accomplishments he has never been allowed to forget even years after Earl's death in 1945; in Watertown he has never been Fred Exley but always Earl Exley's son. The father makes the son's predicament worse when the Watertown junior varsity basketball team plays an old-timers' team and thirteen-year-old Fred has to guard thirty-nine-year-old Earl who scores three baskets in two minutes against his son: "all the way home I had had to repress an urge to weep, to sob uncontrollably, and to shout at him my humiliation and my loathing. 'Oh, Jesus, Pop! *Why? Why? Why?*' I have always been sorry I didn't shout that humiliation. Had my father found the words to tell me why he so needed The Crowd, I might have saved my soul and now be a farm-implement salesman living sublimely content in Shaker Heights with my wife Marylou and six spewling brats." Exley inherits his need for success from his father: "I suffered myself the singular notion that fame was an heirloom passed on from my father. . . . like him, I wanted to have my name one day called back and bantered about in consecrated whispers."

The second symbol of success in *A Fan's Notes* is Frank Gifford, an all-American football player during Fred's days at Southern California and later a star with the New York Giants when Exley goes to Manhattan after college to fulfill his dream of success. Gifford began to become a hero for Exley when Fred, as a campus intellectual resentful of dumb jocks, tried to insult him by sneering at him at a hamburger joint only to receive a friendly smile in return: "With that smile, whatever he meant by it, a smile he doubtless wouldn't remember, he impressed upon me, in the rigidity of my embarrassment, that it is unmanly to burden others with one's grief." Exley comes to identify with Gifford: "Where I could not, with syntax, give shape to my fantasies, Gifford could, with his superb timing, his great hands, his uncanny faking, give shape to his. It was something more than this: I cheered for him with such inordinate enthusiasm, my yearning became so involved with his desire to escape life's bleak anonymity, that after a time he became my alter ego, that part of me which had its being in the competitive world of men; I came, as incredible as it seems to me now, to believe that I was, in some magical way, an actual instrument of his success. Each time I heard the roar of the crowd, it roared in my ears as much for me as him; that roar was not only a promise of my fame, it was its unequivocal assurance."

Exley is not only devoted to Gifford but to the Giants as well, his father having taught him early to love the team. Football gives the alcoholic Exley a focus missing elsewhere in his life: "Why did football bring me so to life? . . . Part of it was my feeling that football was an island of directness in a world of circumspection. In football a man was asked to do a difficult and brutal job, and he either did it or got out. There was nothing rhetorical or vague about it. . . . It smacked of something old, something traditional, something unclouded by legerdemain and subterfuge. It had that kind of power over me, drawing me back with the force of something known, scarcely remembered, elusive as integrity—perhaps it was no more than the force of a forgotten childhood. Whatever it was, I gave myself up to the Giants utterly. The recompense I gained was the feeling of being alive." Football players, regardless of how much they play, regardless of their statistics, regardless of their team's success, are winners by the simple fact that they are athletes;

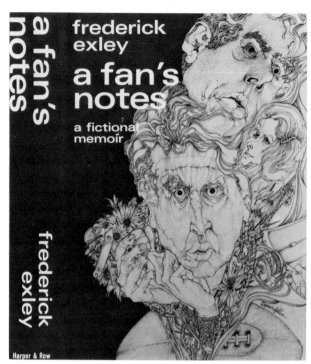

Dust jacket for Exley's first novel

they have achieved something which always eludes the Exleys of the world.

A Fan's Notes is primarily the story of Exley's quest for the American Dream. When he first arrives in New York he confesses, "I wanted the wealth and the power that fame would bring; and finally, I wanted love—or said that I did, though I know now that what I wanted was the adulation of the crowd, and that *love* was just a word that crowded so many other, more appropriate words off the tongue." The quest of this "self-destructively romantic man" leads him to Bunny Sue Allorgee, the Daisy Buchanan for this Jay Gatsby. Bunny Sue not only represents what Exley longs for but what he fears: "I was afraid—scared to death. I had waited too long for her, lived with the dream of her for always, and the thought of actually grasping it struck me, cruelly and ironically, impotent, in words to say, in motions to make, in every possible way."

If Exley's impotence with Bunny Sue suggests his doubts about the dream, the object of his unfulfilled desire has no qualms at all. In fact, she is willing to marry him not despite his impotence but apparently because of it. Exley understands her need for his weakness when they visit her parents in a plastic Midwestern suburb and he sees how Bunny Sue's mother dominates her husband, the father "docilely permitting his own emasculation." Poppy is permitted pride in the reception of his television set and in gadgets such as a garage-door opener but little else: "the thought that this might indeed be my heritage, my fate, struck me all the more impotent." Exley is unable to take any solace in his rejection of life with Bunny Sue (with her suggestive initials) since he has no alternate view of life to escape to: "did I really know that I would have been unhappy, or should I say any less happy, in that life? . . . I do know that the road I was to take would prove neither particularly pleasant nor edifying nor fruitful."

Exley gradually retreats from life into heavy drinking (about which he is unapologetic), passivity (lying on a couch in his mother's house, reading or watching television), and, finally, madness. Exley presents mental instability as a necessary by-product of the American pursuit of success, almost as an alternative way of life. He never sentimentalizes his fellow "inmates" at Avalon Valley but sees them as America's losers whom society wants to hide from sight: "We had failed our families by our *inability to function properly in society* (as good a definition of insanity as any); our families, tears compounded by self-pity in their eyes, had pleaded with the doctors to give us the goals that would set our legs in motion again. The goals—a wife and family, a vice-presidency, a Cadillac—varied only with the imper-

ceptibility, the bland vision of the relative."

Exley tries to impose some order on the chaos of his life by writing, but he has to burn his manuscript "because on every page I had discovered I loathed the America I knew." He is constantly torn between accepting America's middle-class values and rejecting them. His dilemma is dramatized in a recurrent dream with which he ends the book. Exley is walking beside a highway and is passed by a group of drunken college boys in a white convertible who hurl beer cans and obscenities at him. When their car breaks down behind him, Exley turns and runs toward them only to be beaten. He tries to alter the outcome of the dream only to have it recur exactly as before, again and again. C. Barry Chabot, whose essay Exley considers the best analysis of his work, writes that here Exley "shoulders his personal responsibility for the cultural brutishness he has analyzed in such anger. Thus implicating himself in his critique, Exley accepts sin and remorse, transgression and guilt, as inescapable baggage in human life. . . . Exley eventually sees the very capacity for feeling guilt (not guilt itself) as the grounds of our common humanity." By accepting this responsibility and common humanity and turning it into art, Exley gives up being a fan to become, finally, the hero of his life. It is this conviction that the Great American Loser is entitled to and

Frederick Exley

can earn his dignity that gives *A Fan's Notes* much of its vitality and emotional strength.

For a novel rejected by fourteen publishers, *A Fan's Notes* had a surprising success with its reviewers. Mike McGrady in *Newsday* called it "the best novel written in the English language since *The Great Gatsby*." In the *Hudson Review* J. Mitchell Morse called it "one of the best new novels I have read in a long time; Exley the character is worthy of comparison with Antoine Roquentin, Zeno Cosini, and Thomas Mann's Dilettante." *Newsweek*'s Jack Kroll wrote that Exley "has the Fitzgerald-like gift to wrap up the aching vision of beauty . . . the funnily maladroit failure to possess that beauty, and the overwhelming despair that follows the entire process—all in a single tone of narrative accuracy whose authentic sweetness is the measure of its truth-telling. His book . . . is a welcome reminder of what the basic business of literature, and of living, really is." *A Fan's Notes*, according to the *Times Literary Supplement*, "is not a manic cry of anguish and self-pity; self-examination is what Mr. Exley is about. . . . the wry, sometimes painfully funny events are kept from becoming maudlin, but retain the poignancy of a confession which, told solely to amuse, gains sympathy for that reason." Other reviewers, however, responded like the editors who rejected the book. In *New Statesman* Stanley Reynolds called it "rambling, unclear, repetitious, and written in that curious overblown American style. . . . The effect . . . is rather like getting button-holed by a drunk in a bar who grips you by both lapels, breathing whisky and polysyllables into your face, and never uses two words where he can possibly find 10 that'll do." Most of the literary establishment obviously felt differently, for *A Fan's Notes* won the William Faulkner Award as the best first novel of 1968 and the National Institute of Arts and Letters's Richard and Hinda Rosenthal Award for "that work which, though not a commercial success, is a considerable literary achievement."

The reviews and awards, however, were not enough for Exley. In *Pages from a Cold Island* (1975) he writes that awaiting the publication of his first book he "fell asleep to dreams of a fame that never came." "Despite some unanticipated generous reviews," the book did not sell well: "I'd made little money; my life style of lugging my own soiled sweat shirts and skivvies to the laundromat and lunching on cheeseburgers and draft beer had altered not a whit." His fame amounted only to "a certain limited and somewhat dopey cult following among university students."

Exley has retreated from public indifference, a failed marriage, and other disappointments to his "cold island," Singer Island, Riviera Beach, Florida, where he "dwelt in that oddly euphoric languor of a man with no place but up to go." Amid a group of beach bums and prostitutes who take pride in being "all on a slow boat to nowhere," Exley cultivates his malaise and paranoia: "With Beckett (the literary not the historical) I hold it as axiomatic that rather than a deadly sin torpor and sloth comprise a spiritual condition insulating one from life's crippling hurts called disenchantments, a condition out of which there stands revealed, finally, the heart's epiphanies." Once, however, the epiphanies are not there, and Exley, for the second time in his life, decides to commit suicide. After calling James Dickey to apologize because the poet-novelist had helped him obtain a $10,000 Rockefeller Foundation grant, he gets out his Magnum but cannot go further: "I do not know what saved me. At some point I began to laugh, riotously. Suicide presupposes that something is being eliminated. With a silver-inlaid shotgun Hemingway blows away the back of his head, and when the world recovers it finds itself able to remark, 'What a man!' But what precisely was being eliminated in my case? Certainly not a man. Whatever I was eliminating was so inconsequential as to make the gesture one of trifling and contemptible ease and I began to think how much more felicitous the act would be if I sobered up, as best I could healed my mind and body, then erased some bone and tissue that at least conspired to resemble the human. Only then, I thought, might the gesture take on a certain flair or style."

The main cause of Exley's despair is his inability to make *Pages from a Cold Island* work; his 480-page manuscript has stayed in the trunk of his Nova for three years. This book, as with the early version of *A Fan's Notes*, fails because it is "so unrelievedly desolate": "In those pages I'd put down one American's journey through the Sixties and especially his reaction to what historians call 'the great events.' If I had entered the Sixties more given to dark derogation than to joyous celebration, I'd at least been an articulate, relatively hopeful creature. But I had crawled out of the period on my knees, a simpering, stuttering, drunken and mute mess." Though the book is publishable, it is not the book he wants published. Then two days after contemplating suicide, he reads a magazine article about feminist Gloria Steinem and decides that she can save his book: "I thought if I could look right through that lovely placid mask and understand why Steinem so *cared* . . . I might then introduce her into the pile of desolation . . . and thereby lift the pages into those

2-2

Hannibal, with that uncanny animal instinct of his, sensed

some hanky-panky and placed his six-feet, seven-inch 275-pound,

utterly lean and bemuscled frame directly between Jim's and

my line of vision. Not that Jim picked up on anything anyway.

In distress he has a nervous habit of twitching his mustache

and blinking his own eyes, perhaps the ~~poor~~ guy ~~m~~an thought I was

mocking him, perhaps he feels I suffer the same distracting

tic and that we are brothers in affliction. Whatever, his

ministrations completed, Jim gave me a hail-fellow, jovial

poke between my shoulder blades and assured me it was only

a minor crack and that I'd be back on the golf course within

ten days to two weeks.

God of Israel, Sophia, if I am forced one more time

to play 18 holes with ~~with~~ O'Twoomey, Hannibal and Toby I

shall go round the bend completely, though my so-called oldest

pal in the world, Wiley Hampson, about whom you've heard so

much from me, says I'm that anyway, the worst--"the most

mental," he called it--he's ever seen me. One night when

he was drunk the bastard actually had the audacity, in oh-

so-high-and-mighty and self-righteously slurring tones, to

tell O'Twoomey that I was the most paranoid Wiley had ever

seen me and that if O'Twoomey were really my pal he'd get

me institutionalized in some swanky joint Wiley knows of

on Oahu.

"Tut, tut, Wiley," said the totally insane O'Twoomey,

"My dear Frederick shall prevail. Yes, Frederick shall pre-

vail."

Wiley is so busy, so obsessively absorbed in building

Revised typescript page from "Last Notes from Home"

heady regions I felt worthy of offering to my peers."

Exley's December 1971 interview with Steinem is the comic highlight of a frequently funny book and illustrates what Exley the writer does best with Exley the character. Alternately painfully shy and arrogantly brash, eloquent and incoherent, worshipful and lustful, Exley turns the interview into an embarrassing disaster at times. When things go badly, Exley, without understanding why, presses on: "I guess I stayed partly out of courtesy, partly because I can't help being a creature of somewhat frayed hopes, partly because I believed my life style with women was a shambles and thought I might yet take something from Gloria to abet me on my farcical journey in search of my destiny or salvation or whatever preposterous thing I imagined myself in search of."

If Steinem does not quite succeed in "saving" *Pages from a Cold Island*, Edmund Wilson does. Exley is drawn to "America's last preeminently civilized man" because they are both autobiographical writers and both deeply love upstate New York; moreover, Wilson succeeded in living the meaningful, reasonably ordered life Exley feels he has been denied. He also credits reading Wilson for the first time during his "'insane' period" with "having no less than saved my life," by teaching him how to read and, in the process, what literature is so that in "a vast world a man might have something worthy of his attention." When Wilson dies in 1972, Exley feels a compelling need to write something about the great man with whom he has had one brief telephone conversation, and he interviews Wilson's secretary, Mary Pcolar, and his daughter Rosalind Baker Wilson, failing to get the latter to talk about her father. In his quest for "something of Wilson to carry with me," Exley discovers his subject's complexities, contradictions, and humor and shows how movingly he can write about someone other than Frederick Exley.

In *Pages from a Cold Island*, Exley refers to a letter about *A Fan's Notes* from a psychiatrist who "sent me reeling with a truth about myself I had never before articulated when he told me he had never before encountered 'a man so haunted by sense of place.' In this regard he cited my love for my hometown of Watertown, for the neighboring St. Lawrence and its idyllic green islands, for my mother's lovely limestone farmhouse, for the room I had built for myself therein . . . and for Edmund Wilson's Talcottville stone house which even in those pages I had mentioned in passing." In learning about Wilson, Exley learns about himself as well, learns how true the psychiatrist's observation is:

"Watertown is not in my marrow, it is my marrow."

Alfred Kazin, claiming to have liked *A Fan's Notes*, said in the *New York Times Book Review* that in *Pages from a Cold Island* "Exley cares for nothing but storytelling, has evidently read nothing but novels, and wouldn't recognize the unfabled, unvarnished, non-smart truth if it hit him. Like so many new American writers, he grew up on 20th-century novels, he would rather be Nick Carraway than anyone else, he often confuses himself with Herzog. Through such a film of famous characters, scenes, narrative techniques, he no longer knows his life from the book he has made of it." For Kazin, Exley's second book is "a magazine-smart piece of writing by a very good writer who is afraid of letting us see the dilemma that made this book necessary."

Calling Kazin's assessment "monumentally wrong-headed," Jonathan Yardley praised Exley in the *New Republic*: "Readers who aren't interested in the workings of his mind probably won't be interested in his books, but what strikes me as singularly impressive in both of them is that he *makes* the reader interested. . . . He matters . . . because beneath the sad surface of a life seemingly given over to too much booze and too much random sex and too much aimlessness, there is a true writer, an artist unseduced by fad and fashion, pressing on to the fulfillment of his vision. *Pages from a Cold Island* is real progress toward that goal." Exley also matters, as Richard P. Brickner observed in the *New Leader*, because "he reminds us that a large part of the trouble he discovers is trouble we, too, have had, and that much of the rest is trouble we haven't the nerve to seek. . . . He is a kind of redeemer, exonerating our mischievous wishes, and less frequent acts, while experiencing them. He operates with a helpless force of Id that carries us, as readers, beyond embarrassment for him and for our own desires and crudities, to a state of amused, relieved acceptance."

"Last Notes from Home," excerpts from which have appeared in *Rolling Stone* and *Inside Sports*, deals with, among other subjects, his relationships with his brother Col. William R. Exley, veteran of three wars, dying of cancer in a Honolulu hospital in 1972, and with Robin Glenn, a stewardess he meets on his flight to Hawaii, beginning a five-year affair. In Robin, Exley comes across someone whose excesses, sexual and emotional, surpass his own. Robin, who once hurled a double-pronged steak fork into Exley's chest, sees him "as a writer first, perhaps as just another screw second, and possibly even as a fellow human being third. Thus I suspect Robin believed she would show up 'enshrined' among the pages of this book." Despite Robin's neuroses, Exley loves her: "In all the sad and illusory, the laughable and perspicacious, the unbearable and joyous days of my life, I have never addressed myself more urgently to love." Exley's portrait of Robin Glenn makes clearer that all of his writing is about varying kinds and degrees of love—for Gifford, Wilson, friends, relatives, wives, mistresses, places, and, perhaps, even Exley himself. This love, this ability to forgive in others what he cannot usually forgive in himself, is what keeps both Exleys, the writer and the character, going.

Periodical Publications:
"Poem from a Man at Middle Age," *Esquire*, 79 (May 1973): 234;
"Last Notes from Home," *Rolling Stone*, 30 June 1977, pp. 79-84;
"James Seamus Finbarr O'Twoomey," *Rolling Stone*, 5 October 1978, pp. 58-61, 63-64, 67-68;
"Ms. Robin Glenn," *Rolling Stone*, 22 February 1979, pp. 44-49, 93;
"Holding Penalties Build Men," *Inside Sports*, 3 (November 1981): 105-109.

Interview:
Mary Cantwell, "The Sad, Funny, Paranoid, Loving Life of a Male American Writer—Frederick

Exley," *Mademoiselle*, 82 (June 1976): 63-68, 126.

References:
William Burke, "Football, Literature, Culture," *Southwest Review*, 60(1975): 391-398;
C. Barry Chabot, "The Alternative Vision of Frederick Exley's *A Fan's Notes*," *Critique*, 19, no. 1 (1977): 87-100;
Donald R. Johnson, "The Hero in Sports Literature and Exley's *A Fan's Notes*," *Southern Humanities Review*, 13 (1979): 233-244;
Steven Shoemaker, "Barth, Schleiermacher, and a New York Giants Fan," *Religion in Life*, 41 (Spring 1972): 18-28;
Phillip Sterling, "Frederick Exley's *A Fan's Notes*: Football as Metaphor," *Critique*, 22, no. 1 (1980): 39-46;
Tony Tanner, *City of Words: American Fiction 1950-1970* (New York: Harper & Row, 1971), pp. 316-317;
Wiley Lee Umphlett, *The Sporting Myth and the American Experience: Studies in Contemporary Fiction* (Lewisburg, Pa.: Bucknell University Press, 1975; London: Associated University Press, 1975), pp. 184-188.

Papers:
All of Exley's manuscripts are located at the University of Rochester.

Ken Follett
(5 June 1949-   )

Michael Adams
Louisiana State University

BOOKS: *The Big Needle*, as Simon Myles (London: Futura, 1974); republished as *The Big Apple* (New York: Kensington, 1975);
The Big Black, as Simon Myles (London: Futura, 1974);
The Shakeout (London: Harwood-Smart, 1975);
The Bear Raid (London: Harwood-Smart, 1976);
The Secret of Kellerman's Studio (London: Abelard-Schuman, 1976);
The Power Twins and the Worm Puzzle, as Martin Martinsen (London: Abelard-Schuman, 1976);
Amok–King of Legend, as Bernard L. Ross (London: Futura, 1976);

The Modigliani Scandal, as Zachary Stone (London: Collins, 1976);
Paper Money, as Zachary Stone (London: Collins, 1977);
Capricorn One, as Bernard L. Ross (London: Futura, 1978);
Storm Island (London: Macdonald & Jane's, 1978); republished as *Eye of the Needle* (New York: Arbor House, 1978);
The Heist of the Century, by Follett and Rene Louis Maurice (London: Fontana, 1978); republished as *The Gentlemen of 16 July* (New York: Arbor House, 1980);

Triple (London: Macdonald & Jane's, 1979; New
    York: Arbor House, 1979);
The Key to Rebecca (New York: Morrow, 1980; Lon-
    don: Hamilton, 1980).

"If Frederick Forsyth could write as well as he
can plot and if John Le Carré could plot as well as he
can write, one of them might have produced *Eye of
the Needle*," wrote Roderick MacLeish, in *Book World*,
of the first of three best-sellers by British spy
novelist Ken Follett. *Eye of the Needle*, *Triple*, and *The
Key to Rebecca* have established Follett as the most
popular and most interesting writer of spy thrillers
to appear since the generation of Le Carré, Forsyth,
Ian Fleming, and Len Deighton.

Kenneth Martin Follett was born and raised in
Cardiff, Wales, the son of Martin D. and Lavinia C.
Evans Follett. His father was an internal revenue
clerk, who now lectures at a school for tax inspec-
tors. While he was a student at the University of
London, Follett married Mary Emma Ruth Elson
on 5 January 1968. Their son Emanuele was born
later that year and their daughter Marie-Claire in
1973. Mary Follett worked as a bookkeeper so that
her husband could continue his schooling. After
graduating with a degree in philosophy in 1970,
Follett worked as a reporter and rock music columnist for the *South Wales Echo* in Cardiff until 1973,
when he became a crime reporter for the *Evening
News* in London. He quit journalism in 1974 to enter
publishing in London with Everest Books Limited,
attaining the position of deputy managing director
before leaving in the late 1970s to write full time.

While working for the *Evening News*, Follett
was compelled by financial need to write his first
novel, *The Big Needle* (1974), a mystery about drug
dealers. A fellow reporter had just made some quick
money by selling a mystery novel, and when Follett's
car broke down just after the birth of his daughter
and the purchase of a new house, he wrote a mystery to pay his repair bill. *The Big Needle* did not sell
well, however, and Follett joined Everest Books for
his "literary education: to learn how and why books
became best-sellers." At Everest, Follett wrote nine
more novels—mysteries, thrillers, and two children's mysteries—using pseudonyms for six of
them "because my agent suggested I might write
better books in the future." Follett describes these
early novels (excepting the juveniles), each of which
earned him around $5,000, as "very racy, with a lot
of sex." He told the *Los Angeles Times* that he learned
how to write good books "by writing mediocre ones
and wondering what was wrong with them." Follett
tried to make his first spy novels, *The Shakeout* (1975)

and *The Bear Raid* (1976), however mediocre, at
least different: "The spy story has been done by so
many authors that it seems difficult to produce
anything fresh. My solution was to write about industrial espionage."

Eye of the Needle, which fulfilled Follett's desire
for a best-seller, resulted from his attendance at a
sales conference held by Futura Publications,
Everest Books's distributor. Anthony Cheetham,
Futura's managing director, asked him to write an
adventure novel having something to do with
World War II. *Eye of the Needle*, which sold five
million copies worldwide, and *Triple*, Follett's second best-seller, earned him $2.5 million, a three-
book, $3-million deal with New American Library
and the title, according to his publishers, of the
world's youngest millionaire author. His sudden
wealth forced him into the eighty-three-percent tax
bracket and, ironically for the son of a tax official,
into leaving Great Britain. The Folletts now live in
Grasse, France.

"I'm not under the illusion that the world is
waiting for my thoughts to appear in print," Follett
says. "People want to be told a story, and that's what
I'm up to. I think of myself as a craftsman more than
an artist." He admits that his books "are rather
calculated. I'm not an inspirational writer." He
works out a detailed outline of each of his
thrillers—he prefers this term to *novel*—and revises
it with the help of his agent, Albert Zuckerman of
Writers House, and his editor, Pat Golbitz of William Morrow. Follett feels that collaboration to
some degree is helpful for a writer who wants to
reach and entertain as many readers as possible.

Follett sets forth his theory of fiction in his
1979 essay "Books That Enchant and Enlighten."
He says that most popular writers aim too low, while
most serious writers are too concerned with "the
trivia of middle-class life." In the essay, Follett asserts "our profession won't produce too many great
writers while we continue to opt either for exciting
trash or thoughtful tedium. . . . So long as they gave
us thrilling tales the great mass-market writers,
from Edgar Rice Burroughs to Dennis Wheatley,
were permitted cardboard characters, sloppy writing, and texture as bland as Formica. The elite, who
could get away with none of that, were allowed to
dispense with plot, story, excitement, sensation, and
the world outside the mind, so long as they were
deep." As a solution to this problem, Follett pro-
poses that each type of writer, to improve his fiction,
should incorporate the elements of both approaches. To the would-be mass-market writer, he
points out that "the underwater knife fight is more

exciting, not less, if it's described in graceful, powerful prose; the plot has more drama if it depends on character development as much as external events; the romance is more thrilling if the tall dark hero nurses a genuine, credible sadness behind that handsome-but-cruel smile." According to Follett, "Writing successful fiction is a matter of getting lots of different things right (which is why there's no formula for a best seller) and the way to get better . . . is to discover new things to get right."

Follett clearly shows in his three best-sellers that he has taken his own advice. In these exciting, intelligent, generally well-written spy thrillers, not only are the major characters well developed, but the minor characters are given attention as well. The reader is always able to understand all the characters' political, social, economic, and sexual motives. Follett makes certain that even his villains have sympathetic sides; he does not want to elicit a stock Nazi-equals-evil response. Moreover, Follett, as a calculating surveyor of the mass market, also realizes that while the loyal spy-novel readership is predominantly male, female readers are needed, as they always have been, to insure best-sellers. As a result, his heroines are realistically portrayed women who have led fairly ordinary lives but who are capable of heroics when needed. (The heroine saves the day in each of the novels.) He also reveals a thorough understanding not only of the history and techniques of espionage but of the intertwining complexities of twentieth-century world politics. Equally important is the skill of his plotting. While spy fiction is frequently complex and bewildering to the reader, Follett's work is consistently clear and easy to follow. This skill is evident in his first best-selling novel.

Eye of the Needle (1978) concentrates on the efforts of British Intelligence in 1944 to catch the Germans' best spy, Heinrich von Müller-Güden, whose code name is Die Nadel. Referred to in the novel as Henry Faber, one of his British aliases, Die Nadel has discovered that the Allied base in Norfolk is a fake, full of skeleton barracks and wooden and rubber planes and ships. The location of this base is intended to make the Germans think that the coming invasion of the continent will be at Pas de Calais. Hitler's astrologer swears that the Allies will land at Normandy, and Faber has to take his photographic evidence to the contrary to the Fuehrer in person. The British must stop him before he reaches the U-boat sent somewhere off the coast of the United Kingdom to pick him up.

Faber, who has been operating undercover in England since before the war, is not a typical Ger-

man spy. He has never joined the National Socialist party, has disdain for his commanders, includes sarcastic remarks in his reports, and gives false information to keep Saint Paul's Cathedral from being bombed. Although he is not reluctant to use his stiletto to protect his identity, he always vomits after killing someone. Faber tries to turn his weaknesses into strengths: "Fear was never far from the surface of his emotions; perhaps that was why he had survived so long. He was chronically incapable of feeling safe. He understood, in that vague way in which one sometimes understands the most fundamental things about oneself, that his very insecurity was the reason he chose the profession of spy; it was the only way of life which could permit him instantly to kill anyone who posed him the slightest threat. The fear of being weak was part of the syndrome that included his obsessive independence, his insecurity, and his contempt for his military superiors."

Leading the efforts to catch the spy are Prof. Percival Godliman, who "knew more about the Middle Ages than any man alive," and his legman, Frederick Bloggs, a former Scotland Yard inspector. Like Faber, Godliman and Bloggs use their work as a substitute for the emotional lives they should be living. Godliman had retreated into his medieval studies after his wife's death, but "the war had brought him back to life; revived in him those characteristics of dash and aggression and fervor that had made him a fine speaker and teacher and the hope of the Liberal Party." Bloggs is devoted to his wife, a heroic ambulance driver, but she is killed by German bombs. Indirectly, he blames Faber for her death. Yet, ironically, he likes and needs the war: "Bloggs realized suddenly that he did not want the war to end; that would make him *face* issues. . . . The war made life simple—he knew why he hated the enemy and he knew what he was supposed to do about it." Follett shows how war brings people together and brings out the best in them: "War was grueling and oppressive and frustrating and uncomfortable, but one had friends."

The fourth and pivotal major character is Lucy Rose, whose husband, David, had lost both legs in a traffic accident on their wedding night in 1940. With their son, Jo (conceived before the wedding), and an elderly shepherd, they live and raise sheep on isolated Storm Island off the coast of Aberdeen: "It is for places like this that the word 'bleak' has been invented." (The original English edition of the novel was entitled *Storm Island*.) The Roses' marriage is both loveless and sexless because of David's self-pity. Lucy is reconciled to this life, however, because "she had nowhere else to go, nothing else to do with her life, nobody else to *be* other than Mrs. David Rose."

A crucial development comes when the escaping Faber is washed ashore alive on the island during a storm. Faber, who has been celibate for seven years, has a torrid affair with the neglected Lucy. Their idyll is soon shattered when the very outcome of the war comes to a bloody showdown between the world's greatest spy and the housewife who has managed to break down the defenses Faber has carefully built up over the years.

Follett's plot is always believable and entertaining, his characters, including Faber, recognizably human and appealing, and his style economic and very readable. The fast pace, however, is slowed by the obligatory scenes setting up the Roses' relationship.

Reviewers greeted *Eye of the Needle* with enthusiasm rare for spy novels. In the *New York Times Book Review*, Richard Freedman called it "a thriller that really thrills, on both the visceral and intellectual levels." It was called "quite simply, the best spy novel to come out of England in years" by Roderick MacLeish in *Book World*. "It is a story," MacLeish added, "that isn't ashamed to use all the traditional thriller devices of entertainment to serious ends— ideas about war, love, disappointment and hope." Peter S. Prescott of *Newsweek* wrote, "It is not credible, none of these stories is, but it is more than tolerable: it represents a triumph of invention over convention. Follett appears to rejoice in the cliches he has inherited from 'The Day of the Jackal,' yet his story, though ultimately as rubbishy as its canine progenitor, improves upon it by virtue of its remarkable pace, its astute use of violence, its sense of particular environments and its occasionally felicitous prose." Even the dissenting critics did so half-heartedly. "The book is so well done and so enjoyable," wrote Michael Wood in *Saturday Review*, "that I was surprised to find myself not liking it more than I did. There is something unusually heartless about it that comes . . . from playing the shrewd and disabused British sensibility across the heroic days of World War II. Follett seems to suggest that the Germans really deserved to win because Hitler's bunch was right about Normandy and because the Germans were not so sloppy or self-satisfied as the English."

Triple (1979), Follett's second best-seller, begins quietly enough with an Oxford tea in 1947 that introduces five characters who will be involved years later in an explosive international spying operation: Englishman Nat Dickstein, Russian David Rostov, Palestinian Yasif Hassan, Dickstein's American friend Al Cortone, and the hosts' five-year-old daughter, Suza Ashford, whose Lebanese mother both Dickstein and Hassan love.

By 1968, Dickstein has become an Israeli agent, Rostov a Russian spy, and Hassan a businessman who spies for Egypt but is a double agent working for the Fedayeen. The Israelis learn that Egypt is constructing a secret nuclear-power station which will allow it to develop nuclear weapons. Israel must develop its own bomb quickly, and Dickstein is ordered to steal sufficient uranium. He must also make the uranium appear to be lost. With the help of Cortone, now a Mafia don, Dickstein develops a complicated scheme for hijacking a shipload of uranium in the Mediterranean. In the course of planning the hijacking, Dickstein meets Suza for the first time since 1947, and she is just as beautiful as her mother but warmer. They fall in love, but love makes the spy careless; the Russians and Palestinians find out about his plans and set up their own complex counterattack. Suza, whom the

Israelis suspect of being an Arab agent, gets caught up in all these machinations and courageously saves the day.

Triple is notable for Follett's usual fast-paced excitement; there are fewer romantic and domestic scenes than in *Eye of the Needle* or *The Key to Rebecca* and more action. To the adventure Follett adds a sophisticated understanding of the complexities and ambiguities of Middle Eastern politics. We see Hassan as a villain because he is an obstacle for the hero, but we also understand his need for revenge against those who took everything—money, property, nation, dignity—away from his family in 1948.

Dickstein is the most sympathetic of the protagonists in Follett's three best-sellers and provides the focal point for the novel. The forty-three-year-old Dickstein knows he is a good spy and is needed by his country, yet he remains a reluctant agent bothered by the "continual deceit" and constantly afraid of being discovered. He is perturbed by a world which necessitates spying: "It did not seem possible to live honorably. Even if he gave up this profession, others would become spies and do evil on his behalf, and that was almost as bad. . . . He had long ago decided that life was not about right and wrong, but about winning and losing. Still there were times when that philosophy gave him no consolation." He explains his feelings about Israel in the manner of a man who has seen and done everything but realizes that he can never fully understand the implications of his experiences: "I never try to argue the moral rights and wrongs of the establishment of Israel. Justice and fair play never entered into it. After the war . . . the suggestion that the concept of fair play had any role in international politics seemed like a sick joke to me. I'm not pretending this is an admirable attitude, I'm just telling you how it is for me." Like all Follett heroes, however, Dickstein is a romantic whose vision of the world changes when he falls in love. It is this sense of relative notions of good and evil, of moral and political complexities and ambiguities, that makes Follett's world of spies more than just a source of entertainment. Perhaps *Triple*'s only major weakness is that Suza Ashford is not as fully developed as she needs to be; she falls in love with Dickstein too quickly and easily.

The strengths of *Triple* were noted by the reviewers. Anatole Broyard in the *New York Times* wrote that it "is eminently qualified for . . .popularity, for its behind-the-scenes interpretation of contemporary events includes everything in the political and emotional spectrum." In the *New Republic* Lisa Derman observed that "the technical and political details, plus the requisite romance and sex

scenes, fill out the book nicely, without the padding that clouded *Eye of the Needle*."

Follett wrote *Eye of the Needle* in three months and *Triple* in nine but took a year to complete *The Key to Rebecca* (1980). The extra care shows in the maturity of his style and his even greater emphasis on character over plot. Inspired by a reference in Anthony Cave Brown's *Bodyguard of Lies* (1975) to German-Egyptian spy John Eppler's using Daphne du Maurier's novel *Rebecca* (1938) as the basis of a code, *The Key to Rebecca* returns Follett to World War II exploits. Alexander Wolff, a thirty-four-year-old German with an Egyptian stepfather, is the Nazis' main spy in Cairo. He acquires and transmits British battle plans to Field Marshal Erwin Rommel (also a minor character in *Eye of the Needle*) with a code based on du Maurier's novel. Trying to catch Wolff is Maj. William Vandam of British Military Intelligence. Elene Fontana, an Egyptian Jew, agrees to help Vandam in exchange for the right to emigrate to Palestine. Wolff is attracted to Elene and introduces her to Sonja, a belly dancer he uses to discover British secrets. Complicating matters are the efforts of anti-British Egyptians led by Anwar el-Sadat, then a twenty-two-year-old army captain, to aid the Germans. Another complication is that Elene and Vandam, whose wife was killed by a stray German shell on Crete in 1941, fall in love. When Wolff realizes what Vandam and Elene are up to, he kidnaps her and Vandam's young son, taking with him secrets which will assure Rommel's victory: "This would be remembered as the greatest espionage coup of the century." As in Follett's previous novels, the woman's heroic actions save civilization.

While Follett's other spies are perfect in their work and almost perfect as people, Vandam smokes and drinks too much, makes mistakes in his work, and is haunted by self-doubt: "I wonder whether perhaps I've never really been any good at my job, and then I wonder if I'm any good for anything at all." Wolff seems to be an efficient spy except for his willingness to play Sonja's sex games but turns out to be quite mad. By giving the German a name which could be English and the Englishman a name which could be German, by making both spies use women rather ruthlessly, and by having their minds work so similarly, Follett clearly shows how alike the antagonists are, the thin line separating hero from villain. Vandam, Wolff, and Elene have an even greater depth and believability than Follett's previous characters. His other heroines have been less complex than they should have been, but Elene is effectively developed as a three-dimensional character, a woman who is forced to use sex to raise herself from the gutter and hates herself for doing so.

292

looking at pictures.'

'You were with a man.'

Papa said: 'Oh, no. Charlotte, what is all this?'

'He's just somebody I met,' Charlotte said. 'You wouldn't approve of him.'

'Of course we wouldn't approve!' Mama said. 'He was wearing a tweed cap!'

Papa said: 'A tweed cap! Who the devil is he?'

'He's a terribly interesting man, and he understands things - '

'And he holds your hand!' Mama interrupted.

Papa said sadly: 'Charlotte, how vulgar! In the National Gallery!'

'There's no romance,' Charlotte said. 'You've nothing to fear.'

'Nothing to fear?' Mama said with a brittle laugh. 'That evil old Duchess knows all about it, and she'll tell everyone.'

Papa said: 'How could you do this to your Mama?'

Charlotte could not speak. She was close to tears. She thought: I did nothing wrong, just held a conversation with someone w to talks sense! How can they be so - so brutish? I hate them!

Papa said: 'You'd better tell me who he is. I expect he can be paid off.'

Charlotte shouted: 'I should think he's one of the few people in theworld who can't!'

'I suppose he's some Radical,' Mama said. 'No doubt it is he who has been filling your head with foolishness about suffragism. He probably wears sandals and eats potatoes with the skins on.' She lost her temper. 'He probably believes in Free Love! If you have - '

'No, I haven't,' Charlotte said. 'I told you, there's no romance.' A tear rolled down her nose. 'I'm not the romantic type.'

Typescript page from **The Man From St. Petersburg,** *forthcoming 1983.*

Follett's writing is always cinematic, and *The Key to Rebecca* has two of his best-written slam-bang action scenes, in which Wolff has Arab thieves create diversions so that a British Army briefcase can be stolen and in which Vandam, on a motorcycle, chases Wolff, who is on foot, through the streets of Cairo. Follett is also more serious minded here with frequent implied criticisms of men's manipulative attitudes toward women and sex and with criticisms, which appear occasionally in the other two books, of British politics and class consciousness: "People like Sonja looked at Egypt under British rule and felt that the Nazis had already arrived. It was not true, but if one tried for a moment to see the British through Sonja's eyes, it had a certain plausibility: the Nazis said that Jews were subhuman, and the British said that blacks were like children; there was no freedom of the press in Germany, but there was none in Egypt either; and the British, like the Germans, had their political police. Before the war Vandam had sometimes heard Hitler's politics warmly endorsed in the officers' mess: they disliked him, not because he was a Fascist, but because he had been a corporal in the Army and a house painter in civilian life. There were brutes everywhere, and sometimes they got into power, and then you had to fight them."

In the *Times Literary Supplement*, T. J. Binyon summed up the strengths and weaknesses of *The Key to Rebecca*: "A carefully researched, carefully written novel, which holds the attention not only through the suspense engendered by the plot, but also through a certain depth of characterization and description. But one would prefer more concentration on intelligence work, and less on sexual perversion." Allan J. Mayer, in *Newsweek*, wrote that Follett "knows his people and his territory; his evocation of wartime Cairo is a marvel of concise atmospherics." *Time*'s Michael Demarest praised Follett's women: "The most romantic of all the top espionage thriller writers, he understands and sensitively portrays the women who come in and out of his cold. When the belly dancer and the courtesan appear onstage, Rommel seems almost irrelevant." In the *New York Times Book Review*, however, Peter Andrews wrote, "My capacity for junk novels is enormous, but I cannot recall a work as unremittingly stupid as 'The Key to Rebecca.' Coincidences and absurdities are part of any espionage story, of course, but it is outrageous to give us a book in which the characters carry on like The Three Stooges and expect us to take them seriously."

A suit was brought against Follett in 1980 by Leonard Mosley, who claimed that characters and events in *The Key to Rebecca* were similar to those in his *The Cat and the Mice* (1958), an account of the exploits of John Eppler, the real-life model for Alexander Wolff. Mosley voluntarily dropped the suit in January 1981. Ironically, Follett lost a suit of his own in 1980. He had edited an English translation of a French account of the $10-million bank robbery in Nice in 1976. The book had been written by three French journalists under the pseudonym Rene Louis Maurice. Follett and his new publishers, New American Library and Morrow, sought to prevent his former publisher, Arbor House, from listing Follett as principal author of the book, published in America as *The Gentlemen of 16 July*. But U.S. District Judge Robert W. Sweet ruled that Follett had made significant changes in the English translation and should be considered an author of the book. He further ruled that Arbor House had to give equal attribution to Rene Louis Maurice and Ken Follett, in that order, and to indicate that the work was nonfiction.

Follett, whose next novel is a "thriller centering on an English family in the summer of 1914," says, "I don't kid myself that I write as well as Le Carré, though I may get that good one of these days, but my stories are better than his and I certainly write a hell of a lot better than Forsyth does." Yet he does not expect that he will write thrillers forever and looks forward to a long career. "If I live, I have about forty years of storytelling ahead of me."

Periodical Publications:
"Books That Enchant and Enlighten," *Writer*, 92 (June 1979): 9-11, 29.

Interviews:
Carol Lawson, "Behind the Best Sellers: Ken Follett," *New York Times Book Review*, 16 July 1978, p. 24.
Fred Hauptfuhrer, "Out of the Pages: When It Comes to Cliff-Hanging, Ken Follett Has, at 29, Clawed into Competition with Le Carré," *People*, 10 (25 September 1978): 107-108, 110;
Barbara Isenberg, "No Cheap Thrillers from Follett Pen," *Los Angeles Times*, 1 October 1980, VI: 1, 5.

References:
Thomas Lask, "Publishing: The Making of a Big Book," *New York Times*, 12 May 1978, III: 26;
Donald McCormick, *Who's Who in Spy Fiction* (London: Elm Tree Books/Hamilton, 1977), pp. 76-77.

Elaine Kraf

(21 February 1946-   )

Martin Altman
Maspeth, New York

BOOKS: *I am Clarence* (Garden City: Doubleday, 1969);

The House of Madelaine (Garden City: Doubleday, 1971);

Find Him! (New York: Fiction Collective/Braziller, 1977);

The Princess of 72nd Street (New York: New Directions, 1979).

In Elaine Kraf's novels, a major concern of her life, self-knowledge through creative expression, is the dominant and recurring theme. Raised in the Bronx, New York, by a father, Harry Kraf, who was an ambitious local politician, and mother, Lena Rosenfeld Kraf, a schoolteacher, Kraf grew up torn by a conflict between the expectations of a conventional middle-class community and her early and unwitting concept of herself as an independent-minded artist.

Though she took piano lessons at age eight, her first self-motivated artistic pursuit was painting, which she studied in her adolescence at the Museum of Modern Art and The Art Students League of New York. Increasing dedication to painting led her, in 1960, to the Pennsylvania Academy of Fine Arts and in 1964 to Hunter College where she received an A.B. in art in 1965. In 1976 and 1978 she had one-woman exhibits of her box-collages at Ward-Nasse Gallery in Soho.

At the time she was developing her skills in other art forms, she became interested in writing. In 1964, after art education in Philadelphia, she attended Kenneth Koch's poetry class at the New School in New York City. Koch's method, based on surrealist ideas, was to free the mind from ordinary, everyday reality or to transform daily reality. For example, his students made poems from the newspaper society page or compared love with tastes of food. As well as finding a method enabling her to release her creative unconscious, she found an atmosphere of encouragement. Gradually Kraf turned from poetry to prose poems and finally to the novel, integrating her interests in various art forms. *Find Him!* (1977), for example, includes as part of the text music she composed on a small electric organ. Two other novels include poetry

written by her characters. All of her writing is lyrical, rhythmic, and concerned with color. Starting in 1967, Kraf attended various workshops, conferences, and residences, including the Aspen Workshop of 1967 and the Bread Loaf Writers' Conference in 1969. She won a fellowship to the Mac-Dowell Colony in 1974 and residencies to the Yaddo Colony in 1971, 1973, 1977, and 1978. During these years she completed three of her four published novels, two unpublished novels, and many stories, one of which, "Westward and Up a Mountain," won the National Endowment for the Arts grant, 1969-1970.

Concurrently, Kraf's interest in the problems of child development grew. This interest has been a rich source of material for her novels and has led to her dedicated work with the mentally retarded and the physically and emotionally handicapped. She received a master's degree in special education from Queens College in 1978 and presently teaches at United Cerebral Palsy in Queens, New York.

Kraf's first novel, *I am Clarence* (1969), and her third one, *Find Him!*, reflect her preoccupation with the retarded and the handicapped. The main characters in *I am Clarence* are an unnamed mother and Clarence, her brain-damaged, deformed child. They share a poetic reality that unifies them and separates them from the rest of the world. The mother speaks her own vision of the world as well as Clarence's, and the visions tend to merge: "Where we walk, where we sit in silence. We like the luncheonette on Sixty-fifth Street; clockless, rugged, with white wrought-iron chairs. It doesn't matter how long it takes us. The waiters are polite in mustard-colored jackets with red lapels. We are handed menus like everyone. People live in the building above, in combinations we know nothing about. They wonder politely seeing us there day after day. But we live far away."

In *Find Him!* the narrator is again an unnamed woman in a profoundly regressed physical and psychological state who is reared by a man named Oliver. As in her first novel, Kraf is dealing with states of consciousness, identity, and reality. In one person, the unnamed woman, a thwarted, limited consciousness (not unlike Clarence) and a visionary

Elaine Kraf

poet are combined. Unable to chew, defecate, or speak, she is able to see the process of life, and growth, the basis of love and hate, with extraordinary precision: " 'Flush the toilet,' directed Oliver, placing my hand under his and pulling a long braided rusty chain. Deep dark whirling in all directions with sounds of sucking me inside. I held my hands over my ears, eyes shut. Oliver laughed gently, absently—the old Oliver. 'We won't fall into it—it's too small. Look.' I think he said 'we' rather than 'you.' Busy in a carnival of 'we' *then*—whirling toilet, twirling potato skins knifed off in a slow deliberate turn, blue purple yellow flames up and down under yellow eggs, guggle gugle hsssss pah pah. Ch ch ch ts ts ts of salt and pepper falling on flat gold circles. All this a circular laughing dance of water, flamestove sounds as surprising and new as your early rains on springgreen leaves spun from sleeping yellow buds. Innocent." Her whole life is centered on Oliver, and the entire book takes place within the claustrophobic house.

The House of Madelaine (1971), based on a dream, has no comforting poetic vision. The main characters enter a strange, isolated house, a nightmare world unto itself that does not operate according to natural laws. A magician who speaks a

Unicyclist, *an assemblage by Kraf*

59

I am touring my kingdom. It is like taking a long voyage. I am
not sure that I have been here before. I wear a long floorlength
skirt patterned with flowers/ abstract designs. Hanging from my
neck is a huge silver owl. I am dressed to fulfill a title, I think.
I pass many huge shiney plastic bags filled with garbage. Days pass
and no garbage truck appears. However they look elegant sometimes
standing in a long row giving off rotting odors. I enter the Argo
Luncheonette and sit down at the counter. It is on the corner of
72nd Street and Columbus. At one of the tables sits an actor,
a black policeman on one of the ABC television soap operas. He looks
out the window at the line of garbage bags. Two opera tenors are
eating and passing a score of music back and forth.

"They have closed my record store." It is the Argentinian
pianist who sits down on the stool beside me.

"Are you feeling well?" I ask remembering that he looked pale
the last time I saw him.

"Well. Who could look well without money. Noone wants to
spend money on good records anymore. You used to come in. Noone
comes in anymore. I sold it...that's life I guess. You take the
bad and the good when it comes. My wife isn't so well either. It
aggravates her...you look nice as usual."

"I'm sorry if you won't be here anymore," I say feeling
that it is my fault. I haven't been inside the store for a long
time.

"At least the summer is over. It was such a hot summer,"
Socrates says. "So what are you standing there for. Go wait on that
lady he says to a handsome Greek waiter who is standing with his hands
on his hips looking at the women passing outside. He says something
in Greek and laughs. Socrates looks out of the window and laughs
also. The woman sees them and waves. She has big breasts and wears
tight pink pants which outline her buttocks (Men with their darting
eyes, spinning thorny eyes.)

"So how are you Tony?" Socrates extends his hand to a
little old man.

"The season's over. Men are getting laid off...an old
man like me...I don't know..." He sees me sitting there.

I remember suddenly with heart beating fast. I remember
someone else, not me lying in Tony's arms with the tin foil crown
on his head, watermelon pits all over the florr, bursting red. I

A revised typescript page from **The Princess of 72nd Street**

nonsense tongue, as well as a host of obnoxious and sinister characters, brings to mind the flavor of Lewis Carroll's *Alice in Wonderland*, the book that influenced Kraf's undertaking. In this novel the protagonist must journey through confusion and surrealistic terror in order to capture her identity. "I would rather stay here, where veils still give me some respite from the clear light and mutilated faces outside. Yes, I have reclaimed my own fantasies, and returned the identities I had fused with or stolen—except for one. I will miss the color of my madness. The image of the powerful magician has gone. Time, even here, is ticked off into my ear second by second, minute by minute until I scream."

Similar to her other novels but with different emphasis is her last work, *The Princess of 72nd Street* (1979). (Kraf lived on West Seventy-second Street in New York City for eight years.) The areas of exploration—identity, poetic states of consciousness, and reality—are the same, but the setting and the characters of this novel are more realistic. The title character has two personalities: Princess Esmeralda is a poetic visionary who rules West Seventy-second Street and loves life; Ellen, her other half, is brutalized and depressed by life. When one is defeated, both are defeated. For self-protection Ellen moves into the world of marriage, of ordinary things. She is safe and unhappy, neither overwhelmed by reality nor liking it. As in *I am Clarence* and *Find Him!* there is a dichotomized vision of life, split between a vision of beauty and a realization of unalterable reality.

Critical reaction to Kraf's work has varied. *I am Clarence*, reviewed in the *New York Times Book Review*, was called "an extraordinary achievement" and was praised for its "poetic language." Her second novel, *The House of Madelaine*, was not reviewed by any major publication. However, British author Christina Stead, in a letter to Cyrilly Abels (who was at that time Kraf's agent), called this novel "a true experience and in several ways a triumph, of artistry and feeling. Artists have done this before—a few artists—a story of their life in their other world." *Find Him!* was praised in the *Los Angeles Times Book Review* for "its intrinsic interest and for solving the problem of combining fantasy and realism while still grabbing the reader." In contrast, *Kirkus Review* saw *Find Him!* as "so private it seems almost impolite to enter." In the *San Francisco Review of Books*, *The Princess of 72nd Street* was compared to "old-fashioned Expressionism: the hard city turns into an organic landscape of soft sand and sea, a man becomes a 'spice-smelling crawling vine trying hard to grow all around me and inside.' " *Booklist* called it a "serious important piece of contemporary fiction," and praised Kraf for "considerable accomplishment," while the *American Book Review* said it was a book "with good intentions which has gone astray."

Kraf's contribution to literature stems from her concern with identity: she has argued that one must understand the larger world within. She has explored human nature revealed by the most extreme states: psychosis (*Find Him!*), mental retardation (*I am Clarence*), hallucinations (*The Princess of 72nd Street*), and dreams (*The House of Madelaine*). We must understand these states to know ourselves, she maintains. Individuals are defined not by their pasts or by group affiliations but by a thwarted, confused, unceasing process of searching.

Other:

"Westward and Up a Mountain," in *American Literary Anthology 3*, edited by George Plimpton and R. Afdery (New York: Viking Press, 1970);

"Why Was It?" in *Bitches and Sad Ladies*, edited by Pat Rotter (New York: Harper's, 1975);

"Windows," in *Triquarterly 35*, edited by E. Anderson and Robert Coover (1976);

"Men," in *Statements 2*, edited by J. Baumbach and Peter Spielberg (New York: Fiction Collective, 1977).

Benn Wolfe Levy

(7 March 1900-7 December 1973)

Susan Rusinko
Bloomsburg State College

PRODUCTIONS: *This Woman Business*, 18 October 1925, Royal Theatre, London; 15 April 1926, Haymarket Theatre, London, 187 [performances];

A Man with Red Hair, adapted from Hugh Walpole's novel, 27 February 1928, Little Theatre, London;

Mud and Treacle, or The Course of True Love, 9 May 1928, Globe Theatre, London;

Mrs. Moonlight: A Piece of Pastiche, 5 December 1928, Kingsway Theatre, London;

Art and Mrs. Bottle, or The Return of the Puritan, 21 October 1929, Empire Theatre, Southampton; 12 November 1929, Criterion Theatre, London;

The Devil: A Religious Comedy, 12 January 1930, Arts Theatre, London; produced again as *The Devil Passes*, 4 January 1932, Selwyn Theatre, New York, 97;

Topaze, adapted from Marcel Pagnol's play, 8 October 1930, New Theatre, London;

Ever Green, book by Levy, music and lyrics by Richard Rodgers and Lorenz Hart, 3 December 1930, Adelphi Theatre, London, 254;

The Church Mouse, adapted from Siegfried Geyer and Ladislaus Fodor's play, 16 April 1931, Playhouse Theatre, London;

Hollywood Holiday: An Extravagant Comedy, by Levy and John van Druten, 15 October 1931, New Theatre, London;

Springtime for Henry, 9 December 1931, Bijou Theatre, New York, 1931; 8 November 1932, Apollo Theatre, London, 104;

Young Madame Conti: A Melodrama, adapted by Levy and Hubert Griffith from Bruno Frank's play, 19 November 1936, Savoy Theatre, London;

The Poet's Heart: A Life of Don Juan, 1937, Bristol University, Bristol;

Madame Bovary, new version of Gaston Baty's play adapted from Flaubert's novel, 16 November 1937, Broadhurst Theatre, New York;

If I Were You, by Levy and Paul Hervey Fox, 24 January 1938, Mansfield Theatre, New York, 8;

The Jealous God, 1 March 1939, Lyric Theatre, London;

Clutterbuck: An Artificial Comedy, 14 August 1946, Wyndham's Theatre, London, 366;

Return to Tyassi, 29 November 1950, Duke of York's Theatre, London;

Cupid and Psyche, 31 March 1952, King's Theatre, Edinburgh;

The Rape of the Belt, 12 December 1957, Piccadilly Theatre, London;

The Tumbler, 24 February 1960, Helen Hayes Theatre, New York, 5;

Public and Confidential, 17 August 1966, Duke of York's Theatre, London.

SELECTED BOOKS: *This Woman Business* (London: Benn, 1925; New York: French, 1925);

A Man with Red Hair, adapted from Hugh Walpole's novel (London: Macmillan, 1928);

Mud and Treacle, or The Course of True Love (London: Gollancz, 1928);

Mrs. Moonlight: A Piece of Pastiche (London: Gollancz, 1929);

Art and Mrs. Bottle, or The Return of the Puritan (London: Secker, 1929; New York: French, 1931);

The Devil: A Religious Comedy (London: Secker, 1930); republished as *The Devil Passes* (New York: French, 1932);

Hollywood Holiday, by Levy and John van Druten (London: Secker, 1931);

Springtime for Henry (New York & London: French, 1932; London: Secker, 1932);

The Poet's Heart: A Life of Don Juan (London: Cresset Press, 1937);

Young Madame Conti: A Melodrama, adapted by Levy and Hubert Griffith from Bruno Frank's play (London: French, 1938);

The Jealous God (London: Secker, 1939);

Clutterbuck: An Artificial Comedy (London: Heinemann, 1947; New York: Dramatists Play Service, 1950);

Return to Tyassi (London: Gollancz, 1951);

Cupid and Psyche (London: Gollancz, 1952);

The Great Healer (London: French, 1954);

The Island of Cipango (London: French, 1954);

The Rape of the Belt (London: MacGibbon & Kee, 1957);

Britain and the Bomb: The Fallacy of Nuclear Defense

212

(London: Campaign for Nuclear Disarmament, 1959);
The Member for Gaza (London: Evans, 1968).

Benn Wolfe Levy left a substantial legacy of plays that are varied, literate, witty, and well shaped in their pleas for a rational humanism. Publisher, dramatist, play and film director, and political activist Levy wrote twenty-two produced plays, sixteen of which appeared during the 1920s and 1930s. He continued to explore themes of his early plays during the remaining three decades of his life.

A critic of the boulevard theater, fashionable at the time, he wrote comedies that even at their sunniest contain twists of stark naturalism or, at least, wryly ironic turns. Several of his plays are adaptations of other writers' novels and plays, and one of his unproduced plays, "A Tap on the Door," he acknowledges to be derived from Samuel Beckett. On the matter of writing, he states in the program note to this play that "once a play is fighting to be born, it is futile to call upon its forefathers. . . . Derivations may have an honourable place in all the arts but just as it is vain (in both senses of the word) to deny them, so it is disastrous to rely upon them."

The son of Octave and Nannie Joseph Levy and the grandson of the Honourable J. Levy of New South Wales, Levy was born in London. He was educated at Repton and, after World War I, at University College, Oxford. Soon after completion of his studies, he entered publishing and later became managing director of Jarrolds Publishers. His attention turned increasingly to the theater, and in 1925 his first play, *This Woman Business*, was produced. Expanding his interests to play directing and writing for films, he wrote with Charles Bennett the script for Alfred Hitchcock's *Blackmail* (1929), generally regarded as England's first talking cinema. He continued to write screenplays, which included *The Gay Diplomat* (1931); *Lord Camber's Ladies* (1932); *The Old Dark House* (1932), in collaboration with R.C. Sherriff; *The Devil and the Deep* (1932); and *Loves of a Dictator* (1935).

In 1933 he married American-born Constance Cummings, a well-known actress. She appeared in most of his subsequent plays, often directed by him, and was frequently acclaimed for her performances.

Levy served as a sublieutenant in the Royal Navy during World War II, and he was wounded in the Adriatic. In 1944 he was awarded the order of MBE. His duties earlier had included work in British Intelligence, for which he was based in a hotel in mid-Manhattan. He participated with many famous theatrical personalities, such as Noel Coward, in a project to shake public belief in the invincibility of Adolf Hitler.

Levy's return to England was followed by election to parliament on the Labour ticket in 1945. Representing the Eton and Slough constituency, he served for five years. Although he continued writing and directing, he spent most of his time in politics and in work on the arts, particularly the theater. Levy was active in the postwar years as a supporter of liberal causes such as antinuclear proliferation. He served as an executive council member of the Arts Council (1953-1961), and as chairman of the executive committee of the League of Dramatists (1946-1947, 1949-1952). Consequently, his dramatic output after 1939 was approximately one-third that of his pre-World War II period. He died in 1973 and is survived by his wife and their adopted son and daughter, Jonathan and Jemima. Constance Cummings continues an active career in the theater.

Levy's first play, *This Woman Business*, concerns a group of misogynists who retreat to a country setting to pursue their respective interests free from female distractions. Varying in age, marital status, and professions, they discuss their common bond at great lengths. But their objections diminish slowly until they prove to be little more than lies or self-deceptions. At first glance, the comedy seems a replay of James M. Barrie's *What Every Woman Knows* (1908), until a female thief intrudes on the male paradise to prove herself indispensable to the inhabitants. What most critics noted was the seeming lack of action, making the plot appear, according to a 1926 *New York Times* review, a "Chekhovian design to pack the story between the lines." Feminist in its stance, the play begins a long series of Levy's dramas in which sympathetic female roles become increasingly strong.

Levy followed *This Woman Business* with the Gothic melodrama, *A Man with Red Hair* (1928). Adapted from Hugh Walpole's novel, it is a character study of Crispin, an obsessive sadist from whom everyone and everything in the drama radiate. He talks endlessly about the benefits of enduring pain and about the necessity and beauty of that endurance. The psychological Hitchcockian discussions carried on almost exclusively by this madman, who holds two men and a girl prisoner, replace the conventional Gothic stage business of a horror play. Charles Laughton, with his bodily and facial movements, created a "fanatic who has raised a lust for the infliction of pain to the level of a faith," according to a 1928 London *Times* review. Varying shades and proportions of the grotesquerie of Crispin recur in Levy's dramas.

Indeed, the prologue of his next play, *Mud and Treacle, or The Course of True Love* (1928), is devoted to a description of a room in which the body of a dead woman hangs over a chair. From the start, the audience knows the outcome of the play. Polly Andrews, polyandrous by nature, bored by two men of her own class, falls in love with Solomon, an idealist and a misfit in Victorian society. A remote relative of Polly's mother, he is a former clergyman who has actively espoused socialism. When Polly invites Solomon to kiss her, he strangles her instead, in a grotesque twist reminiscent of endings in Browning's "Porphyria's Lover" and "My Last Duchess." He realizes that although Polly is intrigued with the mud, she must also have her treacle. Melodramatic action and discussions of ideas are the substance and style of the drama.

Levy utilized fantasy and myth in his next play, *Mrs. Moonlight: A Piece of Pastiche* (1928). The drama is a variation of the Tithonus legend about a human who wishes to live forever. Mrs. Moonlight desires to remain beautiful during her normal life span, but with the fulfillment of her wish grows the terror that she will be desired by men long after her own desire has died. Critics, who likened *Mrs. Moonlight* to the works of Barrie, praised the play's expertly woven fabric and commended the performances by Leon Quartermaine and Joan Barry in London and Leo G. Carroll in New York.

Illusions about love are the subject of *Art and Mrs. Bottle, or The Return of the Puritan* (1929), which marked the return of Irene Vanbrugh to the London stage. Mrs. Bottle has left her husband, a sanitary engineer. Fantasy gives way to reality as Mrs. Bottle returns to her mate, convinces her daughter to abandon an artist who had formerly been Mrs. Bottle's lover, and persuades her son not to become an artist. As situational humor and witty dialogue are replaced by philosophical disquisitions about art, the play becomes increasingly ironic.

The Devil (1930) presents a familiar Levy situation: a host entertaining guests. One of these guests is a young curate, the Reverend Nicholas Lucy, who suggests that they play Truths, in which each confesses what he most wishes to achieve or become. The game climaxes in the Reverend Messiter's obsession to declare publicly "God to be the mad, malignant bully that he is." The devil takes on the guise of a clergyman through Nicholas Lucy (Lucifer or "Old Nick") to tempt people to make choices for good and evil. Unaware, Lucy does God's work, as the "good in man far outweighs the

evil." As in earlier plays, witty dialogue eventually shifts into a serious discussion.

Produced in 1930, *Topaze* is adapted from Marcel Pagnol's drama. The play is a character study of a schoolmaster who has lived in ignorance of the corruption of the outside world. Akin to stupidity, his innocence becomes the basis for entering a life of crime, which brings him security, respect, and love denied him by his earlier honest and cloistered life.

Contrasting sharply with preceding plays, three of Levy's next four plays are pure entertainments, uncomplicated by shifts from comedy to thesis play. With Richard Rodgers and Lorenz Hart as lyricist and composer, Levy wrote *Ever Green* (1930), a musical spectacular produced by C.B. Cochran. The second of these entertainments is a farce, *Hollywood Holiday* (1931), in which a winding plot impudently develops a joke on the American film industry. Critic W. A. Darlington described the play as "the best laugh I have had for months." The third entertainment, *Springtime for Henry* (1931), demonstrates Levy's genius for comedy. After its initial success it became a perennial on the road and in summer theaters. Edward Everett Horton traveled with the play for a record eighteen years before returning it to New York where he continued to play Henry Dewlip. Twenty years later the comedy appeared to have lost none of its original zaniness and provided Horton with what seemed a lifetime career.

In the play a seemingly chaste secretary who insists on the "decent thing" when propositioned by the hero, turns out to be a husband murderer, and her revelation brings the profligate Dewlip to his senses, after which he resumes his favorite pastime of cuckolding his best friend, Jelliwell. The action, all farcically handled, represents Levy's "cock-eyed" world at its most comically logical.

The Church Mouse (1931), the fourth play of this period, is an adaptation of a Viennese play by Siegfried Geyer and Ladislaus Fodor. A mousey secretary gradually convinces a rakish baron, president of the Universal Bank, to violate his firm intention never to allow romance and business to mix. It is the only one of the 1931 dramas in which the opening comic mode is not sustained.

All in all, 1931 was a vintage year for Levy. *The Devil Passes* and *Springtime for Henry* were running concurrently in New York. Involved increasingly in directing plays, he spent much time in New York. Constance Cummings performed in most of his remaining plays, beginning with *Young Madame Conti* (1936), a courtroom drama adapted from Bruno

Constance Cummings and Benn Wolfe Levy

Frank and written in collaboration with Hubert Griffith. Although subtitled *A Melodrama*, the play limits conventional melodramatic theatricality to the prologue and epilogue, thereby focusing on the trial in a discussive rather than histrionic fashion. Madame Conti, a prostitute, finds herself degraded by a conversation she overhears in which her lover admits to a friend that the motive for his interest in her is money. She shoots him and then directly admits the shooting to the authorities. The mood of the play is hard, in spite of the sympathetic reaction of the judges to the defendant.

Nella Conti is akin to Madame Bovary in Levy's 1937 play by that title, an adaptation of Gaston Baty's dramatization of Flaubert's novel. Lifted from Flaubert's long prose descriptions of Emma's weaknesses as well as her appealing romantic fantasies, Levy's Emma becomes a character of cameo daintiness. Although closer in sympathy to Flaubert than to Baty in his view of Emma's "romantic

stupidity," Levy created an Emma in whose character, according to some critics, the stupidity is missing and with it the Flaubertian deadly balance. Even with the sympathetic version of Emma, however, Constance Cummings as Emma and Eric Portman as Rodolphe received strong praise for outstanding performances.

Concluding the series of plays of the 1920s and 1930s, *The Jealous God* (1939) was given a strong production in London, with Constance Cummings and Irene Vanbrugh in the leads. The bleak comedy portrays a quartet of principal characters—an idealistic woman, her uncomplicated husband, her lover, and an artist who is a conscientious objector to military service. Throughout the play their liberal attitudes become bogged down in a swamp of indecisiveness about what they are going to do with their lives. In the last act, Kate Settle returns to her now dead husband's old home only to find the remaining characters still clinging to their liberal principles although a bit more disillusioned in heart and mind. Similar to Terence Rattigan's *After the Dance*, also produced in 1939, it is permeated with the grayness and indeterminateness of that year in English history. On viewing the play, F. Majdalany called Levy an angry playwright.

Only one new play by Levy was produced in the 1940s. *Clutterbuck* (1946) thrives upon the geometrical design of two wives who discover that they had in their past shared the same lover, Clutterbuck; similarly, their two husbands discover that they had enjoyed the same mistress, Melissa. In the tradition of stylized, artificial comedy, revelations occur when the two couples find themselves aboard the same ocean liner as Melissa and Clutterbuck (now married). Ironic reversals, repetitions, secrets disclosed, and witty dialogue sustained the comedy from start to finish and assured it long runs and frequent revivals in the 1940s and 1950s.

After retirement from parliament in 1950, Levy wrote *Return to Tyassi* (1950), a play that focuses on the troubled conscience of a main character. According to the *Manchester Guardian* critic, the drama is a "penetrating study of a woman offered a second chance of romance who yet arrives at some saner and safer terms of reconciliation within a loveless marriage." The woman-with-a-past theme is thoughtfully explored as a conflict between civilized and natural virtues. Directed by her husband, Constance Cummings again received high praise for her performance.

If *Return to Tyassi* is Levy's serious view of his own generation, *Cupid and Psyche* (1952) is a comic view of the contemporary generation. Mildred, a model, up-to-date on the latest Freudian ideas and jargon, initiates a Canadian geneticist into the rites of Psyche and Cupid.

Five years later Levy reworked another myth, the Antiope legend, in *The Rape of the Belt* (1957). Themes from earlier plays are full-blown here, and comic reversals become an integral and effective part of this feminist thesis comedy. Kenneth Tynan placed the play "squarely in the great tradition of Shaw and Giraudoux" as a "playful philosophic debate." T. C. Worsley applauded its well-chosen theme, its splendid comic reversal, and its adult, civilized comedy. Its kinship to Giraudoux's *Amphitryon 38* was noted in reviews, and with its illustrious cast headed by Constance Cummings and Kay Hammond, the play was a resounding success, running in London for eleven months.

In 1960 *The Tumbler*, a verse drama about a prodigal daughter's return home and her brief liaison with her stepfather, progresses from its opening romance to family melodrama and then into stark naturalism. Despite performances by Rosemary Harris and Charlton Heston and direction by Laurence Olivier, it drew mostly unfavorable notices and closed shortly after its New York opening.

Levy's last produced play, *Public and Confidential* (1966) published in 1968 as *The Member for Gaza*, dramatizes a conflict in the conscience of a politician. A penetrating character study, Malkin is the male counterpart of protagonist Martha Cotton in *Return to Tyassi*. Intent on exposing a political scandal in his party, Malkin risks his impeccable reputation. Cover-ups, national security as excuses for covert actions, communist scare tactics, blackmail, and taping are part of the corruption Malkin plans to expose. Critics described the play as absorbing, intelligent, and civilized.

Levy has said that with his rational turn of mind he "sometimes allowed reason to lead, under the delusion that it could strengthen illumination instead of dimming it. To a rationalist and a convinced partisan like myself neutrality seemed a double betrayal." Perhaps in a play like *Madame Conti*, rationality won too handily over human emotion. In his farces and in his melodramas or thesis plays, the verbal and behavioristic logic, once it begins its course and establishes its premise, continues to its conclusion.

Levy exhibited firm structural control, skill in dialogue, and keen observation of the foibles of humanity. He frequently defended his strong practice of the traditional conventions of the theater, particularly against those who derogatorily labelled his plays well made. Levy stated, "*Waiting for Godot* is

a superbly well-made play. So are the plays of Pinter. *Saint Joan* could not carry the weight of its discursiveness nor *The Three Sisters* its burden of inertia nor *Lear* its narrative puerilities nor *Hamlet* its exploratory diffuseness, if their authors had not been by inalienable instinct master-mechanics of the theatre."

Writing squarely in the traditions of James M. Barrie (*This Woman Business*, *Mrs. Moonlight*, *Art and Mrs. Bottle*), Noel Coward (*Clutterbuck*), Eliot (*Return to Tyassi*), George Bernard Shaw and Jean Giraudoux (*The Rape of the Belt*), and Restoration comedy (*Springtime for Henry*), Levy exhibits firm structural control, skill in dialogue, and a keen observation of the foibles of humanity. His hallmark lies in his direction of the opening situation, serious or comic, toward a strange or unresolved ending, even when the structure is traditionally complete. Many of his plays have enjoyed substantial popularity in England and the United States with long runs and numerous revivals.

Screenplays:

Blackmail, by Levy and Charles Bennett, BIP, 1929;

The Gay Diplomat, RKO, 1931;

Lord Camber's Ladies, RKO, 1932;

The Old Dark House, by Levy and R. C. Sherriff, Universal, 1932;

The Devil and the Deep, Paramount, 1932;

Loves of a Dictator, Ludovico Toeplitz, 1935.

Television Script:

Triple Bill: The Great Healer, The Island of Cipango, The Truth About the Truth, BBC, 14 September 1952.

Radio Script:

Anniversary, or The Rebirth of Venus, BBC, 1941.

Periodical Publications:

"Shaw," *Tribune*, 17 November 1950;

"The Mirage of the Floating Voter," *Tribune*, 15 October 1951;

"Some Lessons for the New Year," *Tribune*, 26 December 1952;

"Cause Without a Rebel," *Encore* (London) (June 1957): 13-35;

"The Gulf Between," *Tribune*, 23 January 1963.

References:

Barrett H. Clark and George Freedley, *A History of Modern Drama* (New York: Appleton-Century, 1947), pp. 196-208;

Robert Burns Mantle, *The Best Plays of 1931-32* (New York: Dodd, Mead, 1932), p. ix.

Thomas Merton

Victor A. Kramer
Georgia State University

BIRTH: Prades, Pyrennes-Orientales, France, 31 January 1915, to Owen Heathcote Merton and Ruth Jenkins Merton.

EDUCATION: Lycee de Montauban, France, 1926-1928; Oakham, England, Higher Certificate, 1929-1932; Clare College, Cambridge, 1932-1933; B.A., Columbia University, 1938; M.A., 1939.

AWARDS: Medal of Excellence, Columbia University, 1963; Honorary LL.D., University of Kentucky, 1964; National Catholic Book Award for *Life and Holiness*, 1964, *Contemplative Prayer*, 1970, and *The Asian Journal*, 1974.

DEATH: Bangkok, Thailand, 10 December 1968.

SELECTED BOOKS: *Thirty Poems* (Norfolk, Conn.: New Directions, 1944);

A Man in the Divided Sea (Norfolk, Conn.: New Directions, 1946);

Figures for an Apocalypse (Norfolk, Conn.: New Directions, 1948);

Exile Ends in Glory (Milwaukee: Bruce, 1948; Dublin: Clonmore & Reynolds, 1951);

The Seven Storey Mountain (New York & London: Harcourt, Brace, 1948);

What is Contemplation? (Holy Cross, Ind.: St. Mary's College, 1948; London: Burns, Oates & Washbourne, 1950);

Seeds of Contemplation (Norfolk, Conn.: New Directions, 1949);

The Tears of the Blind Lions (New York: New Directions, 1949);

The Waters of Siloe (New York: Harcourt, Brace, 1949; London: Hollis & Carter, 1950);

Selected Poems (London: Hollis & Carter, 1950);

What Are These Wounds? (Milwaukee: Bruce, 1950);

A Balanced Life of Prayer (Trappist, Ky.: Abbey of Gethsemani, 1951);

The Ascent to Truth (New York: Harcourt, Brace, 1951; London: Hollis & Carter, 1951);

The Sign of Jonas (New York: Harcourt, Brace, 1953; London: Hollis & Carter, 1953);

Bread in the Wilderness (New York: New Directions, 1953; London: Hollis & Carter, 1954);

The Last of the Fathers (New York: Harcourt, Brace, 1954; London: Hollis & Carter, 1954);

No Man Is an Island (New York: Harcourt, Brace, 1955; London: Hollis & Carter, 1955);

The Living Bread (New York: Farrar, Straus & Cudahy, 1956; London: Burns & Oates, 1956);

Praying the Psalms (Collegeville, Minn.: Liturgical Press, 1956);

The Silent Life (New York: Farrar, Straus & Cudahy, 1957; London: Burns & Oates, 1957);

The Strange Islands (Norfolk, Conn.: New Directions, 1957);

Thoughts in Solitude (New York: Farrar, Straus & Cudahy, 1958; London: Burns & Oates, 1958);

Nativity Kerygma (Trappist, Ky.: Abbey of Gethsemani, 1958);

The Secular Journal of Thomas Merton (New York: Farrar, Straus & Cudahy, 1959; London: Hollis, 1959);

Selected Poems of Thomas Merton (New York: Laughlin, 1959);

Spiritual Direction and Meditation (Collegeville, Minn.: Liturgical Press, 1960; London: Burns & Oates, 1961);

Disputed Questions (New York: Farrar, Straus & Cudahy, 1960; London: Hollis & Carter, 1961);

The Behavior of Titans (New York: New Directions, 1961);

The New Man (New York: Farrar, Straus & Cudahy, 1961; London: Burns & Oates, 1961);

New Seeds of Contemplation (Norfolk, Conn.: New Directions, 1961; London: Burns & Oates, 1961);

Original Child Bomb (New York: New Directions, 1962);

Clement of Alexandria (New York: New Directions, 1962);

A Thomas Merton Reader (New York: Harcourt, Brace & World, 1962);

Life and Holiness (New York: Herder & Herder, 1963; London: Chapman, 1963);

Emblems of a Season of Fury (Norfolk, Conn.: Laughlin, 1963);

Seeds of Destruction (New York: Farrar, Straus & Giroux, 1964); abridged and republished as *Redeeming the Time* (London: Burns & Oates, 1966);

The Way of Chuang Tzu (New York: New Directions, 1965);

Seasons of Celebration (New York: Farrar, Straus & Giroux, 1965);

Raids on the Unspeakable (New York: New Directions, 1966);

Conjectures of a Guilty Bystander (Garden City: Doubleday, 1966);

Mystics and Zen Masters (New York: Farrar, Straus and Giroux, 1967; London: Burns & Oates, 1968);

Cables to the Ace (New York: New Directions, 1968);

Faith and Violence (Notre Dame, Ind.: University of Notre Dame Press, 1968);

Zen and the Birds of Appetite (New York: New Directions, 1968);

My Argument with the Gestapo (Garden City: Doubleday, 1969);

The Climate of Monastic Prayer (Spencer, Mass.: Cistercian, 1969; London: Irish University Press, 1971); republished as *Contemplative Prayer* (New York: Herder & Herder, 1969; London: Darton, Longman & Todd, 1973);

The Geography of Lograire (New York: New Directions, 1969);

Opening the Bible (Collegeville, Minnesota: Liturgical Press, 1970; London: Allen and Unwin, 1972);

Thomas Merton: Early Poems/1940-1942 (Lexington, Ky.: Anvil Press, 1971);

Contemplation in a World of Action (Garden City: Doubleday, 1971; London: Allen & Unwin, 1972);

Thomas Merton on Peace (New York: McCall, 1971);

Pasternak/Merton: Six Letters (Lexington, Ky.: University of Kentucky/King Library, 1973);

The Asian Journal of Thomas Merton (New York: New Directions, 1973; London: Sheldon, 1974);

Ishi Means Man (Greensboro, N.C.: Unicorn Press, 1976);

The Monastic Journey (Mission, Kans.: Sheed, Andrews, McMeel, 1977; London: Sheldon, 1977);

The Collected Poems of Thomas Merton (New York: New Directions, 1977; London: Sheldon, 1979);

Love and Living (New York: Farrar, Straus & Giroux, 1979; London: Sheldon, 1979);

Thomas Merton on St. Bernard (Kalamazoo, Mich.: Cistercian Publications, 1980; London: Mowbray, 1980);

The Literary Essays of Thomas Merton (New York: New Directions, 1981).

Thomas Merton's dual career as a cloistered monk and prolific writer, a career of silence yet one which allowed him to speak to thousands of readers worldwide, was a paradox. Merton can accurately be described as a compulsive and habitual writer with wide-ranging interests. He attracted a broad audience composed of Christians and non-Christians, readers of traditional and experimental poetry, and readers on subjects as diverse as contemplation, violence, solitude, war, liturgy, literature, Eastern thought, and mysticism. At the core of this varied writing is Merton's own experience, an autobiographical vein which perhaps best accounts for his appeal. His life was largely a quest for God, and his spiritual journey, from his earliest years to his last months in Asia, was reflected in his writing.

Merton's formative years provide most of the narrative for his famous autobiography, *The Seven Storey Mountain* (1948), which offers insight into his spiritual quest. His parents were unusual in their single-minded dedication to what they considered important, and Merton's subsequent intensity reflects their strong will. The fact that his father, Owen Merton, was from New Zealand and that Ruth Jenkins, his mother, was from Ohio, and that they had met in Paris suggests the complexity of Merton's background. Because his mother died when he was only six years old, his memories of the earliest years with parents and grandparents and his reconstruction of those years in *The Seven Storey Mountain* emphasize the strength which he gained from his father. Merton depicts his father as a dedicated artist who possessed strength, discipline, and courage to pursue art within a society where art was little honored. Even when he could not support himself fully as a painter, Owen Merton was a model for his son. When Thomas was ten years old they returned to southern France to live a simple life so that his father could pursue a career as a painter. Owen Merton's dedication to quality in art obviously made a lasting impression on his son. When Merton was fifteen his father died of a brain tumor, just as he had begun to be recognized as an artist of note.

Merton's adolescence in France was an extremely influential time in his life. Of those years he recalled children who could be extremely cruel to one another, but also devout Catholics who provided a strong influence on the writer of many years later. His recollection of his stay in the village of Murat with the Privat family exemplifies the importance which that period retained for him and suggests how Merton sought to recognize that all events work together to the good. In *The Seven Storey Mountain* he recalls how, in conversation with the extremely conservative Privats, the question of the validity of Protestantism came up. The Privats were so firm in their faith that they would not even consider arguing with the young boy. While this happened when Merton was an adolescent, the ring of Monsieur Privat quietly speaking, "*Mais c'est impossible*," remained clearly fixed in his mind, a strong reference point for the subsequent spiritual journey.

During the years after his father's death he attended the Oakham School in England from 1929 to 1932 and won a scholarship to Clare College, Cambridge. His year at Cambridge, however, proved to be a severe disappointment because of what he later described as its decadent atmosphere. In fact, as Monica Furlong's biography makes clear, he made many mistakes during these years—mistakes for which he was later very sorry. In his

autobiography Merton offers those crucial years of his young adulthood as a symbol for those who attempt to live in the absence of God. With reflection he realized that God's presence had always been available, yet he lamentably chose to ignore that fact. Several circumstances—including the fathering of an illegitimate child—led to his eventual separation from Cambridge. (The mother and child were later killed in a London firebombing.) When his godfather informed him that it would not be wise to stay on at Cambridge, the young Merton decided it would be more sensible to move back to America and live with his grandparents. This began a new phase in his life, the first of a series of reassessments which changed the course of his future.

Ten years later, Merton realized it had been fortuitous that in the mid-1930s he should have gone to New York City. His decision to live with his grandparents on Long Island and to transfer to Columbia College was invigorating: "Compared

Thomas Merton

with Cambridge, this big sooty factory was full of light and fresh air. There was a kind of genuine intellectual vitality in the air."

Between 1935 and 1938 Merton made many friends who shared his literary interests; he also ran cross-country (without training), flirted with the Communist party, and, most important, became involved with various literary projects. He edited *Columbian*, the college yearbook, and was the art editor for *Jester*, as well as a writer for the campus newspaper and the literary quarterly. Serious study also changed the course of his life. His acquaintance with Daniel Walsh, who taught at Columbia and introduced him to Thomistic philosophy, and his friendships with Mark Van Doren and classmate Robert Lax were crucial elements in his intellectual and artistic formation. These friendships would continue throughout his life to reinforce his literary talents.

During this period both his grandparents died—his grandfather in the fall of 1936 and his grandmother in the summer of 1937—and Merton found himself very much alone. Being an undergraduate at Columbia, he recalls, was in many ways genuinely enjoyable, but by 1938 he sensed that he needed much more if he was to make sense of his life. The period of the late 1930s marks the turning point in his career.

Having no family except his younger brother and approaching the end of his undergraduate years, Merton began a gradual reassociation with the Catholic church. His conversion is, predictably, the central theme of the autobiography, and how he chose to use the experiences of these years in various literary works (poems, journals, essays, fiction) is an important part of his subsequent literary career.

Conversion to Catholicism made it increasingly difficult for Merton to think only in terms of an academic life or a writing career. Religious questions became more important and choosing a vocation dominated his life. He decided writing would have to be subordinated to search for answers to these questions, though his earliest poetry documents this period.

In 1939 Merton decided he should enter the Franciscan order, although shortly thereafter he concluded that this could not be his vocation. By late summer 1940 he had decided instead to become a lay Franciscan and took a job teaching at Saint Bonaventure University. During the summer of 1941, when he was still trying to decide how best he could be both a Christian and a good writer, he composed a novel for which his working title was

"Journal of My Escape from the Nazis." Although it was not published until just after his death, careful study of this novel, which Merton retitled *My Argument with the Gestapo* (1969), makes it clear that many of the threads associated with the mature Merton were present in his earliest writing. Yet only this one book of fiction exists; other manuscripts were destroyed when Merton decided to become a Cistercian monk. In December 1941, at the age of twenty-six, he entered the Cistercian Abbey of Gethsemani near Louisville, Kentucky.

The decision to become a monk might have seemed the end of Merton's physical journey, but in terms of his combined spiritual and literary career, it was actually the beginning. The years Merton spent from 1941 to 1968 as a cloistered monk are best characterized as a continual and systematic investigation of ways to combine contemplation and writing. Much of his journal, *The Sign of Jonas* (1953), treats this question. Ultimately the activities of the contemplative and the writer reinforced each other, for while he entered a monastery he would never forget that he was by temperament an artist. He gradually developed ways to combine his artistic talent with his intense desire to move closer to God. His awareness of the power of language and of its limitations when used poorly is evident throughout his work; he often stressed that while language could express much, many aspects of spiritual experience could never be explained through language.

The Secular Journal of Thomas Merton (1959) is the earliest sustained record of Merton's spiritual pilgrimage and its relation to his interest in language. The journal records his literal pilgrimage beginning in 1939 from New York to Saint Bonaventure University, to Cuba, and then to the Abbey of Gethsemani in 1941. It is a record of Merton's sifting away the unnecessary and a movement toward the decision to spend life as a contemplative. It also affirms his realization that words could relate only limited aspects of the spiritual quest.

Almost twenty years later, in his *Thoughts in Solitude* (1958), he wrote that life should be a spiritual pilgrimage in which man can have little idea of his destination. Such a metaphor hints about the life of a priest-writer full of surprises. His early travels within France and England of the 1920s and between the European and American continents presaged the restlessness and intensity which continued into his literary career.

The journey to the monastery which would become his permanent home was a crucial new beginning; Merton was convinced that he had been given a grace simply in being able to live at Gethsemani. As a novice monk he felt so comfortable in the regular routine of the monastery that he soon was able (in at least one part of his mind) to forego the pleasure of writing verse. One passage in *The Seven Storey Mountain* recounts that while still a new member of his community he discovered that in the interval after the night office, between four and half-past five on feast days, when his mind was "saturated" with the peace of the liturgy and as dawn was breaking, poems seemed to come almost by themselves. However, he wryly qualifies without resentment, "that was the way it went until Father Master told me I must not write poetry."

Becoming a monk at Gethsemani in 1941 was in some ways like stepping back into nineteenth-century France, and the contrast with the hustle and bustle of the activities in New York City as compared to this new quiet he never forgot. Merton's enthusiasm for the atmosphere of Gethsemani is reflected in much of the poetry which grew out of this period, and in *The Waters of Siloe* (1949), his history of the Cistercians, he wrote with great affection of the monastery. It seemed to him that he had discovered a still center in rural Kentucky, a place of fundamental forces which held the modern world together. One early poem, entitled "A Letter to My Friends," was apparently written shortly after he entered and in it he reflects upon his becoming a part of the monastery, a house of God, and metaphorically the "Nazareth, where Christ lived as a boy." This was the house where he now hoped to grow in spiritual awareness, a new home in close harmony with its surrounding landscape: "Fields are the friends of plenteous heaven, / While starlight feeds, as bright as manna, / All our rough earth with wakeful grace." Such was the beginning of his religious life, a life which promised little time for the aspiring writer he had been a short time earlier.

Merton's master's thesis at Columbia had been a study of the poetry of William Blake, and his proposed doctoral topic was on Gerard Manley Hopkins. While Merton was not to continue academic work, his subsequent life and literary career ultimately place him within the ranks of these religious poets. Literary development was to come slowly, however, for if the physical odyssey to Gethsemani had taken years of questioning, the questioning itself was to continue throughout his life, and as Merton continued in his quest toward God, he often wondered if he should even write at all.

At first Merton thought perhaps he must not write, especially if this seemed to be a distraction. Acceptance of monastic anonymity meant there was the real possibility that the schemes which he had earlier conceived for literary work would never be realized. But the atmosphere of the monastery, which might in some ways seem like a fortress to those unfamiliar with it, was not a refuge for him but a place of nourishment: its very atmosphere generated writing. Moreover, this young monk, well educated and gifted in languages, readily came to be recognized, and before long he was being asked to do various "writing jobs" including historical writing and translating.

He spent his first several years at Gethsemani in seclusion with a minimum of contact with the outside world. During that time, he was obligated to several writing jobs, and he also wrote poetry and the autobiography. He pruned down his long manuscript for *The Seven Storey Mountain* and, to his surprise, it soon became a best-seller. In an entry of 1 May 1947 within the journal *The Sign of Jonas* he lists twelve different writing projects in which he was then involved.

It might have seemed during the late 1940s that Merton would make a career of "religious" writing, yet already during those years he realized he was apparently trying too much to be in control of the various projects in which he was involved, and he was learning that his primary responsibility was to accept God's will; the writing was secondary. This realization opened up a new phase in his career and thereby provided other material for writing. His own existential experience, not history, biography, or abstract "religious" devotional subjects, became fundamental to his work. Thus, while he wrote about his earlier life in *The Seven Storey Mountain* and as he prepared for his ordination, his desire to write autobiographically became a matter of communicating how he experienced God. As the religious life developed and he assumed greater responsibilities in relation to his fellow monks, he became intrigued with the fact that his contemplation was the most basic element in his existence. Paradoxically, this led to still more writing so he could inform the world of the peace and happiness which he had found.

During his earliest years in the monastery Merton established a reputation as a poet. Several of his books were published in the 1940s. They too can be seen as a compressed history of his life and as a reflection of a man who was constantly asking himself "How can I best live?" The first published book, *Thirty Poems* (1944), consists of poems written both before he became a monk and during the first few years in Kentucky. His friends Mark Van Doren and Bob Lax helped to get this book published. An example of the calmness and serenity reflected in these poems is "Song for Our Lady of Cobre," a celebration of life written after Merton had traveled to Cuba: "The white girls lift their heads like trees, / The black girls go / Reflected in the street." A second volume, *A Man in the Divided Sea* (1946), suggests by its title Merton's feeling of deliverance. The next collection of poetry, *Figures for an Apocalypse* (1948), was more intense: its title poem sets the tone. The poet announces the approaching end: "Come to your doors, rich women. . . . Weep for the bangles on your jeweled bones." But in 1949, when Merton published a slim volume, *The Tears of the Blind Lions*, he still wondered if he could reconcile the dual role of contemplative and poet.

During the late 1940s and the early 1950s Merton's public reputation developed as a writer of both poetry and prose. This was, as well, the period when he had most doubts concerning how to combine contemplation and poetry although such questions continued well into his mature career in the late 1950s.

From 1941 to the late 1940s Merton prepared for the priesthood and was ordained on 26 May 1949. Gradually Father Louis (as Merton was known at Gethsemani) assumed more duties within the monastery—as teacher, as master of students, and then as Master of Novices. His years there had been times of considerable change both for him and for his monastery. Due partly to changes in the mood of the country following World War II, but also perhaps because of the very success of Merton's own writing, enormous numbers of men had entered Gethsemani. For him, the time up to 1951 was a decade of preparation for an even more intense period of activity which was to include both more writing and more immediate contact through teaching other men in the monastery.

Merton's role was a complex one during this middle period. He continued to write poems and to keep a journal, but he also became involved at the discretion of his religious superiors in many other types of writing. His book *The Ascent to Truth*, written during this period, is his only systematic theological treatise. Published in 1951, it is a competent study of the doctrine of John of the Cross, but in comparison with Merton's later writings on mysticism and contemplation it lacks force partly because it is so systematic. *The Ascent to Truth* was completed in 1950, just before he became Master of Studies; his duties in this position continued into 1955, when he assumed an even greater religious responsibility.

Beginning in 1955, and for ten years thereafter, Merton served as Novice Master at Gethsemani. His duties were demanding, yet his literary output was greater during these years than in the initial magnificent outpouring of the middle and late 1940s. As Novice Master, Merton might have been content with passing on traditional knowledge of monasticism, but his urge to write and to experiment also encouraged him to produce considerable original work. His teaching, his contact with novices, and his reading obviously stimulated his writing. In *The Strange Islands* (1957), his poetic skill was still developing. This volume contains both the stark, meditative "Elias—Variations on a Theme," which is chiefly about learning to be alone—"not alone as busy men are / But as birds"—and the verse play "The Tower of Babel." Such diversity signals Merton's skill both as celebrator of the contemplative life and as a questioner of a society which so resembled Babel.

During this period he also produced books about silence, meditating, and monasticism and was drawn to produce various literary experiments as his studies brought a stronger awareness of the relevance of historical and mythical figures in understanding contemporary Christianity. Finally within this extremely productive period Father Louis (no longer the pious Merton of *The Seven Storey Mountain*) turned toward the East. His tremendous energy and discipline allowed him during this period to clarify both the nature of the monastic life and its relationship to the wider culture outside Gethsemani's walls.

From 1955 to 1965 Merton wrote on a wide range of subjects: race, war, violence, as well as spirituality and renewal within and outside the contemplative tradition. The stylistic variety of his writing expanded while he asked more questions about the secular world. The range of subjects reflects his integrated life and his concern for the entire world, a world which he felt had in large part forgotten how to live. Three books with related titles suggest some of the significant changes in awareness basic to his career. The first, *Seeds of Contemplation* (1949), is an inward turning set of meditations about the contemplative life. *New Seeds of Contemplation*, a greatly expanded version of the earlier book, appeared in 1961, twelve years after the original edition. The changes which Merton brought to *New Seeds of Contemplation* reflect even greater concern for the problems of living in the world as well as his developing appreciation of meditative traditions beyond the Christian. It is as though in the revised version Merton sought ways to move out from the monastery, whereas in the earlier book it sometimes appears he felt the world might adopt the patterns of a contemplative monk. The third book, *Seeds of Destruction* (1964), is a collection of essays which confronts many of the most divisive problems of the contemporary world, including racism and lack of religious belief. In this collection Merton examines what happens in a world which has lost contemplative awareness. Another collection of essays, *Disputed Questions* (1960), is a document which demonstrates changing attitudes about the world and about the writer's responsibility; there he considers questions about repression, totalitarianism, and modern man's need to love. *The Behavior of Titans* (1961) is another example of the monk-poet and scholar-writer who exposes the connections he sees between the contemporary world and earlier eras. Ideas sketched in *The Behavior of Titans* are developed into an extended essay in *The New Man* (1961), where Merton's major focus is upon modern man's mistaken Promethean drives. *The New Man* combines an intense awareness of the need for a contemplative way of life along with a concern about a world caught up in its frantic activities.

Another book which provides evidence of Merton's continuing development during his period as Novice Master is his journal which he entitled *Conjectures of a Guilty Bystander* (1966). This journal covers the years when Merton was changing most. In it he stresses the dual responsibility which he increasingly felt both to live a quiet life but also to speak out on issues of crucial importance for his fellow men who were often so accepting of the drift of Western civilization.

During the late 1950s and early 1960s, Merton also became involved in many writing projects having to do with his opposition to war and violence. A book he edited, *Breakthrough to Peace* (1963), and his collection of essays *Faith and Violence* (1968), provide glimpses of this contemplative who now felt that he had to take a stand on issues in a world which seemed to have lost its contemplative dimension. During these years, Merton frequently asserted that separation of spirituality from questions about the world was not only undesirable but hardly possible. Books such as *Disputed Questions*, *The Behavior of Titans*, *Seeds of Destruction*, and *Conjectures of a Guilty Bystander* are indications that he was now convinced that he had a responsibility to draw as many connections as possible, yet he also continued to reiterate his belief that some separation from the world was essential. His eventual choice to live as a hermit grew out of this phase.

The last three years of Merton's life are the culmination of over twenty years of preparation as a monk and are the final stage of his career. In 1965 he was given permission to live in a hermitage on the grounds of the monastery; there he found a degree of the solitude for which he had longed during more active years. His concern with various Eastern traditions intensified, and during these years most of his books about the East were published. His other literary productions of this period reflect widening interests in terms of awareness of cultural problems and, simultaneously, an intensification of the appreciation of solitude. He also began to write a considerable amount of poetry again (sometimes a variety of what he called "anti-poetry").

Merton chose to live alone in an isolated building which had been constructed for conferences. He had begun spending some time there by day early in the 1960s, but by 1965 he was allowed to live alone permanently. Although Merton did not cut himself off from the other members of his religious community he had more free time than before because he was released from regular duties in the monastery, and his writing flourished.

From the isolation of his hermitage, Merton sought to build further connections between the contemplative life and the needs of the world. These connections are clear in essays in the books already discussed; it is apparent also in a book he edited, *The Wisdom of the Desert* (1960), a collection of the sayings of fourth-century monks. They were explored further in his edited collection of pieces by Mahatma Gandhi about nonviolence. This concern for the world developed in his poetry as well.

Merton's poetic production of the 1950s was not as prolific as in the preceding decade, but by the time he gathered pieces for his volume *Emblems of a Season of Fury* (1963) the change in his interests is clear and presages the poems of the last period. Related to his *Original Child Bomb* (1962), about the atomic bomb, these poems are frequently about a problematic world. At the same time, he included poems which stress an awareness of the beauty of simplicity and the need to cultivate such an awareness, as demonstrated in "Grace's House." He writes of the simplicity reflected in a child's drawing, yet he realizes "There is no path to the summit— / No path drawn / to Grace's House." His poems in *Cables to the Ace* (1968) are a continuation of such themes. *Cables to the Ace* is the work of a writer who is confident in the contemplative life, but feels he must at the same time not abandon the world. These poems are experimental, often ironic approaches to the fact that man lives in a world so cluttered with noise that he

TRUTH AND VIOLENCE

(NOTES on an Interesting Era)

B.   AN INTERESTING ERA

> AN oriental wise man always used to ask
> the Divinity in his prayers to be so kind as
> to spare him from living in an interesting
> era. As we are not wise, the Divinity has
> not spared us, and we are living in an interesting
> era.
>
>   ALBERT CAMUS.

(Go right on with text

Fr. M. Louis
Abbey of Gethsemani
October 1963

1.   We live in crisis, and perhaps we find it interesting to do so.

Yet we are guilty about it, as if we ought not to be in crisis. As if we
were so wise, so able, so reasonable, that crisis ought to have been impossible

It is doubtless this "ought", this "should" that makes our time so interesting

that it cannot possibly be a time of wisdom, or even of reason.

We know what we ought to be doing, and we see ourselves

move with the inexorable deliberation of a machine that has gone

wrong do the opposite.

A page from the first draft of Conjectures of a Guilty Bystander can no longer focus on what is essential. Nevertheless, through irony, parody, wordplay, an intricate reverberation of sound, and literary allusion, Merton reminds readers that the wholeness of God's universe remains and can be experienced if man will but take the time.

His book-length poem, *The Geography of Lorgraire* (1969), is an even more inclusive consideration of such a realization. This poem is a record of Merton's reading, an examination of his personal myth-dream, and an indictment of Western civilization, which he felt so often had not paid attention to the people from other cultures. He called *The Geography of Lograire* a "purely tentative first draft," yet it is more than that. The poem is a crafted set of experiments designed to make the reader wonder about many events in the drift of history which are often ignored.

Merton's many essays about Eastern thought also reveal his increasing awareness of the needs of the modern person. *Mystics and Zen Masters* (1967) and *Zen and the Birds of Appetite* (1968) provide evidence of a writer who is becoming more and more interested in concentrating upon what is of most value. Just as in earlier essays about Pasternak or Gandhi, Merton's main concern as his life drew to a close was with how man might gain truer insight into what was most important.

Parallel developments of Merton's thought can also be traced in terms of his interests in calligraphy and photography. In these instances of visual art we have evidence of an "amateur" who pursued artistic methods of appreciating the immediate as caught with a brush or lens. During the brief years of isolation Merton's correspondence was immense, people sought him out, his amount of writing increased, he became fascinated with photography, and he also continued to provide a weekly talk for novices and other members of his monastic community. He regularly gave these talks on Sundays, and many of these afternoon conferences were recorded. These tapes of Merton speaking in an informal manner to members of the Gethsemani community are an invaluable record of the diversity of his mature interests. They range in subject from technical questions about the monastic life, education, and Cistercian history to commentary about modern literature and renewal in the Church. Thus, although a hermit, Merton severed many connections with the world while in artistic ways he was extending connections. The large amount of poetry, correspondence, and essays of these final years manifests Merton's use of this newfound quiet and, paradoxically, the realization that such sol-

itude strengthened ties with the world. His ties with the world outside monastic life in this period extended to such things as editing four issues of a literary magazine, writing *Monks Pond* (1968), and becoming seriously involved with the peace movement arising from resistance to the war in Vietnam.

This final period of Merton's life is a natural outgrowth of all the preceding stages in his vocation. His writing, which already covered a wide range, now was centered on the subjects which interested him most. Relieved of the daily responsibilities within the monastery, he was able to study, meditate, and simply wonder in ways which he had not been able to do earlier. Living as a hermit was not a radical change in Merton's life, but a natural progression which grew out of all earlier choices.

Merton's life was cut short while he was on a trip to Asia. During his final months Merton had spent some weeks in California and then made an extended trip to Asia. He had been invited to address a conference of Asian religious superiors and had been given permission to combine that trip with investigation for a more secluded hermitage, perhaps in California or Alaska. Preceding his departure for Asia he sent the manuscripts for several new books to his editors, a gesture reminiscent of that time in 1941 when he left for Gethsemani and sent several manuscripts to Mark Van Doren. Being a habitual writer, he was also at the time keeping several notebooks—travel, personal, reading notes—and that material has been edited into *The Asian Journal of Thomas Merton* (1973). When he died, various books which were in the hands of his editors and subsequent volumes of collected essays were published, demonstrating the type of thinking and writing which preoccupied Merton during the final years of his life.

While the trip to Asia was the culmination of his earthly life, that journey's many connections—people, thoughts, places, books—reflect the wide range of his interests in all the years preceding. His final weeks in Asia—observing airports, holy men, art objects, trains, temples, landscapes, and ordinary people—are symbolic of what he had already accomplished with his active pen for three decades. The posthumous *Asian Journal of Thomas Merton* is a specific record of reading, thoughts, and movements during these months. Just as Merton strengthened ties with the world after he was allowed to become a hermit, *The Asian Journal of Thomas Merton* shows he was able to focus more clearly on spiritual matters during the time when he was able to travel. Although it is not a finished composition, it reflects the writer's constant enthusiasm as he becomes more aware of the value of looking, seeing, observing a world so very different from the West.

Merton's death took place on 10 December 1968. He was attending a religious conference of Benedictine and Cistercian superiors of Asia in Bangkok, Thailand. The death was accidental and mysterious. He was found alone in his room late on the same afternoon he had delivered a talk on "Marxism and Monasticism." He had apparently touched the exposed wire of an electric fan.

Books which have been posthumously published, both by and about Merton, add to the significance of his literary career. *Contemplative Prayer* (1969, first published as *The Climate of Monastic Prayer*) is an outline of his mature thoughts on the difficulties encountered by those who wish to be contemplative. In essays collected in *Contemplation in a World of Action* (1971) Merton explores various approaches to demonstrate that contemplation remains necessary in a world of action—the contemplative dimension is part of man's fundamental need. These essays stress a concern for spiritual integration. The collection *Love and Living* (1979) provides still more connections about the needs of contemporary man.

In 1977 *The Collected Poems of Thomas Merton* was published. This book of over 1,000 pages collects almost all of Merton's poetry and also includes some fragments which were left in manuscript. His enormous poetic output is made clear in this inclusive volume. Merton's collected literary essays were published in 1981.

Merton's writing is being scrutinized in many valuable ways. There are two book-length bibliographies, and the bibliography by Marquita Breit is currently being revised. Books which examine Merton's writings range from general studies to specialized ones about social criticism, prayer, and mysticism, many of which had already appeared by the mid-1970s. Among the most useful of these studies are those by James Baker and Raymond Bailey. It should be noted that because Merton wrote on so many subjects, his many critics can, and do, employ different approaches. Many of the books which appeared in the early 1970s have value as introductory studies or as an overview of aspects of Merton's thought. During the past several years more specialized books have begun to appear, while others are in progress. Labrie's study of Merton's art, Woodcock's consideration of the monastic backgrounds, Thérèse Lentfoehr's study of the poetry, and Elena Malits's examination of the themes of "transforming journey" each provide

important access to Merton's thought and writing. Unpublished materials by him also continue to appear at regular intervals. The most complete biography presently available is Monica Furlong's *Merton, A Biography* (1980). A definitive authorized biography is yet to appear.

Merton's career is difficult to summarize, but the total corpus is one which demonstrates that he never ceased to ask how he could both continue his journey to God and share that journey with others. Merton's writing is a reminder to all mankind not to waste time on frivolity and change, but rather to continue to seek the essential and unchanging. His journey is one into quiet and solitude. He wrote that his life was a journey about which he knew not the destination, but through the writing we see how the life fed the writing. From early questions to moments of doubt and then acceptance, and finally to his celebration of immediacy, Merton's life and literary career blend to give us insight into the journey through life which all men must make.

Other:

The Wisdom of the Desert, edited by Merton (New York: New Directions, 1960);

Breakthrough to Peace, edited by Merton (New York: New Directions, 1963);

Gandhi on Non-Violence, edited by Merton (New York: New Directions, 1965);

A Hidden Wholeness/The Visual World of Thomas Merton, photographs by Merton and John Howard Griffin (Boston: Houghton Mifflin, 1970);

Geography of Holiness, The Photography of Thomas Merton, edited by Deba Patnaik (New York: Pilgrim, 1980).

Translations:

The Soul of the Apostolate (Trappist, Ky.: Abbey of Gethsemani, 1946);

The Solitary Life, A Letter of Guigo (Worcester, Mass.: Stanbrook, 1963).

Letters:

A Catch of Anti-Letters, by Merton and Robert Lax (Kansas City: Sheed Andrews & McMeel, 1978).

Bibliographies:

Marquita Breit, *Thomas Merton: A Bibliography* (Metuchen, N.J.: Scarecrow, 1974);

Frank Dell Isola, *Thomas Merton, A Bibliography* (Kent, Ohio: Kent State University Press, 1975).

Biographies:

Edward Rice, *The Man in the Sycamore Tree, The Good Times and Hard Life of Thomas Merton, An Entertainment* (Garden City: Doubleday, 1970);

James Forest, *Thomas Merton, A Pictorial Biography* (New York: Paulist, 1980);

Monica Furlong, *Merton, A Biography* (New York: Harper & Row, 1980).

References:

Daniel J. Adams, *Thomas Merton's Shared Contemplation, A Protestant Perspective* (Kalamazoo, Mich.: Cistercian Studies, 1979);

Raymond Bailey, *Thomas Merton on Mysticism* (Garden City: Doubleday, 1975);

James Baker, *Thomas Merton–Social Critic* (Lexington, Ky.: University of Kentucky, 1971);

James Finley, *Merton's Palace of Nowhere* (Notre Dame, Ind.: Ave Maria, 1978);

Patrick Hart, ed., *The Message of Thomas Merton* (Kalamazoo, Mich.: Cistercian Studies, 1981);

Hart, ed., *Thomas Merton/Monk* (New York: Sheed & Ward, 1974);

John J. Higgins, S. J., *Merton's Theology of Prayer* (Kalamazoo, Mich.: Cistercian Studies, 1971);

Frederic J. Kelly, *Man Before God, Thomas Merton on Social Responsibility* (Garden City: Doubleday, 1974);

Ross Labrie, *The Art of Thomas Merton* (Fort Worth, Tex.: Texas Christian University Press, 1979);

Thérèse Lentfoehr, *Words and Silence: On the Poetry of Thomas Merton* (New York: New Directions, 1979);

Elena Malits, *The Solitary Explorer, Thomas Merton's Transforming Journey* (New York: Harper & Row, 1980);

Dennis Q. McInery, *Thomas Merton, the Man and his Work* (Kalamazoo, Mich.: Cistercian Studies, 1974);

William H. Shannon, *Thomas Merton's Dark Path, The Inner Experience of a Contemplative* (New York: Farrar, Straus & Giroux, 1981);

Gerald Twomey, ed., *Thomas Merton: Prophet in the Belly of a Paradox* (New York: Paulist, 1978);

George Woodcock, *Thomas Merton, Monk and Poet* (New York: New Directions, 1978).

Richard Price
(12 October 1949-   )

Brooks Landon
University of Iowa

BOOKS: *The Wanderers* (Boston: Houghton Mifflin, 1974);
Bloodbrothers (Boston: Houghton Mifflin, 1976);
Ladies' Man (Boston: Houghton Mifflin, 1978).

With his first three books, *The Wanderers* (1974), *Bloodbrothers* (1976), and *Ladies' Man* (1978), Richard Price has, at the age of thirty-two, achieved remarkable success as a novelist. *The Wanderers* and *Bloodbrothers* have been made into major films, and all of his novels have been warmly received by critics. Price writes with dark humor and undeniable power about people trying to survive the fear, loneliness, and brutality of blue-collar lives in New York City. The uncompromising, sometimes heightened realism of his novels captures enough violence, sex, and graphic language to make them a high-school librarian's nightmare, but as critic Roger Sale has noted, Price's "respect for his characters dignifies everything." His writing has not only earned Price an underground following and prominence in countercultural circles, but has also earned him impeccable credentials with the literary establishment. Interviews with Price can be found in *New York Rocker*, which called him "the premier rock and roll novelist of the day," as well as in the *Nation* and *American Literary Review*. While Price's writing most often appears in popular publications such as *Rolling Stone, Village Voice, Playboy,* or *Penthouse,* he was also one of the featured readers at the 1980 Modern Language Association convention. Praise for his books has come, predictably enough, from gritty, hard-edged writers such as William S. Burroughs (*Naked Lunch*) and Hubert Selby, Jr. (*Last Exit to Brooklyn*), but it has also come from John Fowles and can be found in the pages of the *New York Review of Books, The New Republic,* and *Atlantic Monthly*. Price's writing has earned him an MFA degree at Columbia, the Mirriless Fellowship in Fiction Writing at Stanford, a Mary Roberts Rinehart Foundation Grant in Fiction Writing, a MacDowell Colony Fellowship, and two fellowships to the Yaddo Writers' Colony. His recent awards include a New York State CAPS Grant (1981), a National Endowment for the Arts Grant for fiction (1981), and a Playboy Award for Best Nonfiction (1979). He has taught fiction writing at numerous universities, including Hofstra, State University of New York at Binghamton, New York University, Columbia, and Yale.

All of this attention is for what Richard Todd has aptly called "a good old-fashioned young novelist." Comparisons with James T. Farrell, author of *Studs Lonigan*, are inevitable because Price sets his young characters in a naturalistic world where environment shapes and often dooms them, and he writes a very traditional narrative. But any naturalistic bleakness in Price's fiction is constantly lighted by flashes of wild humor and, while his characters see the doors of their lives closing fast, those doors do exist. Escape from their brutal and empty lives is unlikely but not necessarily impossible: whatever the odds against them, Price's characters can make choices that will change their lives. In this sense, and in his respect for wit and spirit, Price is more like another ambivalent naturalist, John Steinbeck, than Farrell. An even better comparison might be made with Nathanael West. If West is remembered as the first explorer of mass loneliness, Price may be the best current explorer of the lonely individuals lost in the gangs, the housing projects, and the singles bars of New York City. All of Price's novels portray the despair and consequent rage of the middle-class people whom West called "the cheated," but Price's works do so with a focus on friendship and the family not to be found in West. Perhaps more than any other novelist now writing, Price shows that his first allegiance in his writing is to the popular culture that molded him—to television, records, radio, and movies—rather than to the high culture of literary tradition.

When Price's first novel, *The Wanderers,* was published in 1974, he became something of a media figure, for exactly the wrong reasons. The novel, set in the early 1960s, describes the painful coming of age of five teenage friends, members of a Bronx street gang named after the Dion song "The Wanderer." Price was born and spent his first eighteen years in the Bronx, and some elements of the press insisted on portraying him as a street punk made good. Although he admits that his writing of the

Richard Price

book was almost automatic and refers to it as "romanticized semi-autobiography," Price labored in vain to convince journalists that he was not such lurid copy. That he had been raised in a middle-class Jewish family (his father owned a hosiery store), that he had not been a member of a gang, that he had gone to Bronx High School of Science and graduated with a BS in labor relations from Cornell, seemed to escape them. Price laments, "everybody was writing about me like I was Johnny Boy out of *Mean Streets*. Out of Odyssey House. Nah. I went to Stanford and Cornell."

For Price's main characters—Richie, Joey, Perry, Buddy, and Eugene—being a "Wanderer" means everything and nothing: the gang offers them friendship, an identity, and an ironic refuge from the rage and violence of their families, but it falls apart when they are forced to break away from home into disappointing jobs and pointless marriages. The Wanderers try to shape their lives with the lyrics of popular songs and with macho cliches and posturing, but they are basically unequipped for the transition from adolescence to adulthood. Roger Sale pinpoints their dilemma: "the Wanderers are good, lonely friends, unable to confer manhood on anyone because Price knows it can't be done, at least not as an act." The novel consists of twelve loosely connected incidents, most of which deal with individual members rather than with the gang together. What these incidents have in common are circumstances that inevitably point toward the breakup of the gang: Perry will have to move away; Buddy will get married; Joey will run away from his sadistic father; and Eugene will join the Marines, looking for validation of his manhood after stumbling across and running away from a black man with a razor who was raping Eugene's girl. However, underlying these physical changes is a psychological change that stalks the Wanderers—the discovery that life is more serious than they want to admit.

Eugene is the first to have this awful epiphany, after getting accidentally knocked out by a playfully-thrown Coke bottle: "something had happened to him when he was coming to, when he didn't know if he was dreaming or awake, when he saw not the Wanderers but a painting of the Wanderers, when above their unreal faces he saw the giant lights of the parking lot—at that moment he'd realized that some day, like Sloopy, he Eugene Caputo, was going to die. And it scared him shitless. It wasn't pain that made him wobbly-legged, but terror.

"His reflex protective impulse was to watch TV. And he watched TV for hours and hours with a savage concentration until his neck muscles felt like pincushions. When only test patterns were on he turned off the TV and turned on the radio. When the radio signed off, he turned on his record player, dressed up in his sharpest clothes, and practiced dancing as if as long as Kookie Byrnes or Cousin Brucie or Mad Daddy or Babalu or Murray the K or Dion or Frankie Valli could be heard, as long as there was some kind of hip ditty bop noise, as long as there was boss action, as long as there was something to remind him of the nowness and coolness of being seventeen and hip, he was safe. At six in the morning he collapsed, trembling with exhaustion. It was no use. He couldn't dance it out of his system. He couldn't stick two fingers down his throat and puke it up like too much Tango. Death was for keeps. He fell asleep and dreamed he was a rock-and-roll star."

"I'm writing about the brutalization process most kids have to go through in order to grow up," Price has written of *The Wanderers*. "On paper the novel deals with a teenage gang but on the gut level I'm talking about the inner struggle between growth and deterioration, between finding one's humanness and becoming one of the living dead." As Price suggests, the Wanderers live in a rough world but one whose real violence is rarely of their making or within their ability to control. In the one gang fight in the book, Ducky boys, a gang of short, terrifying, Irish madmen who make up in swarming numbers and viciousness for what they lack in size, descend upon a football game between teams associated with the Wanderers and the Del-Bombers. The fight is brutal and inconclusive, proving only that for the Wanderers, the "fear of violence was less than the fear of losing face." In the world of the Wanderers, a mother's best advice is "Some day, my son, you are going to learn that the two greatest joys of being a man are beating the hell out of someone and getting the hell beaten out of you. . . ."

Bloodbrothers, Price's second novel, shifts focus but not locale, moving from the dynamics of a group of adolescents to the pathology of the De Cocos, a hard-hat family living in Co-Op City in the Bronx. Stony De Coco is eighteen, caught between a desire and natural talent for working with abused kids and relentless family pressure to join the electrician's union like his grandfather, father, and uncle before him. Stony seems "a son-and-a-half" to his father, a man whose interests have narrowed to drinking and extramarital sex, but Stony thinks and feels in ways beyond his father's imagination. His father agrees to let Stony work for two weeks in the children's ward of a hospital on the condition that he then spend two weeks working with his father and uncle as an electrician. Stony tries to explain this arrangement to his employer at the hospital: "I get more outta jivin' aroun' with these kids for one hour than I would in *ten years* doin' construction. . . . It's my *life* we're talkin' about! I don't wanna be one of those lames that lives for the weekend, you know? I wanna live seven days a week. I wanna go home everyday feelin' like I accomplished somethin'. . . . But look, I gotta pay the devil his due. I gotta give my old man his two weeks, than I got him off my back, he can't say nothin'. . . . I fulfilled my end an' that's that, I'm free as a bird."

Of course, Stony is anything *but* free: complicating his decision is his love for his eight year old brother, Albert, terrified into anorexia by an almost psychopathic mother. Only the mother's fear of Stony keeps her from driving Albert further into terror; only his worship of Stony enables Albert to keep going. Stony knows that if he goes against the wishes and expectations of his father and uncle, he will begin to drive a wedge that will certainly force him to leave home, to leave his brother, and to turn his back on all the macho cliches of his upbringing. He understands that he must leave if he is to avoid the empty, bitter lives of his father and uncle, but he cannot turn that understanding to action. His best friend, Albert's wise doctor, and the most mature girl he has ever been involved with all try to give Stony the strength to follow his heart and mind rather than the blind dictates of blood. However, his father and uncle smother him with demands on his love, inexorably trapping him in the cycle of drinking, violence, and disappointment he so desperately wants to escape.

Much more unified than *The Wanderers*, *Bloodbrothers* was hailed by critics as a large step forward for Price. While the novel is perhaps a bit too heavily plotted, the authenticity of its characters and themes is striking. It gives the reader, noted Richard Todd in the *Atlantic*, a sense "of traveling in unfamiliar territory with someone who knows his way around." Todd also called attention to what is surely one of Price's greatest strengths, his ear for dialogue: "Price writes in a heedlessly old-fashioned naturalistic way: a style prone to sloppiness (and to romantic raunchiness) but also, exuberant, vigorous, tough. His sentences are studded with freshly heard speech and memorable bits of observation." The only harsh note in the critical reception for *Bloodbrothers* was sounded by Richard Ellmann, one of Price's former teachers at Columbia. Ellmann's *New York Times Book Review* article bears noticing for a tone that pauses only briefly at criticism on its way to invective. Whatever the reasons for Ellmann's spleen (he terms Price's handling of his characters "a sin against talent, and art, the eye, the ear, the emotions"), his review contains several obvious misreadings of the book.

Price's most recent novel, *Ladies' Man*, is also his most successful and his most mature since it allows him to develop and sustain a single voice, that of Kenny Becker, a thirty-year-old door-to-door salesman whose life seems to be collapsing on all fronts. That he is thirty panics Kenny, because in place of all the things he feels he should have—a wife, kids, a comfortable relationship with his own parents, a real profession—he has only a growing sense of loneliness and isolation. Kenny could be an older version of the Wanderers or an older and much wittier Stony De Coco, but he lives on the Upper West Side of New York and is a creature of Manhattan rather than of the Bronx. *Ladies' Man* gives Kenny's view of seven searing days in his con-

fused life: first his girl leaves him, then he quits his job, then he begins to feel loneliness coming down on him like some claustrophobic fog. Although he observes that "if you came on friendly to most people they would walk your dog through a mine field for you," Kenny has run out of friends.

When he bumps into a couple of old friends from high school, Donny and Candy, Kenny tries to recapture their old feeling of camaraderie, but when they return to their old neighborhood he recognizes: "It was over. It had been the best and now it was over and nothing had ever felt as good. We had peaked back then, and all we'd been doing since was dying. . . . If any of us had had anything *real* going on in our lives we never would have come back." Like all of Price's central characters, Kenny seems trapped in a realistic twilight zone between a nostalgic but irrecoverable past and a lonely and unbearable future.

In desperation, Kenny tries to lose himself in any activity. He does sit-ups until he drops from exhaustion, stays up all night watching anything on television, tries to psych himself up with records. He endures the absurdity of singles bars, only to wind up for a frustrating night with a woman who makes him feel even more lonely and lost. Then he discovers that Donny, his best friend from high school, is now gay, and after an embarrassing adjustment to that news, Kenny accepts Donny's offer of a tour through gay bars. What follows, Robert Towers wrote in the *New York Review of Books*, "seems to have been designed by Price to gouge out the eyes of any inhabitant of the Bible belt who might accidentally pick up the book."

What saves this tour from sensationalism is that it is narrated in Kenny's hyperbolic, desperately riffing, wisecracking voice. Kenny describes their second stop: "The minute we walked in I realized we'd landed on another planet. I started wigging. I was scared. No lie. . . . The place was mobbed with giants in leather, shades, chains, shaved heads, boots, Fu Manchus. It was a cocktail party in hell. Grim dudes with crook-necked vulture postures stood motionless against walls. Suspended from the ceiling were straps, harnesses, and assorted metal and leather objects which looked like they might be used for either torture or training race horses. I felt like any second someone was going to come up and hurt me." After Donny explains to him that most of what he sees is only expensive posturing, Kenny tries to think of the scene "as if the Junior Chamber of Commerce had dropped acid and threw a Walter Mitty party," and he tries to convince himself "that half these guys are doing

2

So there we were. Me, I was doing my usual 150 sit-ups. My
feet were jammed under the couch for leverage and I was holding a
five-pound barbell behind my head like an iron halo. La Donna was
in her black Danskins sitting by the wall doing dancerizes. I had
a stomach that looked like six miniature cobblestones. La Donna was
so limber that standing and without bending her knees, she could
work her head down between her legs and kiss her own ass. How very
nice for the both of us. She was a twenty-eight-year-old bank clerk
would-be singer; I was a thirty-year-old Fuller Brush Man and we both
walked around all day like Back to Bataan.

When I was doing my sit-ups I liked to watch TV -- Lucy or Fonzie,
whatever reruns I could get a hold of. That was not allowed when
La Donna was around. She needed silence to stand there, pull one foot
backwards, up over her shoulder and tap the base of her skull with her
heel. I could have worked out when she wasn't around, but six weeks
before, on a Sunday morning after she finished her ~~yoga~~ dancercizes she came over
to where I was doing sit-ups and just sat on it. There are ~~these~~
aborigines in New Guinea who have been ~~standing~~ Squatting by an airstrip since
1943 because a plane once landed and dropped off food. Six weeks ain't
that long. Meanwhile, if I needed extra money I could do exhibitions,
have two-ton semis drive over my stomach at state fairs.

Ladies' Man, revised typescript

Disneyland in their heads." But mixed with Kenny's revulsion and amusement is an undeniable excitement, and the prospect of some human connection, even a homosexual one, seems more attractive to him than the emptiness that is tearing him apart. The book ends with Kenny giving Donny a confused call for a dinner appointment.

With *Ladies' Man* Price showed that he is not limited to becoming "the voice of the Bronx" (one of his fears when *The Wanderers* first appeared) and that his mature characters can have the immediacy and intensity of his adolescents. As was true of his earlier work, his ear for dialogue and his gusto for language are superb. If there is a significant criticism of his work it is that he has yet to draw a fully realized female character—although La Donna, Kenny's lover in *Ladies' Man* and Annette, Stony's lover in *Bloodbrothers*, offer his readers glimpses of complicated, interesting women. Certainly, one of the central concerns of Price's fiction is the refutation of what Price sees as the central myths of masculinity, the equation that "to be a man is to be brutal, is to be callous, is to be insensitive."

Richard Price's fiction employs many things he has done or seen or heard in his own life. While he was never a member of a Wanderers-style gang, Price has worked construction, has been a door-to-door salesman, and has worked in a hosiery shop—experiences all put to good use in his novels. However, a much more significant autobiographical factor underlies every word he writes: Price's sensibility has been molded by popular music, by television, and by movies just as surely as it has been molded by his Bronx childhood. To read one of his novels is to see and to hear flashes of city life rather than to be asked to think about it. This is no accident, as Price explains: "I grew up on television and movies. I don't do it on purpose but I can't help it, my frame of reference for telling a story is visual. I'm very influenced by the five senses as opposed to titillating the intellect. I'm not into a lot of what would be considered super fiction, the new fiction, say Robbe-Grillet, Barthelme, Barth, Pynchon. . . . Basically what I'm doing is the old-fashioned socio-realist novel, sort of the documentary novel. I'm not trying to blaze any trails, I'm just trying to make as vivid a picture as I can. . . . If I had a choice between being a painter and a photographer, I'd prefer to be a photographer. I'm much more interested in capturing reality than re-interpreting it into something else."

Price acknowledges his literary influences, crediting Ronald Sukenick, his creative writing teacher at Cornell, as being the most important. He also dutifully lists "Joyce, Miller, Selby, Rechy, James M. Cain, Max Frisch, James T. Farrell, George V. Higgins, Flannery O'Connor—not in any order." But a more immediate influence may be Price's perception that "every American born since 1947 cut his teeth on the tube seven days a week, with Saturday afternoons off to go to the movies." Accordingly, Price envisions a very untraditional audience: "I won't reduce my books to 'Popcorn Lit' (what one critic called an addicting page turner with no nutritional value) to get my audience, but I *am* gunning for that kid who hates to read but can memorize every cereal jingle in a four-hour sitdown with the tube. Because I'm on his case. I've been there, mainlining TV ever since I could say 'Clarabell.' I've been bored by as many books as he and when I started writing I automatically screened out whatever bored me in others' books. What you can't read, you can't write. My writing is a product of being a tube child and is geared towards other tube children, at least stylistically. In other words, even though that jingle-drenched kid might not care a rat's ass about books right now, I'll hook the little booger before I'm through. Ex-junkies can make good drug counselors." Sounding very much like Nathanael West who counseled that "the writer has only time to explode," Price spelled out his credo in a 1976 article for the *Village Voice*, "Aim for the Throat": "To nail this generation coming up, there will be a need to be direct as a heart attack; there will be a need for passion and integrity, an immediacy and urgency as if the writer were sitting naked on a hot stove and couldn't jump off until the story was finished. Spit has got to fly."

Any critical assessment of Price's career should note the progression of both substance and style in his three novels, the consistent genius of his dialogue, and authenticity of his characters and setting. His greatest strength is also his greatest weakness, as the exuberance of his language sometimes overshadows all other concerns. Somewhere in Richard Price is a stand-up comic wanting to get out. But he seems to recognize this danger and, as *Ladies' Man* suggests, has decided to confront the tendency head-on. He has just finished a novel that may be even more direct, to be published in March 1983 by Simon and Schuster. The novel covers "nineteen years (ages 11-30) in the life of a middle class urban kid as he goes from class clown to successful narrative comic."

Play:

"Murphy," Southampton, New York, Fourth Wall
    Repertory Company, July 1976.

Periodical Publications:
NONFICTION:
"Aim for the Throat: Advice to Young Writers,"
    Village Voice, 26 April 1976, p. 65;
"Bear Bryant's Miracles," *Playboy* (October 1979):
    126ff;
"Hell Week," *Penthouse* (October 1979): 154ff;
"The Fonzie of Literature," *New York Times Book
    Review*, 25 October 1981, p. 14ff.

Interviews:
Albert Auster and Leonard Quart, "Studs Lonigan
    in the Bronx," *Nation*, 11 June 1977, pp. 725-
    727;
"Interview with Richard Price," *American Literary
    Review* (Fall 1979): 41-48;
Dennis Paul Wilken, "An Interview with Richard

Price," *Clifton* (University of Cincinnati) (Au-
    tumn 1979): 42-45.

References:
Martin Duberman, Review of *Ladies' Man*, *New Re-
    public*, 6 (January 1979): 30-32;
Charles Michener, "Bronx Bombshell," *Newsweek*
    (13 May 1974): 125-126;
Roger Sale, "The Dangers of Nostalgia," *New York
    Review of Books*, 27 June 1974, pp. 24-26;
Hubert Selby, Jr., Review of *The Wanderers*, *New
    York Times Book Review*, 21 April 1974, p. 38;
Richard Todd, "Two Good Old-fashioned Young
    Novelists," *Atlantic Monthly* (May 1976): 104-
    107;
Robert Towers, "Wanderers," *New York Review of
    Books*, 25 January 1979, pp. 15-17.

May Sarton
(3 May 1912-   )

Jane S. Bakerman
Indiana State University

BOOKS: *Encounter in April* (Boston: Houghton
    Mifflin, 1937);
The Single Hound (Boston: Houghton Mifflin, 1938;
    London: Cresset, 1938);
Inner Landscape (Boston: Houghton Mifflin, 1939;
    London: Cresset, 1939);
The Bridge of Years (Garden City: Doubleday, 1946);
The Underground River: A Play in Three Acts (New
    York: Play Club, 1947);
The Lion and the Rose (New York: Rinehart, 1948);
Shadow of a Man (New York: Rinehart, 1950; Lon-
    don: Cresset, 1952);
The Leaves of the Tree (Mount Vernon, Iowa: Cornell
    College, 1950);
A Shower of Summer Days (New York: Rinehart, 1952;
    London: Hutchinson, 1954);
The Land of Silence (New York: Rinehart, 1953);
Faithful Are the Wounds (New York: Rinehart, 1955;
    London: Gollancz, 1955);
The Birth of a Grandfather (New York: Rinehart,
    1957; London: Gollancz, 1958);
The Fur Person (New York: Rinehart, 1957; London:
    Muller, 1957);
In Time Like Air (New York: Rinehart, 1958);
I Knew a Phoenix: Sketches for an Autobiography (New

York: Holt, Rinehart & Winston, 1959; Lon-
    don: Owen, 1963);
Cloud, Stone, Sun, Vine: Poems, Selected and New (New
    York: Norton, 1961);
The Small Room (New York: Norton, 1961; London:
    Gollancz, 1962);
Joanna and Ulysses (New York: Norton, 1963; Lon-
    don: Murray, 1963);
Mrs. Stevens Hears the Mermaids Singing (New York:
    Norton, 1965; London: Owen, 1966);
Miss Pickthorn and Mr. Hare (New York: Norton,
    1966; London: Dent, 1968);
A Private Mythology (New York: Norton, 1966);
As Does New Hampshire and Other Poems (Peter-
    borough, N. H.: Smith, 1967);
Plant Dreaming Deep (New York: Norton, 1968);
The Poet and the Donkey (New York: Norton, 1969);
Kinds of Love (New York: Norton, 1970);
A Grain of Mustard Seed (New York: Norton, 1971);
A Durable Fire (New York: Norton, 1972);
As We Are Now (New York: Norton, 1973; London:
    Gollancz, 1974);
Journal of a Solitude (New York: Norton, 1973);
Collected Poems (1930-1973) (New York: Norton,
    1974);

Punch's Secret (New York: Harper & Row, 1974);

Crucial Conversations (New York: Norton, 1975; London: Gollancz, 1976);

A Walk Through the Woods (New York: Harper & Row, 1976);

A World of Light (New York: Norton, 1976);

The House by the Sea (New York: Norton, 1977);

A Reckoning (New York: Norton, 1978; London: Gollancz, 1980);

Selected Poems of May Sarton, edited by Sue Hilsinger and Lois Byrnes (New York: Norton, 1978);

Halfway to Silence (New York: Norton, 1980);

Recovering (New York: Norton, 1980);

Writings on Writing (Orono, Maine: Puckerbrush Press, 1981).

For well over forty years, May Sarton has been a serious, prolific writer of poetry, novels, memoirs, personal journals, and children's stories. Though she was long ignored by well-known literary critics, Sarton has in recent years been the subject of new evaluations and more careful critical analyses not only because of the steadily high quality of her work but also because of the fresh interest in women's writing rising from the women's movement. Always read and admired by a large public, Sarton is now recognized as an important author on the American literary scene.

Sarton's novels are explorations of love, friendship, the development of self, and the joys and obligations rising from intense commitment to one's work which also reveal her love of nature and her sensitivity to social and political trends. They are portraits of twentieth-century men and women seeking lives of personal and professional fulfillment against settings which reflect contemporary life here and abroad with insight and skill. Many of the same themes appear in her poetry, which is written in forms ranging from the traditional to free verse. Though Sarton prefers to write in traditional forms, she is at home and successful with more experimental verse as well. In her journals, she uses events in her own life—the purchase of a house, a difficult love affair, a change in life-style—to examine the problems of the individual, particularly the single woman or the female artist.

Born Eléanore Marie Sarton in Wondelgem, Belgium, Sarton is the daughter of talented parents. Her father, George Sarton, was a renowned scholar; his ground-breaking work in the history of science is still highly esteemed. He founded *Isis*, a journal of the history of science and civilization, in 1912, the year of his daughter's birth, and he spoke of them as twins. This remark illustrates George

Sarton's intense commitment to his work, a passion around which the household was organized. Mabel Elwes Sarton, an Englishwoman, was lesser known, but she was an artist of great ability; trained as a portraitist, she later worked in furniture and fabric design. Her interest in gardening is shared by her daughter, who often uses plants and flower arranging as symbols in her writing.

Driven out of Belgium by World War I, the Sartons moved to the United States in 1916 and eventually settled in the Boston-Cambridge area. Sarton became a naturalized citizen in 1924. In Cambridge she attended the Shady Hill School and the Cambridge High and Latin School. She received her only formal education at these schools, save for a year abroad at the Institut Belge de Culture Fran-

çaise, where she studied during her twelfth year.

Both Sarton's parents were committed to excellence and work well done, a passion they transmitted to their daughter. This concept was further nurtured at the Shady Hill School and the Institut Belge de Culture Française, as well as by the men and women who influenced her. Many of these people—her parents, teachers Mary Hotson and Agnes Hocking of Shady Hill, poets Jean Dominique and Eva Le Gallienne, for example—and places are memorialized in *I Knew a Phoenix* (1959), which traces her early years and which explores an important Sarton theme: the importance of sound, supportive friendships. This theme and another Sarton motif, the potential value and fruitfulness of life as a single person, appear again in *A World of Light* (1976), portraits of people who shaped her thought and standards, such as Celine Limbosch and Elizabeth Bowen.

Shortly after her graduation from high school in 1929, Sarton became an apprentice to Eva Le Gallienne at the Civic Repertory Theatre in New York, where she remained until 1934. During the mid and late 1930s she founded the Apprentice Theatre at the New School for Social Research and directed several productions there. Subsequently she founded the Associated Actors Theatre in Hartford, Connecticut, and served as a director there. Though Sarton's first profession was the stage, from the age of twelve she thought of herself as a writer too, and during her years in the theater she was also writing poetry.

In the late 1930s, Sarton produced two collections of poetry, *Encounter in April* (1937) and *Inner Landscape* (1939), and *The Single Hound* (1938), her first published novel, which introduces one of her most important themes: the idea that physical passion is often at war with artistic commitment. The book recounts the relationship between a young writer, Mark Taylor, and an older woman, Doro, a poet whose reputation is firmly established. This type of relationship is echoed in the much later and more important *Mrs. Stevens Hears the Mermaids Singing* (1965).

For many years, Sarton shared a house in Cambridge with a friend, Judith Matlack, who figures in several of the journals. This household is obliquely depicted in *The Fur Person* (1957), the story of an adventurous tomcat. Whimsical in tone, the book illustrates Sarton's love of household animals and her ability to perceive them as contributors to the steadying routine of a home and to the balance of their human companions; this concept is also important in several of the journals, particu-

larly *Journal of a Solitude* (1973), in which a family of wild cats that Sarton tries to tame becomes the symbol of her own loneliness and untamed emotions.

During World War II, Sarton worked for the Office of War Information as a scriptwriter for documentary films. In 1949 she became Briggs-Copeland Instructor in English Composition at Harvard University and remained there until 1952. During the early 1950s, she was also a lecturer at Bread Loaf Writers' Conference (1951-1953) and Boulder Writers' Conference (1954). She continued to write both poetry and fiction. Her volumes of poetry from this period include *The Lion and the Rose* (1948), *The Land of Silence* (1953), and *In Time Like Air* (1958). *The Bridge of Years* (1946), a novel, recounts the story of a Belgian family in the years between the two world wars. Melanie, the heroine, is one of Sarton's best portraits of the strong, nurturing wife-mother. *Shadow of a Man* (1950) reflects Sarton's own dual heritage. Her protagonist, Francis Chabrier, is half-American, half-French, and the novel demonstrates the author's ability to portray male characters effectively. *A Shower of Summer Days* (1952) is important as a study in setting, for Dene's Court, an Irish great house, shapes the relationships of three people: Charles and Violet Gordon and Violet's niece, Sally.

In 1955, one of Sarton's most important novels, *Faithful Are the Wounds*, was published. The title comes from Proverbs 27:8, "Faithful are the wounds of a friend." Based partially on real events, the novel explores the effects of the suicide of Edward Cavan, a victim of the McCarthy era, on his friends. Initially, it has been Cavan who most feels the threat to freedom that stems from compromises made under the pressures of the period. It is Cavan, a remote scholar, who best understands that great minds must come firmly to grips with the political issues of their day. His life and death are symbolized by a great, damaged tree, and though his suicide, which springs from a terrible sense of isolation, leaves a permanent gap in his social and intellectual circle, it forces the friends who have failed him in life to achieve greater understandings of themselves and of Cavan's values. The novel also presents an intriguing view of the Cambridge intellectual community, and Sarton comments upon good teaching, a topic which becomes central to *The Small Room* (1961).

Isolation and friendship are also important topics in *The Birth of a Grandfather* (1957). In this novel, the middle-aged Sprig Wyeth, offspring of an established family and himself the father of bright, able children, is generally considered to be successful, but he is alarmed to find that he wants to abandon his family and run off to Japan. Frances Wyeth senses her husband's emotional detachment but seems unable to deal with it. Both find their answers through accepting the deaths of senior family members and through their efforts to help friends going through difficult periods. As Frances seeks to understand her own marriage, she supports and is supported by Lucy, a friend of long standing who is going through a difficult divorce; both women learn a good deal about dependence and independence through their shared experiences: "As always when she was with Lucy, Frances found all kinds of ideas and sensations opening up inside her. . . . There were no barriers. The exchange was everything. . . . For this reason their hours together had the taste of eternity, were consoling like pure poetry." Sprig's friend Bill is dying of cancer, and as Sprig learns to accept his friend's approaching death, he also learns to accept himself. Both Frances and Sprig learn that continued growth is a key to the worthwhile life, and Sprig is saved from the devastating isolation which destroyed Edward Cavan. He understands, at last, the necessity of vital, worthwhile work and undertakes the task of creating accurate, freshly conceived translations of Greek plays.

Acceptance of self, development of self, and commitment to hard, exhilarating work are also important motifs in *The Small Room* (1961). Here, as in *Faithful Are the Wounds*, Sarton depicts the tensions and joys of teaching. The novel is set at Appleton, an excellent New England women's college where Lucy Winter is undertaking her first year of teaching, having just been jilted by her fiance. Lucy's efforts to understand her colleagues reveal a whole gallery of academics, many of them single women committed totally to their work. Chief among them is Carryl Cope, a distinguished professor who is noted for her ability to inspire students to excellence. Lucy also teaches Carryl Cope's current protegee, Jane Seaman, and the major plot complication is Jane's plagiarism to protect her reputation as an outstanding student. Jane and many of the other characters consider isolation the price of excellence, and Sarton grants that a certain isolation *is* almost always the price of absolute commitment (a theme taken up again in *Mrs. Stevens Hears the Mermaids Singing*), but she also points out the bonds that professional excellence forges. This idea is supported by frequent allusions to the works of Simone Weil, woven into the fabric of the book, which is one of Sarton's finest to date.

In 1958, Sarton bought and renovated an old house in Nelson, New Hampshire. Between 1958 and 1973, the Nelson period, she not only wrote major novels stemming directly from her Nelson experience, but also produced a steady stream of good poetry: *Cloud, Stone, Sun, Vine* (1961), *A Private Mythology* (1966), *As Does New Hampshire* (1967), *A Grain of Mustard Seed* (1971), and *A Durable Fire* (1972). Sarton's pattern of producing one book annually, usually alternating between poetry and prose, was rarely broken during these highly productive years. Meanwhile, she was also lecturing, giving readings, and teaching at Wellesley and Lindenwood colleges.

One's obligation to self and one's obligation to others, explored in *The Birth of a Grandfather* and *The Small Room*, become the central themes of *Joanna and Ulysses* (1963). Sarton uses a domestic animal, Ulysses, the donkey that Joanna rescues from pain and abuse, as her chief symbol. In learning to care for Ulysses, Joanna also learns about her responsibility to herself and her talent—she is a painter—and a good deal about independence. These lessons enable her to understand that she cannot live a life subordinate to the life of her father, that she must abandon her dull office job and turn to her real work.

Many critics consider *Mrs. Stevens Hears the Mermaids Singing* (1965) Sarton's most important novel to date. The plot revolves around Hilary Stevens, who is based upon Sarton herself. While preparing for an interview with journalists from a national magazine and while talking to them, Hilary reviews her life and work. This self-analysis is not always comfortable but it is rewarding, for the poet-novelist comes to a fuller understanding of herself and the sources of her work. A subplot concerns a young poet friend, Mar, who is trying to come to terms with his homosexuality and with his own creative talent. Hilary's newly achieved understanding of herself enables her to help Mar. In the course of the novel, Hilary remembers and reevaluates the men and women who have been the objects of her love; she recognizes all of them as important, but she also notes that it is the women who have inspired her. Her male lovers have, for the most part, nurtured her but they have not inspired her work. She reaffirms, as a result of this evaluation, what she has always known: that it is love itself that is important, not the sex of the loved one. Hilary concludes that she regrets nothing and comments that "it hurts to be alive, and that's a fact, but who can regret being alive and being for others, life-enhancing?" For Hilary, as for Sarton, marriage is not a viable option for the poet, for writing demands attention that cannot be shared with a mate.

After her move to Nelson in 1958 Sarton began working in a new form. In 1968, she produced *Plant Dreaming Deep*, the first of her memoirs, an account of her finding, renovating, and discovering the meaning the Nelson house has for her. Her reports of the daily chores and pleasures in her new home brought Sarton even closer to her large following, for readers felt that they knew the house and its furnishings, its gardens and its guests, and that they knew Sarton very well indeed. In this volume, as in all her journals, Sarton embeds short, informal essays—on the nature of friendship, the joys of homemaking, the responsibilities of the artist. The tone is conversational, her insights moving. Sarton begins this journal with an account of her hanging the portrait of an ancestor in one of the nearly finished rooms of the house, then recalls her efforts in selecting and refurbishing the house, and ends with the town's annual Old Home Day celebration. In the course of the book, the loss of a great maple tree parallels the loss of one of Sarton's first Nelson friends, Albert Quigley, whose work as a painter enabled him to understand Sarton's work as a writer. Toward the end of the journal, an arduous well-drilling operation stands for personal difficulties and their ultimate resolution. All the book's facets point to the human effort to grow and develop throughout life.

A kind of sequel to *Plant Dreaming Deep*, *Journal of a Solitude* (1973) is a less optimistic book. Themes of the memoir reappear here, but Sarton also recalls a difficult love affair. Her Nelson neighbors continue to appear, and she writes movingly about Perley Cole, a handyman and co-worker who helped her clear the fields around the house. Perley, who had given her supportive (if sometimes prickly) friendship, understood nature and seemed to have enduring physical strength. His final sickness and death represents the loss, loneliness, depression, and alienation which also inhabit the Nelson homestead.

Perley's story is part of the inspiration for *As We Are Now* (1973), Sarton's indictment of American attitudes toward the old and the infirm. This novel is the story of Caroline Spencer, condemned at the age of seventy-six to a home for the old and the ill. The operators of Twin Elms immediately set about undermining Caro's independence in order to make her more docile, while she struggles to maintain her identity and to prepare herself for death. The novel contrasts the devastating effects of the proprietors' actions to the supportive love of a local minister, his daughter, and a remarkable woman who is a temporary helper at Twin Elms. Caro calls herself and this woman "two women who understand each other. The relief of that! . . . It *affirmed* our humanity and regard for each other." The forces of love cannot overcome the destructive treatment of the owners, however, and the novel ends ironically with Caro's burning down the nursing home, behaving with the very destructiveness she has scorned. Like Hilary Stevens, Caro Spencer is one of Sarton's excellent portraits of an older woman.

Kinds of Love (1970) is more panoramic than Sarton's other novels, sketching the lives of several generations in Willard, a New Hampshire town much like Nelson. The book's central characters are also older women. Here, Sarton unites her portrayal of strong elderly women with the themes of friendship and of the constant "making" of the self. The chief focus of this novel is the sixty-year-long friendship between Christina Chapman and Ellen Comstock. Christina is one of the city people who come to Willard to summer for generation after generation, and Ellen is a year-round inhabitant; the women's life-styles differ and their personalities sometimes clash, but together they depict elements of New England's (and America's) strength. Other characters such as Jane Tuttle, Sarton's portrait of the perfect friend, and Old Pete, who abdicates responsibility, illuminate the Chapman-Comstock relationship. Subplots tell the stories of Christina's granddaughter and Ellen's son. All these threads are woven together by means of the various characters' preparations to participate in Willard's bicentennial celebration, and in this way the town itself becomes an important character in the novel.

In 1973, Sarton left Nelson and moved to Wild Knoll, a house situated high on a cliff on the Maine coast. In *The House by the Sea* (1977) she recounts the impact of this move and her search for peace despite loneliness and for inspiration from her new surroundings. Though *The House by the Sea* is the longest of Sarton's journals, it is also, in some ways, the most intense, for it recounts the loss of dear friends and the writer's fear of an arid period. Again, animals play an important part. Sarton has brought with her Bramble, the last of the tamed Nelson wild cats, who represents the continuing frustrations and tensions which can never be wholly banished. On the other hand, the writer's new life is represented by her first dog, Tamas, a Sheltie. As in the other journals, daily events—a fall, walks with the animals, trips into town for the mail, illnesses—trigger comments about responsibility to others, to oneself, and the duty of the artist to seek perfection.

Recovering (1980), Sarton's latest journal, complements *The House by the Sea* in much the same way *Journal of a Solitude* completes *Plant Dreaming Deep*. Here again she explores the "landscape of the heart," and once more she confronts the "monsters" which grow within from lack of love. The title refers not only to Sarton's recovery from a mastectomy which she writes about in the journal, but also to her reawakening to love, her reevaluation of love's meaning, and the presence of a companion who has lately come to Wild Knoll to live; the journal ends on a note of hope and deepening understanding of the human condition.

The novels that have appeared during the Wild Knoll period have been less successful than the journals. *Crucial Conversations* (1975) is somewhat less skillfully wrought than most of Sarton's fiction. Yet, this novel is of interest to the student of Sarton's works. Throughout her fiction, Sarton has examined marriage. In *Crucial Conversations*, Poppy Whitelaw has decided in mid-life to leave her husband, Reed, and turn her attention wholly to sculpting. American attitudes toward the war in Vietnam and toward the Watergate scandal have spurred Poppy toward her decision. In this way *Crucial Conversations* is reminiscent of *Faithful Are the Wounds*. The series of conversations which is the unifying device of the novel slows the action it should dramatize, but though *Crucial Conversations* is not a perfect novel, it is a demanding and worthwhile book.

A Reckoning (1978) is a sound novel which seems not to have been fully understood by reviewers. The account of Laura Spelman's fatal bout with cancer, the novel is important for its treatment of differing attitudes toward death, as well as for its portrayals of the friendship between Laura and Ella and of the relationships between Laura and her mother. Laura is a thoughtful woman who is unafraid to face the final venture. Like Caro Spencer, Laura Spelman wishes to evaluate her life and her relationships. Unlike the heroine of *As We Are Now*, she has the time and the atmosphere in which to accomplish her purpose.

One of the most distinctive features of Sarton's prose is its cool, reflective tone. This attribute is the source of both positive and negative criticism. Elizabeth Janeway charges that *The Birth of a Grandfather* lacks force and "rather gives the

impression of floating in space," but Francis Keene finds it and all the other works "alive with their own kind of tension, drama, and suspense." Critics such as Francis Murphy comment upon the intensity of the prose, which "rises to the beauty which poetry alone can deliver." Though Richard McLaughlin reports a "certain chilliness in the writing," Sylvia Stallings, noting a "cool flow of imagination which invigorates and refreshes," offers a contrasting insight.

Since her move to Wild Knoll, Sarton has also produced two volumes of poetry, *Halfway to Silence* (1980) and the important *Collected Poems, (1930-1973)* (1974). Not surprisingly, many of the themes important to her prose also appear in the poetry. Her sensitivity to places, for example, so important to her fiction and journals, is also evident in many of the poems. "Boulder Dam" (*The Lion and the Rose*) praises human creativity, the ability to work with rather than against nature:

> Not built on terror like the empty pyramid,
> Not built to conquer but to illuminate a
> > world:
> It is the human answer to a human need,
> Power in absolute control, freed as a gift,
> A pure creative act, God when the world was
> > born!

"Italian Garden" (*The Land of Silence*) uses the description of a very old, very formal garden to comment upon traditional poetic forms. A series of poems in *A Private Mythology* reveals the inspiration afforded by a trip to Japan, and in other cases, single poems capture single moments in Sarton's travels. One example is "At Chartres" (*A Grain of Mustard Seed*), in which she compares the cathedral to an open door through which one may glimpse faith, aspiration, and creative ability:

> Here we are measured by our own creation.
> Against this little anguish, this short breath,
> These choirs of glass rise up in an ovation,
> Ourselves so small, this house so huge with
> > faith.
> Here we are measured against the perfect
> > love,
> Transparent flowing walls define and free.
> The door is open, but we cannot move,
> Nor be consoled or saved. But only see.

In "Kot's House" (*The Leaves of the Tree*, 1950) Sarton joins the sense of place with a tribute to the personality and standards of an early mentor, S. S.

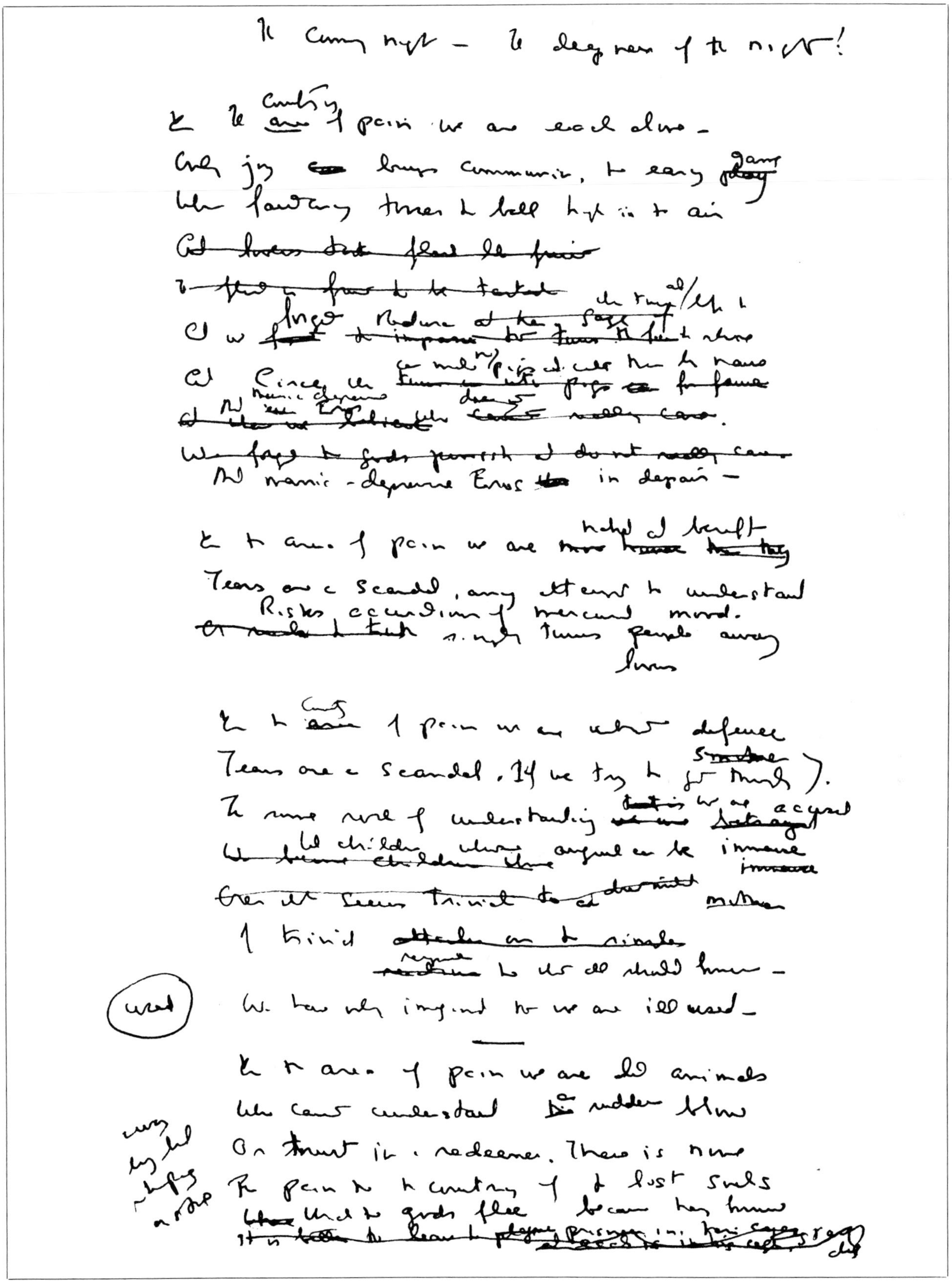

"To Coming Night. . . ," manuscript

Koteliansky, whom she later wrote about in *A World of Light*. "A Celebration for George Sarton" extols the lifelong vitality of her father, once again pointing out his intense commitment to his work and to excellence. "Elegy for Louise Bogan" (*A Durable Fire*) mourns the loss of a friend and fellow poet (also discussed in *A World of Light*), but reminds readers of Bogan's continuing presence through her work.

Love appears often in the poems, and "A Divorce of Lovers" (*Cloud, Stone, Sun, Vine*) is among the most important. The twenty-sonnet sequence traces the persona's progress through tension, anger, and pain toward acceptance and healing, stressing, as always, the need to grow, develop, and learn through even the most difficult experience. In contrast, "The Other Place" (*In Time Like Air*), a peaceful lyric, reports lovers breaking through conflict into total unity of "pure thought." In another poem, "First Snow" (*Encounter in April*), Sarton compares the snowfall to biting, stiffening, despairing love.

"Winter Night" (*As Does New Hampshire*), which describes the gathering darkness and then the starlight on the snow-covered earth and comments on ways of looking at one's natural and personal worlds, demonstrates the unity of thought and device in Sarton's prose and poetry. In *As We Are Now*, the first snow represents the deadline Caro Spencer has set for herself, the end of the bitter autumn of her days. In the journals and in *Kinds of Love*, the isolation the snow creates can suggest loneliness or can signify a welcome respite, a time for contemplation.

Sarton's ability to treat a body of significant themes in several genres and with diverse effects is one of her strongest characteristics as a writer. The resulting variety within unity has won her the respect of an enormous readership.

Periodical Publications:
The Writing of a Poem, Scripps College Bulletin, 31 (February 1957);
The Design of a Novel, Scripps College Bulletin, 37 (July 1963);
"Homeward," *Family Circle* (June 1968-June 1969).

Interviews:
Paula Putney, "Sister of the Mirage and Echo," *Contempora,* 2 (Spring 1972):1-6;
Barbara Bannon, "PW Interviews: May Sarton," *Publishers Weekly,* 205 (24 June 1974): 25;
Jane S. Bakerman, "A Conversation with May Sarton: 'Work Is my Rest,' " *Moving Out,* 7, no. 2/8, no. 1 (1979): 3-12, 87.

Bibliography:
Lenora P. Blouin, *May Sarton: A Bibliography* (Metuchen, N.J.: Scarecrow Press, 1978).

References:
Dawn Holt Anderson, "May Sarton's Women," in *Images of Women in Fiction,* edited by Susan K. Cornillon (Bowling Green, Ohio: Bowling Green University Popular Press, 1972), pp. 243-259;
Jane S. Bakerman, " 'Kinds of Love': Love and Friendship in the Novels of May Sarton," *Critique,* 20 (1979): 83-91;
Agnes Sibley, *May Sarton* (New York: Twayne, 1972).

Carol Sturm Smith

(28 October 1938-   )

Richard Ziegfeld
University of South Carolina

BOOKS: *For Love of Ivy* (New York: Avon, 1968)—novelization based on screenplay by Robert Alan Aurthur;

The Complete Kitchen Guide, by Smith and Lillian Langseth-Christensen (New York: Grosset & Dunlap, 1968; revised in new format, New York: Grosset & Dunlap, 1977);

The Complete Kitchen Library, by Smith and Langseth-Christensen, 18 volumes (New York: Walker, 1968-1969);

What's Up, Doc? (New York: Avon, 1972)—novelization based on screenplay by Buck Henry, adapted from a story by Peter Bogdanovich and others;

The End (New York: Avon, 1978)—novelization based on screenplay by Jerry Belson;

Fat People (New York: Fiction Collective, 1978);

The Child and the Serpent, by Smith and Sy Cook (New York: Seaview, 1980);

Fever (New York: Savonne, forthcoming 1982)—novelization of *General Hospital*;

Renewal (New York: Ballantine, forthcoming 1982);

Right Time (New York: Ballantine, forthcoming 1982).

Carol Sturm Smith is the author of a serious novel—*Fat People* (1978)—and a member and former codirector of the Fiction Collective, an alternative publishing arrangement for serious fiction writers. She has also been involved in some of the publishing industry's recent commercial successes (as author of novelizations, as ghostwriter, and as line editor). Smith is an anomalous figure in American literature because she has engaged in serious and commercial projects simultaneously, yet unlike most other writers she feels no obligation to disparage either pursuit.

Smith was born in Trenton, New Jersey. Her father died when she was seven and her mother when she was in her twenties. She started writing early—she had a play entitled "Alice in Bookland" produced when in the second grade and published stories and poems in elementary and high-school publications. In high school she wrote a long, rhymed, dramatic poem which was staged by dancers. She attended Bucknell for one and one half years (1957-1958) as a premedical student. When she realized she was not interested in medicine but was not certain what she wanted, she left Bucknell to work for a language research project at RCA (Astro-Electronics products division) in Hightstown, New Jersey (1958-1959), and took evening courses at Trenton Junior College. In 1959 she returned to college full time at New York University, from which she received a B.A. in English in 1961, after working with M. L. Rosenthal on *Apprentice,* the literary magazine, as an editor during her senior year.

From N.Y.U. in 1961 Smith went to work for a series of publishers, including Coward-McCann/Putnam (1961-1964) and New American Library (1965-1966), where she wrote copy, presented projects at sales conferences, supervised production, and edited and copy edited numerous manuscripts, including the first American edition of John Le Carre's *The Spy Who Came in From the Cold.* In the mid-1960s she turned to free-lance work, as well as doing research and her first ghostwriting assignment. She began several editing and writing projects, including work with researchers who did the early writing on psychedelic drugs, Timothy Leary and Donald B. Louria, then head of the New York State Commission on Drug Control. As house editor in 1964 she supervised publication of David Solomon's *L.S.D.: The Consciousness-Expanding Drug* and in 1966 *L.S.D.* by Lawrence Schiller, Richard Alpert (now Baba Ram Dass), and Sidney Cohen.

In 1966 she married Stanley Palmer Smith, painter and animator, with whom she has maintained a good friendship despite a long-term separation and a recent divorce. In 1981 she renewed a high-school romance and married Wesley E. Beaumont, who tunes, repairs, and restores pianos.

In 1967 Smith, working full time as a free-lance editor, began an association with Peter Mayer, Robert Wyatt, and Nancy Coffey at Avon Books, where this group contributed significantly to the development of one of the most dramatic innovations in commercial publishing during the twentieth century: original paperbacks. At this time she also began collaborating with Lillian Langseth-Christensen (for whom she was editor at Coward-

Carol Sturm Smith

McCann) on a kitchen source book and a series of specialty cookbooks, both of which were published in formats and sizes that were unusual at the time.

Nineteen sixty-eight was a watershed year during which her daughter, Sharian Dove Smith, was born and during which she wrote *For Love of Ivy*, a novelization of the movie. Novelization was a new phenomenon during the 1960s, and when *For Love of Ivy* appeared on paperback best-seller lists a trend was established. Smith considers this project a turning point in her career because it was her first full-length piece of writing.

During the early 1970s her work pace slowed when she made two moves (in 1970 she moved to Millerton, New York; in 1971 to Richmond, New Hampshire) and her marriage broke up. Soon, however, she became involved with a second ongoing body of editorial work, this time line editing original historical romances, a genre that would produce several of the most successful commerical books in publishing history. During these years, while writing her second novelization from a movie (*What's Up, Doc?*, 1972) and beginning *Fat People*, she did the line editing for *Sweet Savage Love* and *Dark Fires* by Rosemary Rogers and *The Flame and the Flower* and *Shanna* (an industry trend setter, pub-

lished as a trade paperback) by Kathleen E. Woodiwiss.

Fat People to a large extent grew out of Smith's participation in the late 1960s in a women's group which met for several years and included, among others, Kristen Booth Glen (now Judge Glen, elected to the Civil Court of New York in Manhattan), Gloria Stern (now a psychiatrist), Louise Bernikow (poet and novelist), Erica Jong, Alice Kessler-Harris (academic), Margot Lewitin (director of the Women's Inter-Art Center), and Susan Kleckner (photographer and filmmaker).

On the basis of forty-eight pages of *Fat People*, editor Aaron Asher contracted the book for Holt, Rinehart and Winston, although he was to leave there before the project was completed, a situation which was to contribute to *Fat People*'s seven-year cycle from inception to publication by the Fiction Collective in 1978.

From 1973 until the completion of the novel in the fall of 1975, living on partial payments of her Holt advance and money from free-lance editing, Smith wrote *Fat People* while traveling extensively. She lived a nomadic existence, rarely staying in one place more than two or three months: Richmond, New Hampshire; Hillsdale, New York; Boston; New Orleans; Baton Rouge; the MacDowell Colony in Peterborough, New Hampshire; the writer's colony at Ossabaw (off the coast of Georgia); London; and New York City.

In 1975 Holt delivered Smith a devastating blow. It decided not to publish *Fat People*, despite payment of two thirds of her $15,000 advance—a rejection which included neither suggestions for changes nor an opportunity to revise, although Smith did rework material prior to publication by the Fiction Collective. There were many more rejections—approximately thirty-five—during the next few years.

Smith offers the following hypotheses about why Holt may have decided not to publish *Fat People* and why the book encountered such problems with other publishers. The manuscript was late, and in the mid-1970s there was a sudden spurt of women's books. *Fat People* was only 164 printed pages, which is considered short for commercial purposes. Moreover, it is always difficult commercially to market a first novel, especially in this case, in which the protagonist is an unsympathetic, self-centered woman whose strength may threaten many males. Finally, Smith introduced a four-letter reference to sex in her book's first paragraph, a highly risky venture for a woman in the 1970s. No one of these factors poses a serious problem, but the combina-

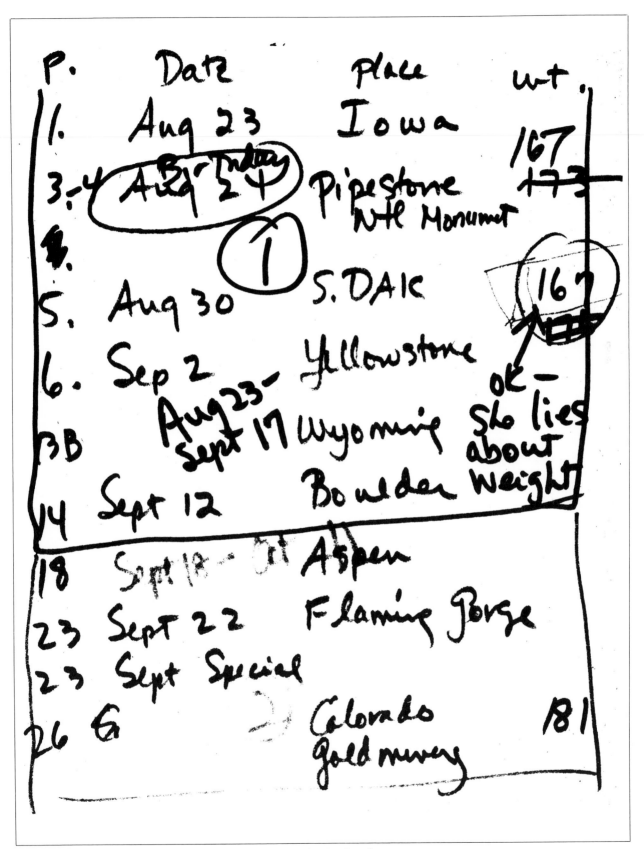

tion, she felt, eliminated the possibility of commercial publication.

Additional line editing on two more bestsellers—the enormously successful *Sacajawea* (1978) by Anna Lee Waldo, Smith's favorite editing project, and *Gypsy Lady* (1977) by Shirlee Busbee—and work on her second novel, "Cosmic Clowns," filled the next few years. During this period she also developed an interest in music, especially in learning to play the guitar and to write songs.

In the meantime, a fire on 9 December 1976 destroyed all of Smith's possessions (including completed manuscripts and works in progress) and nearly took her life. The fire left her in a state of ecstasy for a while, awed by her own courage in managing to survive such an experience. Emergency space was made for her at the MacDowell Colony, where she renewed work on the lost opening of "Cosmic Clowns."

The nonprofit Fiction Collective accepted *Fat People* in 1977. At this point, without asking to recover its advance, Holt, Rinehart, and Winston released her from the original contract. After *Fat People* was published, members of the Fiction Collective approached her about taking on the codirectorship of the group. Feeling a responsibility as a member of the collective, she accepted a position, along with Raymond Federman, as an unpaid codirector, a position she held from 1977 to 1979, overseeing the production of two lists, including the fifth anniversary series. During this time, she wrote and published her third novelization of a movie, *The End* (1978), from a screenplay by Jerry Belson (one of the original scriptwriters for *All in the Family*). The work at the Fiction Collective was supposed to be part-time, but Smith found herself devoting nearly forty hours per week to the duties, making it difficult to complete the work on her next project, *The Child and the Serpent* (1980).

She has completed three additional books that await publication: *Fever* is a novelization based on the television soap opera *General Hospital*; *Renewal* and *The Right Time* are romances. She anticipates that the realistic adult romance genre will break ground in the 1980s, as historical fiction did in the 1970s. In her romances she has complete freedom in character and story development, the only restrictions being length (50,000-60,000 words) and the ending, which must conform to the romance genre.

She is working on two long-term noncommercial projects. One involves research on a historical novel set in and around Trenton, New Jersey, her childhood home. The other undertaking is a continuation of her trilogy on power struggles, begun with *Fat People*. "Cosmic Clowns," the work in progress, deals with power struggles in a group situation. Fat Sarah from *Fat People* will appear in "Cosmic Clowns" "from the outside," thanks to the presence of a first-person narrator. Volume three, "Mal de Mere," dealing with struggles in a family situation, will also feature Sarah, both younger and older than she was in the first novel. Smith continues to work as both a writer and a publishing professional, preferring to be able to choose her projects freely.

Important influences upon Smith have included not only writers but work situations and social forces: Nathanael West, Irish poets, the literature and poetry of the 1920s (Joyce, Eliot, Stein, and others), the Fiction Collective, people at the writing colonies, the isolation of New England, and the women's movement and consciousness-raising sessions.

Smith's only serious novel, *Fat People* is a character study concerned with one year and a day in the life of Sarah Campbell, who is trying to put her life back together after her husband, Sweep, leaves her. In parts one and two, Sarah is alternately on the road or back East, frequently indulging in unimpassioned sex (with whomever happens to be available), eating voraciously to add protective fat, complaining about her lack of energy, and "digesting" her experiences. In part two Sarah learns a significant lesson about herself: experience alone will not release her from her monotonous but desperate quest for meaning (suggested most clearly by lines from T. S. Eliot's *Four Quartets* used by Smith at the beginning of part two: "You say that I am repeating Something I have said before. I shall say it again"). In part three Sarah ends her travels across the country to settle down in the East and try to come to terms with her realization that experience will not lift her out of her horrid depression.

The narration in *Fat People* jumps back and forth between the past and the present, leading to time disjunction, an indication that Sarah's energy is so drained by her attempt to understand events of the past that she is unable to absorb and understand the present.

Fat People has three interrelated thematic issues: the power struggle between men and women, the role of creativity in relation to the power struggle, and the integration of a seriously divided personality. The theme of the male-female power struggle begins when Sarah takes flight upon being abandoned by Sweep in order to try to understand her rejection. The following passage vividly illus-

Toot-toot! Toot-toot! What else is there to say? That
there was no trouble ~~with~~ working out the vehicle exchange? That is a lie.
That the sound of ~~Chestnut's voice~~ spurred out settling of
details? Well, ~~suggestion automatic?~~ That is certainly true enough. ~~A~~ A single moan
through the metal of the van and the idle sounds of the Porsche.
It was urgent, and could not be denied.

~~"Her labor pains are still irregular," and her water~~
~~bag is intact," Benjamin said.~~

~~"I'll back the Porsche up and give us some light."~~

~~"I'll have to get her out the side. Neither of The~~
~~front windows work, driver's door doesn't open."~~

"How fast are the pains coming?" I said, as ~~"Has her water bag broken?" I say,~~ as if I ~~can~~ (could) make use
of the information. said.
"They're still pretty irregular," Benjamin ~~says.~~ "Look,
~~"Now look,~~ how about backing up and giving us some
light? I"ll have to get her out through the side door. The
door on this side doesn't open."

~~"_____"~~

It was not until Chestnut had been
helped on to solid ground that I was
able to get a look at her; I was
struck with the insight that I have
not often been curious about a woman
if there was a man around.

Revised typescript page for Fat People

trates Sarah's dilemma: "Mostly there is a kind of numbness, as if the half year from the time Sweep split until I split is my only reality. I can't even think about Sweep. I don't understand what happened, why I can't control this incredible self-destructiveness. I know its [sic] self-destructive, but that doesn't seem to matter at all. I eat, and I drive, and I turn on, and I eat, and I drive, and I check into a motel and I drink and there you are." Sarah is in a classical depressive state, characterized by her numbness, low energy level, flight patterns, avoidance of contact with the person who hurt her, suppression of pain, a hard, hollow state, and mindless activity to try to create a fire in her psyche—through sex, eating, and driving.

The second theme emerges when Sarah learns to play the guitar, an activity that allows her to express her creativity, as the drum (used primarily as an outlet for aggression and frustration), her previous instrument, never did and as her obsessive pursuit of sex never could. The more involved she becomes with the guitar, the less interested she is in sex and food. She remains fat (parity with males), but more importantly the music clearly allows her to integrate her personality so that she is capable of feeling. She is now highly conscious of her energy and in a jam session with three males she charges the atmosphere to such an extent that one of the musicians comments on her ability to create electricity. For an indication that Sarah has found a means of transferring her pain from the interior (suppressed) to the exterior (her fingers become very sore after extensive picking exercises) and has emerged from the numbness of her depressed state, a scene with Sam, her guitar-maker friend, is symbolic of her condition. He says of her tender fingers: "The pain's good. . . . It means you're learning to use new muscles and doing it right." At the novel's end, Sarah is well on her way to a vital existence because she now accepts herself—she is in no rush—and because she has her music (questing has ceased).

The male-female power struggle from the past led to the dissolution of her identity and sense of self-worth. The fat allows her to recover from the blow of Sweep's rejection. The guitar, however, offers her an outlet for creativity and tenderness that transforms her sense of self and her relations with men. Several writer friends suggested to Smith that in part three Sarah is not as strong as she was in the first two parts. In fact, Sarah is stronger. She has moved from negative passivity in her dependence on a male to negative aggression to a combination of positive aggression and positive passivity that will eventually lead to psychological health. A hard-hitting, earthy account of life for a depressed woman who is in some respects myopic and self-centered, *Fat People* is a good, psychologically acute novel that offers measured optimism about the human capacity to recover from deep hurt and rejection.

The book has not received much critical attention, but those notices it has garnered have been generally positive. Stephen Phelps in the *Minnesota Daily* found it accessible and engaging, but he called the structure unwieldy. E. M. Broner in *Woman's Times* liked the book because of its concern for a woman's perspective; she was disturbed, though, by Sarah's myopia about life and her lack of interaction with women. David Press in the *Cream City Review* found the plot restrictive, but he appreciated Smith's narrative ability: "Her consciousness as a storyteller suffuses her tale, so that the meaning of her fiction is most often found in her innovative telling." The most enthusiastic response came from *Kirkus Reviews,* which found the book "very very polished, impressively so." The Kirkus reviewer was struck by the development of Sarah's state of mind, commenting: "Still, in her diffidence, Sarah's that rare thing in a fictional character—reluctant. Not raging, not renouncing, not riled, just not quite *ready*—and the delicacy of that state takes a real writer to produce. Smith *is* one."

Smith collaborated with Sy Cook to produce a novel about Nazi experimentation with cruel behavior-modification techniques that enhanced a baby's innate psychokinetic powers. The novel, *The Child and the Serpent*, is a well-crafted tale of intrigue concerning the extraordinary results achieved by Alfred Volte, the Nazi scientist, that have been kept secret for forty years, but as the tale opens, Adam Keyes, the child on whom Volte performed the psychokinetic enhancement tests, is beginning to discover the reason for his unusual power.

The novel functions on one level as a fast-paced story of adventure and revenge. On another level, it taps the current interest in the Holocaust. On yet another level, the tale concerns the nature, enhancement, and exploitation of psychokinesis. The detail about the experimentation is credible, even captivating. However, the description of Adam's destructive use of his seemingly superhuman power is tantalizingly vague. Once the destructive feature of Adam's power—and its potential for misuse—is recognized, it would seem important to work out some of the ramifications.

However, since minimal space is devoted to the negative aspect of his power, several significant moral and social issues are unexplored.

Smith came to the project through her agent, Charles Neighbors, who had agreed to handle Cook's novel. Cook had a 600-page manuscript, which included an extensive family history for Adam. Smith agreed to function as line editor on the book, which had structural problems: it was overloaded with family history; Lena, Adam's foster mother, was unsatisfactorily developed; and Adam did not have a proper place in the dramatic action. Cook had a fascinating tale to tell, but he needed a professional writer to shape it for him. Cook's role changed from writer to storyteller, and Smith became a collaborator. The result is a riveting tale.

During Carol Sturm Smith's twenty-year ap-

prenticeship as editor, ghostwriter, and author, she has learned her trade well (she is able to shape a good suspense tale and sketch engaging characters quickly) and has made a promising start in her investigation of power struggles, creativity, and identity.

Other:

Lucius von Frieden, *Mushrooms of the World,* edited by Smith (New York: Bobbs-Merrill, 1967).

Periodical Publications:

"Fat People" [excerpt], *Center,* 9 (December 1976): 49-51;

"Cosmic Clowns" [excerpt], *Center,* 13 (June 1981): 80-81.

Peter Spielberg
(2 July 1929-   )

Jane Schwartz
Brooklyn College, City University of New York

SELECTED BOOKS: *Bedrock: A Work of Fiction Composed of Fifteen Scenes from my Life* (Trumansburg, N.Y.: Crossing Press, 1973);

Twiddledum Twaddledum (New York: Fiction Collective/George Braziller, 1974; London: Sidgwick & Jackson, 1979);

The Hermetic Whore (New York: Fiction Collective/ George Braziller, 1977).

Although Peter Spielberg arrived in America in 1939, at the age of ten, in many essential ways he remains a refugee. A sense of impermanence pervades his work; stripped of his culture and his past, he has developed a heightened sense of the irrationality and absurdity of the modern world. Born in Vienna to middle-class Jewish parents, Henry and Erna Kulka Spielberg, he and his older sister were spirited out of the country after *Anschluss* in August 1938 and hidden with their maternal grandmother in Czechoslovakia. Later they were joined by their parents and together the family escaped to New York, where Spielberg has lived, with brief exceptions, ever since.

Supporting himself by a variety of odd jobs—

short-order cook, truck driver, packer in the garment district—Spielberg put himself through college at New York's City College (graduating with a B.A. in 1952) and went on to gain an M.A. at New York University (1957) and a Ph.D. in literature from the University of Buffalo (1961). His dissertation on Joyce's manuscripts was later published as a book. He has been married to Elaine Konstant since 1956 and they have two children.

Along with a European graciousness and charm, Peter Spielberg maintains a sense of privacy that borders on reclusiveness. Because of this, he has sometimes been misunderstood by his colleagues and at one point in his teaching career was referred to as "Surly Spielberg." He feels very strongly that biographical information adds nothing to his fiction; in fact, it may restrict the reader. Thus, he prefers to keep his personal life as far away from the reader as possible.

Spielberg can be considered a "late bloomer" in terms of his publishing history: he has been writing fiction since the early 1950s; a few stories came out in the 1960s; but he did not receive any critical recognition until the 1970s, when all three of his

books appeared, first *Bedrock* (1973), then *Twiddle-dum Twaddledum* (1974) and *The Hermetic Whore* (1977). In 1979 he received his first grant for fiction writing, an NEA Fellowship. This allowed him to take a leave of absence from Brooklyn College, where he has been teaching literature and creative writing since 1961; during this leave he completed two novels, "Play Dead," which he had been writing and revising off and on for almost ten years, and "Crash-Landing."

With a group of other writers, Spielberg founded the Fiction Collective in January 1974, and he continues to sit on its board of directors. The collective was organized as an alternative to traditional publishing houses, which the group felt often imposed a commercial censorship on innovative works that might not have mass appeal by refusing to publish them either because of their experimen-

tal forms or their subject matter, or, as in Spielberg's case, both.

Although his fiction is hardly conventional, Spielberg differs from certain postmodern experimentalists in that there is always at least the germ of a real story in his work; the thread of recognizable human experience is never snapped, although it is often stretched near the breaking point by wild exaggerations, fantasies, dreams, and distortions. Some critics and readers have objected not to his form, but to what they see as his "lack of taste": his fascination with all bodily functions, including eating and excreting as well as various sexual pleasures.

However, his overriding concerns spring more from his continuing perspective as a refugee than from anything else. He is not simply an outsider, someone who has escaped a repressive family or a narrow-minded small town; he is a survivor of one of the century's greatest evils—the Holocaust. Though Spielberg never refers to this event by name, not even in the novel that unfolds in its shadow, its presence can be felt in much of his work. The Holocaust has become the prototype of all evil, especially the small, everyday evils that accumulate over a lifetime and from which no one ever truly escapes. Mistrust and betrayal; inexplicable separations and abandonments; the constant humiliations of the powerless, especially children and lovers; harsh, arbitrary authorities; the lack of connection between human beings; the inability to love; and the overwhelming guilt of those who survive—these are the recurring themes in his work. For Spielberg's characters *do* survive: they are maimed and mutilated; they wander over bleak urban landscapes; but they survive.

Fortunately, there is comic relief in his work. Spielberg has developed and refined an outrageous gallows humor apparent in each of his books, and it is as refreshing as it is unexpected. His black comedy has come to be accepted as his signature.

In addition to the thematic concerns arising from his experience as a refugee, his attention to language is itself an outgrowth of his past, and his wordplay has become increasingly clever and sophisticated. He deftly bends and folds the language into puns, allusions, and double entendres. Critics have compared his verbal manipulations to Joyce, and his vision is seen as the American offspring of Beckett, Ionesco, and Kafka.

Bedrock, Spielberg's first book, is unorthodox in form, composed of "fifteen scenes from my life." These scenes are grouped into three sections— "birth," "copulation," and "death"—after the line from T. S. Eliot's *Sweeney Agonistes* which serves as an epigraph for the book: "That's all the facts when you come to brass tacks: / Birth, and copulation, and death." This book is neither a novel nor a collection of short stories in the conventional sense. It is a series of scenes: nightmares, distorted memories, darkly comic sketches, and fantasies. The unfeeling authoritarian father reappears in various guises, most notably in the fragment titled "Hide and Seek," where he says of his small son, who is terrified of being left by himself in a strange hotel room, "He has to learn to be by himself, just like the rest of us." This sets the tone of the opening section. With typical irony, Spielberg has used "birth" to signal not new life or hope, but the beginning of awareness of the horrors of the world. The young man in "Morning Sickness" explains, "What made my stomach turn was the dread of having to live

through the day that was at hand then and there." Anxiety pervades the book. The section entitled "copulation" portrays sex as pursuit, humiliation, and even castration—yet it unfolds as a series of modern cautionary tales, erotic, absurd, sad, and funny at the same time. Yet the futility of existence is never really doubted. In "The Last Day of Winter" a husband who is mistaken by his own wife as her lover enjoys an afternoon of passion before going out into the freezing winter streets. He slips on the ice and slides down a sewer, but even as he is heading toward his ignominious doom he realizes who is to blame and why: "It was his own fault. He had been looking up into the blue instead of at the treacherously slippery ground before him." The message is clear: sex is always punished, and constant vigilance is the price of making it to the corner. Interspersed throughout such absurdity are touches of gentle, poetic writing. The last line of this scene, as the husband vanishes into the depths, is "The white steam of the sewer rose to meet him with a deep breath."

Finally, in a segment called "Sickness Unto Death," Spielberg comments on his own craft. He recreates the journal of a writer who has decided to stop writing. This writer writes (the ironies abound), "Writing is a frustrating business at best. The strain of trying to squeeze the chaotic raw material of life into the orderly strait jacket of linear, two-dimensional words takes superhuman nerves." But, the writer concludes, writing about the chaos is the only thing that allows him to survive, and survival is the heart of Spielberg's concern.

Twiddledum Twaddledum, published in 1974, is Spielberg's second book and the one that most resembles the traditional novel, the Bildungsroman. Divided into two sections, the first part chronicles the coming of age of Pankraz, a young Viennese boy, during the late 1930s. *Anschluss* is mentioned only by oblique references to the terrors, displacements, and disappearances that the boy witnesses but does not understand. His heretofore sheltered but not very loving world is ripped apart, and a long series of humiliations culminates in a night spent with his ex-governess Lotte, on whom the boy has had a hopeless, adolescent crush. Lotte, who sometimes poses as her own identical twin (the real world is not to be trusted), seduces Pankraz one night after his parents have vanished, never to return—a fact which the boy suspects but guiltily refuses to believe—only to humiliate and betray him the following morning by turning him over to the authorities, who shove him aboard a crowded death train bound for some undisclosed "camp" in the distance. All his life, Pankraz has been shuttled about by "authorities" of one sort or another; he moves uncomprehendingly through a forest of Kafkaesque irrationality. This time, survival becomes as inexplicable as death: the train veers to the left instead of the right at a switch, and, through some fluke, becomes the *Through-Train-Special/Le Havre-Amerika/Non-Stop-Express*. Pankraz winds up in the Bronx and is born again as Paul, given a second chance at survival with an American family.

The second part of the book deals with Paul, who has survived Pankraz just as Pankraz had earlier survived an identical twin who shriveled up and died a few days after birth. Events begin to repeat themselves. Paul struggles against the authority of the family, becomes involved in yet another sadomasochistic sexual relationship with an older woman, finds himself generally humiliated and willingly victimized, encounters more "doubles," and finally, once again, is shoved onto a crowded train—the same train, really—and bound for another new life, a third chance for survival. This ending was initially misread by some who thought it signified hope and renewal. In fact, it is only another repetition of the cycle in which Pankraz/Paul—now metamorphosed into Peter—is trapped. This "new" life in the West will be the same life. For the refugee, the survivor, the landscape never changes: it is always guilt, standing out against a background of betrayal, humiliation, and death. Life in America has relieved Pankraz/Paul/Peter of the terror of the Holocaust, but the horror of everyday life persists—the isolation, the meaninglessness—and there is no train he can board that will spare him the modern world.

The form of the book distances the reader to some extent, as one never loses sight of the author's manipulations. Artifice is evident throughout. Doubles appear and disappear, events repeat, long lists become biting satires of everyday life, puns and allusions that inject literary and political history into the bloodstream of the book are commonplace. Form is crucial and always apparent, for this is not the usual novel about growing up: it is the superstructure of a nightmare.

His third book, *The Hermetic Whore*, like his first, is also a collection of scenes or short fictions that continue to explore new variations of the old nightmares. The biggest difference is that the humor of the earlier works, especially the satirical shadings, has ripened, providing a witty, sometimes hilarious counterpoint that makes the bleakness and the emptiness at once more bearable and more poignant, for it allows a more emotional connection between the reader and the characters. In the title story, the Department of Social Services endorses an enlightened program of masturbation for senior citizens to prevent the onset of boredom and loneliness, feelings which have resulted in hordes of senior citizens congregating in the Port Authority Bus Terminal and taking up all the seats. The finely observed ironies and deadpan presentation, including a list of ten tried-and-true methods, all supported by pseudosociological and pseudopsychological jargon, make this piece a masterful satire. In another story, "Jumping Joan, Sonny, Mother & I," children sue their parents for divorce. Case studies from a popular woman's magazine are cited as precedent. So-called authorities—a civil libertarian, a sociologist, a representative of the Church—all comment on the case in a parody of traditional divorce as it now exists and in a wistful understatement about innocence lost and children who must inevitably grow and change. Spielberg dedicates this book to his two children, with the proviso: "Not to worry. It's only a story." But this, too, is ironic, a father's ultimately futile reassurance, for Spielberg sets out to disturb, to shake up the more complacent reader, to unsettle the foundations. To some extent, this approach has limited his readership. Those looking for straightforward

Title page for Spielberg's Viennese bildungsroman

plots and likable heroes will be disappointed. These are stories of survival, but they do not have happy endings.

Spielberg seems to be moving in the same general direction with his recent works, two completed but as yet unpublished novels. "Play Dead" is about the death of a nuclear family by "natural" causes: boredom, longings, anger, fears, and self-deception. It, too, has its doubles and imposters and twins, and even a retired homicide detective who investigates real and imagined domestic crimes. In "Crash-Landing" Spielberg finally attempts to end on a happy note the only way he knows how: by working backward through time from a contemporary divorce to the passionate beginning of a couple's love affair twelve years earlier.

Spielberg remains dissatisfied with traditional realistic fiction, but he is equally dissatisfied with clever experimental fiction that is full of verbal manipulations but has no soul, no story. He tries to reflect ordinary, recognizable human experience through a funhouse mirror that lies, distorts, invents, and disturbs.

Periodical Publications:

"Laissez Faire," in *Statements* (New York: George Braziller, 1975), pp. 164-180;

"Prognosis," *New York Arts Journal*, 19 (September 1980): 14-15.

References:

Larry McCaffery, "The Hermetic Whore, Peter Spielberg," *American Book Review*, 1 (April-May 1978): 1-3;

Barbara McDaniel, "Peter Spielberg, The Hermetic Whore," *West Coast Review*, 12 (January 1978): 59-60.

Ronald Sukenick
(14 July 1932-   )

Timothy Dow Adams
McMurry College

BOOKS: *Wallace Stevens: Musing the Obscure* (New York: New York University Press, 1967; London: University of London Press, 1969);

UP (New York: Dial Press, 1968);

The Death of the Novel and Other Stories (New York: Dial Press, 1969);

Out (Chicago: Swallow Press, 1973);

98.6 (New York: Fiction Collective, 1975);

Long Talking Bad Conditions Blues (New York: Fiction Collective, 1979).

Although best known as an innovative novelist, Ronald Sukenick is also a provocative critic of modern poetry and postmodern fiction, a professor of creative writing and literature, publisher of the *American Book Review,* and a cofounder of the Fiction Collective, a group of writers who publish experimental fiction considered financially risky by commercial publishing firms.

Sukenick was born in Brooklyn, New York, received a B.A. degree from Cornell University in 1955, and went on in 1962 to obtain a Ph.D. in English at Brandeis University, where he wrote a doctoral dissertation on the modern American poet Wallace Stevens. His first major book was a revision of his dissertation, published in 1967 as *Wallace Stevens: Musing the Obscure,* in which, after a brief analysis of Stevens's literary theory, Sukenick provides close readings of many of the poems whose complexities, Sukenick claims, have caused earlier critics to "explain the obvious lines and skip the difficult ones." Reviews of the book were varied. Denis Donoghue wrote in the *New York Review of Books,* "Mr. Sukenick's readings are remarkably acute, so that even to disagree with them is exhilarating," while Joseph Riddel, writing in *American Literature,* thought the book "had almost nothing to commend it to anyone in the least acquainted with Stevens."

In 1961 Sukenick married Lynn Luria, who now teaches at the University of California at Irvine. (Her first book of poems, *Houdini,* was published in 1973.) She is a major character in Sukenick's first novel, *UP* (1968), a parody not only of literary criticism, but also of academics, book publishing, and the literary life. The novel's major character is

SANTANA 70

leadership and responsibiltiy, you know ~~naturexabhe~~ power

abhors a vacuum. If I don't use it somebody else will.

Somebody worse. You ke p mak*ing* tactical reappraisals.

In the sixties it's radicalism now it's something else,

so what. The point is to make things happen, "where such an

one is needed such am I,"X that's what one of those Greeks said,

Aristotle or somebody, so keep your eye on the ball kid, and

don't leave anything to ~~m~~luck. The weak need luck, the

powerful have other resources. ~~HistoryXis~~ ~~IXXXXIXXXXX~~ History is a ~~biech~~

belch in the boardroom. . . . Clover will be wearing a

modest grey sheath, trying to dress down . . . Roy: I came

in my new old beat pickup truck, eyes bugging, lip licking:

Heel, Drackenstein will say to ~~k~~oy. Roy: ~~How do you mean~~

~~that, Rod?~~ . . . Get Roxoff, somebody will say ~~at some point~~

~~in the evening~~x . . . Then, seeing how she'd be ~~dealing with~~

Miracle, Drackenstein will start looking at ~~m~~Clover in a new

way: I always thought you were stupid, he'll tell her.

Clover: I am stupid Rod. Everybody knows my ~~xaienixisxix~~brains

are in my tits and ass, don't ~~try~~ to blow my scene . . . For

the first time Rod ~~starte~~ will start getting really horny for

her. It wouldn't be that he'd never fucked her before of

course he'd fucked her before but that was just routine, in

fact he had the impression ~~m~~she could barely keep her hands

off him and that tur~~m~~ed him off, but now he'll see the

~~possibly~~ possibility that was just what she wanted him to

think and that turned him on . . . unlike Ccrab who has a

taste for women who are vulgar and simple, women like the

younger Cathy June emerging from her teen age hooker days

when she fell under Ccrab's psychic influence, ~~unless she~~

"Santana," revised typescript

"Ronald Sukenick," who is writing a novel called *UP* while holding a college teaching position. The fictional "Ronald Sukenick," like the actual Ronald Sukenick—who was a professor of writing and literature at Sarah Lawrence College in 1968-1969, and writer-in-residence at Cornell in 1969-1970—struggles to balance his novel and his teaching, worries about *UP*, and imagines the kind of reviews his writing will receive. "Ronald Sukenick" writes a mock review in *UP*, arguing that the novel fails because its major character is too closely identified with its author, thereby anticipating the actual reviews that the novel *UP* received. *UP* ends with a description of the real Ronald Sukenick, his real friends, and his real wife at a party celebrating the publication of the novel in which these people are both literary characters and themselves. Lynn Sukenick complains that one of the female characters is not as pretty as she had imagined, and her husband reminds her that it is only a novel. This blurring of nonfictional and fictional characters has become one of the trademarks of Sukenick's writing. When it first appeared, *UP* seemed startlingly innovative in its parodic use of the old Victorian novel's device in which the author stepped back from the story to comment editorially on its progress, though by now this technique has become commonplace. John Fowles, Norman Mailer, and Kurt Vonnegut are only a few of the authors who make cameo appearances in their own novels. Although still energetic, innovative, and funny, *UP* now seems dated.

Sukenick's second work of fiction, published in 1969, was a collection of six short stories called *The Death of the Novel and Other Stories*. In the title story a mock-autobiographical character named Professor Sukenick, teaching a college seminar on the death of the novel, reflects on the irony of teaching such a course—if the novel form is really dead how can a course be taught about it?—while trying to cope with social cleavages of the Vietnam era. Another story from this collection, "Roast Beef: A Slice of Life," which is in the form of a tape-recorded dinner-table conversation, was done in collaboration with Lynn Sukenick. The story parodies realism's call for a "slice of life" by pretending to be a documented tape recording of the Sukenick family as they eat dinner, discuss their daily life, and wonder whether this semifictional discussion will be publishable. The last story—often anthologized—in the collection is "The Birds," about which Sukenick said, "the story is the purest improvisation and I had no idea where it was going until the fragments started coming together pretty much of their own accord towards the end." "The Birds" is a collage of narrative fragments, birdsongs, newspaper stories, scraps of a letter about the French student uprisings, and even a brief mid-term examination on the story itself, complete with both short answers and essay questions. Many of the stories in this collection make use of such typographical devices as side-by-side conversation, marginal comments on the text, fragments and fused sentences, and minimal punctuation.

The Death of the Novel and Other Stories remains Sukenick's major literary effort to date. The stories reflect a variety of innovative techniques, yet each stands on its own. Narrative innovation is integral to each story, but these short pieces are not merely technically interesting; they continue to engage the reader's imagination in a deeper and more lasting way than his novels because Sukenick is able to sustain his improvisational style in the stories. The techniques these stories employ do not overpower the natural attraction of Sukenick's ironic ruminations, believable characters, and compelling writing style.

In 1970, while writer-in-residence at the University of California, Irvine, Sukenick began publishing selections from *Out*—which was to be his second novel—in literary magazines. At the same time his statements about the postmodernist novel and its tendency toward plotless, fragmentary, ironic self-consciousness were being printed by journals devoted to literary criticism. When *Out* was published in 1973, it was clear that the typographical playfulness and improvisation common to his earlier writing had become a major part of his style. Each of the ten chapters of *Out,* except the first, is arranged on the page in ever-decreasing lines corresponding to the chapter number. Chapter six, for instance, is printed as a group of six-line prose stanzas, chapter three as three-line stanzas, and so on.

Characters in *Out* change names and identities within sentences. Sukenick appears in many forms, changing from Harold to Nick to Carl, who says of himself, "I'm just a character trying to be a person the strain is terrific." By the last chapter (called "Chapter One"), the characters have been reduced to initials, the one-line stanzas have become increasingly more abstract, and the reader has been propelled toward the last page, on which only the letter *o* appears, the rest of the word *out* having disappeared into the void. The modern *no exit* has become the postmodern *this way out.* Despite the strict formality of *Out*'s spatial format, the narrative itself becomes more and more discontinuous, the threads of the plot unraveling as the novel progresses.

By 1974 Sukenick's writing had become too experimental for even Swallow Press, traditionally among the more innovative publishing companies, so he joined with other writers whose work had been labeled experimental to form the Fiction Collective, which included among its early members Jonathan Baumbach, Peter Spielberg, Steve Katz, and B. H. Friedman. Larry McCaffery, in *Contemporary Literature,* called Sukenick's third novel, *98.6,* "the collective's most significant book." Published in 1975, *98.6* is divided into three sections. The first, "Frankenstein," is an extended metaphor in which the random, senseless combinations of violence, war, and ordinary life in America in the 1960s—a decade in which the temperature of the times was certainly *not* normal—are represented by juxtaposed newspaper articles, nonfictional accounts of such atrocities as the Manson murders, and other fragments, patched together like Dr. Frankenstein's monster. The next section, "The Children of Frankenstein," focuses on a commune whose members seek refuge from the monstrous reality of the world described

in the novel's first section. Among the commune members is Ron Sukenick who is trying to write a novel about the communal experience as a way of ordering the chaos of the world. In the last section of *98.6,* "Palestine," the author presents an imaginary Israel where the chaos of both the real world and the commune's misguided attempt to escape it are resolved by application of "The Mosaic Law—a way of dealing with parts in the absence of wholes." Containing Sukenick's usual metamorphosis of character, *98.6* includes the author himself appearing in many forms, ranging from Roland Sycamore to Professor Sukenick to R. Thomas LeClair, in the *New York Times Book Review,* thought "Sukenick's achievement is making curiosities into concepts and freaks into human figures. . . .Because he sees life as continual invention, he can get at the imaginative bases of the alternative culture with sympathy and humor without trapping himself in hip cliches."

In 1979 Ronald Sukenick published his latest novel, *Long Talking Bad Conditions Blues.* Unlike his earlier works, this novel has not been sympathetically reviewed. The fragmentary style, which accurately reflects the 1960s, does not seem appropriate for the 1980s. Sukenick has returned to the lyricism that characterized much of the writing in his short-story collection. The typographical experimentation is still there: there is no conventional punctuation, though Sukenick's skillful transitions and use of blank space make the book's single 114-page sentence easily understood. *Long Talking Bad Conditions Blues,* set in the futuristic world of "The Island," takes the form of what music scholars call a "talking blues," a half-sung, half-spoken documentary account of both individual problems and historical disasters such as floods, crop failures, labor strikes, and other hard times. Like traditional blues music, it employs puns, topical references, and sexual metaphors. Early on in this rhythmically pulsating "talking blues" a character named Carl describes the way the book is written: "He had no taste for prophecy and was content to be a camera without film the very presence of the camera being in his mind monitor enough to establish the integrity of certain blocks of data."

Although the critical consensus is that Sukenick's writing has begun to repeat itself, and that his lack of conventional structures, characters, and themes is both too rarified and too numbing, he has firmly established himself as an important figure in the writing, publishing, and analyzing of what has come to be called postmodern fiction.

Sukenick is currently professor of English and

creative writing at the University of Colorado, Boulder, where he is at work on a new novel about "Los Angeles, fortune telling, and films." He is the publisher of the *American Book Review*, which appears every two months in tabloid form, an alternative to the *New York Times Book Review* and the *New York Review of Books*.

Other:

"The New Tradition in Fiction," in *Surfiction*, edited by Raymond Federman (Chicago: Swallow Press, 1974), pp. 35-45;

Statements: New Fiction From the Fiction Collective, introduction by Sukenick (New York: Fiction Collective, 1975).

Periodical Publications:

"On the New Cultural Conservatism," *Partisan Review*, 39 (Summer 1972): 448-451;

"Twelve Digressions Toward a Study of Composition," *New Literary History*, 6 (Winter 1975): 429-437;

"Eight Digressions on the Politics of Language," *New Literary History*, 10 (Fall 1979): 467-477.

Interviews:

Joe David Bellamy, ed., "The Tape Recorder Records," *Falcon*, 2-3 (April 1971): 5-25;

Bellamy, "Ronald Sukenick," in *The New Fiction: Interviews with Innovative American Writers* (Urbana: University of Illinois Press, 1974), pp. 55-74.

References:

Timothy Dow Adams, "The Mock-Autobiographies

of Ronald Sukenick," *Critique*, 20 (1978): 27-39;

Alan Cheuse, "Way Out West: The Exploratory Fiction of 'Ronald Sukenick,'" in *Essays on California Writers*, edited by Charles L. Crow (Bowling Green, Ohio: Bowling Green State University Press, 1979), pp. 115-121;

Denis Donoghue, Review of *Wallace Stevens: Musing the Obscure*, New York Review of Books, 1 February 1968, p. 24;

Ihab Hassan, "Reading *Out*,"*Fiction International*, 1 (Fall 1973): 108-109;

Jerome Klinkowitz, "Getting Real: Making it (Up) with Ronald Sukenick," *Chicago Review*, 23 (Winter 1972): 73-82;

Klinkowitz, "Literary Disruptions; or, What's Become of American Fiction?," in *Surfiction*, edited by Raymond Federman (Chicago: Swallow Press, 1974), pp. 165-179;

Klinkowitz, "A Persuasive Account: Working it Out With Ronald Sukenick," *North American Review*, 258 (Summer 1973): 48-52;

Klinkowitz, "Ronald Sukenick and Raymond Federman," in his *Literary Disruptions: The Making of a Post-Contemporary American Fiction* (Urbana: University of Illinois Press, 1975), pp. 119-153, 228-230;

Thomas LeClair, Review of *98.6*, New York Times Book Review, 18 March 1975, p. 6;

Daniel Noel, "Tales of Fictive Power: Dreaming and Imagination in Ronald Sukenick's Post-Modern Fictions," *Boundary 2* (Fall 1976): 117-135;

Joseph Riddel, Review of *Wallace Stevens: Musing the Obscure*, American Literature, 40 (1965): 47-48.

Peter Taylor

(8 January 1917-   )

Victor A. Kramer
Georgia State University

A Long Fourth and Other Stories (New York: Harcourt, Brace, 1948);

A Woman of Means (New York: Harcourt, Brace, 1950);

The Widows of Thornton (New York: Harcourt, Brace, 1954);

Tennessee Day in St. Louis: A Comedy (New York: Random House, 1957);

Happy Families Are All Alike: A Collection of Stories (New York: McDowell, Obolensky, 1959);

Miss Leonora When Last Seen and Fifteen Other Stories (New York: Obolensky, 1963);

The Collected Stories of Peter Taylor (New York: Farrar, Straus & Giroux, 1969);

Presences: Seven Dramatic Pieces (Boston: Houghton Mifflin, 1973);

In the Miro District and Other Stories (New York: Knopf, 1977).

Peter Hillsman Taylor's writing reflects a knowledge and love of his home state, Tennessee, and the people of his and earlier generations. Part of his success can be explained by the fact that he was born into a family of storytellers at a time when close ties of kinship and friendship were valued in small Tennessee towns. He used the stories he was told to create a fictional world with universal implications. Although some of his stories reflected the tales he heard as a child, he never is content merely to repeat; he imagines incidents, suggests the complexity of various relationships, and interprets the past. His stories often examine the difficulties of adjustment characters face as they become aware of what other generations hold dear.

Taylor's family history has the makings of a story in it. He was born in Trenton, Tennessee, 8 January 1917, to Matthew Hillsman Taylor and Katherine Baird Taylor (her maiden name also) Taylor. It is from his mother perhaps more than from anyone else that he developed his love of listening to tales. His maternal grandfather, Robert L. Taylor, served as United States congressman, three-term governor, and finally as United States senator. In the gubernatorial campaign of 1886, two of his mother's brothers and their father contended for the governorship of Tennessee. Taylor's

father also was involved extensively in the political life of the state before assuming the presidency of a life insurance company in St. Louis.

Although Taylor's family left Trenton when he was seven, the small town inspired his work, particularly the stories in which he used the fictional towns of Chatham and Thornton. The family resided in several different cities while he was growing up: Nashville, from 1924 to 1926, St. Louis, from 1926 to 1932, and Memphis, from 1932 to 1937. Taylor's childhood and adolescence allowed him the opportunity to observe upper middle-class life when it is transplanted from a familiar, small Southern town setting to new urban ones.

Almost instinctively Taylor knew early that he would write fiction. To this day, however, he maintains he is not a professional writer concerned about producing work and meeting deadlines, but rather an amateur, in the sense of someone who cultivates a love of language and storytelling.

Taylor's formal education had a significant influence upon his subsequent literary activity. He studied one year at Vanderbilt University (1936-1937), but declined to continue there when John Crowe Ransom moved to Kenyon College. In Memphis he attended Southwestern College (1937-1938) where he studied with Allen Tate. As Taylor's composition teacher, Tate announced that there was little he could do after a few weeks to teach such a gifted writer. Taylor studied with a series of teachers connected in one way or another with the Vanderbilt-Agrarian movement, and those associations helped Taylor in two ways. First, they reinforced his appreciation of the rapidly changing culture of the middle South and Midwest as those areas were moving away from their agrarian bases. Second, because several of his teachers were interested in poetry, early in his career he strengthened his awareness of the delicacy and nuance possible when the writer uses language precisely.

After a year in Memphis, Taylor went on to Kenyon College (1938-1940), where he received a B.A., and there, with Ransom, his decision to be a writer was solidified. It was also at Kenyon that Taylor entered into lifelong friendships with Randall Jarrell and Robert Lowell. Their ability as poets and Taylor's interest in poetry may help to explain why he chose to be a short-story writer rather than a novelist. The compression and tightness of poetry have influenced all his prose.

In the fall of 1940, Taylor enrolled as a graduate student at Louisiana State University.

was stationed in Georgia and later in England. In 1943 he married poet Eleanor Lilly Ross of Norwood, North Carolina. After the war Taylor's life gradually developed into that of teacher-writer. He began teaching at the University of North Carolina at Greensboro in 1946 and taught there intermittently through 1966. He has held numerous other

Peter Taylor

During his brief stay there he studied with both Cleanth Brooks and with a former member of the Vanderbilt-Agrarian group, Robert Penn Warren. However, as Warren remembers the period affectionately, it did not take Taylor long to realize that he was far more interested in being a good writer than in pursuing graduate work. His subsequent awards to support his writing showed that others appreciated Taylor's talent. He received a Guggenheim Fellowship in 1950; a National Institute of Arts and Letters award in 1952; a Ford Foundation fellowship and a Rockefeller Foundation grant in 1966.

He served in the army from 1941 to 1945 and

appointments at colleges, including Indiana State University (1948-1949), the University of Chicago (1952), Kenyon College (1952-1957), Ohio State University (1957-1963), and Harvard University (1964). In 1967 Taylor moved to the University of Virginia in Charlottesville where he still teaches creative writing and directs the creative writing program. He has arranged his life so he has time to write. In recent years he has steadily produced plays and stories. In the past decade, as has been indicated by his experimental plays in *Presences: Seven Dramatic Pieces* (1973), he seems to have become ever more aware of the sound of language and the relationship of prose and poetry.

In Warren's introduction to Taylor's first book, *A Long Fourth and Other Stories* (1948), he identifies the milieu of Taylor's stories: "the contemporary, urban, middle-class world of the upper South." He also suggests the themes: the disintegration of family life and "the attrition of old loyalties, the breakdown of old patterns, and the collapse of old values." Warren sees Taylor's sensibility as ironic, not an easy irony but one which discovers extraordinary significance in the "small collisions" of everyday life. Reviewers agreed with Warren that *A Long Fourth and Other Stories* was a brilliant work by a gifted writer. Warren's comments have also proved to be of considerable importance in setting the tone and mode of inquiry for subsequent criticism. In that first volume (and in subsequent work), Taylor's stories often take the city as their subject; and it is correct, as Walter Sullivan has stated, that Taylor is the first Southern writer who recognized the value of the city as subject matter. What happens, Taylor asks, when characters raised in one set of circumstances suddenly find themselves in another? Taylor frequently examines the effect of such changes upon often idealized views of the past. The pain and anguish which follow when those who try to live in the past cannot accommodate themselves to the present provide the impetus for the title story, "A Long Fourth," a study of expectations, disappointments, and stresses that exist just below the surface of life. Other stories reveal Taylor's ability to imagine characters in situations where the past influences the present. "Allegiance," for example, is told from the point of view of an American soldier who visits an aunt in London. He wonders if his interpretation of events which occurred years before between his mother and his aunt will change for he had been led to dislike his aunt. Yet the impression is created that whatever change might be in process will be a gradual one.

Taylor's second published work, the novella *A Woman of Means* (1950), did not meet with the same critical acclaim accorded to *A Long Fourth and Other Stories*. The 30,000-word narrative traces an adolescent boy's growing awareness of the disintegration of his father's second marriage and the descent of his stepmother into madness. For most critics, *A Woman of Means* is in large part a study of how the young narrator is caught between opposing forces—the rural and urban, the masculine and feminine, the age of childhood dependence and the inevitable independence that brings pain and loneliness. Taylor's method of using a young narrator who speaks obliquely allows him to present a view of the world in the process of its unfolding.

The joy of the novella is its indirect revelation about the character of the narrator, who, like an artist, carefully observes his surroundings. While this narrator might be described as "unreliable," Taylor's arrangement of the narrative provides a picture both of what is seen and of the child-narrator in the process of maturing as he makes those observations.

In his next book, *The Widows of Thornton* (1954), eight stories and one short play are unified by two themes. The first concerns families or individuals who have migrated from a country town to cities of the South or Midwest but whose values and behavior are determined by older provincial patterns. The second theme involves a figurative definition of widowhood; most of the women in these stories have been widowed not by the deaths of their husbands, but by the male's desertion of the old, shared, domestic life for the competitive, masculine world of business and commerce. For the critics this volume provided proof that Taylor had mastered the short-story form.

With the publication of *Happy Families Are All Alike* (1959) and *Miss Leonora When Last Seen and Fifteen Other Stories* (1963), Taylor's high reputation as a writer of short fiction was secure. Two of the best stories he has ever written, both in his estimation and that of the critics, appear in *Miss Leonora When Last Seen*, "Venus, Cupid, Folly and Time" and "Miss Leonora When Last Seen." Both chronicle a particular time, but are, as well, complex psychological studies.

The entire body of Taylor's stories could profitably be classified in relation to how they reflect his knowledge of cities, but that is just the starting point for his study of the human condition. He uses his settings to illustrate points about life. In "Promise of Rain" (collected in *Happy Families Are All Alike*), a story set in Nashville, he allows the father-narrator to dwell on the fact that he and his teenage son, although they live together, seem to inhabit two completely different cities. In other words, each life is unique in its perceptions.

As in *The Widows of Thornton*, a sense of community remains the source of values and beliefs for many of his characters when they find themselves in new environments, both Southern and Northern. Taylor does not, however, merely stress positive values associated with a small community, for such places do make it difficult for persons to adapt to change. Sometimes Taylor's characters are trapped by their past. "Venus, Cupid, Folly and Time," for which Taylor won an O. Henry award in 1959, suggests the complexity of adapting to change within radically altered circumstances. The story is about an eccentric old bachelor and his spinster sister who are socially prominent in a small town. They only mix with their neighbors once a year when they host an exclusive party for young socialites who dread the event, but feel attendance is mandatory. One year the dance is crashed by an outsider, and, after hints of their incest, the hosts never invite guests to their home again.

Taylor frequently stresses the influence of the past upon the present within small communities, and thus, in one of his most frequently anthologized stories, "What You Hear From 'Em?" (*Miss Leonora When Last Seen*), he provides glimpses of the past through an old black character, Aunt Munsie, who has lived into the twentieth century almost as an anachronism, and as a testimony to the love which binds people. The story creates no quaint, nostalgic picture of the past; rather it demonstrates that each human relationship is important. Although the two white boys Aunt Munsie raised leave Thornton for Memphis and Nashville, she continues to love them and to hope they will return to stay. Taylor's chronicles of such enduring love demonstrate gradual cultural changes from an awareness of community to other more impersonal values.

"The Death of a Kinsman" (*The Widows of Thornton*) was Taylor's first dramatic venture. It was followed by *Tennessee Day in St. Louis: A Comedy* (1957). "A Stand in the Mountains" (*Kenyon Review*, March 1968), and *Presences. Presences*, a collection of one-act plays, most of which are about ghosts, or the presence of a character from an earlier time, extends themes Taylor touches on in many of his earlier stories. He is especially concerned that people may have completely different interpretations of events. His devotion to the theater is genuine; citing the examples of Chekhov and Pirandello and the short story's inherent dramatic quality, he claims that the play rather than the novel is the writer's natural domain. While some of his plays have been successfully produced, they are for the most part closet dramas. Critics, such as Brainard Cheney and Albert J. Griffith, have been responsive to Taylor's plays, noting similarities between them and his fiction, but they generally have considered the dramatic pieces artistically inferior. It should be noted, however, that most of the plays treat themes which have assumed an increasing significance for the mature Taylor who delves into the complexity of motivation—often unconscious—of his characters.

The publication of Taylor's last two works of fiction, *The Collected Stories of Peter Taylor* (1969) and *In the Miro District and Other Stories* (1977), has al-

lowed critics an opportunity to reevaluate an author who had previously been described as the finest living short-story writer in America. The new stories of *The Collected Stories* are not startlingly different from many early ones. What is evident, however, is Taylor's gradual refinement of technique. Over the years he seems to have become more attentive to the complexity of fictional situations, and especially to the intricacies of the individual psyche and to how language reveals this complexity.

Some critics have been puzzled by the verse-narratives of *In the Miro District*, finding no good reason for abandoning prose as the narrative mode. The development of this new form of a modified, stressed verse, however, allows an intimacy not possible with conventional narrative prose. The verse form in these stories seems to work best in revealing the complexity of a narrator's involvement in the tale. An example of its success as an experimental technique is the story "Three Heroines," which Taylor constructed from his memory of his mother. Its verse pattern allows him to emphasize the narrator's involvement in the storytelling itself:

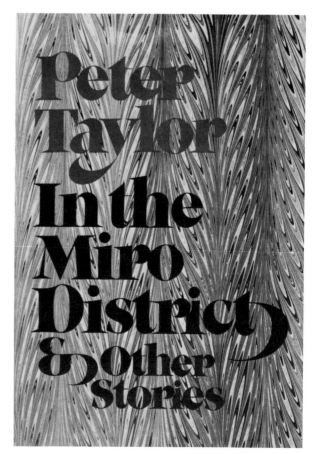

Dust jacket for Taylor's collection of verse-narratives

Home at last, yes,
And I have almost forgotten whether
It is my mother I am with
Or my Great-grandmother Haynes.
Though I have heard it all recited before
Time and again, and in the same words,
It never seemed so real.
The two women never seemed so nearly one.

This is not only an example of Taylor's refinement of technique, but also an illustration of his use of material he had lived with for decades.

Four approaches can be detected in a review of the criticism of Taylor's work. The first and earliest approach, explored by such critics as Robert Penn Warren, Ashley Brown, Barbara Schuler, and others, emphasized what they believed was Taylor's essential theme: the dissolution of family and community in the contemporary world. This avenue of criticism inevitably produced its antithesis, those who discern in Taylor's irony an implied attack not only on family and community, but also on veneration of the past and respect for traditions. A third attempt at an overview is the synthesis most recently suggested by Jane Barnes Casey (*Virginia Quarterly Review*, Spring 1978) and Alan Williamson (*Shenandoah*, Fall 1978). For Casey the tension between order and disorder and "the great modern problem of how to incorporate the most vital but also the most archaic urges into civilized life" constitutes the real subject of Taylor's fiction, and it is only in the stories of the last volume, *In the Miro District*, that a proper equilibrium between these forces has been struck. Williamson's position differs from Casey's in that he sees the opposing forces which seek resolution as "the wider eros," which directs men outward to achieve social, ethical, and even transcendent relationships, and on the other hand the need to satisfy the narrow drive of "self-love." Refraining from seeking synthesis or an overview of Taylor's work, a fourth group of critics, represented at their best by Morgan Blum and Kenneth Cathey, has been content with a formalistic approach. Examining structure, texture, point of view, irony, and symbolism in various stories or groups of stories, these critics have contributed valuable insights into Taylor's fictional devices and techniques. Taylor's

reputation has also been enhanced by Albert J. Griffith's *Peter Taylor* (1970), the only book-length study to date. In addition to an intelligent, judicious interpretation of individual works, Griffith provides a scholarly investigation of Taylor's most characteristic narrative habits: his digressive-progressive development of the memoir story, his employment of the unreliable narrator, and his ironic qualifications, intended to reflect the involutions of human experience.

Taylor's recent story about Memphis, "The Old Forest," (*The New Yorker*, 14 May 1979), extends his best qualities. It catches nuances of the social differences between classes in Memphis during the 1930s. Taylor's ironic vision also is clearly evident in this narrative. Critics who continue to write about Taylor should remember Griffith's observation that even though Taylor's opus is small, his stories frequently have the complexity, the density, and the scope of novels. There is also the attractive challenge of trying to sum up an ever-elusive Taylor, who in each story appears to examine old problems from a new perspective. For example, in his most recently published story, "The Gift of the Prodigal" (*The New Yorker*, 1 June 1981), he returns to a former theme, but in a new posture. Narrated by a father who in the process of telling about his son reveals the depth of his own needs, this story confronts facts of loneliness and alienation in a contemporary setting, yet succeeds without stereotypes and cliches. Taylor continues to look carefully at the present moment, document it, and thereby suggest mystery as he has done in his best work for forty years.

Other:

Randall Jarrell, 1914-1965, edited by Taylor, Robert Lowell, and Robert Penn Warren (1967).

References:

James Boatwright, ed. "A Garland for Peter Taylor," special Taylor issue, *Shenandoah*, 28 (Winter 1977);

Albert J. Griffith, *Peter Taylor* (Boston: Twayne, 1970).

John Kennedy Toole

(1937-26 March 1969)

Joan Bobbitt
Clemson University

BOOK: *A Confederacy of Dunces* (Baton Rouge: Louisiana State University Press, 1980).

The 1980 Pulitzer Prize for Fiction was awarded posthumously to John Kennedy Toole for his novel, *A Confederacy of Dunces*, written almost twenty years before. The circumstances of its publication and the life of the author are at least as remarkable as the work itself.

Toole was thirty-one years old when he died on 26 March 1969. The son of Thelma and John Toole, a car salesman, he spent much of his life in New Orleans, the city whose people and moods he so skillfully evokes in his novel. As a child he was intelligent, imaginative, and precocious. Like his literary creation, Ignatius Reilly, he disdained the company of his classmates and the quality of his education. He skipped the first and fourth grades, completed high school early, and entered Tulane University. Though only sixteen at the time, he had already written his first novel, still unpublished, titled "Neon Bible." Toole graduated from Tulane in 1958, and left New Orleans for New York where he earned his master's degree in English at Columbia University the next year. He then spent a year teaching at the University of Southwestern Louisiana. There he purportedly got the idea for the character of Ignatius Reilly, who is believed to be modeled on an English department colleague and friend.

Toole began writing *A Confederacy of Dunces* in 1962 while doing a stint in the army in Puerto Rico. He was twenty-four years old. Upon completing the novel in 1963, he began negotiating with Simon and Schuster for its publication. The exact nature of these negotiations remains unclear, but Toole apparently corresponded with Robert Gottlieb (editor-in-chief from 1955-1968) for a number of years, during which Toole revised the manuscript several times. The contact ended in 1966 when the novel was finally rejected. Evidently he did not pursue any plans for publication elsewhere.

Following his army discharge, Toole returned to New Orleans, where he lived with his parents while teaching at Saint Mary's Dominican College and working toward his Ph.D. at Tulane University.

In December 1968 he resigned from his job and left New Orleans. For several months he traveled around the country, paying visits to Hearst's Castle in San Simeon, California, and Flannery O'Connor's home in Milledgeville, Georgia. Shortly thereafter, he was found dead in his car in Biloxi, Mississippi, the victim of self-induced carbon-monoxide poisoning.

With her son dead, Thelma Toole took it upon herself to get his novel published. Over the next few years she sent a single carbon copy manuscript to more than half a dozen publishing houses; it was rejected by all of them. It was not until 1976 that her efforts began to pay off. Through sheer fortitude, she managed to get Walker Percy, then teaching a seminar at Loyola University, to read *A Confederacy of Dunces*. As Percy explains in the book's introduction, his initial reluctance gave way to unqualified enthusiasm as he realized what a masterpiece it was. He immediately made an effort to get the novel accepted by his own publisher, Farrar, Straus and Giroux. When it was refused, he took the manuscript to L. E. Phillabaum of the Louisiana State University Press, which was just beginning to publish high quality fictional works. Phillabaum was astonished by it, and the book was quickly accepted. *A Confederacy of Dunces* came out in May 1980 and began at once to garner rave reviews. It was picked up as an alternate selection by the Book-of-the-Month-Club, Grove Press snapped up the paperback rights, and Twentieth Century-Fox secured an option for the film version. Less than a year later, more than 40,000 hard cover copies had been sold. In April 1981, the novel received the Pulitzer Prize, and John Kennedy Toole's work was vindicated.

Reviews of *A Confederacy of Dunces* have been uniformly positive. Alan Friedman, in the *New York Times Book Review*, calls it "nothing less than a grand comic fugue," while the *New Republic* finds it to be "without question, one of the funniest books ever written." The *Virginia Quarterly Review* terms the novel "a superb mock-heroic tale . . . full of the exuberance—and the profound solitude—of life." At its center is Ignatius Reilly, Toole's finest comic creation and the orchestrator of most of the work's hilarious misadventures. A gargantuan, unemployed thirty-year-old, Reilly lives at home with his long-suffering mother. Indeed, he spends most of his life there, alternately eating, watching television, and expounding his personal philosophy in Big Chief notebooks. In the evenings he goes to the movies. The novel's intricate plot line is spawned by Mrs. Reilly's attempts to get her son to find a job, not an easy task. As becomes apparent in the opening scene, despite his master's degree, Ignatius is not the kind of person to inspire trust in a prospective employer. While waiting for his mother at that traditional New Orleans meeting spot, the clock in front of D. H. Holmes, he is taken for a suspicious character and almost arrested by an overly zealous policeman. Dressed in baggy tweed trousers and a green hunting cap with earflaps, his standard garb, Reilly, through his physical appearance, aptly reflects his emotional separation from the rest of the world. Both literally and philosophically, he looks down on those around him, searching in vain for the requisite "theological and geometrical standards" which he demands. He is further debilitated by a number of phobias, the worst centering on his sensitive pyloric valve, which responds to the vagaries of the world by snapping shut at the slightest provocation. Worse yet, Ignatius feels compelled to inform everyone of his condition in a most ponderous and erudite manner. Mrs. Reilly ultimately prevails, however, and despite his personal liabilities, Ignatius is "forced to function in a century which he loathes."

Reilly's previous job record has been nothing short of disastrous. His career as a teacher ended abruptly when his students joined forces in a demonstration demanding that he grade and return their papers; he refused. Later he was fired from the New Orleans Public Library for spending all day pasting only three or four slips in the backs of new books, insisting all the while that the quality and integrity of his work were more important than the quantity. Under pressure from his mother, Ignatius manages to get a job as a clerk at the floundering firm of Levy Pants, where he copes with his filing duties by putting the files in the trash. Instead of working, he devotes his time to boosting the morale of the office by improving its atmosphere. To that end, he spends days painting assorted cardboard signs, including one of a crucifix, and growing bean plants which eventually entwine themselves around the handles of the empty file drawers. However, "Fortuna," as Ignatius calls it, is no more kind to the fledgling employee than she has been before. Ignatius's peaceful days at Levy Pants are destined to end when he decides to organize an employee re-

John Kennedy Toole

bellion in order to prove to Myrna Minkoff that he is not without a social conscience. In one of the novel's funniest episodes, Ignatius leads a group of reluctant factory workers in a Crusade for Moorish Dignity against the company's "exploitive" management, represented by the kindly, innocuous Mr. Gonzales. Prodded along, the troops march on the office, holding aloft the yellow-stained bedsheet which their leader has fashioned into a banner. However, the uprising proves abortive when the workers refuse to obey Ignatius's order to beat Mr. Gonzales over the head with their pipes and chains, taking a half hearted swipe at his posters and bean plants instead. Thus another page in Ignatius's employment record comes to a close.

After his ignominious dismissal from Levy Pants, the only job he can get is selling hot dogs for Paradise Vendors, Inc. Not only is an educated man reduced to peddling "weenies" on the street, as his mother puts it, but he seldom sells enough to make up for the number he eats. The owner keeps him on only because he feels sorry for "the boy" because of his drunken mother and his defective pyloric valve. Even the kid who rents the bun compartment of his weenie wagon to store pornographic playing cards

Dust jacket for Toole's Pulitzer Prize-winning novel

pities Ignatius, whom he sees as the victim of too much schooling. Never very promising, Reilly's vending career is cut short when he is indirectly involved in a police arrest, and a picture of him and his overturned wagon lying in the street appears in the newspaper.

In his quest for permanent but effortless employment, Ignatius comes in contact with a cross section of New Orleans's geographical and human landscape. As Alan Friedman points out, "A dozen characters bounce off each other, physically and verbally, through a plot of such disarming inventiveness that it seems to generate itself effortlessly. . . . The plot, as it spins, also generates the city of New Orleans in hot, sharp, solid, ethnic detail." Ignatius's peregrinations take him from the Irish Channel around Magazine Street to Bourbon Street and Pirate's Alley in the French Quarter to the run-down warehouse district along the Industrial Canal. It is a picaresque journey that Toole uses to introduce a gallery of originals. There is Patrolman Mancuso, Ignatius's nemesis, who is assigned to undercover duty in a stall of the bus station men's room as punishment for not making enough arrests. One of his near arrests is Claude Robicheaux,

Mrs. Reilly's elderly suitor, who suspects everything and everyone, including the police, of being "communiss." There is also Jones, the "colored dude" who is forced to take a sweeping job below the "minimal" wage to avoid arrest for "bein vagran." His coworker, Darlene, is a B-girl at the Night of Joy bar who reads *Life* magazine for self-improvement and dreams of having a striptease act with her pet cockatoo. At Levy Pants there is senile Miss Trixie, who insists on calling Ignatius "Gloria," the name of a previous employee, and who wants nothing more than to be retired and to get her long overdue Easter ham. She is kept employed against her will by Mrs. Levy, the owner's wife, who has taken on Miss Trixie's welfare as a personal project, the result of having completed a correspondence course in psychology. All of their diverse stories converge at some point in the novel, usually with Ignatius as the catalyst.

Although he is responsible for much of the novel's humor, Ignatius is also the source of its philosophical inconsistencies. As Paul Gray observes in *Time*, ultimately "the world he howls at seems less awful than he does." By his own admission, he is an anachronism in an age which he regards as an "abortion" and an "abomination." Ironically, he insists on a standard of "taste and decency" which he himself shockingly violates. Though he rejects manufactured foods as a modern "perversion," he consumes vast quantities of pastries and Dr. Nut, his favorite soft drink. While he regards commerce and industry as a blight, he initially envisions himself as Levy Pants's savior, seeking to make it "become more militant and authoritarian in order to survive in the jungle of modern commercialism." Slovenly, lazy, and self-indulgent, Ignatius is nevertheless rigid and unbending ideologically. He rejects his religion because the pope is no longer sufficiently authoritarian to suit him, citing as evidence the meager penance the parish priest gives his mother for an equally minor transgression. "You should have been lashed right there in the confessional," he complains. He watches American Bandstand each weekday because it confirms his belief that the ideas of the Founding Fathers have failed and that the country would be better off with a "good, strong monarchy." Before he is forced to work, Ignatius's infrequent excursions outside the house serve only to reinforce his narrow vision. Indeed he seeks out precisely those sources of entertainment which he knows will activate his disgust.

All of his responses are equally negative. As Ignatius tells his mother, "I refuse to 'look up.' Optimism nauseates me. It is perverse." Even his ill-fated Crusade for Moorish Dignity is explicable only as an act of spite, a means of "assaulting the effrontery of M. Minkoff." Additionally, Ignatius seeks the betterment of the workers at the expense of Mr. Gonzales's skull; when thwarted there, he quickly offers the workers the adoring Miss Trixie's head as a substitute. Not surprisingly, none of Ignatius's actions ever succeeds. Even the magnum opus in which he records his world vision amounts to no more than "six paragraphs monthly." As with most of his inconsistencies and failures, Ignatius rationalizes the situation: "He could not even remember what he had written in some of the tablets, and he realized that several were filled principally with doodling. However, Ignatius thought calmly, Rome was not built in a day."

Ignatius's character would not pose a problem except that his vision is often indistinguishable from the narrative voice of the novel. At times it is not clear whether Toole believes him to be a prophet or a buffoon; indeed the comedy itself tends to overshadow and blur such philosophical considerations. Finally, though, it is hard to accept Ignatius as a lone, sane voice crying in the wilderness. As Paul Gray notes, "He is too grotesque and looney to be taken for a genius." Such a view is supported by Mrs. Reilly's growing disenchantment with her son throughout the novel. Though he depends on his mother for everything, he offers nothing in return. In fact, he ridicules her publicly and privately and then capitalizes on her feelings of failure as a parent. When she begins to make a few friends and enjoy an occasional night out, he responds with childish indignation, insisting that she stay home with him. When he learns that she is being courted, he asks in disgust, "Do you mean to tell me that you have been permitting some old man to paw all over you?" Though she explains that she only "wants to be treated nice by somebody," he accuses her of forgetting "his dear departed father barely cold in his grave," though Mr. Reilly has been dead twenty-one years. Even the most simple demonstration of kindness is beyond him. When, for example, the doctor recommends massage as therapy for his mother's elbow, he responds characteristically: "I hope you don't want me to do that. You know how I feel about touching other people." In fact, Ignatius has a distinct loathing of the human body, reflected in his obsessive concern with his own physical functions. (Interestingly, this attitude extends to the novel's narrative imagery where the human body is often described in unflattering terms.) For all practical purposes, he is a eunuch, which explains his rejections of Myrna Minkoff's attempts to involve him in a sexual relationship and his aversion to any reminder of his mother's womanhood. As her own world expands, however, Mrs. Reilly's tolerance for such abuse decreases and she comes to face what she has long suspected—that her son has a "heart of ice." A user and a deceiver, he is finally incapable of any emotion which is not self-serving. As she observes near the end of the novel, "You learnt everything Ignatius, except how to be a human being."

Though such a resolution is not really supported thematically, the novel does end happily for most of its characters. Patrolman Mancuso makes an arrest and becomes a hero. Jones is given a reward and a decent job. Darlene and her bird get their act. Miss Trixie is retired at last, and Mr. Levy takes a new interest in Levy Pants. Mrs. Reilly finally decides to have her son committed to a mental ward and to pursue a life of her own. Ironically, Fortuna even smiles on Ignatius, despite his sins. As the men in white coats descend on him, he is whisked away from New Orleans by his nemesis turned savior, Myrna Minkoff. Though he is seemingly unchanged, he nonetheless takes Myrna's pigtail in his hand "gratefully" and presses it "warmly to his wet moustache"—an uncharacteristic gesture and perhaps a sign of hope.

References:
Alan Friedman, Review of *A Confederacy of Dunces*, *New York Times Book Review*, 22 June 1980, p. 7ff;

Phelps Gay, Review of *A Confederacy of Dunces*, *New Republic*, 183 (19 July 1980): 34;

Paul Gray, Review of *A Confederacy of Dunces*, *Time*, 115 (2 June 1980): 78;

Review of *A Confederacy of Dunces*, *Virginia Quarterly Review*, 56 (Autumn 1980): 140;

David Roberts, "Genius Among Dunces," *Horizon*, 23 (September 1980): 4ff.

John Varley
(1947-   )

J. D. Brown
University of Oregon

BOOKS: *The Ophiuchi Hotline* (New York: Dial/James Wade, 1977; London: Sidgwick & Jackson, 1978);

The Persistence of Vision (New York: Dial/James Wade, 1978);

Titan (New York: Berkley/Putnam's, 1979);

The Barbie Murders (New York: Berkley, 1980);

Wizard (New York: Berkley/Putnam's, 1980).

John Varley first made his mark as a talented science-fiction writer with a series of short stories, beginning with "Picnic on Nearside" in *Magazine of Fantasy and Science Fiction* (August 1974). Five years later, at age thirty-two, he received the two highest awards in the field, the Nebula and Hugo, for "The Persistence of Vision" published in *Magazine of Fantasy and Science Fiction* (March 1978). Varley's rise to prominence was due in part to his mastery of the demanding short-story form as well as to the subjects he handled in a fresh, inventive manner. He explored feminism (his central character was usually a highly capable woman), sexuality (from lesbianism to intercourse with alien life forms), and genetic engineering (cloning was an essential feature of the future that Varley envisioned). Beyond craft and subject, Varley exhibited a third special quality: a positive view of the individual in the future. This optimism was neither simpleminded nor unadulterated; ultimately, it was an expression in the science-fiction genre of individual idealism and transcendental vision, common elements in mainstream American literature. Born in Texas, the son of oil worker John E. Varley and Joan Boehm Varley Litel, Varley spent a year and a half at Michigan State University in the mid-1960s before moving to San Francisco. He married Anet Mconel in 1970; they have three children: Maurice, Roger and Stefan. Struggling to earn a living by his writing, he moved his family from one of the rougher sections of the Bay Area to western Oregon in 1975. The move apparently suited his literary endeavors, for most of his writing dates from that period.

Varley's writing career can be divided roughly into two phases. In the first phase (which includes the novel *The Ophiuchi Hotline*, 1977, and the short stories collected in *The Persistence of Vision*, 1978, and *The Barbie Murders*, 1980) Varley creates an account of man's progress 500 years in the future. Expelled from Earth by alien Invaders, the human survivors have colonized the solar system. In the second phase (which begins with the novel *Titan*, 1979, continues in a sequel, *Wizard*, 1980, and is not yet completed), Varley narrates the epic adventures of a crew caught in the interior of an immense, living alien body which orbits Saturn. While there are significant differences between the two phases, there are strong elements of continuity as well, which give Varley's brief literary career a compelling consistency.

The finest segments of Varley's initial vision of the future of civilization are collected in *The Persistence of Vision*. The stories are "hard" science fiction, employing extraterrestrial settings and projected technologies, but the style and themes continue in the later phase of Varley's work. From the first sentence of "The Phantom of Kansas," the first story in this collection, the reader is entranced by a new voice in the genre, a direct, humorous colloquial voice: "I do my banking at the Archimedes Trust Association. Their security is first-rate, their service is courteous, and they have their own medico facility that does nothing but take recordings for their vaults." The world Varley invokes in this passage seems similar to our own, yet there is a shocking difference: this bank of the future is a repository for individual personality and memory, computerized and paired with tissue samples so that the insured customer can be cloned in the event of death. In this instance, Varley transforms a novel idea into a mystery story. The heroine, Ms. Fox, a successful female artist, is murdered and remurdered, cloned and recloned. She seeks to identify her murderer. The culprit is a criminal outcast and her alter ego—a male clone of Ms. Fox which went awry. Victim unites with murderer through sexual intercourse; they then plot their escape from an oppressive solar system. The ending is a happy, transcendent one: the unified self heads out for a new frontier among the distant stars.

Most of the stories from Varley's first phase are set in the same future which receives expanded treatment in his first novel, *The Ophiuchi Hotline*. This future has several positive features—sexual equality and freedom, interplanetary mobility, and immortality through cloning. On the other hand, there is a raft of negative features mankind must contend with in this imagined future. The individual is prohibited from full expression: first, by strict controls placed on population (the most basic rule is "One Person, One Child"); second, by laws against genetic manipulation ("If there was a taboo in human society which had taken the place of sex, it was human genetics . . . human DNA was inviolate"). On a larger scale, the human race itself has been severed from its home, its spiritual source; the Earth has been usurped by an invisible, insurmountable horde of Invaders (come to save the whale and dolphin, considered higher intelligences than man). The survivors of the invasion have fled to the moon and other planets, their migration aided by technological information supplied through a one-way interstellar transmission of unknown origin. The negative aspects of this future are consistently defined as any force or law which curbs free individual expression and exploration.

The main character of *The Ophiuchi Hotline* is Lilo, an Enemy of Humanity sentenced to permanent death for genetic experiments she carried out on herself. She escapes her death sentence and rebels, cloning herself several times over, so that in the course of the novel there are three heroines of the same name and personality, each leading a separate life in a different region of the solar system. Lilo has a double task: first, to break all bonds which imprison her and to achieve freedom; second, to unite her various selves and become whole again. Like Varley's other heroines, she lives her life (or lives) in pieces until she achieves a triumphant, transcendent end.

The novel's structure enhances the heroine's quest. Each time Lilo is cloned, a new narrative thread begins, separate but parallel with others in the novel; the main character of each thread is the same, but not the same; and in the end, the discontinuities of place, event, and identity literally and figuratively merge. The threads are tied off and the Romantic impulse—"a vaguely defined but compelling vision of the human race," Varley explains, "scattered to the stars, redefined, transformed"— achieves its full expression.

Although it received little critical attention, *The Ophiuchi Hotline* was one of the finest science-fiction novels of the decade. Yet Varley's short stories—rich in invention, gripping in plot, often splendid in characterization—outweigh his first novel. The colloquial voice is especially compelling in the short narratives, as disarming and striking as a latter-day Mark Twain's. "Never buy anything at a secondhand organbank," a typical story, "In the Bowl," begins. "And while I'm handing out good advice, don't outfit yourself for a trip to Venus until you *get* to Venus." Varley's surrealistic, frank, comic vision comports with his vernacular voice.

Varley's sheer inventiveness is most dazzling in his short narratives. In "Overdrawn at the Memory Bank," for example, the hero's memory and personality are withdrawn by a computer and placed in a lion who roams a lunar amusement park, the "Kenya Disneyland." This therapeutic vacation turns into a nightmare when the hero's body is misplaced. His mind must be stored in the computer until his body is located. The computer becomes a holding tank for the disembodied. Stored there, the hero sets out to "edit his world." This threatens to destroy the computer itself and the individual mind imprisoned within it. The world inside the computer is a frustrating, hallucinatory analogue of analogues from which the hero eventually escapes. The story is a satire on technology and bureaucratic bungling, subtly linking solipsism with the nightmare of a computerized society.

The Ophiuchi novel and stories are an exceptional beginning for Varley's fictional world; a bizarre future is fully imagined and made plausible.

Moreover, he develops coherent, universal themes from that projected future, implicitly linking the future to the present and the present to the past. The individual struggle for autonomy and wholeness is not only timeless but, Varley seems to say, within our determined grasp.

This vision also underlies the second phase of Varley's career, which in most other respects represents a new direction. In *Titan* and *Wizard*, Varley combines the trappings of science fiction with those of a swashbuckling fantasy. He now has less concern with a mad technology; instead, he turns to epic adventure. These novels resemble sagas, cycles in a vast heroic fantasy. The heroine of *Titan* is Captain Cirocco Jones, a third-world figure descended from Varley's previous line of independent feminists, but she is now endowed with a harder, more complex character. The world which entraps Cirocco and her space crew is Gaea, a living creature orbiting Saturn. Gaea, as her name suggests, is indeed an earth mother. She swallows the wandering earth-

lings and they are reborn within her, a band of Jonahs who set out to chart a new world, naming its strange denizens and geographical features from Greek mythology. Cirocco's goal, of course, is to free herself and her crew from the dangerous belly of this alien whale.

To reach her goal, Cirocco makes a literal journey to the Goddesshead. The internal stairway of her ascent is fraught with heroic adventure— monsters, wars, and extended detours into exotic, somewhat symbolic regions. Accordingly, Cirocco's motives—and perhaps those of the author and intended reader—are rendered as nothing more profound than a basic desire for adventure: "It had driven her all through her life, from the first comic book she opened, the first space documentary she had watched as a wide-eyed child, the first old black and white flat-screen swashbucklers and full-color westerns she saw," Varley explains. "The thirst to do something outrageous and heroic had never left her. It had pushed her away from the singing career her mother wanted, and the housewife role everyone else thrust at her. She wanted to swoop down on the base of the space pirates, lasers blasting, to slink through the jungle with a band of fierce revolutionaries for a night raid on the enemy stronghold, to search for the Holy Grail or destroy the Death Star." If this be Cirocco's thirst, it is quenched in the narrative. *Titan* is a feminist space epic, readable, wildly inventive, complex in plot, consistent in characterization. When the heroine completes her quest, she rejects the offer of freedom; she becomes the divine representative of Gaea in the closed world below, drawn by the promise of unending adventure—"a life you won't find on earth, the kind of life you knew you wouldn't find in space but hoped for anyway."

In the sequel, the novel *Wizard*, Cirocco has matured, and her thirst for adventure has been refined and dramatically altered. Now a confirmed drunk, this representative of the Goddess recognizes the injustices of the world. Prodded by her loyal companion Gaby, she plots the overthrow of Gaea. Gaea has meanwhile opened herself to a handful of carefully selected tourists from Earth. Exhibiting a weakness for heroic individuals, Gaea rewards those pilgrims who prove themselves worthy in her domain. Two young adventurers (a lesbian separatist and a withdrawn epileptic man) become such heroes, but their intricate journeys are subservient to Cirocco and Gaby's anarchistic schemes. Attempting to recruit the rebellious regional brains of an aging Gaea and thereby overthrow "the arbitrary power that held sway over her

```
                        Blue Champagne
                             by
                        John Varley


     Megan Galloway arrived in the Bubble with a camera crew of three. With her
breather and her sidekick she was the least naked nude woman any of the lifeguards
had ever seen.
     "I bet she's carrying more hardware than any of her crew," said Glen.
     "Yeah, but it hardly shows, you know?"
     Q.M. Cooper was thinking back as he watched her accept the traditional bulb of
champagne. "Isn't that some kind of record? Three people in the camera crew?"
     "The Queen of England brought twenty-nine people in with her," Anna-Louise
observed. "The President of Brazil had twenty-five."
     "Yeah, but only one network pool camera, for each of them."
     "So that's the Golden Gypsy," Leah said.
     Anna-Louise snorted. "More like the Brass Transistor."
     They had all heard that one before, but laughed anyway. None of the lifeguards
had much respect for Trans-sisters. They were all young, and preferred to go out
and do things for themselves. Yet Cooper had to admit that in a profession that which
sought to standardize emotion, Galloway was the only one who was uniquely herself.
The others were as interchangeable as News Anchors. And there was no denying she had
clout. The board of Blue Champagne Enterprises was stingy with press passes, not
wishing to clutter the Bubble with hardware. Cooper was wondering why he had not
been notified of the visit when Galloway gave them all a second surprise. A voice
started whispering in their ears, over the channel that was supposed to be reserved
for emergency announcements and warnings.
     "Entering the Bubble now is Megan Galloway, representing the Feelie Corporation,
a wholly-owned subsidiary of GWA Conglom. Feeliecorp: bringing you the best in
experiential tapes and erotix. Blue Champagne Enterprises trusts you will treat her
just as you would any other patron, asks you not to impede the taping, and regrets
any disturbance."
     "Commercials, yet," Glen said in disgust. To those who loved the Bubble-- which
included all the lifeguards-- this was something like using the walls of the
Taj Mahal for the Interconglomerate Graffiti Championship finals.
     "Stick around for the yacht races," Cooper said. "They should have at least told
us she was coming. What about that sidekick? Is it a hazard to other swimmers? Or
Should we know anything about it if she gets into trouble?"
     "Maybe she knows what she's doing," Leah said, earning sour looks from the other
four. It was an article of faith among them that nobody on a first visit to the
Bubble knew anything about what they were doing.
     "You think she'll take her sidekick into the water?"
     "Well, she sure isn't going to take it off," Cooper said. "Stu, you call up
operations and ask them why we weren't notified. Find out if we need to take any about
special precautions. The rest of you get back to work. A.L., you take charge here."
     "What will you be doing, Q.M?" Anna-Louise asked, arching one eyebrow.
     "I'm going to get a closer look." He ignored it when her eyebrow went even higher,
pushed off, and sliced air toward the curved inner surface of the Bubble.

     The Bubble was the only thing Q.M. Cooper had ever encountered which had caught
his imagination, held it for years, and did not prove a disappointment when he finally
saw it. In fact, it exceeded his expectations. It was love at first sight.
     It floated out there in lunar orbit with nothing to give it perspective, a
preposterous object when seen for the first time. Under those conditions the eye can
```

"Blue Champagne," revised typescript

life and those of everyone dear to her," Cirocco utterly fails. Stripped of her high position and of her faithful friend Gaby, the woman she could not fully love but could hardly live without, Cirocco transforms herself from wizard to demon (insuring another sequel in this Titanic saga).

A decided twist in Varley's usual plots, *Wizard* is more tragic than comic. Under the darkly glittering surface, Varley is once again tapping psychological impulses. Cirocco becomes a fully drawn character—a sad but honorable figure, a loner hardened by a lifetime in an alien world who summons from within the power to break the bonds of her despair. Her allegiance to the demonic is a more desperate solution than any Varley has offered before, but it is consistent with his romanticism and may open up a fresh vein of creative energies for this author. Certainly the elaborate sexuality of *Wizard* provides a solid basis of motivation for the conflicts and interactions of the characters. The baroque mating customs of the Titanides (the centaurlike creatures fashioned by Gaea) and the sexual activities between humans and aliens create an appropriate atmosphere for the demonic theme of Varley's narrative.

Titan and *Wizard* have been better received by critics outside the science-fiction field than by those within. They have also reached a far larger audience than the lightly promoted *The Ophiuchi Hotline*. While Varley's first novel was more innovative in structure, *Titan* and *Wizard* form a larger, richer canvas on which an enclosed, logically consistent world flowers and enchants us. The skillful mixture of plausible science and anthropology, swashbuckling romance and dream quest reminds one of science fiction by Frank Herbert and Robert Heinlein, just as Varley's earlier work reminds us of many writers from Damon Knight to Philip José Farmer. Varley feels that Heinlein exerted the single strongest influence on his art, an accurate appraisal.

Yet it is still Varley's short works which stand out. The narratives collected in *The Persistence of Vision* and *The Barbie Murders* often seem closer to our world; certainly they possess immediate power, astonishing invention, and irresistible delight. Varley's most honored story is "The Persistence of Vision," and it relies little on the trappings of science fiction, belonging neither to the Ophiuchi narratives of the first phase nor the Gaean sagas of the second phase. The time of the story is the late decades of our century, but the setting is clearly the America of the present or the recent past. The unemployed first-person narrator (a projection, perhaps, of Varley himself) goes "on the road" during the latest of a nagging series of economic downturns. After stops at several communes in the Southwest, he stumbles into the walled settlement of blind and deaf utopians in New Mexico. Members of this group communicate through touch and an advanced form of body language. They have refined such transactions of the flesh to the point of transcendent vision. The narrator becomes part of this intimate commune, but not a full member; like

the children of the commune (one of whom he falls in love with) our visitor can see and hear, and he cannot become a complete participant in their more ethereal forms of communication. The story is a fine variation on H. G. Wells's classic fable of the seeing man who is at an ironic disadvantage in the kingdom of the blind. Varley's story, however, is more complex and detailed. After a thorough analysis of this special social organism, the outsider leaves. He becomes a success in his world, a world which is in shambles by the year 2000. In the midst of disintegration and a loveless society, the narrator returns to the commune, a pastoral world where human values still prevail. There he discovers that the elders have disappeared; the suggestion is that they have so refined their communication and ritual that they have elevated themselves into another realm. The children left behind have gradually chosen to blind and deafen themselves. The narrator has little choice; he, too, blinds and deafens himself to the world he has rejected in order to feel more meaningful and fulfilled. This wonderfully concrete, ambiguous tale is not told in the tragic mode of *Oedipus Rex*, but in the serious-comic mode Varley typically employs. Rebellion, self-discovery, and personal transcendence again underlie Varley's narrative.

Currently, Varley's career is taking a new turn, toward the cinema. He has completed the first revised script of his short story "Air Raid," and has indicated that if this venture is rewarding he may do more work in this medium, provided he can gain greater control over script and film production. As a screenwriter, Varley has often commuted between Los Angeles and his home in Oregon.

Varley is presently working on the third, possibly concluding, volume of his Gaean saga in which he plans to trace the fortunes of Cirocco Jones and others in the war against the world which holds them. It would be foolish at this early point in Varley's promising career to predict its later phases, but it would not be surprising if the victories of the individual over oppressive environments continued to be a controlling idea in his work. This theme is an enduring one in every genre of American literature; subject to countless variations in imaginative form, it requires continual testimony and renewal. In this view, it is the special achievement of John Varley's fiction to test and validate the tradition of individual idealism under the most extreme circumstances imaginable.

Derek Walcott

(23 January 1930-   )

Dennis Jones
Luther College

SELECTED BOOKS: *Twenty-Five Poems* (Port of Spain, Trinidad: Guardian Commercial Printery, 1948);

Epitaph for the Young–A Poem in XII Cantos (Bridgetown, Barbados: Advocate, 1949);

Poems (Kingston, Jamaica: City Printery, 1953);

Ione (Mona, Jamaica: University College of the West Indies, 1957);

In a Green Night: Poems 1948-60 (London: Cape, 1962);

Selected Poems (New York: Farrar, Straus & Giroux, 1964);

The Castaway and Other Poems (London: Cape, 1965);

The Gulf and Other Poems (London: Cape, 1969); republished as *The Gulf* (New York: Farrar, Straus & Giroux, 1970);

The Dream on Monkey Mountain and Other Plays (New York: Farrar, Straus & Giroux, 1970);

Another Life (New York: Farrar, Straus & Giroux, 1973);

Sea Grapes (New York: Farrar, Straus & Giroux, 1976);

The Joker of Seville & O Babylon! (New York: Farrar, Straus & Giroux, 1978);

The Star-Apple Kingdom (New York: Farrar, Straus & Giroux, 1979).

PRODUCTIONS: *Henri Christophe: A Chronicle*, Castries, St. Lucia, 1950; London, 1951;

Wine of the Country, Whitehall Players, Mona, Jamaica, 1953;

The Sea at Dauphin, Whitehall Players, Mona, Jamaica, 1954; London, 1960;

Ione, A Play with Music, Little Carib Theatre, Port of Spain, Trinidad, 1957;

Ti-Jean and His Brothers, music by André Tanker, Little Carib Theatre, Port of Spain, Trinidad, 1958; Delacorte Theatre, New York, 20 July 1972, 15 [performances];

Drums and Colours, Royal Botanical Gardens, Kingston, Jamaica, 1958;

Malcochon; or, Six in the Rain, St. Lucia Arts Guild, Castries, St. Lucia, 1959; produced again as *Sin in the Rain*, London, 1960; produced again as *Malcochon* in *An Evening of One Acts*, New York, 25 March 1969, 32;

The Dream on Monkey Mountain, Toronto, Ontario, 1967; St. Mark's Playhouse, New York, 9 March 1971, 48;

In a Fine Castle, Little Carib Theatre, Port of Spain, Trinidad, 1971;

The Joker of Seville, Little Carib Theatre, Port of Spain, Trinidad, 1974;

The Charlatan, music by Galt MacDermot, Los Angeles, 1974;

O Babylon!, Little Carib Theatre, Port of Spain, Trinidad, 1976;

Remembrance, Dorsch Centre, St. Croix, Virgin Islands, 1977;

Pantomime, Little Carib Theatre, Port of Spain, Trinidad, 1978.

At age fifty-two, Derek Walcott has established himself as an important literary artist. The quantity of his work is in itself impressive. He has written fifteen plays which have been produced and published and ten volumes of poetry, seven of which must be called major collections. Publication of another volume of poetry is imminent, and his work appears regularly in the *New Yorker*. In 1981, besides preparing the new volume of poetry for publication, Walcott has lectured at Columbia University, composed lyrics for a production of *The Little Prince* (by Antoine de Saint Exupéry), and helped in direction of his own play, *Remembrance*. His creative energy is great and his productivity seems unabated.

Derek Walcott was born 23 January 1930 in Castries on St. Lucia, a small island in the West Indies that contains a varied and complex ethnic and linguistic community common to islands of the region. The sun was rapidly setting on this part of the British Empire as Walcott grew up. He was keenly aware of this phenomenon, and "the twilight," becomes a major theme in his art. English was the language of his family, of his schooling, and officially of his country, but the common folk of the island, the fishermen and the people of the back country who appear in many of his plays, speak a mixture of languages including standard and patois French. These folk, their manners and customs, their language, their struggle to survive, and their battle to give their lives some degree of human dignity, figure importantly in Walcott's drama and his poetry. He, however, does not see his role as artist to be primarily that of reflector of experience. In his autobiographical reflection, *Another Life* (1973), Walcott gives the artist the role of namer and quotes Malraux's comments on the pioneer realist, Giotto, to suggest that art, not life, is the prime mover of the artist.

Walcott, as the child of European and African parents, embodies one of the prime tensions of the West Indian experience. He is the "divided child," or as he calls the phenomenon in "What the Twilight Says," *the* cultural schizophrenic. But unlike many of his contemporaries, he has chosen not to jettison any of his cultural legacies—not the European, not the African, nor even the island mixture he calls schizophrenia. All the legacies play a significant role in the development and ultimate achievement of his artistry, and herein lies much of what is so special about his contributions to the new Caribbean literature.

The poet's father was English, and though he died when Walcott was too young to have any direct memories of him, the family's consciousness of Warwick Walcott remained very strong. It was enough to inspire Derek Walcott to dedicate his first volume of poems to his father's memory. The poet's early image of himself as a painter could well have stemmed from an urge to emulate his father, whose primary vocation seems to have been the visual arts. This, of course, is speculation, but art was in any case a significant matter to the Walcott household, in part as a legacy from the father, in part through active participation in things artistic by the mother.

The Walcott children grew up in a family with an unusual position in St. Lucian society. They were second generation immigrants in a time-worn settlement, Protestants in a dominantly Catholic community, a family that was linked by the color of their skin to the ruled and linked by culture to the rulers. This circumstance allowed Walcott to identify with common people and write about them while maintaining a degree of artistic detachment. His mother, Alix, a teacher, was actively involved in amateur theater, and according to her son, she kept a houseful of books. Walcott's early impetus to read and to write came principally from her.

Walcott's formal education, first at St. Mary's College, Castries, St. Lucia (where he received a B.A. in 1953) and then at the University of the West Indies in Mona, Jamaica, followed a classical British curriculum with major emphasis on the Latin and French languages and on English and other western European literatures. He developed a special love for Shakespeare and the great Jacobean playwrights, and his early efforts in this medium were frankly imitative of these masters of poetic drama. Considering this influence, it is not surprising that his first effort at playmaking was a historical piece presented in verse. *Henri Christophe: A Chronicle* was produced first in Bridgetown, Barbados, as radio theater in 1950; later that year it was staged in St. Lucia, and the following year in London. "The Jacobean style, its cynical, aristocratic flourish came naturally to this first play—the corruption of slaves into tyrants," Walcott writes in "What the Twilight Says: An Overture." According to the poet, Christophe had produced the only "noble ruin in the archipelago," and while "it was a monument to egomania," it was also "the summit of the slave's emergence from bondage."

History, however, was not to become a frequent subject of Walcott's plays. After one other venture into this genre, he left it to return only under commission to write an epic for the opening of the First Federal Parliament of the West Indies. The result of the commission was *Drums and Colours*, which was produced at the Royal Botanical Gardens

Derek Walcott

in Kingston, Jamaica, in April 1958. The play focuses on four historical figures: Columbus, the discoverer; Raleigh, the conqueror; Toussaint, the rebel; and Gordon, the martyr to constitutional rights. The likenesses of the piece to seventeenth-century court masque were most certainly a result of conscious choice by the author, for he was making celebrative, ritual drama to deal with his people's response to history, a subject that was to continue to trouble him. He sees that response as a constant stimulus to division in the Caribbean consciousness, and division is to him a problem, not a solution. This idea is clarified in his later poetry and finally in a 1978 essay entitled "The Muse of History." But one can see evidence of his concern about the effect of this early historical play in the words he gives the chorus to introduce it:

> Before our actors praise his triumph, Time
> Shows his twin faces, farce and tragedy;
> Before they march with drums and colours by
> He sends me, his mace-bearer, Memory.
> To show the lives of four litigious men,
> The rise and ebb of cause and circumstance,
> For your delight, I raise them up again,
> Not for your judgment, but remembrance.

The judgmental response, which is a prime source of divisiveness, is what Walcott asks his audience to avoid.

The 1950s were a productive, formulative period for Walcott. During the first part of the decade, Jamaica was home base to him while he taught, wrote, and found a stage and players for his "fisherfolk" plays with the Whitehall Players at Mona. There he produced *Wine of the Country* (1953), and *The Sea at Dauphin* (1954). Errol Hill was active in this company, and *The Sea at Dauphin*, which Hill produced, is dedicated to him.

This play is representative of the direction of Walcott's work at this time. It is a short, powerful piece that makes a rather harsh, humanistic statement. Afa, its hero, is a defiant Job figure who "must curse or he will cry." The play develops around Afa's dogged facing of the sea on one particularly violent day and his promise to face it in the future despite his knowledge that the sea has killed his bravest friends and despite his uncertainty of what his efforts will amount to in the end, a question posed through the suicide of an old man who can fish no more and who refuses to beg. Platitudes pale before the roar of Afa and the sea.

The major change that *The Sea at Dauphin* signals lies in what happens with the language of the play, which is English and French, both and neither. It is a language of cultural synthesis, an effort of the divided heart to reach beyond itself. Even more, it is the language of the people, not strictly imitated, but made eloquent, as the common folk represented in the work are made noble, by the magic of the artist. In a later poem, Walcott concludes that "To change your language you must change your life." *The Sea at Dauphin* seems to be a part of such a process.

In 1957 Walcott joined the Little Carib Theatre Workshop in Port of Spain, Trinidad, as its director. A short time later he received the commission for *Drums and Colours* and from that came the recognition which gained him a Rockefeller Fellowship to study theater in the United States. For the next two years, 1958-1959, he was in the United States studying with José Quincero at the Circle in the Square and Stuart Vaughan at the Phoenix Theatre.

Meanwhile, in 1958, the Little Carib Theatre produced *Ti-Jean and his Brothers*. Over the next twenty years this place and its company were very important to Walcott. After his two years in the United States, he returned to Trinidad and organized the Trinidad Theatre Workshop. He worked closely with the Little Carib, which produced five more of his plays. During the 1960s, Walcott was much involved in the total life of the new nation of Trinidad/Tobago. Besides his work in the theater, he was a regular art critic and reviewer for the *Trinidad Guardian* and a feature writer for the political journal, *Public Opinion*. The essays in these journals have not been collected.

Ti-Jean and his Brothers demands some attention, for it is a work with some special qualities. Its language and the people that it treats show continuity with *The Sea at Dauphin*, but the tone of the work is radically different. *Ti-Jean and His Brothers* is a morality play, a folk fable (truly something of both forms), in which animals speak and the devil appears onstage with cloven hoof and stiff tail. The play presents folk beliefs without apology or condescension, attesting to their reality and their force in everyday life. Ti-Jean, who shows respect for all creatures small or great, is an Anansi-like trickster-hero who succeeds through his native wit where gross strength and pretentious intellect fail. A less apparent but just as real part of the play, though, is its comment on the exploitation (complete with racial overtones) of the have-nots by the haves.

Walcott's folk drama culminates in the masterful *Dream on Monkey Mountain*. Unlike many of his other plays, this one seems to have been a long time in the making. The author tells us that he began work on it while he was in New York during the late 1950s, yet it was not staged until 1967 in Toronto. He brought *The Dream on Monkey Mountain* to New York in 1971 where it earned the Obie Award as the outstanding Off-Broadway production of the year. *The Dream on Monkey Mountain* is a very ambitious work, for it creates a metaphor of the colonized consciousness in the acting out of the hallucinations of an old charcoal maker and vendor. The question of what is dream and what is reality hovers before the audience from beginning to end. What should be reality is presented in the prologue and the epilogue. The setting for these parts of the play is a prison where Makak, the charcoal vendor, is incarcerated for a night and released at the end to return to Monkey Mountain. At the first and at the last Makak is in conflict with the "brown" corporal who has totally accepted the values of the colonizers and assumed the role of defender of the "Roman-English" law. In the middle of the play the reader is carried to Monkey Mountain to enter the dream. Makak insists in more than one place that the dreams are not dreams, and in the sense that they project the reality of his inner self, they are indeed something more than fantasy. Clearly, Makak has some connection to the man in prison that Franz Fanon says dreams of walking on water or of flying. It is most important, though, that Makak's dreams connect to the past, and it is in that past kept alive in the dreams of the folk that an element of freedom is maintained in the colonized world.

Walcott was active in theater during the 1960s, writing for and directing the Trinidad Theatre Workshop and producing *The Dream on Monkey Mountain* and several other plays toward the end of the decade. But in some respects this period is more important to his development as a poet. From 1962 to 1969 he published four major volumes of verse and received notable critical recognition for each. *In A Green Night: Poems 1948-60* (1962) drew high praise from Robert Graves and was honored with the Guiness Foundation Award. *The Castaway and Other Poems* (1965) received the Heinemann Award, and *The Gulf and Other Poems* (1969) was recognized with the Cholmondeley Award. His poetry was also awarded second prize at the Pan-African literary festival in Dakar, Senegal, in 1965, and he was invited along with three other English and American poets to read in the Poetry International Festival in London in 1969. The corpus of Walcott's poetry published in the 1960s is large; the themes are rich and varied and the formal qualities are interesting.

In a Green Night draws its title from a poem by Andrew Marvell, indicating the importance of seventeenth-century literature to Walcott. The opening poem, "Prelude," in its parade of sensuous images, reminds one of early Eliot, a link through modern poetry with Walcott's favorite literary era. Walcott always sees himself working out of the "great tradition," noting in this poem that

> . . .my life, too early for the profound
>
>   cigarette,
>
>   . . . . . .
>
> . . .must not be made public
> Until I have learned to suffer
> In accurate iambics.

The forms of the poems in this volume are in many respects quite traditional, with a sequence of ten sonnets entitled "Tales of the Islands" set at its center. John Figueroa, who has written a book-length study (awaiting publication) of Walcott's poetry, has suggested that these poems are among Walcott's highest achievements in poetry to this point in his career. The poet varies line length, rhyme scheme, and meter but does so within limited bounds so that a fresh experience is created while the audience relaxes among comfortable, familiar forms.

One of the major themes that emerges in *In a Green Night* is that of the dying Empire. In "Ruins of a Great House," the poet detects "A smell of dead limes [which] quickens in the nose / The leprosy of Empire." And when a wind shakes the lime trees he hears "What Kipling heard, the death of a great empire, the abuse / Of ignorance by bible and by sword."

The theme takes a different turn in the second of "Two Poems on the Passing of an Empire" when Walcott shows a pensioner of the African campaign lifting his "cropped wool" head to squint with his one eye at children who ignore the somber warning of the flag made from his empty sleeve.

Walcott understands himself as a child of the Empire, as well as a child of those ruled and exploited by it, and this division of origin, sentiment, and allegiance is thematic throughout his poetry. In "A Far Cry from Africa," he acknowledges that he is "poisoned by the blood of both" the Kikuyu (Mau Mau) avenger and the "drunken officer of British rule." He will not, cannot, reject either.

In "Chapter X" of "Tales of the Islands" Walcott speaks of leaving home, a theme particularly important to his generation of West Indian artists and intellectuals since so many have found expatriation necessary to their development and recognition. (Walcott is exceptional because he has made the islands home base during most of his career.) From the perspective of a rising aircraft, the poet sees the roads "twine" about the mountains and feels his "fidelity strained." The experience calls emotional commitment to the surface and provides a basis for labeling special elements of value in island living; it also sets up the later, most important theme of homecoming.

In *The Castaway and Other Poems* certain other significant and continuing Walcott themes show themselves. Central to the poetry in this volume is the shipwreck vision of the modern world which Walcott sees dramatized in the stories of Crusoe and Prospero. "Crusoe's Journal" and the title poem are representative.

The shipwreck is not ultimately a negative image to Walcott. The encounter of the light and the dark, the Western dualism that this event brings into focus, is finally a historical phenomenon. It sets up the dialectic and allows the new search for synthesis to begin. Much of Walcott's succeeding poetry can be seen as a part of this quest for synthesis. There is, though, an element of anger at the pervasive racism of the Occident in such poems as "Goats and Monkeys" and "Laventille." This theme becomes much more evident in his next volume, *The Gulf and Other Poems*.

In this collection of poems, Walcott demonstrates more awareness than before of his (and the archipelago's) linkage with the American continents. The title poem is a statement from America of the 1960s with references to Lyndon Johnson campaigns, violence in the cities, and the assassination of John F. Kennedy. The leaden Gulf is an image of separation—separation of black and white, as well as of northern and southern continents. Other poems in the volume respond to the blues world, to Washington, to Boston, and to the Middlewest. Yet the poet's identification with his subjects seems to strengthen as he goes south and writes of Che in a poem of that name and as he moves across the South American continent in a series of responses to such places as Georgetown, Guyana.

The motif that dominates this volume, though, is that of homecoming. "Homecoming: Anse La Raye," dedicated to his childhood friend Garth St. Omer, introduces the idea, and several other poems develop it through allusions to experiences, hopes, and visions of an earlier time. The poet seems to have left intending to return with wisdom; he does not return so much to find meaning as to try to give it. *The Gulf and Other Poems*, like *In A Green Night*, is dedicated to Walcott's wife, Margaret, and the several latter poems in both volumes which use personal love relations as a means of ordering the fragmented archipelago of his imagination seem to draw heavily on a satisfying marital relationship.

In 1970 *The Dream on Monkey Mountain and Other Plays* was published and Walcott introduced the collection with an essay entitled "Twilight: An Overture." It is a reflective prose piece which employs a compact, metaphoric style that allows him to describe in less than forty pages a spiritual, intellectual, artistic odyssey of thirty stormy years. He speaks of fevered ("malarial") purpose inflamed by the desire to escape colonial bonds, of the anger at first awakening to the legacy of bondage, of indulgence in the satisfying sensuality of a paradise home, of glorifying and idealizing Africa, of discovering the power in the theater of everyday life. He describes the recognition of a people lost, a history and landscape failed, but finally moves beyond all this, beyond the "self-appointed schizoid saint," to a kind of stasis in a vision of a city devoted to art. This is a powerful essay, describing a powerful imagination which defies all manner of limiting paradigms of the age in its rage to find a satisfying order. It marks the end of one phase of Walcott's career and the beginning of another.

This new beginning has a more personal quality to it and finds its clearest expression in what may well be Walcott's most important poetic statement, the long lyrical poem *Another Life*. Here the poet, moving toward and past forty years of age as he writes (he identifies 1965 to 1972 as the period of composition), sets himself at midpoint in his life and reflects on where his own story has begun, on what he is as artist, and on why he is what he is. The poem is set in four parts with each section dominated by a significant figure in the poet's past. The first section, "The Divided Child," establishes the poet himself as its image: Derek Walcott caught between two worlds and propelled by the very division of selfhood into an especially powerful artistic urge for synthesis. There is reconciliation in this world as he relates the legacy of the West, particularly classical mythology, to figures in his everyday childhood experiences.

"Homage to Gregorias," the second section, is centered on the image of the artist Gregorias, who is obviously based on Garth St. Omer, a friend of Walcott's. The friends vow to capture "in paint, in words, / As palmists learn the network of a hand," this island, this landscape. But while Gregorias pro-

22

Europa

This full moon is so fierce I can count the
coconuts' cross-hatched shade on bungalows,
their white walls raging with insomnia.
The stars leak drop by drop on the tin plates
of the sea-almonds to the jeer of clouds
as luminously rumpled as bed-sheets.
The surf, insatiably promiscuous,
groans through the walls, so I let my mind
whiten to moonlight, altering a form   *that*
which ~~that~~ daylight unambiguously designed
from a tree to a girl's body bent in foam;
~~then~~ *and*, treading close, the black hump of a hill,
its nostrils softly snorting, nearing the
naked girl splashing her breasts with silver.
~~yet,~~ they'd have kept their proper distance still
would if the chaste moon hadn't swiftly drawn the drapes
of a dark cloud, coupling their shapes.

She teases with those flashes, yes, but once
you yield to human horniness, you see
all that through ~~legendary~~ moonshine what they were,
those gods as seed-bulls. gods as ~~rutting~~ swans,   *fucking*
an overheated farmhand's literature
~~whose vision hooks her pale arms round his horns,~~
~~clamps her thighs white in their slow-plunging ride,~~
~~sees, in the hiss of the exhausted foam,~~
~~her body breaking into phosphorous,~~
~~as in salt darkness beast and woman come:~~
A wedge of the salt drops glittering on his matted hide,   *Nothing is there,*
foam ~~then nothing there,~~ just as it always was,
~~but the foam's wedge~~ to ~~low~~ horizon-light,   *the*
~~and,~~ wire-thin, the studded armature
then of hoof and horn-points anagrammed in stars.

Whoever saw her pale arms hook
his horns,
her thighs clamped white in their
deep-plunging ride,
watched ~~heard~~, in the hiss of the exhausted
foam
her body breaking into phosphorous
as in salt darkness beast and woman
come?

"Europa," corrected galley proofs

duces seascapes, the poet can only produce poetry
". . .full of spiders, / bones, worms, ants things eating up each other." The poet yearns to embrace his
friend's romantic vision but reality continually en-
croaches on his sensibilities and at the end the fire
comes ". . . .with the fierce rush of a furnace door /
suddenly opened, history was here." The third section, "A Simple Flame," opens with *Inferno* imagery. The Beatrice-figure, Anna, becomes the major
image of this part. She is not the ultimate syn-
thesizer, though, for that role remains for Margaret, the Madonna who provides means for over-
coming "The Estranging Sea" in the final section of
the work. "Holy were you, Margaret, / and holy our
calm."

Two volumes of verse that follow *Another Life*
carry forward the personal vein that typifies much
of Walcott's poetry in the 1970s. *Sea Grapes* (1976) is
a collection of short pieces, responding to a broad
spectrum of experiences in settings from Ohio to
London. The five "Sainte Lucie" poems, which are
in the middle of the volume seem the strongest. The
last of this group, "For the Altarpiece of Rouseau
Valley Church, Saint Lucia," responds to a painting
by St. Omer. "The valley of Roseau is not the Gar-

Dust jacket for collection of short lyrics written in the 1970s

den of Eden," the poet tells us. But Adam is there,
not an Adam of innocence but one tired from many
trials, returning to where "your faith like a canoe at
evening [is] coming in, / like a relative who is tired of
America, / like a woman coming back to your
house." "Names," a poem dedicated to Edward
Brathwaite, makes a powerful statement about the
motive for Walcott's art. The sea bird, the osprey,
cries out with "that terrible vowel, / that I!" to utter
the poet's own need for expression and
recognition—his need to *be*.

The Star-Apple Kingdom (1979) puts the poet's
image into a narrative structure moved along by the
island wanderings of the schooner *Flight*. This tale
of the West Indian wanderer has strong parallels to
the Jonah story. The Shabine, the "red nigger,"
carries bad luck with him, and we hear part of the
story from his point of view and in his language. He
is a folk character reminiscent of those in the early
dramas. The sea in this poem is the repository of
history, and coral reefs cry out with the horror of
sunken ships packed with human cargo. After the
middle passage and the era of slavery comes the
long colonial era when "seven prime ministers" cut
up the Caribbean like bolts of "aquamarine with lace
trimmings."

Walcott produced five new plays in the decade
following the great success of *The Dream on Monkey
Mountain* (he produced *Ti-Jean and His Brothers* out-
doors in Central Park, but the response to it was not
nearly as favorable as to *The Dream on Monkey
Mountain*). One of the new plays, *The Joker of Seville*,
produced in 1974, was a translation commissioned
by the Royal Shakespeare Company. Walcott admits
there are problems with this play because of his
efforts to reproduce some of the quality of the
original verse, a problem linked somewhat to his
lack of facility with Spanish. The lyrics in parts of
the works are lively and interesting, but the general
movement of the action is hampered by the sameness of some of the joker's antics.

O Babylon!, produced in 1976, is a more interesting piece. It is a play based on an actual community of believers who speak in a melodic language of rhetorical negatives that obviously in-
trigues Walcott. They are the "true Rastafari," who
believe that Haile Selassie is God and have faith in
peace and love. Babylon is Kingston, but it is also the
cities of New Jersey that promise even more satisfaction of the flesh; it is the whole of the decadent
modern world that these believers are rejecting.
The end of the play sets the spirit of Babylon in the
chorus against the visionary Aaron who speaks for
the new and glorious Zion. However surprising, it is

Dust jacket for Walcott's narrative poem of the West Indies

satisfying to witness Aaron's victory.

Walcott's final two plays of the decade are *Remembrance*, produced in 1977, and *Pantomime*, produced in 1978. Both works use the differing perspectives of major characters as a means of commenting on foibles of middle- and upper-class Trinidadians. *Remembrance* is playful in the beginning but painful in the end. Albert Perez Jordan, a "retired schoolteacher, aged sixty-five," faces an interview on Remembrance Day. As the play develops the audience slowly gets a full picture of this great dreamer who, in his youth, had set hopes in a vision of "an archipelago in a beautiful sea. Cities where all the races joined to make one race. Athens." Now, though, he nears death having lost one son to "Black Power riots" and must struggle to keep his own sanity while dealing with the madness of another son who rejects his father's dream of racial integration and paints an American flag on his father's roof. The elder Jordan has long ago embraced the values, language and literature of the Empire, but the expected results of this commit-

ment are unrealized. He can only write "Christmas-cardish" poetry and seek to justify the way he once taught Gray's "Elegy Written in a Country Churchyard."

The primary tension which enlivens the play results from the contrasts between the romantic vision of Jordan and the hard-nosed realism of his editor friend, Ezra Pilgrim. Pilgrim had opened his library to Jordan's rebellious son and encouraged him to read Cesaire, Marx, and Fanon. There is likeness here to the differing perspectives of Gregorias and the narrator in *Another Life* and likeness, too, in the resolution in which the realist must save the dreams of the dreamer for the sake of both. The problem of *Pantomime* seems to be to see if "any black man should play Robinson Crusoe," or Columbus or Sir Francis Drake. Jackson Phillips, the retired calypsonian who now serves Harry Trewe, a retired English actor, can obviously handle these roles and more. There are only two actors in this play, but with all the reversals and additions of roles, the stage sees many characters. The drama is not a tour de force; it is a very serious statement about stereotype, mask, and racial discrimination, presented in a comic mode.

Since the mid-1970s Walcott has spent much of his time in the United States. He has taught at Hollins College, New York University, Yale, and Columbia. He was named an honorary member of the American Academy of Arts and Letters in 1979 and in 1980 received the Welsh Arts Council's International Writer's Prize.

Special recognition of Walcott's talent came in the spring of 1981 when he was chosen one of the select group of recipients of the first John D. and Catherine B. MacArthur fellowships intended to "free from financial burdens for five years or longer" research scientists, composers, poets, and "other exceptionally talented people." Walcott's achievement and promise make him a most worthy choice.

References:

Edward Baugh, ed. *Critics on Caribbean Literature* (New York: St. Martin's Press, 1978);

Lloyd W. Brown, *West Indian Poetry* (Boston: G.K. Hall, 1978);

Benjamin DeMott, "Poems of Caribbean Wounds," review of *The Star-Apple Kingdom*, *New York Times Book Review*, 13 May 1979, pp. 11, 30;

"Derek Walcott," in *Caribbean Writers: A Bio-Bibliographical-Critical Encyclopedia*, edited by

Donald E. Herdeck (Washington, D.C.: Three Continents Press, 1979);

Irma E. Goldstrau, *Derek Walcott: A Bibliography of Published Poems* (St. Augustine, Trinidad: University of West Indies Press, 1979);

Louis James, ed. *The Islands in Between: Essays on West*

Indian Literature (London: Oxford University Press, 1968);

Bruce King, *The New English Literature* (New York: St. Martin's Press, 1980);

"Man of the Theater, an interview with Derek Walcott," *New Yorker*, 47 (26 June 1971): 30-31.

James Whitehead
(15 March 1936-   )

Michael Adams
Louisiana State University

BOOKS: *Domains* (Baton Rouge: Louisiana State University Press, 1966);
Joiner (New York: Knopf, 1971);
Local Men (Urbana: University of Illinois Press, 1979).

James Whitehead's two books of poetry, *Domains* (1966) and *Local Men* (1979), and his novel, *Joiner* (1971), have demonstrated his promise in both genres. Whitehead writes with passion, humor, and insight about the South, about its violence, ignorance, racism, and ambiguous morality. Yet he is far from being simply a regional writer, for his work focuses on the alienation and despair of twentieth-century man, on the social, political, historical, and sexual forces, which can sometimes be understood but rarely controlled.

Born in St. Louis, the son of Dick Bruun Whitehead, a bacteriologist, and Ruth Ann Tillotson Whitehead, a social worker, Whitehead grew up in Jackson, Mississippi. He played football at Vanderbilt University, where he received a B.A. in 1959 and an M.A. in 1960. He taught at Millsaps College in his hometown from 1960 to 1963 and then went to the University of Iowa to study in the writers' workshop. Whitehead received an M.F.A. from Iowa in 1965 and since then has taught at the University of Arkansas. He is married to Gen Graeber, and they have seven children, Bruun, Kathleen, Eric, Joan, and triplets Philip, Edward, and Ruth.

According to Whitehead, "When I first started writing poetry, I was influenced by stream of consciousness, impressionistic, surrealistic poets like Dylan Thomas and the early Robert Lowell. I thought that I could write that kind of poetry, but, in fact, I couldn't because what I did was essentially

write bad imitations of Dylan Thomas." Whitehead says that he learned how to "objectify" his poetry by reading Robert Frost, Robert Penn Warren, and, especially, the Welsh poet R. S. Thomas. He decided that he "wanted to work within something both economical and dramatic. And I played with the idea of little stories, sometimes anecdotal material in some fairly traditional forms, to see if I could sort of tell a story in a sonnet, for example." The result, *Domains*, "is essentially a dramatic, objective, narrative collection in which scene, character, action, grammar—everything—is highly logical and highly moral. The poems dramatized my aversion to racism."

The forty-three short narrative poems in *Domains* present Whitehead's responses, both positive and negative, to sex, violence, politics, and racism in a South resistant to change. Typical is "The Politician's Pledge" in which the politician-narrator blames racism primarily on preachers: "They whine in the dusk for Zion's flames." He resolves never to stoop to what the voters have traditionally demanded: "Make me an out-of-work mechanic / And bring my whole family down sick / If I ride one nigger again." In "The Young Deputy," butchered parts of Negroes' bodies are found in a river, and the narrator voices his hopes for the future:

> There'd be, I thought, if things were right,
> a fine day of picnicking,
> preaching to a big mixed audience,
> and in the nearest pine one buzzard,
> glossy, hunkering, with a confused gaze.

The reader is reminded of man's bestiality throughout *Domains*.

"Floaters," one of many poems which employ the river as a symbol of death, describes bodies washed miles and miles down the river:

> Like a glove
> Full of mother's cold dishwater, or maybe
> fudge
> Left out a week and getting whitish from
> sugar
> Crystals, they were pulled onto our sand bar.

Rather than life-giving and cleansing, Whitehead's rivers represent open sewers of destruction running throughout the South.

Domains is about not just racial violence but everyday emotional violence. "Desertion" examines a husband whose wife has left him, leaving behind an empty house containing "her rooms where the drawers / Are still open like stunned mouths." "Leavings" criticizes how easy it is to become engulfed in banalities:

> I hesitate to enter rooms
> Where friends intend to be themselves;

I find myself afraid of wives
Who never mention sex until
Their husbands have gone to pee. But still
I move right in among those breasts
They say are only for baby. If

I run I'll never understand
Illogical tales, bad jokes, and men
Who horrify themselves until
They leave marks on public walls.

Yet even the quest for truth can meet with disaster, as in "First Lecture," a portrait of a teacher gone insane:

He knew nine languages
By heart and tried to read each line of poetry
As if it were the last the man had said.
He wanted to know what caused a hand to
push pen
Or to type, he wanted to know why any man
Felt wise enough to speak
At all. This led to his fall.

While Whitehead is driven to criticize man's social and political fallibilities, he also knows that these fallibilities are part of what makes man human, as in "Domains":

I stagger with my banner everywhere
Toward a better state
But always lovely hair
Long limbs negotiate
To turn my mind from taxes
And jack the old reflexes.

Whitehead's first book was well received by reviewers. "These poems bite hard, without pretense of being hard-bitten," wrote Christopher Ricks in *Southern Review*. Whitehead's debut was called "exciting" by *Virginia Quarterly Review*: "Like Goethe's Faust, he is truly aware and concerned with those two natures of man which share our flesh and lives, forever contending and never content. His poems ravel and unravel the tangled truths of our warring natures with real and impressive success." Ernest Kroll, in *Michigan Quarterly Review*, praised Whitehead for confronting "the horror of existence with a great calm remarkable for a young poet," adding that he writes "the kind of verse that Faulkner might wish to have written in his own flirtation with the art." *Domains* won Whitehead a Robert Frost Fellowship in Poetry to the Bread Loaf Writers' Conference of Middlebury College.

One of Whitehead's major virtues as a poet is his ability to create a wide range of believable narrative voices. The voices in *Local Men*, his second collection, include those of bankers, lawyers, judges, red-necks, drunks, and migrant workers. These fifty poems are again primarily concerned with the nature of the South and its inhabitants, but the horrors of domestic life, rather than racism, are the most frequent topic.

Local Men, even more than *Domains*, is notable for Whitehead's remarkable descriptive skills. In "The Plain Story of Macintosh the White Cropper Who Never Stopped Talking Until He Got to Death," he vividly evokes Macintosh's voice:

Someone a half mile down the road could
hear
Himself addressed before he saw the old man
Boiling off through the heat
Alive with Macintosh's history—
In broad sunshine a voice more furious
For ears than brigades of Turks—
A redneck Odyssey afloat on air
Like brigantines across a wild catarrh—
A voice fired through light like Minie balls or
flak.

Dust jacket for Whitehead's second collection of poems about the South and its inhabitants

A LOCAL MAN ESTIMATES WHAT HE DID FOR
HIS BROTHER WHO BECAME A POET
AND WHAT HIS BROTHER DID FOR HIM

I shot the chicken in the tree above
Where Herbert stood howling after I'd shot.
Bitterly he cried so loud & feathers have
Itself became involved, 'lord, lord, the fit
He threw was terrible. He said his head
His sacred head — was dandered for poetry —
He said my cruelty would make him mad —
He said it was a ritual catastrophe.

Herbert was splattered with old chicken blood
and pink feathers from eyes to knees, He said
later, twelve years later, that he was sad
God'd frightened me. Within a month he died.
On his deathbed he reached out for my hand
and said we come from where we get the wound,

From _Local Men_ , U of Illinois Press, 1979

James Whitehead

Manuscript for a poem from Local Men

Whitehead is an economical storyteller, especially in "He Remembers Something From the War," in which the violence a boy's father faced in World War II is made graphic when a murderer leaves a bloodstained car in the alley beside the boy's home.

The most frequent subjects in *Local Men* are loneliness and desperation. The narrator of "A Local Contractor Flees His Winter Trouble and Saves Some Lives in a Knoxville Motel Room," restraining himself from making his violent dreams come true, says "Everybody longs for where they began / Or where they've never been, you better believe. / You better believe we all end up alone." In "The Country Music Star Begins His Politics," the singer-narrator is depressed by his audience:

> I am paid to strum
> And make up songs that help grown children
> play.
> The thing I do has prospered and gone
> wrong.
> Lord, we are multiplied and we mean well.
> There's murder in the darkness I can't kill.

But Whitehead's vision of the world is not completely negative. "A hopeful life is possible out here," says the narrator of "He Loves the Trailer Park and Suffers Telling Why." There are virtues in the simplified, as opposed to simple, life: "still we have more fun than we do wrong. / We take a simple pleasure from the rain." Another weapon against the violence and stupidity of the world is self-knowledge, as Whitehead suggests in "I Write in a Peculiar Mood Unworthy of the Trust," a poem for his children:

> Your father is a tulip,
> A withdrawn man who won't outgrow his
> fears
> Of pleasant husbandry and ignorance.
> Learn to avoid his awkward mental dance.
>
> He's liliaceous to a fault. Say that
> He fumbled daily in the words for it.

Whitehead's major achievement is clearly *Joiner*, in which Eugene "Sonny" Joiner, native of Bryan, Mississippi, former pro football player and ex-husband, tries to create some order out of the excessive chaos of his life. The six-foot-seven-inch, 300-pound Joiner is a larger-than-life creation, a man of enormous passions who makes enormous mistakes in his relationships with those he cares about. The themes of Whitehead's poems about the South are brought together and intensified in his novel.

Joiner's story of how he has failed all his friends and relatives and how they have let him down as well is told against the background of the changes brought about by the civil-rights movement of the late 1950s and early 1960s. Joiner examines his relationships with his civilized, peaceful parents, with childhood friends Coldstream Taggart and Royal Carle Boykin, with his wife April, son Aubrey, and mistress Mary Ann, with his teammates at Southern Mississippi and with the Dallas Bulls of the National Football League, and with the white and black citizens of his hometown—attempting to explain the parts all these people have played in creating the man he has become, to explain himself to himself, to understand why and whom he has failed, and to understand why he has killed two men.

Joiner's "diary and massive autobiography" is a journal which seems to jump about randomly in time. Joiner, whose parents, mistress, and favorite college professor all want him to be a teacher, quotes extensively from his favorite historians and philosophers. The novel's excessive, frequently obscure allusions perhaps hinder the reader's understanding of Joiner more than they help; yet both writer and narrator seem aware of the problem: once Joiner says, "I promise that's the last quotation." Joiner tries to use the history of Western civilization to make some sense of his own history: "The great Vico knows: there is no true wisdom except for the sweet patterns you yourself have made. Understand the configurations of your own dear, meaty life and times, and you've got the bitch by the bush. Blake said that."

Joiner, who was a standout offensive tackle in high school and college and never wanted to do anything but play professional football, makes his dream come true in his rookie year with Dallas until he breaks his arm. Football has always been an outlet for this man of violence: "I'll admit it ain't half bad to be knocking people down, on the football field." He longs to be a star but forces himself to admit that he is only "competent": "if you see you're just another jock in the game, you get out and go on to something else." He learns that love and death, guilt and responsibility are tougher to deal with than charging linemen.

Whitehead, who also wanted to be a professional football player until an injury ended his college career, presents football as being a form of religion in the South: "Our new stadium . . . was cockpit, amphitheater, and bawdy house to all the citizens of Bryan, and on Friday nights I was Saint Henry Suso drinking Christ's blood from all five wounds." Because Joiner is a football hero, the community overlooks his faults, but his feelings of guilt increase after he kills man with one punch during a prank which goes out of control. Whitehead's Bryan is a town with as little civilization as the people can get by with: "People who will shake a coon twenty feet out of a tree onto the hard ground, and then wrestle it into a sack, will do anything."

The savagery of Bryan takes its most extreme form in racism, ranging from that of the middle-class, content to shoot their television sets the first time Sammy Davis, Jr., appears on *The Ed Sullivan Show*, to that of red-necks, who resort to violence to try to make up for their inadequacies: "it's no god-damned fun to shoot a nigger if nobody respects you for it." Joiner prides himself on being "a niggerlover true and blue": "I come from good people who know there's damn well trouble enough in the world without making up more over skin." He has sufficient self-knowledge to realize that his feelings for blacks are not entirely the result of the goodness of his heart, that they are partly a way of getting back at the world, of being an individual: "to make much of my emotions would be wrong, be-cause the emotions weren't in the best objective sense political, or social, or even what you'd call humane. No way." After leaving the National Foot-ball League, Joiner joins with a group of blacks who attack the county courthouse to protest the murder of an elderly Negro, and he kills a second man, the ringleader of the local racists. Ironically, Joiner's victim, Foots Magee, is a former pro football star who, like his killer, has been unable to adjust to the real world. Joiner's guilt and remorse come quickly, and he kisses the head of his enemy moments after he has shot him.

Joiner resolves never to resort to violence again, although he wants to kill his ex-wife and former best friend after they become engaged. Writing his story is one means of reforming himself. Teaching at an experimental elementary school in Fort Worth is another: "I'm finally suffering my way back to sanity in a sixth-grade classroom. I'm teaching my little ladies and gentlemen to love de-tails." He sees teaching as life enhancing in a way playing football could never be and realizes that work can be the best weapon against chaos: "one thing I know is that what you do for a living is important. Maybe it's the only important thing." As his name suggests, Joiner has gained the ability to bring things—physical skills, ideas, emotions—together to make an integrated whole, both on per-sonal and social levels.

The reviewers who liked *Joiner* liked it a great deal. In the *New York Times Book Review*, R. V. Cassill wrote, "What Whitehead has achieved is to sound the full range of the Deep South's exultation and lament. . . . His tirade makes an awesome, fearful and glorious impact on the mind and ear." Accord-ing to Jonathan Yardley in *Life*, "there seems a good chance that James Whitehead has . . . taken south-ern fiction in new and potentially exciting direc-tions. In many ways *Joiner* is a great sprawling mess of a book, but it is also a work of power and even daring, and it explores aspects of the South that have up to now been touched, if at all, only tenta-tively." The "great sprawling mess" Yardley refers to bothered many critics. "One of the main prob-lems with this book," wrote L. J. Davis in *Book World*, "is that there is just too much *stuff* in it. . . . The effect is rather like being trapped for ten hours on a cross-country bus with a loquacious non-stop egoist and non-stop storyteller, an impossible mixture of good ole boy and pedant."

Whitehead may try to encompass too much in *Joiner*, and his hero's rantings do get tiresome at times; but the novel's excesses support the writer's portrait of a man who has allowed himself to be defined by his excesses all his life and who must learn to control them if he is to become the worth-while citizen he wants to be. Both Whitehead and Joiner are artists who must plow through a great deal of chaos in order finally to reach some unified vision of the world. *Joiner* succeeds because Whitehead succeeds in creating in Bryan, Missis-sippi, not only a convincing, unsentimental portrait of the South, but a microcosm of any society torn by irrational hates and ambiguous loves.

Whitehead intends *Joiner* to be the first novel in a Bryan trilogy with the other two to focus on Joiner's friends Taggart and Boykin. Besides the novel "Coldstream," his other work in progress is "A Radical Tolerance," a third collection of poems.

Interviews:

Marda Burton, "An Interview with James Whitehead," *Notes on Mississippi Writers*, 6 (1973): 71-79;

John Graham, "James Whitehead," in *The Writer's Voice: Conversations with Contemporary Writers*, edited by George Garrett (New York: Mor-row, 1973), pp. 183-199.

Reference:

David L. Vanderwerken, "From Tackle to Teacher: James Whitehead's *Joiner*," *North Dakota Quar-terly*, 47 (Autumn 1979): 35-42.

Appendices

Literary Awards and Honors Announced in 1981

AMERICAN ACADEMY AND INSTITUTE OF ARTS AND LETTERS

AWARDS IN LITERATURE
Louise Gluck, Gail Goodwin, Howard Frank Mosher, James Salter, Elizabeth Sewell, William Stafford, Hilma Wolitzer, Jay Wright.

AWARD OF MERIT MEDAL
John Guare.

HAROLD D. VURSELL MEMORIAL AWARD
Edward Hoagland.

MORTON DAUWEN ZABEL AWARD
Guy Davenport.

RICHARD AND HINDA ROSENTHAL FOUNDATION AWARD
Jerome Charyn, for *Darlin' Bill* (Arbor House).

ROME FELLOWSHIP IN CREATIVE WRITING
Edward Field.

RUSSELL LOINES AWARD FOR POETRY
Ben Belitt.

SUE KAUFMAN PRIZE FOR FIRST FICTION
Tom Lorenz, for *Guys Like Us* (Viking).

WITTER BYNNER FOUNDATION PRIZE FOR POETRY
Allen Grossman.

AMERICAN BOOK AWARDS

NATIONAL MEDAL FOR LITERATURE
Kenneth Burke.

AUTOBIOGRAPHY/BIOGRAPHY
HARDCOVER: Justin Kaplan, for *Walt Whitman* (Simon & Schuster).
PAPERBACK: Deirdre Bair, for *Samuel Beckett* (Harvest).

CHILDREN'S BOOKS
FICTION HARDCOVER: Betsy Byars, for *The Night Swimmers* (Delacorte).
FICTION PAPERBACK: Beverly Cleary, for *Ramona and Her Mother* (Dell Yearling).
NONFICTION HARDCOVER: Alison Cragin Herzig and Jane Lawrence Mali, for *Oh, Boy! Babies!* (Little, Brown).

FICTION
HARDCOVER: Wright Morris, for *Plains Song* (Harper & Row).
PAPERBACK: John Cheever, for *The Stories of John Cheever* (Ballantine).

FIRST NOVEL
Ann Arensberg, for *Sister Wolf* (Knopf).

GENERAL NONFICTION
HARDCOVER: Maxine Hong Kingston, for *China Men* (Knopf).
PAPERBACK: Jane Kramer, for *The Last Cowboy* (Pocket Books).

HISTORY
HARDCOVER: John Boswell, for *Christianity, Social Tolerance, and Homosexuality* (University of Chicago Press).
PAPERBACK: Leon Litwack, for *Been in the Storm So Long: The Aftermath of Slavery* (Vintage).

POETRY
Lisel Mueller, for *The Need to Hold Still* (Louisiana State University Press).

SCIENCE
HARDCOVER: Stephen J. Gould, for *The Panda's Thumb* (Norton).
PAPERBACK: Lewis Thomas, for *The Medusa and the Snail* (Bantam).

TRANSLATION
Francis Steegmuller, for *The Letters of Gustave Flaubert* (Belknap/Harvard University Press), and John E. Woods, for *Evening Edged in Gold*, by Arno Schmitt (Harcourt Brace Jovanovich).

BANCROFT PRIZES
Ronald Steel, for *Walter Lippmann and the American Century* (Little, Brown), and Jean Strouse, for *Alice James: A Biography* (Houghton Mifflin).

BOLLINGEN PRIZE IN POETRY
Howard Nemerov, May Swenson.

BOOKER PRIZE FOR FICTION
Salman Rushdie, for *Midnight's Children* (Knopf).

CALDECOTT MEDAL
Arnold Lobel, for *Fables* (Harper & Row).

CAREY-THOMAS PUBLISHING AWARD
Avon Books, for the Bard series.

CLARENCE E. HOLTE PRIZE
Ivan Van Sertima, for *They Came Before Columbus: The African Presence in Ancient America* (Random House).

DELMORE SCHWARTZ MEMORIAL POETRY AWARD
Constance Urdang.

EDGAR ALLAN POE AWARDS
GRAND MASTER AWARD
  Stanley Elkin.
NOVEL
  Dick Francis, for *Whip Hand* (Harper & Row).
FIRST NOVEL BY AN AMERICAN
  K. Nolte Smith, for *The Watcher* (Coward, McCann & Geoghegan).
SHORT STORY
  Clark Howard, for "The Horn Man," in *Ellery Queen's Mystery Magazine*.
ORIGINAL SOFTCOVER NOVEL
  Bill Granger, for *Public Murders* (Jove).
JUVENILE MYSTERY
  Joan Lowery Nixon, for *The Seance* (Harcourt Brace Jovanovich).
FACT CRIME
  Fred Harwell, for *A True Deliverance* (Knopf).
CRITICAL/BIOGRAPHICAL
  John Reilly, for *Twentieth Century Crime and Mystery Writers* (St. Martin's).

EDWARD MACDOWELL MEDAL
John Updike.

ERNEST HEMINGWAY FOUNDATION AWARD
Joan Silber, for *Household Words* (Viking).

FRANCIS PARKMAN PRIZE
Charles Royster, for *A Revolutionary People at War: The Continental Army and American Character, 1775-1783* (Norton/University of North Carolina Press).

GOLD MEDAL OF HONOR
Leon Edel.

HUGO AWARDS
NOVEL
  Joan D. Vinge, for *Snow Queen* (Dial).
NOVELLA
  Gordon R. Dickson, for *Lost Dorsai* (Ace).
NOVELETTE
  Gordon R. Dickson, for *The Cloak and the Staff*.
SHORT STORY
  Clifford D. Simak, for "Grotto of the Dancing Bear."
NONFICTION BOOK
  Carl Sagan, for *Cosmos* (Random House).
PROFESSIONAL EDITOR
  Ed Ferman, editor of *Fantasy and Science Fiction*.
FANZINE
  Locus, edited by Charles Brown.
FAN WRITER
  Susan Wood.
JOHN W. CAMPBELL AWARD
  Somtow Sucharitku.

INTER NATIONALES AWARD FOR LITERATURE AND ARTS
Helen Wolff.

IRITA VAN DOREN BOOK AWARD
New York Times Book Review, edited by Harvey Shapiro.

IRMA SIMONTON BLACK AWARD
William Steig, for *Gorky Rises* (Farrar, Straus & Giroux).

JANET HEIDINGER KAFKA PRIZE FOR FICTION
Anne Tyler, for *Morgan's Passing* (Knopf).

JERUSALEM PRIZE
Graham Greene.

LEONORE MARSHALL/SATURDAY REVIEW PRIZE FOR POETRY

Sterling A. Brown, for *Collected Poems of Sterling A. Brown* (Harper & Row).

NATIONAL BOOK CRITICS CIRCLE AWARDS

FICTION
John Updike, for *Rabbit Is Rich* (Knopf).
GENERAL NONFICTION
Stephen J. Gould, for *The Mismeasure of Man* (Norton).
POETRY
A. R. Ammons, for *The Coast of Trees* (Norton).
CRITICISM
Virgil Thomson, for *A Virgil Thomson Reader* (Houghton Mifflin).

NATIONAL JEWISH BOOK AWARDS

JEWISH FICTION
Johanna Kaplan, for *Oh My America!* (Harper & Row).
THE HOLOCAUST
Randolph L. Braham, for *The Politics of Genocide: The Holocaust in Hungary* (Columbia University Press).
JEWISH HISTORY
Mark R. Cohen, for *Jewish Self-Government in Medieval Egypt* (Princeton University Press).
JEWISH THOUGHT
Isador Twersky, for *Introduction to the Code of Maimonides* (Yale University Press).
CHILDREN'S LITERATURE
Leonard Everett Fisher, for *A Russian Farewell* (Four Winds Press).
POETRY
Louis Simpson, *Caviare at the Funeral* (Franklin Watts).

NEBULA AWARDS

BEST NOVEL
Gregory Benford, for *Timescape* (Pocket Books).
BEST NOVELLA
Suzy McKee Charnas, for *The Unicorn Tapestry*, in *New Dimensions II*, edited by Robert Silverberg and Marta Randall (Pocket Books).
BEST NOVELETTE
Howard Waldrup, for *The Ugly Chicken*, in *Universe 10*, edited by Terry Carr (Doubleday).
BEST SHORT STORY
Clifford D. Simak, for "Grotto of the Dancing Deer," in *Analog* magazine.

NEWBERY MEDAL

Katherine Paterson, for *Jacob Have I Loved* (Harper & Row).

NOBEL PRIZE FOR LITERATURE

Elias Canetti.

O. HENRY AWARD

Cynthia Ozick, for "The Shawl."

P.E.N. FAULKNER AWARD

Walter Abish, for *How German Is It* (New Directions).

PRESENT TENSE MAGAZINE AWARD FOR FICTION

Johanna Kaplan, for *O My America!* (Harper & Row).

PULITZER PRIZES

FICTION
John Kennedy Toole, for *A Confederacy of Dunces* (Louisiana State University Press).
BIOGRAPHY
Robert K. Massie, for *Peter the Great: His Life and World* (Knopf).
GENERAL NONFICTION
Carl E. Schorske, for *Fin-de-Siècle Vienna: Politics and Culture* (Knopf).
HISTORY
Lawrence A. Cremin, for *American Education: The National Experience, 1783-1876* (Harper & Row).
POETRY
James Schuyler, for *The Morning of the Poem* (Farrar, Straus & Giroux).

WILLIAM CARLOS WILLIAMS AWARD

Brewster Ghiselin.

The American Writers Congress:
A Report on Continuing Business

On 15 December 1981, The American Writers Congress circulated to its members a report on its recent activities and the texts of twenty-two resolutions presented—but not voted on—at the general session of the Congress on 10 October 1981 (see pp. 3-8 for a report on that meeting). Members were asked to vote by mail.

The nature of the American Writers Congress and the scope of its members' concerns is perhaps best revealed by these resolutions.

December 15, 1981

TO: American Writers Congress Participants

FROM: Ann Marie Cunningham and the Congress staff

It's been two months since the Congress convened in New York. We want to report to you exactly what has been accomplished, what we hope to accomplish, and how you can help.

But first, our appreciation: thanks to your participation and that of thousands of other writers, the American Writers Congress was, as *Newsweek* put it, "an enormous success." Over 3,000 writers attended, about 40 per cent from outside New York.

The primary goal of the Congress was to serve as a catalyst for collective action, and that objective was achieved in three ways. At the plenary session on Sunday, October 11, the Congress endorsed 1) the principle of a national writers union; 2) an alliance of existing national writers organizations; 3) the inauguration of the American Writers Congress as an ongoing national organization. In short, the Congress confirmed that there is indeed—in the words of keynote speaker Toni Morrison—the potential for "a heroic writers' movement" in this country today.

You are a vital part of this movement; you will be called upon in the future for your judgment, your ideas, your time, and your support. To start, we've asked you to complete the unfinished business of the plenary by mail. Because time ran out, the en-closed resolutions were not brought up for consideration on October 10. Please cast your vote for these resolutions on the enclosed tally sheet.

We have also sent you both the original and new versions of a resolution that was passed at the plenary, but whose authors wished to reword it for reasons of style and/or clarity. Please read each version carefully, and then vote for the version you prefer by marking your choices on the tally sheet. When you have finished voting, mail the tally sheet back to us in the enclosed envelope.

We have also enclosed a short questionnaire designed to assemble your views on your own needs, and those of local and national writers' organizations, and your reactions to and hopes for the Congress. Please fill out the questionnaire, add your comments on the back, and return it to us with your voting sheet. The questionnaire will help us determine the direction and the structure of the Congress' organization and of future Congresses.

Now, a summary of the American Writers Congress since October 10. . . . . .

The plenary session on Sunday, October 10, saw 14 resolutions introduced, all of which passed. The resolutions endorsed: 1) First Amendment rights; 2) the principle of a national writers union; 3) the need for an alliance of writers' organizations; 4) defense for writers threatened with libel suits; 5) gay and lesbian writers' rights; 6) the formation of a literary defense network, uniting writers, publishers, distributors, librarians, and booksellers against censorship; 7) a communications bill of rights; 8) increased distribution of small press poetry; 9) minority writers' rights; 10) imprisoned writers' rights; 11) support for journalists in El Salvador; 13) support for liberation struggles in Southern Africa; 14) support for feminist writers.

On Monday, October 12, the Congress *Continuations Committee* (open to all interested participants) met at the New School for Social Research in downtown Manhattan, and elected a national *Executive Committee*. The Executive Committee is charged with the responsibility of setting up the structure and the direction of the Congress as a continuing organization. The fifteen-member Executive Committee represents the widest possible spectrum of writers' genres, and ethnic and geographic orientation. It includes members from San Francisco, Los Angeles, Chicago, Atlanta, Washington, D.C., Boston, and New York, plus three representatives of The Nation Institute. The Executive Committee has asked The Nation Institute to temporarily house the ongoing work of the Congress. The Executive Committee will meet again on February 5 and 6, 1982, to set up the Congress' structure and agenda. Your questionnaire will be a big help to them, so please return them as soon as possible.

The future program of the Congress will include:
—spreading the word about the work of the Organizing Committee for a National Writers Union. You'll find a message from OCNWU on the last page of this newsletter, and we've enclosed some material about how to join the union and how to start a local in your home town.

—assisting the Literary Defense Network, which has won the endorsement of the Midwest Booksellers Association. . . .

—helping local writers organize follow-up meetings to report on the Congress. Such meetings have already taken place in Chicago, Albuquerque, Houston, Washington, and San Francisco.

—helping with plans for regional Congresses. There's considerable interest in holding them in the South (possibly in Nashville), in the Midwest, and on the West Coast. Once completed, the film about the Congress will be a fundraising tool for regional Congresses, in addition, of course, to distribution on cable, public, and commercial television.

—publishing the Congress proceedings through South End Press in Boston.

—exploring and aiding efforts of writers organizations to form an alliance, either through the Council of Writers Organizations or through some other mechanism.

—a "Washington Writers Watch" on legislation that affects other writers, which we'd conduct in conjunction with other writers organizations. PEN and the ASJA have already expressed interest. The "Watch" might be inaugurated with a rally and/or hearings, like those held at the Congress, to help save the Freedom of Information Act.

—exploring the possibility of a Writers Political Action Committee. . . .

R-5 RESOLUTION ON SOUTHERN AFRICA
(original version)

The American Writers Congress urges the U.S. Congress to provide material and military aid to all organizations genuinely in support of the South African Liberation struggle against colonialism, racism, censorship, and apartheid.

The American Writers Congress urges the U.S. to cease trade with South Africa, to retain the ban on the sale of military equipment to South Africa and to isolate it politically, economically, culturally, and militarily. Since South Africa's racist policies allow 4.5 million whites to dominate over 20 million blacks, the U.S., in order to end racist oppression, should actively support black majority rule in South Africa.

The American Writers Congress joins with those organizations genuinely in support of the South African Liberation struggle against colonialism, racism, censorship, and apartheid for a boycott of all writers, entertainers, media people, sports figures, and artists who go to South Africa or who by word or deed lend credibility to South Africa's attempts to lessen its isolation and to create a favorable international image for its apartheid regime.

The American Writers Congress urges the U.S. government to demand South African withdrawal from Namibia, and illegally occupied territory, to support the implementation of the United Nations resolution to sponsor U.N. sanctioned and supervised elections in Namibia and that there be no allowance for a residual South African security force once Namibia is an independent nation.

The American Writers Congress urges the U.S. Senate and the House of Representatives to thwart covert U.S. involvement in Angola and South African intervention in Angola's internal affairs by:

(1) retaining the Clark Amendment proscribing U.S. aid to guerrilla forces working to overthrow the government of Angola.

(2) insuring that the territorial integrity of Angola be respected and protected from invasion by South African military forces by the U.S. and its allies.

The American Writers Congress will investigate conglomerates whose holdings include publishing houses for any connection with South Africa related to military equipment, ammunition and defense systems. In the case of Gulf & Western and ITT who, according to research done by the *American Committee on Africa* and the *Southern Africa Report*, have a possible military connection to South

Africa's defense systems, the Congress should call on these conglomerates to prove that these charges are false. And if this is not done to the Congress's satisfaction, the Congress should call on writers and the general reading public to boycott publishers owned by Gulf & Western, ITT, and any other conglomerate, if divestiture is not completed before a certain period of time.

The American Writers Congress will establish a working alliance with all organizations genuinely in support of the South African Liberation's struggle against colonialism, racism, censorship, and apartheid.

R-5 RESOLUTION ON SOUTHERN AFRICA (revised version)

The American Writers Congress urges the U.S. Congress to provide material aid to the liberation movements of the peoples of Southern Africa.

The American Writers Congress urges the U.S. to cease trade with South Africa, to retain the ban on the sale of military equipment to South Africa, and to isolate it politically, economically, culturally, and militarily. Since South Africa's racist policies allow 4.5 million whites to dominate over 20 million blacks, the U.S., in order to end racist oppression, should actively support black majority rule in South Africa.

The American Writers Congress joins with the United Nations in calling for a boycott of all entertainers and sports figures who go to South Africa to perform, thereby lending credibility to South Africa's attempts to lessen its isolation and to create a favorable international image for its apartheid regime.

The American Writers Congress urges the U.S. government to demand South African withdrawal from Namibia, an illegally occupied territory, to support the implementation of the United Nations resolution to sponsor U.N. sanctioned and supervised elections in Namibia and that there be no allowance for a residual South African security force once Namibia is an independent nation.

The American Writers Congress urges the U.S. Senate and the House of Representatives to thwart covert U.S. involvement in Angola and South African intervention in Angola's internal affairs by:

(1) retaining the Clark Amendment proscribing U.S. aid to guerrilla forces working to overthrow the government of Angola.

(2) insuring that the territorial integrity of Angola be respected and protected from invasion by South African military forces by the U.S. and its allies.

The American Writers Congress will investigate conglomerates whose holdings include publishing houses for any connection with South Africa related to military equipment, ammunition, and defense systems. If such a connection is *clearly* established, the Congress should call on writers and the general reading public to boycott publishers owned by these conglomerates, if divestiture is not completed before a reasonable period of time.

The American Writers Congress will endorse and implement those resolutions pertaining to writers passed at the Conference in Solidarity with the Liberation Struggles of the Peoples of Southern Africa, held October 9-11, 1981, at the Riverside Church in New York City, which call for:

(1) working to counter South African propaganda in the U.S. media.

(2) working to counter the influence of South African propaganda which is distributed free of charge in the U.S. public school system.

(3) lending its support to Dennis Brutus and other South African writers who face the threat of deportation from the U.S.

(4) lending its support to alternative news sources on Southern Africa and publications by the liberation movements, by acting as distributors and conducting circulation drives.

(5) working to increase the dissemination within the U.S. of the work of black Southern African writers.

R-6 RESOLUTION ON IRANIAN WRITERS

Iranian writers have for the past several months become the targets of a brutal campaign of terror. With the closing of all avenues of free expression in Iran, writers, who had helped lead resistance to the Shah, have been tortured, have disappeared, and have been executed under the new regime.

In June of 1981, Saeed Soltanpoor, the Iranian poet and dramatist, was arrested at his own wedding and executed for no other crime than that of being a writer. In late September, several prominent members of the Iranian Writers Association were arrested at their hiding places and face possible execution; their whereabouts are unknown at this writing. The group includes Mostofa Rahimi, Homa Nategh, Alinaghi Monzavi, Morteza Ravandi, and Bagher Parham, some of whom were members of the Committee of Progressive Writers.

Ironically, all six were imprisoned while the Shah ruled.

These are not isolated instances of terror and brutality. Rather, they are part of a systematic campaign of violence by the government against its opponents. According to Amnesty International, at least 1800 people, many of them leftists, have been executed since June.

The American Writers Congress deplores the deterioration of human rights in Iran and notes with particular concern the situation of writers. The only crime of most of these writers has been their artistic imperative: to speak and write the truth as they perceive it. This resolution is not meant as an endorsement of the political beliefs of anyone named in this resolution, nor is it meant to pass judgment on their guilt or innocence. Its only purpose is to mobilize American and international public opinion in a protest to save the lives of imprisoned Iranian writers and to safeguard human rights in Iran. We urge the United Nations to investigate the human rights situation in Iran as soon as possible and to focus particular attention on those people, particularly writers, who have "disappeared".

Copies of this resolution will be forwarded to the Secretaries of the U.N., the Iranian delegation at the U.N., and the President and Prime Minister of Iran.

R-7 RESOLUTION ON JACOBO TIMMERMAN

The American Writers Congress publicly thanks and praises the American government for its 1979 role in helping to free publisher Jacobo Timmerman from the Argentine neo-Nazis. In preventing his murder, the fate of so many other Argentine writers, his supporters have alerted the world to the Mussolini-type tyranny which has usurped control of what was once one of the most advanced nations in Latin America.

R-9A RESOLUTION IN SUPPORT OF AIR TRAFFIC CONTROLLERS

Seventy-seven air traffic controllers have been indicted on felony charges for advocating and participating in an illegal strike, and their freedom of expression has been seriously threatened. The Reagan Administration's attack on labor is part of a larger right wing offensive against civil rights, freedom of expression and freedom of information whose consequences will affect American writers as severely as trade unionists.

We believe that the actions of the Reagan Administration against the air traffic controllers strike represent a very serious challenge to basic human and trade union rights which, if successful, will undermine the bargaining and organizing strength of the whole labor movement. The American Writers Congress therefore supports the Professional Air Traffic Controllers Organization (PATCO) in their struggle to win a decent contract, including safer conditions that will protect all air travelers.

R-8 RESOLUTION ON PEACE

The U.S. bombs dropped on Hiroshima and Nagasaki opened a new era in history, signalling above all that there can be no victory in nuclear war, the only possible war between the great powers, the U.S. and the Soviet Union, in the first place. We writers gathered at the American Writers Congress recognize our responsibility to promote peace with freedom and justice. We are horrified at the worldwide escalation of the arms race, and the fact that we can no longer be silent about the existence of 10,000 nuclear warheads in the United States.

Therefore the American Writers Congress demands that:

The government of the U.S. resume serious talks for disarmament with the Soviet Union and all nuclear weapons states.

The government of the U.S. transfer the billions of dollars budgeted for weapons and death to health care, housing, education, jobs, the arts and humanities, etc.

War industries be converted to useful and peaceful purposes, including retraining and placement of affected workers.

There be no MXs, neutron bombs, "first use" diplomacy or advocacy, new weapons of mass destruction of any kind (including biochemical) produced, stockpiled, or installed by the U.S. or the Soviet Union, or by any other country.

A clear schedule for the destruction of all existing nuclear weapons in all countries be adopted with haste and urgency, and that there be an end to all nuclear testing.

International issues be settled through negotiations, not militarily, and that our government, in the United Nations, take a positive position on questions related to peace, freedom and justice, the Third World, equality among nations, general and complete disarmament, and the relaxation of international tensions.

Only by taking these steps is it possible to end the pervasive deterioration in the lives of the great majority of U.S. citizens, including writers, and to allow the nation to advance on all fronts—economic security, racial equality and justice; also, to achieve the full emancipation of women; and political democracy for all citizens.

Finally, the American Writers Congress empowers the Continuations Committee to establish a task force to organize and administer a "Writers for Peace" network which would work to fulfill the spirit and demands of this resolution.

R-9B RESOLUTION ON GOVERNMENT REPRESSION IN UNIONS

We have embarked on an historical effort to fight the wideranging attacks on writers' freedom of expression and their livelihoods. We are confronted by the reality that the Reagan Administration is carrying out a step-by-step campaign of New McCarthyism, already more dangerous than in the 50s. This campaign has taken its heaviest toll in the union movement.

The Reagan Administration used the full power of the federal government to crush the Professional Air Traffic Controllers' strike, including illegal phone taps and secret indictments. *We support PATCO and all workers' right to strike.*

The FBI employed an agent provocateur in interfering with legal union activities at the National Steel and Shipbuilding Company (NASSCO) in San Diego, the largest defense shipyard on the West Coast. *We support the Congressional investigation of the FBI's and the National Security Agency activities proposed by Congressman Ron Dellums of California.*

R-10 RESOLUTION ON MULTIRACIAL AND MULTICULTURAL AMERICA

The American Writers Congress recognizes that the American writer is a multiracial and multinational aggregate and that America embraces a geographic boundary that extends hemispherically, and that all Congress bodies must reflect this reality as well as all genres of writing, from children's books to specialized fields.

R-10.5 RESOLUTION ON A NATIONAL BLACK ARTISTS CONFERENCE

The American Writers Congress joins in sup-
port with the National Black United Front, the Black Writers Union and the Black Caucus at this Congress to call for regional Black Artists Conferences throughout the U.S. by 1982 and the National Black Artists Conference by 1984.

R-11 RESOLUTION ON NEH AND NEA

The American Writers Congress, while recognizing the urgent need to correct the racist funding patterns of NEA and NEH, opposes any governmental attempts to further weaken their funding capacities, particularly those agencies that focus on the needs of oppressed nationalities, artists and scholars.

R-12 RESOLUTION ON POLITICAL PERSECUTION

The American Writers Congress stands in full opposition to the continued political persecution of all nationally oppressed writers, such as Amiri Baraka (United States) and Dennis Brutus (Union of South Africa).

R-13 RESOLUTION IN SUPPORT OF THE SOCIALIST WORKERS' PARTY

The Socialist Workers' Party, like many other dissenting political organizations in the United States, has been victimized by government wiretapping, mailcovers, harrassment of members on the job and at home, and other disruptive activities.

The Socialist Workers' Party has filed a $70 million law suit against the federal government seeking damages for this disruption campaign and a permanent injunction against further such activities.

Writers, as much as all Americans, have a great personal and professional interest in the maintenance of the Bill of Rights, many of the provisions of which are directly threatened by the government through political disruption campaigns.

The American Writers Congress endorses the law suit filed by the Socialist Workers' Party against the United States Government.

R-14 RESOLUTION ON SOUTHERN WRITERS

Writers from the South who want to be published by a major publishing house have always had to send their manuscripts North, usually to New York or Boston. In many instances Southern writers are forced to portray Southern life in its most bestial and backward aspects in order to appeal to their editors' and publishers' preconceived notions of the South.

Southern writers are forced to cater to the stereotyped conceptions of the major publishers; Southern Black, Indian and Appalachian writers face almost total exclusion from the large publishing houses, which generally accept the dominant opinion that their literary and artistic contributions are inferior and unimportant.

This backward and reactionary demand for conformity prevents a larger body of Southern writers from participating in national organizations that seek to protect the interest of all writers.

The American Writers Congress proclaims that it will begin to undertake the difficult task of drawing more Southern writers, and especially Southern writers from oppressed nationalities, into its fold. The American Writers Congress directs the Continuations Committee to establish a body of writers from the South that will work to bring Southern writers into the American Writers Congress.

R-15 RESOLUTION ON WRITERS' WORK

A writers organization based only on a group of successful writers is doomed, from the start, to failure. The American Writers Congress directs its Continuations Committee to take any and all steps necessary to seek out less recognized writers; to aid these writers in their creative and publishing endeavors; and to draw these writers into the work of the organization. The Congress will promote the fullest participation of writers in the financial and creative wealth they create, and attention to the work of regional writers.

R-16 RESOLUTION ON CONSUMER SERVICES

The American Writers Congress, through its Continuations Committee, will investigate the feasibility of offering consumer services to members, such as group insurance, discounts on professional materials, group charter flights, and a credit union.

R-17 RESOLUTION IN SUPPORT OF ALTERNATIVE CHANNELS FOR THE PUBLICATION, REVIEW AND DISTRIBUTION OF BOOKS

The American Writers Congress resolves to establish an ongoing committee to develop and support alternative channels for the publication, distribution and review of books and periodicals. The committee should investigate methods for doing this which include but are not limited to the following:

1. Established authors should be encouraged to publish with independent presses, and means should be found to facilitate communications and negotiations between such authors and institutions. In addition, a fund should be established to provide advances to authors, first-time or otherwise, who publish with alternative institutions. This would be a revolving fund to be repaid out of royalties.

2. A network should be formed to assist in the promotion and distributon of books and periodicals from alternative publishers. Such a network should plan the formation of a cooperative national distributor, assist bookstores in advertising and sponsoring book parties and in maintaining stock. It should also assist authors to promote their works through the mass media and through authors' tours.

3. An "authors' review of books" should be established, to be financed solely through subscriptions, direct sales over the counter, foundation support, and perhaps a generalized royalty on major publishers' promotion budgets. Such a review would have an editorial policy free from the constraints imposed by the need to attract advertising and could therefore give space to first-time and controversial authors.

R-18 RESOLUTION ON A BOOKSTORE

RESOLVED, that the American Writers Congress Continuations Committee work to establish and operate a non-profit bookstore specializing in university and alternative press books and materials, in a few major cities starting with New York.

R-19 RESOLUTION ON THE PUBLISHING CONTRACT

The standard book publishing contract is unjust in several particulars to authors. It is desirable that fairness characterize all publisher-author dealings, and in particular the publishing contract which defines the publisher-author relationship and sets forth the terms of manuscript preparation, writing, publishing, distribution, compensation and proprietorship. The inequities arising from these unjust parts of the publishing contract have long been a source of discord and writer distress.

The American Writers Congress demands that the publishing community, individually and collectively, take the following steps to improve the publisher-author relationship and the publishing process:

1. Eliminate from the publishing contract all provisions obliging the author to indemnify the publisher for liabilities incurred by the publisher.

2. Eliminate so-called "satisfactory manuscript" provisions which permit a publisher to withhold or demand the return of an advance, or portion of an advance, for frivolous, capricious or otherwise unfair reasons.

3. Revise the provision which permits the publisher to retain a so-called "reasonable" part of royalties, purportedly to protect him against possible return of unsold books so that any sums so withheld become truly reasonable and fair to both parties.

4. *Establish a PUBLISHER-AUTHOR ARBITRATION COUNCIL to settle disputes.* The expense of litigation effectively discourages authors from seeking legal redress for their grievances and encourages publishers to interpret the contract's provisions to suit their convenience and benefit. Members of the PUBLISHER-AUTHOR ARBITRATION COUNCIL would be drawn from publisher, writer and legal organizations.

R-20 RESOLUTION ON PAPERBACK RIGHTS

The American Writers Congress will investigate the possibility of formulating a clause to be inserted in the standard author's contract by which the hardback publisher binds her/himself to insure that the purchaser of paperback rights contribute a percentage of the purchase price to a fund, to be administered by the Writers Congress with the aim of either establishing the Writers Congress as a permanent organization with lobbying powers, or setting up an independent noncommercial publishing house, or both.

R-21 RESOLUTION ON BOOK BURNING

The American Writers Congress strongly protests the Bloomfield, N.M., School Board's burning of books written by prominent New Mexico author Rudolfo Anaya. This action is a slap in the face to the best cultural traditions of the Southwest. Reminiscent of Nazi Germany, it signals a bleak future for progressive literature unless firmly opposed.

R-22 RESOLUTION ON THE WILLOW DECLARATION

The American Writers Congress supports the following Declaration on media control and the democratization of communication:

We are a group of artists, educators, researchers, film and video producers, electronic technicians, social scientists, and writers united in our support for democratic communications. The economic, cultural and spiritual welfare of humanity is increasingly tied to the structure for production and distribution of information. Most communications today is one-way, from the center of power to passive audiences of consumers. We need a new information order here in the U.S. to give the power of voice to the unheard and the disenfranchised. We strongly support freedom of the press, but we see that in our own country, this freedom now exists mainly for huge corporations to make profits, to promote socially useless consumption and to impose corporate ideology and agendas. As workers who produce, study and transmit information, we pledge to change this reality. We will work to preserve and encourage face-to-face communication: people can speak best for themselves without the intervention of professionalism or technological mediation. We support that technology which enhances human power and which is designed and controlled by the communities which use it. We support the participation of workers and non-professionals in media production and the use of media for trade union and community organizing. We support the development of community channels for programs, news flow and data exchange. We support popular access to and control of media and communications systems. We support the internationally guaranteed right to reply and criticize and deplore the fact that this right is being attacked now in the U.S. by efforts in Congress to eliminate the Fairness Doctrine and public interest broadcast regulations. While these laws have been underutilized and difficult to apply, they have been the principle tools for forcing even token public debate. We who live and work in the U.S. pledge ourselves to struggle for the democratization of communications within our communities, our places of work, and our political institutions. We support the further inquiry by international organizations such as UNESCO into the social relations of the electronic environment. We hope that these discussions will continue and will resonate among and between nations and peoples.

R-23 RESOLUTION ON SUPPRESSED BOOKS

The American Writers Congress calls for all writers and their literary agents to put in their contract with publishers

1. that authors should be fully and immediately informed of any interference with their books.

2. that authors be informed of the projected first year sales estimate for their book at the time of the publisher's sales conference and the projected advance sales target. (Example: the projected first year sales estimate may be 15,000 books; the advanced sales target—books sold in advance of official publication date—may be half that amount, or 7,500 books).

3. that authors be informed of the advertising and promotional budget of their book, prior to and after publication date.

4. that authors be informed of achieved advance sales of the book.

5. that authors be informed of any changes made to the advertising or promotional budget and reasons for these changes.

R-24 RESOLUTION ON FREE-LANCE WRITERS AND MAGAZINE EDITORS

The American Writers Congress demands more equitable bargaining power rights for free-lance writers vis-a-vis kill fees, time tables for accepting or rejecting manuscripts, publication of pieces, payment for work, etc.

Checklist: Recent Contributions to Literary History and Biography

This checklist is a selection of new books on various aspects and periods of literary and cultural history; biographies, memoirs, and correspondence of literary people and their associates; and primary bibliographies. Not included are volumes in general reference series, literary criticism, and bibliographies of criticism.

Abse, Joan. *John Ruskin: The Passionate Moralist*. New York: Knopf, 1981.

Ackroyd, Peter. *Ezra Pound And His World*. New York: Scribners, 1981.

Allen, Gay Wilson. *Waldo Emerson*. New York: Viking, 1981.

Allen, Michael J. B. and Kenneth Muir, eds. *Shakespeare's Plays in Quarto: A Facsimile Edition*. Berkeley: University of California Press, 1981.

Anderson, G. L. *Asian Literature in English: A Guide to Information Sources*. Detroit: Gale Research, 1981.

Andrews, Wayne. *Voltaire*. New York: New Directions, 1981.

Arndt, Walter, ed. and trans. *The Genius of Wilhelm Busch*. Berkeley: University of California Press, 1981.

Arthurs, Peter. *With Brendan Behan: A Personal Memoir*. New York: St. Martin's Press, 1981.

Ascher, Carol. *Simone de Beauvoir: a Life of Freedom*. Boston: Beacon, 1981.

Baker, Carlos, ed. *Ernest Hemingway: Selected Letters, 1917-1961*. New York: Scribners, 1981.

Bander, Edward J. *Mr. Dooley & Mr. Dunne: the Literary Life of a Chicago Catholic*. Indianapolis: Bobbs-Merrill, 1981.

Barron, Neil, ed. *Anatomy of Wonder: Science Fiction*, revised and enlarged edition. New York: Bowker, 1981.

Bates, Susannah. *The Pendex: An Index of Pen Names and House Names in Fantastic, Thriller and Series Literature*. New York: Garland, 1981.

Battiscombe, Georgina. *Christina Rossetti: A Divided Life*. New York: Holt, Rinehart & Winston, 1981.

Benedict, Stewart, ed. *The Literary Guide to the United States*. New York: Facts on File, 1981.

Bennett, Patricia. *Talking with Texas Writers: Twelve Interviews*. College Station: Texas A&M University Press, 1981.

Betts, Glynne Robinson. *Writers in Residence: American Authors at Home*. New York: Viking, 1981.

Blackbeard, Bill. *Sherlock Holmes in America*. New York: Abrams, 1981.

Borst, Raymond R. *Henry David Thoreau: A Descriptive Bibliography*. Pittsburgh: University of Pittsburgh Press, 1982.

Brabazon, James. *Dorothy L. Sayers*. New York: Scribners, 1981.

Brady, John. *The Craft of the Screenwriter*. New York: Simon & Schuster, 1981.

Brenman-Gibson, Margaret. *Clifford Odets: American Playwright, the Years from 1906-1940*. New York: Atheneum, 1981.

Brinnin, John Malcolm. *Sextet: T. S. Eliot & Truman Capote & Others*. New York: Delacorte/Seymour Lawrence, 1981.

Bruccoli, Matthew J. *James Gould Cozzens: A Descriptive Bibliography*. Pittsburgh: University of Pittsburgh Press, 1981.

Bruccoli. *Some Sort of Epic Grandeur: The Life of F. Scott Fitzgerald*, with a genealogical afterword by Scottie Fitzgerald Smith. New York & London: Harcourt Brace Jovanovich, 1981.

Bruccoli and Margaret M. Duggan, with Susan Walker. *Correspondence of F. Scott Fitzgerald*. New York: Random House, 1980.

Bynner, Witter. *Selected Letters*. Edited by James Kraft. New York: Farrar, Straus & Giroux, 1981.

Cannon, John. *The Road to Haworth: The Story of the Brontës' Irish Ancestry*. New York: Viking, 1981.

Carey, John. *John Donne: Life, Mind & Art*. New York: Oxford University Press, 1981.

Carpenter, Humphrey. *W. H. Auden: A Biography*. Boston: Houghton Mifflin, 1981.

Carpenter, with Christopher Tolkien, eds. *The Letters of J. R. R. Tolkien*. Boston: Houghton Mifflin, 1981.

Carroll, Jock. *The Life and Times of Greg Clark: Canada's Favorite Storyteller*. Garden City: Doubleday, 1981.

Cendrars, Blaise. *The Astonished Man, The Knockabout, The Severed Hand*, 3 volumes. Translated by Nina Rootes. New York: Stein & Day, 1981.

Cole, Lester. *Hollywood Red: The Autobiography of Lester Cole*. Palo Alto, Cal.: Ramparts Press, 1982.

Conrad, John. *Joseph Conrad: Times Remembered*. Cambridge: Cambridge University Press, 1981.

Cook, Ann Jennalie. *The Privileged Playgoers of Shakespeare's London, 1576-1642*. Princeton: Princeton University Press, 1981.

Cook, David A. *A History of Narrative Film*. New York: Norton, 1981.

Coser, Lewis A., Charles Kadushin, and Walter W. Powell. *Books: The Culture and Commerce of Publishing*. New York: Basic, 1981.

Darlington, Beth, ed. *The Love Letters of William and Mary Wordsworth*. Ithaca: Cornell University Press, 1981.

Davies, W. H. *Young Emma*. New York: Braziller, 1981.

Davis, Robert Murray. *A Catalogue of the Evelyn Waugh Collection at the Humanities Research Center, the University of Texas at Austin*. Troy, N.Y.: Whitston, 1981.

de Mallac, Guy. *Boris Pasternak: His Life and Art*. Norman: University of Oklahoma Press, 1981.

De Mille, Agnes. *Reprieve: A Memoir*. Garden City: Doubleday, 1981.

Dillon, Millicent. *A Little Original Sin: the Life and Work of Jane Bowles*. New York: Holt, Rinehart & Winston, 1981.

Dinesen, Isak. *Letters from Africa, 1915-1931*. Edited by Frans Lasson, translated by Anne Born. Chicago: University of Chicago Press, 1981.

Donaldson, Gerald and Elizabeth Donaldson, eds. *Books: Their History, Art, Power, Glory, Infamy and Suffering According to their Creators, Friends and Enemies*. New York: Van Nostrand Reinhold, 1981.

Dooley, Roger. *From Scarface to Scarlett: American Films in the 1930s*. New York & London: Harcourt Brace Jovanovich, 1981.

Dreiser, Theodore, *American Diaries, 1902-1926*. Edited by Thomas P. Riggio and others. Philadelphia: University of Pennsylvania Press, 1982.

Dukore, Bernard F., ed. *Bernard Shaw's "Arms and the Man": A Composite Production Book*. Carbondale & Edwardsville: Southern Illinois University Press, 1981.

Eagle, Dorothy and Hilary Carnell, eds. *The Oxford Illustrated Literary Guide to Great Britain*, enlarged edition. London & New York: Oxford University Press, 1981.

Elborn, Geoffrey. *Edith Sitwell: A Biography*. Garden City: Doubleday, 1981.

Evans, William R. *Robert Frost and Sidney Cox: Forty Years of Friendship*. Hanover, N.H.: University Press of New England, 1981.

Fairbairn, Douglas. *Down and Out in Cambridge*. New York: Coward, McCann & Geoghegan, 1982.

Ferlinghetti, Lawrence and Nancy J. Peters. *Literary San Francisco*. San Francisco: City Lights Books/San Francisco, Cambridge, Hagerstown, Philadelphia, New York, London, Mexico City, São Paulo & Sydney: Harper & Row, 1981.

Findlater, Richard. *At the Royal Court: Twenty-five Years of the English Stage Company*. New York: Grove, 1981.

Fletcher, Marilyn P. *Science Fiction Story Index, 1950-1979*. Chicago: American Library Association, 1981.

Floyd, Virginia, ed. *Eugene O'Neill at Work*. New York: Ungar, 1981.

Frappier, Jean. *Chrétien de Troyes: The Man and His Work*. Translated by Raymond J. Cormier. Athens: Ohio University Press, 1982.

Fraser, Russell. *A Mingled Yarn: The Life of R. P. Blackmur*. New York & London: Harcourt Brace Jovanovich, 1981.

Furnas, J. C. *Fanny Kemble: Leading Lady of the Nineteenth-Century Stage*. New York: Dial, 1982.

Gérard, Albert S. *African Language Literatures: An Introduction to the Literary History of Sub-Saharan Africa*. Washington, D.C.: Three Continents Press, 1981.

Gérin, Winifred. *Anne Thackeray Ritchie: A Biography*. London & New York: Oxford University Press, 1981.

Glendinning, Victoria. *Edith Sitwell: A Unicorn Among Lions*. New York: Knopf, 1981.

Goodman, Michael Barry. *Contemporary Literary Censorship: the Case History of Burroughs' "Naked Lunch."* Metuchen, N. J.: Scarecrow Press, 1981.

Goorney, Howard. *The Theatre Workshop Story*. New York: Methuen, 1981.

Grant, Michael. *Greek and Latin Authors, 800 B.C.-A.D. 1000: A Biographical Dictionary*. New York: Wilson, 1981.

Green, Benny. *P. G. Wodehouse*. New York: W. H. Smith, 1981.

Green, Stanley. *Encyclopaedia of the Musical Film*. New York: Oxford University Press, 1981.

Greenberg, Martin H., ed. *Fantastic Lives: Autobiographical Essays by Notable Science Fiction Writers*. Carbondale & Edwardsville: Southern Illinois University Press, 1981.

Grimes, Janet and Diva Daims, with Doris Robinson. *Novels in English by Women, 1891-1920: A Preliminary Checklist*. New York: Garland, 1981.

Haining, Peter. *Mystery! An Illustrated History of Crime and Detective Fiction*. New York: Stein & Day, 1981.

Halaas, David Fritdjof. *Boom Town Newspapers: Journalism on the Rocky Mountain Mining Frontier, 1859-1881*. Albuquerque: University of New Mexico Press, 1981.

Hall, Donald, ed. *The Oxford Book of American Literary Anecdotes*. New York: Oxford University Press, 1981.

Hamalian, Leo. *D. H. Lawrence in Italy*. New York: Taplinger, 1981.

Hamilton, Nigel. *The Brothers Mann: The Lives of Heinrich and Thomas Mann*. New Haven: Yale University Press, 1981.

Hayman, Ronald. *Kafka: A Biography*. New York: Oxford University Press, 1982.

Heffernan, Thomas Farel. *Stove by a Whale: Owen Chase and the* Essex. Middletown, Conn.: Wesleyan University Press, 1981.

Hill, Mary A. *Charlotte Perkins Gilman: The Making of a Radical Feminist, 1860-1896*. Philadelphia: Temple University Press, 1981.

Hingley, Ronald. *Nightingale Fever: Russian Poets in Revolution*. New York: Knopf, 1981.

Hirschhorn, Clive. *The Hollywood Musical*. New York: Crown, 1981.

Hoge, James O., ed. *Lady Tennyson's Journal*. Charlottesville: University Press of Virginia, 1981.

Holme, Timothy. *"Vile Florentines": The Florence of Dante, Giotto and Boccacio*. New York: St. Martin's Press, 1981.

Honan, Park. *Matthew Arnold: A Life*. New York: McGraw-Hill, 1981.

Hone, Ralph E. *Dorothy L. Sayers: A Literary Biography*. Kent, Ohio: Kent State University Press, 1981.

Horwitz, Rita and Harriet Harrison, with Wendy White, comp. *The George Kleine Collection of Early Motion Pictures in the Library of Congress: A Catalog*. Washington, D.C.: U.S. Library of Congress, 1981.

Hyde, H. Montgomery. *Oscar Wilde*. New York: Plenum/Da Capo, 1981.

John, Arthur. *The Best Years of the Century: Richard Watson Gilder, Scribner's Monthly, and the Century Magazine, 1870-1909*. Urbana: University of Illinois Press, 1981.

Johnson, Dorris and Ellen Leventhal, eds. *The Letters of Nunnally Johnson*. New York: Knopf, 1981.

Kafka, Franz. *Letters to Ottla and the Family*. Translated by Richard and Clara Winston, edited by N. N. Glatzer. New York: Shocken, 1982.

Kanin, Garson. *Together Again: The Stories of the Great Hollywood Teams*. Garden City: Doubleday, 1981.

Keller, Karl. *The Only Kangaroo Among the Beauty: Emily Dickinson and America*. Baltimore: Johns Hopkins University Press, 1981.

Klein, Marcus. *Foreigners: The Making of American Literature, 1900-1940*. Chicago: University of Chicago Press, 1981.

Kramer, John E., Jr. *The American College Novel: An Annotated Bibliography*. New York: Garland, 1981.

Kramer, Leonie, ed. *The Oxford History of Australian Literature*. Melbourne: Oxford University Press, 1981.

Lang, Cecil Y. and Edgar F. Shannon, Jr., eds. *The Letters of Alfred Lord Tennyson, Volume I: 1821-1850*. Cambridge: Harvard University Press, 1981.

Langguth, A. J. *Saki: A Life of Hector Hugh Munro, with Six Stories Never Before Collected*. New York: Simon & Schuster, 1981.

Lees-Milne, James. *Harold Nicolson: A Biography, 1886-1929*. Hamden, Conn.: Archon/Shoe String Press, 1981.

Lindop, Grevel. *The Opium-Eater: A Life of Thomas De Quincey*. New York: Taplinger, 1981.

Lockwood, Allison. *Passionate Pilgrims: the American Traveler in Great Britain, 1800-1914*. East Brunswick, N.J.: Cornwall/Fairleigh Dickinson University Press, 1981.

Lopez, Enrique Hank. *Conversations with Katherine Anne Porter: Refugee from Indian Creek*. Boston: Little, Brown, 1981.

MacShane, Frank, ed. *Selected Letters of Raymond Chandler*. New York: Columbia University Press, 1981.

Marchand, Leslie A., ed. *Byron's Letters and Journals, Volume II: For Freedom's Battle*. Cambridge: Harvard University Press, 1981.

Mariani, Paul. *William Carlos Williams: A New World Naked*. New York: McGraw-Hill, 1981.

Mason, Hayden. *Voltaire: A Biography*. Baltimore: Johns Hopkins University Press, 1981.

Mendelson, Edward. *Early Auden*. New York: Viking, 1981.

Milosz, Czeslaw. *Native Realm: A Search for Self-Definition*. Garden City: Doubleday, 1981.

Mitchell, Donald. *Britten and Auden in the Thirties: the Year 1936*. Seattle: University of Washington Press, 1981.

Mordden, Ethan. *The American Theatre*. New York: Oxford University Press, 1981.

Mordden. *The Hollywood Musical*. New York: St. Martin's Press, 1981.

Muhlenfeld, Elizabeth. *Mary Boykin Chesnut: A Biography*. Baton Rouge: Louisiana State University Press, 1981.

Mumford, Lewis. *Sketches from Life: The Autobiography of Lewis Mumford, The Early Years*. New York: Dial, 1982.

Nadel, Ira Bruce. *Jewish Writers of North America: A Guide to Information Sources*. Detroit: Gale Research, 1981.

Nelson, Raymond. *Van Wyck Brooks: A Writer's Life*. New York: Dutton, 1981.

Osborne, John. *A Better Class of Person*. New York: Dutton, 1981.

Parish, James Robert and Gregory W. Mank. *The Best of MGM: The Golden Years*. Westport, Conn.: Arlington House, 1981.

Partridge, Frances. *Love in Bloomsbury: Memories*. Boston: Little, Brown, 1981.

Paton, Alan. *Towards the Mountain: An Autobiography*. New York: Scribners, 1981.

Perelman, S. J. *The Last Laugh*. New York: Simon & Schuster, 1981.

Perry, Lilla S. *My Friend Carl Sandburg: The Biography of a Friendship*. Edited by E. Caswell Perry. Metuchen, N.J.: Scarecrow Press, 1981.

Plimpton, George. *Writers at Work: The Paris Review Interviews*, Fifth Series. New York: Viking, 1981.

Plummer, William. *The Holy Goof: A Biography of Neal Cassady*. Englewood Cliffs, N.J.: Prentice-Hall, 1981.

Rafroidi, Patrick. *Irish Literature in English: the Romantic Period (1789-1850)*, 2 volumes. Atlantic Highlands, N.J.: Humanities Press, 1981.

Reilly, John M., ed. *Twentieth Century Crime and Mystery Writers*. New York: St. Martin's Press, 1981.

Reynolds, David S. *Faith in Fiction: The Emergence of Religious Literature in America*. Cambridge: Harvard University Press, 1981.

Rossel, Sven. *A History of Scandinavian Literature*. Minneapolis: University of Minnesota Press, 1981.

Rowse, A. L. *What Shakespeare Read and Thought*. New York: Coward, McCann & Geoghegan, 1981.

Rugoff, Milton. *The Beechers: An American in the Nineteenth Century*. New York: Harper & Row, 1981.

Sartre, Jean-Paul. *The Family Idiot: Gustave Flaubert, 1821-1857*, volume 1. Translated by Carol Cosman. Chicago: University of Chicago Press, 1981.

Schoenbaum, S. *William Shakespeare: Records and Images*. New York: Oxford University Press, 1981.

Schwartz, Nancy with Sheila Schwartz. *The Hollywood Writers' Wars*. New York: Knopf, 1982.

Scott, Sir Walter. *Scott on Himself*. Edited by David Hewitt. Edinburgh: Scottish Academic Press, 1981.

Sennett, Ted. *Hollywood Musicals*. New York: Abrams, 1981.

Sheed, Wilfrid. *Clare Boothe Luce*. New York: Dutton, 1982.

Shi, David E. *Matthew Josephson: Bourgeois Bohemian*. New Haven: Yale University Press, 1981.

Shivers, Alfred S. *The Life of Maxwell Anderson*. New York: Stein & Day, 1982.

Singer, Isaac Bashevis. *Lost in America*. Garden City: Doubleday, 1981.

Smith, Cecil and Glenn Litton. *Musical Comedy in America*, expanded edition. New York: Theatre Arts, 1981.

Stearn, Jess. *In Search of Taylor Caldwell*. New York: Stein & Day, 1981.

Sternburg, Janet, ed. *The Writer on Her Work: Contemporary Women Writers Reflect on their Art and Situation*. New York: Norton, 1981.

Straus, Dorothea. *Under the Canopy*. New York: Braziller, 1982.

Tebbel, John. *A History of Book Publishing in the United States, Volume IV: The Great Change, 1940-1980*. New York: Bowker, 1981.

Tennant, Roger. *Joseph Conrad*. New York: Atheneum, 1981.

Thomas, William F. *Front Page 1881-1981: 100 Years of the* Los Angeles Times. New York: Abrams, 1981.

Thompson, Lawrence and R. H. Winick. *Robert Frost: A Biography*. Condensed into one volume by Edward Connery Lathem. New York: Holt, Rinehart & Winston, 1982.

Thomson, David. *A Biographical Dictionary of Film*, 2nd revised edition. New York: Morrow, 1981.

Thurber, Helen and Edward Weeks, eds. *Selected Letters of James Thurber*. Boston: Atlantic/Little, Brown, 1981.

Tolstoy, Alexandra. *Out of the Past*. Edited by Katharine Strelsky and Catherine Wolkonsky. New York: Columbia University Press, 1981.

Toth, Emily. *Inside Peyton Place: The Life of Grace Metalious*. Garden City: Doubleday, 1981.

Treglown, Jeremy, ed. *The Letters of John Wilmot, Earl of Rochester*. Chicago: University of Chicago Press, 1981.

Vaughn, Jack A. *Early American Dramatists: From the Beginnings to 1900*. New York: Ungar, 1981.

Wagenknecht, Edward. *Henry David Thoreau: What Manner of Man?*. Amherst: University of Massachusetts Press, 1981.

Wagenknecht. *Seven Daughters of the Theater*. New York: Plenum/Da Capo, 1981.

Warner, Sylvia Townsend. *Scenes of Childhood*. New York: Viking, 1982.

Washington, Ida. H. *Dorothy Canfield Fisher: A Biography*. Shelburne, Vt.: New England Press, 1982.

Watson, George, ed. *The Shorter New Cambridge Bibliography of English Literature*. Cambridge: Cambridge University Press, 1981.

White, Patrick. *Flaws in the Glass: A Self-Portrait*. New York: Viking, 1982.

Wilbers, Stephen. *The Iowa Writers' Workshop: Origin, Emergence, and Growth*. Iowa City: University of Iowa Press, 1980.

Winston, Richard. *Thomas Mann: The Making of an Artist, 1875-1911*. New York: Knopf, 1981.

Woodward, C. Vann, ed. *Mary Chesnut's Civil War*. New Haven: Yale University Press, 1981.

Yeats, W. B. *The Death of Cuchulain: Manuscript Materials including the Author's Final Text*. Edited by Phillip L. Marcus. Ithaca, N.Y.: Cornell University Press, 1981.

Young, Thomas D. and John J. Hindle, eds. *The Republic of Letters in America: The Correspondence of John Peale Bishop and Allen Tate*. Lexington: University Press of Kentucky, 1981.

Ziff, Larzer. *Literary Democracy: The Declaration of Cultural Independence in America*. New York: Viking, 1981.

Contributors

Michael Adams ....*Louisiana State University*
Timothy Dow Adams...*McMurry College*
Martin Altman ....*Maspeth, New York*
W. R. Anderson ....*Huntingdon College*
Jane S. Bakerman...*Indiana State University*
Joan Bobbitt...*Clemson University*
Ashley Brown ....*University of South Carolina*
J. D. Brown ....*University of Oregon*
Robert E. Burkholder ....*Pennsylvania State University, Wilkes-Barre*
George F. Butterick.......................................*University of Connecticut*
Ann Charters...*University of Connecticut*
Bill Crider ....*Howard Payne University*
Scott Donaldson...*College of William and Mary*
Richard A. Fine ....*Virginia Commonwealth University*
Joseph M. Flora.............................*University of North Carolina at Chapel Hill*
Daniel Fuchs...*Los Angeles, California*
George Garrett ....*York Harbor, Maine*
Sinda J. Gregory ....*San Diego State University*
Elizabeth B. House ....*Augusta College*
Dennis Jones...*Luther College*
Victor A. Kramer...*Georgia State University*
Brooks Landon...*University of Iowa*
Richard Layman ....*Columbia, South Carolina*
John R. May...*Louisiana State University*
Larry McCaffery ....*San Diego State University*
John Ower...*University of South Carolina*
Donald G. Parker ....*Orange County Community College, State University of New York*
Jean W. Ross ....*Columbia, South Carolina*
Hugh M. Ruppersburg.......................................*University of Georgia*
Susan Rusinko ....*Bloomsburg State College*
Jane Schwartz.............................*Brooklyn College, City University of New York*
Robert L. Sims ....*Virginia Commonwealth University*
Jon Christian Suggs ....*John Jay College, City University of New York*
Margaret A. Van Antwerp ....*Columbia, South Carolina*
Holly Mims Westcott ....*Florence, South Carolina*
Alden Whitman...*Southampton, New York*
Rhoda H. Wynn ....*Paul Green Dramas*
Dana Yeaton ....*Middlebury, Vermont*
Richard Ziegfeld...*University of South Carolina*

Yearbook Index: 1980-1981

Yearbook Index: 1980-1981